Denominação de Origem (DOC) areas of Portugal

1 Vinho Verde
2 Trás-os-Montes
3 Douro/Porto
4 Távora-Varosa
5 Lafões IPR
6 Bairrada
7 Dão
8 Beira Interior
9 Encostas de Aire
10 Óbidos
11 Alenquer
12 Arruda
13 Torres Vedras
14 Lourinhã
15 Bucelas

16 Carcavelos
17 Colares
18 Ribatejo
19 Setúbal
20 Palmela
21 Alentejo
22 Lagos
23 Portimão
24 Lagoa
25 Tavira
26 Madeira
27 Madeirense
28 Biscoitos IPR
29 Pico IPR
30 Graciosa IPR

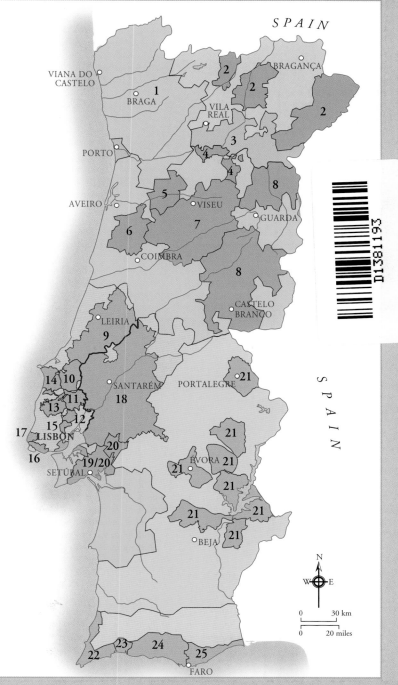

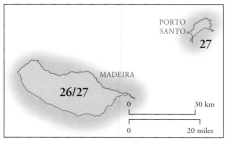

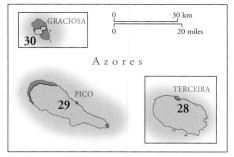

Published by **Inn House Publishing**
Old Inn House, London Road,
Balcombe, Haywards Heath RH17 6JQ, UK
Email: office@innhousepublishing.com

First published 2007
Revised and updated 2008

© Inn House Publishing

ISBN 978-0-9557069-0-5

British Library Cataloguing in Publication Data.
A catalogue record for this book is available from
the British Library.

Depósito Legal 264544/07

© Charles Metcalfe and Kathryn McWhirter are
hereby identified as the authors of this work in
accordance with Section 77 of the Copyright,
Designs and Patents Act 1988.

Design, layout and production: Sarah Moysey,
sarah@moysey.biz

All maps ©2007 Wendy Price Cartographic Services,
Inverness, IV1 3XQ, Kathryn McWhirter and
Charles Metcalfe. Digital Terrain Modelling by
Geo-innovations (www.geoinnovations.co.uk)
Information kindly supplied by Instituto Geográfico
Português (www.igeo.pt), Automóvel Club de
Portugal and El Corte Inglés.

Researchers: Bill Reed, José Ramos, Mónica Braz,
Ben Campbell-Johnston

Index: Ben Campbell-Johnston, Kathryn McWhirter

Printed in Portugal by Printer Portuguesa (Arvato).

ACKNOWLEDGEMENTS

Our sincere thanks go to Vasco d'Avillez (of ViniPortugal) and
António Silva (of AICEP), without whose initiation and support
this book would not exist – Vasco especially, for his constant
patience and help with research; Sarah Moysey, for brilliant design,
cool-minded execution and loyal friendship; Wendy Price and Helen
Sterling for patient and painstaking map-making; Robert Joseph for
the original concept; Bruce Hawker, for publishing and distribution
wisdom; Luís Pais, Filipe Neves, Rui Leal and Graham Smith in
particular for excellent photography; Mark Harding for his
contributions to the Explore sections of the Lisboa-Ribatejo and
Beiras chapters, and Judy Sharp for writing the Explore section of
the Alentejo; Christina Hippisley and Martin Symington, for
helping us to find them; Damian Warburton and Neal Tomlinson,
for IT support; Chris Foulkes & Carrie Seagrave, for patient
publishing advice; Mary Anne Stilwell d'Avillez, Dave Cartwright,
Mónica Braz, Emma Dalton, Natasha Hughes, Adrian Bridge,
Nicholas Faith, Paul and Philippa Reynolds, Michael Hopkins and
Norman McWhirter, for reading proofs; Dora Simões, Marcio Ferreira,
Ana Sofia de Oliveira (of ViniPortugal) for driving, companionship
and help throughout; Filipe da Mota Neves, Luís Gaspar, Rosario
Silva and Rui Cordovil (of AICEP) for friendship, information and
help; Mark Rowlinson, our golfing guru; all the Portuguese wine
and food producers, restaurateurs and hoteliers who received us, sent
us their wines and gave us information, in particular Nuno Araújo,
Miguel Azevedo, Vasco Croft, Pedro Rodrigues, Vasco Magalhães
and Filipa Pato, all hugely generous with their time and knowledge;
Margarida Andrade of CVR Beira Interior for her exceptionally
efficient and cheerful help with maps and pictures; Fátima Silva and
Henriques Soares (Rota dos Vinhos de Setúbal), Silvia Monteiro
Novais (CVR Algarve), Carlos Manuel Tiago Mesquita and Helena
Cardoso (CVR Trás-os-Montes), Helena Ribeiro (Lisbon Tourist
Office), Sandra Dart (Isla de Horta Tourist Office), Ana Isabel Talus
(Azores Tourist Office), Cristina Machado (Câmara Municipal de
Vila Nova de Gaia), Madalena Barreiros (Hotel do Colégio, São
Miguel), Gebhart Schachermayer (Vila Joya, Abufeira), and Pedro
Vihena (Hotel da Cartuxa, Évora); David Lopes Ramos (of *Público*)
for help with restaurant reviews; Luís Lopes (of *Revista dos Vinhos*),
Rui Falcão (of *Blue Wine*) and Richard Mayson, for wine advice; Dave
Cartwright, for keeping the garden under control, unaided; and
Rachel, Sarah and Oliver, for discovering even greater independence
as we concentrated on this book, rather than on them.

We dedicate this book to our children.

THE WINE AND FOOD LOVER'S GUIDE TO

Portugal

Best wishes,

Charles Metcalfe & Kathryn McWhirter

INN
HOUSE
publishing

Foreword

Charles and Kathryn are some of my oldest friends in the wine world. No, hang on. Charles is *the* oldest wine friend I have, the original. If I hadn't shared a shower with him at the Oxford Playhouse Theatre and helped him scrub the artificial blood off his back (no, you *don't* want the details) I might never have got involved in wine at all.

He came from a wine family, I didn't. He knew all the wine people at Oxford, I didn't know any of them.

But I told him I longed to learn about wine. And within a day he'd swept me off to start me on my quest. We learnt about wine together, teaching each other, challenging each other. We went on our first wine trips together and did our first vintage together (I picked, he actually helped make the stuff). But we didn't get beyond the Pyrenees – well, not initially. Yet you can't stand gazing south at those majestic peaks and not long to know what lies the other side. So we soon got to Spain, and, finally made it all the way to Portugal, the land of fly droppings, dog strangler and the little red Bastard. These are all names of Portuguese grape varieties, by the way, and such oddities seemed entirely apt in a country that appeared at that time to devote all its passion to being different from the rest of Europe, living then in a state of inspired chaos afloat in a sea of uniquely anachronistic flavours.

Well, that's not quite fair. Portugal was a very early convert to the idea that wine production needed rules and controls. But Portugal *was* not, *is* not now (and hopefully never will be) a slavish follower of the ebb and flow of international fashion. On our first trip, we stood in the cobwebbed gloom of Caves São João, tasting a range of Dão and Bairrada reds that ran back through 20 vintages. Suddenly, at twenty summers old, the wines blossomed and revealed a personality and haughty beauty completely unrelated to any other European wine. 'It takes 20 years,' the owner said. 20 years of investment. 20 years of nodding and humming and waiting. Till it's ready. That was Portugal. The grand old Portugal Charles and I discovered together.

Luckily, the new Portugal is just as proud, just as idiosyncratic, just as unwilling to submit to international opinion. The wine world may swoop and sway like mackerel shoals as it attempts to please whatever opinion-former is currently in fashion. Portugal swims in a different tide, as modern as any country needs to be, as outrageously proud of its traditions, its potential, and its God-given duty to stand as a fiery beacon of individuality raging against the insidious ooze of globalisation. And if this is why we know less of Portugal's treasures than her quality deserves, then Portugal clearly needs chroniclers who are no slaves to fashion, but have a deep passion for the individual, the courageous, the rare, and the delicious.

Charles may have been my first and finest friend in wine, but Kathryn was my first editor (firm but fair, fair but firm...). What a combination. Just what Portugal needs.

à vossa

Oz Clarke

Contents

How this book works

A personal selection No one has paid anything to be included in this book. Our principle has been to choose producers, restaurants and places to stay that we truly wanted to recommend, rather than including many and criticising some.

Regional chapters The book's first emphasis is wine, and our chapters divide Portugal into the regions that were chosen for the Vinho Regional wines (which in places are slightly different from the administrative regions). But sometimes it was clearer and more logical to call the chapters by a region's more familiar name: for instance we have chapters called Douro (not the VR name Duriense) and Trás-os-Montes (not the VR name Transmontano). One chapter combines the VR regions of Lisboa and Ribatejo. The chapters travel through the wine regions west to east, north to south. There are also two city chapters: Lisbon and Porto/Gaia.

Maps and listing order Ours is the best wine mapping of Portugal to date. As a starting point, many individual regions could give us only the vaguest of maps, although of course they knew where their boundaries were, from lists of parishes and part-parishes… Our maps have relief, to give some idea of the lie of the land. Apart from showing the whereabouts and boundaries of the wine areas, the purpose of the maps is to locate visitable wineries, and places to eat and stay, linking over to the town or district names in the text. In this respect they are deliberately simplified maps, showing only the towns, villages and city districts mentioned in the book. You will still of course need a larger scale road map, or a city plan, in conjunction with the book maps to find your way.

Alphabetical by place Entries are listed in alphabetical order of their town or village; in the case of the Lisbon and Porto/Gaia city chapters, listings are by area of the city. Search via the maps or the index.

Wineries and wines All the wines in the book have been tasted by Charles, plus many more that we chose not to include. Of course, there are other good wineries out there that we have yet to discover, or whose wines will have come of age in time for the next edition. A remarkable number of wineries welcome visitors. Some wineries are seriously set up to receive unannounced visitors at any time of the working day, offering tours and tastings, and maybe meals or even accommodation. We have indicated where you should book in advance – when they are not receiving visitors, producers may of course be out tending their vines and wines, or selling them, or generally going about their other business! It would be courteous, especially in smaller places, to make a purchase, at least a little one. Wineries that are not visitable at all by the general public appear in a coloured box.

Eat Our starting point in seeking and selecting restaurants was the Portuguese wine industry: producers, marketing and sales people all over Portugal, as well as wine journalists, restaurant reviewers and our own spontaneous discoveries. In the Algarve, Lisbon and Porto-Gaia we have listed 'modern Portuguese' and 'good traditional' restaurants separately, and in all regions we have marked these two styles of restaurant separately on the map. Elsewhere the modern ripples are spreading out from these gastronomic centres – maybe in future editions we shall make the same divide elsewhere. In each region or city, we have tried to include at least one vegetarian restaurant. We have also included a small selection of bars, wine bars, cafés, tea houses, markets, wine and food shops. We phoned the restaurants to check details, including average prices of a three course meal plus wine, for one. It is clearly difficult to pin down a figure, especially in a country where set meals are rare: prices are intended as a helpful indication of how much you might expect to pay.

Explore These sections are not meant to be a comprehensive guide – just a quick touristic run through each region or city to help you get your bearings; and a few pointers to non-culinary things we have enjoyed and that you might not want to miss.

Sleep Again, we were guided initially by friends in the wine trade. We have sought out characterful places at a range of price levels, many of them conveniently placed for winery visits, or restaurants. Portugal has a complicated classification system for accommodation, which we won't go into here, nor have we fussed too much about numbers of stars. Our suggestions range from grand old manor houses to farms, from starry hotels to little inns, plus

occasionally houses, villas or flats to rent. We have also selected some of the *pousadas*, a growing range of smart hotels in historic monuments – convents, monasteries, castles – or modern buildings in beauty spots. Once government owned, they were recently privatised, mostly belonging to a group, though two stand alone. Our prices are normally for a double or twin room with breakfast.

Grape varieties Portugal has a number of really fine, flavoursome grapes that can stand up proudly to the likes of Chardonnay and Cabernet Sauvignon. Wines are often a blend of two or more varieties. To get to grips with the grape flavours and characteristics, *see page 428*.

The language The Portuguese are good linguists, but you will need some Portuguese. Get started on *page 434*.

A spot of architecture between meals Manueline pillars, Pombaline streets, Baroque churches... If you're at all confused or lost in time, consult our bite-sized architectural guide, *page 432*.

Photos Much of the wine photography is by Luis Pais, who travelled with us. For photo credits *see page 438*.

LISTINGS AND SYMBOLS

♟ Used for restaurants with a particularly good wine list (judged within their price and category) or for a place-to-stay that offers particularly good wine to guests.

✗ In places-to-stay, you can assume that breakfast is available, and included in the price, unless the text says otherwise. ✗ means that other meals are also available, often by prior arrangement in the case of bed and breakfast places.

V Vegetarian options available. It is rare in Portugal for menus to include a vegetarian option. We include a *V* if restaurants said they would prepare something specially if asked. However, it is always best to phone ahead, whether to a humble or a grand establishment.

V! means serious catering for vegetarians.

€ *Restaurant prices* are estimates (mostly suggested by the restaurants themselves) of the cost of a three-course meal for one, with wine. It's a kind of typical, average price, dependent of course on choice of wine and food, and can only be an indication.

€ *Prices of places to stay* Price ranges indicate probable cost of a double or twin room with breakfast for two; we show the lowest winter price and the highest summer price.

🛏 In a 'sleep' entry, this shows the number of bedrooms for two; in a winery or restaurant entry, this symbol means that accommodation is available in-house

[S] Suites

[SC] Self-catering; [SC] *2(4&2)* means two self-catering units one sleeping four, one sleeping 2; [SC] *1(4+2)* means one self-catering unit sleeping four with a possible extra two on a sofa bed.

No credit cards Simpler restaurants and bed and breakfast places, even in fine manor houses, are less likely than you might imagine to take credit cards. We asked everyone. Where it doesn't say 'no credit cards', you should be safe, but do check in simpler establishments.

Emails We have listed email addresses for bookings, but be slightly wary. If there is no confirmation, check by phone. Emailing should be safe in smart restaurants or big hotels. But not everyone seems to check their emails in Portugal, and not everyone seems to see a need to respond, at least with any speed.

🏊 Swimming pool

♨ Spa

🏋 Gym

🧖 Steam room/sauna

☀ Solarium

🎾 Tennis courts on site

🏸 Squash courts on site

⛳ A golf course actually attached to the hotel

About the authors

Charles Metcalfe and Kathryn McWhirter wrote their first book on Portuguese wines over 20 years ago, and are still at it. Charles is one of the most spontaneous and amusing wine critics in Britain, and a well-known face on British television, having been part of the ITV *This Morning* team for 12 years. He was a co-founder of *WINE International* magazine, and is co-chairman of the International WINE Challenge, the world's biggest wine competition. Before turning to wine, he was a professional singer. You can read Charles regularly in *Blue Wine* (if you speak Portuguese!) and he is the UK correspondent for *Wine Business International*. Kathryn was drinks correspondent for the *Independent on Sunday* for nine years, sometimes also writing about food. She wrote and edited the *Which? Wine Guide* and *Good Wine Bar Guide* for the Consumers' Association, as well as wine list reviews for the *Good Food Guide*, and was editor of *Wine & Spirit* magazine. Together Charles and Kathryn have written wine and wine-with-food books for Sainsbury's, Tesco and Marks & Spencer, as well as other publishers.

We'd value your views for future editions of *The Wine and Food Lover's Guide to Portugal*. Do write to tell us of experiences (good, we hope) of the wines, winery visits, restaurants or places to stay in this book; or of others you consider worthy of inclusion.
Inn House Publishing, Old Inn House, London Road, Balcombe, Haywards Heath, RH17 6JQ
E charles&kathryn@innhousepublishing.com
W www.innhousepublishing.com

It's not just beaches

Beaches are only the beginning. Inland, Portugal has some of the world's most beautiful scenery, mountains, lakes, reservoirs, rivers, waterfalls, forests of chestnut, pine and cork oak, citrus and olive groves, ancient hill villages, castles and monasteries... Most tourists go to the Algarve, Madeira, Lisbon, Porto-Gaia, but this book also takes you beyond. It focuses first upon Portugal's wineries – and not just wineries that privileged wine-writers can visit. Portugal's wineries are eager to show their new, fine wines to the world, and most of the wineries in this book can be visited. Amongst gastronomes in Portugal there is a real culture nowadays of wine appreciation, as well as the marriage of the characterful modern Portuguese wines with food both traditional and new wave.

The Portuguese are welcoming to visitors, and patient and appreciative if you speak a bit of their tricky language (novices might get to work on *page 434*). Portugal has been open to all kinds of foreign influences throughout its history, from early occupation to the Age of Discoveries. But the *modern* outward-looking spirit – embracing amongst other things wines, food, restaurants, and places to stay – is new. Portugal lived under a dictatorship for 48 of the middle years of the 20th century, and then a left-wing, collectivising revolution put another kind of brake on development for a while. Portugal joined the EU as one of its least developed, poorest members. And suddenly the infrastructure improved. Wineries and food manufacturers were amongst the beneficiaries, financed to upgrade their facilities, often with impressive results. Further efforts were required to provide for the influx of football fans to this football-mad country for Euro 2004, and facilities poured into parts of Portugal other tourists had not yet reached.

But even if new roads and ideas have penetrated the most remote of places, ancient traditions are still held dear. Family life and family meals are deeply important, and so is religion: most people are Catholic, more devout in the north, though religion is losing its grip a little amongst city dwellers and the young. There are several sites of serious annual pilgrimage; saints' days are celebrated with enthusiasm, beginning perhaps with mass but ending in street parties, dancing, music and feasting, all washed down with quantities of wine. Superstition and ancient

rites mingle with religion, especially at *festa* time. Churches are often richly decorated, with blue and white *azulejo* tile designs, or with gilded carvings paid for with the wealth that flooded into Portugal from its 'discovered' colonies. Centuries of war with Spain gave rise to a string of medieval hill-top castles and fortified villages along the border.

The north and east of the country have the most dramatic hills and mountains – and the majority of the top vineyards. The highest range is the wild and beautiful Serra da Estrela in the Beiras, home of Portugal's most famous ewe's milk cheese. But it's difficult to select a 'most beautiful' mountain area. It could be the Douro Valley, one of the world's great beauty spots and source of port and a vast number of fine unfortified wines; or the high, remote Trás-os-Montes area in the north-east with its wild, stark beauty; the dramatic Peneda and Gerês ranges in the the Vinho Verde country of the Minho; the spectacular mountains of inland Madeira, and the Azores islands with their peaks and crater lakes. In the lower-lying southern half of Portugal, there are the limestone mountains of the Serras de Aire and Candeeiros north of Lisbon, and the Serra de São Mamede, on whose foothills the grapes for some of the Alentejo's most elegant

wines are grown. And, unbeknown to many beach-based tourists, there are lovely mountains of outstanding beauty in the Algarve, just a short drive inland from the crowded central coastal strip. For the energetic, there's fantastic mountain walking and riding, parachuting and climbing.

For city breaks, the obvious first destinations are Lisbon and Porto/Vila Nova de Gaia, concentrated centres nowadays of the new-wave restaurants listing extensive ranges of fine Portuguese wines. Lisbon is a fascinating city, its quarters ranging from Moorish to modern, stuffed with museums and monuments, character and atmosphere. Porto's old quarters are a delightful hillside medieval jumble topped with grand, wealthy streets and monuments of later ages. Gaia, a city in its own right across the River Douro, offers the port experience – a mind-boggling choice of tastings and visits to most of the major names in port. Gaia is also planning a serious revamp in the next few years, some of the old wineries and more run-down areas turning into boutique hotels and restaurants, leafy parks and promenades. Historic Coimbra, an ancient university city alive with students, has beautiful, hilly, narrow streets and stairways, fine buildings, churches, monasteries and cathedrals, gardens, and some good restaurants and cafés. Just to the south are the impressive Roman ruins of Conimbriga, just to the north are the wine regions of Bairrada and Dão, the magical Buçaco forest and hotel, and various spas; and the Serra da Estrela lies to the east.

Of course, with the prospect of a little wine and food on the side, you may be here mainly for the world-class golf –

PORTUGUESE NATIONAL HOLIDAYS

Many restaurants and tourist attractions close for public holidays, so you need to be aware of these dates:

JANUARY
New Year's Day

FEBRUARY/MARCH
Carnival Tuesday, the day before Ash Wednesday

MARCH/APRIL
Good Friday and **Easter Sunday**

APRIL
Liberty Day Celebrating the 1974 revolution, 25 April

MAY
Labour Day 1 May

MAY/JUNE
Corpus Christi Ninth Thursday after Easter

JUNE
Portugal Day (Camões/Community Day) 10 June

AUGUST
Assumption 15 August

OCTOBER
Republic Day Commemorates the declaration of the Portuguese Republic in 1910, 5 October

NOVEMBER
All Saints' Day 1 November

DECEMBER
Independence Day, celebrates the 1640 restoration of independence from Spain, 1 December
Immaculate Conception 8 December
Christmas Day

in which case you will probably be based around the Algarve, or somewhere in a wide arc around Lisbon, though fine golf courses are scattered elsewhere, including the islands. Which brings us back to the beaches. For many people, that will cue images of the highly developed tourist strip of the central Algarve with its dunes, white sand, golden cliffs, caves and rock formations, hotels and international resorts. And this is indeed a magnet also for lovers of fine food and wine: a lot of Portugal's top gastronomic restaurants are here, along with wonderful seafood restaurants, and night life at all levels of sophistication, some very exclusive. The same goes for the beaches around Lisbon, though these and the nearby restaurants are peopled more by the leisure-loving Portuguese. But Portugal has 960 km of beaches, long stretches of them undeveloped and often deserted even in summer, including many wild surfing beaches in the north, and down the long western coastline, away from the capital. Sailors and intrepid wind surfers enjoy some beaches that most tourists miss, accessible by land down long, unmade tracks. All of the south-west coast from the tip of the Algarve nearly up to the Setúbal Peninsula is now a natural park, protected from development.

Wherever you are around the coast, head for a plate of gloriously fresh and delicious seafood or fish. And toast your holiday with a glistening glass of chilled white wine. Now, what should it be... a subtly aromatic Alvarinho Vinho Verde? Or maybe a characterful Douro white; a steely white from Bairrada, Dão or Bucelas, or a rich but sprightly Antão Vaz from the Alentejo...

Wine in Portugal

If it's a while since you tasted Portuguese wines, you're in for a big surprise. Twenty years ago, in our first book, we wrote this: 'The potential for producing fine table wines in Portugal is enormous…but most of the Portuguese table wine industry has been behind the times for years, and traditional domestic demand has meant that winemakers have had no need to adjust to the outside world. The Portuguese knew what they liked and drank it all.' That was a polite way of saying there was too much awful wine in Portugal. Now Portugal has definitely found the plot. The main change has been one of attitude. For the last 15 years, Portuguese winemakers have been striving to make wines that can compete in a world arena, both at the cheaper, everyday end, *and* up there with the world's finest wines.

What has not changed is Portugal's palette of unique, flavoursome indigenous grapes. Backed by modern growing and winemaking skills, these can now shine, in ever more varied locations. And the best of the local grapes are ousting the lesser ones. In the lush, green country of Vinho Verde, the aromatic Loureiro has taken over as main grape. More and more vineyards of Touriga Nacional, Touriga Franca and Tinta Roriz have been planted in the schistous wonderland

of the Douro Valley, giving rich, powerful reds, as well as ever-better port. And winemakers have discovered that the Douro's traditional white grapes – Viosinho, Malvasia Fina, Gouveio and Rabigato – can make subtle, elegant whites.

Bairrada and Dão, the best-known wine regions in the Beiras, both had quality problems two decades ago. Bairrada's recent revolution freed it from the shackles of the Baga grape, which ripened only four years in ten. Now Bairrada has a new two-track system, one for traditional Baga, one for 'imported' varieties, and both offer some fantastic wines. Dão remains under-rated, its granite soils producing some of Portugal's most thrilling reds and steely whites. The mountain country of the Beira Interior also deserves to be discovered, by wine-hunters as well as tourists.

Most of the wine from Lisboa and Ribatejo is knocked back in bars, or makes brandy, but there are really notable exceptions, some producers there making truly exceptional wines, others carefully crafting mid-range wines for export. Terras do Sado is perhaps the least changed – because things were already pretty good 20 years ago. The Alentejo has hugely increased its range of fleshy, generous reds, new vineyards flourishing between the cork forests.

Portugal nowadays has a huge number of wine estates making and selling their own wine – that's another big difference from 20 years ago. Then, in our first book, there were 50 recommendable producers of unfortified wines. Now the Beiras region alone has more. Where have they all come from? Most are grape-growing families who used to sell their grapes or the wine they made from them to big exporting companies, or send them to co-operatives, usually for very little return. More recent generations have chosen to do their own thing – and to do it well. Young wine makers have studied to degree level and beyond, and many have travelled. The index of this book is liberally peppered with the names of the best performers.

The large merchant companies still control most of the exports – good wines right across the price range. Many small estates do export their wines, but it's not easy. Portugal's quality revolution is only just beginning to be noticed by the wine-drinking world outside Portugal – and by the people in export markets who should, by all rights of quality, be selling these wines in restaurants, wine bars, supermarkets, shops and mail order... Even when a supermarket recognises quality and value and puts a wine on sale, customers haven't yet the confidence that a Portuguese wine will be good – and the wine is sadly prone to disappear from the shelves. A big PR job is ahead for the producers, for ViniPortugal, the constantly beavering wine promotion company sponsored by the producers, and for ICEP, the government organisation that promotes the country's exports.

When we ask not particularly winey friends what they know about Portuguese wines, their first and sometimes only thought is often Mateus Rosé. Made by the big, quality-conscious Sogrape, Mateus Rosé is still Portugal's largest volume wine export, although the origin is blurring with the recent introduction of pink Mateus wines from elsewhere. The major companies are responsible for some of Portugal's élite wines, too: Sogrape's Barca Velha, José Maria da Fonseca's Hexagon, Bacalhôa Vinhos de Portugal's Palácio de Bacalhôa, Esporão's Reserva, Aliança's T de Terrugem, for example. There have been changes in recent years amongst the big companies, notably the arrival of José Berardo as the largest single investor in the Portuguese wine industry. Having bought the majority share of what used to be called João Pires in 1998 (now Bacalhôa Vinhos de Portugal), he also owns slices of Sogrape, Aliança and Henriques & Henriques (in his native Madeira). Coming up fast on the outside is Companhia das Quintas, a new, quality-minded company

THE MAIN PORT PLAYERS AND THEIR LABELS

Fladgate Partnership Taylor's, Fonseca, Croft, Delaforce
Sogevinus Cálem, Burmester, Barros Almeida, Kopke, Gilbert's
Sogrape Ferreira, Sandeman, Offley, Robertson
Symington Family Estates Dow's, Graham's, Warre's, Smith Woodhouse, Gould Campbell, Quarles Harris, Quinta do Vesúvio

owning estates around the country, and keen to develop export markets.

The port industry has changed, too. Some changes are technical – improved viticulture, robotic *lagares*, better choice of fortifying spirit – all leading to better ports. There have been changes of ownership, too. Sogevinus, a company formed by a Spanish bank, now owns Cálem, Burmester, Barros Almeida and Kopke. Symington Family Estates (owners of Dow's, Graham's and Warre's, among other port labels) now have more vineyards in the Douro than any other company, since their acquisition in 2006 of Cockburn's estates and wineries. The Fladgate Partnership (owners of Taylor's and Fonseca) also added Croft and Delaforce to their portfolio, and Sogrape did the same with Sandeman and Offley.

If you're getting the idea that this means most port is produced by a small number of large companies, well, in terms of numbers, that's probably true. But this reckons without all the smaller estates that have sprung up since the relaxation in 1986 of the rule that obliged all port destined for export to be shipped out of the town of Vila Nova de Gaia, opposite Porto. Now any estate that wants to export direct from the Douro is allowed to do so, and many do. Best known of these is Quinta do Noval, but many of the top estates for unfortified wines are selling ports as well.

Elsewhere, too, politics kept the lid on small estates until recent years. In Dão, legislation favoured the co-ops in the era of the dictator Salazar (the whole middle part of the last century) and the left-wing, collectivist period that followed; only one estate (Casa de Santar) was bottling its own wine a couple of decades ago. Between Dão and Bairrada, the Buçaco Palace Hotel was bottling and selling wines, as it continues to do today. In Bairrada, Luís Pato was one of the few individuals bottling wine from his vineyards. A handful of estates bottled their own wine in the Alentejo, including the then newly replanted, giant Esporão property, Mouchão, the Fundação Eugénio de Almeida, José de Sousa Rosado e Fernandes (belonging to José Maria da Fonseca) and Quinta do Carmo. Only in Vinho Verde country and Lisboa were there numerous growers making, bottling and selling their wine (most of them from old land-owning families, living in splendid manor houses).

Now individual wine estates are popping up too fast to keep count. The Douro charge was led by Miguel Champalimaud's Quinta do Côtto and by Ramos Pinto, and the second wave was the Douro Boys *(see box)*,

WINEMAKERS UNITED

Some producers have formed their own marketing groups. The most important of these are:

G7 (Grupo dos Sete) Six of Portugal's largest companies: Aliança, Aveleda, Bacalhôa, Esporão, José Maria da Fonseca and Messias. (Yes, *sete* does mean seven: Sogrape left in February 2007.)

IWA (Independent Winegrowers Association) Six companies from northern Portugal (Vinho Verde, Minho, Douro, Bairrada and Dão): Quinta do Ameal, Casa de Cello, Quinta de Covela, Alves de Sousa, Quinta dos Roques, Luis Pato.

The Douro Boys Five of the best new-wave Douro producers: Quinta do Vallado, Niepoort, Quinta do Vale Dona Maria, Quinta do Vale Meão, Quinta do Crasto

Wine Friends from Portugal A trio of producers from different regions: Quinta da Ribeirinha (Ribatejo), Hero do Castanheiro (Terras do Sado), Quinta do Barranco Longo (Algarve).

Quinta da Gaivosa, Quinta de la Rosa, Real Companhia Velha, and many others. The most recent arrivals are among the best. The Beiras brigade has blossomed, with companies such as Dão Sul, Alvaro de Castro, Luis Lourenço and many others, not forgetting the many good wines made by Luís Pato, Sogrape, Aliança, Borges, Messias and Caves São João. In Dão particularly, new wines arrive on the market with bewildering frequency, maybe a reaction to the years when the co-ops ruled all. The same applies in the Ribatejo and Lisboa: as the co-ops wane, the single estates have to fend for themselves. In the Alentejo, further large estates have decided to go it alone, aware of their neighbours' success. Again, several of the newer arrivals are making some of the best wines.

One key to the success of these single-estate labels has been the work of a very bright generation of consultant winemakers, often working for several estates at once. Amongst the first in the field was João Portugal Ramos, now with his own substantial businesses in the Alentejo and Ribatejo. Rui Moura Alves, Jorge Borges, Rui Cunha, Luís Duarte, Paolo Laureano, Anselmo Mendes; Rui Reguinga and António Saramago are some of the busiest at the moment. Others have gone before, and there is an eager generation of younger winemakers also starting to work as consultants, António Maçanita and others.

Least impressive performers in the past two decades have been some of the wine co-ops, most set up in the 1950s, and only latterly able to invest in the modern equipment necessary for making high-quality wines. Two have shut up shop since our first book, and a few others are paying little if anything to their members for their grapes – always a worrying sign. But there are co-op out-performers as well, ones that have moved with the times, hired winemaking consultants, and taken advantage of EU grants and loans to re-equip with modern machinery. The co-ops of Monção, Santo Isidro de Pegões and Borba are three of the most savvy producers in Portugal.

Traditional winemaking techniques have either been replaced or adapted to advances in knowledge. *Lagares* (traditional, wide, low winemaking troughs) are still used for port and for red wines, and not only in the Douro. In some wineries, the old granite *lagares* have been replaced by stainless steel versions, complete with full cooling equipment (and sometimes robotic 'treaders' that mimic the action of the human feet of previous centuries). In the Alentejo and Algarve, a few wineries still ferment in large clay amphorae, but with the back-up of modern cooling systems, in case things get over-heated.

Everywhere, the best producers are using modern knowledge in vineyard and cellar to get the most out of Portugal's twin strengths, its dazzling array of native grapes and wonderfully varied vineyard terrain. A huge range of flavours and styles comes from the clay and chalk mix of Bairrada, the windy slopes of Lisboa, the fertile river valley of the Ribatejo, the ancient sands of Terras do Sado, the rolling plains of the Alentejo; and heading upwards, from the contoured, schistous valleys of the Douro and its tributaries, the granite mountains of the interior (in Dão, northern Alentejo or the Beira Interior, and the green northern hillside of Vinho Verde). Portugal's unique vine varieties have rarely escaped the borders (though they deserve to be planted elsewhere), and that means that Portugal's wines taste different. Some of the flavours may not turn out be your favourites, but we defy anyone not to appreciate the herby scent of Touriga Nacional, the fresh, bright fruit of Trincadeira, the aromatic minerality of Alvarinho, the steely crispness of Arinto…

Add the investment that membership of the European Union has brought, in roads, bridges and new vineyards and winemaking equipment, a new generation of winemakers that has travelled the world in search of knowledge and experience their fathers and grandfathers never had, and it's a heady mix. Of course you can still find poor wine in Portugal, but there's so much good wine around that it's a shame to waste drinking time on the mediocre. And many of these good wine producers welcome visitors, proud to show you their immaculate vineyards and cellars and eager to sell you bottles for your holiday drinking. Our aim is to select the best in every area. All you need is a car and a good road map.

Food in Portugal

What do we choose to bring back in our suitcase at the end of a visit to Portugal? There'll certainly be a jar of *marmelada*, the wonderful, firm, sweet quince paste, to eat with cheese, or on toast for breakfast. And a packet of the addictive Elvas plums *(ameixas de Elvas)*, sugar-preserved greengages from the Alentejo, their sweetness balanced by acidity and fine flavour. Our children will fight over the *doce de abóbora* – subtly flavoured, orange-coloured pumpkin jam, which the Portuguese often serve as a pudding or at breakfast with a wedge or mound of sheeps' milk ricotta *(requeijão)*. We pack bread when returning from northern regions: huge, round loaves of coarse-ground corn bread *(broa)*; and the similar but finer-ground *bolo de milho* corn bread from the Azores. There'll be a sumptous, soft-centred cheese or two, usually Queijo da Serra from the Beiras, or the similar Queijo de Azeitão from the Setúbal Peninsula or Queijo de Serpa from the Alentejo.

Lucky we don't pack too many clothes, because there has to be room for a bottle or two of single-*quinta* olive oil, and some *presunto de porco preto bolota*, the richest of the cured hams from the Alentejo's acorn-fed black pigs.

Back home we'll need to slim, so too bad that we packed a little box of *doces conventuais*, the expensive but delicious little egg-yolk sweets. Case checked in, we might in season still be nursing a bag of Alcobaça peaches.

And what will we miss, fresh home from the Portuguese coast? Seafood, of course, all kinds, simply cooked, super-fresh. And amongst Portugal's plethora of fishes, perhaps most of all the flavoursome red mullet – *salmonete*. Meaty delights we'd lust after would include Bairrada crispy roast suckling pig *(leitão)* and the wonderful roast pork or sausages from the *porco preto* – those Alentejo black pigs again.

And we also leave Portugal, every time, with a growing list of new, world-class restaurants. Travellers of old may have filed Portugal away under R for rustic, and maybe also S for stodgy. Things have changed, and are changing. The R-word still applies of course, in local restaurants, and portions are usually huge. But now there are modern restaurants in abundance in the Algarve, Lisbon and Porto, and scattered here and there elsewhere. A new generation of top chefs has travelled abroad, absorbed ideas and skills, and come back to reinterpret Portuguese

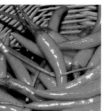

From Portuguese outposts in Brazil, Angola, Mozambique, Goa, Macau, the Azores and Madeira, spices arrived. Cinnamon *(canela)*, discovered in India, is still sprinkled on every imaginable pudding, cake and sweet, and a cinnamon stick is a regular alternative to the spoon for stirring coffee. Cumin *(cominhos)* is a frequent flavour, especially in Vinho Verde country and the Azores. Paprika and sweet peppers are used everywhere. *Piri-piri* – a very hot chilli – arrived from Angola, made into a simple sauce that still enlivens fish and chicken all over Portugal, especially in the Algarve. Saffron *(açafrão)* features less than in Spain, but you'll come across curry *(caril)*, always used mildly. The explorers also brought turkeys, tomatoes, potatoes and corn, cocoa and coffee. It was apparently the Portuguese who first introduced tea to the English aristocracy, when Catherine of Braganza married Charles II in 1662.

cuisine, making creative new use of fine local ingredients but never quite abandoning familiar culinary themes. This is, after all, a land that values and loves its traditions.

Many of those traditions arrived in Portugal in two distinct periods in the past. Medieval Moors brought almonds, rice, coriander *(coentros)*, dishes based on chickpeas, lentils and dried beans, and stewy-soupy dishes thickened with breadcrumbs and slices of bread. They introduced fritters, the wonderful quince paste *(marmelada)*… and the national sweet tooth. Later, the Age of Discoveries brought all kinds of new ingredients and influences that infused Portuguese cuisine for ever.

This is a conservative nation, and until the current influx of ideas the cuisine has not developed greatly over the intervening centuries – though traditional local dishes have spread around the country as transport and communications have opened up. It's a tradition based on meat and fish (where available and affordable), heavily backed up by carbohydrate staples. You won't go hungry in Portugal. Meat or fish dishes in a traditional restaurant will often come with rice *and* potatoes. And of course there's always bread.

There are rice producers small and large all the way down the plains and estuaries of the west coast, but rice still has to be imported. The Portuguese eat more rice than any other country in Europe. Local rice *(arroz)* is traditionally medium grain, increasingly joined by long-grained varieties, and it's almost always white: self-caterers in search of brown rice *(arroz integral)* may strike lucky in a good deli. Firm, creamy rice pudding *(arroz doce)* is a national dish, flavoured with lemon, enriched with egg

yolks and decoratively sprinkled with cinnamon – it's on every menu, and at birthdays, weddings, Christmas…

The potatoes that arrived on the discovery ships were viewed at first with suspicion, and indeed were used as animal feed until the end of the 18th century, whilst inland, humans far from the rice fields used chestnuts as a staple (delicious chestnuts are still much used in the rural north) as well as potatoes, boiled, fried, roasted, or maybe baked and then crushed, sprinkled with garlic and doused with olive oil – *batatas a murro (a murro* means punched). Potatoes are often the thickener for soups.

Our favourite breads are corn breads *(broa, pão de milho* or *bolo de milho)*, famous in the north, Ribatejo and the Azores, and the rye breads, such as *pão centeio do Sabugueiro* from the Serra da Estrela in the Beiras; tourist restaurants may serve boring white rolls; but *pão caseiro* – baked on the premises – should be something else. And bread gets into soups and all kinds of other dishes. *Açorda* (originally a southern dish) was a moist peasant dish of lumps of stale bread boiled with water, olive oil, herbs and garlic; now restaurants everywhere add meat or seafood, and maybe tomatoes, onions and beaten eggs, and it can taste good – or, well, like boiled bread. Portuguese infants used to eat a lot of this, and, like rice pudding, it can trigger sentimental memories. Another common bread concoction, *migas*, is usually drier, sometimes more of a

SOME TOP OLIVE OIL PRODUCERS

DOURO/TRÁS-OS-MONTES CARM, Sardeiro, Val d'Ondel, Niepoort, Quinta do Crasto, Taylors, Ramos Pinto, Romeu ALENTEJO Esporão, Cortes de Cima, Casa Aragão, Quinta do Côa, Quinta das Marvalhas, Quinta da Urze, Quinta Calábria RIBATEJO Quinta Vale de Lobos

side-dish, bread soaked in water and olive oil, with garlic and perhaps meat, maybe offal, and vegetables; it may be a thick mush, or presented as fried crumbs (*migas* literally means 'crumbs') or fried like an omelette. The distinction between *migas* and *açorda* sometimes blurs. Bread also appears in *ensopados* – stews containing fried or toasted bread. All kinds of nibbles contain bread, from cod balls to prawn rissoles *(rissois de camarão)*. There are bread-crusted pies *(folares* or *bolas)*, savoury and sweet, sold like sandwiches for outdoor eating. And on festival days, sardines and other street food are likely to come on a bread 'plate'.

Whatever the day, from spring to autumn all around the coasts, the smell of grilling sardines will never be far away – and that includes Lisbon and Porto. On bread they are finger food, on a plate they often come with roasted red peppers and boiled potatoes. The small ones are most appreciated. (There's a chauvinistic Portuguese saying about women and sardines – it boils down to 'the thinner the better'.) Tuna, however, have disappeared from Algarve waters, no longer spawning in the Mediterranean. Why? Tuna mature sexually only after having put on a large number of kilos, which takes several years. Over time, all the large, mature and profitable fish were caught, no eggs were laid, no new tuna were spawned. Tuna is still popular in the Algarve, now brought in mostly from Madeira, where tuna steaks *(bifes de atum)* are on every menu. In traditional restaurants, tuna tends to be cut

thin and cooked until grey and solid – ask for it *'muito mal passado'* and mime a quick flip in the pan if you like it rare.

BELOVED BACALHAU

It was traditional to dry octopus as well as cod for the long sea voyages, and for consumption inland, and the taste has stuck, especially in remoter inland areas. But dried salt cod *(bacalhau)* has stuck most firmly. Salt cod is on the menu by the sea as well as inland, delicately presented in modern restaurants upon its bed of wilted spinach, chunkily prepared in countless well-loved ways in local restaurants everywhere. Once cheap, it is now expensive, and eaten at home for special occasions. The Portuguese did a deal to fish for cod in English waters in 1353, and moved on in the early 16th century to the *'Terra dos Bacalhaus'* (Newfoundland). With cod fishing now banned there, the fish is sourced nowadays ready-salted in Norway, Iceland and Denmark, and brought to Portugal for drying. Once upon a time *bacalhau* was home-made. Twenty years ago, from March to September, you could still see cod drying commercially on racks or hurdles all down the Portuguese coast. Nowadays almost all drying is done in controlled factory conditions indoors. The most prized and the most expensive is still the *bacalhau de cura amarela*, dried in the traditional way in the open air, mainly around the city of Aveiro.

Bacalhau has a slightly chewy aspect and a dangerous, gamey taste that some foreigners find difficult to acquire. The Portuguese love nothing better than a big fat chunk of *bacalhau*. First encounters are easier with dishes in which it is flaked, sauced and mitigated by other ingredients. If you buy some to cook yourself, you may want to wrap it well, as its powerful aroma easily migrates to other food! Rinse it and soak it in frequent changes of cold water for 12 to 14 hours depending on the thickness – it should still be somewhat salty at the end. You may then want to scale and bone it, but without the skin it flakes apart. Once soaked, it cooks more or less like fresh fish.

The choice of fish is huge – main ones are listed on *page 436* – but for us the stars are red mullet *(salmonete)*, monkfish *(tamboril)*, sea bass *(robalo* – which may be farmed but still good), skate *(raia)*, wreckfish *(cherne)*, sea bream *(pargo)*, 'Dover' sole *(linguado)*, and, on the mainland, scabbard fish *(peixe espada)* – not the bland fish of the same name in Madeira. Swordfish *(espadarte)* can be good though dry if overcooked. Fish stew or *caldeirada* can be delicious – containing a mixture of fish and shellfish, onions, garlic, tomatoes, peppers, potatoes and possibly bread, wine and maybe *piri-piri*. The name comes from *caldo* meaning broth or stock.

The *cataplana* is also a mixed seafood dish, this time shellfish, usually with *chouriço*, onions, potatoes and other vegetables; *cataplana* is also the name of the almost clam-shaped cooking vessel, traditionally copper, with two halves that form a vacuum and steam the contents. Everywhere on Portugal's coasts there's a glorious choice of seafood. Amongst the clams, the one we like best is the *conquilha*; other more common species of clam *(ameijoa)* are also delicious, as is the cockle *(berbigão)*. Clams often come cooked *à Bulhão Pato*, steamed with garlic, olive oil and white wine, liberally sprinkled with chopped coriander leaves.

Most expensive of the crustaceans are the lobsters: the *lavagante* is the common European lobster, with claws, the *lagosta* the clawless spiny lobster – both delicious. There are lovely, expensive prawns *(gambas)* of various sizes and species. The common crab, with the familiar large claws, is

a *sapateira*; the *santola* is a spider crab, a bit rare nowadays in Portuguese waters – you may unwittingly devour a Cornish import. Weirdest of the crustaceans are the goose-necked barnacles *(perceves)*, like scaly fingers ending in a 'hoof', broken off their rocks. Though edible raw, they are best when cooked – peel off the skin and bite the lovely sweet, sea-tasting flesh. There are also wonderful little cuttlefish *(choquinhos)*, and well as the larger *chocos*, squid *(lulas)* and octopus *(polvo)*.

Meaty highlights begin with roasts of baby animals – kids, veal, young lambs, and often most delicious of all, the suckling pigs, no more than a month old, fed only on their mothers' milk. Bairrada in the Beiras is the place to find specialist restaurants, but *leitão* is to be found all over Portugal, the best having thin, very crispy skin, with meltingly tender flesh underneath. The other really flavourful pork meat to seek out is the *porco preto* – black pig – from the Alentejo, a

lean, long animal left to roam the cork oak groves, its food including the nourishing acorns; and the *bísaro*, a black and pink mottled pig with floppy ears, slow-growing and flavourful, mainly from Trás-os-Montes in the north-east. Nearly half of the meat eaten in Portugal is pork.

Offal is a favourite all over the country. Do try tongues (*línguas*) – truly one of the great meats – and gooey, delicious pigs' trotters (*pèzinhos* or *pés de porco*) and calves' feet (*mãozinhas* or *pés de vitela*). Ears are a bit crunchy, and snouts, brains and tripe? Anything with *cabidela* in the name includes blood. And to get it all over in one paragraph, snails are a delicacy here, too – *caracóis*, often served in a broth flavoured with garlic, bay and oregano.

The Portuguese eat a lot of chicken, from succulent young roast chickens with hot *piri-piri* sauce on the Algarve beaches to flavoursome stews of free range mountain hens; also ducks, often served in rice as *arroz de pato*. In season, game includes wild boar, hare, and pheasant, partridge and quail. Most Portuguese like their meat well cooked, and little birds in traditional restaurants may disappoint if you like them pink. The same goes for beef steaks, which tend to be thin-cut, and well cooked except in modern restaurants. There are a lot of one-pot dishes (*pratos completos*). The winter dish *cozido à portuguesa*, boiled meat and veg, is likely to include chicken, pigs' trotters or ears, pork, black pudding, sausages, beef, potatoes and rice, cabbage, chickpeas, carrots and turnips.

Which brings us to vegetables. It's hard here to eat your greens – unless you do what the locals do, and eat soup.

SAUSAGES AND HAM – ENCHIDOS AND PRESUNTO

Alheira Light-coloured, garlicky, bready sausage, served hot. A 16th century invention of 'undercover' Jews who had been forced to convert ostensibly to Christianity; it looked like pork but was made of game and poultry – but now occasionally contains some pork.

Chouriço Dry-cured, smoked sausages made from pork, pork fat, red-pepper paste, wine, garlic and herbs. Eat it sliced, raw, as a nibble before a meal, or to add flavour to cooked dishes.

Farinheira Meatless, light-coloured sausage made from pork fat bound with flour and flavoured with spices, wine and garlic.

Fiambre Boiled or roast ham.

Linguiça a thinner version of *chouriço*, often used in soups or stews.

Morcela Black pudding, blood sausage. Also known as **chouriço mouro**, or **chouriço de sangue**.

Presunto Dry-cured smoked hams, of varying origins, qualities and prices. They are served thinly sliced, usually as a pre-meal nibble, best at room temperature. The finest are made from two breeds of pig: the *porco preto* (black pig) of the Alentejo, the *bolota* quality *(page 342)* being especially rich and delicious; and from the Bísaro pig of the upper Douro Valley and Trás-os-Montes *(page 69)*. Occasionally made from *javalí*, wild boar. Elsewhere in Portugal, cheaper *presunto* is likely to be made from ordinary pigs. *Presunto serrano* simply means that the pig was raised in the mountains. *Pata negra* (black foot) is not an official term, often used for *porco preto* but also for another, less interesting beast. (For a *presunto* map of Portugal, *see www.idrha.min-agricultura.pt/produtos_tradicionais/presuntos/ index.htm*.)

Salpicão Small smoked sausage, like a thick but lean *chouriço*, made from pork tenderloin marinated in white wine, garlic and paprika. Also known as **Paio**.

At home in Portugal, meals are likely to start with a vegetable soup. Signature soup of the north is *caldo verde*, cabbage, onions, potato and *chouriço*. Sometimes there may be a tiny, mixed, undressed salad – dress it yourself with the olive oil and vinegar you'll find on the table. If there is a vegetable on the side in a traditional restaurant, it's likely to be cabbage, carrots or green beans, the latter sometimes battered and deep fried and euphemistically called 'little fish from the garden' *(peixinhos da horta)*. Just about everything contains onions and garlic, sweet peppers abound, and carrots and turnips turn up in stews and braises. Turnip tops *(nabiças)* are a worthy delicacy, as are the the flowers of cabbage plants *(grelos)*, and Algarve sweet potatoes are delicious. Dried pulses are a vital part

of the diet – chickpeas, broad beans, butter beans and haricot beans appear in soups and bean-based stews *(feijoadas)*. Herbs are less used than you might expect – bay leaves and parsley are common, oregano and mint used a little, and coriander *(coentros)* is very widely sprinkled upon fish, seafood and other dishes in the Alentejo and Algarve. Vegetables may pop up unexpectedly, however, in jams – carrot or tomato jam, for instance, or scrumptious pumpkin jam, flavoured with cinnamon.

Fruit and nuts are the obvious substitute if you are missing vegetables. There are wonderful almonds and walnuts, fresh, ripe figs, oranges, cherries, apricots, plums, peaches, quinces and of course grapes.

Sweet-toothed visitors will have landed amongst friends. The Portuguese have developed a dangerously tempting range of sweets, cakes and puddings over the years, egged on initially by the Moors. Later inventions were based on egg yolks left over after fining wines with the whites (uncommon nowadays), and after the wimples and habits of nuns had been stiffly starched with a mix of egg whites and flour. Some of the sweets and cakes were invented in convents, confections of egg yolks, ground almonds, sugar, honey, cinnamon, sometimes lemon or pine nuts. Hence heretical-sounding names such as angels' tummies *(papos d'anjo)*, heavenly lard *(toucinho-do-ceu)* or nuns' bellies *(barrigas de freira)*. The little ex-convent egg sweets are known as *doces conventuais*. You will probably meet 'egg ribbons' *(fios de ovos)* as a garnish or filling for puddings, cakes and sweets, made by pouring a thin stream of egg into hot sugar syrup.

Portuguese cheeses are mostly ewe *(ovelha)* and goat *(cabra)* or a mix of the two. There are cow's milk cheeses *(vaca)* as well as sheep and goat in the north, and especially from the lush pastures of the Azores. Cheesemaking is mostly a cottage industry, and country people still make soft, white, fresh cheese *(queijo fresco)* at home, to eat as a pre-meal nibble, or for breakfast. Some of the best cheeses are out of season in the summer months. You will meet cheese at breakfast, fresh as well as ripened *(curado)*, and cheese will generally appear as a pre-meal nibble on traditional restaurant tables, sliced or cubed. The cheeses listed here all have official, protected and highly regulated DOP status, but there are other interesting cheeses to explore.

Queijo da Serra da Estrela (BEIRAS) This is Portugal's star cheese – so we've put it first and, exceptionally, out of alphabetical order. The pale, gloopy paste inside the soft, smooth, yellow rind has an irresistible, buttery-lactic flavour. Queijo da Serra is a mountain sheep's cheese, in season from December to April, and made with the milk of particular breeds of sheep, curdled with thistle extract rather than animal rennet. It is usually eaten after four to six weeks' ripening, spooned out through the sliced-off lid

– our children call it 'lid cheese'. Serra Velho, aged for five months or more, is firmer and stronger in flavour, and more expensive. Some distinctly lesser cheeses are sold as 'Tipo Serra', while some are naughtily passed off as the 'real thing'. These can be very boring, so beware.

Amarelo da Beira Baixa (BEIRAS) Semi-soft cheese similar to Castelo Branco *(below)* but from a wider surrounding area, made of ewe's milk alone, or mixed with goat, and curdled with animal rennet. The matured Velho is darker, stronger, firmer.

Azeitão (TERRAS DO SADO) A fine ewe's milk cheese, based on Queijo da Serra, made for nearly 200 years in the Arrábida hills of the Setúbal Peninsula.

Beira Baixa (Queijos da) (BEIRAS) Global DOP covering three cheeses with their own sub-DOPs in the south-east of the Beiras: Queijo de Castelo Branco, Queijo Amarelo da Beira Baixa and Queijo Picante da Beira Baixa.

Cabra Transmontano (TRÁS-OS-MONTES AND DOURO) Hard goat's cheese made with animal rennet.

Castelo Branco (BEIRAS) Serra-like ewe's milk cheese from Castelo Branco in south-east Beiras, semi-soft, whitish-yellow and smooth. The 90-day-matured Velho version is darker and stronger flavoured. Thistle-curdled.

Évora (ALENTEJO) Historic little pale yellow cheeses from a large area of central Alentejo. They are salty, semi-hard and crumbly, made from ewe's milk occasionally mixed with goat. Harder, mature, stronger versions are aged for up to a year. Curdled with thistle extract.

Mestiço de Tolosa (ALENTEJO) A small, semi-soft cured cheese from sheep and goats in the northern Alentejo; same areas as Nisa. It is thistle-curdled, its yellowy-orange paste sometimes unctuous, and pleasantly sharp. The rind is wrinkled because rather than being made with salty curd, it is salted from the outside.

Nisa (ALENTEJO) Whitish-yellow, cured, semi-hard pure sheep's cheese from the northern Alentejo, from a

Far left Queijo da Serra da Estrela is lusciously gooey when young

Right There's a wealth of delicious fresh goat and ewe's cheese

Far right The producers!

DOP AND IGP

Denominação de Origem Protegida (DOP) is the food equivalent of DOC for wines, an appellation of origin with strict quality, production and geographical requirements, intended to guarantee quality to the consumer as well as to protect fine products from look-alikes made by dubious interlopers from elsewhere.

Indicação Geográfica Protegida (IGP) is like Vinho Regional, a broader appellation with less stringent rules. Both categories cover select cheeses, meat, charcuterie, fruit, olives, olive oil, chestnuts, honey, pine nuts, *marmelada*… around 90 different food products are currently certified.

large area surrounding Nisa and Portalegre. Thistle-curdled.

Picante da Beira Baixa (BEIRAS) From the same large demarcated area around Castelo Branco as the Queijo Amarelo (opposite), a smooth, hard or semi-hard cheese, sharply salty, with a wrinkly, greyish rind. Made with goat's or ewe's milk, it can be powerful when aged.

Pico (AZORES) A historic cured cow's milk cheese from the Island of Pico. Rounded and shallow, with a soft, pale paste, creamy and piquant.

Rabaçal (BEIRAS) Small but chubby squashed white balls of cheese from south of Coimbra, gentle and semi-hard; or ripened, firm and stronger flavoured. Legally, it has to be 20-25% goat, 75-80% ewe.

Saloio A mild, firm cheese made in the south of the Lisboa VR area, formerly only from ewe's milk, but now more often from a mix of sheep, goat and cow. Small and cylindrical, it's fresh and white and often cubed or sliced as a pre-prandial nibble. *Saloio* means 'country bumpkin'.

São Jorge (AZORES) Made from cow's milk from the island of the same name, in big truckles. Firm, pale yellow, like a soft Cheddar, and indeed introduced long ago by the English.

Serpa (ALENTEJO) Excellent, mild, Serra-type cheese from the southern third of the Alentejo, lusciously buttery. Ewe's milk only, and curdled with thistle extract. Serpa Velho with extra ageing is very strong and hard. They can be small or quite large.

Terrincho (TRÁS-OS-MONTES AND DOURO) Squat, paprika-coated, firm, pale yellow cheese made from ewe's milk in Trás-os-Montes. Smooth and rich.

Ricotta – *Requeijão* Not strictly a cheese, soft, fresh, white *requeijão* is made from the whey of ewe's milk, heated until the proteins coagulate. There are DOP versions: Requeijão da Serra da Estrela and Requeijão da Beira Baixa. It is delicious eaten for breakfast, topped with sugar and cinnamon; on bread with quince paste *(marmelada)*, pumpkin jam *(doce de abóbora)* or honey; as a dessert with caramelised pumpkin, or pumpkin jam; or it might come in restaurants as a pre-meal nibble, to spread on bread. It is also used a lot in cheesecakes and cheese tarts *(queijadas)*.

ON THE CHEESE MAP

See individual regional chapters for further details, and for a cheese map of Portugal, *see www.idrha.minagricultura.pt/ produtos_tradicionais/queijos/index.htm.*

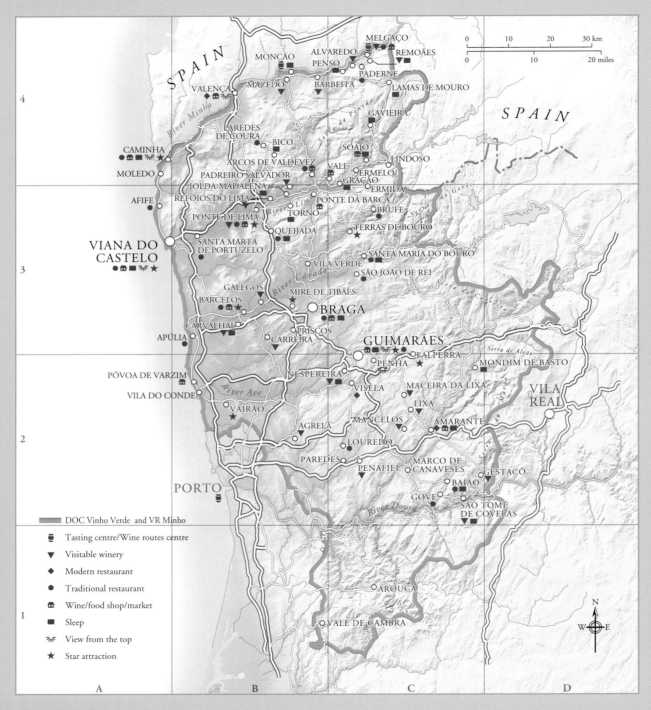

SPAIN

SPAIN

MELGAÇO
ALVAREDO   REMOÃES
MONÇÃO   PENSO
PADERNE
VALENÇA   MAZEDO   BARBEITA
LAMAS DE MOURO
GAVIEIRA
PAREDES
DE COURA   BICO
SOAJO
CAMINHA   ARCOS DE VALDEVEZ   LINDOSO
MOLEDO   PADREIRO SALVADOR   VALE
ERMELO
JOLDA-MADALENA   GRAÇÃO   ERMIDA
AFIFE   REFÓIOS DO LIMA   PONTE DA BARCA
BRUFE
PONTE DE LIMA   TORNO
QUEIJADA   TERRAS DE BOURO
VIANA DO   SANTA MARTA
CASTELO   DE PORTUZELO   SANTA MARIA DO BOURO
VILA VERDE
SÃO JOÃO DE REI
GALEGOS   MIRE DE TIBÃES
BARCELOS
BRAGA
CARVALHAL   PRISCOS
APÚLIA   CARREIRA   GUIMARÃES
FALPERRA   MONDIM DE BASTO
PENHA
PÓVOA DE VARZIM   NESPEREIRA   MACEIRA DA LIXA   VILA
VISELA   REAL
VILA DO CONDE   LIXA
VAIRÃO   MANCELOS   AMARANTE
AGRELA
LOUREDO   MARCO DE
PAREDES   CANAVESES   GESTAÇO
PENAFIEL   BAIÃO
PORTO   GOVE   SÃO TOMÉ
DE COVELAS

AROUCA

VALE DE CAMBRA

0   10   20   30 km
0   10   20 miles

River Minho
Serra da Peneda
Serra do Gerês
River Lima
River Cávado
Serra da Cabreira
Serra de Alvão
River Ave
Serra do Marão
River Douro

N
W   E
S

DOC Vinho Verde and VR Minho

Tasting centre/Wine routes centre

Visitable winery

Modern restaurant

Traditional restaurant

Wine/food shop/market

Sleep

View from the top

Star attraction

Vinho Verde and Minho

Cool and moist, green and fertile except for its mountain uplands, the land of Vinho Verde is densely populated and intensively forested and farmed. Smallholders – of which there are many – still sometimes train their vines in high canopies around and over crops of maize, wheat and long-stalked cabbages. But modern vineyards are trained in rows, and the grapes ripen all the better for it.

The VR Minho region has exactly the same outer boundaries as DOC Vinho Verde, and this is the area covered in this chapter. Once upon a time, the northern part was a province called the Minho, the southern part the Douro Litoral. Nowadays the administrative areas are Viana do Castelo, Braga and Porto, and the wine area of this chapter also dips into a chunk of the Aveiro district, which administratively is in the Beiras. Confused? Relax, take a soothing sip of Vinho Verde, and trust the map.

If you plotted the actual distribution of Vinho Verde vineyards, the result would look not dissimilar to the darker green, lower-lying areas on the map opposite, the coastal strip excepted. Vines follow the nearly parallel river valleys that slice through from the eastern mountains to the sea, including the valley of the Minho, which forms the border with Spain in the north. The rivers are fish-filled, popular with anglers and canoeists. Walkers can head for the hills all the way down the eastern border, where mountain ranges divide this rainier coastal area from the hotter, drier interior. The Parque Natural do Alvão has spectacular waterfalls and thatched stone houses. In the north-east swathe of the Parque Nacional da Peneda-Gerês, there are wooded valleys, meadows and craggy upland moors. Maps may prove harder to track down than the wolves and eagles.

The mountain population is declining rapidly, but in other rural areas of the VR Minho, the farming and hard-working populace is much better off than pre-EU, and better connected now that motorways span the region. Religion still flourishes, as do costumed folk festivals, which erupt at regular intervals, especially in summer. The occasional ox cart still holds up traffic. But there is wealth here too, past and present: maritime trade with the New World-funded palaces, white-painted, granite-framed manor houses (often nowadays with rooms to rent), and the church brought riches of its own. Braga was the seat of Portugal's bishops for seven centuries, Guimarães the medieval capital of Portugal.

Vinho Verde and VR Minho

Vinho Verde can be one of the world's most delightful aperitifs, crisp, aromatic, with the lightest imaginable prickle of fizz, and sometimes a hint of sweetness. It can also be one of the few wines in the world to match really successfully with oily fish such as grilled herrings, mackerel or sardines, and it's a perfect partner for a high-acid dish such as ceviche: fish marinated in citrus juice with onions. It can be dry and creamy, and totally free of fizz, perhaps rounded by a short stay in oak barrels – a good wine to serve with lightly sauced fish and seafood dishes. Or it can be mouth-filling, with a steely backbone of minerality, a complex yet understated aromatic white wine. And that's not the end of the range. There's rosé Vinho Verde and sparkling Vinho Verde Espumante, introduced in 1999, and there's red Vinho Verde.

It could be seen as an advantage that Vinho Verde is so diverse, but most people don't realise this diversity exists. The popular image of Vinho Verde is of an inexpensive, sweetish, slightly fizzy white wine, packaged in a Mateus Rosé-shaped flagon or a tall, slim green bottle. The very name, Vinho Verde ('green wine', referring to wine's youth, not its colour), is not helpful, as it's the only name among Portuguese wine regions with no geographic association.

Everyone in Portugal knows where the Vinho Verde region is, in the north-western corner. But even the Portuguese might be uncertain what to expect from each of the nine sub-regions, sometimes named after the river that runs through them, sometimes after the principal city. Starting in the north, inland Monção is, famous for its Alvarinhos; then come Lima, Cávado and Ave, where the floral Loureiro rules; Bastos, where vineyards start to climb into the Serra de Alvão; Sousa, densely populated, with some of the most modern viticulture in the region; Amarante, close to the Serra de Marão and famous for its reds; Baião, furthest to the south-east, and straddling the Douro river; and Paiva, south of the Douro river, best-known for its reds.

Different grapes provide diversity as well. Alvarinho is one of the country's best white grapes, and it is beginning to find successful locations outside the northern sub-region of Monção.

> **Wine regions**
> DOC Vinho Verde
> Vinho Regional Minho
> **Main local grapes**
> *Red* Vinhão, Espadeiro, Borraçal
> *White* Loureiro, Azal Branco, Arinto, Trajadura, Alvarinho
> *For details of grapes see page 428.*

Above A decorative take on the old *ramada* system of vine trellising, shading the driveway to a modern wine estate

Right Vinho Verde comes in more styles and colours than you might expect

The delightfully floral Loureiro is now the most widely-planted grape in the entire region. It's a great improvement on Azal Branco, a grape that needs warm weather to ripen fully, but is rarely more than crisp and neutral. Trajadura is often a companion grape to Alvarinho, providing more aroma and steely backbone in a blend. The mineral Arinto (or Pedernã, as it's known here) is better in warmer areas. Avesso is a grape with great potential, creamy and mineral, at home in Baião, and particularly good for sparkling Vinhos Verdes.

Fully sparkling wines are a welcome addition to the Vinho Verde list, and vary from perfectly pleasant, slightly neutral fizz to wines of real quality and personality. Most *rosado* Vinho Verde samples we have tasted have been unimpressive. And red Vinho Verde is, with few exceptions, an acquired taste.

Until the latter part of last century, more red Vinho Verde was made than white. Then the proportions changed in the 1970s. Red Vinho Verde is dark coloured, with high acid and low alcohol. Acid is high because Vinhão, the main

red variety in the region, ripens very late. So why plant it? Because it is one of the rare red wine grapes that has red flesh (and so red juice), and this gives more colour to the wine. (For the same reason, it is increasingly planted in the Douro region, where it is called Sousão.)

Red Vinho Verde is very popular in Northern Portugal, but struggles to sell anywhere else. Yet 40% of the wine produced in the region is still red. And small producers have recently been planting more red grapes than white, because of the demand from traditional restaurants in the region. Do try it! It really is brilliant with sardines.

The improvements over the last two decades have mostly been in the vineyards. In our first book 20 years ago, it was still appropriate to illustrate the Vinho Verde section with pictures of people up ladders picking grapes from vines trained up trees or on high trellises. There are still quite a lot of vines bordering cereal plots, particularly in the north, but professional grape growers have replanted and restructured their vineyards.

As in many other Portuguese regions, some of the best producers choose not to submit to DOC rules, but to take the VR path, with its greater flexibility. They may be small in number, but some of our favourite wines from this part of Portugal are made as VR Minho. This allows them to use other grape varieties, and make the wine they think will best express the potential of their vineyards.

Left and right Many smallholders still train their vines up trees, or around their fields or vegetable plots, but wine estates now plant in modern rows. The result is much riper grapes.

AGRELA B2

Vercoope This is a super-co-op, an agglomeration of seven other co-ops to take advantage of economies of scale in vinification, blending, marketing and distribution. It was founded in 1964, in the decade after most Portuguese co-ops were set up. Seven Vinho Verde co-ops (Amarante, Braga, Guimarães, Famalicão, Felgueiras, Paredes and Vale de Cambra) contribute wine to Vercoope. If all the members of the associated co-ops are taken into account, about 5,000 growers contribute grapes to the wines Vercoope sells. As well as helping to market and distribute the brands made at these co-ops, Vercoope has its own brands, Pavão and Via Latina. The top wines are sold under the Via Latina label. The **Via Latina Loureiro** is a bright, fresh, aromatic wine, with quite a prickle of fizz and lively acidity. It's off-dry, but well-balanced. **Vial Latina Alvarinho**, from the Monção sub-region, is aromatic, with hints of lemon and apricot, and some minerality.

Rua 25 de Abril 691, Agrela,
*   4825-010 Santo Tirso*
T+351 229 698 180
E uniao.adegas@vercoope.pt
W www.vercoope.pt
Visits phone to arrange

ALVAREDO C4

Quinta de Soalheiro The further from the Atlantic, the warmer and drier the weather becomes. So this estate, almost

50km from the sea and 5km west of Melgaço, is distinctly warmer and drier than the vineyards round Monção. It's owned by António Cerdeira,

who qualified as a winemaker at Vila Real University, then worked in Burgundy for a while. He is passionate about the 10ha of vineyards he controls (6ha belong to him, the rest are leased), and works hard to grow the best grapes he can. He started the business in 1982, when, as he says, there were only four different brands of Alvarinho. He now counts himself among 'the biggest of the small producers'.

Cerdeira is a believer in wines that can be kept. So he harvests his grapes relatively early, certainly before the likely rains of the equinox, and aims for 12.5% alcohol, maximum 13%. He makes only one wine, and on the evidence of the wines he showed us, it's probably worth keeping it for at least a year after you buy. Not that you can't drink it earlier! **Alvarinho Soalheiro** is lean and mineral at the outset, with youthful intensity, then develops to citrussy, eventually toasty flavours.

Visitors are welcome to see the cellar, and taste the latest release, free of charge.
Alvaredo, 4960-010 Melgaço
T+351 251 416 769
E quinta@soalheiro.com
W www.soalheiro.com
Visits Mon-Fri 10-7

Quintas de Melgaço This was started in 1990 by a local businessman, Amadeu Abílio Lopes, to provide a winery to process local growers' grapes. Six years later, having got the company up and vinifying on behalf of numerous grower-shareholders with small shareholdings,

Lopes decided to bow out, handing over his majority shareholding to the town of Melgaço. So, with 430 shareholders today, it is effectively a Melgaço co-op in nature, if not name. There have been ups and downs in its fortunes, but today Quintas de Melgaço is making good wines, and has recently entered into a promotional partnership with Pousadas de Portugal, which could do sales a lot of good (as long as the promoting doesn't cost too much!).

They are happy to receive visitors, if possible with previous notice, and can sometimes manage an appointment at weekends by prior arrangement. You will see their winery and taste some wines, and the cost will depend on what you taste.

Their **Torre de Menagem** is almost all Alvarinho, with a dash of Trajadura, crisp, aromatic and ripe-fruited. The real star is the **QM Alvarinho Reserva Bruto Natural**, a terrific, completely dry sparkling wine made from Alvarinho. It's rich and toasty, with real Alvarinho aromas – fascinatingly different!

Ferreiros de Cima, Alvaredo,
*   4960-010 Melgaço*
T+351 251 410 020
E quintasdemelgaco.info@sapo.pt
Visits Mon-Fri 9-12.30, 2-6.30
*   appt preferred € variable*

BARBEITA B4

PROVAM (Produtores de Vinhos Alvarinhos de Monção) This is a highly quality-conscious mini-co-op, just to the east of Monção. It was started in 1992 by ten growers who wanted to get better prices for their grapes than the Monção co-op was offering, and decided to pool their resources to invest in a really up-to-date winery. 15 years on, their company is one of the best producers of Alvarinho, helped by the advice of the

VINHO VERDE TASTING CENTRES

Two new tasting centres are planned in Vinho Verde country for the near future, one in the historic centre of AMARANTE, overlooking the Church and the Hotel Casa da Calçada, the other in the centre of MARCO DE CANAVESES. The following three centres are already in action:

Rota dos Vinhos Verdes The multi-lingual Vinho Verde Wine Routes office in Miragaia, Porto, is in a 19th house on a slope overlooking the Douro, near the Port Wine Institute and the Solar do Vinho do Porto *(see Porto chapter page 120)*. You will be offered two or three wines to taste on a balcony overlooking the river. They can organise self-drive tours incorporating visits to wineries and other points of interest, and will book or suggest restaurants and hotels or bed and breakfast in the region. You can choose from 67 wineries, from small producers to large estates to co-ops. They have also developed a tutor-supported 'e-course' in English called Knowing Vinho Verde – Level I, which includes tasting suggestions. *Rua da Restauração 318, 4050-501 Porto T+351 226 077 300 E rota@vinhoverde.pt W www.vinhoverde.pt Open Mon-Fri 9-5.30 Sat 9-1 Closed Sun, public hols*

MELGAÇO **Solar do Alvarinho** Within the lovely, arched council building in the historic centre of Melgaço, the Alvarinho tasting centre offers free tastings, as well as selling local Alvarinho wines, hams and charcuterie, corn bread *(broa)* and crafts. They will direct you to producers if you want to visit. *Rua Direita-Vila T+351 251 410 195 Open Sun-Thu 10-8, Fri & Sat 10-2*

MONÇÃO **Paço do Alvarinho** Tasting room and information centre. *Casa do Curro, Praça Deu-la-Deu Open every day 9.30-12.30, 2.30-6*

ever-thoughtful winemaking consultant Anselmo Mendes. As the company has grown, they have had to seek more grapes than they themselves can produce, and 70% of the grapes they process they now buy from local growers.

Everything they do is carefully considered for its impact on raising

quality. Alvarinho grapes have very aromatic skins, and more of these aromas can be extracted into the juice if the skins are allowed to macerate in the juice for a limited time before pressing – a delicate operation, as harsh, undesirable skin components might also be extracted. PROVAM macerate only grapes picked in the morning, when temperatures are low, and the grapes lose fewer aromas through respiration. After pressing, the juice is left for two days to settle before a long, slow, low-temperature fermentation. CO_2 is used when pumping wine from one vat to another, to avoid contact with the air. The wines are left on their lees for four months after fermentation, with *bâtonnage* (stirring once a week to help release extra

flavour from the lees). Most wines are steel-fermented, but one is fermented in oak.

There are two sparkling Vinhos Verdes. **Castas de Monção Espumante** has 30% of the less aromatic Trajadura in the blend; it is pleasant, with a hint of fragrance and a lively mousse. **Côto de Mamoelas Espumante** is pure Alvarinho, with a good sparkle, lovely, honeyed, toasty flavour and a hint of minerality. The still range starts with **Varanda do Conde**, a Vinho Verde made from half and half Alvarinho and Trajadura, lean and citrussy, with highish acidity. **Alvarinho Portal do Fidalgo** is the main brand, lean, mineral and citrussy, very fine and elegant. The oak-fermented **Alvarinho Vinha Antiga** has slightly more exotic aromas, but is not at all overtly oaky, more subtle and long, with a lovely balance between bready lees flavours and fruit.
Cabo, Barbeita, 4950-045 Monção T+351 251 534 207 E comercial@provam.com W www.provam.com Visits Mon-Fri 9-12, 2-6 appt only, 1 week's notice Closed Sep

CARREIRA B3

Quinta de Santa Maria If you're interested in roses, camelias, fruit trees or other trees, this is the wine visit for you. As well as vineyards and wines, Quinta de Santa Maria has a nursery that sells plants. There are in fact two estates under the same ownership, Quinta de Santa Maria (21ha) and Quinta do Tamariz (14ha). Lúcia Borges married into the Vinagre family, and was given Quinta de Santa Maria by her father in 1926. Quinta do Tamariz was bought a few years later, in 1939. The company is now run by Lúcia's grandson, António Vinagre. The predominant grape in the vineyards

is Loureiro, very much at home in the Cávado sub-region. What is less usual is Alvarinho. There's also Arinto, a little Trajadura, and various red grapes, including Touriga Nacional. Our favourite wines are the **Quinta de Santa Maria Alvarinho Loureiro**, a VR Minho, floral, fragrant, lemony and full-bodied, and the **Quinta do Tamariz Loureiro**, a Vinho Verde with classic Loureiro floral perfume and good, citrussy acidity.

You will be welcome to visit the cellar and estate, and have a tasting, and there is an attractive shop *(above)* where you can buy wine, brandy and vinegar. And you might stock up on Portuguese plants, too.
Rua Arquitecto Borges Vinagre 555,
  Carreira, 4775-058 Barcelos
T+351 252 960 140 / 968 582 857
E quintadesantamaria@oninet.pt /
  antonio.vinagre@sapo.pt
W www.quintadesantamaria.com
Visits Mon-Sat 8-12, 1-5
Closed public hols
€5

CARVALHAL B3

Quinta da Franqueira Piers and Kate Gallie live in a wonderful 16th century convent about 3km south-west of Barcelos. It was bought in 1965 by Piers's father, in a very dilapidated state, and is being slowly restored to its former glory. As well as planting a 6ha vineyard from 1981 to 1985, the Gallies rent beautifully furnished rooms in the convent *(page 61).*

When Piers is there, the tour will include a look at the vineyard, the 16th century font over a holy spring, and a tasting in the cloister with bread and cheese. But you have to phone ahead to book.

The vineyard is planted with Loureiro and Trajadura, and two wines are made, in a modern winery, finished in 1991. **Quinta da Franqueira Reserva** is a blended Vinho Verde, usually 70% Loureiro and 30% Trajadura, very dominated by fragrant Loureiro, crisp, fresh and appealing. **Quinta da Franqueira Rosé Reserva** is a pale, redcurranty Vinhão rosé, with a very lively acidity.
Carvalhal CC 301, 4755-104 Barcelos
T+351 253 831 606
E piers@quintadafranqueira.com
W www.quintadafranqueira.com
Visits 11-12, 3-5 appt only €5 🛏

GALEGOS (SÃO MARTINHO) B3

Quinta de Paços Along with Quinta da Boavista *(page 41),* this estate has been owned by the same family for 400 years (and 15 generations). It is in Loureiro country just east of Barcelos. There are references to the vineyards as far back as the 16th century. It's a 200ha farm, with cereals and forest as well as vineyard.

Casa de Paços Loureiro and Arinto is a Vinho Verde, two-thirds Loureiro and one-third Arinto, bright and aromatic, with a gentle, rose-petal fragrance. **Casa de Paços Arinto Reserva**, on the other hand, has opted for the VR Minho route, as half is fermented in French oak barrels (and half in stainless steel), and it's all aged in oak on the lees for six months,

with *bâtonnage*. The result is rich, tangy and creamy, but it still has the steely, mineral backbone of Arinto.
Rio Côvo Santa Eulália, 4750-484 Barcelos
T+351 253 897 109
E quintapacos@gmail.com
Visits Sat 10-12, 3-7 appt only

GESTAÇÔ C2

Quinta do Ferro This is a relatively young company, in the Baião sub-region close to the Douro. It is owned by Carlos Fonseca, who also has a shoe business. Although much of the estate is devoted to 12ha of vines, there are also 2ha of walnut trees. The vineyards are planted with Avesso and Arinto, the local hero grapes, used for both still and sparkling wines. Carlos Fonseca has invested both in replanting the vineyard and equipping the winery (particularly for sparkling wines), and the results already look good. The **Quinta do Ferro Bruto**, based on Avesso, is a good, crisp, appley Vinho Verde bubbly. The still **Quinta do Ferro Avesso** is crisp and mineral, with typical Baião region Avesso creaminess. Not yet released as we write, the **Quinta do Ferro Arinto** is fresh and flinty, with an almost Sauvignon-like aroma.
Lugar da Igreja, 4640-230 Gestaçô
T+351 254 881 975
E geral@quintadoferro.pt
W www.quintadoferro.pt
Visits appt only

LAMA
Quinta de Azevedo This is Sogrape's headquarters in Vinho Verde country, and responsible for the production of Gazela, a large Vinho Verde brand, and Quinta de Azevedo, made only from the estate's grapes. (Sogrape's other Vinho Verde, **Morgadio da Torre Alvarinho**, is a fragrant, peachy Alvarinho and has by law to be made in the Monção sub-region. It is made under Sogrape supervision, at the very good Monção co-op.)

The house at Quinta de Azevedo is a lovely building, part dating from the 11th century, and has been carefully and sensitively restored. Unfortunately, neither the house nor winery and estate are visitable under present Sogrape policy. The estate has almost 37ha of vineyard, split between the Azevedo vineyard and another estate over the road (literally), Quinta da Covilhã, which also belongs to Sogrape. Azevedo is almost entirely planted with Loureiro (with small patches of Trajadura, Arinto and Azal Branco), and Covilhã with Arinto (with a tiny amount of Loureiro). In total, there's more Loureiro than Arinto (known locally as Pederna), as is typical in this Cávado sub-region of Vinho Verde. The Azevedo winery is ultra-modern, all stainless steel, with temperature control and very gentle presses. No oak is used.

Gazela is a successful modern Vinho Verde, mainly Loureiro, fresh and bright, with lemony acidity and a hint of sweetness. It is made partly from estate grapes, partly from local growers **Quinta de Azevedo** is made entirely from estate grapes, 70% Loureiro and 30% Arinto, lively and aromatic, just off-dry, with good notes of citrus, and some minerality.

LIXA C2
Quinta da Lixa The Meireles brothers, Óscar and Alberto, have achieved a lot with this company in the past 20 years. They have other business interests, shoes, textiles and construction, but have always had vineyards as well. They started selling wine in bulk in 1986, made from vineyards they owned near the little town of Lixa, just to the south-east of Felgueiras, and soon realised they would have to bottle the wine to achieve real quality. They bought Quinta da Lixa, with 7ha of vines, and started selling bottled wine in 1988. A new winery was built ten years later, and another estate, Quinta de Sanguinedo, bought in 1999, with another 20ha of vines. They now have 42ha in total, which supplies about a third of their needs. They buy in grapes from other growers in the area. Almost all the wine they produce is white, with small amounts of rosé and red (the red only sold locally). The latest experiment is a plantation of Vinhão and Touriga Nacional, the vines only three years old at present, destined maybe to make 'a different style of red'.

They have plans to convert four houses for wine tourism, which will give 22 rooms to let. But that's not ready yet. At the moment, they are happy to receive visitors, and offer tours of the cellar and estates. The price of the tasting will depend on what you want to taste.

Even the basic **Terras do Minho** is crisp and clean, with some aromas, and just off-dry. The **Quinta da Lixa Trajadura** is a very aromatic version of this grape, with citrus and exotic fruit flavours, and dry; as is the **Quinta da Lixa Loureiro**, which has amazing aromas of lychee, grapefruit and rose-petal. The blended **Quinta da Lixa** is half and half Trajadura and Loureiro, dry again, with citrussy length and brisk acidity. They also have a rich, aromatic, peachy **QL Alvarinho** (not from the estate, but from Monção grapes), and a soft, berry-fruited, just off-dry, pink Vinho Verde, **QL Espadeiro**.
Rua Monte, 4615-658 Lixa
T+351 255 490 590
E info@quintadalixa.pt
W www.quintadalixa.pt
Visits Mon-Sat 9-12, 2-6 Sun appt only
€5-€15

MACIEIRA DA LIXA C2
Quinta de Simães As well as having 40ha of vines, Quinta de Simães is also one of the two vinification centres of Vinhos Borges. It lies a scant 5km south-east of Felgueiras, and is responsible for some of the biggest-volume brands in the Borges range, such as Gatão Vinho Verde and Fita Azul sparkling wine. But as well as being a centre for wine production, Quinta de Simães is a flagship Vinho Verde estate, the first in Portugal to use a Y-shaped system of vine training called *'lys'*,

which produces much riper grapes than before. One year, in fact, their Arinto reached 14.5%, tricky when the top alcohol level allowed in a bottled Vinho Verde is 13%!

Arinto is the backbone of Quinta de Simães, although Avesso works well, too, and they have Trajadura and Alvarinho for aromas. Most of the estate can be machine-harvested, which means grapes are picked when the winemakers want them, rather than when the personnel manager can organise 50 pickers for four weeks.

Back in the 1980s, Gatão was the best-selling Vinho Verde in the UK. It's still a well-made wine, with crisp, lemony fruit, and acidity that successfully disguises the residual sugar. **Quinta de Simães** really is the new face of Vinho Verde, a blend of Arinto, Avesso and Trajadura, clean and mineral, with fresh acidity and real elegance. The gently aromatic, mineral **Borges Alvarinho** is made for the company in Monção, by the renowned Anselmo Mendes, ex-winemaker at Borges, and still consultant. The two sparkling wines are the fresh, lemony, attractive **Fita Azul**

Reserva, and the very good, toasty, complex, mineral *Real Senhor Velha Reserva*. Borges also has an estate in Dão *(page 173)*.

You can visit the Lixa production centre, and Quinta de Simães itself. It's best to make an appointment by email or phone. The cost will depend on what you want to do.
Rua Marco de Simães, 4615-414 Macieira da Lixa
T+351 255 490 790
E turismo@vinhosborges.pt
W www.vinhosborges.pt
Visits Mon-Fri 9-5 € variable

MANCELOS C2

Quinta de SanJoanne About 12km west of Amarante, these 14ha of family-owned vineyards have been much improved since João Pedro Araujo took over a decade ago. He has slightly changed the varietal balance to favour the more aromatic grapes, introducing Loureiro and Chardonnay, and doubling the proportion of Alvarinho, whilst reducing the non-aromatic Azal Branco and Arinto. A firm believer in the virtues of blends, he makes no single variety wines. Anselmo Mendes, one of the region's best winemaking consultants, is his adviser. The family also owns Quinta da Vegia, a Dão estate *(page 175)*.

The *quinta* is really called Casa de Cello but 'Cello' had already been

registered by Sogrape, so Casa de Cello labels its wines as 'Quinta de SanJoanne'. It's a lovely estate, with forest and a lake, as well as vineyards. You must make a prior appointment to tour the winery and vineyards, with a tasting of five of the estate's wines, for €10 per person.

Casa de Cello makes both classic Vinhos Verdes and VR Minho wines, preferring, in the latter category, to offer full-bodied, higher alcohol wines, made from fully ripened grapes. There are also a couple of sparkling Vinhos Verdes. **Leira Mancas** is a blend of Avesso and Arinto, creamy but crisp. **Quinta de SanJoanne Vinho Verde** is mostly Avesso, with about a third of aromatic Loureiro, lemony-creamy, with a hint of fragrance. The sparkling Vinhos Verdes are also differentiated by variety: **Quinta de SanJoanne Vinho Verde Espumante** is a traditional blend, of Arinto and Azal, fresh, crisp and mineral, and **Quinta de SanJoanne Vinho Verde Espumante Reserve** is Chardonnay and Avesso, resulting in a creamier, more full-bodied fizz. The two VR Minho wines are modern and interesting. **Quinta de SanJoanne Escolha** is a white blend of Alvarinho fermented in old oak barrels, Avesso and Chardonnay, rich, honeyed and savoury. The new, beautifully balanced **Quinta de SanJoanne Superior** is a ripe blend of Alvarinho and Malvasia Fina.
Mancelos, 4605-118 Vila-Meã
T+ 351 226 095 877
E quinta@casadecello.pt
W www.casadecello.pt
Visits appt only €10

MAZEDO B4
Adega Cooperativa Regional de Monção OK, so we confess a weakness for Alvarinho, but this is a very good co-op, nonetheless. It has grown from the original 25 growers who founded it in

1958, to over 1,700, farming over 1,000ha, when we visited in 2006. It's not all new and gleaming – there are epoxy-lined cement vats for some of the fermentations – but most of the equipment is sparkling new stainless steel. And they're about to build a new bottling line. There is also a winery in Melgaço for grape reception and vinification, so the grapes don't have to travel that extra 30kms before being processed.

The Monção co-op belongs to the Vinho Verde Route, and they say they receive visitors for tours of cellar and vineyards. They have a good display of old wine machinery – pumps, filling machines, corkers and destalkers – in an area on the lower ground floor.

Alvarinho is what they do best, but they have other wines to offer as well. The **Adega de Monção Vinho Verde** is pleasant, crisp and florally aromatic. **Muralhas de Monção** is a blend of about half and half Alvarinho and Trajadura, fragrant, with apple and apricot aromas and freshness. They make two versions of the Alvarinho Deu La Deu, with and without oak. (Deu-la-Deu Martins was a 14th century heroine who tricked the Spanish who were besieging Monção into giving up the siege.) The **Alvarinho Deu La Deu** is wonderfully fragrant, with aromas of violets, peaches and lemons, and great length. The oaked **Alvarinho Deu La Deu Casco de Carvalho** is rich, smoky and creamy, less fragrant, with highish acidity. Their red **Adega de Monção Vinho Verde Tinto** is a bracing blend of Brancello, Pedral and Vinhão (known locally as Pedral). It's inky and high in acidity, but not under-ripe.

Cruzes, 4950-279 Mazedo
T +351 251 652 167 / 251 653 114
E adegademoncao@mail.telepac.pt
W adegademoncao.com
Visits Mon-Fri 9-12, 2-5

Quinta da Boavista Like Quinta dos Paços *(page 38)*, this estate has belonged to the Ramos family for 400 years. Quinta da Boavista has the magnificent 17th century Casa do Capitão-mor, the old house belonging to the local military governor, as well as 12.5ha of land, of which 8.5ha are vineyard. This being in the northern sub-region of Monção, the vines are Alvarinho, and responsible for one of the most highly-regarded local wines, the **Alvarinho Casa do Capitão-mor**. It has bright, tropical fruit aromas, with a palate that combines crisp acidity, minerality and soft fragrance.

Quinta da Boavista is signed up to the Vinho Verde Route, and receives visitors for tours of the vineyard and cellar, and wine tastings.
Mazedo, 4950-277 Monção
T +351 251 651 288 / 226 101 838
E quintapacos@gmail.com
Visits Sat 10-12, 3-7 appt only

MELGAÇO

Anselmo Mendes The man most closely identified with the revival of Alvarinho-based wines in the northern Minho is undoubtedly Anselmo Mendes. A consultant to several companies (including Borges and Domingos Alves de Sousa, as well as estates in the Douro, Dão, Ribatejo and Alentejo), he advises others here in the Minho, and also makes some of the best Alvarinho Vinhos Verdes on his own account. He used to make his wines in other people's wineries, but his own new winery will be in action for 2008. His crisp, aromatic **Muros Antigos Alvarinho** is a benchmark for the region (he also has very good **Muros Antigos Loureiro** and **Avesso**), and his **Muros de Melgaço Alvarinho** (in a rather curious bottle) is probably the best oak-fermented Alvarinho around. He makes wine in the

Douro and Alentejo as well, and has a 30ha estate in Dão, as he feels Dão has as yet huge, unrealised potential (we agree). Watch out for these wines, under the **'ONLY by Anselmo Mendes'** label.
Zona Industrial do Penso,
4960-310 Melgaço.
T +351 22 712 85 41
E anselmo.mendes@netcabo.pt
Visits appt only

NESPEREIRA C2

Casa de Sezim This estate about 6km south-west of Guimarães is a fully registered member of the Vinho Verde Wine Route, and a historic house, with a cellar dating back to 1396. It was given to the ancestors of the present owners in 1376. It's the kind of place sometimes used for state meetings, and has some original hand-painted early 19th century wallpapers in some of the main rooms that depict scenes of contemporary life in Portugal and other countries. And they have lovely rooms to rent *(page 62)*. You can visit the winery and have a tasting free of charge. Look at the website or ring for instructions on how to get there: it's not easy.

The 32ha vineyard has recently been replanted and retrained, with Loureiro and Arinto (locally known as Pedernã). Everything is hand-picked, and the ancient winery filled with gleaming, ultra-modern equipment. **Sezim Branco** is a fragrant Vinho Verde, a blend of Loureiro and Arinto, with marked CO_2 and a little sweetness, but well-balanced. **Casa de Sezim Grande Escolha** is totally dry, very fragrant, and will develop in bottle.
Apartado 2210, 4811-909 Guimarães
T +351 253 523 000
E geral@sezim.pt
W www.sezim.pt
Visits Mon-Sat 9-12, 2-5
Sat appt only

Afros/Casal do Paço Vasco Croft has great plans for his new winery, which should be in place by 2009 including a visitor centre. For the time being, he is happy to receive visitors by appointment. We're sure you will be received warmly. Make sure you have plenty of time! Vasco is an architect who has turned to furniture design and wine. He is passionate about his vineyard and the wines he makes. You may alternatively be received by his estate manager, Alberto Araújo, whose French is better than his English!

Casal de Paço is in the early stages of conversion to biodynamics, and Vasco intends to erect signs explaining the grape varieties in the different plots, their ages and characteristics, and the use of plants in the vineyard and infusions made from them. It should be a very informative visit for anyone interested in learning more about biodynamic viticulture. You will be shown the vines as well as the garden, orchards, and ancient trees near the house, the processes of biodynamic agriculture, and be given a tasting of the two basic Afros wines, free of charge.

Afros (from Aphrodite) is the name Vasco has given to his wines. The whites are Loureiro (the top local grape), the red, Vinhão. The **Afros Loureiro** is a high acid, aromatic Vinho Verde, with a hint of sweetness. The **Afros Escolha** is Loureiro again, this time mostly fermented in two to three-year-old French oak barrels, and

aged for six months. It's bright, lively and fragrant, with a creamy texture, and settles down to fragrant intensity with a few months in bottle. The **Afros Bruto Vinho Verde Espumante** is savoury and aromatic, with crisp acidity and creamy fizz. The real surprise for us was his red **Afros Tinto Vinhão**. This is hugely better than most red Vinhos Verdes, with intense, raspberry fruit and high acidity – and brilliant with grilled sardines.

Casal do Paço, Padreiro-Salvador,
4970-500 Arcos de Valdevez
T +351 914 206 772
E vcroft@afros-wine.com
Visits Mon-Sat 9-7 appt only

Aveleda If you'd enjoy wandering among 30ha of delightful, shady gardens, admiring early-20th century follies (including a goat-tower – every garden should have one), then a visit to Quinta da Aveleda could be just the thing for you and the family. There aren't that many Portuguese wineries that are so child-friendly. Just keep them out of the various ponds and lakes! And while the children are admiring ducks or chickens, you can take turns to nip off for a wine-tasting.

The Guedes family have owned Quinta da Aveleda since the 17th century, and have been bottling their wines for over 100 years. It was Don Manuel Pedro Guedes da Silva da Fonseca who first took the estate's vineyards in hand. He planted vineyards varietally (as opposed to the usual jumble of mixed varieties in the same block) in 1860, and his efforts were rewarded with a Gold Medal for one of the Aveleda wines at the 1889 Paris Exhibition. After this success, he went all out for export markets, starting with Brazil (not easy in the days when the only Portuguese wine anyone had heard of

outside Portugal was port). The growth was gradual to start with, but succeeding generations have continued the expansion, and Aveleda is now one of Portugal's largest exporters.

Located as it is in a very accessible part of Vinho Verde country, directly east of Porto, it's hardly surprising that most of Aveleda's production is of Vinho Verde, 13 million bottles per year, in fact, making them the largest Vinho Verde producer. And the 160ha of vineyard at Quinta da Aveleda are immaculately planted, as indeed they were when we first visited 20 years ago. This supplies about 10% of their total production, the rest is bought in as grapes. The only exceptions to this are Aveleda Alvarinho, and Charamba, a Douro red first produced in 1992. Both are made from bought-in wine.

In 1998, the three Guedes brothers who now run Aveleda (António, Luís and Roberto) bought Quinta d'Aguieira, in Bairrada, already planted with Cabernet Sauvignon and Touriga Nacional, and sold as VR Beiras. They retrained the vines in modern style on the 25ha of vineyard three years later. After experimenting with different vines and rootstocks, they decided to grow Chardonnay and Maria Gomes (aka Fernão Pires) for whites, and Touriga Nacional, Cabernet Sauvignon and Tinta Roriz (Aragonez) for reds. They planted more Touriga Nacional. Now the Aguieira grapes go into the latest Aveleda creation, the Follies range. And with the change of the Bairrada wine rules in 2003 *(page 160)*, the wines are perfectly acceptable now as Bairrada.

The Follies range appeared in 2006, the result of co-operation with an English label designer, Abigail Barlow, who was

very taken with the many whimsical buildings in the Quinta da Aveleda garden and park.

Casal Garcia is the biggest-selling Vinho Verde, crisp, off-dry and commercial. **Grinalda** is a definite step up, made only from the estate's grapes, a blend of two aromatic grapes, Loureiro and Trajadura, a bright, aromatic, floral and near-dry Vinho Verde. **Quinta da Aveleda** is just over half Loureiro, with the balance in Trajadura plus 10% Alvarinho. It's a crisp, creamy Vinho Verde, the citrus elements joined by a richer, exotic fruit character. They have a very creditable **Aveleda Alvarinho**, steely, peachy and mineral. **Charamba Tinto** is a bright, modern, raspberry-fruited Douro red. There are five wines in the Aveleda Follies range. Our favourites are the fragrant, citrussy, intense, **Aveleda Follies Alvarinho**, the peachy, balanced, appealing **Aveleda Follies Chardonnay Maria Gomes**, the explosively fruity, blackcurranty, firm-tannined **Aveleda Follies Cabernet Sauvignon Touriga Nacaional**, and the subtle, harmonious, herby **Aveleda Follies Touriga Nacional**.
Apartado 77, 4564-909 Penafiel
T+351 255 718 200
E info@aveleda.pt
W www.aveleda.pt
Visits Mon-Fri 9-12, 2-5
€2.50/€4

PONTE DE LIMA B3

Adega Cooperativa Ponte de Lima
We picked this co-op out as the best in the Vinho Verde region when we wrote our book 20 years ago. It was the quality of their pure Loureiro wine that impressed us then, and it's still good. They started in 1959 with 47 grower-members. Now they have over 2,000. Not surprisingly, they make a lot of wine, about 50,000 hectolitres a year. If that were all sold in bottle (which it isn't), it would add up to over 6.5 million. That's a lot of wine to sell! As is often the case with large companies, if you stick to their top wines, you should not be disappointed. The elegant **Vinho Verde Loureiro Colheita Seleccionada** is citrussy, with lean acidity. The **Vinho Verde Espumante Loureiro Colheita Seleccionada** fizz is the other one to look out for, with intensity and fragrance, and some sweetness.
Rua Conde de Bertiandos,
*   4990-078 Ponte de Lima*
T+351 258 909 700/2
E secretariado@adegapontelima.pt
Visits phone to arrange

REFÓIOS DO LIMA B3

Quinta do Ameal Pedro Araújo is a meticulous winemaker. He crops his vines at about 6 tonnes to the hectare in a region where the average yield is nearer 15 tonnes. That means he is restricting his yield per hectare of vineyard to 5,600 bottles rather than 14,000. No wonder the Quinta do Ameal wines have more flavour than many others in the region. He also farms his vines completely organically, with no herbicides, insecticides or fungicides. Whatever your views about organic versus conventional farming, there is no doubt that the organic route makes for an environment richer in insect, bird and plant life. It's also much harder work.

Quinta do Ameal sits on the north bank of the river Lima, with 800m of river-front. There's a bit of work to be done on clearing the river-bank, but it's a lovely spot, with 8ha of mixed oak, walnut and stone-pine forest running down to the river. The Lima sub-region is where the Loureiro grape is most widely planted, and Loureiro is a speciality of this estate. Pedro Araújo has devoted much time to work on how to maximise the aromatic potential of Loureiro. The answer seems to be hard work in his gently sloping vineyards, pruning shoots, trimming the vines mechanically later in the season and leaf-plucking to ensure the grapes ripen.

For a while, Quinta do Ameal has produced two wines, a pure Loureiro Vinho Verde, and a special selection Loureiro fermented in new French oak barrels. He is about to add two other wines to the line-up, a pure Arinto Vinho Verde and a sparkling Vinho Verde, which will be mainly Arinto with a touch of Loureiro. His **Quinta do Ameal Loureiro** is fragrant and pineappley, with a rich, creamy character and lovely acidity. The **Quinta do Ameal Escolha** is even better, though a bit oak-dominated when young. It's bready and rich, with good acidity and some fragrance, and develops beautifully in bottle. In fact, both the Quinta do Ameal wines age very well, to a lean, fragrant toastiness reminiscent of the best Semillons from the Hunter Valley in New South Wales!
4990–707 Refóios do Lima, Ponte do Lima
T+351 258 947 172 / 938 546 278
E quintadoameal@netcabo.pt
W www.quintadoameal.com
Visits Mon-Sat appt preferred

Quinta do Reguengo A country hotel as well as a wine producer, this 17th century manor house has its vineyards virtually overlooking the River Minho, and over to Spain on the other side. It is 2km west of Melgaço, with 10ha of very stony Alvarinho vineyards. The wine is made only from the estate's grapes. **Alvarinho Reguengo de Melgaço** is beautifully balanced, between crisp and creamy, with appealing Alvarinho aromatics and steely, mineral length.
4960-267 Paderne MLG
T+351 251 410 150
E geral@hoteldoreguengo.pt
W www.hoteldoreguengo.pt
Visits phone to arrange

SÃO TOMÉ DE COVELAS C2

Quinta de Covela You can see the south bank of the river Douro from Nuno Araújo's estate. Quinta de Covela occupies a south-facing amphitheatre overlooking

the river. The soils are a mix of the granite of the Minho and the schist of the Douro. You wouldn't expect this property to produce classic Vinho Verde, and it doesn't. There are several reasons for this, not least the kind of wines Nuno wants to make (we'll come to that later). The first, fundamental factor is geographic. This is the south-eastern sub-region of Baião, renowned for rich, creamy whites based on Vinho Verde's non-aromatic grapes, particularly Avesso. The weather is hotter and drier than it is further north and nearer the coast. Grapes ripen further than they do elsewhere in the Minho VR region.

The next reason is that this estate is farmed organically, and is in process of conversion to biodynamic farming, advised by Bordeaux consultant Daniel Noël. Why? It's not just so he can call the wines organic, Nuno explains, but to protect the place itself. He explains how he was amazed by the life on the estate when he bought it 20 years ago, families of partridge, hawks with their young, crickets, rabbits (but not too many, because of foxes), rats (but snakes as predators). Last year he added chickens. Being organic is about protecting life, not just the life of the vines.

He also decided he didn't want to produce Vinho Verde. Nor did he want to make Douro wine (he can't, anyway, being outside the boundaries). He wanted to explore the possibilities of Covela, try different grapes, and go with what worked best. And Quinta de Covela now has an entirely eclectic range, incorporating grapes such as Chardonnay, Gewurztraminer, Chenin, Semillon, Viognier and Avesso for whites, and Cabernet Franc, Cabernet Sauvignon, Merlot, Syrah and Touriga Nacional for reds. The two Portuguese grapes are always in the blends.

The results are very successful, and completely individual. All are VR Minho wines, as all incorporate non-traditional grapes. They are most easily identified by the colours of the labels. The **Covela Escolha Branco** (green label) is fresh and citrussy, with a hint of fragrance from the small proportion of Gewurztraminer in with the Avesso and Chardonnay. Wine in shorts, summer wine, Nuno calls it. **Covela Branco Seco Colheita Seleccionada**

(orange capsule and label lettering) is the oaked white, half-and-half Avesso and Chardonnay, ripe, peachy and honeyed, with a hint of toffee. The **Covela Escolha Palhete Seco** is the rosé (pink label), Touriga Nacional, Cabernet Franc and a little Merlot, dry and herby, with pleasing berry fruit. **Covela Escolha Tinto** (purple label) is the unoaked red, Touriga Nacional, Cabernet Franc, Merlot and Syrah, brightly aromatic and herby, with smooth tannins and black cherry and chocolate flavours. The **Covela Tinto Colheita Seleccionada** (red label) is Touriga Nacional, Cabernet Sauvignon and Merlot, with 12 months' ageing in French barrels, rich, elegant and restrained, with herby aromas and berry fruit flavours.

Visits and tastings are by appointment only, and you can have an explanation of organic and biodynamic farming methods, if you want. There is also a delightful house for rent *(page 63)*.
4640-211 São Tomé de Covelas
T+351 254 882 412 / 917 557 447
E covela@gmail.com
W www.covela.pt
Visits Mon-Fri 9-4 appt only €25

WATCH OUT FOR THESE WINES

Paço de Teixeró *(page 91)*
Alvarinho Quinta da Brejoeira (Palácio da Brejoeira)
Alvarinho Rebouça (Luís Euclides Fernandes Rodrigues)
Casalinho Arinto (Caves do Casalinho)
Arca Nova Rosé (Quinta das Arcas)
Almagrande Branco, VR Minho (Cavipor)
Alvarinho Quinta de Carapeços

Eat in the VR Minho region

You won't go hungry in the north west. Restaurant portions are huge; the local people eat out a lot – and we could have recommended more traditional-style restaurants than we could fit into our allotted space, though restaurants serving truly *modern* food are rare. The corn bread *(broa de milho)* is delicious. Local meat is usually excellent, and offal is a big favourite hereabouts. Down the coast there is the usual wonderful fish, but there's also fish from the region's numerous rivers, plus the highly-prized, seasonal lamprey and shad (neither of which is amongst our favourites). And the Minho has added several famous dishes, both savoury and sweet, to the national repertoire.

Most famous is probably *caldo verde* – a soup of finely-sliced cabbage with a piece of *chouriço* in a thin, puréed base of potato and onion. The cabbage should be added at the last stage of cooking, and still be green when served. *Caldo verde* appears on menus all over Portugal, but it started here, and only in the Minho is it made with the right kind of cabbage. You'll spot the *couve galega* sold loose-leaved or machine-shredded in markets, and growing

Left Sometimes you can have just too many oranges…

Right Tender young roasts have always been a speciality

Below A cluster of *espigueiros*, used to store the corn that makes the wonderful *broa de milho*

on its long stalks in vegetable patches. Vegetables come mostly in soups – another Minho speciality is *rancho à moda do Minho*, a chunky soup containing chickpeas, onions, chilli, potatoes, pasta, beef, bacon and *chouriço*. *Tomatada com batatas* (not a soup) cooks together tomatoes, sweet peppers and potatoes. Cumin and coriander seeds flavour many Minho dishes.

Wood-fired ovens are a Minho tradition, meat roasts a highlight, especially on Sundays and feast days; the meat is often very young and tender: kid *(cabrito)* sometimes goes in the Minho by the even more diminutive name *cabritinho*, and there's roast lamb, suckling pig and free-range veal.

The region has three DOP *(Denominação de Origem Protegida)* meats, two of them from rare breeds of cattle. You will see the Arouquesa cow in the south of the Vinho Verde area and over into the Beiras, brown and long-horned, renowned for succulent steaks. The Cachena is very small, pale brown with corkscrew horns; it grazes the Peneda-Gerês National Park, spending May to September on high pastures. Fine Barrosã beef also comes over the mountains from Trás-os-Montes. The third local DOP is for a breed of goat descended from the now-extinct wild goats of the Gerês mountains: on menus you might see the kid, *Cabrito das Terras Altas do Minho*, which can come from any of the mountains along the Minho's eastern 'border'. Many small-scale farmers keep free-roaming chickens and ducks, and a pig. The rare breed Bísaro pig of northern Portugal is also very special.

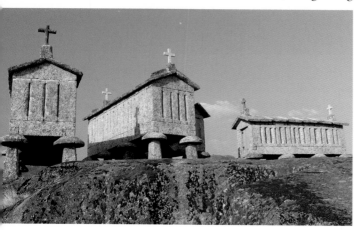

Far left Nibble some cod balls *(pasteis de bacalhau)*

Left If lamprey tickles your fancy, visit between February and April

Right and below Charcuterie *(enchidos)*, another pre-meal nibble

There is good ham *(presunto)*, not just from the regions to the east, but local, too – try the smoked hams from Melgaço. Minho *bicas* are not small cups of black coffee as in the south, but small, cumin-flavoured blood sausages bulked up with maize flour. Pigs' ears and lungs, stomachs and other bits are favourite ingredients! You will certainly meet *rojões à minhota* – chunks of usually quite fatty pork marinated and cooked in red Vinho Verde, cumin, coriander, garlic and bay, with pieces of liver, tripe, black pudding, *chouriço* and fried potatoes, sometimes chestnuts. The port of Viana do Castelo was the origin of *papas de sarrabulho*, various boiled meats, sausage and potatoes, moistly thickened with bread and pig's blood and flavoured with cumin; the mix may also include liver, kidneys, tomatoes and red Vinho Verde. *Arroz de sarrabulho* is similar, with rice replacing bread.

Viana do Castelo is one of the last places in Portugal where you can still see *bacalhau* drying in the sun. *Pastéis de bacalhau*, little deep-fried cod, onion and potato balls bound with egg, are a common nibble, and almost every restaurant has its *bacalhau* dishes. Lovely fish fresh from the sea includes seabass *(robalo)*, wreckfish *(cherne)*, hake *(pescada)*, and sole *(linguado)*. Shad *(sável)* swim up the Minho in May to spawn – to our palates they are rather bony and not very exciting. Lamprey *(lampreia)* is a rich, dense, eel-like fish with, to us, a slightly muddy flavour – and it's expensive. A primitive parasite, sucking the blood of other fish, it lives in the lower reaches of the Minho and may be eaten fresh only from February to April. It is greeted with glee, and mostly cooked in a wet rice dish *(arroz de lampreia)* or in a red Vinho Verde sauce *(lampreia à bordalesa)*; the locals drink red Vinho Verde with this too: not a combination we would recommend, but one of those things that one maybe ought to try once.

The local salmon and trout may be safer choices. Trout is likely to come with ham *(presunto)*, or cooked in bacon fat. There are lots of fish soups, risottos and stews.

Room for a pudding? Arouca in the south of the Vinho Verde region, and Amarante in the east are famous for their *doces conventuais*, confections of egg yolks, sugar and ground almonds, but these convent sweets will tempt you in your tracks in tea houses and pastry shops all round the

region. Portugal's beloved rice pudding *(arroz doce)* is said to have originated in the Minho, along with *rabanadas* – sweet eggy fried bread with cinnamon and red wine sauce. And the famous Pudim do Abade de Priscos is a sort of milk-free *crème caramel* invented by a 19th century priest of Priscos, just south of Braga; it's made with egg yolks, sugar, port, lemon zest and cinnamon – oh, and bacon. Sounds yummy? Then the *manjar de língua de Arouca* might just be for you – it's a blend of rice, flour, eggs, sugar and ox tongue!

RESTAURANTS

AFIFE A3

Casa Mariana A high quality local restaurant, here for nearly 50 years opposite the track to the sandy surfing beach of Afife, just up the coast from Viana do Castelo. It's a friendly place with long pine tables, benches and panelling, specialising in simply-cooked fish and seafood, but

offering good meat dishes too. Start perhaps with the delicious clams *(ameijoas à Bulhão Pato)*, goose-neck barnacles *(percebes)*, prawns or crab, and move on to the speciality of the house, steamed seabass on seaweed *(robalo com algas)*. Finish with excellent, lemony *crème brûlée (leite creme)*. Wines are safe, middle-of-road, with Alvarinhos the interesting options.
Lugar de São Roque
T+351 258 981 327
€20 V
Closed Tue; 2nd half May, 2nd half Sep;
*   24 & 25 Dec*

AMARANTE C2

Largo do Paço Young chef Ricardo Costa has been heading the renowned restaurant of the Hotel Casa da Calçada since

September 2006, and is establishing a firm reputation for creative, accomplished cooking. The tasting menus are the highlight, four courses for €45, six courses €65, but an à la carte menu is also available. You might be served a citrus-lacqered duck breast stuffed with *foie gras* accompanied by a carrot and turnip risotto perfumed with eucalyptus; or *bacalhau* tempura with cod's roe *açorda*, green asparagus and hot coriander foam. There are good vegetarian options on the menu, and longer-term vegetarian guests will be specially catered for. The menu suggests wine pairings. A very good Portuguese wine list has most of the top names, at reasonable prices; over 30 wines are listed by the glass – but you can order *anything* by the glass (the bottles preserved after opening under inert gas). In 2002, the hotel replanted a historic 5ha vineyard up the hillside at the rear, and the list offers the resulting wines, still and sparkling Vinhos Verdes called Quinta da Calçada, made with the advice of one of the area's top consultants. There are monthly wine tasting dinners. Dining room decor is warm and elegant, furnishings antique, with comfortable, fabric-draped armchairs. Take a trip out from Porto, call in on your way up the Douro or up or down the Minho, or make this your destination *(details of the hotel on page 60)*.
Largo do Paço 6
T+351 255 410 830
E mail@casadacalcada.com
W www.casadacalcada.com
€55 ☿ V! ⌦
Closed 7-27 Jan

APÚLIA B3

Camelo Although most of the restaurants in this area are good for fish, this is the smartest one… but not too pricey. It's practically on the beach, just where the fishing boats come in. Seafood and fresh fish are the mainstay, plus octopus and *bacalhau*, and the famous lamprey when in season, as well as meat and various types of bean dish *(feijoada)*. The wine list is good, majoring on Vinhos Verdes and particularly Alvarinhos. On the coast south of Esposende, this is the second Camelo restaurant – find the first, also good, in Santa Marta de Portuzelo *(page 50)*.
Rua do Facho
T+351 253 987 600
E ocamelo@mail. telepac.pt
W www.ocamelo.pt
€15-€20 ☿ V
Open every day Closed 1st week Jun

ARCOS DE VALVEVEZ B4

Costa do Vez Master of the house João Correia da Costa is president and main sponsor of the local orchestra, and runs his restaurant at perfect pitch, in precise rhythm, with not a hint of syncopation in the nifty service. Stone walls, *azulejos* and close-packed tables make for a rustic atmosphere, and the fine local cooking is renowned hereabouts. Try the wonderful fried octopus with a wet rice stew of beans and vegetables *(arroz de feijão)*, tender local beef steaks *(posta barrosã)*, roast veal and kid, excellent hotpot *(cozido)*, and very fresh fish. The *bacalhau à lagareiro* comes with flavoursome olive oil from Miranda. Over 200 wines span the country; the house Alvarinho/Trajadura is good.
Quinta de Silvares, Salvador, EN 101
T+351 258 516 122
E costa.do.vez@clix.pt
W www.www.costadovez.pt
€23 ☿ V Closed Mon; 1st half Oct

ARCOS DE VALDEVEZ B4

O Lagar Join the many local people who come here for lunch, and enjoy the very warm, smiling service and very good, inexpensive Minho cooking. It's a small, cosily rustic restaurant, with white-pointed stone walls, wood and local artefacts as decoration. There are few tables, and benches rather than chairs. Wines are mainly Vinhos Verdes.
Rua Dr Vaz Guedes
T+351 258 516 002
€15 V Closed Sat except in Aug

BAIÃO C2

Pensão Borges This inexpensive hotel *(page 60)* serves very good, traditional Portuguese food in a dining room of rough-hewn granite. Roasts in the wood-fired ovens are a speciality, the Sunday baby lamb (kid in season) and braised rice *(arroz de forno)* a point of pilgrimage. Meat is well sourced, there are home-made sausages *(alheiras)*, and good *bacalhau* dishes. Local wines served in good glasses include the excellent Quinta de Covela, made 15 minutes' drive away *(page 44)*.
Rua de Camões, Campelo
T+351 255 540 278 or 255 541 322
E reservas@residencialborges.com
W www.residencialborges.com
€25 ♀ V ⊟ No credit cards – but soon

BARCELOS B3

Bagoeira In a very old building right in the centre of Barcelos, a hotel with nine different dining rooms, ranging from cosy to barn-like, and serving good, hearty local cooking. There's always roast chicken, lots of fish, *bacalhau* and octopus *(polvo)* cooked in various ways, chunks of belly pork *(rojões)*, and on Friday market days and weekends an excellent *cozido*. Try the tongue stewed with peas *(língua estufada com ervilhas)*. There's a very

extensive range of Vinhos Verdes, with Alvarinhos from most producers of this lovely grape, and there are good wines from elsewhere in Portugal, too. Service is friendly and efficient.
Avenida Sidónio Pais 495
T+351 253 811 236
E restaurante@bagoeira.com
W www.bagoeira.com
€25 ♀ V ⊟ Open every day

BARCELOS (PEDRA FURADA) B3

Pedra Furada Just outside Barcelos via the medieval bridge on the road to Barcelinhos, this is a pleasantly old fashioned restaurant, smart-rustic, friendly and welcoming, with polished-wood ceilings and tiled floors. Cooking is good, solid local fare, fresh fried fish as well as traditional dishes, including roasts in the wood-fired oven – roast kid on Sundays. A good, long wine list spans Portugal's wine regions, with lots of Vinho Verde, of course.
Rua Nova, Pedra Furada
T+351 252 951 144
€18 ♀
Closed Mon din; last week Aug; 25 Dec, 1 Jan, Easter Sun

BRAGA B3

O Arcoense A relaxed, friendly restaurant serving seriously good local food near the River Este. The cooking is accomplished, with a touch of originality, but not complicated, made with fine products drawn from the owner's farm and elsewhere. Most tempting option may be the mixed roast *(assado misto)*, which includes fine *porco preto* from the Alentejo, kid *(cabritinho)* and ribs of veal from the Serra do Barroso *(costela mindinha barrosã)*; there's risotto of octopus or game, or a delicious sea bass dish, *cataplana de robalo*. There may be

no written menu, portions will certainly be copious, and pre-prandial nibbles may arrive in profusion – beware eating your fill before the meal has even begun! A good wine list is especially strong on Alentejo and Douro.
Rua Engenheiro José Justino Amorim 96, São Victor
T+351 253 278 952
€30 ♀ V Closed Sun

Inácio A narrow, stone-walled, oak-beamed restaurant in the old part of the city, popular locally for its Minho cooking and roasts in a wood-fired oven. The wine is mostly Vinho Verde.
Campo das Hortas 4
T+351 253 613 235
€15-€20 V
Closed Tue; 9 days after Easter; 2 weeks Sep; Christmas

BRUFE C3

Abocanhado Shockingy modern in design, surprisingly excellent, Abocanhado nestles into the terraces 800 metres up in the Serra Amarela, on the edge of the village of Brufe, west of the Serra do Gerês – in the middle of nowhere, in fact, but with amazing views over everywhere around from the big picture windows. A short menu is based around excellent local meat including game, kid and veal. Watch out for goats and horses in the road on the way down!
Brufe, Terras do Bouro
T+351 253 352 944
E info@abocanhado.com
W www.abocanhado.com
€25 V No credit cards Closed Mon, Tue

CAMINHA A4

Solar do Pescado Tucked down a side street on the way from the river to the main square, this little restaurant is

renowned for its fish and seafood, a great place in season (spring) to try the local specialities shad *(sável)* and lamprey *(lampreia)* from the River Minho. The squid is excellent. Other specialities are lobster risotto *(arroz de lavagante)* and seabass *cataplana* with clams *(robalo na cataplana com ameijoas)*. The meat is good, too, including wild boar *(javali)*. There are lovely tiles, arches, white-painted walls, deep blue tablecloths.
Rua Visconde Sousa Rego 85
T +351 258 922 794
€25 ♀ V
Closed Sun din, Mon; 2nd half May,
  2nd half Nov

GOVE C2

O Almocreve A welcoming, rustic restaurant in an old stone building serving very good local and Portuguese dishes, and Sunday roasts of lamb, kid or veal from the traditional wood-fired ovens. Service is excellent, the wine list strongest on Douro wines. Gove is a little village 4km south of Baião by the EN 108, the old panoramic road linking Porto to Régua along the right bank of the Douro.
Portela do Gove
T+351 255 551 226
E oalmocreve@hotmail.com
W www.sblog.noite.pt/oalmocreve
€12 V Closed Christmas

GUIMARAES C2/3

Valdonas Don't be put off by the slightly gaudy Valdonas posters as you walk up and into the old town centre – you'll probably vet the menus all round town then come back here. Valdonas has good regional food, both fresh fish and meat, plus some specialities such as rabbit in red wine sauce *(coelho à bordalesa)*. Portions are large – order in moderation! Their *bacalhau* gets rave reviews. With the

exception of the occasional exposed stone wall, the 16th century building has been painted white, right up to the enormous ceiling beams. Furniture is minimalist, however. For summer there are outdoor courtyards, one of them mediaeval.
Rua Val das Donas 4
T +351 253 511 411
E info@valdonas.com
W www.valdonas.com
€25 V

LOUREDO C2

Cozinha da Terra A beautiful old granite farmhouse cooking excellent traditional dishes and roasts in a wood-fired oven. Service is friendly and welcoming. A short wine list has some good bottles. Find Louredo just north of the motorway, 20km east of Porto.
Casa de Louredo, Lugar da Herdade 8
T+351 255 780 900
E casalouredo@iol.pt
W www.netmenu.pt/cozinhadaterra
€28 V
Closed Sun din, Mon; last week Aug, 1st
  week Sep; Easter, Christmas & New Year

MELGAÇO C4

Restaurante Panorama Adelino Lindo is well placed to buy choice fresh produce for his restaurant, which you will find within Melgaço's modern covered market. And there are indeed panoramic views down over the River Minho. Lindo is a character, and a renowned and talented chef, his cooking centred mainly around traditional northern dishes. Choose from a multitude of starters, followed perhaps by fresh grilled fish, *bacalhau*, lamprey *(lampreia)* when in season, chunks of fried belly pork and offal in a spicy red wine sauce *(rojões)*, or roast kid or veal. Excellent cheeses include *Queijo da Serra*, and home-made puddings are out to

tempt. A wide-ranging, discerning collection of wines is arrayed on shelves around the walls, but there is no wine list.
Mercado Municipal de Melgaço
T +351 251 410 400
E restaurante.panorama@sapo.pt
W www.restaurantepanorama.eu
€25 ♀ V
Closed Sun din, Mon; Wed & Thu din in
  winter; 2 weeks Oct, 2 weeks May, 24 &
  25 Dec

PADERNE C4

Adega do Sossego Just south of Melgaço, a typical Minho granite house has been turned into an intimate restaurant, full of little corners. Admire the lovely old wooden ceiling. Excellent Minho fare includes ham and charcuterie, and the boiled meat and vegetables *(cozido)* gets rave reviews. There's usually roast kid on Sundays, and it's a place of pilgrimage in the lamprey season. Some dishes must be ordered in advance. The wine list is attractive, service helpful. Book by phone, email is less certain.
Lugar do Peso, Estrada Nacional 301 km 4
T +351 251 404 308
E geral@adegadosossego.com
W www.adegadosossego.com
€25 ♀
Closed Wed; 1st half May, last week Sep,
  1st half Oct; 24 Dec din, 25 Dec, 1 Jan

PAREDES DE COURA B4

O Conselheiro Sit comfortably in the cool, leafy interior, or on the terrace, take a trip around Portugal, menu in hand. You might choose a bean-based stew from Trás-os-Montes, *tripas à moda do Porto*, stuffed squid Algarve style, meats various cooked Minho style in red Vinho Verde, trout from the River Coura, or particularly succulent kid *(cabrito)*. Some dishes must be ordered in advance. Find it 15km south

of Valença. Lunch will see you through till bedtime...
Largo Visconde de Moselos
T+351 251 782 610
E contacto@cm-paredes-coura.pt
€25 ⚲ Closed Mon; also Sun din in
winter; Oct; 24 Dec

PENSO C4

Jardim A simple, rustic, friendly place near Melgaço, by the side of the N202, up by the Spanish border. Cooking is good and local, and you should not be disappointed by the house wine.
Canhoto, Penso
T+351 251416303
€15 No credit cards
Closed Mon din; last 3 weeks Sep

PONTE DE LIMA (ARCA) B3

Bocados In the countryside 2km outside Ponte da Lima, this friendly little restaurant is unique, and a delight. With only 30 places per sitting, on the ground floor and sometimes in the garden of the owners' old granite house, it is imperative to book. The atmosphere is very homely and cosy, bright ochre walls hung with pictures.You will be given no menu – little portions *(bocados)* will arrive, made according to the inspiration of the day – expect perhaps seven little starters, a main course and a pud, sophisticated-traditional in style. There may be seafood, lamb cooked in red Vinho verde, Bísaro pork, and in season game or lamprey. You do get to choose the wines you drink, from a 200-strong list where Alentejo and Douro reign, at very reasonable prices.
Carreiros, Arca
T+351 258 942 501
E bocados@sapo.pt
W www.bocados.pt.vu
€33 ⚲ V
Closed Sun; Jul-Sep; Easter; 25 Dec; 1 Jan

PONTE DE LIMA B3

Carvalheira A cosy, friendly restaurant, tastefully renovated, with granite walls and a big old fireplace for winter. Lots of little starters and very good charcuterie are followed by generous portions of delicious traditional food – *bacalhau com migas* is the signature dish. A very good, long, fairly-priced wine list has more Douro, port and Alentejo than local wines. Find it just across the river from Ponte da Lima.
Antepaço, Arcozelo
T+351 258 742 316
E restcarvalheira@hotmail.com
€25-€30 ⚲ V
Closed Mon; 11-31 Oct; 25 Dec

QUEIJADA B3

Cozinha Velha Come here for the roast kid or suckling pig *(leitão)*, or well-cooked Minho dishes – and a fascinating list of over 300 wines. Wooden wine cases piled between the tables subtly divide the space. It's a small country house restaurant by the roadside south of Ponte de Lima, with a beamed ceiling, soft but cheerful colours, a cosy traditional atmosphere with a light, modern touch.
Queijada, Cangosta
T+351 258 749 664
€20-€25 ⚲
Closed Tue

SANTA MARIA DO BOURO C3

Pousada de Santa Maria do Bouro The candle-lit dining room of this *pousada* was once the kitchen of the old Cistercian monastery, which opened as a hotel in 1997 *(page 62)*, just north-east of Amares. Well-cooked local dishes come in large portions, including veal steaks, roast kid, *rojões, bacalhau* or simply cooked fish fillets. The dessert buffet of course includes the wonderful *doces conventuais*, and a tempting range of local cheeses. There's a

good wine list, and service is attentive.
Bouro, Santa Maria, 4720-688 Amares
T+351 253 371 970
E recepcao.bouro@pousadas.pt
W www.pousadas.pt
€40-€50 ⚲ V 🛏
Open every day

SANTA MARTA DE PORTUZELO B3

Camelo Just east of Viana do Castelo, on the 202 to Ponte de Lima, this is one of the area's most popular restaurants, and despite its size you need to book, especially at weekends when the place is buzzing with whole families of local folk. Portions of hearty, tasty northern cuisine are huge, raw materials chosen with care. Come for the famous *cozido* on the second Sunday of the month, or enjoy the local charcuterie and hams, fish or lamprey in season, mixed pork grill *(parilhada de carnes de porco)*, tripe in red wine *(tripa de porco estufada em vinho tinto)*, and tempting home-made puddings such as *rabanadas* – like French toast smothered in syrup and sprinkled

with cinnamon. Wines are mainly Vinhos Verdes. The dining rooms are simple and modern, or eat in summer under a leafy trellis.

Rua Santa Marta 199
T+351 258 839 090
E camelosantamarta@megamail.pt
€25 V
Closed Mon

São João de Rei C3

Restaurante Victor In a remote little village amidst the vines east of Braga, this is a very special, homely place with blue-checked table cloths and a warm, happy atmosphere. At its heart are the characterful Senhor Victor and his family. It is he who will greet you in the rustic dining room or leafy conservatory, where you might choose the speciality, *bacalhau com batatas a murro* (with crushed roast potatoes), charcuterie or meat from the Barroso mountains of Trás-os-Montes, or kid roasted in the wood-fired oven. The wines are as good as the views.

Lugar do Laranjal, São João de Rei
T+351 253 909 100
E restaurantevictor@net.sapo.pt
W www.ovictor.web.pt
€25 ♀
Closed 25 Dec

Valença (Urgeira) B4

Quinta do Prazo Do make a detour to this very special restaurant, right up by the Spanish border, where cooking by Amaya Guterres is modern, creative and beautifully presented, accompanied by a stunning wine list. The list is very long – even the fortified wine section has over 100 entries – with a good selection of foreign wines as well as Portuguese, at very fair prices. There are specific glasses for wine styles, knowledgeable wine service, food and wine pairing suggestions on the menu, and a good selection of wines by the glass. The setting is an imposing Minho country house, old stone walls tastefully offset by modern furnishings, touches of red amidst the granite and wood. As well as three dining rooms, there's a wine bar, and a big conservatory has views over a lake where black and white swans glide. This is a new gastronomic star.

Urgeira
T+351 251 821 230
E quintadoprazo@mail.pt
€30 ♀ V
Closed Sun din, Mon

Viana do Castelo A3

Casa d'Armas In the former stables of a manor house by the port of Viana, this family-run restaurant produces gently creative traditional dishes, with an accent on fish and seafood. A short but good wine selection includes some old vintages of famous wines.

Largo 5 de Outubro 30
T+351 258 824 999
E casadarmas@hotmail.com
€30 ♀
Closed Wed except in Aug; 3 weeks Nov;
*   24 Dec din; 25 Dec; 1 Jan*

Taberna do Valentim A small, simple, inexpensive restaurant with very good, fresh fish, simply grilled, served with boiled potatoes and vegetables, or as risotto or soup – try the fishermen's broth *(chorinha)*. Wine is not the strong point. You must book, and be aware never-theless that the restaurant may not open in stormy weather if the fishing boats could not put out.

Rua Monsenhor M Machado
T+351 258 827 505
€15 V
Closed Sun, public hols

Vizela (Moreira de Cónegos) C2

São Gião You wouldn't expect to find one of Portugal's finest restaurants in an industrial area by a football stadium, and even the façade blends in with the unprepossessing surroundings. But inside, São Gião is unexpectedly spacious and contemporary, elegant but relaxed, with dark wooden floor, beams and pillars offset by ochre and white. Chef-owner Pedro Amaral Nunes is a self-taught, inspired, accomplished cook, combining elements of Portuguese, Spanish and French cooking with culinary ideas of his own. Ingredients are top quality, sometimes home-smoked: hams, salmon, duck breast, or loin of Bísaro pork. In season there will be wild mushrooms and game. Seaweed often features with fine fish including bacalhau in various guises. There may be fresh goose liver with mango sauce, snail and rice stew *(arroz de caracóis)*, or roast kid *(cabrito)*. The long and interesting wine list has some of Portugal's best wines, as well as good foreign wines. Find it east of Vizela.

Avenida Comendador Joaquim Almeida de
*   Freitas 56, Moreira de Cónegos*
T+351 253 561 853
E geaomoreiraconegos@mail.telepac.pt
W www.sgiao.com
€35 ♀ V
Closed Sun din, Mon; last 3 weeks Aug,
*   23 Dec-1 Jan*

AMARANTE C2

Doces conventuais These little eggy delights are a great speciality of Amarante. To try them, eat-in or take-away, head for **Confeitaria Tinoca** *Rua 31 de Janeiro 62*, **Confeitaria da Ponte** with terrace overlooking river and bridge *Rua 31 de Janeiro 1-5,* or **Doçaria do Mário** *Rua Cândido dos Reis 137*

Market on Wednesday and Saturday.

ARCOS DE VALDEVEZ B4

Doçaria Central A small shop selling traditional sweets. Try the huge, colourfully-wrapped *rebuçados dos Arcos,* made from sugar and honey, or the scrumptious *charutos de ovos moles,* filled with a mix of egg paste *(doce d'ovos)* and pumpkin jam *(doce de abóbora). Rua General Norton de Matos 18/20*

Market on alternate Wednesdays

BARCELOS B3

Feira The Thursday morning market and agricultural fair in the town centre, on the huge, tree-shaded Campo da República, is one of Portugal's biggest and best, the perfect place to stock up on all kinds of fresh food products and many other things.

Pecados e Sabores
A good range of Portuguese wines. *Largo da Madalena 110*

BRAGA B3

Frigideiradas do Cantinho Shop selling traditional local cakes and pastries as well as antiques. Glass panels in the floor reveal Roman excavations. *Largo São João de Souto*

Loja dos Vinhos Good wine range. *Rua Dr Francisco Duarte*

Terra Mãe A smart new wine shop upstairs, and downstairs a delicatessen, just by the cathedral. Apart from a good selection of Portuguese and foreign wines, plus port and some spirits, there's cheese, charcuterie, truffles, chocolates, coffee, and numerous products from Hédiard. *Rua Dom Frei Caetano Brandão 120-122*

CAMINHA A4

Garrafeira Baco In a historic former bar, under a vaulted ceiling, this welcoming family wine shop has an excellent and extensive range of Portuguese wines, port and Madeira, including old and rare, plus a small selection of top deli products, fine ham *(presunto)* and cheeses, CARM olive oil… *Rua São João 42*

GUIMARÃES C2

Casa Gourmet Good wines and a tempting selection of gourmet products. *Rua Manuel Saraiva Brandão 217*

MELGAÇO C4

Solar do Alvarinho The best place to buy wine in Melgaço, also some traditional food *(page 37).*

Mercado Municipal The covered market, apart from produce stalls, has the excellent Panorama restaurant *(page 49)* **Open-air market** Along the river on Fridays.

PONTE DA BARCA B3

Market on Wednesdays

PONTE DE LIMA B3

Market Fortnightly on Mondays, a big, atmospheric open-air market by the riverside.

PÓVOA DE VARZIM B2

Garrafeira do Alberto Famous old wine shop with a good range spanning all the Portuguese regions. *Rua Gomes de Amorim*

SOAJO C4

Market on the first Sunday of the month in this beautiful mountain village east of Arcos de Valdevez. There's not only food. Just about anything domestic or agricultural is on sale, even tiny stills to turn your own wine into brandy *(left)* – though we don't know what the customs officers would say when you arrive back home.

VALE C4

Quinta do Cruzeiro Emília Vasconcellos has no shop as such, but from her farmhouse you can buy a fine selection of home-made jams, fruits in syrup, and *fumeiros* – smoked sausages, *alheira, salpicão, chouriça, chouriça de sangue....* Find her east of Arcos de Valdevez. *Vale, 4970-705 Arcos de Valdevez*

VALENÇA B4

Aromas do Vinho Lovely shop within the fortress, with a particularly good range of Douro reds and ports, including some very old vintages, *colheitas* and aged tawnies *(top right).* There are good Bairradas and Dãos, and a decent selection of Vinhos Verdes, plus a big range of wine accessories. *Rua Apolinário da Fonseca 55-63*

Garrafeira Vasco da Gama An impressive selection of vintage ports as well as other wines. *Centro Comercial Alvarinho*

VIANA DO CASTELO A3

Tertúlia do Vinho A new, modern wine shop and delicatessen in the town centre with a good range from across Portugal. *Rua Mateus Barbosa 8*

Garrafeira do Martins In the main avenue, an interesting selection of wines, port, whiskies and accessories. *Avenida dos Combatentes 248*

Friday market A large, all-day agricultural market selling everything from furniture to birds to all kinds of fresh food. *Campo da Agonia*

Casa Melo Alvim Next to and connected with the Estalagem Melo Alvim, in partnership with Sogrape, this new wine shop sells the excellent Sogrape range plus other wines and some deli products such as olive oil and *compotas. Avenida Conde da Carreira 28*

Explore the VR Minho region

Let's start in the little port of CAMINHA in the far north west, facing the hills of Spain across the wide Minho Estuary. The scenery along the winding riverside road to VALENÇA is stunning. On a hilltop over the river, Valença has an old quarter and two latter-day fortresses set within double, fortified walls, around which you can walk. The old town is full of Spanish shoppers, and surrounded by modern sprawl – but enjoy the views across the river. From here we're heading for the Alvarinho country around MONÇÃO, a remote and charming fortified town with hot spas, mosaic paving and cobbles, and MELGAÇO, also a spa town, in the Minho's north-east corner, looking out across the river and into the Serra da Peneda. The highlight is the old castle at its centre. South of Melgaço is Portugal's only National (as opposed to Natural) park, the **Parque Nacional da Peneda-Gerês**, an area of high peaks, lush valleys, lakes, streams and wild beauty *(page 57)*.

Moving south, the next major river to cut through the region is the Lima. VIANA DO CASTELO, on the north bank of its estuary, is a lively, sophisticated ship-building town with architecture from grand Baroque to Art Deco – to modern industrial around the edges. Portuguese adventurers left from here to discover the New World, and during the 16th and 17th centuries trade with Brazil brought great prosperity, fine new manor houses and religious buildings. Viana has beautiful squares, smart shops, nightlife and theatre, and in August the biggest and perhaps the most vibrant of the region's summer festivals *(page 59)*. There's a lovely, golden bay only a short ferry-ride across the Lima.

Follow the River Lima upstream on the old road and you arrive in the beautiful old town of PONTE DE LIMA. It was once an important stop-off on the pilgrim way north to Santiago de Compostela, and used to be a serious river port until the river silted up. The long, arched granite bridge is part Roman, part 14th century. Apparently a Roman army nearly mutinied here and refused to cross, a rumour having got about that the Lima was the legendary, memory-stealing River Lethe – an old *azulejo* panel within the town depicts the story. There are imposing buildings, narrow cobbled streets, and pretty public gardens, with an imposing backdrop to the north-east of the Serra de Arga mountain range.

Ponte da Barca is another attractive town along the River Lima, nestling by its 16th century bridge. The oldest quarter still has a medieval air. A tree-hung riverside park

Far left Green and fertile: the Minho has Portugal's highest rainfall

Left Walk beneath the trees in Ponte de Lima

Right The castle in the centre of Melgaço

Above Waterfalls and streams from the eastern mountains feed the region's main rivers

Right Sunset over the Minho Estuary and the hills of Spain on the far bank of the river

GRANITE GRAIN STORES

Exploring the Peneda-Gêres Natural Park, you'll see curious tall, narrow, grey structures, raised on granite columns and built of granite or wood, with slatted sides. Topped with a cross, they look like massive tombs. They are in fact grain stores *(espigueiros)*, keeping the corn ventilated and more or less out of reach of marauding rats and birds. The very pretty villages of Lindoso and Soajo (both east of Arcos de Valdevez) are the best place to find whole families of *espigueiros* – Lindoso has an amazing 60!

Left The iconic bridge and imposing riverside houses of Amarante

Right The famous castle of Guimarães

Below Bridge across the peaceful River Vez at Arcos de Valdevez

is a popular bathing spot in summer. Modern Ponte da Barca is up the hill. North from here, up the River Vez, ARCOS DE VALDEVEZ is a quiet and untouristy town, bordering on the National Park.

Next river south is the Cávado. The old city of BARCELOS, 10km upstream, has two culinary claims to fame. The first is its spectacuar weekly market *(page 52)*, the second its historic roasted cockerel. The legend goes that a cockerel that had been cooked for a royal banquet stood up and crowed to save an accused man from execution. The good yarn is still spinning profits for the townsfolk of Barcelos, whose many potteries turn out gaudy tourist cockerels – as well as more distinguished wares. The city's attractive old quarter leads down towards the river.

Barcelos has numerous fine churches, but BRAGA seems to have a church at every turn. It was the seat of Portugal's archbishops from the 11th to 18th centuries, and the town amassed great wealth, especially ecclesiastical, manifested also in fine mansions, fountains, palaces and gardens beautifully restored in recent years. It is lively and youthful thanks to its university. Right in the heart of the region, GUIMARÃES is also a university town and was the secular capital of Portugal in medieval times. The old town centre is a very special place, with atmospheric little streets full of characterful buildings. It is now a UNESCO World Heritage

Site, and blissfully car-free. Down-country a little more, the River Ave flows into the sea by the quiet fishing port of VILA DO CONDE with its narrow, cobbled streets. PÓVOA DO VARZIM, just up the coast, is a lively seaside town with wind-swept, sandy beaches, and nightlife.

The Vinho Verde region skirts around Porto. From Porto and Gaia, the River Douro dives southward for a while, so the westward artery at this point is not a river but a new motorway, crossing the region from north of Porto to Vila Real, with exits to PAREDES, PENAFIEL and AMARANTE. Amarante is a very pretty town of grand, balconied old houses dominated by its church and monastery. The River Tâmega flows peacefully through the town, spanned by a lovely bridge of pale stone. Do buy some of the delicious little local eggy sweets *(page 46)*, and then tackle some of the town's steep slopes, or hire one of the brightly-coloured boats on the river, and burn off the calories before heading south, maybe, to the monastery of AROUCA, to taste the rival eggy wares.

BETWEEN MEALS

❧ VIEW FROM THE TOP ❧

Natural *miradouros* in the verdant, forested mountain regions and the national park are plentiful and often stunning. A few of the more outstanding top spots partly engineered by man are as follows:

GUIMARAES **Castelo de São Miguel** Climb steeply up for fine city views from the restored square keep of the 10th century castle. *Rua Conde Dom Henrique Open Jun-Sep 9.30-5 Oct-Jun 9.30-12.30, 2-5*

PENHA There's a rocky picnic area with great views over Guimaraes from the highest point in the countryside south-east of the city. It's a long, cobbled walk or a ten-minute ear-popping ride in a cable car from the Parque das Hortas.

VALENÇA Marvellous views across the River Minho to Galicia from the city walls.

VIANA DO CASTELO **Monte de Santa Luzia** Drive or take the funicular to this famous viewpoint on a church terrace 400m above sea level and look down upon the town, the sandy beaches

along the coastline, and the Lima valley, especially from the roof of the Templo do Sagrado Coração de Jesus. *Apr-Sep 8-7 Oct-Mar 8-5*

Parque Nacional da Peneda-Gerês

If fell-walking is your thing, head up to the fabulous swathe of mountains around the Minho's north-eastern corner. Four mountain ranges form the Peneda-Gerês National Park: the Serra da Peneda, Serra do Soajo, Serra Amarela and (peaking at 1,545m above sea level) the Serra do Gerês. Between the peaks are forested valleys and mountain pastures, up high it's moorland, heather and gorse. Take your waterproofs, because this is Portugal's wettest corner, with the highest rainfall, six reservoirs, and a multitude of springs, rivers, waterfalls and streams. But what's a bit of rain, in such magical surroundings? Access to some of the highest land is restricted by the park authorities for reasons of conservation. No one lives in the highest reaches, except maybe in summer, when flocks and herds move up to high pastures, and some of the mostly elderly farmers and shepherds move with them to high summer houses known as *brandas*. In places it is possible to rent these little mountain houses *(page 61)*. The highlands are not very adequately

mapped, and a compass and proper equipment is vital. There are wild boar, wildcats, golden eagles, and wandering ponies, goats, sheep and brown, long-horned cattle – and wolves. Numbers of the once endangered Iberian wolves are now increasing, but the human population is dwindling, even in the more accessible lower reaches, as the young leave the mountains. The little mountain villages are lost in time: ERMELO, ERMIDA, BRUFE and LINDOSO are all a delight; as are SOAJO, LAMAS DE MOURO and GRAÇÃO, which have already adapted somewhat to the new world of tourism *(page 63)*. In the inhabited areas, the footpaths are increasingly well marked: good walking leaflets are available from the office of Adere-PG in Ponte da Barca. Mountain trekking on Garrano horses, a small, strong breed, is organised by the Centro Hípico do Mezio; and wolf observation (on horse or foot), also local dance and music, by ECOTURA. *Adere-PG Largo da Misericórdia 10, Ponte da Barca T+351 258 452 250 W www.adere-*

pg.pt Open Mon-Fri 9-12.30, 2.30-6; Centro Hípico do Mezio Vilar de Suente, Soajo T+351 258 526 088 ECOTURA T+351 251 465 025 / 934 671 393 E ecotura@sapo.pt

MIRE DE TIBÃES **Mosteiro de São Martinho de Tibães** This large Benedictine monastery is one of Portugal's finest religious sites. It grew and developed from the 11th century to the 18th. The church is completely lined with dazzlingly beautiful gilded wood. An atmospheric cloister has *azulejos* and a central granite fountain. There's a baroque garden with fountains and water channels, and a mini-replica of the stairs of the Bom Jesus sanctuary near Braga. *Mire de Tibães Open spring/summer Tue-Sun 10-1, 2-6.30 autumn/winter Tue-Sun 9.30-1, 2-5.30 Closed Mon, 1 Jan, Easter, 1 May, 25 Dec*

MUSEUMS & GALLERIES

BARCELOS **Museu de Olaria** In this town famous for its pottery, a museum of both local and national pottery, permanent and touring exhibitions. *Rua Cónego Joaquim Gaolas Open Tue-Sun 10-12, 2-5.30 Closed Mon, 1 Jan, Good Fri, Easter Sun, 1 May, 1 Aug, 25 Dec*

BRAGA **Museu de Arte Sacra** The Museum of Sacred Art in the cathedral reflects Braga's sumptuously wealthy religious heritage in a collection of vestments and silverware, statues, carvings and fine *azulejos*. *Largo da Sé Open summer Tue-Sun 8.30-6.30 winter 8.30-5.30*
Palácio dos Biscainhos Anthropological and arts museum in a 16th century manor house west of the pedestrian centre. Exhibits include Portuguese and foreign furniture, art, sculpture, glassware, textiles and clocks. The house itself has impressive stucco ceilings and *azulejos*, and the Baroque gardens have deliciously shady, mature trees. *Rua dos Biscainhos Open Tue-Sun 10-12.15 2-5.30 Closed Mon; 1 Jan, Good Fri, 1 May, 25 Dec*

GUIMARÃES **Museu de Alberto Sampaio** In a magnificent old monastery, a museum of religious artefacts, ceramics, silverware, paintings and *azulejos*. *Rua Alfredo Guimarães Open Tue-Sun 10-12.30, 4-5.30 Closed Mon; public hols Free Sun am*
Museu Martins Sarmento Archaeological museum in a convent, named after the archaeologist who excavated the 150 Iron Age houses on the site of Citânia de Briteiros 15km north of Guimarães. *Rua Paio Galvão Open Tue-Sun 9.30-12, 2-5 Closed Mon, public hols*

PONTE DE LIMA **Museu Rural** Museum of winemaking, agriculture, linen and corn production and traditional cooking, set in gardens. Spot the *espigueiro* perched high outside. *Largo do Armado Open Wed-Sun 2-6*

TERRAS DE BOURO **Museu Etnográfico de Vilarinho das Furnas** In 1972 the village of Vilarinho das Furnas in the

valley between the Amarela and Gerês mountains was submerged under the waters of a new reservoir. Displaced villagers used stones and other building materials from their lost village to build a museum in Terras de Bouro, detailing their former community. In the drought of 2005 the drowned and dilapidated village temporarily reappeared. *São João do Campo Open Wed-Fri 8.30-12, 2-5 Closed Mon*

VAIRÃO **Museu do Vairão** Small museum of linen and wine production. *Centro de Formação do Vairão, Rua da Agrária, Lugar do Crasto Open 10-12.30, 2-5.30*

VIANA DO CASTELO **Museu do Traje** Museum of the heavily-embroidered local costumes, and linen production, from field to loom, attractively exhibited. *Praça da República Open Sat & Sun Jun-Sep 10-1, 3-7, Oct-May 10-1, 3-6 Closed Mon*
Museu Municipal Worth visiting for the 18th century palace in which it is partially housed, with its impressive *azulejos*, as well as for its china and furniture, art and local archaeology. *Largo São Domingos/ Rua General Luís do Rego 219 Tue-Sun 9.30-12.30, 2-5.30 Closed Mon, public hols, 20 Aug*

CHURCHES

BARCELOS **Igreja de Nossa Senhora do Terço** *Azulejos* depict the life of St Benedict around the walls of this former convent. *Avenida dos Combatentes da Grande Guerra Open every day 10-12, 2-5*

BRAGA **Bom Jesus do Monte** Just east of Braga, on a forested hill, a seemingly never-ending double-zigzag Baroque staircase climbs past chapels, fountains and statues up to a small church that is much less interesting than the approach. The devout sometimes climb the 1,000 steps on their knees, but second time round might be obliged to take the creaky 19th century funicular... It is quieter during the week. *Bom Jesus, Tenões Open 9am-8pm*

Sé Braga's cathedral is a charming mix of styles and periods from the 12th to the 18th century, elegantly plain here, ornate there. The west door and southern portal are the oldest parts. Don't miss the Manueline font with its twisted carvings, the golden baroque organs and gilded choir stalls, and the frescoes in one of the chapels. The mummified body of Archbishop Dom Lourenço Vicente has lain in state in another of the courtyard chapels since the 14th century. Visit the Museu de Arte Sacra, up the cloister stairs *(page 58). Rua Dom Paio Mendes Open May-Oct 8.30-6.30 Nov-Apr 8.30-5.30*

CAMINHA **Igreja Matriz** Beautiful carved maplewood ceiling and *azulejos. Rua Ricardo Joaquim*

FALPERRA **Igreja de Santa Maria Madalena** *Azulejo*-rich Baroque church approached by a wide staircase in this village 6km south-east of Braga.

GUIMARÃES **Igreja de São Francisco** Built in 1400 in Gothic style, this was embellished in the 18th century with *azulejos* showing scenes from the life of Saint Anthony. There's a delightful cloister, and painted ceilings. *Largo de São Francisco Open Tue-Sat 9.30-12, 3-5 Sun 9.30-1*

FAIRS & FESTIVALS
This north-western corner of Portugal is famous for its festivals, most of them religious in origin but jollied along with plenty of food and Vinho Verde, and traditional and modern dancing and music – all a good excuse to bring out the colourfully embroidered local costumes.

Summer is the festival high season. Here are some top ones:

MAY BARCELOS **Festa das Cruzes** Back in the 16th century, a Barcelos cobbler had a vision of Christ's cross engraved into the ground. The miraculous moment has been commemorated ever since. The festival, one of Portugal's biggest, lasts for five days. On 3 May, the processional route to the church is spectacularly carpeted with flowers; there's a country fair with lots of pottery, eating, Vinho Verde, dancing and music, and a fine firework display illuminates the old centre and river banks.

JUNE AMARANTE **Festa de São Gonçalo** Religious and folk festival in honour of the patron saint of this pretty town. The saint's stone hands and feet in the Igreja de São Gonçalo have been practically worn away by centuries of bachelors and spinsters in search of a speedy spouse; he is also reputed to cure diseases. Young unmarrieds exchange phallic-shaped cakes on the first weekend of June, there's folk dancing, a farmers' market, a battle of flowers, bullfighting, fireworks on the Saturday night and a procession on the Sunday.
BRAGA **Festa de São João** Porto *(page 129)* is the top place to party on June 23-24, Saint John's Eve, but Braga is also a fun place to be: musical, cultural and folk events in the week leading up to all-night street parties and fireworks on the 23rd.
PONTE DE LIMA **Festas do Vinho Verde** Wines to taste from a large number of Vinho Verde producers, as well as charcuterie and other regional products, and a folk festival. Mid-month.

JULY MONDIM DE BASTO **Festas de Mondim de Basto** This pretty mountain town in the Parque Natural do Alvão attracts thousands of visitors for its annual festival and pilgrimage. There are five days of music and partying near the end of the month, fireworks on the penultimate evening, and on the final day a mass and procession through the forest to the high mountain chapel of São Cristovão, from which there are stunning views.

AUGUST GUIMARÃES **Festas Gualterianas** On a weekend early in the month, the medieval city gets dressed up and illuminated for 'The Festival of Saint Walter', and enjoys a procession of giants, a torchlight procession, concerts both rock and traditional, dancing, bullfights, fireworks, a fair, and lots of food and wine. This has been an annual event since 1452.
VIANA DO CASTELO **Romaria de Nossa Senhora de Agonia** The biggest of the region's folk festivals, three days in the third week in August, has processions, stunning local costumes, music and dancing and much feasting, culminating with fireworks on the bridge.

SEPTEMBER PONTE DE LIMA **Feiras Novas** The 'New Fairs' were new back in 1125 but are still going strong, attracting huge numbers of visitors over the three days around the third Sunday in August. It all centres on the pretty river bank, a huge fair and market, regional dishes and Vinho Verde, a folk festival, bands, and fireworks, of course.

Sleep in the VR Minho region

AMARANTE C2
Hotel Casa da Calçada An imposing former palace overlooking the old town centre and the river Tâmega, the hotel was sensitively and luxuriously restored in 2002. Service is excellent, decor classic, colours warm, and rooms are large, some with fabulous city views. The Largo do Paço restaurant has creative cooking *(page 47)*, and the bar/café has panoramic

views. In mature gardens you will find two pools – and up the hill behind the hotel a new vineyard has been planted, which provides the house wine. There may be art exhibitions, or classical concerts. The hotel owns tennis courts and an 18-hole mountain golf course 15 minutes' drive away. It's only 30 minutes' drive from Oporto's new airport, on the motorway that leads to Vila Real, and the Douro.
Largo do Paço 6
T +351 255 410 830
E reservas@casadacalcada.com
W www.casadacalcada.com
€170-€220
🛏26 [S]4 ♀ ✕ ⚓ 🏊 ✓ ♞
Closed 7-27 Jan

BAIAO C2
Casa de Cochêca A large, stone and white-painted manor house with its own small chapel, overlooking its own vineyards, orange groves and peaceful, terraced farmland near the River Douro. The decor is charming, rooms very comfortable, and there is a big pool on the lawn. As well as breakfast, you can order lunch, evening meals, barbeques, snacks and drinks.

A large cottage with a private garden sleeps up to ten.
Cochêca, 4640-360 Mesquinhata
T +351 255 551 174
E reservas@cocheca.com
W www.cocheca.com
€100, cottage €160-€320
🛏3 [SC]1(8+2) ✕on request ⚓
No credit cards Min nights 2

BAIÃO (CAMPELO) C2
Pensão Borges The views are simply stunning from the bedroom balconies of this inexpensive yet comfortable and welcoming hotel. The restaurant is very good too *(page 48)*. Campelo is part of the small town of Baião. This is a useful base for visits to some excellent local wineries, whether in Minho or Douro.
Rua de Camões, Campelo, 4640-147 Baião
T +351 255 541 322
E reservas@residencialborges.com
W www.residencialborges.com
€40
🛏14 ♀ ✕ *No credit cards*
Closed Sep; 23 to 26 Dec; Mon after Easter

BICO B4
Casa das Cerejas In a tranquil spot south-east of Paredes de Coura on the western side of the Corno de Bico mountains, 'The Cherry House' is a lovely granite farmhouse dating back to the late 17th/early 18th century and set in 2ha of gardens and farmland. It has been recently renovated by a geologist couple. The main

house has charming bedrooms with exposed stone walls and en-suite bathrooms, dining room and sitting/television/games room, and there's a pool in the garden.
Quinta da Portela, 4940-061 Bico,
*   Paredes de Coura*
T +351 251 780 040
E casadascerejas@sapo.pt
W www.casadascerejas.com
€55-€65 🛏3 [S]3 ✕on request ⚓

BRAGA B3
Albergaria Bracara Augusta Brilliant value, friendly, small hotel in an attractive old house in the pedestrian zone of this quiet town. Rooms are modern. The restaurant gets good reviews, for meals as well as breakfast. Staff are very friendly and helpful. There's underground parking two minutes' walk away.
Avenida Central 134, 4710-229 Braga
T +351 253 206 260
E bracara.augusta@mail.telepac.pt
W www.bracaraaugusta.com
€59-69 🛏17 [S]2 ✕

CAMINHA A4
Casa da Eira de Moledo Just a few minutes from the ferry that crosses the estuary of the Minho into Spain, and 2km from the wide and sandy Moledo beach, three lovely farmworkers' cottages to rent, beautifully renovated, with fine sea views. There are pretty gardens with a beautiful swimming pool, and orchards of apples, pears, apricots, oranges and hazels.
Bookings Avenida da Boavista 3523 3º
*   Sala, 303 4100-139 Porto*
Houses Rua do Ingusto 274, Gateira-
*   Moledo, 4910-255 Caminha*
T +351 226 183 907 / 919 847 131
E reservas@casadaeira.com
W www.casadaeira.com
€60-€80 [SC]3(2&2+2) ⚓
No credit cards Min nights 2

Quinta do Convento da Franqueira
On a wine estate *(page 38)* between Braga and the coast, surrounded by vines and woodland, this enchanting old monastery has cosy en-suite rooms and apartments to let. Built in the 1650s, it has been renovated by an English family, and comfortably furnished with English and Portuguese antiques. A spring-fed swimming pool 300m from the house overlooks the vines, with distant views of the Gerês mountains. One of the apartments is the gatehouse above the main gate to the patio and cloister gardens; it has its own entrance, and terraces with barbecue and fine views of the *quinta*.
Carvalhal CC301, 4755 Barcelos
T+351 253 831 606
E piers@quintadafranqueira.com
W www.quintadafranqueira.com
€100 SC €560–€700 per week
🛏3 ⓢ 1 SC 1(2+1) ♀ 🏊
Closed Nov–May Min nights 2

GAVIEIRA C4
Hotel da Peneda Beside a serious waterfall, backed by a steep slope and a mountain top, within the Peneda-Gerês National Park, this imposing granite building with arcaded ground floor was modernised in 2005. Decor is bright, airy and modern. Ten of the rooms are in an annexe of attractive, more classic design, and a smart, modern self-catering building, the Abrigo, can house up to 24 in dormitories with bunk beds. There's a bar and restaurant.
Gavieira, Peneda, 4970-150 Gavieira
T+351 251 460 040
E geral@hotelpeneda.com
W www.hotelpeneda.com
€60 🛏30 SC 1(12-24) ✗

GRAÇÃO C3/C4
Casas de Além In the middle of a little mountain village, on the edge of the National Park, two simple, modern, wood-panelled chalets with reed-shaded terrace decking have fabulous views over the Lima River, lake and mountains *(below)*. Ideal for a couple or families. The chalets share a swimming pool with the owner. There are fabulous walks, natural pools for bathing…
T+351 917 540 404
E info@casasdealem.com
W www.casasdealem.com
€70 for two, + €25 additional people
SC 2(4+2) ♀ 🏊 *No credit cards*
Min nights 2 (7 in summer)

GUIMARAES C2
Pousada de Guimarães, Santa Marinha A former monastery built in the 12th century on a hill with sweeping views of the city. Public rooms are very grand, some with vaulted ceilings and *azulejos*, all furnished with antiques and rich drapes. Balconies, terraces and lots of little reading spots overlook the city and mature, formal gardens. Some rooms are

air-conditioned, some are spacious, some are, inevitably, the size of a monk's cell; rooms in the old wing have city views. There are

wild gardens as well, and a big swimming pool. The restaurant may disappoint.
Largo Domingos Leite Castro,
*   4810-011 Guimarães*
T+351 253 511 249
W recepcao.stamarinha@pousadas.pt
🛏49 ⓢ2 ✗ 🏊

Pousada Nossa Senhora da Oliveira
Beside the Praça da Oliveira, the main medieval square, this is a historic building with particularly fine wooden ceilings, simply furnished with old pieces and antiques. Good breakfasts can be taken in fine weather on the terrace overlooking the square (but meals are otherwise not the strongest point). Rooms are air-conditioned, windows recently double-glazed, making for quieter nights. It's a 100m walk from the car park through the pedestrian city centre. You can use the

pool at the other pousada, a €3-€4 taxi-ride up the hill.
Rua de Santa Maria4801-901 Guimarães
T+351 253 514 157
E recepcao.oliveira@pousadas.pt
W www.pousadas.pt
€120-€198
🛏10 ⓢ6 ✗ 🏊 *at the other pousada*

JOLDA-MADALENA B3
Paço da Glória Paço means 'palace', and this is indeed a palace, of the fairytale variety. Between Ponte de Lima and Arcos de Valdevez, overlooking the Lima Valley, it is set in a park with ornamental pools, mature trees, vineyards and gardens.

It was built in the 18th century, with beautiful architectural detail both inside and out, and is furnished with antiques. The two bedrooms in the main house are splendid, and there are more modest rooms in the former stables around a courtyard with lemon trees. There's a chapel, tennis court, swimming pool, games room with billiards and table tennis, and a beautiful terrace with stone arches where breakfast is taken on fine mornings.
Lugar de Novais, Jolda-Madalena
*   4970-205 Arcos de Valdevez*
T+351 226 102 494
E home@ges-exportadores.pt
€80-€110 🛏9 ✗*on request* 🏊 ℗
No credit cards Closed Christmas

LAMAS DE MOURO C4
Casa da Bica/Casa Forte do Carvalhinho In the heart of the Peneda mountains, south of Melcaço, two granite cottages with beautiful wood panelling and exposed granite interiors. Branda da Aveleira is a small group of individual old mountain cottages or brandas, little houses to which local people once transferred when spring came, moving with their animals to higher pasture.
Branda da Aveleira, 4960-160 Gave
T+351 251 487 360 / 933 894 259
E rasa199494@hotmail.com/turismorural
*   @brandadaaveleira.com*
W www.brandadaaveleira.com
€70 SC *2(4+1) No credit cards*
*   Min nights 2*

MONÇÃO B4
Casa de Rodas A delightful old manor house with many period features and beautiful furnishings in Alvarinho country only 1km outside Monção, owned by the

same family since 1500. Surrounded by woods and vines, with mature gardens, woods, and a pool bordered by an *espigueiro* – one of the region's historic and emblematic grain stores.
T+351 251 652 105
€80 🛏10 🏊 *No credit cards*
Min nights 2

MONDIM DE BASTO C2
Quinta do Fundo High-trellised vines surround a swimming pool and tennis court, shade the pretty patio and driveway and twine onto the house. Simple, rustic rooms have en suite bathrooms and central heating. It's a tranquil spot beside the Tâmega and Cabril rivers, with views over vineyards to the Alvão mountains. The spectacular Fisgas de Ermelo waterfalls are only a few kilometres away. There are horses, and bicycles to borrow.
Vilar de Viando, 4880-212 Mondim de Basto
T+351 255 381 291
E fernandobouca@quintadofundo.com
W www.quintadofundo.com
€50 🛏5 S *2* ✗ 🏊 ℗ *No credit cards*
Closed Jan; 24 & 25 Dec
Min nights July & Aug 2

NESPEREIRA C2
Casa de Sezim South of Guimaraes, this 32ha wine estate *(page 41)* has been in the family since 1376. The current house with its 18th-century façade is built around a courtyard. It's an atmospheric place, with wonderful wood floors and ceilings, antiques, rugs and drapes, and original French murals showing scenes of early 19th century Portugal and the New World. Some of the bedrooms have four-poster beds. There's a covered terrace, sitting room, dining room and games room with billiards table and table tennis. Formal and semi-formal gardens have a pool on a sheltered lawn, and a tennis

court. There may be cookery courses, and you can join in the grape-picking, visit the vineyard and taste the wines.
Apartado 2210,
*   Santo Amaro,*
*   4810-999 Guimaraes*
T+351 253 523 000
E geral@sezim.pt
W www.sezim.pt
€110 🛏6 S *2* ℗ ✗*on request V!* 🏊 ℗

REMOÃES C4
Hotel Rural Quinta do Reguengo On the banks of the Minho just along the border from Melgaço, a 17th century manor house amidst vineyards that make a very good Alvarinho Vinho Verde *(page 44)*. There are wonderful polished wood floors, and a mix of modern and classic furnishings, comfortable rooms in the house, and two suites in an annexe, each with a kitchenette. Beautiful views over the Peneda-Gerês mountains.
Remoães, Paderne 4960-267 Melgaço
T+351 251 410 150
E geral@hoteldoreguengo.pt
W www.hoteldoreguengo.pt
€75 🛏11 S *2* ℗
Closed 25 Dec; Easter Mon

SANTA MARIA DO BOURO C3
Pousada de Santa Maria do Bouro In a small, unspoilt village, this magnificent 12th century Cistercian monastery makes a wonderful base from which to visit the Peneda-Gerês National Park. The ruined building was lovingly converted,

modern materials sensitively inserted into the imposing granite shell. Though very comfortable, the pousada retains a certain monastic austerity with, on the ground floor, bare stone walls and flagged floors and an ancient central cloister planted with orange and lemon trees. Decor is modern, minimalist and smart. A broad, grassed terrace with ancient water tank runs the length of the building at the rear, overlooking the green valley – do pack some insect repellent... There is no formal planted garden. Below the hotel are agreeably untended grounds and a secure car park. Air-conditioned bedrooms are minimalist-modern, full of light, sometimes large, sometimes within the relatively small confines of a former cell, but all have great views. The dining room, converted from the original monastery kitchen, is a spectacular place to breakfast and dine *(page 50 and pictured on page 9)*.
Bouro, Santa Maria, 4720-688 Amares
T+351 253 371 970
E recepcao.stamarinha@pousadas.pt
W www.pousadas.pt
€150-€250 🛏49 Ⓢ2 ✗ 🏊

São Tomé de Covelas C2
Quinta de Covela Enchanting former vineyard workers' house for rent in the centre of the excellent Quinta de Covela organic wine estate, just west of the Douro DOC boundary and in theory within the Vinho Verde DOC, but in practice making modern, unconventional, very appealing wines blended from Portuguese and international grapes *(page 44)*. The stone building has been sensitively renovated and decorated, with modern comforts. There are three double bedrooms leading to a first floor veranda, two bathrooms, kitchen, living room with open fire, and a large, wisteria-hung terrace with dining tables overlooking the vineyard. It's a tranquil spot

with beautiful views – the River Douro is just a few hundred meters below. A secluded pool is shaded by citrus trees.
T+351 917 557 447
E covela@gmail.com
W www.covela.pt
€564-€1,050 per week Ⓢ*1(6)* 🍷 🏊
Closed Sep-Apr

Soajo C4
Casa da Eira da Lage/Casa do Cavalheiro A stone house built in the early 19th century for the parish priest of this remote and lovely mountain village, arranged around a courtyard and now divided into two, and modernised. One house has one double bedroom, the other three, all with en-suite bathrooms, and they share a sitting room, kitchen and barbecue.
Lage Soajo 4909-600
T+351 258 576 165
E casas_turismo@hotmail.com
W www.casasdesoajo.com
€45-€50 🛏*4 or* Ⓢ*2(2&6) No credit cards*

Torno B3
Casa de Juste A stunningly beautiful manor house amidst vines, woods and formal walled gardens with pools and a Baroque chapel. The kitchen of the main house was a fortified tower in the 15th century. There are seven rooms in the main house and its outbuildings.

A converted barn beside the garden sleeps up to ten, self-catering. There's an organic vegetable garden; the property makes its own wine and cheese, and a little shop sells estate and local produce.
Torno 4620-823 Lousada
T+351 255 821626 / 914 788 866
E casadejuste@casadejuste.com
W www.casadejuste.com
€90 SC €250/day €1,500/week
🛏*7* Ⓢ*1(8+2)* ✗*on request* 🏊
Closed Nov-Feb except for groups

Viana do Castelo A3
Casa Melo Alvim A five-star hotel beautifully inserted into a historic building near the centre of this attractive seaside town. The house was built in 1509 in

Manueline style, and much added to over the years, with some oriental influences. Beneath ornate battlements, within the white and granite façade, new materials and design contrast with old. Each bedroom is different, styled for a particular century or period right up to the 21st, with an Indo-Portuguese and a 'rustic' room as well; all are spacious and comfortable. The Conde do Camarido restaurant serves traditionally-based food with modern influences. Staff are extremely helpful.
Avenida Conde da Carreira 28,
 4900-343 Viana do Castelo
T+351 258 808 200
E hotel@meloalvimhouse.com
W www.meloalvimhouse.com
€115-€175 🛏*16* Ⓢ*4* ✗

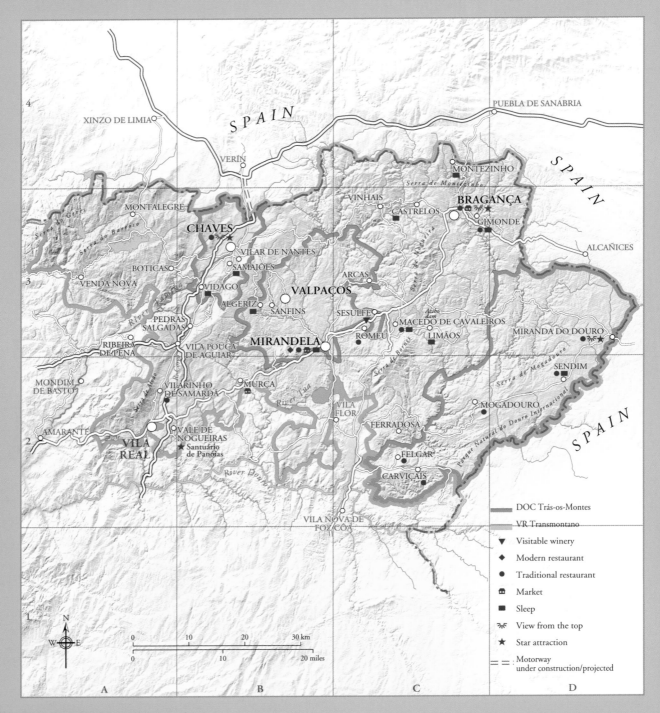

SPAIN

4

XINZO DE LIMIA

VERÍN

PUEBLA DE SANABRIA

SPAIN

MONTEZINHO

Serra de Montezinho

VINHAIS

BRAGANÇA

MONTALEGRE

Serra do Barroso

CASTRELOS

GIMONDE

Serra do Gerês

CHAVES

VILAR DE NANTES

ALCAÑICES

3

BOTICASO

VENDA NOVA

SAMAIÕES

VIDAGO

ARCAS

Serra de Nogueira

VALPAÇOS

ALGERIZ

SANFINS

SESULFE

River Tâmega

River Rabaçal

PEDRAS
SALGADAS

MIRANDELA

MACEDO DE CAVALEIROS

Azibo dam

LIMÃOS

MIRANDA DO DOURO

RIBEIRA
DE PENA

VILA POUÇA
DE AGUIAR

ROMEU

Serra de Bornes

SENDIM

Serra de Mogadouro

MONDIM
DE BASTO

VILARINHO
DE SAMARDÃ

MURÇA

River Tua

VILA
FLOR

MOGADOURO

SPAIN

2

AMARANTE

Serra do Alvão

VILA
REAL

VALE DE
NOGUEIRAS

★ Santuário
de Panóias

FERRADOSA

Parque Natural do Douro Internacional

River Douro

FELGAR

CARVIÇAIS

VILA NOVA DE
FOZ CÔA

	DOC Trás-os-Montes
	VR Transmontano
▼	Visitable winery
◆	Modern restaurant
●	Traditional restaurant
🏚	Market
■	Sleep
✻	View from the top
★	Star attraction
= =	Motorway under construction/projected

1

N
W E
S

0   10   20   30 km

0   10   20 miles

A   B   C   D

Trás-os-Montes

The remote beauty of Portugal's north-eastern uplands was pierced in the 1990s by a forked motorway system. To the west it snakes up from Vila Real, past Chaves, soon to join the motorway that runs along the north of Spain; the other fork heads off east from Vila Real, past the little towns of Murça, Mirandela and Macedo de Cavaleiros to the chunky, fortified capital of Bragança in the far north-east. Now another motorway penetrates from the Douro Superior through the Serra de Bornes, also heading for Bragança. Bragança and the small spa town of Chaves are becoming more sophisticated. And thanks to local and EU support for agriculture and business, the flow of young people out of Portugal's poorest region is slowing.

But the population is still an ageing one, and local people still lead a traditional life. North of the Douro valley, east of the Minho, they are *trás os montes*, behind the mountains, of Gerês, Alvão and Marão. People here have historically been cut off from the rest of Portugal, whilst belligerently braced against their long, curved, mountainous border with Spain. The dialects and traditions of Trás-os-Montes are quite distinct. Out in the mountains, people are independent-minded, conservative, soberly proud of their region, and generally warmly welcoming to visitors. Religion is very important, mingled at festival times with devils, masks and other echoes of pre-Christian times. Fortified medieval towns and villages have cobbled streets and stone houses with wooden balconies and roofs of slate or thatch. Some more remote villages have been abandoned.

There are many smallholdings, often with squat, whitewashed dovecotes (*pombais* – the birds are raised for food), and curious, narrow, stone granaries (*espigueiros*), built on stilts. The mountains are grazing grounds for long-horned cattle, sheep and goats. In the river valleys and plateaux there are vines, rye, corn, wheat, olives, almonds, potato fields and vegetable gardens, as well as forests of sweet chestnut, oak, walnuts and eucalyptus. Higher up is rocky moorland, heather, broom, and in spring an unbelievable wealth of wild flowers. Three mountain ranges – Montesinho, Alvão and Gerês – have been singled out as natural or national parks.

Tourists are still select and few, mainly hill-walkers, horse-riders, hang gliders, and hunters in pursuit of the plentiful local game. Some come for the hot spring waters and spas of Chaves, Pedras Salgadas and Vidago.

Wine in Trás-os-Montes

In this high, hard place of schist and granite rocks and laborious agriculture, much of the country lies at altitudes of between 500 and 600m. There is serious snow in winter. In the summer, baking days are mercifully followed by cool nights – a good thing for grapes, helping them to retain their flavours and aromas. Whilst Vinho Regional wines can be made throughout the region shown in our map, the DOC areas are confined to the two river valley areas of Valpaços and Chaves in the centre and east, and Planalto Mirandês, based around the high plateau of the Serra de Mogadouro in the south east.

Regional names have changed recently up in these parts. The VR region is now known as VR Transmontano (it used to be 'VR Trás-os-Montes'), and it no longer includes the Douro region (now known as 'VR Duriense'). The DOC region confirmed in November 2006 has taken over the 'Trás-os-Montes' name, with three sub-regions that are, in fact, the ex-IPR regions (determined in 1989). So the new DOC Trás-os-Montes consists of three sub-regions, Chaves, Valpaços and Planalto Mirandês.

It is now quite confusing to find pre-2006 bottles labelled 'VR Trás-os-Montes', but coming from the Douro part of the old VR region. Many of the best-known of these wines (such as Ramos Pinto Bons Ares and Real Companhia Velha Quinta do Cîdro) will be labelled 'VR Duriense' in future vintages, as they come from the area around the Douro but do not comply with the DOC rules.

> **Wine regions**
> DOC Trás-os-Montes
> Vinho Regional Transmontano
> **Main local grapes**
> *Red* Touriga Nacional, Touriga Franca, Tinta Roriz (Aragonez), Tinta Amarela, Trincadeira
> *White* Côdiga de Larinho, Malvasia Fina, Síria, Boal Branco
> *For details of grapes see page 428*

Wines, more red than white, are mostly made from varieties found in the neighbouring Douro region. It's a pity that grapes such as Cabernet Sauvignon and Syrah have not been incorporated into the new DOC regulations. These are planted in the vineyards of the two wineries whose wines have impressed us most. (They will therefore be labelling wines made from these varieties as VR Transmontano.) The politics of wine legislation in the region has always been driven by the co-operative wineries in Valpaços and Chaves, and what counted was what their members have in their vineyards. Sogrape has a winery in Trás-os-Montes, where it processes red grapes for use in the production of Mateus Rosé. With rare exceptions, wines produced in Trás-os-Montes are not often seen outside the region. Both of our top wineries are to be found in the central part of the region, near Valpaços.

Above and opposite
A mix of Portuguese and international grape varieties on part of Valle Pradinhos' 400ha estate

Right New oak barrels, vats and tanks in the Valle Pradinhos winery

WINERIES

SESULFE

Casal de Valle Pradinhos It was the hunting that first attracted Manuel Pinto de Azevedo, who bought this estate and various parcels of land surrounding it in 1913. He would bring guests up to shoot over the 400ha of the property, and planted vines so he had wine from the estate to serve at meals. His chosen mix of local and international grapes remains unchanged: the wines here are made from Cabernet Sauvignon, Touriga Nacional, Tinta Roriz and Tinta Amarela, Riesling, Gewurztraminer and Malvasia Fina.

The estate is now run by his great-grand-daughter, Maria Antónia Pinto de Azevedo Mascarenhas. There are 32ha of vineyard, 80ha of olive trees and about 200ha of cork oaks. And yes, there is still hunting. Of the vines, 8ha are about 30 years old, mostly Cabernet Sauvignon, and it is these that go into the estate's top wine, **Valle Pradinhos**. The rest of the grapes, from vineyards replanted more recently, are used to make **Porta Velha**, the estate's second label. The cellar has also been re-equipped, with modern stainless steel everywhere and a new bottling line. Rui Cunha, one of northern Portugal's best consultant winemakers, is in charge of the wines. You can tour the vineyard and winery, and have a taste, but you must make an appointment in advance.

In 1952, the family also started a hotel for hunters, the Estalagem do Caçador. You don't have to arrive with a gun these days, and it has been considerably smartened up, but still has much of the charming old furniture and décor *(page 78)*.

The white **Valle Pradinhos** is a real surprise, an aromatic, citrussy, off-dry blend of 70% Riesling with Malvasia Fina and Gewurztraminer. **Porta Velha**, the second-label red, is mainly Tinta Roriz, with some Touriga Nacional, soft and ripe, with bright red berry fruit. The red **Valle Pradinhos** steals the show, a blend of Cabernet Sauvignon, Touriga Nacional and Tinta Amarela, full of dense, dark, herby, red and black fruit flavours, with very firm tannins. Valle Pradinhos is always released before Porta Velha, as its reputation means it's snapped up fast.
Sesulfe, 5340-422 Macedo de Cavaleiros
T+351 278 421 716 / 916 593 802
E valleppradinhoswines@sapo.pt
Visits appt only

Quinta do Sobreiró de Cima This estate has been owned by the same family for over 120 years. It's in the hot part of Trás-os-Montes, the *Terra Quente*, and has 42ha of vines and 17ha of 350-year-old olive-trees. Up until 2000, António Teixera, the present owner, delivered the grapes from his 10ha of old vines to the local co-op, but he decided to go it alone in 2001. Since then, he has bought 32ha more, some old vines and some new. 20ha of vineyard are on granite soils near the estate, the rest on schistous soil in the Rio Torto area. All are farmed without the use of herbicides or pesticides, and the grapes are hand-picked into small plastic crates.

The winery has been modernised, to include small stainless steel vats and a sorting belt, where four women check that only the best bunches make it into the wine. In 2007, work started on an entirely new winery, which will have a tasting room for the first time. It should be finished in 2009, and the hope is to receive visitors from then on. Until then, you'll just have to look for the wines if you're in Trás-os-Montes. Rui Cunha and Raquel Cruz are the winemakers.

The **Quinta do Sobreiró de Cima Rosé** is herby, dry and attractive, made from Touriga Nacional and Syrah. The young red, **Quinta do Sobreiró de Cima Tinto**, is bright, rich and herby, with firm but ripe tannins, a blend of Touriga Nacional, Tinta Roriz and Trincadeira. The oldest vines go into the **Quinta do Sobreiró de Cima Tinto Reserva**, mainly Touriga Nacional, but with quite a bit of Trincadeira, and some other grapes, as is usually the way with old vines. It's serious wine, with black fruit flavours and dense, high tannins.

Eat in Trás-os-Montes

It would seem that even two millennia ago, pork was a vital part of the diet in these mountains – ancient, crudely fashioned stone pigs have been found all around the area (now most often in museums). It's hard around here to avoid pork, and pork fat vies with the local olive oil for cooking. Anyway, most visitors will relish the tasty meat of the Bísaro pigs, a rare breed still common in the north east. The region is famous for its sausages and cured hams, sometimes smoked over oak, or sometimes chestnut. This is a cuisine firmly based on meat, and next on the menu are the various breeds of long-horned cattle. *Posta Mirandesa* is a huge steak of beef or veal, served with

potatoes roasted in their skins, in garlicky olive oil. Mountain goats feature strongly too, often as kid *(cabrito)*. The partridge season runs from October to December, and woodcock shooting goes on until February. Other game specialities are roebuck and wild boar.

Country soups and stews are the mainstays. *Cozido à portuguesa* (a pot-boiled dish of beef, pork, chicken, *chouriço*, onions, potatoes and various vegetables, *pictured opposite*, is eaten now all over Portugal, but it started here, where it's the celebration dish of choice. *Feijoada à Transmontana* is a delicious stew made of dried beans with all kinds of pig's offal, from trotters to smoked ears,

KNOW YOUR SAUSAGES

Some Trás-os-Montes sausages, particularly those of the small town of Vinhais, in the Serra de Montesinho west of Bragança, and Montalegre, in the far north-west of the region, have protected and regulated status. Those from Vinhais and Montalegre all have to be made from pure-bred Bísaro pigs, or crosses of the Bísaro with another breed. *Alheiras* need cooking; *chouriças*, *butelo* and *salpicão* can be eaten as they come, or cooked.

Alheira de Barroso – Montalegre Thin, yellowish or brownish, fine-textured sausage from around Montalegre, made from pork, chicken, duck, rabbit, bread, garlic, hot and sweet paprika, onion and local olive oil.

Alheira de Mirandela Similar to the Barroso version above, but it may contain ham, beef or veal as well, and the pork does not have to be Bísaro. Its regulated status is not yet rubber-stamped. *(Pictured right)*

Alheira de Vinhais A smooth, smoked pork sausage containing local wheat bread and olive oil. (*Alheiras* were originally developed in this region by Jewish refugees obliged by the Inquisition to make at least a show of eating pork; the Jewish *alheiras* substituted chicken and game.)

Butelo de Vinhais A chubby smoked sausage made with pork meat and fat, along with garlic, paprika and local wine.

Chouriça Doce de Vinhais Well, you'd never know to look at it, but the *chouriço* has had a sex change around these parts.

This 'Sweet Chouriça' is an exotic creature, containing local honey, nuts, olive oil and bread, as well as not-too-fatty, partly-cooked pork. It is usually cooked, but can be served cold, cut into thin slices.

Chouriça de Carne de Barroso – Montalegre Dark red, thin, fatty smoked sausage with Bísaro pork meat, wine, garlic and hot and/or sweet paprika.

Chouriça de Carne de Vinhais/Linguiça de Vinhais Dark red, thin, fatty smoked sausage made from pork, pork fat, local wine, garlic, bay and paprika. Sometimes spicy.

Chouriço Azedo de Vinhais Smoked sausage made from cooked pork and pork fat, local wheat bread, olive oil, paprika and garlic.

Salpicão de Barroso – Montalegre Big salami-sized sausage made from pork and pork fat, garlic, wine and paprika. Can be produced in Boticas, Chaves and Montalegre.

Salpicão de Vinhais Lean smoked sausage made from pork tenderloin, broad in diameter (15-20cm), flavoured with local wine, garlic, bay and paprika.

THE HAMS OF TRÁS-OS-MONTES

The ancient *Porco Bísaro* used to be farmed more widely. Now it is more or less limited to the mountains and hills of Trás-os-Montes and the upper Douro. It's a slim, arched-backed animal with big, floppy ears and long legs, mottled black and pink. It is slow-growing, its diet, like that of its owners, traditionally including chestnuts, pumpkins and potatoes. Its hams *(presuntos)* are distinctive, always dark from liberal use of paprika and long smoking. Being produced in limited quantities, these hams are inevitably expensive. The most reputed hams are from Vinhais, west of Bragança, Chaves, Murça (and Lamego, down in the Douro Valley, out of bounds for this chapter!).

The cool mountain autumns and springs, and the cold winters, are perfect for the preparation of fine cured ham. The legs are dry-salted at a low temperature for around 30 days. They can be flavoured at this stage – maybe with cumin, saffron, garlic, red or white wine and paprika – before being hung up to dry in a place where the air is free to circulate. The ideal temperature is between 3° and 6°C – often achieved nowadays in refrigerated, aerated rooms. The hams lose up to 15% of their initial weight. Summer heat, or a simulated version, makes the hams sweat, allowing the melted fat to penetrate the meat and the flavour to spread throughout the ham. At this point hams may get a few days' smoking over oak or chestnut fires. The best will then continue to age for 12 to 24 months, the flesh darkening with age, but cheaper hams are saleable after four months.

maybe with some *presunto*. *Coelho de cebolada* is a rabbit and onion stew. Dried fish (*bacalhau* and octopus) has been a special treat for centuries. Boiled octopus is eaten at Christmas, and the local *bola de bacalhau* is a simple codfish, onion and garlic pie made with yeasty pastry.

Trás-os-Montes keeps Portugal supplied with chestnuts *(castanhas)*, which appear in many local dishes, sometimes as the main staple – as indeed they traditionally were. They are also eaten on their own, boiled in water with aniseeds, then roasted. The *Transmontanos* eat lots of potatoes too, and excellent bread made from rye, corn, wheat or a mixture. The delicious local corn bread is known as *broa*.

Mountain honeys are on sale everywhere, some with special denominations: Mel do Baroso, Mel do Parque de Montesinho and Mel da Terra Quente are all highly regulated. Cheeses are mainly goat and sheep: you will meet **Terrincho**, a firm, smooth, rather oily, pale yellow sheep's cheese, squat in shape and coated in paprika; and **Cabra Transmontano**, a hard goat's cheese.

PICK OF THE EXTRA VIRGINS

The traditional olive oils tend to be rather rustic, though they are improving. These two are world-class quality, however.

Romeu Excellent, characterful, slightly exotic-flavoured organic oils from near Mirandela.

Val d'Ondel/Sardeiro Very good organic olive oils from Quinta do Carrascal in the south-east of Trás-os-Montes.

BRAGANÇA C3

O Geadas A large, friendly restaurant with views from its big windows and terrace over the River Fervença. They serve good local cuisine, including lots of game. Puddings are a speciality. Portions are generous, so you might prefer to go easy on the nibbles, which arrive unordered and in profusion.
Rua do Loreto 32/Rua da Fervença
T+351 273 326 002
E ogeadas@hotmail.com
W www.geadas.net
€25 ♀
Open every day Closed 24 & 25 Dec

Solar Bragançano A smart yet inexpensive restaurant in an 18th century town house on the cathedral square, with original features, open fires in winter, and a wood-fired oven. One of the two dining rooms looks out on the romantic garden terrace. Cooking is good and local, with lots of appealing game dishes, *posta mirandesa*, and home-made sausages.
Praça da Sé 34
T+351 273 323 875
E admr.sb@gmail.com
€20 ♀
Open Jul-Sep every day Closed Oct-Jun Mon

CARVIÇAIS C2

O Artur A favourite of wine people from the Douro as well as locally, this remote, cosy, rustic restaurant is hung, pub-like, with all kinds of interesting objects, from mandolin-shaped Portuguese guitars to hats and bits of harness. Food is good, traditional and home-made, with game a speciality in season, as well as wild boar *(javali)*, roast kid *(cabrito)*, and *posta mirandesa;* the roast potatoes are scrumptious. And the wine is very reasonable. Find it in a little old village right down in the south-east of the Trás-os-Montes VR, or approach it from the Douro Superior, on the twisty road between Torre de Moncorvo and Freixo de Espada à Cinta. They have eight rooms to let.
Lugar do Rebentão, Estrada Nacional 222
T+351 279 939 184
E arturgordete@hotmail.com
W www.restauranteoartur.pa-net.pt
€40 ♀ V 🍴 No credit cards

CHAVES B3

Adega Faustino Sit on the little wooden stools and eat *petiscos* or well-cooked traditional dishes in this simple but atmospheric restaurant. This used to be a winery, just off the main street in the old centre of town. Lovers of *bacalhau* will be spoilt for choice. There may be exhibitions of local art, or live music.
Travessa do Olival
T+351 276 322 142
€15 V No credit cards
Closed Sun; Jan

Aprígio A bit hard to find, near the new hospital, an inexpensive, welcoming family-run restaurant with simple decor, green gingham tablecloths, and good, local cooking, which might include calves' feet with chickpeas *(mãozinhas de vitela com grão)* or roast kid *(cabrito).*

Trás do Calvário
T+351 276 321 053
E aprigiochaves@hotmail.com
€15 No credit cards
Closed Sun din

Carvalho Opposite the spa, this is a slightly formal restaurant with very good local cooking, a good wine list, and friendly, attentive service. There is always fresh fish and seafood as well as meat and sausages, and their desserts have won prizes – you might be tempted by the *doces conventuais*.
Alameda do Tabolado, Bloco 4
T+351 276 321 727
€20 ♀ V
Closed Mon; 1 week around Carnaval

FELGAR C2

Casa de Santa Cruz In a pretty little village just this side of the invisible border between the Douro and Trás-os-Montes VR regions, near Torre de Moncorvo, the Casa de Santa Cruz is a small inn with very good local cooking and simple rooms.
Rua Cimo do Lugar 1
T+351 279 928 060
E mail@casadesantacruz.com
W www.casadesantacruz.com
€30 No credit cards
Open every day

GIMONDE C3

Dom Roberto Heading east out of Bragança towards Spain, in a little village on the edge of the Parque Natural de Montesinho, this is an old inn with exposed schist walls hung with agricultural tools and bits of harness, and lots of atmosphere. Very good local cooking includes nourishing soups, game risottos, *porco bísaro* suckling pig *(leitão)*, excellent local lamb, and veal and *porco bísaro* steaks. The wine list is good, too. A shop sells

local produce, and there's accommodation *(page 78)*.
Estrada Nacional 218, km 7
T+351 273 302 510
E droberto@amontesinho.pt
W www.amontesinho.com
€20 ♀ *V if ordered in advance* 🛏
Open every day

MACEDO DE CAVALEIROS C3

Estalagem do Caçador A smart but relaxed restaurant in this historic town-centre inn, where game is the speciality, expertly cooked. You might enjoy hare *(lebre)*, wild boar *(javali)*, or stewed calves' feet *(mãozinhas de vitela estufadas)*, or phone ahead and pre-order the partridge with chestnuts *(perdiz com castanhas)*, or game-based sausages. There's a very well-chosen wine list – the owners are wine producers, from one of the region's top estates, Casal de Valle Pradinhos *(page 67)*. The inn has 25 rooms *(page 78)*.
Largo Manuel Pinto de Azevedo
T+351 278 426 356
€30 ♀ *V* 🛏
Closed Mon; 24 & 25 Dec

MIRANDA DO DOURO D3

A Balbina An attractive, smart but remarkably inexpensive restaurant in the old town centre, decorated in pretty blue and white, with plants. A Balbina has a good wine list matched by accomplished traditional cooking and efficient and friendly service. Balbina Porto Rodrigues is the owner and chef, and has cooked here for nearly 40 years.
Rua Rainha Dona Catarina 1
T+351 273 432 394
€20 ♀ *V*
Closed 24 Dec din, 25 Dec & Easter Sun

MIRANDELA B3

Flor de Sal Opened in July 2004 by a local olive oil producer, gastronome and wine lover, João Paulo Carlão, Flor de Sal

serves inventive, modern dishes such as *carpaccio de porco bísaro*, based on excellent local ingredients, as well as a separate menu of very good local food. With a big terrace right on the bank of the River Tua, and huge windows overlooking the water, the modern building is attractively designed, the interior smart and minimalist, with marble floors and angular fittings, large but still intimate. Tasting menus (including an olive oil menu) offer five dishes with accompanying wines. A very good wine list is particularly strong on the Douro and Trás-os-Montes, but in addition has some very interesting wines from elsewhere in Portugal and abroad. There are good wines by the glass, and wine is served with knowledge and flair.
Parque Dr José Gama 348
T+351 278 203 063
E joaopaulo@flordesalrestaurante.com
W www.flordesalrestaurante.com
€27 ♀ *V*
Open every day

O Grês This is the place to go in Mirandela to eat fresh fish and seafood, as well as the more usual *bacalhau* and local meat dishes, in two big, bright dining rooms with high ceilings, remarkably large old windows, and the kitchen in view. The local sheep's cheese is very good.
Avenida Nossa Senhora do Amparo
T+351 278 248 202
€18 *V*
Closed Sun din; 1st 2 weeks July

MOGADOURO D2

A Lareira On one of the main streets of Mogadouro, the easternmost town just before the Spanish border, 'The Hearth' combines classic French sauces with local dishes, game and wild mushrooms, and local meat grilled in the restaurant's

71

centrepiece, the old brick oven. You might choose local sausage, kid *(cabrito)*, lamb *(borrego)*, or veal steaks. There's a terrace, and a big, simple, rustic dining room. The Douro-based wine list is quite good. There are ten en-suite rooms above the restaurant.
Avenida Nossa Senhora do
Caminho 58-62
T+351 279 342 363
E a.lareira.mogadouro@gmail.com
€20 ⚘ *V* 🛏
No credit cards
Closed Mon; Jan

Maria Rita In a picturesque village half way between Mirandela and Macedo, Maria Rita has long been famous for its very good regional and Portuguese cooking. A very sweet old stone building *(below)*, beautifully renovated, has three cosy and atmospheric dining rooms. Music is classical or jazz, the tone calm and friendly.
Rua da Capela
T+351 278 939 134
E meneres@quintadoromeu.com
W www.quintadoromeu.com
€20 ⚘ *Closed Sun din, Mon*

Gabriela Through three generations of owners, the spacious, friendly restaurant of the Residencial Gabriela has been renowned for its excellent traditional cooking (especially the *posta à Gabriela* steaks). There is also very good charcuterie, and home-made preserves and liqueurs. There are rooms to let *(page 79)*. Find it by the village church, the Igreja Matriz de Santa Maria de Sezim.
Largo da Igreja 27
T+351 273 739 180
€20 🛏 *No credit cards*
Closed 24 & 25 Dec

Passos Perdidos Simple, attractive, spacious restaurant, with a terrace, in a little old village 11km north of Vila Real, on the road to Chaves. A friendly place recommended by numerous Douro wine producers. The food is very traditional and quite heavy but well cooked, and very copious.
Casa da Coutada
T+351 259 347 322
E passos-perdidos@sapo.pt
€18
Closed Tue, Sun din

MARKETS

Mercado Municipal This new, modern block has a traditional market selling smoked hams, charcuterie, meat, fish and seafood, bakery, fruit and vegetables, as well as a modern shopping centre and CyberCentro! *Forte São João de Deus*

Farmers' markets on the 3rd, 12th and 21st of most months, or the following Monday if these fall at a weekend

Mercado Municipal Covered market, especially Thursday, but other mornings

too. **Farmers' markets** Big events, on the 3rd, 14th and 25th of most months.

Mercado 13th or 28th of most months, all kinds of food including ham, sausages, goat's cheese and honeys.

Explore Trás-os-Montes

Dominating a broad, high plateau in the far north-east, surrounded by mountain ranges, the city of BRAGANÇA has the feel of a solid, mountain market town. Historically, Bragança was a strategic border fortress. It was also the origin of the Portuguese royal house of Bragança, which ruled the country from 1640 to 1910, and provided a queen, Catherine of Bragança, for Charles II of England. The square towers of the medieval *citadela* stand above on the hilltop, ringed by sturdy city walls. Within, old whitewashed houses are tightly tucked between cobbled streets and stairways. The city expanded westwards beyond the walls in the 15th century, tumbling down towards and along the River Fervença. Imposing granite houses were added in the 18th century, and the 20th century surrounded it all with an urban sprawl.

Left Walking in the Montesinho mountains

Right One of the towers that dominate Bragança

Below Bragança has the feel of a market town, but it has latterly become more sophisticated

Always the administrative and cultural capital of Trás-os-Montes, important also for its university and its agricultural markets, modern Bragança is a place of growing enterprise and sophistication, the motorway bringing business, tourists, and the return of at least some of the younger citizens who had emigrated to more lucrative lives elsewhere.

It's worth taking a leisurely day or two to explore the historic buildings and streets in and around Bragança's citadel. The town is also a good base for exploring the forested hills, heathery uplands and delightful little villages of the **Parque Natural de Montesinho**, which borders Spain to the north. West of Bragança, through woods and hilly pasture, you come to VINHAIS, a ribbon town likewise on the southern edge of the Natural Park, with lovely castle ruins. Stop to buy some hams and sausages.

CHAVES lies west again, 10km south of the Spanish border, in a wide, fertile valley that leads from Spain down into the interior of Trás-os-Montes. As well as having great potential for winemaking, the eastern side of the Tâmega valley from Chaves southwards has a fault line that gives rise to hot springs (70°C) of strongly mineralised water. The spa water is still used today to treat rheumatism and hypotension, on doctors' orders, as well as being bottled (in places where it emerges in more palatable form) for the table. Accommodation can be hard to find in Chaves in the summer months as a result of this 'medical tourism', so book well in advance. Chaves is a pretty town, its long, 20-arched Roman bridge still in use; gardens surround the

UPGRADING THE SPAS

Trás-os-Montes is soon to have 'two of the finest thermal centres in Europe', according to the big drinks company Unicer (producers of Super Bock beer). The Tâmego valley from Chaves southwards has long been famous for its hot springs, but the spas have been stuck in the past. Now Unicer is spending over €45m to create up-to-date spa facilities, both medicinal and recreational, in two separate locations. In VIDAGO, south of Chaves, the **Vidago Palace Hotel & Spa** is due to re-open in spring 2008, promoted to five stars, its 9-hole golf course expanded to 18. The grand, pink edifice had a faded elegance and beauty even before the renovation; it dates from the turn of the 19th century and is surrounded by 40ha of grounds and forest. Its new thermal spa will be a serious, medical affair, as well as a recreational facility for the hotel. 9km south of Vidago in PEDRAS SALGADAS, Unicer are building a completely new 115-room hotel and spa, this one intended more for fun and relaxation. It should be ready by summer 2009. Also in the Parque Termal de Pedras Salgadas will be the first regional offshoot of Porto's famous gallery of modern art, the Museu de Arte Contemporânea da Fundação de Serralves *(page 128)*.

remnants of the 14th century *castelo*, and there's an atmospheric medieval quarter.

Heading down the valley, perhaps nowadays by motorway, VIDAGO is a quiet spa town, whose grand Vidago Palace Hotel is soon to re-open with expanded golf course and top-class spa. PEDRAS SALGADAS, south again, is likewise getting a makeover, and VILA POUCA DE AGUIAR is an interesting medieval village, famously surrounded by dolmens. Another of the region's natural parks now looms ahead, the **Parque Natural do Alvão**, its main tourist attraction being the spectacular waterfall near the sweet old village of Ermelo.

Seduced by the motorways, we temporarily missed MONTALEGRE, on a plateau up in the north-west by the Serra do Gerês. Montalegre itself is not an exciting town. It sits on a hill, topped by an impressive, much-renovated but unvisitable medieval castle. But the surrounding moorland attracts hill walkers – take advice and maps from the Montalegre tourist office. South of Montalegre is the heathery, mountainous area known as the **Barroso**, where sheep and oxen graze, and reservoirs attract fishing

Opposite Dovecote near Macedo dos Cavaleiros and *left* a nearby farm

Right Castle tower of Mogadouro and bridge over a rocky stream in the Serra do Gerês mountain range

and watersport enthusiasts, as well as walkers.

The towns that link Vila Real (in the Douro chapter) to Bragança are of course more accessible now. Neatly modern MURÇA (half in the Douro, half in Trás-os-Montes) is famous for its Roman bridge and the Porca de Murça, a giant granite Iron Age pig in the main square (the largest of these Trás-os-Montes *berões* or sows). MIRANDELA draws its tourists from the motorway now that the branch line of the Douro railway has closed for good. It's a market town with a fine old bridge. MACEDO DE CAVALEIROS has the **Azibo Dam** for watersports and swimming, and shortly golf, and exciting hang gliding on the **Serra de Bornes**.

Towns off to the south-east are still far from everywhere. Twitchers are in their element – the **Serra de Mogadouro** and **Parque Natural do Douro Internacional** support a wealth of bird life, from black storks to vultures. MOGADOURO itself is a sleepy market town. MIRANDA DO DOURO holds more interest for visitors, though also quiet. High on a cliff, Portugal's eastern-most city (yes, it is a city, though very small), has a lovely old centre with cobbled streets, old white houses, and great views into and across the canyon of the 'Douro Internacional'. An 80m-high road crosses the hydro-electric dam from Miranda to Zamora, in Spain.

✹ VIEW FROM THE TOP ✹

Natural *miradouros* lie around every corner in the mountains of Trás-os-Montes. Here are a few more, architecturally enhanced.
BRAGANÇA **Citadel** The best thing about the military museum in the keep is the wonderful view from the battlements over the city to the surrounding hills. *Open 9-11.45, 2-4.45 Closed Thu; public hols.* **Mosteiro de São Bartolomeu** On the other side of the river, the *miradouro* by the monastery on the hilltop has great views of the *cidadela*.
CHAVES **Torre de Menagem** Fine views from the roof of the military museum in the castle keep, and from the remnants of the castle walls. *Open Mon-Wed, Fri-Sun 9-12, 2-5.30 Closed Thu; public hols.*
MIRANDA DO DOURO **Cathedral terrace** Terrifying views over the Douro gorge and dam.

BRAGANÇA Domus Municipalis
Portugal's oldest town hall, though of uncertain date, a pentagonal Romanesque building whose ceiling is supported by carved stone heads. Find it behind the *cidadela*, within the walls. *Open Fri-Wed 9-4.45 Closed Thu*

Parque Natural do Alvão North of Vila Real, this is Portugal's smallest Natural Park, spanning the ridge of the Serra de Alvão, between the rivers Tâmega and Corgo. The lower slopes are farmed. There are long-horned cattle, some houses are thatched, and the higher reaches are wildly beautiful. The main destination of

intrepid tourists is the 300m waterfall on the River Olo at Fisgas de Ermelo, a 6km climb into very rocky terrain. The park's visitor information centre in Vila Real provides limited leaflets about walks, in Portuguese mainly, and the footpaths are in any case not well mapped. *Visitor Information, Praça Luis de Camões 2, Vila Real*

Parque Natural de Montesinho One of the wildest parts of Europe, between Bragança and the Spanish border, a vast and powerful granite landscape with rivers and lakes, where red-coated Iberian wolves apparently still roam. The Serra de Montesinho is gentle at lower levels, with little villages and farms, meadows and deciduous forests of ancient oaks and sweet chestnuts. Higher, by the Spanish border, it becomes wilder, a land of heather and broom, granite and schist, wolves, falcons and golden eagles. Atmospheric little stone villages are a delight for visitors, but some have been partially or totally deserted by local people tired of a hard and isolated mountain life. Spring is a good time to visit, as the wild flowers are wondrous. The park offices in Bragança and Vinhais can advise walkers and motorists. *Casa do Povo, Rua Dr Álvaro Leite, Bragança; Rua Cónego Albano Falcão 5, Vinhais Open (both) Mon-Fri 9-12.30, 2-5.30*

Serra do Gerês (Parque National da Peneda-Gerês) The drier, eastern side of the Serra do Gerês lies in Trás-os-Montes (the rest of it is in the Minho). The park is highly protected for conservation purposes, and there are no-go areas for walkers, and roads where stopping is not allowed, but there are good walking paths through the forests, hillsides and pasture of the lower, more inhabited areas. For more on the National Park and details of the helpful information centre in Ponte da Barca, *see page 57.*

VALE DE NOGUEIRAS Santuário de Panóias Also called Fragas (rocks) de Panóias. On the way from Vila Real to Sabrosa, but in an enclave of the VR Trás-os-Montes, this National Monument consists of three big boulders, visitable

with the aid of fixed ladders. 'Bowls' of various sizes were hollowed out at some point in the distant past, possibly to contain blood and entrails following human or animal sacrifices. One rock bears Greek and Roman inscriptions. *Vale de Nogueiras Open Tue 2-5 Wed-Sun 9-12.30, 2-5 Closed Mon, Tue am, 1 Jan, Easter Sun, 1 May, 25 Dec*

Igreja Santa Maria The charming 16th to 17th century Baroque church within the *citadela* walls has a peeling *trompe-l'oeil* ceiling, and carved vines twist around pillars at the entrance *(below)*.

CHAVES **Igreja da Misericórdia** *Azulejo*-clad walls, painted ceiling and gilded altar. *Praça de Camões*

MIRANDA DO DOURO **Sé** The imposing square-towered cathedral, built in the 16th century, has fine wood carvings, including a figure of the boy Jesus, the *Menino Jesus da Cartolinha*, whom the townspeople still dress in an ever-changing wardrobe of clothes, a tradition that began after a siege in 1711, when the figure apparently helped the inhabitants hold out against the Spanish.

FAIRS & FESTIVALS
JANUARY
MONTALEGRE **Feira do Fumeiro e Presunto do Barroso** Big charcuterie fair, second to third week of the month.

FEBRUARY
VINHAIS **Feira do Fumeiro** A festival of smoked charcuterie, early in the month. Lots of sausages, ham, music, folklore, a bullfight, fireworks, and festivities.

MUSEUMS & GALLERIES
BRAGANÇA **Museu Abade de Baçal** The Abbot of Baçal was a local scholar and historian. This serious, wide-ranging museum is housed in Bragança's 16th century Bishop's Palace. See a collection of the region's famous stone pigs *(berrões)*, plus coins, paintings dating from the 18th century to the present day, local costumes and instruments of torture. *Rua Conselheiro Abílio Beça Open Tue-Fri 10-5 Sat & Sun 10-6 Closed Mon; public hols*

MIRANDA DO DOURO **Museu da Terra de Miranda** Evocative museum of local domestic and farming life – regional costumes, kitchen utensils, furniture and farming tools, and archaeological finds. *Domus Municipalis, Praça Dom João III*

Open Summer Tue 2.30-6 Wed-Sun 9.30-12.30, 2-6 Winter Tue 2.30-6 Wed-Sun 9-12.30, 2-5.30 Closed Mon

CHURCHES
BRAGANÇA **Igreja de São Bento** *Trompe-l'oeil* and carved, Arabic-style ceilings are the high point of this beautiful church. *Rua São Francisco*

Igreja de São Vicente Romanesque to 18th century church combining giltwork and *azulejos*. This is the church where Pedro I is said to have married his lover Inês de Castro in 1354 before she was murdered by his father *(page 196). Largo de São Vicente*

Sleep in Trás-os-Montes

ALGERIZ B3

Casa da Aldeia In a little mountain village west of Valpaços, this big, white country house overlooks the village and mountains, out to the horizon. It is for rent as a whole self-catering unit rather than as bed and breakfast rooms. Beautifully renovated, preserving period detail and furniture, it is very well appointed and equipped. It has two double bedrooms, two quadruple and one single, two bathrooms, three living rooms, open fires, a huge old kitchen with traditional fireplace, and long, shady terraces upstairs. Outside is a garden terrace, nature and peace. The helpful owners live just alongside. Everyone who stays there loves it.
Algeriz, Valpaços
T+351 962 056 663/934 200 382
E aglobo@gmail.com
€630-€950 per week [SC] *1(9-13)*
Min nights 3 No credit cards

ARCAS C3

Solar das Arcas A grand, historic manor house on the biggest farm in Trás-os-Montes (600ha), which grows organic olives and fruit, especially cherries. There's woodland, a lovely garden, a pool and barbecue in a walled courtyard, fine mountain vistas, and a friendly welcome in this very small mountain village.

Spacious, rustic houses and studios in the outbuildings have kitchenettes, and central heating. If so inclined, you can help on the farm, and they have another 800ha of land for hunting. Find it east of Valpaços.
Arcas, 5340-031
Macedo de Cavaleiros
T+351 278 400 010
E solardasarcas@solardasarcas.com
W www.solardasarcas.com
€130 for houses sleeping 4, €65 for studios
sleeping 2 or 3 (without breakfast)
[S] / [SC] *6(4&2+1)*
[X]*on request* [≈] *No credit cards*
Min nights (2 in Aug)

CASTRELOS C3

Moinho do Caniço Historic stone watermill (self-catering), just west of Bragança on the banks of the river Baceiro. Cosy and atmospheric, it has two bedrooms, double and twin, two bathrooms, kitchen-dining room and sitting room. Castrelos is on the brink of the Montesinho Natural Park, perfectly placed for walking, trout fishing, peace and quiet.
Ponte de Castrelos, 5300-471 Castrelos
T+351 273 323 577
E moinho@bragancanet.pt
W www.bragancanet.pt/moinho
€80-€100 [SC] *1(4+2) No credit cards*
Min nights 2 (1 at short notice)

GIMONDE C3

A Montesinho Grupo Scattered around a village on the edge of the Parque Natural de Montesinho, rooms in seven holiday houses in very different styles, from old farmhouse to sleek and modern. Connected with the very good local restaurant, Dom Roberto *(page 70)*. Rooms can be rented individually, sharing kitchen facilities with other guests, or you can rent whole units.
Rua Coronel Álvaro Cepeda, Gimonde,
5300-553 Bragança
T+351 273 302 510
E info@amontesinho.pt
W www.amontesinho.com
€46-€56 (€40-€50 without breakfast)
[⌂]*22* [SC] *6(4, 4+1, 6, 10+1, 10+5)* [Y] [X]

LIMÃOS C3

Casa dos Pinelas Old village house beautifully renovated with lots of exposed stone walls. The modern woodwork and furniture tastefully integrated with original features. There is a shared sitting room with wood-burning stove, a pool surrounded by lawns, a rocky terrace, and a smart new tennis court.
Rua do Outeiro, Limãos-Salselas,
5340-400 Macedo de Cavaleiros
T+351 278 441231 / 967 713 661
E casa@casadospinelas.pt
W www.casadospinelas.com
€50-€60 [⌂]*8* [X]*on request* [≈] [⚲]
No credit cards

MACEDO DE CAVALEIROS C3

Estalagem do Caçador The smartly traditional 'Hunter's Inn', with its excellent restaurant *(page 71)*, is right in the centre of this small hill town. It has the feel of a country house, with hunting pictures and trophies, plentiful antiques, and comfy sofas (by the fire in winter). And if you are keen to visit the local wineries, our two top choices are within easy reach. Indeed the 'Hunter's Inn' is owned by the Pinto de Azevedo family of Casal de Valle Pradinhos *(page 67)*, just 7km away. As you would expect, the wines are good. Rooms are comfortable and homely. There's a garden where you can

eat out in summer, and an outdoor pool in a flowery pink courtyard. The surrounding country has good walks, a top-class local hang gliding centre, and an 18-hole golf course is to open in 2008 at the nearby Azibo Dam.

Largo Manuel Pinto Azevedo, 5340-219
  Macedo de Cavaleiros
T+351 278 426 356
E estalagemdocacador@sapo.pt
€85-€98 🛏25 ⚐ ✗ 🏊
Closed 24 & 25 Dec

MIRANDELA (CHELAS) B3

Quinta Entre Rios There are seven en-suite rooms in the 18th century farmhouse, three in the annexe of this organic 'Farm Between Rivers' – the Tuela and the Rabaçal, 2km outside Mirandela. The house was tastefully renovated at the turn

of this century. Guests have the use of a long first-floor terrace, sitting and dining rooms, games room and library. The farm grows mainly olives in the hills. Breakfasts include home-made bread, ewe's milk cheese and sausages. There's an outdoor pool and tennis court, bicycles and horses.

Chelas, 5370-070 Mirandela
T+351278 263 160
E quintaentrerios@sapo.pt
W www.quintaentrerios.do.sapo.pt
€60-€75 🛏9 ✗ 🏊 ♞ *No credit cards*
Min nights 2 (1 at short notice)

MONTESINHO C4

A Lagosta Perdida It would be hard to find a more perfect base for a holiday in the Serra de Montesinho. Sally Godward and Robert Van der Vliet and their young son left their home in the Isle of Skye to transform this charming mountain house in the village of Montesinho. The road stops at the village. It's a 2km walk or a 5km drive to the Spanish border, a 13km drive south to Bragança. The characterful old house with its thick stone walls and tiny windows has been lovingly restored. Rooms are simple and delightfully rustic. Guests share the terrace, garden, games room and library. There's table tennis, mountain bikes to borrow, a reservoir nearby, and the swimming pool at 1,000m, is thought possibly to be Portugal's highest!

Aldeia de Montesinho, 5300-542 Bragança
T+351 273 919 031
E lagostaperdida@lagostaperdida.com
W www.lagostaperdida.com
€90-€120 inc breakfast and din for 2
🛏6 ✗ *on request including V!* 🏊

SAMAIÕES B3

Hotel Rural Casa de Samaiões An imposing, low-built manor house, four centuries old, in a village only 5km from Chaves, this was extensively modernised and opened as a hotel in 2001 by the Pereira Machado family. There's a gym, sauna, outdoor swimming pool, plus a little pool for children, a grassy football

pitch, tennis, archery and organised walks in and around the 100ha estate. And beautiful views all around.

Samaiões, 5400-574 Chaves
T+351 276 340 450
E info@hotel-casasamaioes.com
W www.hotel-casasamaioes.com
€72-€93 🛏18 S 2(4) ✗ 🏊 🛁 🕴 ♞

SENDIM D2

Residencial Gabriela This old inn in a village to the south-west of Miranda do Douro makes a good base for visiting the Parque Natural do Douro Internacional – all the more so because its restaurant is famous hereabouts *(page 72)*. It's a nice old building by the village church, a first floor terrace supported by pillars. Enjoy the home-made preserves for breakfast.

Largo da Igreja 27, Sendim,
  5225- Miranda do Douro
T+351 273 739 180
€40-€50 🛏10 S 1 ✗ *No credit cards*

VIDAGO (MATOSINHOS) B3

Quinta do Real An aristocratic country house built in the late 17th century, Quinta do Real has style and rustic elegance. Some bedrooms (all with private bathroom) are in the main house, some in outbuildings, but all have use of the two sitting rooms, one grand, one more cosy, with a wood-burning stove, as well as a bar and games room and a lovely inner courtyard with stone table. There's a pool in the garden, forest round about, and the possibility of mountain bikes, quad-biking, horses and paint ball – it is best to book these in advance.

Matosinhos, 5400-740 Chaves
T+351 276 966 253
E quintadoreal@sapo.pt
W www.quintadoreal.com
€50-€65 🛏9 ✗ *packed lunches* 🏊
No credit cards Min nights 2

Douro

Source of the grapes for port, and for many of Portugal's finest unfortified reds, the Douro is also one of the world's most beautiful wine regions, with its winding river, sculptured terraced hillsides and wild hill vistas rolling out to the horizon. From its source in Spain, the Douro meanders 200km east-west across northern Portugal to its estuary in Porto, through deep ravines and dams, past schist and granite hillsides and terracotta-tiled white farmhouses. Famous port names stand out in large, white capitals amidst the vines. Quintas and vineyards cling to precipitous slopes along the main river, while more vines and most of the villages are tucked up the tributaries. The way man has tamed the rugged countryside, with hundreds of kilometres of contoured dry-stone terraces, has earned the upper Douro its place as a UNESCO World Heritage Site.

Until recently, the Douro was a beautiful back-water, reached only by the wine trade and the hardiest of tourists. All that is changing (except for the beauty), and the Douro Valley is slowly becoming a smart tourist destination – though you still won't meet hoards of fellow travellers. Comfortable, atmospheric old manor houses and quintas are turning into guest houses, with pools and stunning views. There are even some brand-new boutique hotels. Where once you would have satisfied your hunger with goat stew and cabbage soup, now suddenly there are also a few truly gastromic restaurants. And it's easier to get here, now that the motorway whisks you up from Oporto to Vila Real.

Even the river has changed. It used to flow tumbling and crashing towards the Atlantic ocean, and notorious rapids claimed the lives of those unlucky enough to misjudge the currents. Nine dams, built in the mid-20th century, have calmed the Douro. Up to that time, *barcos rabelos* (flat-bottomed sail-boats) used to carry pipes of port precariously down to be matured in Vila Nova de Gaia. Now the Douro is a pleasure-river, where stately cruisers glide. And port shippers can zip safely around on speedboats to follow the progress of the harvest.

For active tourists there are castles galore, and archaeological sites. There's fishing, windsurfing and canoeing, and the tributaries provide safe bathing. Hardy hill walkers and bird-watchers will be in their element. The further east you go, the wilder and rockier the terrain, and the hotter and drier the climate. And everywhere there are vines.

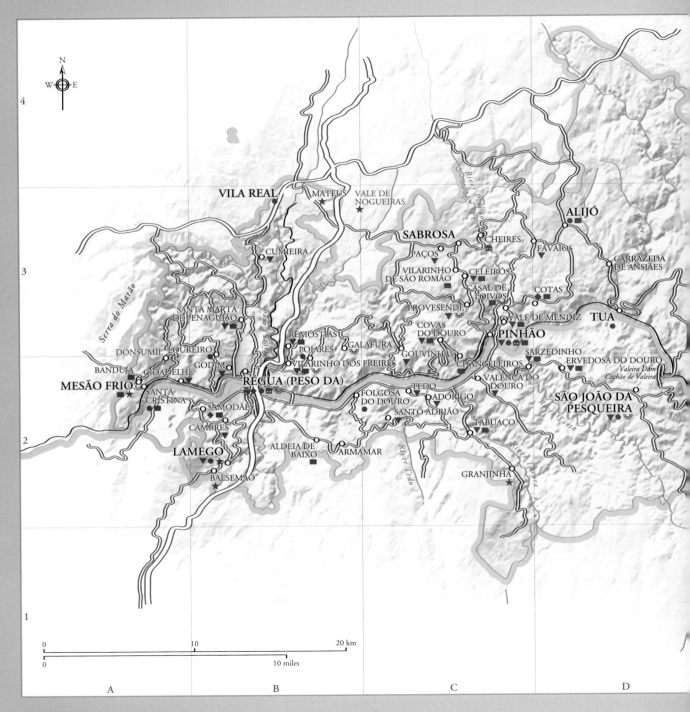

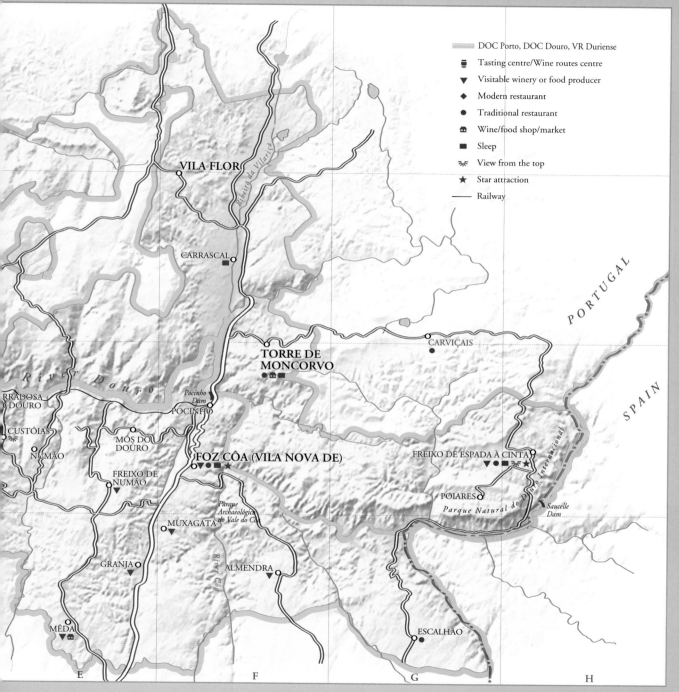

	DOC Porto, DOC Douro, VR Duriense
🍷	Tasting centre/Wine routes centre
▼	Visitable winery or food producer
◆	Modern restaurant
●	Traditional restaurant
🏪	Wine/food shop/market
■	Sleep
⚘	View from the top
★	Star attraction
—	Railway

PORTUGAL

SPAIN

VILA FLOR

CARRASCAL

CARVIÇAIS

TORRE DE MONCORVO

River Douro

Pocinho Dam
POCINHO

 RRADOSA
O DOURO

CUSTÓIAS

MÓS DO DOURO

FOZ CÔA (VILA NOVA DE)

FREIXO DE ESPADA À CINTA

Rio Douro Internacional

NUMÃO

FREIXO DE NUMÃO

POIARES

Saucelle Dam

Parque Archaeológico do Vale do Côa

Parque Natural do Douro Internacional

MUXAGATA

River Côa

ALMENDRA

GRANJA

MÊDA

ESCALHÃO

E F G H

Wine in the Douro

The Douro is one of the world's great wine rivers, up there with the Rhine, the Rhône, the Loire and the Mosel. Whilst most of northern Portugal sits directly upon granite, the Douro gorge is remarkable for its thick upper layer of schist. Indeed, the boundary of the port region encloses the area in which schist predominates – along the main river and a little way up the many tributaries. This hard, dark, multi-layered rock is important for the vines in two respects. Firstly, it absorbs and then radiates heat; and it also allows the limited rain water to seep down, and vine roots to delve deep between rock layers that were once horizontal, but were then wrenched by earth movements into more vertical planes.

The demarcated wine areas for DOC Port, DOC Douro wine and Vinho Regional Duriense all start 100km inland from Porto, a couple of kilometres downstream of the little village of Barqueiros, near Mesão Frio, and finish at the Spanish border. Within the map area, there are some no-go areas for port grapes – these are outcrops of granite or mixed granite/schist terrain, as well as fertile and floodable lowlands. The port vineyards are officially classified into five different qualities, A to F. There are also some areas not considered acceptable for DOC Douro wines either – but table wine is less restricted than port. The VR region covers 45,580ha, the DO Douro wine area 38,057ha, and the DO Port area just 32,290ha.

The western part of the region is known as the Baixo Corgo (Lower Corgo) which runs almost as far as the River Tedo, and includes the towns of Mesão Frio, Lamego and Peso da Régua (generally known simply as Régua). The Baixo Corgo is sheltered from most of the maritime influence of the Atlantic by the massive Serra do Marão range, but this is still the wettest and coolest part of the Douro wine region. Wines and ports here have a softer, gentler profile than those made from grapes at the other end of the region up by the sweltering Spanish border.

Next comes the Cima Corgo (Upper Corgo), which includes the towns of Pinhão and Tua on the river, Tabuaço and São João da Pesqueira south of the river and Alijó and Sabrosa north of it. Here in the historic heartland of the port industry there's a healthy debate over whether to use prized patches of old vines for port or for rich, complex table wines.

The Douro Superior (Upper Douro) goes from Numão up to the Spanish border, taking in Vila Nova de Foz Côa (Foz Côa to the locals), Torre de Moncorvo and Freixo de Espada à Cinta. Bitterly cold winters, the hottest of summers and poor roads gave the port producers of old little incentive to plant here. But the Douro Superior is suddenly sprouting all over with vines – mostly for DOC Douro wines. In what is known as the 'International

> **Wine regions**
> DOC Port
> DOC Douro
> Vinho Regional Duriense
>
> **Main local grapes**
> *Red* Tinta Roriz (Aragonez), Touriga Nacional, Touriga Franca, Tinta Barroca, Tinto Cão and Sousão (Vinhão)
> *White* Viosinho, Malvasia Fina, Gouveio, Rabigato and Côdega (Siria)
> *For details of grapes see page 428*

Opposite The road to Lamelas, Quinta de la Rosa's rentable farmhouse

Left Terrace steps at Quinta do Noval

Right Terrace steps, and pressing business at vintage time

Douro', with Portugal on one side and Spain the other, the Portuguese side is filling up with vineyards wherever planting is possible, while the Spanish side remains wild and uncultivated. It's almost another 100km till you reach Toro, the first official Spanish wine region the other side of the border.

THE PAST OF PORT

For about 300 years, port has been much the same style it is today. How it came to be a fortified wine nobody knows precisely. Some say it was a couple of young Englishmen from Liverpool who first shipped Douro wine fortified with brandy out of Porto in 1678, unwittingly inventing what became a world-renowned style. Whoever started it, the reason is clear: it was much more stable and kept longer if brandy had been added.

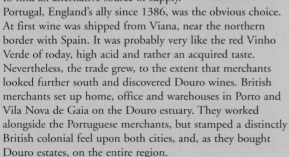

Why Englishmen? Rows and wars between England and France had resulted in a ban on imports of red Bordeaux – claret – and the English wine trade had to find an alternative source of supply. Portugal, England's ally since 1386, was the obvious choice. At first wine was shipped from Viana, near the northern border with Spain. It was probably very like the red Vinho Verde of today, high acid and rather an acquired taste. Nevertheless, the trade grew, to the extent that merchants looked further south and discovered Douro wines. British merchants set up home, office and warehouses in Porto and Vila Nova de Gaia on the Douro estuary. They worked alongside the Portuguese merchants, but stamped a distinctly British colonial feel upon both cities, and, as they bought Douro estates, on the entire region.

For 300 years, the region's fame has rested upon its fortified wine, *vinho do porto* – port. Now the emphasis is shifting, or at least, we are seeing double. The muscular, modern DOC Douro reds are regularly ranked among Portugal's finest. And red grapes from vineyards at higher altitudes (which can be up to 700 metres above sea level), or facing north, are increasingly valued for making more elegant styles of DOC Douro. There's also growing acclaim for the dry, sophisticated whites. Cinderella vineyards of old white-grape vines are at last being sought out by young winemakers. The grapes that used to disappear into white port (improved by ice and tonic) are now used for a new generation of elegant, complex, barrel-fermented DOC Douro whites. There are even a few sweet Muscats, and good sparkling wines.

Vineyard creation and cultivation have been hugely simplified by modern machinery. The wonderful stone-walled terraces (mostly in the Cima Corgo) are preserved by the area's World Heritage Site status, but the new vineyards are different. Where the gradient is gentle enough, vines are planted in rows up and down slopes, rather than following round the contours of the hills. The other modern terraces *(patamares)* are dynamited out of the hillsides, then carved by bulldozers, to allow one or two rows of vines, the earth then sloping steeply down to the terrace beneath. The vinescape has changed, but the effect is still breathtaking.

We take for granted in northern Europe that vineyards are planted by grape variety. Vineyards in the Douro were

Barão de Forrester You can't fail in these parts to come across the charming and opinionated Joseph James Forrester. Born in Hull in 1809, he emigrated in 1831 to work in his uncle's firm Offley Forrester & Co. He was popular for his humour, charm and kindness, and made friends across the divides of class, politics and nationality. But he declined to conform, and in 1844 famously and publicly berated his fellow merchants

and the port wine officials for adulterating their wines with inferior wine from the Beiras, plus sugar and elderberry juice, to satisfy a demand for darker, sweeter wines in Britain. His other contention was that the wines of the Douro should be natural and unfortified – a man before his time. Eventually, the King of Portugal made him a baron, for services to port wine. He loved the Douro, and travelled the hills and rivers, visiting farmers, meticulously mapping the region for the first time, and painting. His watercolours include a view of the Cachão da Valeira, a gorge of wild waters now tamed by a dam. Tragically, he drowned there in 1862, when his *barco rabelo* overturned after a lunch at Quinta de Vargellas. His body was never found, thought to have been weighed down by the money-belt he carried to pay farmers for wine.

Dona Antónia Adelaide Ferreira The serious, kindly eyes of Antónia Adelaide Ferreira will look down upon you if you visit the Ferreira port lodge in Vila Nova de Gaia *(page 134)*. Born in Régua in 1810, she married her cousin, António Bernardo Ferreira. Whilst he enjoyed the business and social life of Porto, building a palace there, his small, reserved but charismatic wife loved the Douro. Together they founded the huge Quinta do Vesúvio estate, and she spent 13 years overseeing the terracing and planting. When she was widowed at 33, left with a young daughter, she not only took on her husband's business, but set about buying and developing vineyards throughout the Douro, finally owning 30 *quintas*. She also used the ensuing wealth to improve the social conditions of the Douro farmers, building hospitals, nurseries, schools and roads. Much loved, she was affectionately nick-named A Ferreirinha (The Little Ferreira Girl). Dona Antónia was also in the boat with Barão de Forrester the day he was lost. But she floated on, buoyed up by her crinoline dress, and was washed up on a sandbank. She died in 1896 at the age of 86.

always planted with a complete jumble of different vines. In 1981, after five years of experimentation at Ramos-Pinto's Quinta do Bom Retiro, five of the region's 80 or so varieties were selected as the best ones to plant. And varietal planting began. The study impressed the World Bank, who financed the planting of 2,500ha in the Douro. Those grapes were Tinta Roriz (Aragonez), Touriga Nacional, Touriga Franca, Tinta Barroca and Tinto Cão. Now, as priorities change, there's more concentration on the first three of these. Sousão (known as Vinhão elsewhere) is the other grape being planted, for its colour (it has red flesh, thus red juice even before the skins give up their colour) and high acidity, being a late ripener.

The traditional picture of port-making shows a shallow, rectangular granite *lagar* with a row of treaders marching back and forth, arms linked, up to their thighs in the squelchy pulp. Pickers trod at the end of a long, hot working day. It's a practice that still goes on – indeed if you arrive at a *quinta* (wine estate) at the right moment in September, you may be invited to don some shorts, wash your dusty feet, and jump in. So why has foot power survived in the Douro? In the first instance, there was little choice. 'Normal' winemaking would use pumps to spray the juice back over the cap, keeping it moist and extracting colour, flavour and tannins. But electricity took a long time to reach the outposts of the Douro – even though Vila Real was the first town in Portugal to install electricity in 1895. It was only the building of the dams on the Douro in the 1960s that provided easily available hydro-electricity to the *quintas*. As the 20th century progressed and labour became a problem, producers used an ingenious vat design from Algeria (the auto-vinificator) that sprayed juice over the cap every 15 minutes or so, powered by the formation of carbon dioxide during fermentation.

But foot-treading served the wine-makers' purpose for another reason. Making port presents the winemaker with problems that don't apply to table wines. To make port, you have to stop the fermentation before it has finished. You run off the part-fermented juice after two or three days and add alcohol, which kills the yeasts and stops the

Opposite Quinta de Roriz, perched on a fold of the riverbank 10km upstream from Pinhão

Right Ancient rafters soar above the *toneis* (big, horizontal barrels) at Wiese & Krohn

fermentation. (This is why port is always sweet, and has high alcohol.) When making red wine, on the other hand, you can allow more time to get the colour, tannins and flavouring out of the grape skins. Often, table wine winemakers will finish the fermentation, then leave the young wine in contact with the skins for still longer to extract more flavour and tannins. In the port-making process, winemakers must make the most of the shorter period for extraction.

Besides foot treading, you will still see autovinificators if you visit the Douro at vintage-time. You might also see modern open, shallow rectangular *lagares*, made of stainless steel, with cooling equipment attached to slow down the fermentation. Some are fitted with robotic 'treaders', or plungers, that mimic the action of the human foot treading the grape-mush. The robots don't need an accordion player or occasional swigs of *bagaceira* (brandy made from skins and pips) to keep them going. More efficient, but less fun.

When the port wine has been made, it must be matured and blended. The same applies to DOC red and white. Traditionally, all port had by law to be shipped from Vila Nova de Gaia, opposite Porto near the mouth of the Douro *(page 120)*. Now that the law has changed, and it's possible to build fully air- and humidity-conditioned cellars, Douro estates are maturing and bottling wines right by their vineyards. And as roads to the Douro have improved, more port and wine producers have opened up their estates to interested visitors.

(Peso da) Régua

Solar do Vinho do Porto Wine bar cum port promotion centre representing all producers and selling by the bottle or by the glass. An attractive, modern space in a converted warehouse. There are also books about port, advice and information, a small museum exhibition area, and sometimes music events.
Rua de Ferreirinha Open Mon-Sat 10-1, 2-7 Closed Sun, public hols

Rota do Vinho do Porto The Port Wine Routes centre near the station is run jointly by local tourist and wine authorities. It is open all year, fixing up accommodation and visits to a selection of producers large and small. They can offer guided tours, and even arrange hands-on visits, where you help in the vines or winery – or wade into the fermentation lagar to join the foot-treaders at vintage time!
Largo da Estação, Apartado 113, 5050-237 Peso da Régua T+351 254 324 774 E reservas@rvp.pt

BARCA VELHA AND CASA FERREIRINHA

Barca Velha is still Portugal's most famous red wine, even if others have now overtaken it in price. The name means 'Old Ship', and it is indeed a very old brand, launched more than half a century ago, the vanguard of the whole movement towards modern unfortified red Douro wines. It was the idea of the young Fernando Nicolau de Almeida *(below right)*, wine-maker-to-be at the Ferreira port company, after a trip to Bordeaux to study winemaking techniques. He was convinced he could make great red wines from Douro grapes, up till that time destined only for port. He realised he had somehow to cool the fermentations in the late summer heat of the Douro Superior (40° to 45°C in the shade). This being before the arrival of electricity, he had blocks of ice brought up from Porto to place around the fermentation tanks. He tried different varieties, grapes from different altitudes, and experimented with ageing the wines in new (Portuguese) oak barrels. Tinta Roriz (Aragonez) finally formed the heart of the blend, and stainless steel vats proved best for fermentation. The first vintage of Barca Velha was 1952. (In an uncanny parallel, Max Schubert created Australia's most famous red, Penfold's Grange, in 1951, also after a visit to Bordeaux.) Even now, Barca Velha is released only in the best years – there have been a mere 15 vintages in total. It is notable above all for its complexity, not a huge wine, despite its origins in the Douro Superior, but always dense, sweet-fruited and very long-lived.

Fernando Nicolau de Almeida made Barca Velha at Quinta do Vale Meão in Foz Côa, owned then as now by the descendants of Dona Antónia Adelaide Ferreira. In 1987, the Ferreira family sold the business (but not Quinta do Vale Meão, *page 95*) to the large, quality-minded firm of **Sogrape**. Sogrape continued to make Barca Velha in the same way for another decade, a blend of Aragonez, Touriga Nacional and Tinta Barroca from the Quinta do Vale Meão, though now the barrels were of French oak. But in 1998, the owner of Quinta do Vale Meão decided to stop selling his grapes to Sogrape.

Barca Velha and the other Sogrape Douro wines are now made at a winery built in 2001 at Quinta da Leda, another Douro Superior estate, in Almendra. (You can't visit Quinta da Leda.)

The latest **Barca Velha** vintage released, 1999, has more Touriga Nacional, Touriga Franca and Tinto Cão and less Tinta Roriz. It is soft, rich and aromatic, with dense, ripe tannins and berry fruit length. In vintages when no wine is selected as Barca Velha, the top wines are released under various **Casa Ferreirinha** labels. Foremost of these is **Casa Ferreirinha Reserva**, a slightly bigger, richer style than Barca Velha. (This will be known as **Reserva Especial** from the 2007 vintage, because of EU regulations.) Then comes **Casa Ferreirinha Colheita**, for the years when the style of the vintage seems to dominate more than the 'Barca Velha character'. **Planalto Reserva** is a Douro white made with grapes from high altitude vineyards, a crisp, unoaked, aromatic blend. **Vinha Grande Branco** is a bright, lemony, subtle white, all fermented in oak, a quarter of which is new. **Vinha Grande Tinto** is rich, dark and serious, with good black-fruit flavours. **Quinta da Leda** (made of equal parts of Touriga Nacional, Touriga Franca and Tinta Roriz) is intense and aromatic, with smooth tannins. There are now two single vineyard wines from Quinta da Leda, the aromatic, dense, Touriga Nacional-dominated **Vinha da Ribeira**, and the bright, thick-fruited, aromatic **Vinha do Pombal**. Callabriga, the new Sogrape range from the Douro, Alentejo and Dão, has a very accessible, herby **Callabriga Douro**, and **Callabriga Douro Reserva**, richer and denser than the normal, with impressive length.

W www.sogrape.pt No visits

CHRYSEIA AND ALTANO

Symington Family Estates is the largest vineyard owner in the Douro. The extended Symington family has been a hub of the port trade for generations. Their port portfolio currently includes Dow, Warres, Graham's, Quinta do Vesuvio, Smith Woodhouse, Quarles Harris and Gould Campbell *(for details of their ports, see page 140)*. They own the Madeira Wine Company, too. But they came quite recently to DOC Douro wines. Their first serious attempt was in 1999. The reason? If they wanted to buy the best grapes for port from a grower, they had to buy all the others as well, including those not suitable for port. So the Symingtons started making unfortified wine. For a few years, their Altano wines were adequate rather than awesome. Then, in 1998, they got together with Bruno Prats, ex-owner of Château Cos d'Estournel in Bordeaux, to start a joint wine project.

The result was Chryseia 2000, made in a specially built micro-vinification area of the Symington winery, Quinta do Sol in Parada do Bispo, not far upstream from Régua. A Bordeaux winemaker collaborates with Pedro Correia, the Symington red winemaker. **Chryseia** is wonderfully elegant, with raspberry perfume and smooth tannins. It is made mainly from Touriga Nacional, Touriga Franca, Tinta Roriz and Tinto Cão. In 2002, they didn't feel the wine was quite up to standard for Chryseia, so created **Post Scriptum**, a second label. It has the same smoothness and elegance as Chryseia, but a slightly fresher, more accessible style. This work on the Prats & Symington project has had a beneficial effect on Altano as well. Altano is now rich, ripe and up-front, and Altano Reserva is fresh, aromatic and densely textured, with lovely, creamy oak.

ADORIGO C2

Quinta de São Luiz Quinta de São Luiz is right opposite Quinta do Crasto, on the south side of the Douro. Bought by the Barros port company in 1922, it has taken in neighbouring estates over the years to bring it to 125ha, 90ha of which are planted with vines. The main grapes are Touriga Nacional and Tinta Roriz (about a quarter each), with smaller amounts of Touriga Franca and Tinta Barroca, and then the usual jumble of other varieties in the old vineyards. A new winery was built in 1998, incorporating such things as steel tanks with pneumatic plungers, and this is what you will be shown round, normally on Saturday afternoons in the spring and summer, with a tasting, of course.

The estate's grapes are made into DOC Douro and port under the Kopke and Barros labels, although most go into ports. The unfortified **Kopke Tinto Reserva** is all from São Luiz, with good berry fruit and fresh acidity, and the **Barros Touriga Nacional** even better, herbily aromatic, with rich, ripe tannins. Best of the DOC Douro wines from São Luiz is the **Barros Grande Escolha**, almost all Touriga Nacional, which develops rich, meaty complexity if given age in bottle. The **Kopke Vintage Port** is all from São Luiz grapes, again beautifully aromatic, with firm tannins.

5120-012 Adorigo, Tabuaço
Visits Sat 2-5 May-Sep appt only
T +351 223 746 660
E turismo@sogevinus.com
W www.sogevinus.com

ALMENDRA F1

CARM – Casa Agrícola Roboredo Madeira The Madeira family own six estates up in the wild east, with breathtaking views over the Douro Superior countryside. Some of their 500ha of vines, olive and almond trees are well away from the river Douro, one looking out on the river Côa. This is the driest part of the Iberian peninsula, with less rain than the Sahara, and in summer it gets very hot indeed. The advantage for the grapes is that there is little threat from moulds; it was therefore relatively easy for Celso Madeira to convert (in 1995) to organic farming. Now all the wines are made from organic grapes. The winery, built in 2004, is immaculate, with stainless steel *lagares* with robotic 'treaders'. Celso's son Rui looks after the wine side *(above left, with brother Filipe)*. For such a remote spot, visits have to be by appointment, but are offered throughout the year. You can take a tour around the Quinta das Marvalhas, see the winery, and taste.

CARM's only white wine is the rich, complex **CARM Reserva Branco**, made from 60 year-old mixed vines. **CARM Rosé** is herby, elegant and dry, and then you're into reds. The **Quinta do Côa Tinto** is soft and elegant, and the basic **CARM Tinto** dense and herby. The **CARM Grande Reserva** is even better, aromatic, with fine, ripe tannins and lovely length. Best is the **CARM CM** (named after Celso Madeira), dense, but fresh and vigorous,

with lovely acidity and great length. CARM also produce almonds, and some of the finest olive oils in Portugal *(page 106)*.
Rua de Calábria, 5150-021 Almendra
T +351 279 718 010
E sales@carm.pt
W www.carm.pt
Visits 9-6 all year appt only

CAMBRES B2

Quinta de Monsul Quinta de Monsul is the Douro headquarters of Porto Rozès, with a recently-opened, state-of-the-art winery and bottling plant. Porto Rozès was started in 1855 by a Frenchman, Ostende Rozès, to import Port into Bordeaux. The headquarters are now in Vila Nova de Gaia, and it's no longer owned by the Rozès family, but still by a French company, Vrancken-Pommery Monopole (V-PM), best known for their Champagnes. When V-PM bought Rozès in 1999, Monsul was the only quinta the company owned. Since then, V-PM has bought several more, including the wonderful Quinta do Grifo right up by the Spanish border, where griffon vultures glide, borne high on hot air currents. Monsul is the only estate at which Rozès receives visitors, and it's much more accessible than Grifo, being halfway between Régua and Lamego, about 10km south of the Douro. It's a historic estate, having belonged in the 12th century to Afonso Henriques, first King of Portugal. You'll tour vineyards and winery, and be given a tasting.

If you're in Barca de Alva, by the way, particularly in the heat of summer (probably over 40°C in the shade), drop in to the gloriously air-conditioned Dom Rozès, a wine-bar just above the quay where cruise-boats put in. There you can taste the full range of Rozès ports and DOC Douro wines (or, if you fancy a change, Champagnes from the parent company). Our choice would be the **Quinta do Grifo Reserva Tinto**, bright and herby, with Touriga Nacional length. Or you could have a **Rozès White Reserve Port** and tonic, to aid the chilling process.
5100-381 Cambres
T +351 223 771 680
E angelica.gomes@rozes.pt
W www.rozes.pt
Visits Mon-Fri 10-5 appt only

CELEIRÓS C3

Quinta do Portal Portal burst upon the Douro wine scene at the beginning of the 1990s. They have four Douro wine estates, making very good, modern wines. A purpose-designed visitor centre offers tastings, a restaurant serves good meals (by prior arrangement), and there's a modern guesthouse, Casa das Pipas – 'House of Barrels' *(page 115)*. The company is owned by the Branco family, and one of the estates, Quinta dos Muros, has been in the family for over a century. Quinta

do Portal, site of the winery, visitor centre and guesthouse, is up near the village of Celeirós, at about 500m altitude. Most of Portal's vineyards lie at highish altitudes for the Douro, so escaping the incessant summer heat at least by night, and producing grapes that make wines of freshness and elegance. Quinta da Abeleira, one of the five estates, is near Favaios, a village known for its Moscatel wines, so Portal has access to Moscatel grapes for fortified and unfortified wines.

From the beginning, the Brancos realised they would do best to concentrate on DOC Douro wines. But as their only experience was of growing grapes for port, they consulted Pascal Chatonnet, a well-known Bordeaux oenologist. And the results have been terrific. The top-of-the-range Portal wines and ports have won very high awards in international competitions. Even the **Quinta do Portal Branco** is bright and fresh, with a telling hint of Moscatel perfume, and the **Quinta do Portal Rosé** is dry, with a rosehip perfume. The single variety **Quinta do Portal Touriga Nacional** is herbily aromatic, with high ripe tannins, and the **Quinta do Portal Grande Reserva** is discreet, with red fruit flavours and ripe length. **Auru**, made from 25 year-old vines in Quinta dos Muros, has bright, herby aromas and firm tannins. The finish is delicious, but it needs time in bottle.

For a company specialising in DOC Douro wines, the ports are good, too. The **Portal LBV** is easy, with structure and freshness, and the **Portal Vintage** is dark, ripe and appealing. In 2003, they released **Portal+ Vintage**, more restrained than the normal Vintage, with black fruits and lovely Touriga Nacional perfume. And then there are the **Moscatels**. These are probably the best examples of fortified Moscatel you'll find in the Douro, definitely worth trying if you're a Muscat fan.

EN 323 Celeirós do Douro, PO Box 2,
*   5060 Sabrosa*
T+351 259 937 104
E frebelo@quintadoportal.pt
W www.quintadoportal.pt
Visits Wed-Sun 10-12.30, 2.30-6.30
 ⊨ ✕ *by prior arrangement*

CIDADELHE A2

Quinta do Côtto Miguel Champalimaud, owner of Quinta do Côtto, is not a conformist. It was he who pioneered the shipping of good red DOC Douro wine from his estate, when all around were making port. Recently, he has become the first Portuguese producer to switch to screwcap closures for two of his wines in protest at the variability of cork. In the world's largest cork-producing country, that was high treason. And the wines are good, the estate worth a visit. It's a handsome 18th century manor house perched high above the surrounding countryside, with 50ha of vineyards and wonderful views. You need an appointment to visit at weekends, but otherwise they are well prepared for visitors, and will show you round the winery and give you a tasting for no charge.

Champalimaud's white wine does not come from Quinta do Côtto, but from another estate, the 12ha Paço de Teixeró. **Paço de Teixeró** is in the Vinho Verde DOC, but only about 200m from the river Douro, and more like a white Douro than a Vinho Verde in character. The principal grape is the creamy, full-bodied Avesso, which combines well with the fragrance of Loureiro and Trajadura. It's not sold as Vinho Verde, but as Vinho Regional Minho, to make the point that it's different from most Vinhos Verdes. **Quinta do Côtto** red has good, straightforward berry fruit and savoury concentration. **Quinta do Côtto Grande Escolha** is the wine that has made Côtto's reputation, a rich, complex red,

with considerable ageing potential. And the **Champalimaud Vintage Port** is good, in the raisiny Lower Corgo style.
Cidadelhe, 5040-154 Mesão Frio
T+351 254 899 269
E inform@quinta-do-cotto.pt
W www.quinta-do-cotto.pt
Visits Mon-Fri all year 10-12, 2-5
*   Sat/Sun appt only*

COVAS DO DOURO C3

Quinta do Infantado In 1979, Quinta do Infantado was the first Douro estate for about 50 years to start bottling and selling its ports from the estate. Other quintas were selling their wines to the well-known port shippers, who would transport them to Gaia, blend, mature and sell them, very often to export markets. All port destined for export had to be shipped from Gaia, by law – it was illegal to export a wine direct from the Douro. To Luis Roseira, one of the brothers who own the *quinta*, this seemed unfair and protectionist, as anyone who had no warehouse in Gaia was excluded from exporting port. When Portugal joined the European Community in 1986, this law was thrown out, and Quinta do Infantado exported its first port soon after.

The estate has about 40ha of vines, half old, half renewed within the last 20 years. Since 1990, they have been converting to organic. João Roseira, in charge of winemaking at the estate, believes in fermenting his ports (in *lagares*) further towards dryness than most other producers before stopping the fermentation with brandy. He feels this achieves something closer to unfortified wine, and means there's less sugar to obscure the flavours. Since 2001, they have been making DOC

Douro wines as well. Their **Quinta do Infantado Reserva** was first made in 2003 from old vines, and has lovely, flamboyant, red-fruit flavours. Their **LBV Port** is rich and subtle, with smooth, cedary fruit, and the **Tawny 10 Years Port** is nutty and intense, with a real feeling of age. The Roseiras are an interesting family, and Infantado's wines reflect that. They are very happy to offer a tasting if you make an appointment. You will not regret it.
5085-217 Covas do Douro
T+351 254 738 020
E info@quintadoinfantado.pt
Tasting Mon-Fri 9-6 (except week of 15
* Aug) appt only*

Covas do Douro C3 *(continued)*
Quinta Nova de Nossa Senhora do Carmo As you travel along the river from Régua to Pinhão, Quinta Nova is one of those estates that catches your eye on the left-hand, northern bank, perched high above the river. And you think you'd love to spend a night or two there, amid the sights and sounds of this wonderful landscape. Well, you can. Quinta Nova, as well as having 85ha of vineyards, is a wine hotel *(page 116)* with a restaurant and wine bar, offering wine courses, grape-picking at harvest time, wine tastings and much more. It is owned by the Amorim family, big manufacturers of wine corks. Their DOC Douros are hugely improved. The **Quinta Nova Tinto** is smooth, rich and red-fruited, and the **Quinta Nova Grande Reserva**, dark and intense, with overtones of herbs and tayberry. **Quinta Nova LBV Port** is sweet, rich and modern (though foot-trodden), and the **Quinta Nova Vintage** is bright, floral and accessible, again, in the modern style. And since their business is looking after guests, tours of estate and winery are well-planned. If you're not staying at the hotel, make an appointment.

5085-222 Covas do Douro
T+351 254 730 430 / 969 860 056
E hotelquintanova@amorim.com
W www.quintanova.com/hotel
Visits 9-6 appt only

CUMIEIRA B3
Quinta da Gaivosa Four generations of the Alves de Sousa family have grown and made wines. Domingos Alves de Sousa was already qualified and working as an engineer before the pull of the Douro became too strong to resist. In 1987 he returned to the family estates, now joined by his son, Tiago. They have five estates, totalling 110ha of vineyard. The winery is at Quinta da Gaivosa, and that's where you should go for visits. In the vineyards you will learn about the varieties of grape grown in the Douro, the viticulture and the soils. Then it's back to the winery for an explanation of the winemaking process, and maybe a tasting of some wines from barrel, and a selection of three to five wines in bottle, including single-variety wines, classic Douro blends and a port.

Since the winery was built by Domingos' father in the 1950s, much has been changed. They no longer use their *lagares*, preferring temperature-controlled stainless steel tanks, pumping the wine back over the skins to extract colour. The real secret of this excellent range of wines is in the vineyards, and their old vines. Nearly 50ha of the Gaivosa and Vale da Raposa vineyards are over 60 years old, most planted by Domingos' father in the 1940s. Some are around 100 years old. The Alves de Sousas have done a lot of replanting, too, selling the grapes from vines under 20 years to port shippers. But that still leaves 95ha of vines over 20 years old. The **Alves de Sousa Reserva Pessoal Branco**, rich, complex, creamy and

mineral, is made from 80-year-old mixed vines. The single variety **Quinta do Vale da Raposa** reds are lovely, especially the violetty, aromatic **Touriga Nacional** and the restrained **Tinto Cão**, reminiscent of red fruits. The **Alves de Sousa Reserva Pessoal Tinto** is another old-vine red, ripe, bright-fruited and substantial. There are two wonderful single-vineyard old-vine reds, the intense, complex, powerful **Vinha de Lordelo** at Gaivosa and the spicy, meaty, intense **Vinha do Abandonado** at Vale da Raposa. The limited number of ports they produce are good, particularly a richly fruity, velvety **Vintage**.
Pousada da Cumieira, Apartado 15,
* 5030-055 Santa Marta de Penaguião*
T+351 254 822 111 / 914 082 322
E info@alvesdesousa.com
W www.alvesdesousa.com
Visits 9.30-6 all year appt only

ERVEDOSA DO DOURO D2
Quinta das Carvalhas (Real Companhia Velha) This is the largest of the properties belonging to Real Companhia Velha (RCV), a huge 600ha quinta towering over the Douro directly opposite the town of Pinhão, It has a very

ERVEDOSA DO DOURO
Quinta de Roriz

You can't visit Quinta de Roriz, but keep and eye out for its stunning wines. Half the quinta belongs to João van Zeller, the sixth generation of the van Zeller family to own the estate. The other half belongs to the Symington family, who entered into a partnership with João van Zeller to restore Quinta de Roriz to its former renown. For Quinta de Roriz ports have been famous for over 150 years, sold by name in an 1828 auction at Christie's in London, and much written about through the latter half of the 19th century. The quinta, about 10km up-river from Pinhão, was originally established as a hunting lodge by Scotsman Robert Archibald at the beginning of the 18th century. Symington Family Estates now manages the 40ha estate, and makes wines and ports in the original granite *lagares*. **Quinta de Roriz** used to be mined for tin (and a little gold), and has a reputation of making wines with a strong mineral element! You can see this in Prazo de Roriz, the second wine of the estate, as well as lovely raspberry perfume. **Quinta de Roriz Reserva** is restrained and firm, with notes of tobacco, red and black fruits. You get the mineral twang in the **Quinta de Roriz Vintage Port**, too, mixed with dense, herby flavour and big, chocolatey tannins.

welcoming visitor centre, with a lovely garden (designed by an English garden designer), and a big shop selling ports and DOC Douro wines from the company's large range.

The 'Old Royal Company', to translate RCV's name, is indeed old and historic. It was originally founded by Royal Charter in 1756, and consisted of the principal farmers of the Douro and traders of Porto. RCV drew up the first classification of the Douro region between 1758 and 1761. At that time, RCV acted as a regulator of wine quality and of prices – making sure that farmers were adequately rewarded for their grapes and that traders made money. The company traded port wine with England, Russia and Brazil. In 1865, King Fernando II passed a decree freeing up the trade in port, and RCV became a port shipper competing in an open marketplace. In 1963, RCV entered into a partnership with Real Companhia Vinícola, a company whose major shareholder was Manuel Silva Reis. Now the Silva Reis family controls RCV, and Pedro Silva Reis has taken over from his father.

Despite various moments of crisis in the last 15 years, RCV has recovered, and is one of the largest owners of vineyard land in the Douro, with over 500ha of planted vineyard. Californian winemaker Jerry Luper has been Director of Winemaking since 1999, so it's not surprising if some of the RCV wines have a Californian accent. Many of the best RCV wines are DOC Douro or VR wines. *(For a port selection, see page 138.)* RCV was one of the first companies in the Douro to plant Chardonnay (originally for sparkling wines). They now have a rich, tropically fruity **Quinta do Cidrô Chardonnay**. **Quinta do Cidrô Rosé** is a pleasant, rosehippy, off-dry slurper. **Quinta dos Aciprestes Reserva** is a rich, jammy, herby

blend of the two Tourigas. **Grantom** used to be a blend of Douro and Dão wines. Now it's just Douro, big, soft, ripe and cedary, made from the two Tourigas with some Cabernet Sauvignon. **Evel Grande Escolha** is even bigger, mainly Touriga Nacional. The **Grandjó Late Harvest** is a fully botrytised Semillon (known in the Douro as Boal), creamy and honeyed, with good acidity.

Ervedosa do Douro, 5085 Pinhão
T +351 254 738 050
E rcvelha@realcompanhiavelha.pt
W www.realcompanhiavelha.pt
Visits Mon-Fri 9-6 Sat/Sun appt only
Tasting €2

ERVEDOSA DO DOURO D2
Quinta das Tecedeiras

This is one of two Douro estates that belong to Dão Sul, a young company (founded in 1990) but one that has really advanced wine quality and wine tourism in the Dão region. Tecedeiras is 6km up-river from Pinhão, on the south bank of the Douro. They are very proud of their 5ha of old vines on stone terraces, and it is grapes from these that go into the dense, black cherry and blackberry-fruited **Quinta das Tecedeiras Vintage Port**. The other 10ha are of 20 year-old vines, and they are planting 4ha more. The whole estate is 66ha, much of the rest covered with olive trees.

You have to get in touch with Cláudio Loureiro or Ana Paula Figueiredo at the Dão Sul head office, and they will fix up a visit if possible. Your tour will start at Pinhão, travelling up-river by boat and arriving at Quinta das Tecedeiras by river. (If it's bad weather, you can get there by car.) Then you'll have a tour through the vineyards, followed by the winery, where you'll taste wines from barrels, followed by a tasting of bottled wines. There is no charge for this.

The production of port is tiny, and most of the wine made at Tecedeiras is DOC Douro. The 10ha of 20 year-old vines are planted varietally, and partly go into two single variety wines, a sweet-fruited, smooth-tannined **Quinta das Tecedeiras Tinta Roriz**, and a dark, black-fruited but accessible **Quinta das Tecedeiras Touriga Nacional**. The old vines are used again in the **Quinta das Tecedeiras Reserva**, a wine with firm tannins and typical old-vine intensity.
5130-114 Ervedosa do Douro,
 São João de Pesqueira
T+351 232 960 140
E joaoloureiro@daosul.com
W www.daosul.com
Visits Mon-Fri 9.30-5.30 appt only

ERVEDOSA DO DOURO D2 *(continued)*
Quinta de Ventozelo In 1999, Quinta do Ventozelo was bought by Proinsa, the largest mussel farming business in Galicia. It's a big quinta of 600ha, on the southern bank of the Douro river, just upstream of Pinhão and roughly opposite Quinta da Romaneira. It's not short of vineyards, with 200ha planted, including 10ha of 100-year-old vines and 40ha at 25 to 30 years old. Until the current owners took over, everything was sold off as young bulk port to the shippers. Ports are still made in *lagares*, DOC Douro wines in stainless steel. Production is big – a million bottles of port a year and half a million of DOC Douro. The unoaked, inexpensive **Vinzelo** red has good, bright red-fruit flavours. **Quinta de Ventozelo Reserva Tinto** is smooth and spicy, and the single varietal **Tinta Roriz** and **Touriga Nacional** are both good, the Tinta Roriz brightly red-fruity and the Touriga Nacional herbily aromatic. Ports are impressive, an excellent, blackberry and cedar-flavoured **LBV**, and an intense, herby **Vintage** (made from the

old vines). Ventozelo is a magnificent estate, with wonderful views over to the northern bank of the Douro. The owners are still investing in the winery, and probably the best days are still to come, but you will be welcomed, shown the estate and winery, and given a tasting.
Ervedosa do Douro,
 5130-135 São João da Pesqueira
T+351 254 732 167 / 254 731 181
E info@quintadeventozelo.pt
W www.quintadeventozelo.com
Visits Mon-Fri 11-1, 3-5 appt only
Tasting/visit €5

Quinta do Vale Dona Maria
Cristiano van Zeller has cut a large figure in the Douro since he and his sister Teresa ran the family's Quinta do Noval estate back in the 1980s. When he sold out to AXA in 1993, it was unthinkable that he should leave the wine business. In 1996 he and his wife, Joana, took over the running of Quinta Vale Dona Maria, an estate in the Rio Torto valley that had been in her family for generations. His winemaker there is one of the best in the Douro, Sandra Tavares da Silva. And Cristiano always has several other projects simmering, whether they're wines of his own, making wine for other estates, or advising others on export sales and marketing.

Vale Dona Maria now has 20ha of vineyards, including some very old vines from which he makes a special blend, **CV**. When he and Sandra were originally working on the blend, the wine was so good that Cristiano said: 'This will look good on our CV'. The name stuck. It's rich, dense wine, massively tannic, with amazing intensity and length. **CV** doesn't seem to have detracted from the quality of

the normal **Quinta do Vale Dona Maria**, which is smooth, ripe and impressive. **Casal de Loivos** is an aromatic, densely black-fruited red Cristiano makes for the Pereira de Sampayo family, from their estate overlooking Pinhão. And the ports are good, too, particularly the **Vintage**. Everything is foot-trodden in modern, temperature-controlled *lagares*. Lots of new French oak barrels are used for ageing, but the oak never overpowers as the wine is so rich.

Visitors must give 48 hours' notice, but you will be received by either Cristiano, Sandra or José Carlos, their viticulturalist, if they are there. Expect a full tour of the cellar, with barrel-tastings and a taste of **Quinta do Vale Dona Maria** DOC Douro and **LBV port**. If you want to open other bottles, you'll pay for what is opened – then get to take what's left in the bottle away.
Ervedosa do Douro 5130-055
T+351 223 744 320 / 254 732 375
E cvanzeller@mail.telepac.pt/
 joanavanzeller@mail.telepac.pt
W www.valedonamaria.com
Visits Mon-Fri 10-5 appt only
€12.50 (cash only)
🛏 ✕ *by prior arrangement*

FAVAIOS D3
Adega Cooperativa de Favaios
Favaios is famous for fortified Moscatel (Muscat), a wine rarely made elsewhere in the Douro. The Moscatel vineyards are planted at between 550 and 630 metres altitude, which means conditions are cooler, helping the grapes keep their freshness and perfume through the hot summer months. Almost half the co-op's production is Moscatel do Douro, and these are by far their best wines. The Favaios Moscatels are made by fermenting the whole destalked grapes (without

Foz Côa (Vila Nova de)
Quinta do Vale Meão

Quinta do Vale Meão is one of the great estates of the Douro Superior. In 1877, it was the last land to be bought by the elderly Dona Antónia Adelaide Ferreira *(page 86)*, famous for her vast vineyard and wine holdings in the 19th century. To develop this wild, remote land, she had to wait ten years, until the railway arrived, bringing workers to construct terraces for the vines, and a house. She finished the works in 1895, but spent little time at Vale Meão – she died in 1896, at the age of 86. The 270ha estate still belongs to her descendants, the Olazabal family.

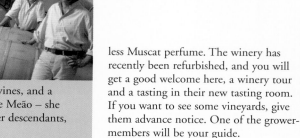

For almost the whole of the second half of the 20th century, Quinta do Vale Meão's grapes went off to form the heart of Barca Velha, the complex and famous forerunner of all the Douro red table wines. But in 1998, Dona Antónia's great-great-grandson, Francisco Javier de Olazabal, persuaded the other Ferreira descendants to sell their shares in Vale Meão to him, and decided to stop selling his grapes. The first vintage of Quinta do Vale Meão red was the 1999, released in 2001, to huge acclaim. His son, also Francisco (but known as Xito, *above, foreground*) is the winemaker.

At the moment, they have 65ha of vineyard, and would like to plant 15ha more. The young vineyards are planted varietally in blocks, of Touriga Nacional, Tinta Roriz, Touriga Franca, Tinta Amarela, Tinta Barroca and Tinto Cão. The massive, granite-blocked winery has been completely converted to modern technology, though the great granite *lagares* are still used for the first stage of fermentation. After foot-treading, the red wines are run off to the lower level of the winery where they finish their fermentations in vats. Two new French oak vats have recently joined the serried ranks of steel ones, and there will probably be more before long. Ports continue longer in *lagares*, human foot-treaders replaced by robotic plungers.

The Olazabals have always received visitors from the wine trade, and are now carrying out work at the estate to enable them to welcome other travellers, but they're not quite there yet. So would-be visitors will have to wait a little longer to admire the great winery, see the estate and taste the Vale Meão wines at the quinta. There are only two DOC Douro reds, the ripe, accessible mulberry-fruited **Meandro**, and the powerful, dark-fruited, aromatic **Quinta do Vale Meão**, with fine-grained tannins. Experiments with Syrah look very promising. Most of the port made on the estate is sold to other shippers, but the **Quinta do Vale Meão Vintage** is bright and red-fruited, with excellent acidity.

5150-501 Vila Nova de Foz Côa
T+ 351 279 762 156
E l.o@quintadovalemeao.pt/
Not yet visitable

removing pips and flavour-rich skins) for three to five days, then stopping the fermentation by adding wine alcohol, leaving a lot of sugar unfermented. Then the grapes are pressed and the wine is matured for at least two years in oak vats. If you like fortified Muscats, try one of the *young* Moscatel wines first. **Favaíto** and the basic **Favaios Moscatel do Douro** both have fresh, orange-and-honey flavours and good acidity. The **Moscatel do Douro 10 Anos** is richer and more intense, and the older, single-year Moscatels have much more of a nutty, creamy smoothness, and less Muscat perfume. The winery has recently been refurbished, and you will get a good welcome here, a winery tour and a tasting in their new tasting room. If you want to see some vineyards, give them advance notice. One of the grower-members will be your guide.

5070-265 Favaios
T+351 259 949 166 / 259 949 172
E geral@adegacooperativadefavaios.pt
W www.adegacooperativadefavaios.pt
Visits 9-12, 2-5.30

Freixo de Espada à Cinta H2

Quinta de Maritávora Maritávora is not a huge enterprise (8.5ha between two quintas), but they have some very bright ideas. It's owned by Maria Isabel and Manuel Gomes Mota, and has been in their family for 150 years. It was only in 2004 that they started bottling and selling their wines. They start off with the advantage of having some old vineyards (the vines for the white wine are over 100 years old). First bright idea: employ a really good consultant winemaker. The Maritávora wines are made by Jorge Serôdio Borges, either at the Maritávora winery way up near the Spanish border, or at his winery in Vale de Mendiz. Second bright idea: a scheme called Vinhomeu ('my wine'), which will allow visitors to make their own wine, from picking to designing the label and bottling. Third bright idea: if Vinhomeu visitors cannot manage vintage time, they will be able to make wine from deep-frozen grapes! An early experiment with white grapes looks promising. The wines Jorge Borges makes for Maritávora are excellent. The **Maritávora Branco Reserva** is an exceptional white, made from those ancient vineyards at 500m altitude, understated, savoury and delicious, with length and elegance. The **Maritávora Tinto** is bright and lively, with lovely raspberry fruit, and the **Maritávora Tinto Reserva** is darker and richer, with smooth, rich tannins and complex length.

EN 221, 5180-104 Freixo de Espada-à-
*   Cinta*
T+351 969 059 324
E mgm@maritavora.com
W www.maritavora.com
Visits appt only

GODIM B2

Caves Vale do Rodo The Cooperativa Vitivinícola do Peso da Régua, Caves Vale do Rodo (CVPR), to give this co-op its full name, is just to the west of Régua. It was conceived in 1950, when 25 growers decided to create better working conditions for themselves and other members. In 1951 the winery was built, and the co-op started with 70 members. In 1982, to get round the law that forbade co-ops to sell wine in bottle, CVPR set up a company with Gran Cruz Porto, as they needed to work with a company who owned a warehouse in Vila Nova de Gaia. At last, in 1987, they bought back the Gran Cruz Porto share, and started shipping from Régua. Red DOC Douro wines are more successful than whites, and the best is **Cabeça de Burro Tinto**, **DOC Douro**, a blend of Touriga Franca, Tinta Roriz and Tinta Barroca, with ripe, thick, raspberry fruit and firm tannins. Pick of the CVPR ports is their thick-fruited, tannic **Vintage Porto**. You can turn up for a winery tour any time during the working week (including Saturday morning). If you want to see some vineyards, get in touch in advance.

Rua da Lousada, Godim,
*   5050-262 Peso da Régua*
T+351 254 320 358
E caves.vale.rodo@mail.telepac.pt
W www.cvpr.pt
Visits Mon-Fri 9-12.30, 2-6 Sat 9-12.30

GOUVINHAS C3

Quinta do Crasto You have to negotiate some pretty unreconstructed Douro roads to get to Quinta do Crasto, but it's worth it. The estate is magnificently sited above the north bank, 10km downriver from Pinhão (and yes, it is easier to get there by boat). Crasto is one of the most dynamic single estate port and DOC Douro producers. It's not surprising to learn that the Roquette family (the owners) have just bought another quinta, Quinta da Cabreira, in the Douro Superior. They have replanted it, and are considering what best to do with the grapes they will produce there – maybe a 'Crasto' wine (without the word 'Quinta' the grapes would not have to come from Quinta do Crasto itself), probably a special Quinta da Cabreira wine as well.

Crasto does receive visitors, but only by appointment – at the moment. They are building a new reception centre and shop, and intend to convert an 18th century house to provide eight rooms to rent. (They have similar plans at Cabreira, but that's a few years away.) But already, pre-opening, you will undoubtedly get a good tour and tasting at Crasto.

The estate has been owned by the de Almeida family since the early 1900s. Leonor de Almeida married Jorge Roquette, and they started bottling and selling their own wine in 1994. They have had tremendous success (thanks to hard work by Jorge's sons Miguel and Tomás), and you can now find Crasto wines all over the world. They are best known for their DOC Douro wines, but make decent ports as well. The **Quinta do Crasto** red is fresh and easy-going, whereas the **Vinhas Velhas**

(old vines) **Reserva** is dense, dark and intense, with considerable length and perfume. There is a lovely, perfumed, herby **Touriga Nacional**, and two magnificent, very old-vine, single vineyard wines, the immense, rich-fruited **Vinha da Ponte** and the huge, dense, intense **Vinha Maria Teresa**. The latest creation is **Xisto**, a joint venture with Jean-Michel Cazes of Château Lynch-Bages. This comes from younger vineyards in the Douro Superior, about one-third each of the two Tourigas and Tinta Roriz, with dashes of Tinta Barroca and Tinto Cão, fresh, aromatic and beautifully balanced.

Gouvinhas, 5060-063 Sabrosa
T+351 254 920 020
E crasto@mail.telepac.pt
W www.quintadocrasto.pt
Winery visits 10-5 appt only

GRANJA E1

Caves Transmontanas (Vértice, Quanta Terra) You may not expect to find fine fizz in a region famous for powerful reds and some of the world's great fortified wines, but these rank amongst Portugal's best bubblies. The company was started by Jack Davies, of Schramsberg sparkling wines in California, who came to Portugal in the late 1980s and decided it would be possible to make good sparkling wine. After three years of experiment, Davies finally plumped for the Douro region, and formed Caves Transmontanas with a local co-op, the Caves Riba-Tua e Pinhão. Winemaker at the co-op was Celso Pereira, still today winemaker at Caves Transmontanas. Davies and his team chose Gouveio, Côdega (alias Síria), Malvasia Fina, Touriga Franca, Viosinho and Rabigato as their varieties, and specified that they must come from high altitudes – 550m above sea-level. The grapes are picked early and the wines

have always been bottled-fermented in the traditional style. Celso uses some not-quite-new Burgundian barrels these days for added complexity. The very functional winery is open for visits and tastings, but do make an appointment. After the death of Jack Davies in 1998, the Davies family sold their shares in the company to the original Portuguese investors.

The **Vértice Reserva** is lean and savoury, and the **Vértice Super Reserva** is the top fizz, toasty and complex, with finesse and length. There are a DOC Douro white and red, **Vértice Branco** creamy but mineral, and **Vértice Tinto** savoury and elegant. Celso Pereira also makes **Quanta Terra Tinto** with Jorge Alves (of Quinta do Tedo). It's a red sourced with grapes from Quinta do Tralhão, north of Tua, dominated by the herby aromatics of Touriga Nacional, with dense, ripe tannins.

Rua São Domingos 22, Granja,
* 5070-092 Alijó*
T+351 259 958 508 / 932 675 164
E ctvertice@sapo.pt
Visits Mon-Fri 9-5.30 appt only

LAMEGO B2

Raposeira Portugal's oldest and largest sparkling wine producer was making little of interest to wine lovers during its 20 years in the ownership of multinational drinks company Seagram. Bought in 2002 by its main local rival, Murganheira *(page 180)*, Raposeira is in the midst of a €2m renovation and expansion programme. Apart from great improvements in the production area, a new wine museum and tasting centre are due to open in 2008. Raposeira are already set up to receive visitors, but you must phone in advance until the works have finished. Founded in 1898, they own no vineyards and make only sparkling wines from grapes they buy in, mostly from Távora-Varosa, some Douro.

Our favourites are the clean, lemony **Raposeira Super Reserva Brut**, a blend of Malvasia Fina, Cercial and a little Chardonnay, with three years on yeast lees; the **Raposeira Velha Reserva**, half Malvasia Fina, half Chardonnay, with five years on lees, fine and lemony, a toasty character; and **Raposeira Rosé**, a blend of Tinta Roriz, Touriga Nacional and Tinta Barroca, very pleasant, with raspberry fruit and gentle acidity.

Lugar da Raposeira, Apartado 9,
* 5101-909 Lamego*
T+351 254 655 003
E cristina.osorio@caves-raposeira.com
Visits Mon-Fri 10-12, 2-5

MÊDA E1

Muxagat Way south of the river in the Douro Superior, the winery is at 800m altitude, among old vineyards of white grapes that used to supply wines for white ports. Now it's the new generation of serious white DOC Douro wines that are more in demand. The partners in the enterprise are Mateus Nicolau de Almeida (son of João Nicolau de Almeida of Ramos Pinto, grandson of Fernando Nicolau de Almeida, creator of Barca Velha) and Eduardo Lopes, whose vineyards supply some of the grapes. They make a red and a white. The **Muxagat Branco** is mineral, rich and creamy, part barrel-fermented, and the **Muxagat Tinto** rich and fresh-fruited, with good acidity from the granite soils of Mêda. The granite winery in Mêda is tiny (garage-sized, indeed), but Mateus is very happy to receive visitors there, take you to a vineyard and give you a tasting. But you have to make an appointment.

Avenida Gago Coutinho e Sacadura Cabral,
* 6430-183 Mêda*
T+351 938 058 077 / 917 260 928
E mateus@muxagat.pt
Visits appt only

MUXAGATA F1

Quinta da Ervamoira (Ramos Pinto)
The firm of Ramos Pinto has been at the forefront of modern quality winemaking in the Douro. Their Quinta da Ervamoira is a lush, green oasis amidst the bare, parched hills of the Douro Superior, not far from the Spanish border. But those healthy vines might by now have been under the waters of a reservoir flooding the valley of the river Côa. The estate was saved by the discovery of the largest open-air Palaeolithic collection of rock engravings in the world, now a UNESCO World Heritage Site, the Parque Arqueológico do Vale do Côa *(page 113)*. Some of the engravings are actually on the estate, others in the surrounding countryside. The museum, opened in 1997, tells the story of the discoveries, of various other archaeological finds on the estate and, of course, the story of Ramos Pinto. The tour (by appointment) includes the museum and vineyards, and a tasting of Ramos Pinto ports – plus the Ramos Pinto DOC Douro, for a few Euros more.

The stirring story of Ervamoira began back in the late 1960s, when José António Ramos Pinto Rosas, then Chairman of Ramos Pinto, became convinced that exceptional wines could be made in the Douro Superior. What he was looking for was somewhere relatively flat, to take advantage of modern mechanised viticulture (and avoid terracing). He came across Ervamoira in 1972 (then known as Quinta da Santa Maria). He persuaded the family who owned it to sell after the 1974 Revolution, and started planting. Ervamoira was used as a pilot scheme for the study to find the grape varieties best adapted to the Douro, a study that eventually resulted in five being chosen, and 2,500ha of new vines being supported by grants from the World Bank.

Then the Portuguese Government decided to dam the river Côa, and Ramos Pinto realised this would completely flood Ervamoira. They tried everything to reverse the decision. They presented awards Ervamoira wines had won. They showed Roman coins and buildings that archaeologists had found on the estate. Nothing was considered important enough. Archaeologists working for the electricity company found the Palaeolithic engravings, but kept quiet about them, and in 1992, the building started.

Then, in 1995, a left-wing government was elected and one year later the dam was abandoned.

Grapes from Ervamoira and another Ramos Pinto estate, Bons Ares, go into the bright, lean, elegant **Bons Ares Branco**, a white VR wine made from Viosinho and Sauvignon Blanc. **Duas Quintas Tinto** DOC Douro is also made from (Touriga Franca, Tinta Roriz and Touriga Nacional) grapes from these two estates, a red with ripe red and black fruit and good length. The **Duas Quintas Reserva Tinto** is even better, serious, sweet-fruited and long-lived. Top of the Ramos Pinto unfortified wines is the **Duas Quintas Reserva Especial**, dense, dark and rich, with savoury black fruit and tremendous minerality. *(For a selection of the Ramos Pinto ports, see page 138.)*
Muxagata, 5150 Vila Nova de Foz Côa
T+351 279 759 229 / 932 992 533
E ramospinto@ramospinto.pt
W www.ramospinto.pt
Visits Tue-Sun 9.30, 11.30, 2.30, 4.30
*   appt only €5*
Closed 1 Jan, Easter, 1 May, 1 Nov, 25 Dec
✗ *lunch by arrangement*

PAÇOS C3
Lavradores de Feitoria In 2000, 15 Douro quintas got together to create a table wine brand. It was to be 'great wine at a reasonable price', made from a selection of their grapes, and would give a better return than they would get by taking their grapes to the local co-operative. From the start they sought the advice of Dirk Niepoort (producer or consultant for numerous Douro wines, as well as of the Niepoort wines and ports). Most of the participating estates are in the central (Cima Corgo) part of the Douro, with a couple just into the Douro Superior and one in the Baixo Corgo. But there are many different soils, altitudes, grape varieties and exposures, and the three Lavradores winemakers have a wide palette to draw on for the blends. Lavradores de Feitoria doesn't take all the grapes from the estates, although it offers viticultural advice through the year. They select what they want, sometimes also making wines from the individual 17 properties the company now includes, then the rest is sold off as grapes or wine by the individual estates. Many of the wines are made in wineries at the quintas, and there is a central cellar in Sabrosa for blending and ageing the wines. This is the winery you can visit, by appointment. They will show you the winery and give you a tasting, the price depending on what you want to taste.

Três Bagos is the main brand, ranging from a steely but ripe, part-barrel-fermented **Sauvignon Blanc** to the serious, perfumed, velvety **Grande Escolha**. Only a few wines from individual quintas are selected by a panel to be released under the Lavradores de Feitoria label each year. **Quinta da Costa das Aguaneiras No 6** is dark, smooth and floral. **Meruge** is elegant, intense and

deceptively powerful. There is also a less expensive but reliable **Lavradores de Feitoria Douro** label.
Zona Industrial de Sabrosa, Lote 5,
*   Apartado 25, Paços, 5060 Sabrosa*
T+351 259 937 380
E lavradores@feitoria.jazznet.pt
W www.lavradoresdefeitoria.pt
Visits appt only

PINHÃO C3
Quinta de la Rosa A lovely estate just above the Douro, five minutes' drive from Pinhão, Quinta de la Rosa is entirely geared up for winery visits, and has bed and breakfast rooms and holiday houses *(page 117)*. Turn up at 11am on weekdays for the tour: vineyards, then the *lagares* where port grapes are foot-trodden in September, the wine cellar, and the wooden vats in which port is matured. Then there'll be a tasting. If you're staying in one of the rooms or houses, it's free.

Quinta de la Rosa has 55ha of vineyards, and is owned by the Bergqvist family, who celebrated 100 years of their involvement with the estate in 2006. Tim Bergqvist's father Eric married Claire Feuerheed, who had been given La Rosa as a christening present in 1906. Tim, daughter Sophia and son Philip still run La Rosa. The Bergqvists started making their own port in 1988, and DOC Douro wine soon followed. Since 2002, both ports and DOC Douro wines have flourished under the care of Jorge

Moreira, one of the Douro's most gifted young winemakers *(below, right)*. Sophia Bergqvist has expanded the portfolio to include red, white and rosé under the Vale de Clara label – for which Jorge can buy in grapes from other local vineyards as no quinta name is specified. In 2005, the Bergqvists bought Quinta das Bandeiras in the Douro Superior. Jorge is determined to keep the wine from Bandeiras separate from the Vale de Clara wines, as he dislikes the 'lack of definition' in cross-regional blends. **Passagem** is the latest wine, an exotic, glowingly ripe red, from Bandeiras and other Douro Superior grapes. The **Vale de Clara Branco** is full bodied and honeyed, with lovely acidity, and the **Vale de Clara Rosé** rich and herby. **Vale de Clara Tinto** has appealingly soft, red fruit flavours. **Quinta de la Rosa red** is rich and serious, with lovely depth. **Quinta de la Rosa Reserva** is a definite step up, dense and smooth, sumptuous but discreet, mostly made from 60 to 70-year-old vines. The **Quinta de la Rosa Vintage Port** is rich and dark, spicy and smooth.
Pinhão 5085-215
T+351 254 732 254
E sophia@quintadelarosa.com
W www.quintadelarosa.com
Visits Mon-Sat 11 or by appt
Wine shop & tastings Mon-Fri 8.30-5.30
*   Sat 9.30-12.30*
Visit & tasting €2.50
🛏 ✕ *by arrangement* ⚓

Quinta do Noval One of the Douro's most beautiful estates with immaculately maintained terraced vineyards, Quinta do Noval is just north of Pinhão on the road to Alijó. All the Noval facilities are now located in the Douro, mostly at the quinta, which makes it particularly worth a visit. A disastrous warehouse fire in Vila Nova de Gaia in 1981 wiped out 350,000 litres

of Noval's stock, destroying the warehouses. Teresa and her brother Cristiano van Zeller, owners at the time, decided to rebuild winery and cellar at the quinta. In 1986, the law forbidding the shipment of port from anywhere other than Vila Nova de Gaia was abolished, and Quinta do Noval was the only major shipper in a position to take immediate advantage.

Noval was bought by AXA (the insurance company) in 1993, and in 1994 started a major vineyard replanting programme. A new vinification cellar has been built at the quinta, together with a warehouse and bottling plant near Alijó. There are now 104ha of vineyard, and the plantings of Touriga Nacional have risen from 3ha before 1993 to over half the estate. One result of this was the release in 2006 of a DOC Douro red, 2004 **Quinta do Noval Tinto**. Herby and spicy, with dark, firm tannins, it's a blend of Touriga Nacional with smaller amounts of Tinto Cão and Touriga Franca.

Quinta do Noval's ports are much improved from 20 years ago. One that has always been exceptional is the amazingly intense, long-lived **Quinta do Noval Nacional Vintage**, a wine made in tiny quantities from ungrafted vines (many of them Sousão). **Quinta do Noval Vintage** is also very impressive, seductive and black-fruited, with lovely freshness. The unfiltered **Late Bottled Port** is exemplary, meaty, cedary and mature. It's hard to choose between the aged tawnies and the colheitas, all are so good. The **Noval 10 Year Old Tawny** is one of the best available, nutty, creamy and long, the **20 Year Old** is toffeed, woody and more elegant, and the **40 Year Old**, intense, immensely elegant and penetrating. The **Colheitas** are

splendid, intense symphonies of nutty, dried-fruit concentration.

Quinta do Silval is not far from Noval, and serves as a label for a more accessible style of vintage, principally for the US market, where vintage ports slip down young and easy. **Silval Vintage** (not all grapes are from the quinta, so it's not Quinta do Silval) is aromatic, very fragrant and ultra-smooth.

The wines of Quinta da Romaneira, a huge quinta of 400ha just over the hill, are also made at Noval at present. Romaneira opened in summer 2007 as a super-luxury hotel *(page 116)*. The vineyards have been extensively replanted, and a new winery is underway. The **Quinta da Romaneira Tinto** is herby and sweet-fruited, and the **Quinta da Romaneira Vintage port** wonderfully aromatic, dominated by Touriga Nacional.
T+351 223 770 270
E noval@quintdonoval.pt
W www.quintadonoval.pt
Visits appt only

PROVESENDE C3

Quinta da Terra Feita de Cima (Poeira) During the day, Jorge Moreira and Olga Martins work for Quinta de la Rosa and Lavradores de Feitoria respectively,  Olga on the commercial side, Jorge making wine – he is one of the Douro's best young winemakers. In the evening they come home here. They bought the 15ha estate in 2001. There were 3ha of old mixed vines, and he has planted five more, mostly of Touriga Nacional and Sousão (on its own roots, not grafted), plus a hectare of Alvarinho. Much of the

quinta faces north, so avoiding the hottest sun of the day. Indeed, the Poeira grapes ripen a fornight after those at La Rosa, just 5km down the road. Dirk Niepoort, friend and mentor to so many of the younger generation of Douro winemakers, has helped them to get going. Jorge and Olga have had their own winery since the 2005 vintage, and now live over the new cellar, with a lovely view over the valley to Vale de Mendiz. They are very happy to receive visitors, show you the winery and vineyards, and give you a tasting, but you must make an appointment. And they make only one wine, **Poeira** ('dust' in Portuguese). (Maybe the Alvarinho will give a white Poeira one day.) **Poeira** is a red that balances subtlety with seductiveness, with silky tannins and lovely acidity. Jorge also has a joint project with a friend making another rich, sumptuous red, **Sirga**, from the Douro Superior near Quinta dos Malvedos.

5060-283 Provesende, Sabrosa
T+351 939 506 699
E poeira@poeira.pt
W www.poeira.pt
Visits appt only

REMÓSTIAS B3

Momentos do Douro A joint project between Luis Soares Duarte *(below)*, winemaker at Quinta do Infantado, and Domingos Silva (MD of Quinta do Lago in the Algarve). Until now, Luis has always collaborated as a winemaker with others – Quinta do Infantado, Bago de Touriga,

Kolheita de Ideias. Momentos do Douro sees him flying solo, with funding from Domingos Silva, a passionate Douro wine enthusiast. There

are two red wines, **Perfil** and **Momentos**, made at a winery near Régua. The permanent home for the enterprise, Casa das Camélias, is being refurbished, and will be ready for the 2008 harvest. The grapes come from three vineyards, in Vale de Mendiz, São João da Pesqueira and near Vila Nova de Foz Côa. The bright, fresh, red-fruited **Perfil** (30,000 bottles to 3,000 of **Momentos**) comes from the Vale de Mendiz vineyards, favouring elegance over power. **Momentos** comes from the other two, from old vines cropped at low yields. It's lovely wine, dense and herbily aromatic, with great length. A rosé and white have recently been added.

Visits to the present winery are possible with a previous appointment, tastings likewise. Casa das Camélias should be finished by July 2008.

Until July 2008: Casa da Calçada,
Remóstias, Peso da Régua
From July 2008: Casa das Camélias, Vila
Seca de Poiares, 5050 Peso da Régua
T+351 917 559 717
E soaresduarte@mail.telepac.pt
Visits Mon-Fri 10.30-12.30, 2.30-5 appt
only

SANTA MARTA DE PENAGUIÃO B3

Caves Santa Marta This is the largest wine co-operative in the Douro, formed by merging with two smaller co-ops (Cumieira and Medrões) in 1986. Founded in 1959, Santa Marta had more of a social than a commercial role, at that time legally obliged to buy grapes from its members, and make them into wine, but not allowed to sell them in bottle. The wines went off to the merchants, and it was they who had the chance of making money out of them. That all changed with the 1974 revolution. Now, Caves Santa Marta has 2,200 members, and produces a tenth of all wine made in the

Douro, some 12 million bottles a year, five million of port, the rest unfortified wines, sparkling wines and brandies. Red wines are the ones to go for here, particularly the fragrant, cedary **Touriga Franca**. Even better is the **Montes Pintados** (named after a book by João de Araujo Correia), a rich, savoury blend of Touriga Franca and Tinta Roriz. Caves Santa Marta are also proud to have produced the first vintage port from a Douro co-op, in 1998. In good years the **Vintage Porto** is sweet and reminiscent of black fruits. Their **LBV Porto** is always good, vigorous and richly fruity. The large shop welcomes ten million customers a year. They also offer tours round a refurbished port warehouse and distillery, part of it converted into a museum.

Apartado 50, 5031-909 Santa Marta de
Penaguião
T+351 254 810 313
E visitas@caves-stamarta.pt
W www.caves-stamarta.pt
Visits Mon-Fri 9-6 Sat 9-12.30

SANTO ADRIÃO C2

Quinta do Tedo In 1989, Vincent and Kay Bouchard visited the Douro for the first time, and fell in love with the region. Vincent (yes, a descendant of Bouchard Père & Fils) had moved from Burgundy to California and started a business selling French oak barrels. He met Kay, a Californian, and they married and have three children. Vincent returned to the Douro, found Quinta do Tedo, and he and Kay bought it in 1992. The estate is on the south bank of the Douro, at its confluence with the river Tedo. There are now 14ha of vineyard (and 8ha of olives), and the Bouchards have repaired the old terraces and replanted some of the vineyards. They have also installed cooling systems in the *lagares*, and still tread the grapes for all their ports. They made their first DOC Douro red in 2003 (and bottled that vintage in port bottles, as no others were available). **Quinta do Tedo Douro Red** is rich and soft, with good fruit intensity. The **Quinta do Tedo Reserva** is even better, dense, but brightly aromatic. Ports are made in a very sweet, easy-drinking style (maybe with an eye to the early-drinking US market). Undoubtedly the best is the **Quinta do Tedo Vintage**, crammed with sweet, blackcurrant fruit, and with very smooth tannins.

The Bouchards and Jorge Alves, their winemaker and estate manager, are used to receiving visitors: at some times of the year they welcome three groups a day from a French cruise operator! (It's a good idea to phone before to ensure you don't clash with one of these.) You'll see the *lagares* and ageing cellar, and have a tasting, which might include the DOC Douro (they don't make much of this), certainly some ports, maybe even their olive oil.
5110-548 Santo Adrião, Armamar
T+351 254 789 543
E info@quintadotedo.com
W www.quintadotedo.com
Visits Mar-Oct Mon-Sat 10-7 Nov-Feb
*   Mon-Fri 10-7*

SÃO JOÃO DA PESQUEIRA D2
VDS – Vinhos do Douro Superior (Castello d'Alba) VDS has changed from being three winemakers and a winery to that plus an estate in the Douro Superior at 650m altitude. The three winemakers are Rui Madeira, João Matos and Joaquim Anacleto, and their winery is in São João da Pesqueira. Their newly-acquired estate is Quinta da Pedra Escrita, near Freixo de Numão, and they are planting 12ha of

white varieties to take advantage of the cool conditions at their high altitude.

The operation used to consist of the three buying up grapes and wines as they went on their rounds as consultant winemakers in the Douro, and putting together blends under the **Castello d'Alba** label. Previous releases of the white wines have been particularly impressive, with both the **Vinhas Velhas Branco** and the **Branco Reserva** showing real Douro mixed white grape flavours, subtlety and elegance. The elegant, spicy, berry-fruited **Tinto Reserva** has now been joined by an unoaked red, called **Un Oaked**! They have added red wines from two single estates to the VDS range, the herby, mineral **Quinta da Cassa Reserva** and the dense, firm, tannic **Quinta do Banco**. Most of their grapes come from the Douro Superior, a region familiar to Rui Madeira, whose family wine company, CARM *(page 90)*, is also at that end of the Douro.
Quinta da Pedra Escrita,
*   5155 Freixo de Numão*
T+351 254 488 070
E ruimadeira@vds.pt/ joaomatos@vds.pt
Visits from 2008, appt only

SARZEDINHO C2
Quinta de Macedos Paul and Philippa Reynolds, an English couple, bought this 150-year-old quinta in 1998, and farm it organically. They took on about 7ha of old vines, planted in 1920 and 1945 on beautiful old stone terraces overlooking

the River Torto. They have replanted patches of vineyard (mainly with Touriga Nacional) where the vines had died. Among the old vines, Tinta Roriz and Touriga Franca dominate a mix of many different Douro varieties. The winery has been refurbished. Grapes are trodden in restored granite *lagares* (now equipped with a cooling system), then aged in French oak barrels. The wines mature in the newly built 'wine lodge' until ready for bottling. Macedos has rooms to rent *(page 118)* and is good at looking after passing visitors too. You will be shown the estate and winery, and given a tasting, although it's best to get in touch ahead to fix a time.

The Macedos wines are made in an uncompromisingly traditional style, magnificent examples of what old vines, organic cultivation and a respect for tradition can achieve. The most accessible is **Pinga do Torto** ('Pinga' means drop), dense and rich, with dark fruit flavours. **Quinta de Macedos** is made only from the 1920 plantings, a wine to keep for five years if you can restrain your curiosity, huge, tannic and mineral, the essence of the stone-walled terraces. If you go there, you might get to taste the **Pinga Rosé**, first made in 2006.
Sarzedinho, 5130-141 Ervedosa do Douro
T+351 254 731 391 (winery)
*   +351 254 738 090 (house)*
E info@quintamacedos.com
W www.quintamacedos.com
Visits Mon-Fri 10-4 Sep every day 10-4
⌷ ✗ by prior arrangement

TEDO C2
Quinta de Nápoles (Niepoort)
Quinta de Nápoles is a relatively recent acquisition for the family-owned company of Niepoort. Niepoort survived for their first 145 years without owning any Douro

estates at all. They were buyers, blenders and shippers of ports, buying wines from growers with whom relationships had deepened through five generations of the Niepoort family. Now they make all of their own wines, and no longer buy wine from growers. But they do still buy grapes.

Quinta de Nápoles (and the neighbouring Quinta de Carril) were bought by Dirk Niepoort's father, Rolf, when he was in charge of the company. Why? Because Dirk felt he needed a base for the winemaking he wanted to do in the Douro, and he needed some vineyards in a prime part of the Douro. So, for almost 20 years, Dirk has been making DOC Douro wines (and some others) at Nápoles, conditions becoming more and more cramped as he tried to squeeze in more vats and barrels. All this has recently changed. Nápoles now has a sleek, stylish, ultra-modern winery, clad in Douro schist outside, and all fed by gravity. Water is heated by solar panels, the air inside cooled by water running down a rock-face deep in the mountain. Make an appointment, and you'll get a good tour of vineyards and winery, and taste some wines.

Quinta de Nápoles is just back from the little River Tedo, which runs into the Douro between Pinhão and Régua almost opposite Quinta do Crasto. There are about 30ha of vineyard on the estate, at ages between nearly 20 and over 70. Height and exposition to the sun vary, too. Altitudes are between 180 and 250 metres, and there are some cooler, north-facing slopes whose grapes Dirk uses to make what he calls his 'wild Douro wine', **Redoma** red, dark with raspberry and black cherry fruit, rich but still elegant. Some Nápoles grapes also go into **Batuta**, a soft, elegant, Burgundy-like red mostly made from Tinta Amarela, Touriga Franca and Tinto Roriz. Dirk's top red is **Charme**, entirely

foot-trodden in old granite *lagares*, an incredibly intense, mineral but elegant wine, made from old vineyards in Vale de Mendiz. His whites, too, are very different from Douro norms, from high, old vineyards. The stars are the lean, appley, steel-fermented **Tiara**, and the mineral, bright, oak-fermented **Redoma Branco Reserva**, with just a hint of toast. For the Niepoort port recommendations, *see page 136*.

As you may have noticed, Dirk Niepoort has moved in a very different direction with his wines from many of his contemporaries. While many have revelled in the power that Douro grapes have to offer, he has sought finesse and elegance. At the same time, he has been an unofficial spokesman and ambassador for a generation of new Douro winemakers. You're more likely to meet him in an airport or a foreign city than in Porto or the Douro – except, of course, at vintage time. And the wines he has created, and inspired in others, are among the best in Portugal.
Tedo, 5110 -543 Santo Adrião
T+351 254 855 436
E quintadenapoles@niepoort-vinhos.com/
* info@niepoort-vinhos.com*
W www.niepoort-vinhos.com
Visits Mon-Fri 9-5 appt only Closed public hols
✗*on request*

Quinta do Passadouro In 1991, Dieter Bohrmann, who lives in Belgium, bought Quinta do Passadouro in Vale do Mendiz, just north of Pinhão in the Cima Corgo. For the first 13 years, he worked with Dirk Niepoort and his then-winemaker, Jorge Serôdio Borges, to make the wines of the estate. Some of the grapes were sold to Niepoort Vinhos, where they formed an important part of Redoma Tinto. In

2004, Bohrmann decided to go his own way. Jorge Borges now works as the winemaker at Passadouro (as well as running his own project, Wine & Soul). There were 16ha of vines originally, now there are 20ha with new plantings. Most of the Passadouro grapes that ended up with a Passadouro label in the Niepoort era were released as port. But Bohrmann had always had a dream to make great red wine in prime port vineyards such as these. Now Passadouro is at least as well known for its DOC Douro reds as for its ports. Both are made very traditionally, foot-trodden in granite lagares, although Jorge uses 'dry ice' (frozen CO_2) in the *lagares* after treading to prevent oxidation.

The Quinta do Passadouro does bed and breakfast *(page 119)*, so you will always find a friendly welcome from Ronald and Jet, who run the accommodation side. You need to make an appointment, but Passadouro receives visitors all year (except for 'a few weeks in the winter'). You will be shown the estate and winery and given a tasting of a red wine and two ports. There's no charge, just 'buy a bottle'! (There will be a charge if you want to taste the more expensive bottles.) The red wines of Passadouro have got better and better as Jorge has matured as a winemaker. The **Passadouro Vinho Tinto** has spicy concentration and firm tannins. The **Passadouro Reserva** is even better, with lush intensity, complexity and glorious length. As you'd expect from this spot and a great winemaker, the **Quinta do Passadouro Vintage** is magnificent, dark, complex yet intensely fruity.
Vale de Mendiz, 5085-101 Pinhão
T+351 254 731 246 / 938 136 067
E info@quinta-do-passadouro.com
W www.quinta-do-passadouro.com
Visits 10-6
🛏 ✗*by prior arrangement*

Wine & Soul (Pintas, Guru) Jorge Serôdio Borges and Sandra Tavares da Silva are both winemakers working for other companies (Quinta do Passadouro, Quinta do Vale Dona Maria and Quinta da Chocapalha) as well as having this tiny but hugely successful business. At the moment, the two wines and one port they produce in this little white-washed winery really are 'garage' wines. There are about 5,000 bottles of **Pintas**, fewer than 1,500 of **Guru** (the white) and about 3,000 of **Pintas Vintage** port. But (as well as just having had their first child), Jorge and Sandra are about to release **Pintas Character**, another red wine whose production could grow from the 7,000 bottles they made in 2005. 'Pintas' means 'spots', by the way, after the ubiquitous wine splashes at vintage.

The chances of getting to visit them are slight, as they both have jobs elsewhere, and do a lot of travelling to promote the wines they make. But it's always worth a try! Maybe the baby will mean they're around more. They're a charming couple, both very talented, and great examples of the younger generation of winemakers responsible for the huge rise of quality in the Douro.

Their first premise is to work with old vines. Pintas 2001 was their first wine, from a 2ha vineyard they succeeded in buying in 2003. By buying small neighbouring parcels of old vines, they now have 3ha for Pintas wine and port, so the number of bottles is strictly limited to what this can give. They buy white grapes for Guru from a 40 year old vineyard near Murça, north of Vale de Mendiz, at 550 metres altitude. The idea of Pintas Character is a wine not limited by vineyard area (as long as they are always grapes from old vines), so the brand can grow if successful (which it is sure to be). The first **Pintas Character**

is bright and red-fruited, with dark, herby intensity. **Guru** is savoury, mineral and amazingly elegant, and **Pintas**, wonderfully expressive, with rich depths and explosive length. **Pintas Vintage** is lovely, as well, with dark structure joined to wonderfully sweet fruit. Jorge also makes **VT**, a very aromatic Touriga Nacional-dominated red, with dark, austere tannins, in partnership with José Maria Cálem and Cristiano van Zeller.

Av. Júlio Freitas, 6, Vale de Mendiz,
*   5085-101 Pinhão*
T +351 936 161 408 / 932 722 700
E pintas.douro@mail.telepac.pt
Visits appt only

VALENÇA DO DOURO C2

Quinta do Panascal This is part of the Fladgate Partnership portfolio of Douro estates. (If that name means nothing to you, the names on the labels of their ports will mean considerably more – Fonseca, Taylor's, Croft and Delaforce.) This is the only Fladgate port estate to receive visitors at present. Quinta do Panascal is a little way up the valley of the river Távora, which flows into the river Douro on the opposite side from Pinhão, about 5km downriver. Of its 78ha, 44 are planted with vines, and it supplies most of the grapes that go into Fonseca's smooth,

easy-going premium reserve port, Bin 27. It's very much the Fonseca quinta, unlike Quinta de Vargellas and Quinta da Terra Feita, both identified more closely with Taylor's.

Fonseca are very proud of their eight-language audio-guide to the quinta, which takes visitors into the vineyards, talks about the Douro region, tells the history of the company and explains how Fonseca wines are made. After the tour, you can watch a video while tasting **Siroco White Port** and **Bin 27**. If you turn up during vintage, you might see treaders at work in the *lagares*. And there's a shop where you can buy Fonseca ports.

Although the company's name has now been shortened to 'Fonseca', the founder was a Guimaraens and members of the Guimaraens family have worked in the company for six generations. David Guimaraens is the current winemaker, following in the footsteps of his father, Bruce. In 1948, Fonseca joined forces with Taylor's in the difficult era after World War 1, but the two co-exist happily, with grapes sourced from different estates, and Fonseca known for its rich, opulent style of port. The two vintage ports lead a very impressive Fonseca line-up, the rich, dense, sweet-fruited **Fonseca Vintage** in the top years, and the smooth, balanced **Guimaraens** in the lesser ones. The aged **Tawnies** (**10 and 20 Year Old**) are also among the best in their categories, and the **Fonseca Crusted** is worth seeking out, full of dark, figgy, cedary fruit. The cedary, refreshing unfiltered **LBV** port is another cracking bottle – just remember to decant it.

Valença do Douro, 5120-496 Tabuaço
T +351 254 732 321 / 223 742 800
W www.fonseca.pt
Visits Apr-Oct Mon-Sun 10-6 Nov-Mar
*   Mon-Fri 10-6 Sat/ Sun appt only*

Quinta do Vallado Quinta do Vallado is one of top DOC Douro performers in the Baixo Corgo, as well as having five beautifully refurbished bedrooms to let *(page 119)*. The estate has been owned by the Ferreira family ever since the time of the famous Dona Antónia Adelaide Ferreira. Wines are made by Xito Olazabal, son of the owner of Quinta do Vale Meão, and a cousin of Vallado's owners, Maria Antónia Ferreira and her son, João Ferreira Álvares Ribeiro. Chico Ferreira, nephew of the owners, manages the estate.

Vallado have 38ha of vineyard, 26 of them old, mixed vines, the rest more recently planted. The brightly orange-painted estate buildings are unmissable from the other side of the valley. Even if you don't do the winery visit, and taste no Vallado wines (which would be a pity), Vallado is worth a visit just for the view from the highest point in the vineyard, looking out over the mouth of the river Corgo as it reaches the Douro. But do visit. They're well prepared for visitors, and interesting tours of the new and old wineries, the ageing cellars and a small museum of historic winemaking equipment. At the end, you can taste five Vallado wines, the white, two reds and two ports.

Quinta do Vallado started bottling and selling their wines only in 1995. Both DOC Douro wines and ports are excellent, starting with a crisp, mineral **Quinta do Vallado Branco**, with just a touch of oak, and a bright, red-fruited, firm **Quinta do Vallado Tinto**. You move up quite a level to the **Quinta do Vallado Reserva**, two-thirds of which come from the old vines at the top of the estate, rich, dark and intense, with a bright note of aromatic Touriga Nacional. Still to come is a wine made from just the old vines (whose name had not yet been decided when we last visited), a real inky, intense powerhouse – typical old-vine Douro red. The **10 Year Old Tawny port** is delicious, too, full of toffee and nut sweetness.

Vilharinho dos Freires,
*   5050-364 Peso da Régua*
T +351 254 323 147
E vallado.turismo@mail.telepac.pt
W www.quintadovallado.com
Visits 9-6 appt preferred
Tasting €6-€11 🛏 ✕

Eat in the Douro

Three new, modern-Portuguese restaurants have recently opened in the Douro valley. A few others had already begun to take a more modern approach. But the Douro is still a land of tradition, still quite isolated. Rustic, stodgy, old-fashioned food abounds, much loved nonetheless by locals. But if you know where to look, some very memorable gastronomic experiences await you in the best of the Douro's traditional restaurants, or the region's many family guest houses.

Highlights of the local fare are game and other roast meats, often young meat including kid *(cabrito)*, lamb *(cordeiro)*, and veal *(vitela)*. Offal dishes will be on many menus, perhaps pigs' trotters *(pézinhos de porco)*, or tripe with beans *(tripas à moda do Porto)*. LAMEGO is famous for its smoked hams *(presuntos)* and sausages. An expensive speciality of VILA REAL is breaded and fried *presunto* steak on a bed of butter beans, rice, onion and tomato *(bife de presunto panado com arroz de feijão)*. The local farmers keep pigs and chickens. They grow vegetables to serve in soups, including the famous cabbage soup, *caldo verde*, and sweet corn to make a delicious corn bread *(brôa de milho)*, or a savoury maize porridge *(papas de milho)*, maybe with turnip leaves stirred in – a delicious discovery. Cumin is a frequent flavour.

Even with the new roads, it's still a long way up the Douro for fresh fish to travel. You may be well advised to save your fish dinners for the coast, though nowadays there *is* fresh fish up here, where once all fish was tinned, dried or salted. But the locals still love their reconstituted dried fish dishes – based on dried cod *(bacalhau)* or octopus *(polvo)*. You will meet tinned fish, too – sardines, octopus, squid... Everything seems to come with rice, corn bread *and* potatoes, and often generous lashings of the local olive oils.

Summers here are bakingly hot, ideal for olive, citrus, fig and almond trees, as well as sweet chestnuts. And of course

vines. In the summer you will find plenty of local fruit, including cherries and oranges (pressed for breakfast if you are lucky, straight from the tree). TORRE DE MONCORVO in the wild east is famous for its sugared almonds, MESÃO FRIO in the more accessible west for its wonderful chestnut cakes *(falachas)*, and nearby DONSUMIL for its lemon and soda cake, *doce de Donsumil*. An old tradition of fining the wines with egg whites has left a tempting trail of yellow cakes and puddings, full of egg yolks, almonds, butter and sugar and dusted with cinnamon. Most famous perhaps is the large, flat *toucinho do céu* cake ('heavenly bacon'). Another local speciality, *Aletria com ovos* – spaghetti cooked in milk and sugar, finished with lemon zest, egg yolks and cinnamon – is a bit of an acquired taste.

Above English-style tea in a shady garden

Left Kid *(cabrito)* makes a regular appearance on menus up the Douro

Right Pick your own lemons – or enjoy the zesty local lemon cakes

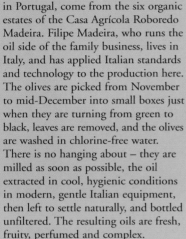

ALMENDRA

CARM Organic Extra Virgin Olive Oil

The Douro's finest olive oils, amongst the best in Portugal, come from the six organic estates of the Casa Agrícola Roboredo Madeira. Filipe Madeira, who runs the oil side of the family business, lives in Italy, and has applied Italian standards and technology to the production here. The olives are picked from November to mid-December into small boxes just when they are turning from green to black, leaves are removed, and the olives are washed in chlorine-free water. There is no hanging about – they are milled as soon as possible, the oil extracted in cool, hygienic conditions in modern, gentle Italian equipment, then left to settle naturally, and bottled unfiltered. The resulting oils are fresh, fruity, perfumed and complex.

The Madeira family has owned land up here on the steep, stony slopes of the Upper Douro since the 17th century. Filipe's father, Celso, began to buy more land about 40 years ago, and has now retired up here amidst the 200 hectares of olive groves. As well as the 'ordinary' CARM extra virgin oils and the more exclusive **CARM Grande Escolha**, there are several single quinta extra virgin and extra virgin reserva oils from **Quinta das Marvalhas**, **Quinta do Côa**, **Quinta de Calábria** and **Quinta do Bispado**, from specified olive varieties. CARM also grow almonds (Almendra, the village name, is the Spanish word for almond), and make excellent wines *(page 90)*.
Rua de Calábria, 5150-021 Almendra
T+351 279 718 010
E sales@carm.pt
W www.carm.pt
Visits 9-6 appt only

RESTAURANTS

ALIJÓ D3

Cepa Torta Right next to the town's wine co-operative, the 'Twisted Vine' was recommended to us by numerous wine people. Fine, traditional cooking (with a modern touch) includes very good veal and roast kid, and octopus rice. The wine list is excellent. Decor is modern, and comfortable.
Rua Dr José Bulas da Cruz
T+351 259 950 177
E arisdouro@arisdouro.com
W www.arisdouro.com/cepatorta.htm
Closed Tue; & Mon in winter
€30 ♀ *V*

COTAS D3

Redondo Opening in September 2008, this is the 'gastronomic restaurant' of Quinta dos Sonhos, the new super-luxury quinta hotel on the Quinta da Romaneira estate *(page 116)*. It is headed jointly by a Parisian chef Philippe Conticini and Miguel Castro Silva from the famous Bull and Bear in Porto. The picture below, looking down on the hotel, is the view from the restaurant's panoramic windows.

Quinta dos Sonhos, Quinta da Romaneira, 5070-000 Cotas
T+351 254 732 432
E info@maisonsdesreves.com
W www.maisondesreves.com
♀ *V!* 🛏

ESCALHÃO G1

O Lagar One of the very best restaurants in the region, with typical local food of the highest standard. The wine list is good, with both national and foreign wines, the wine glasses unexpectedly fine in this remote spot. In a small village 7km outside Figueira de Castelo Rodrigo, O Lagar is a simple, traditional place, cosy and homely, with ancient stone walls and huge olive-press screws harking back to the days when this was an olive *lagar*. The menu is short but tempting, and a further list of dishes can be ordered in advance, including vegetarian dishes. Vegetable soups hail from their own garden, there is wild boar, various bacalhau dishes, and excellent home-made charcuterie including delicious sweet morcela (black pudding). And the magical mayonnaise is made from CARM olive oil.
Rua do Barreiro
T+351 271 346 974
E geral@olagar.com
W www.olagar.com
€25-€30 ♀ *V by prior order No credit cards*
Closed Tue

FERRADOSA DO DOURO E2

Cais da Ferradosa In a lovely spot overlooking the River Douro, this restaurant opened in 2004 in the restored station of Ferradosa. Food is well-cooked traditional, and the wine list is strong on local wines.
Ferradosa
T+351 254 481 024
€15 ♀ *V on request*

FOLGOSA DO DOURO B2

DOC Opened at Easter 2007 on the banks of the Douro, this was acclaimed by one wine trade friend as 'a food and wine lover's dream, up-scale, hip and discreet, ever so good!' It is owned by Rui Cardoso and Cristina Canelas of the Cepa Torta restaurant in Alijó *(opposite)*. Decor is modern, the food traditional with a light, modern touch, the wine list excellent, and long. There's also a terrace right by the river, open till 2am, serving drinks and a selection of small dishes.
T+351 254 858 123
E doc@arisdouro.com
W www.arisdouro.com
€30 ♀ *V*

FOZ CÔA (VILA NOVA DE) F2

Bruiço On the outskirts of the town, heading out towards Guarda, once a disco, now a spacious restaurant, O Bruiço puts a very slightly modern twist on traditional Beiras cuisine. Some dishes have to be pre-booked. Numerous wine trade people recommended this place, but more for the food than the wine. The decor is brightly yellow, blue and white.
Lugar do Frango, Estrada do Poio, EN 102
T+351 279 764 379
€15-€20
Closed Sun din, Mon

LAMEGO B2

Casa Filipe A delightful, simple little restaurant in a little narrow street by the cathedral. Food is good and traditional, and service very friendly.
Rua Trás da Sé
T+351 254 612 428
€15 V on request No credit cards
Closed Sat Oct-Mar; last week Jul

LOUREIRO B3

Varanda da Régua Large, airy restaurant on four floors with terraces, big windows and wonderful views of the vineyards down to Régua and the Bagaúste dam. Tempting and copious nibbles might blunt your appetite for the well-cooked traditional dishes, which include excellent roast kid *(cabrito assado)* and roast veal *(vitelo assado)*. The wine list is good, especially for red Douro wines.
Lugar da Boavista
T+351 254 336 949
E restaurante@varandadaregua.com
W www.varandadaregua.com
€15 ♀ *V*

MÓS DO DOURO E2

Petiscaria Preguiça A simple, rustic place renowned for its *petiscos* (little dishes or *tapas*) in a tiny old village south of the river, north-west of Vila Nova de Foz Côa. Worth the wiggly drive!
Mós do Douro
T+351 279 789 432
€8-€12 V No credit cards

PINHÃO C3

Ponte Romana 'The only good place to eat in Pinhão,' according to one wine trade friend. 'You can lunch cheaply if you take the fixed menu with two choices – three courses including coffee for €7! At lunch you have all the local winemaking fraternity there, sampling different wines around the tables. A good atmosphere and a great wine list – this is where we all eat.' Enjoy views over the River Pinhão at its confluence with the Douro. Portions are huge. They also do take-away, to carry off to your eyrie.
Rua Santo António 2
T+351 254 732 978
€20-€25 ♀
Closed Mon

POIARES B2

Repentina Repentina means 'unexpected' and this would indeed have been a happy surprise up here by the Miradouro de São Leonardo de Galafura *(page 112)* – had we not been recommended to it by so many wine trade friends. Simple and rustic, with a wood-fired oven much in service, Repentina is famous locally for its roast kid *(cabrito)*. It is definitely worth booking, and mentioning *cabrito* (not always available) if you want some. If *cabrito* is off, local roast chicken or veal will not disappoint, and bread, olives and house wine are all very good.
Casal de Canelas
T+351 254 906 145
€18-€20 ♀
Closed Mon; Sep

RÉGUA (PESO DA) B2

Cacho d'Oiro In a little cul-de-sac off Rua da Perreirinha, Cacho d'Oiro has good local cooking, simple decor and very friendly service. The menu is long and traditional, the wine list long and good – a comprehensive selection of Douro reds, including Barca Velha, Vale Meão, Duas Quintas Reserva and other good wines, though the whites on the list are less exciting.
Travessa Branca Martinho
T+351 254 321 455
E reservas@restaurantecachodoiro.com
W www.restaurantecachodoiro.com
€18 ♀

Restaurante Douro In The elegant, modern interior and fine views over the Douro river are not the only happy surprises here. Food is imaginatively cooked and presented, with local influences. The wine list includes most of the top Douro red and white wines, often available by the glass.
Avenida João Franco
T+351 916 602 399
E douro-in@hotmail.com
W www.douro-in.com
€30 ♀ *V*

SAMODÃES B2

Almapura The top restaurant of the Aquapura Douro hotel near Régua *(page 117)* serves the accomplished cuisine of Philippe Bossert. Dine in shades of black, white and aubergine beside a wall of water. There are tasting menus, and a long and tempting wine list.
Quinta de Vale Abraão,
T +351 213 660 600
E reservations@aquapuradouro.com
W www.aquapurahotels.com
€60 ♀ *V!*

SANTA CRISTINA A2

Alpoim The restaurant of the grand Solar da Rede *pousada (page 118)* serves good local food. Dine on a terrace with fabulous views down over the swimming pool and vines to the river, or in the old kitchens, which have been converted into an elegant, cosy dining room.
Solar da Rede, Santa Cristina, Mesão Frio
T+351 254 890 130
E reservas@solardarede.pt
W www.pousadas.pt
€35 ♀ *V*

SÃO JOÃO DA PESQUEIRA D2

O Forno A favourite of the local wine trade for its good roasts, including suckling pig *(leitão)* and kid *(cabrito)* – it may be wise to order these in advance. There's also excellent charcuterie, cheeses, fresh home-baked bread and home-made desserts. The decor is fresh, white and attractive.
Largo da Devesa
T+351 254 484 414
€15-€20 No credit cards
Closed Sun, 25 Dec, Easter Sun, 1 Jan

Cantiflas From the front, this looks like a boring bar, but the restaurant at the back has excellent meat dishes, game in season, and certain dishes, including roast kid *(cabrito)* that must be ordered in advance. Wines are well chosen, their glasses are unexpectedly fine, and service of both wine and food is exceptionally skilled and friendly. All this in a simple, spacious village restaurant, with welcome air-conditioning and a TV!
Rua Nova 13, Espinho
T+351 254 484 474
€15 ♀ *V No credit cards*
Closed Mon

TUA D3

Calça Curta Right by the Tua railway station is a wooden prefabricated building housing a café and a remarkably good restaurant, with a terrace and very fine views of the River Douro. Service is young and enthusiastic, and the menu strays from the usual fare to offer stews *(estufados)* and risotto *(arroz)* of wild boar, eel, lamprey, hare, partridge or venison, depending on the season.
Estação de Foz Tua, Carrazeda de Ansiães
T+351 278 685 255
€11 No credit cards
Open every day

VILA REAL B3

Barriguinha Cheia You will indeed leave with a 'Full Tummy', as the name suggests. From the outside, the restaurant is unpreposessing, on the ground floor of a big, modern building. Inside it is pleasantly bright and airy, cool (thanks to air conditioning), friendly and informal. Food is good traditional, based on excellent ingredients both local and from further afield, and they have a very good list of Douro wines. A favouite of Douro wine folk.
Rua Cidade de Espinho 115
T+351 259 321 266
E jjmonteiro@sapo.pt
W www.o-barriguinha-cheia.com
€13 ♀ *Closed Sun*

O Cardoso A very old, characterful, simple place, very inexpensive, serving delicious local meat and snacks such as ham and cheese on toast. Drink beer!
Rua Miguel Bombarda 42-44
T+351 259 325 329
€10 No credit cards Closed Sun

O Espadeiro A smart, slightly formal restaurant with a terrace and two dining rooms, open fires and a friendly welcome. Good traditional cooking in very healthy

portions includes offal dishes, as well as roast kid, good cheeses and charcuterie. The wines are good – this is another wine trade haunt.
Avenida Almeida Lucena
T+351 259 322 302
E respadeiro@onidu.pt
€25-€30 ♀
Closed Sun din; Mon lunch

Museu dos Presuntos Don't be fooled by the name 'Museum of Hams'. The fare here is not just a fine selection of hams – all kinds of excellent, fresh, local produce is on offer, and the cooking is good and local too. This is a friendly, fun restaurant, with narrow wooden tables, and hams hanging above the bar. Prices are very reasonable, and generous half portions allow you to try different things. The wine list is strongest in the Douro and Alentejo sections.
Avenida Cidade Ourense 43
T+351 259 326 017
€15 ♀
Closed Tue & Fri lunch

Terra da Montanha A lovely, atmospheric place in the historic town centre of Vila Real, with tables cosily, romantically and discreetly tucked inside big, varnished wine vats. Good regional cooking, and a very good Douro wine selection, including some lesser-known wines.
Rua 31 de Janeiro 16-18
T+351 259 372 075
E geral@terrademontanha.pt
W www.terrademontanha.pt
€17-€20 ♀
Closed Sun din, public hols

MARKETS, WINE AND FOOD SHOPS

CHEIRES C3
Quinta dos Lagares Deli shop and relaxing tea rooms in an old dovecote *(below)* on a wine estate 10km north-west of Alijó. Apart from their own wines, they sell jams made from different grape varieties, local fruits and nuts, olive oils, herb vinegar, cheeses and honeys. *Casa da Quinta, Cheires, Sanfins do Douro T+351 259 686 167*

MÊDA E1
Vinho & Eventos *(pictured right)* Over to the south-east, near the border with the Beiras, this attractive shop has good wines, especially Douros and Alvarinho Vinhos Verdes, majoring on unfortified wine rather than port. And a great deli, with products from the Douro and beyond. Beautifully designed modern shop with seating areas. Hams and lots of fine charcuterie, olive oils, good cheeses, nuts, Riedel glasses and other wine accessories, wine and cookery books. *Avenida do Parque*

PINHÃO C3
Loja do Vinho, Vintage House Hotel The shop inside this smart hotel, right in the centre of town, is open to non-residents. It sells a big range of ports and table wines from the region, plus olive oils, jams, cheeses and biscuits. You can join short wine courses here, and watch demos of port-making.
Lugar da Ponte

RÉGUA (PESO DA) B2
Avepod-Vinhos de Quinta Shop selling wines and oils of 60 small producers, at good prices. *Rua de Alegria 39*

Market A good one, on Wednesdays and Saturdays.

TORRE DE MONCORVO F2
ArteSabor e Douro Small shop selling local wine and farm produce such as almonds, cheese and preserves. *Largo General Claudino*

Explore the Douro

It takes ages to get anywhere in the Douro – unless a very friendly port shipper scoops you up by helicopter. Driving along the narrow, steep and winding roads may require travel sickness pills, but the views are stunning. Meeting a lorry coming from the opposite direction can be hairy, being stuck behind one can be irritating. You will of course meet lorries and tankers far more frequently at harvest time, but driving apart, harvest is an exciting time to see the Douro. In places, a road runs alongside the river, and occasional bridges permit weaving from bank to bank. The easiest options are public transport. Buses (to various places near and far) are practical if unromantic, but a cruise or the train along the river *(page 114)* is an experience you won't forget.

Nowadays the approach to the Douro is often from the motorway, at VILA REAL. Mountains to the back of it, canyon to the front of it, the university town dominates the lovely vineyards and citrus groves of the Corgo Valley. Known as the Baixo Corgo, this western part of the wine region, with its fertile, rolling hills, is easier to farm than the precipitous slopes to east. Vila Real (Real means Royal) is a modern, industrial city, with a traffic-free old centre and some fine old 16th to 18th century houses and baroque churches. Vila Real is a good base from which to visit the Natural Park of Alvão.

Below left Bridge over the River Pinhão

Right Vineyard scene depicted in *azulejos* on Pinhão railway station

Below Boating up the river from the Casa de Mendiz guest house

Vila Real is also a transport hub, for trains, and buses serving the Douro Valley, up into Trás-os-Montes, down to Coimbra… You can also take the train from here, down to the river, then up to near the Spanish border. Just off to the east of the city in the village of MATEUS, you can visit the baroque Casa Mateus and gardens *(page 113)*.

To the south, the fortified village of MESÃO FRIO marks the beginning of the wine region, and the most beautiful stretch of the river. Just up-river, overlooking the wide valley of the Baixo Corgo at the confluence of the Corgo and Douro rivers, (PESO DA) RÉGUA is the historic centre of the port trade in the Douro. Called simply Régua by the locals, it is not a beautiful place, but you can see the *barcos rabelos* and the long, dumpy port warehouses, and take trains or boats upstream. For a characterful, historic town, head south of the river to

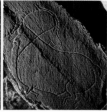
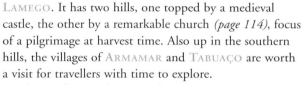

Left Shadowy folds and contours at Quinta de Roriz and goat engraving in the Foz Côa valley

Right Centre of the vineyard area

Below The River Pinhão, lovely walking country

LAMEGO. It has two hills, one topped by a medieval castle, the other by a remarkable church *(page 114)*, focus of a pilgrimage at harvest time. Also up in the southern hills, the villages of ARMAMAR and TABUAÇO are worth a visit for travellers with time to explore.

The small riverside town of PINHÃO is iconic as the heart of the port industry, but again it is not pretty. Its *position* is lovely, facing south cross-river at the confluence of the Rio Pinhão and the Douro. Normally a sleepy place, it is very busy at vintage time. Its railway station is worth a visit even if you are not travelling by train. The walls are liberally decorated with *azulejos* – tiled pictures

of historic harvest scenes and the river before the dams. Many of the famous port quintas are around and above the town. The little village of PROVESENDE is an attractive place to break the winding journey up into the hills north from Pinhão to SABROSA. Sabrosa is famous as birthplace of Fernão de Magalhães (Ferdinand Magellan), who led the first round-the-world sailing in the early 16th century. He would still recognise some of the 15th century manor houses. The fairly large town of ALIJÓ (largely 19th century) is also in the rocky hills north of Pinhão, up a spectacular winding road amongst olive and citrus trees, and vines. There's not much to see once you get there, other than the impressive Pousada Barão Forrester.

To proceed upriver from Pinhão, you have to take to the hills, or go by boat or train, as the road veers way off the river from this point. Next settlement of note is SÃO JOÃO DE PESQUEIRA perched high over the river and the Barragem de Valeira (Valeira Dam). It was in the rapids of this great gorge that British port pioneer Baron Forrester drowned. This was the limit of navigation on the Douro until the 18th century, when a rock wall partially barring the gorge was demolished. Another name the townspeople can drop is Pombal – this

was the early home of the famous politician who rebuilt Lisbon after the earthquake *(page 235)*. São João de Pesqueira has some grand old houses, as well as newer ones. There are watersports by the dam, and one of the Douro's finest viewpoints, São Salvador do Mundo, is nearby.

Further east, olives and almonds used to take over from vines, but recently many new vineyards have been planted. The almond blossom is still a stunning sight in early spring. The ridge-top settlement of VILA NOVA DE FOZ CÔA overlooks the valley of the Rio Côa and the famous rock engravings *(see right)*. TORRE DE MONCORVO and the ancient FREIXO DE ESPADA À CINTA ('Ash Tree of the Girth Sword') are small, fortified towns beside the Spanish border, with narrow, winding streets and dwindling populations. Just beyond Freixa de Espada à Cinta, the Douro flows along between Portugal and Spain, forming the border for 112km, flanked by the Parque Natural do Douro Internacional.

✳ VIEW FROM THE TOP ✳

Climb up just a little way above the river almost anywhere in the Douro Valley for spectacular views. Here are some of the most impressive:

CASAL DE LOIVOS **Miradouro de Casal de Loivos** Just by the cemetery of this village in the hills above Pinhão, stunning views over vineyards, river and hills.

CUSTÓIAS **Senhora do Viso** A chapel has been built to mark this viewpoint, 813m above sea level on top of the Monte do Viso. The view takes in São Salvador do Mundo and the Castelo de Numão.

FREIXO DE ESPADA À CINTA **Vista do Penedo Durão** This is a high, steep hill on the right bank between Poiares and Freixo de Espada à Cinta, from which you can see well into Spain, far around the upper Douro, and down to the Barragem de Saucelle (the Saucelle Dam). A flight of steps leads up to a viewing platform.

GALAFURA (PESO DA RÉGUA) **São Leonardo da Galafura** Half way between Régua and Vila Real, this spot gives one of the best views over the vineyards, the Douro Valley and the Serra do Marão. There's a small chapel, and a picnic area where the locals gather for a communal lunch on the third Sunday in August.

PROVESENDE **Miradouro de São Domingos** In the hills north of Pinhão, half way up to Sabrosa, this is one of the contestants for 'best in Douro' – over to Vila Real, Régua, Mesão Frio, the hill-top church of Lamego, and the hill ranges of the Serra do Marão and Serra das Meadas. There's a camp site nearby.

SÃO JOÃO DA PESQUEIRA **São Salvador do Mundo** This pointed hill has wonderful views over the river gorge, mountains and vineyards. It is a wild, silent place. Witness its pagan past in the granite boulders out of which bowls were carved aeons ago for offerings of oil and wine. In Christian times, little chapels appeared on the hillside, and now there are pilgrimages (with family picnics) in early June, when, harking back to pagan days, local women trying to improve their chances of finding good husbands apparently tie knots in the broom bushes…

VILARINHO DOS FREIRES **Miradouro Vallado** Great views out over the valley of the Corgo from the top of the Quinta do Vallado vineyards.

BETWEEN MEALS

TRAIN JOURNEYS

One of the world's most enthralling rail journeys is on the 175km track

between Porto and Pocinho up by the Spanish border. For 100km it runs right alongside the river, passing through 26 tunnels and crossing 30 bridges. Change at Régua from the ordinary train from Porto. There's a steam train on Saturdays from Régua to Tua, a 1925 engine pulling some of the oldest rolling stock still in action. The 'modern' trains are great fun too. The most scenic section is Pinhão to Tua. Sadly, the branch line from Tua to Mirandela has recently closed. Many stations are liberally decorated with *azulejos* (tiles), and some stations serve the famous port quintas – platform signs may read 'Vargelas' or 'Vesúvio'. *Information from the Portuguese rail company, CP: T+351 213 185 990 W www.cp.pt*

MATEUS (VILA REAL) Casa de Mateus
You may already have met this impressive house on labels of Mateus Rosé, but the wine has never been made here. Sogrape, producers of Mateus, simply thought the house would look nice on the label of their

new wine way back just after the Second World War. They offered the house-owners the choice of a one-off modest payment or lifelong per-bottle royalties. They chose the one-off payment. Sixty years and millions of bottles later, it must be some consolation to live in such a remarkable house and garden. The house was built around 1740 for António José Botelho Mourão, Third Morgado of Mateus, ancestor of the current owners. The style is baroque, the winged form symmetrical and mirrored in a formal lake. Inside there are lots of mirrors too, reflecting carved chestnut and fine paintings. Ten rooms and a library of historic books are open to the public, as well as the gardens. The formal garden has box designs and other topiary, including a 35-meter-long aromatic cedar tunnel planted in 1941 and trimmed using special curved ladders. The garden is surrounded by fields, orchards and vineyards, whose grapes are sold to Lavradores de Feitoria *(page 98)*, some of them to be made into a single-vineyard Mateus wine called Alvarelhão, which you can buy in the shop. There's a programme of concerts – classical, ancient, jazz, opera… from May to early September in a converted barn – starting late, at 9 or 10pm. If you have no car, a bus will take you the 3km from Vila Real on weekdays, but note that the last bus back leaves mid-afternoon. *Fundação da Casa de Mateus,*

5000-291 Vila Real T+351 259 323 121
E casa.mateus@mail.telepac.pt
W www.casademateus.com Open Jan-Feb 9-1, 2-5 Mar-Apr 9-1, 2-6 May-Sep 9-7 Oct 9-1, 2-6 Nov-Dec 9-1, 2-5 Closed 25 Dec

VALE DE NOGUEIRAS Santuário de Panóias Ancient sacrificial site with impressive carved and inscribed rocks. On the way from Vila Real to Sabrosa, but in an enclave of the VR Transmontese, therefore in another chapter *(page 76)*.

VILA NOVA DE FOZ CÔA Parque Arqueológico do Vale do Côa (Archaeological Park of the Côa Valley) The discovery of the world's best example of open-air Stone Age engravings saved this remote valley from flooding. This was to be the site of Portugal's largest hydro-electric power station. After a long battle in the early 1990s, archaeologists v government, the archaeologists at first lost, and the dam was already half built when a socialist government came to power and reversed the decision. The valley is now a National Park, and a UNESCO World Heritage Site. Some of the engravings are nevertheless under water, because a dam further downstream has raised the water level. But the lower 17k of the Côa valley has 28 engraving sites so far identified, some of them quite faint representations of animal and human figures. Their original purpose is unclear – did they have religious or cultural significance, or were they the work of graffiti artists of Upper Palaeolithic and Neolithic times? For reasons of preservation, the sites cannot be

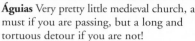

BOAT TRIPS

Boat trips up the Douro leave from the quayside in the Ribeira district of Porto, or from (Peso da) Régua, or Pinhão. There are short outings, day trips, or five or seven-day luxury cruises from Porto to the border with Spain and back, through locks, past dams, with shore hops to wine quintas, restaurants and places of interest. From Pinhão or Porto, you can also take day trips up the river in a *barco rabelo*, now engine-powered, rather than relying on currents and sail.

Cruises and outings: Douro Azul
T+351 223 402 513
E geral@douroazul.pt
W www.douroazul.com
Barco Rabelo trips: Aris Douro
T Pinhão +351 917 933 595
T Porto +351 222 006 418
E geral@douroacima.pt
W www.douroacima.pt

visited unaccompanied, and since daily visitor numbers are limited, it is vital to book with the park office ahead of your visit. Tours lasting about 90 minutes leave from three visitor centres in Vila Nova de Foz Côa, Muxagata and Castelo Melhor to visit three different sites. A visit to the engravings is only for the fit and the well-shod – the guided tours begin with a drive across bone-shaking terrain, and you will continue on foot. Take hats, sunscreen and water in the summer, raincoats in winter – umbrellas are banned. *Avenida Gago Coutinho e Sacadura Cabral 19A, 5150-610 Vila Nova de Foz Côa T+351 279 768 260/1 E pavc@ipa.min-cultura.pt W www.ipa.min-cultura.pt/pavc Open Tue-Sun 9-12.30, 2-5 Closed Mon, 1 Jan, Easter Sun, 25 Dec*
Ervamoira Museum *(page 97).*

MUSEUMS & GALLERIES

LAMEGO **Museu de Lamego** Housed in a magnificent 18th century episcopal palace near the cathedral, this is one of Portugal's top muesums. Highlights are five panels of an altarpiece painted in the 16th century attributed to the famous Portuguese artist Grão Vasco, and some fine 16th century Flemish tapestries. Four baroque chapels have been deconstructed and re-assembled within the museum, and there are sections on jewellery, furniture, archaeology, *azulejos* and religious vestments. *Largo de Camões Open Tue-Sun 10-12.30, 2-5 Closed Mon and some public hols*

CHURCHES

BALSEMÃO (LAMEGO) **Capela de São Pedro de Balsemão** In a little village near Lamego on the Tarouca road, this is thought to be the oldest church in Portugal, the sanctuary probably 7th century Visigothic. *Closed Mon, Tues am, third weekend of month*

FREIXO DE ESPADA À CINTA **Igreja Matriz** 16th century church just below the tower, a mini version of the beautiful Jerónimos monastery church in Lisbon, with elegant interior, twisted pillars, ribbed vaulted ceilings, and Manueline portals and pictures attributed to Grão Vasco.

GRANJINHA **Igreja Românica de São Pedro das Águias** Very pretty little medieval church, a must if you are passing, but a long and tortuous detour if you are not!

LAMEGO **Igreja de Nossa Senhora dos Remédios** Modelled on the Bom Jesus church in Braga (Minho), this hilltop church has an amazing zig-zag double staircase (611 steps), punctuated by terraces with statues, *azulejos* and fountains. For the tired or infirm, a 3km drive takes you to the top, where the church itself is less exciting than the fine views straight down the town's main street. At the annual pilgrimage *(see below)* in late August-early September, pilgrims sometimes climb the steps on their knees. *Open summer 7.30-8, winter 7.30-6*

MESÃO FRIO **Igreja Matriz de São Nicolau** Dating from the 12-13th century, modified in the 18th, this Romanesque-Gothic church is famous for its gilded wood and arched, panelled ceiling.

FESTIVALS

There are lots of local village *festas* in the summer around the saint's day of each village…some can be fun, with fireworks, street processions, local bands and partying, some have loud music and little else…
AUGUST/SEPTEMBER LAMEGO **Festas de Nossa Senhora dos Remédios** From the last Thursday in August to mid-September, thousands of pilgrims (and revellers) invade the town for the *festas*. The most devout climb the 611 steps to the hilltop church on their knees, some in the hope of healing miracles. Meanwhile there are parades, a procession of ox-drawn carts, live music (folk and rock), dancing, a fairground, and a 'battle of the flowers'.

Sleep in the Douro

ALDEIA DE BAIXO B2
Casa de São Miguel

Charming old stone house, beautifully restored, elegantly and comfortably furnished, in a little village up in the hills.
Aldeia de Baixo, Armamar 5110 Lamego
T+351 933 185 391 (English);
*   +351 963 013 935 (Portuguese)*
E geral@casadosarcosboavista.com
€60-€70 🛏8 [SC] *1(2-3)* 🏊 *No credit cards*
Closed Mid-Aug to mid-Sept

ALIJÓ D3
Pousada do Barão de Forrester
The original house was built by the nephew of the famous Baron Forrester *(page 86)*, but it was remodelled and extended in 1996. The result is elegant and comfortable, with spacious rooms, most overlooking the garden.
Rua José Rufino, 5070-031 Alijó
T+351 259 959 467
E recepcao.barao@pousadas.pt
W www.pousadas.pt
€120-€180 🛏21 ✗ 🏊 ⛳

BANDUJA (MESÃO FRIO) A2
Casa de Canilhas
Comfortable family house belonging to a local doctor, offering bed and breakfast up in the vineyards near Mesão Frio. There are fine river views from garden, terraces, pool and long veranda.
Estrada Municipal de Banduja,
*   5040-302 Mesão Frio*
T+351 254 891 181
E info@canilhas.com
W www.canilhas.com
€60-€90 🛏7 ✗ *bar service* 🏊
No credit cards Min nights 2 (weekends and high season)

CARRASCAL F3
Quinta de Santa Luzia
The owners live in the main farmhouse, and five farm buildings have recently been converted into well-equipped, attractive holiday cottages. Three of the cottages can be taken as one, sleeping 12. The garden, with pool and paddling pool, is surrounded by vines, olive and almond trees. This is a remote part of the region, but only 10 minutes' drive from Torre de Moncorvo, and 15 minutes from Vila Flor.
Carrascal, Vila Flor
T+351 254 731 246
E info@quinta-do-passadouro.com
W www.quinta-do-passadouro.com/
*   douropass/quinta-de-santa-luzia*
€545-€745 per week [SC] *5(2-6)* 🏊

CASAL DE LOIVOS C3
Casa de Casal de Loivos
This delightful 17th century manor house on a hill-top above Pinhão probably has the best views in Portugal – over the vineyards to a bend in the river, and the mountains beyond. The lovely, smart, narrow rooms beneath the main house were once the stables. Each has its own bathroom, and leads out through French windows onto the panoramic terrace. There's a honeymoon annexe. The sitting room in the former woodstore has sisal carpets, wood stacked by the stove for cosy open fires in winter. You can breakfast on the table outside your room. Other meals are available on request, around a convivial

table in the main house kitchen, or on a stone table outside, along with excellent wine from the property's own vines. Service is attentive and friendly, and Manuel de Sampaio Pimentel is a charming host. The house stands at the end of Casal de Loivos village, a little place of narrow streets and white houses up a 7km winding road from Pinhão.
5085-010 Casal de Loivos
T+351 254 732 149
E casadecasaldeloivos@ip.pt
W www.casadecasaldeloivos.com
€95 🛏6 [SC] *1(2)* ♀ ✗ *on request* 🏊
No credit cards Closed Jan

CELEIRÓS DO DOURO C3
Casa das Pipas
An impressive, stylish, modern guest house in the middle of the vines on the Quinta do Portal estate, south of Sabrosa on the road down to Pinhão. Bedrooms are large, comfortable and individually designed. A 'panoramic room' on the upper floor has board games, a wine library and a magnificent view over the vineyards. The sitting room has an open fire in winter, and there is a gym, and an outdoor pool.

If visiting the winery is not enough, *(page 90)*, you may be able to roll up your sleeves and join in the vineyard work. There are wine courses, too, and wine weekends including boat trips on the Douro.
Quinta do Portal, Celeirós do Douro,
*   5060 Sabrosa*
T+351 259 937 000
E reservas@quintadoportal.pt
W www.quintadoportal.com
€85-€120 🛏10 ♀ ✗ *on request* 🏊 ⛹

Casa do Visconde de Chanceleiros

This is a magical place, a beautifully restored 18th century summer residence in a small village 5km from Pinhão. The house itself offers casual luxury and elegance, with *azulejos* and lovely spacious rooms, some with open fires and private terraces. The games room has a pool table, and there is a bar. Outside is a flower-filled garden with swimming pool, then olives trees and vines. After tennis, or squash, relax in the jacuzzi, and the sauna, built into a port vat. The views are stunning, and breakfasts are excellent.

Largo da Fonte, Chanceleiros,
* 5085-201 Covas do Douro*
T+351 254 730 190
E chanceleiros@chanceleiros.com
W www.chanceleiros.com
€120 🛏6 ✗ *on request* 🛶 🏰 ⚲ 🏌

COTAS D3

Quinta dos Sonhos This new super-luxury *quinta* hotel is on the beautiful Quinta da Romaneira estate. Farmhouses, an old winery and farm buildings have been converted into very large and very luxurious rooms and apartments, pools, restaurants and spa. Romaneira's 400ha front the River Douro for 7km, the result of the amalgamation of seven farms in the early 20th century. Much of it was abandoned until a consortium came along a couple of years ago to turn it into their third 'House of Dreams' (*Sonhos*) – the other two are in Morocco. The houses here have different styles, from British colonial Porto, to Portuguese colonial, to Douro country manor. Roads have been cobbled, and a sandy and pebbled beach has been created for barbecues, camp fires and canoeing. The price is nearly all-in, including meals and snacks (but not in the top restaurant), all drinks (but not

other producers' wines), as are most of the activities (wine and port tastings, canoe, hammam, gym, mountain biking, walking, chauffeured estate drives in the 4x4, a small cinema, outdoor children's activities). There's a supplement for the spa, in an orange grove on the river bank, and for the top restaurant, Redondo, headed jointly by a top French chef and Miguel Castro Silva *(page 108)*. Although only 30km from Vila Real, this dream-spot lies at the end of a tortuous car journey. Or you can arrive by train to Pinhão, 15 minutes away – or by helicopter! The vineyard (potentially one of the Douro's best sites for port) has also been replanted, and a new winery built *(page 99)*.

Quinta da Romaneira, 5070-000 Cotas
T+351 254 732 432
E info@maisondesreves.com
W www.maisondesreves.com
€1,000-€1,200 (includes meals etc)
🛏14 Ⓢ7 ⚲ ✗ 🛶 ☕ 🏌

COVAS DO DOURO C3

Quinta Nova de Nossa Senhora do Carmo It's well worth the long and wiggly drive to this 'wine hotel' in a beautifully restored 18th century manor house. There are numerous sitting rooms in relaxing shades and combinations of green and wine, deep fireplaces, fine wood-panelled ceilings and oak beams, old prints. Rooms

overlook the vineyards and river, and you need wooden steps to get up into bed. Read outside in secluded corners, swim in the little pool over the vines. A heliport is available, but you may be content with bicycles, and vineyard walks to picnic tables amidst the oranges, almonds, olives and vines. You can buy the home-made wines, olive oil, and herb teas (camomile, heather, lavendar or broom). Breakfasts include scrumptious fig jam. *(See page 92 for wine visits.)*

5085-222 Covas do Douro
T+351 254 730 430
E hotelquintanova@amorim.com
W www.quintanova.com/hotel
€90-€150 🛏11 ⚲ ✗ 🛶

ERVEDOSA DO DOURO D2

Quinta de São José Surrounded by new vineyards on a steep hillside only just above the Douro, this quinta has bed and breakast rooms and three houses, each sleeping four people (but not self-catering). The main house has a sitting room and dining room open to all guests. There are lovely original features, exposed stone walls, terraces and verandas with river views, fireplaces and modern comforts, traditional furnishings, and a pool above the river. Derelict only a few years ago, the farm was taken over by descendants of the Ferreira family, who created the holiday houses and planted 8ha of vines. The quinta makes excellent wine. The owners are keen to help with visits, tasting and meals, and emphasise that this is a quiet, calm spot, unsuitable for children under 15. You can borrow canoes and bikes.

513-123 Ervedosa do Douro
T+351 254 240 000 (Porto 226 186 566)
E sjose.douro@iol.pt
W www.quintasjose.com
€150 🛏10 ⚲ ✗ *prior arrangement* 🛶
No credit cards Min nights 3

FOZ CÔA (VILA NOVA DE) F2

Casa Vermelha Right in the centre of the town and painted red – vermelha – with white windows, this impressive 1920s family house was built by the grandfather of the current owners, who have recently modernised it. It is surrounded by a large garden, with trees and a swimming pool. There's a big terrace, sitting room with fire place, games room, bar, and shop selling regional produce including wine, olive oil, almonds and fruit.

Avenida Gago Coutinho 3,
*   5150-610 Vila Nova de Foz Côa*
T+351 279 76 52 52
E geral@casavermelha.com/ silvia.caceres@
*   mail.telepac.pt*
W www.casavermelha.com
€90 🛏7 ✕*on request; light meals in*
*   summer on terrace* ⚓
No credit cards

FREIXO DE ESPADA À CINTA H2

Quinta do Salgueiro Amidst vines, olive and almond trees – and salgueiro means willow – right up in the Parque Natural do Douro Internacional, this is a fine spot to enjoy some peace and quiet. The 19th century farm has recently been comfortably converted, with simple, fresh en-suite rooms and sitting rooms with open fires. There is a pool, and a garden is underway.

5180-104 Freixo de Espada à Cinta
T+351 279 652 007
E info@quintadosalgueiro.com
W www.quintadosalgueiro.com
€50-€70 🛏7 S1 ✕*on request* ⚓
No credit cards

MESÃO FRIO A2

Casa d'Além The family house of a former port estate, Casa d'Alem was built in the 1920s, and still retains its original decor, its old fashioned charm and elegance. Outside, there are terraces, a pool, tennis, and fine views over the vineyards of the Baixo Corgo.

Oliveira 5040-204 Mesão Frio
T+351 254 321 991
E casadalem@sapo.pt
W www.casadalem.pt
€80 🛏3 ✕*to order* ⚓ ⚲

PINHÃO C3

Quinta de la Rosa Only just above the river, within sight of Pinhão, this wine and port estate has elegant, comfortable rooms down by the river and in the house next to the winery, and terraced gardens with a pool. Breakfast and pre-ordered meals are served on a wisteria-hung terrace, or in a sunny dining room. There are also two lovely farmhouses, Quinta Amarela *(pictured below)*, near the main property by the river, and Quinta de Lamelas, up in the hills, with spectacular views, both also with pools. Visit the winery *(page 98).*

5085-215 Pinhão
T+351 254 732 254
E rooms@quintadelarosa.com or
*   sophia@quintadelarosa.com*
W www.quintadelarosa.com
€75-€100, farmhouses €660-1,400
🛏5 S2 SC2(6&10) ♀ ✕*on request,*
except Sun ⚓

Vintage House This is an eye-catching edifice right on the river bank in the centre of Pinhão. Step off the train or boat and you're right here. Once a port warehouse and house belonging to Taylors, the hotel is big, classy and comfortable. Plush common areas are decorated with frescoes. Big, modern rooms with private balconies all face the river. Terrace, garden and pool stretch out along the river bank. The Restaurant Rabelo serves modern Portuguese cuisine (we have had mixed reports). Breakfasts are good. Try the evening chocolate and port tastings, and Saturday wine tasting courses.

Lugar da Ponte, 5085-034 Pinhão
T+351 254 730 230
E reserva@cs-vintagehouse.com
W www.hotelvintagehouse.com
€119-€186 🛏36 S7 ♀ ✕ ⚓

SAMODÃES B2

Aquapura Douro Hot, moist towels greet you in the vast entrance hall, where the reception desk stands on gnarled and varnished tree trunks. Your bath may lie at the end of your four poster bed, on a wooden floor the colour of port wine. Even the garden is square and angular. Keep fit in the technogym, relax in one of Portugal's best spas, where the sauna has a fine river view; a lovely indoor pool flows through to the garden. There's a top, gastronomic restaurant, Almapura *(page 108),* and a simpler one, Vale Abraão. Breakfasts are excellent. You could splash out on a cookery course with head chef Philippe Bossert.

Quinta de Vale Abraão,
*   5100-000 Lamego*
T+351 254 660 600
E reservations@aquapuradouro.com
W www.aquapurahotels.com
€240-€380
🛏41 S9 SC21(2&4) ♀ ✕ ⚓ ♨ 🤸

SANTA CRISTINA (MESÃO FRIO) A2

Solar da Rede, Pousada de Mesão Frio A hotel of palatial proportions high above the Douro on the road from Mesão Frio to Régua. Under new ownership, this is a pousada but one of two not in the main group. Built in the 18th century as

a stately home, its architecture, decor and furnishings are stunning – including delightful *azulejos*, granite floors, staircases and archways. The old kitchens have been converted into a dining room *(page 108)*, and other public rooms are elegant and spacious, although some of the bedrooms are on the small side. Outside there are lovely gardens, a pool, terraces, and great views over the vines to the river. Arrive if you wish by boat, or helicopter.
Santa Cristina, Mesão Frio, 5040-339
T+351 254 890 130
E reservas@cs-solardarede.com
W www.pousadas.pt
€150-€210 Suite €283 🛏21 ⑤8 ♀ ✕ ⇌

SANTA MARTA DE PENAGUIÃO B3

Casal Agrícola de Cevêr On a small farm, Quinta do Pinheiro, producing port, wine, olive oil and honey, west of the road from Vila Real to Régua, Casal Agrícola de Cevêr is a recently renovated 19th century house with comfortable ground-floor rooms and a turret room with vineyard views. The decor is period, the colours soft, the atmosphere peaceful. There is a shared sitting room for guests, a games room with pool table, a garden and swimming pool in ancient pine woods. You will be encouraged to tour the winery, taste the produce, and even join in the farm work.

Quinta do Pinheiro, Sarnadelo,
*   5030-569 Santa Marta de Penaguião*
T+351254 811 274
E casalagricoladecever@
*   casalagricoladecever.com*
W www.casalagricoladecever.com
€80 🛏4 ⑤1 ✕*on request* ⇌
No credit cards Closed Christmas

SARZEDINHO C3

Quinta de Macedos A 'wine lodge' on a historic wine-making quinta in the beautiful valley of the Rio Torto, this is owned by an English family, who use it themselves in August. The house is elegant, homely and comfortable, with a terrace overlooking the vines. Breakfast is included, dinner on request, prepared by staff who leave at 5pm. Visit the winery *page 101*.
T+351 254 738 090
E info@quintamacedos.com
W www.quintamacedos.com
€50-€60 🛏5 ♀ ✕*on request* ⇌ *Jun-Oct Closed Aug*

Quinta do Vale Dona Maria Once a vineyard workers' dormitory up in the vines above the winery and the Rio Torto, this has been beautifully restored and converted by the quinta's owners Joana and Cristiano van Zeller. There are rustic home comforts, great views from the flowery patio, and delicious wine on hand. Breakfast ingredients are provided. It's only a 15-minute drive up from Pinhão. Visit the winery *page 94*.

Sarzedinho, Ervedosa do Douro,
*   5130-141 São João da Pesqueira*
T+351 223 744 320
E cvanzeller@mail.telepac.pt
W www.quintavaledonamaria.com
€100 🛏3 ♀ ⇌ *No credit cards Min nights 3 Closed Sep-Oct*

TABUAÇO C2

Casa do Brasão A grand and characterful 17th century family house in the hill town of Tabuaço, south of Pinhão. Historic features include octagonal ceilings in the dining room and sitting room, and fine

multicoloured *azulejos*. There is a games room with pool table, and a bar.
T+351 254 780 040
E casadobrasao@gmail.com
W www.casadobrasao.com
€50-€75 🛏2 ⑤3 ✕*on request, min 10 people* ⇌ *No credit cards*

Quinta do Monte Travesso A 200-year-old farmhouse on a working farm offering bed and breakfast in the midst of vines and olives 5km from Tabuaço. Furnishings include old family pieces, and there's a library, a common sitting room, a chapel, lovely gardens, and a chance to experience the wine harvest in September, and the olive harvest in November/December.
5120-082 Tabuço
T+351 919 187 022
E turismo@quintadomontetravesso.com
W www.quintadomontetravesso.com
€60 🛏2 ✕*on request No credit cards*

TORRE DE MONCORVO F2

Quinta das Aveleiras As you leave town heading for Vila Nova de Foz Côa, this is a large farm in a scenic spot amidst woodland, terraced vines and olive groves, on the slopes of the Serra de Reboredo. Numerous farm buildings have been beautifully restored. One of the suites is in a dovecote. Another, the Casa do Retiro, is an isolated retreat house built of schist. Prices below include breakfast ingredients. There's an 18th century chapel and fountain, a garden and lake, swimming pool, tennis court, and bikes to borrow. A magical place.
5160-206 Torre de Moncorvo
T+351 279 252 285 or 258 280
E reservation@quinta-das-aveleiras.com
W www.quinta-das-aveleiras.com
€90-€165 ⓈⒸ *4(2-6)* ✕*take-aways from*
  local restaurants ⚓ ⚲

VALE DE MENDIZ C3

Casa de Mendiz This sensitively and beautifully converted farm/manor house, up in the hills above Pinhão, can be rented as a private holiday house, but the suites may also be available individually. Rooms are delightful – rustic in style but modern and comfortable. Terraces have wonderful views *(one of the terraces is pictured below)*, and there is a garden with a swimming pool, and a games room with pool table.
Apartado 14, Vale de Mendiz,
  5085-909 Alijó
T+351 917 009 055
E info@casademendiz.com
W www.casademendiz.com
€120, €320 for SC house
🛏*4* ⚲ ✕*on request* ⚓ *No credit cards*

Quinta do Passadouro Nestling on a hillside north of Pinhão, this farmouse is part way between between Provesende and Favaios, two of the Douro's historic wine villages. It is surrounded by vines, garden and a terrace for breakfast or outside dining. Passadouro is run by a Dutch couple with background in wine and the hotel business. They have established vineyard walks between the two villages, with optional overnight stays at other quintas or village houses. Visit the winery *page 102.*
Vale de Mendiz, 5085-101 Pinhão
T+351 254 731 246
E passadouro@quintadopassadouro.com
Wwww.quintadopassadouro.com
€62.50 🛏*6* ⚲ ✕*on request*
No credit cards Closed 2-3 weeks Dec/Jan

VILARINHO DE SÃO ROMÃO (SABROSA) C3

Casa de Vilarinho de São Romão In a little hamlet on the right bank of the River Pinhão, outside Sabrosa, this 17th century aristocratic house was much added to in the 18th century. Sensitively renovated with modern comforts, it has large rooms, a lovely terrace and garden, an old chapel, and beautiful views and vineyards all around.
Lugar da Capela, 5060-630 Sabrosa
T+351 259 930 754
E mail@casadevilarinho.com
W www.casadevilarinho.com
€85 🛏*6* ✕*dinner on request* ⚓
No credit cards Closed Christmas

VILARINHO DOS FREIRES B2

Quinta do Vallado This delightful old house on a wine estate just outside (Peso da) Régua, built in 1716, was once the home of the famous Dona Antónia Adelaide Ferreira, and still belongs to her decendants.

It was recently very beautifully and sensitively restored to a comfortable blend of old and new. There are great views, a pool in the terraced garden, snooker, and activities on offer including water-ski and cycling. Visit the winery *(page 104)* and stock up in the smart wine shop.
Vilarinho dos Freires,
  5050-364 Peso da Régua
T+351 254 323 147
E vallado@mail.telepac.pt
W www.quintadovallado.com
€85-€115 🛏*4* Ⓢ*1* ⚲ ✕*on request,*
  min 4 people ⚓
Closed Jan

Porto and Gaia

Where Douro meets Atlantic, the two cities of Porto and Vila Nova de Gaia have an austere, Northern European feel, facing each other across the river under skies that are often grey and hazy. The cities gave their name to the country – for the Romans they were the strategic ports of Portus and Cale; by the middle ages the name Portucale applied to the local region, and then finally, as Portucalia, to the whole kingdom. The age of discoveries, the spice trade and then the port trade brought great wealth – visible today in the grandeur of church interiors, public and private buildings. The river has since silted up, the major port has slipped around the corner, to Matosinhos, and only small craft and pleasure boats sail under the cities' bridges.

Both cities have their sprawling suburbs, but the characterful centre of Porto has always been residential and commercial, the site of tourist hotels and restaurants, while central Gaia played the role of wine merchant, its narrow streets lined with long, red-roofed port warehouses. Gaia now has big plans. Over the next decade, the serious port-production work is to move out to modern, purpose-built premises on the outskirts, whilst the centre is to be spruced up, the historic cellars smartened and still

visitable, and new classy hotels and restaurants built, designed to lure tourists to the south bank.

Both Gaia and Porto have already done a good deal of sprucing in the past few years, especially along the riverbanks, and up along Porto's long, straight Avenida da Boavista, which runs from the centre out to the wealthy seaside suburb of Foz do Douro. There's a fine new metro, one arm of which crosses the top level of the iconic two-tier Dom Luis I Bridge. The bridge and parts of both cities have been classified as a UNESCO World Heritage Site: in Gaia the Convento da Serra do Pilar, and Porto's Ribeira district, with its historic buildings, riverside promenade and cafés, along with the steep hillside behind, where small medieval houses and workshops cling higgledy-piggledy between narrow streets and cobbled steps. There are fabulously ornate churches, and many Art Deco buildings.

The inhabitants, *Portuenses,* have a reputation for being traditional in taste and opinion, as well as organised and hard working. But they are also hospitable, and as expert at partying as they are at relaxing in cafés with a newspaper and a little cup of good coffee.

121

Explore Porto and Gaia

Porto is not a good place to hire a car – unless you are heading straight out of town. Many streets are narrow and congested, or total no-go areas for cars; parking is a nightmare, especially in summer, and few central hotels have their own parking; road signs are sparse, and the one-way systems will turn you round in circles. As most of the tourist venues are fairly central in both Porto and Gaia, you may be better hiring a car only for your onward journey. Porto and Gaia are great cities to discover on foot – but do bring trainers or flat, non-slip shoes for the steep,

cobbled streets and alleys. For late night or longer distances, or when you have faced one hill too many, public transport is good, and taxis are inexpensive.

The first tourist focus of Porto is the spectacular, two-tier Dom Luis I Bridge (Ponte Dom Luis I), spanning the Douro between Porto and Vila Nova de Gaia. The dark, arched iron structure carries two roads, one 30 metres above the other. You can walk or drive across both levels, and Porto's new metro now also runs along the top. It was designed in 1886 by a disciple of Eiffel, with lots of cross-struts to give it strength. Apparently, left-over pieces were

used to build the Elevador de Santa Justa in Lisbon *(page 232 and 235)*. On the northern side of the river, just west of the bridge, the RIBEIRA is another hub of tourist life. *Ribeira* means 'riverside area'. The riverside promenade, the Cais (Quay) da Ribeira, is so broad as to be normally uncrowded, despite the many tourists and locals who head to this lively district at all times of day and night. An ageing population also *lives* here, in the colourful flats and houses that form a backdrop to the Cais. Musicians lay out their hats, and boats dock along the Cais da Ribeira to

WHEN AND HOW

Sundays and Mondays Some tourist sites, including a few port lodges, are closed on Sundays, and many museums and galleries close on Mondays. Some restaurants and bars close on Sundays, especially in the evening, some on Mondays. But there is much more action on Mondays in Porto than in Lisbon.
Meals Lunch is between 1 and 3pm. Dinner out for locals tends to start around 9pm, but you can be served earlier.
Monuments and museums Usually open at 9 or 10am and close at 5pm. Some close at lunchtime.
Shops Usually open 9am-1pm, 3pm-7pm, but are shut from 1pm on Saturday afternoons, and on Sundays; most shopping centres are open 10am-11pm all week.
Transport The same tickets are now valid for all modes of transport in Porto: the fine new metro/light rail network, buses, urban trains, the funicular and few remaining trams. It is much more expensive to buy individual journey tickets; for multiple journeys, buy an **Andante Azul** card from metro stations or Andante kiosks or shops, and load it digitally with the required number of units. The Blue Card itself costs 50c, and can be recharged. Each Andante unit gives you unlimited travel in your chosen zone for an hour or more, depending on zone. 11 journeys cost between €8.50 and €26, depending on zones. An **Andante 24** gives a day's unlimited travel from the first moment of use, for €3 to €9.10. The tourist offices and certain hotels also sell the **Passe Porto**, valid for transport and museums, plus reductions on some river cruises, concerts etc. One day costs €3.50 without transport, €7.50 with transport, 2 days €11.50, 3 days €15.50.

WHEN AND HOW *continued*

The hub of the smart, efficient **metro** is the Estação Trindade, just north of Aliados. The five lines are colour-coded, and will take you over the bridge to Gaia, out to the fish restaurants of Matosinhos, up to the airport, and out north into Vinho Verde country. Metro trains run from 6am-1am. Many **buses** *(autocarros)* leave from the Praça da Liberdade, north-east of São Bento station. Porto has only two tram lines at present, one from Massarelos to Carmo, the other from Infante along the river to the beaches and restaurants of Foz do Douro, starting at 9.15 or 9.30am until 6 or 7pm. But some old tram routes are currently being re-laid. The narrow **Funicular dos Guindais** will hoist you from just east of the Luis I Bridge a short but steep distance up to Batalha, from 8am-8pm, and until midnight on Fridays, Saturdays and festivals. Long-distance **trains** from Lisbon and the south arrive at the Estação de Campanhã, 2km east of the centre; it's a five-minute journey from there to Estação São Bento – this is the starting point for the wonderful train journey up the Douro valley.

From the smart, new **Francisco Sá Carneiro** airport, 19km to the north-west, the **Aerobus** to the city centre is free if you fly TAP, otherwise €2.60 for a ticket also valid on local buses for the rest of the day; or take city buses 56 and 87. The metro is quicker, 30 minutes to the city centre.

Boat Cruises Various companies offer river trips, on pleasure boats, *barcos rabelos* (like the boats that used to transport barrels of young port wine), or small cruise ships, lasting from 50 minutes for a local excursion to several-day cruises up to the Spanish border. Diana Tours offers boat-train combinations to and from Regúa.

Aris Douro T Pinhão Porto T+351 222 006 418
  E geral@douroacima.pt W www.douroacima.pt
Barcadouro T+351 223 722 415 E reservas@barcadouro.pt
  W www.barcadouro.pt
Diana Tours T+351 227 160 624 W en.dianatours.pt
Douro Azul T+351 223 402 513 E geral@douroazul.pt
  W www.douroazul.com

Tourist offices Porto has three Turismo do Porto tourist offices, for info, maps, timetables and Passe Porto transport and museum passes: the main one at *Rua Clube dos Fenianos 25; Ribeira Rua do Infante Dom Henrique; and Terreiro da Sé W www.portoturismo.pt Open summer Mon-Fri 9-7 Sat, Sun and public hols 9.30-4.30 winter Mon-Fri 9-5.30 Sat, Sun & public hols 9.30-4.30*. The tourist office of Vila Nova de Gaia is next to the Sandeman lodge at *Avenida Diogo Leite 242 Open summer 10-7 winter Mon-Fri 10-6.*

pick up river trippers. There's a weekday open air market, souvenir and craft stalls and shops, and many restaurants and bars, some built into the remains of the old city wall. People flock here in the evening for dinner, and then party on into the night, especially in summer. The Ribeira has been gradually cleaned up and restored over the last decade, since it and a small surrounding area became a UNESCO World Heritage Site – but there still remains a lot of renovation to be done.

The Ribeira has two squares: behind the Cais da Ribeira, the Praça da Ribeira, lined with street cafés, and a little way up the hill to the west, the Praça do Infante Dom Henrique (the Infante in question was Prince Henry the Navigator, who was born here in the nearby Casa do Infante in 1394, and later inspired Portugal's voyages of discovery). On this square, it's worth visiting the grand old stock exchange building, the Palácio da Bolsa, and the

Left The famous Ponte Dom Luís I was designed by a disciple of Eiffel

Above The reflective Douro by night

Right Hillside jumble of Porto's Ribeira

Igreja de São Francisco *(page 128)* so shockingly over-gilded that it was deconsecrated. All around this old part of town, steep little cobbled streets and alleyways twist, turn into steps, duck under archways, and soon have you completely lost. Washing flaps between the houses. Elderly residents sit in their windows and chat across the street.

The Sé (Cathedral) district is up above the winding alleys and stairways, dominated by the cathedral's austere granite hulk. Just below to the right is the former Bishop's Palace (a huge, imposing building you cannot visit) and in the angle between them is the Terreiro da Sé, the 'Cathedral Terrace', with an impressive Manueline pillory, and panoramic views. Over slightly to the east, don't miss the amazing Renaissance Igreja de Santa Clara, the church interior dripping with gilt woodwork *(page 128)*, though you would never guess it from the outside. North of the cathedral, street markets sell fruit, veg and fish. A wide avenue sweeps straight up from the top level of the Dom Luis I Bridge through the Sé district to the Belle Epoque railway station (Estação São Bento). Even if you have no need for trains, do wander into the main hall to admire the famous floor-to-ceiling *azulejos*.

RIBEIRA **Sala Ogival**

Not to be missed, within the grand Palácio da Bolsa, this is a drop-in 'educational' tasting centre representing the wine industry of the whole country, where you can taste a regularly changing selection of Portuguese wines free of charge. ViniPortugal's staff will give you an individually-tailored tutored tasting, explaining the wine regions, grape varieties, climate, soil... There are special wine events on the first Sunday in July, the annual Dia do Vinho (Wine Day), and during Essência do Vinho *(page 129)* in February.
Palácio da Bolsa, Rua Ferreira Borges Open Tue-Sat 10-7 Closed Sun, Mon

This is the limit of the World Heritage Site. North of the station is the heart of 19th century Porto, first the Praça da Liberdade around the equestrian statue of Pedro IV (hub of the bus routes), then the civic and financial centre of Porto, around the wide, double Avenida dos Aliados with its promenade, park and cafés. At the top is the city hall, and the main tourist office. Over to the east of this, the BAIXA is the main shopping area, centred on the Rua Sá da Bandeira and parallel to it the long, pedestrianised Rua de Santa Catarina, heading northwards

Above and left The *Sé* (Cathedral) and Bishop's Palace dominate the Porto hillside by day and night

Right The Manueline pillory by the cathedral

Far right Azulejos decorate all kinds of buildings

Diana Tours
Those hills can be tiring. One effortless way to visit the two cities is in the little street-trains of Diana Tours. One tour lasts one and three-quarter hours and takes in a Gaia wine lodge, with tasting (€6, under-3s free); the other is a three and a half hour trip visiting famous monuments (€30, under-7s free, under-13s €15). *Rua Delfim Lima 3551 T+351 227 160 624 W www.en.dianatours.pt*

from the Praça da Batalha. Shops and department stores (some very quaint) sell mainly clothes, jewellery, leather and shoes, but you will also find smart cafés, and shops selling cakes, bread, cheese... and part way up, on the corner with Rua Fernandes Tomás, the wonderful Mercado do Bolhão *(page 151)*, the best place in town for food shopping, though changes are afoot.

West of São Bento station and the Praça da Liberdade, in the CORDOARIA area, is another of Porto's major landmarks, the tall Torre dos Clérigos *(page 127)*, and round the corner to the north, the extraordinarily beautiful, neo-Gothic bookshop, Livraria Lello & Irmão *(page 127)*. The old part of the university is here, surrounded by characterful old shops and 18th century houses on steep streets. Porto's main museum, the Museu Soares dos Reis *(page 128)*, is just over to the west.

The other smart and busy shopping area is along and around the city end of the Avenida da Boavista, and the big Rotunda da Boavista roundabout (really called Praça de Mouzinho de Albuquerque, but that proved too much of a mouthful). The lion squashing the eagle in the centre of the roundabout symbolises the united Portuguese and British defeating the French in the Peninsular War. Further along, the Avenida da Boavista becomes more residential: modern apartment blocks, smart new hotels, and the angular new Casa da Música *(page 127)*; the modern art museum with its park, Fundação de Serralves *(page 128)* is

way along the straight Avenida da Boavista, which ends after 7km at the coast and the military Castelo do Queijo.

Unglamorous, high-rise MATOSINHOS, up the coast from the Castelo, is a working port bristling with seafood restaurants, and nightclubs that were once fish-canning warehouses – easily accessible now by metro or bus. Opposite, and still part of the port, is the small holiday and fishing town of LEÇA DA PALMEIRA, with yet more fish restaurants, and nice, uncrowded beaches. FOZ DO DOURO lies to the south, right on the corner of the estuary – *foz* means the place where a river flows into the sea (or into another river). This is the most expensive place to live in the Porto area, trendy by night, with a lovely seafront, well supplied with palm trees, dunes, wave-washed rocky and sandy beaches, designer shops, smart fish restaurants and bars, some of them on wooden decking on the beach. Foz is very lively in summer, quiet and partially closed out of season. It's a young nightlife spot. Take the tram, or the bus along the river.

VILA NOVA DE GAIA – THE SOUTH BANK

The quickest route from Foz do Douro across the river to VILA NOVA DE GAIA is the Arrábida Bridge (built mid-20th century), at the point where the river begins to widen. Changes are afoot in Gaia. The historic centre of Gaia is, as we write, still the true centre of port production. Port producers struggle with cramped conditions in their *lojas* (Portuguese for 'warehouses' or 'shops' – hence 'lodges'). Lorries squeeze down narrow streets, where tourists also wander. Here and there washing dangles from old balconies, and old men emerge from ancient barbers' shops and little bars.

There have already been changes in Gaia – a new riverside park and promenade, a new complex of shops, bars and restaurants down by the quay, popular particularly with the younger inhabitants. There are new sports and social centres, the convent has been renovated, some new roads are already in use, and work has started on a big pleasure port on Gaia's Atlantic coast. But in the next six years the Gaia city council plans to transform the historic centre into 'the capital of high quality leisure in the northeast of the peninsula', as well as 'the most appealing residential district of the Metropolitan area of Porto'. Their target is 6,400 new residents, and nearly 3,000 new

jobs. They have employed Parque Expo, planners of the wonderful Parque das Nações in Lisbon's eastern dockland *(page 234-235)*, and are seeking international finance to bolster the input from the wine industry, government and the EU. Plans include a new pedestrian bridge across the Douro, better walkways, lifts, escalators and cable-cars; an open air shopping centre, a 'port wine cultural centre', a large theatre, and a Museum of Barcos Rabelos.

The serious cellar work is to move out to purpose-built modern warehouses in an out-of-centre industrial park. The 'ageing population' of the historic centre will be relocated in 'better housing and social conditions', mainly around the station area, along with new residents. There are to be public spaces, gardens, car parks and a new road linking horizontally behind the lodges. These will turn into more efficient tourist museums and tasting rooms, and in some cases boutique hotels (Burmester, Caves Cruz...). The Croft lodges up on the hill will become the Yeatman Hotel, 84-rooms, five-stars, plus spa and wine school.

The political masters of Gaia want to double the number of tourists in the next ten years – and have them stay on this side of the river.

Left A peaceful moment on the Gaia quays

Above and right Gaia's Mosteiro (monastery) da Serra do Pilar gives a fine view over the port lodges, the famous bridge, and the city of Porto

❊ VIEW FROM THE TOP ❊

Of the many views from the hills and buildings of Porto and Gaia, this is a small selection.

CORDOARIA (PORTO, CENTRE) **Torre dos Clérigos** The Baroque granite clocktower of the Igreja dos Clérigos stands at the top of one of one of the hills in the centre of Porto. For €1, climb more than 200 worn steps to see most of the city, river and coast. Too tired? Tower closed? The view is nearly as good from the small square along the Rua da Estrada da Assunção, nearby. *Rua São Filipe de Nery Open Apr-Sep 9.30-12.30, 2.30-6.30 Oct-Mar Mon-Sat 10-11.30, 2-4.30 Closed 25 Dec & 1 Jan*

RIBEIRA & GAIA **Dom Luis I Bridge** Top level pavement – only for the brave.

SÉ (PORTO, CENTRE) **Terreiro da Sé** The traffic-free square outside the main doors of the cathedral has an impressive Manueline pillory and great views of Gaia. Even better, go into the Sé and pay €2 to climb to the upper level of the cloister to admire the 18th century *azulejos* and the view. *Open Apr-Oct 9-12.15, 2.30-6 Nov-Mar 9-12.15, 2.30-5.15*

GAIA (VILA NOVA DE) **Mosteiro da Serra do Pilar** On a steep hill high above the bridge, the monastery terrace has fine views of Gaia, Porto and the river.

MATOSINHOS (PORTO, COAST) **Castelo do Queijo** Built on boulders that resembled holey cheese *(queijo)*. Apart from the sea and coastal views, there's a small bar, and the army is still in residence. *Tue-Sun 1.30-7*

BETWEEN MEALS

RAMALDE (PORTO, WEST) **Casa da Música** A few years late, seriously over-budget, its exterior loved or hated, this impressive, lop-sided building opened in April 2005, providing exciting spaces with great acoustics and unexpected natural light. Performances range from classical to fado to rock. The Italian-fusion Kool restaurant on the 7th floor under the roof is half-named after the building's Dutch architect, Rem Koolhaas. The terrace looks out towards the Rotunda da Boavista and the city. *Avenida da Boavista 610*

T+351 220 120 220
E info@casadamusica.com
W www.casadamusica.com

RIBEIRA **Palácio da Bolsa** Up in the western part of the Ribeira, this large, famous building is sternly neo-classic on the outside, grand and ornate within. It was built as a merchants' guild hall, and has served as law courts, parliament, and as Porto's stock exchange until as recently as 1995. Most memorable are the ornately gilded Arabian room, and the Pátio das Nações, the pink stucco and glass-domed great hall where the stock exchange was housed – and where the annual Essência do Vinho consumer wine fair is now held *(page 129)*. Hear the history of

Porto and Gaia on a half-hourly guided tour in numerous languages. There's a good wine shop inside. *Rua Ferreira Borges Open every day Apr-Oct 9-7 Nov-Mar 9-1, 2-6 Closed 25 Dec & 1 Jan*

VITÓRIA (PORTO, CENTRE) **Livraria Lello** Just up from the Clérigos church, this startlingly beautiful bookshop is not only for bookworms – though you'll find English books amidst the 60,000, new and second hand. It is more a temple than a bookshop, built in 1906 in ornate neo-Gothic style. Admire the stained glass ceiling, intricate stucco and woodwork, sweep up the double staircase to the galleries, and stop for a cup of coffee or glass of port in the tiny café in the upper gallery *(page 151)*. There's a track around the floor along which shop assistants push carts of books. *Rua das Carmelitas 141 Open Mon-Fri 9.30-7 Sat 9.30-1 Closed Sun*

MUSEUMS & GALLERIES
LORDELO DO OURO (BOAVISTA)

Fundação de Serralves Portugal's most prestigious galleries of modern art are set amidst 18ha of French-designed hillside garden with lake and fountains, park,

woods and farmland just south of the Avenida da Boavista. There are two impressive buildings – the big, stark, marble-rich Museu de Arte Contemporânea, opened in 1999, and the pink art deco Casa de Serralves, built in the 1930s, and now housing temporary exhibitions. Sculptures are also dotted outside around the grounds. Don't miss the wisteria-clad restaurant and tea house near the rose garden – the restaurant is good. There are Jazz concerts in the summer. *Rua Dom João de Castro 210 T+351 226 156 500 E balcao.informacoes@serralves.pt W www.serralves.pt Open Museu Oct-Mar Tue-Sat 10-7 Apr-Sep Tue-Fri 10-7, Sat, Sun & public hols 10-8 Casa & park Tues-Sun 10-8 Closed Mon, 1 Jan, 25 Dec €5, free on Sun*

MIRAGAIA (PORTO, WEST) **Museu do Vinho do Porto** New museum in a lovely, vaulted space in the 17th century warehouses originally built to house the wines of the Companhia Geral de Agricultura das Vinhas do Alto Douro, set up by the Marquês de Pombal. There is attractively-presented interactive info on port production and its history, in numerous languages, including braille. Throughout the museum, the imaginary personages Pipas and Sarah Pipas pop up to occupy the children. *Rua de Monchique 45-52 Open Tue-Sun 12-5 Closed Mon €1, free on Sat & Sun*

MIRAGAIA (PORTO, WEST) **Museu Nacional Soares dos Reis** Porto's once dowdy main museum and art gallery re-opened in 2001, renovated, extended and much improved. West of the centre and named after a famous Portuguese sculptor of the 19th century, the pretty pink 18th century building was the royal Palácio das Carrancas. Exhibits range from beautiful Iron Age jewellery to 20th century art and sculpture. *Rua Dom Manuel II Open Tue 2-6 Wed-Sun 10-6 Closed Mon, 1 Jan, Easter Sun, 1 May, 25 Dec*

CHURCHES
RIBEIRA **Igreja de São Francisco** The over-the-top guilded grandeur of this church led to its deconsecration. Originally medieval Gothic, the interior was reworked in the 18th century. Its 'Tree of Jesse' gilded altarpiece (left of the nave) is always considered to be the highlight, but the whole place is amazing, and not to be missed even if churches are not normally your thing. *Rua do Infante Dom Henrique Open Feb-May 9-6 Jul-Aug 9-8 Jun, Sep, Oct 9-7 Nov-Jan 9-5.30 Closed 25 Dec*

SÉ **Igreja do Convento de Santa Clara** In the cathedral district, this lovely renaissance church, simple on the outside, has gilded woodwork covering ceiling and walls – less overdone than the Igreja de São Francisco. One of the best remaining sections of the old city wall is just alongside the church. *Largo do 1 de Dezembro, east of Avenida Vimara Peres Open Mon-Fri 9.30-11.30, 3-7 Closed Sat, Sun, public hols*

FAIRS & FESTIVALS

FEBRUARY

Essência do Vinho Portugal's biggest consumer wine event (variable dates in February, for three days around mid-month). It is held in the spectacular Palácio da Bolsa. There are 2,000 wines to taste from 250 producers from Portugal and abroad. Now, concurrently, there is a consumer food fair, **Essência do Gourmet**, in the nearby Mercado Ferreira Borges, with demos by famous chefs (Portuguese and foreign), and food exhibitors.
W *www.essenciadovinho.com*

JUNE

Festas de São João Porto is the place to be in the last week of June for the Festival of Saint John. This is celebrated all over Portugal, but Porto does it best. The city explodes into a riot of slightly bacchanalian anarchy. It's a strange mix of religion (a bit), partying (a lot) and amusing pagan rituals – this is, after all, also the summer solstice. Streets are decorated, and altars appear throughout the city, along with stalls and stages for live music. It all starts on the day of 23 June, St John's Eve, with a religious-model-making competition between city's districts. People give each other basil plants, representing 'holy

scented herbs', which were believed to bring health and luck in love and business. Then there's an all-night party, the whole town seemingly out in the streets, dancing and singing, with lashings of *vinho verde, caldo verde* soup, sardines, roast kid, roast lamb, roast potatoes... Join local street parties, or you could head for the Ribeira, the best place to see the late-night fireworks, or to the beach at Foz do Douro, where serious, youthful partying goes on all night. The weirdest aspect of the celebrations is people bashing each other over the head with inflatable squeaky hammers – traditionally the chosen

weapons were leeks, and you'll see these too – especially around dawn, when things get *really* silly. People release little paper hot air balloons (an ancient sun-worshippers' ritual), and you may see the youth of Porto leaping over bonfires: an odd number of jumps, but at least three, are said to deflect misfortune in the coming year – but it's really just for fun. On the saint's day itself, people sleep it off, the religious go to church, and in the afternoon there is the annual race of *barcos rabelos* on the river. This is not the time to come to Porto if you want a peaceful visit.

Left Celebrate with sardines and Vinho Verde

Right The annual race of the *barcos rabelos*, culmination of the São João festivities

Below Spectacular fireworks on St John's Eve

Wine in Vila Nova de Gaia

The long, low, tiled-roof warehouses in the town of Vila Nova de Gaia, directly across the river from Porto, have been a crucial staging post in port's journey from the vineyards of the Douro region to the outside world since the 18th century. These buildings, known as 'lodges' (after the Portuguese word *loja*, meaning shop or warehouse), sometimes go down two, even three levels into the hill on which Gaia stands, creating ideal conditions for the storage of port wines. Here ports are matured in large *balseiros* (upright wooden vats), or *toneis* (horizontal vats), or in *pipas* (barrels).

Originally, the young, fortified wines made their journey from the estates in the Douro region on *barcos rabelos*, the boats that now remain moored at the Gaia quayside, waiting for their annual outing on 24 June. Today's wines come down by road tanker, and the steep, cobbled streets of Gaia, designed for nothing larger than ox-carts, are often blocked by bulky modern vehicles.

Between 1926 and 1986, Gaia had a uniquely privileged position. By law, all port that was to be exported had to start its journey here. This meant that all port shippers were obliged to buy or rent warehouses in Gaia. Producers

without premises in Gaia were unable to export their ports, or had to export via a shipper who did have a lodge. When Portugal joined the European Community in 1986, the law was repealed as protectionist. Port producers without lodges in Gaia began exporting their wines direct from estates in the Douro region itself.

But the lodges of Gaia are still where most port is matured, blended and bottled. And since all port producers are legally obliged to sell no more than one-third of their total stock each year, huge amounts of wine lie maturing in lodges awaiting blending. This is a highly skilled job, requiring tasters who can put together an intricate jigsaw of different wines to achieve a consistent style year after year.

Now Gaia is in the process of reinventing itself *(page 126)*, both as a town and as a tourist destination. New hotels and housing are to be built, and the main business of storing and bottling port to be moved out of town to purpose-built facilities. Many lodges already have excellent facilities for visitors. There are sure to be improvements, but it might be fun to experience the town before and after the substantial changes that are to come.

Left A seagull's eye view of the port lodges of Vila Nova de Gaia and the Dom Luís I Bridge

Right Nosing around in the old-fashioned tasting room at Niepoort

STYLES OF PORT

White Made from white grapes, usually medium-sweet or sweet, and sold without much ageing in barrel. Best drunk chilled, even with a slice of lemon or splash of tonic water. A few white ports have extra ageing in barrel, and develop nutty complexity.

Ruby Basic red port, made from lighter wines, so it can be released young and fruity.

Tawny Lighter-coloured port, released young. This can be naturally light-coloured, a blend of red and white ports, or with some colour filtered out of it. (But see 'aged tawny' below, which is something quite different).

Reserve Popular category now, as it takes in ports of better-than-average quality blended to make a consistent style.

Late-Bottled Ports aged in barrel or vat until the fourth or the sixth year after the vintage, then bottled. **Late Bottled Vintage** must come from a specified year. **Bottle-matured** means the wine must have spent at least an extra three years in bottle.

Crusted Port bottled in the knowledge that it will form a deposit (or 'crust') in the bottle if kept for a few years. The wines have to be kept for at least three years after they are bottled before being sold. This will have to be decanted, because of the deposit. Not many are made now, but they're usually good value.

Aged Tawny 'Port with an indication of age': 10, 20, 30 and 40 years are the ages allowed on the labels of these wines. The theory is that these will be blends of wood-aged ports that will correspond roughly to the age stated on the bottle's label. In practice, the wines have to be approved as being typical of their stated ages by the official tasting panel. Aged tawnies are some of the most delicious ports of all, becoming more subtle and complex. They are lighter in colour – tawny – because much of the colour falls out as sediment during their stay in wood.

Colheita Wood-aged, tawny port from a single year. These have to start out as good as the wines that go into vintage port, in order to survive a minimum of seven years' ageing in wood before bottling. Essentially, *colheita* ports are vintage ports aged in wood. Some of the greatest, most complex ports available.

Vintage Whereas all other port styles are aged in wood for varying lengths of time before bottling, vintage port is allowed only two years in wood before being bottled. So it is known as 'bottle-matured' (rather than 'wood-matured'). Most shippers do not 'declare' (release) a vintage port every year, partly because they want it to be a special category, released only in the best years, partly as they want to keep quantities limited and prices high. Most vintage wines are big and deep-coloured, capable of maturing in bottle for decades. The new generation of vintage ports can be enjoyed young, thanks to improvements in viticulture, vinification and a rise in the quality of brandy available for fortification.

Single Quinta Vintage – a vintage wine from a single estate bottled after only two years in wood. Single-quinta wines are usually released in the years between declarations of vintage wines, made from the grapes of the estate that forms the heart of a blend in a vintage year. They are usually ready to drink at a younger age than vintage.

Barros

Barros Almeida & Companhia, to give it its full name, was the latest port company to be snapped up by the Spanish-owned Sogevinus in 2006. Barros had a reputation for making large quantities of inexpensive wine, much of it sold to France, Holland and Germany. In 1998, the Barros group built a new winery at one of their two quintas in the Douro, São Luiz *(page 89)*. Since then, the quality of the wines has definitely improved. The **Barros LBV** is made in a fresh, light, fruity style, which contrasts with the sweet, rich, figgy style of the **Barros 10 Year Old Tawny**. The **Barros Vintage** is aromatic, dense and complex. But the real glories of the house are their complex, intense old **Colheitas**. Barros are also making good Douro reds. The Barros lodge offers no tours, but you can pay to taste in the shop before buying.

Avenida Ramos Pinto 288,
  4400-288 Vila Nova de Gaia
T+351 220 109 015
E turismo@sogevinus.com
W www.porto-barros.pt
Shop Jun-Sept 10-8 Oct-May 10.30-7.30

Burmester

The venerable house of JW Burmester, founded in 1730, is another that has come under the wing of Sogevinus, the Spanish-owned group that also owns Cálem. Burmester was owned by members of the Burmester family or their direct descendants until 1999, then bought by

another family company, Amorim, better known for their cork, finance and property interests. Less than ten years later, in 2005, Amorim sold to Sogevinus. Burmester has always had a reputation for its **Burmester 20 Year Old Tawny** and **Burmester Colheita** wines (aged tawnies from a single vintage). The stocks of these were included in the sale to Sogevinus, so they're still available, and the old ones are absolutely brilliant. The free cellar tour includes a tasting of two ports.

Rua Barão de Forrester 73,
  4400-034 Vila Nova de Gaia
T+351 223 747 290
E turismo@sogevinus.com
W www.burmester.pt
Visits Jun-Sept Mon-Sat 10-6.30
  Oct-May Mon-Fri 10-1, 2-6

Cálem

The new Spanish owners have invested in an outstanding new visitor centre in their lodge on the main riverfront at Gaia – one of the best visitor experiences in Gaia, and definitely one of three or four to choose from if yout time is limited. (They also have another shop and tasting area at their other Gaia lodge, just to the east of the Dom Luis I Bridge.) In 2006, they won a prize for the refurbishment in an international competition 'Best of Wine Tourism', organised in San Francisco. It really is a splendid visit, with a well-lit, modern museum showing the history of the Douro region, how port is made and

Cálem's history. Then you walk through the ageing cellars, past vats and pipes of maturing port, and eventually into a spacious tasting room with refectory tables, in a refurbished ageing cellar. Here you will be offered a pair of ports to taste, red and white. Then it's on to stock up in the Cálem shop.

Founded in 1859, Cálem was owned by four generations of the Cálem family before Sogevinus bought the company in 1998. It was high time for a new owner with ample investment funds, as wine quality had fallen in the years before the takeover. There is a real air of optimism in the company now, and gleaming new equipment in the working parts of the lodges. They have launched two new Douro DOC labels, **Curva** and **Trium** (for single-variety reds). Both are good, with honours going to the Touriga Nacional-dominated **Curva Reserva Tinto**. **Aged tawnies** and old **Colheita** are also good. The quality of **Cálem Vintage** port, made from grapes sourced from farmers in the Upper Douro, is fast catching up with some much better-known names.

Avenida Diogo Leite 26,
  4400-111 Vila Nova de Gaia, &
Largo da Ponte Dom Luis I,
  4430-083 Vila Nova de Gaia
T+351 223 746 660
E turismo@sogevinus.com
W www.calem.pt
Visits May-Oct 10-7 Nov-Apr 10-6
✗

Churchill's

Johnny Graham is a brave man. In 1981, together with his two brothers, he founded the first independent port company to be established in more than 70 years. It was a struggle. Born into a port family who sold the family business, he joined the production side of Cockburn's in 1973, at the age of 21. Seven years later, he was made a director, but decided to leave, and set up on his own. He had seven years of experience in vineyard, winery and blending-room, but no vineyards, no winery and no lodge where he could blend and bottle. He worked as a consultant blender for Taylor's while he started his company. The wines came from three quintas belonging to the Borges de Sousa family, who sold their grapes at good prices to companies such as Cockburn's and Taylor's in vintage years. Johnny Graham offered them good prices every year. And he rented a lodge from Taylor's.

Churchill Graham (Johnny's wife, Caroline, is a Churchill) released Churchill's Vintage, and single-quinta vintage ports from Quinta da Água Alta and Quinta do Fojo. As Churchill's reputation grew, and another generation of Borges de Sousas took over the family estates, Johnny Graham realised he would have to buy his own estates to ensure his wine supply. And he needed more space for storage in Gaia. In 1988, Churchill's bought three ruined lodges. It took two years of restoration before they could be used. Now there is barely enough space for all the vats and barrels, and not enough, unfortunately, to receive visitors. In 1999, Johnny Graham bought two estates, Quinta da Gricha and Quinta do Rio. Together with grapes from another rented estate next door to Quinta do Rio, Churchill's had an assured supply.

The next project was Douro DOC wines. The first **Churchill Estates** red was released in 2002. Now he has three levels of quality, all much better than his first efforts. Our favourite is the aromatic Churchill Estates, dominated by floral Touriga Nacional. The ports are getting better every year: the bright, elegant **Quinta da Gricha** single-quinta vintage, and the darker, richer **Churchill's Vintage**. Churchill's also makes a good **White Port**, one of the best, nutty, herby and quite dry.

Cockburn's

This is a company in transition. In July 2006, Beam Wine Estates (BWE – owners of Californian, Australian and New Zealand wines, and of Courvoisier Cognac) sold all the vineyards, wineries and stock to Symington Family Estates. BWE retained only the Cockburn's brand, and contracted with the Symingtons to supply the wines. But you can still visit the lodge in Gaia, where you will be shown round and given a free tasting.

The Cockburn's ports were based on grapes from four quintas, Quinta dos Canais, Quinta Val Coelho, Quinta do Tua, and Quinta do Atayde (or 'Ataíde' – spellings vary) in the flatlands of the Vilariça valley, north of Torre de Moncorvo in the Douro Superior. Atayde was a pioneering estate in the Douro Superior back in the mid-1970s, part of a 200ha development Cockburn's undertook in the Vilariça valley. Everything was planted by variety (mostly red), and the whole project was co-ordinated by Miguel Corte Real, an eminent viticulturalist. Now the wines made at Atayde are mostly DOC Douro, while most of the Cockburn's ports have been made at Tua.

'Canais' means canals, and these were built in the 19th century to irrigate the olive trees from a waterfall at the top of the estate. Quinta dos Canais is a magnificent estate, more easily reached from the river than by road, and the 300ha of vineyards have the potential to deliver magnificent wines. The DOC Douro wine made from the estate's grapes, a lovely, herby red with dark, smooth tannins, will probably never now reach the public, but be blended away into other brands, as BWE seem interested in Cockburn's and Canais only as port brands. The **Cockburn's 20 Year Old Tawny** is the pick of their aged tawnies, light and elegant, with flavours of nuts and dried fruits. The single *quinta* **Quinta dos Canais Vintage** is a sweet, almost treacley style of vintage, with tea and blackcurrant flavours. **Cockburn's Vintage** has perhaps not lived up to its historic reputation in recent decades, though most recent releases have more intensity and richness.

Rua Dona Leonor de Freitas,
    4400-123 Vila Nova de Gaia
T+351 223 772 326
E coralia.tavares@beamglobal.com
W www.beamglobal.com
Visits Mon-Fri 9.30-12.30, 2.30-4
    Closed Aug

Croft

The present Croft lodge in Gaia is to be converted into an 84-room luxury hotel, the Yeatman Hotel, so visit it now while it still exists! You can visit, without appointment, any day of the year except Christmas Day and New Year's Day. There is a magnificent cellar housing a fabulous collection of old vintage port, and you can taste two of the Croft range free, as well as buying in the shop.

The company was founded over three hundred years ago, in 1678, although it only took the name Croft when John Croft joined the company in 1736. The Yorkshire wine merchant Croft family developed the company for about a century before returning to England, and Croft was bought by Gilbey's in 1911. After another change of ownership in 2001, it is now in the safe hands of the Fladgate Partnership, the family-owned company that also owns Taylor's, Fonseca and Delaforce.

Croft has always been a house dedicated to port. As the late Percy Croft put it: 'Any time not spent drinking Port is a waste of time.' The jewel in Croft's crown since 1875 has been Quinta da Roêda, just up-river from Pinhão. This is sometimes released as a single quinta vintage, **Quinta da Roêda Vintage**, renowned for its sweet, floral fruit. And Roêda forms the backbone of the **Croft Vintage**, sometimes all, dense and ripe, with the sweet, floral character of Roêda running through it. It's worth looking out, too, for the **Croft Late Bottled Vintage**, smoky, sweet and fragrant.

The good news is that Croft plan to open Quinta da Roêda to visitors before long. Thomas Croft, an architect descendant of Sir John Croft, has done the designs.

Largo de Joaquim Magalhães 23,
  4400-187 Vila Nova de Gaia
T +351 223 742 800
E ana.sofia@croftport.com
W www.croftport.com
Visits 10-6 Closed 25 Dec, 1 Jan

Delaforce

You can't visit Delaforce, but it's a company whose wines you should look out for. Delaforce has been associated with Croft since the Delaforce family sold the business in 1968, and the two companies were then acquired by Taylor Fonseca in 2001 to create the present Fladgate Partnership. George Henry Delaforce, of Huguenot origins, started the company in 1868, and it was run by generations of the family until the sale to Croft. Delaforce has always been known as a skilled blender of wine. Even today, the company's strength lies in the aged tawnies and colheitas, particularly two brands created in the 1930s, the nutty, dried fruit-flavoured **His Eminence's Choice 10 Years Old Tawny** and the creamy, nutty, intense **Curious and Ancient 20 Years Old Tawny**. The brilliant **Delaforce Colheitas** combine delicacy with intensity. **Delaforce Vintage** is sweet and dark, with dense, ripe tannins and black fruit flavours.

Ferreira

This company has become so associated with the most famous of the Ferreira family, Dona Antónia Adelaide *(page 86),* that it's sometimes overlooked that the company was actually founded in 1751, almost a century before she was widowed at the age of 33 and took charge. When she died 53 years later, and mainly through her industry, the family company owned over 30 estates in the Douro, an inheritance she passed on to her family. Sogrape bought Ferreira in 1987, and still strives to maintain the company's close links to the land and intimate connection to the culture of the Douro and of port.

The Ferreira lodge you will visit is one of 12 Sogrape owns in Gaia, all linked on a computerised system by stainless steel piping that contrasts strongly with the venerable wooden vats *(balseiros)* in which the ports are matured. Floors in the working sections are made of beaten earth – good for humidity and temperature control – and you'll usually hear a pump ticking away somewhere in the bowels of the lodge. Someone is working, racking, blending or filling. In the lower levels of the lodges, there are what seems like kilometres of tunnels, containing barrels and stacks of maturing bottles. €2.50 gets you the basic tour and a taste of two ports at the end. The 'Dona Antónia' tour costs €10, but is longer and you'll taste more ports.

All the Ferreira ports are good, made in a sweet, gentle, very seductive style. **Dona Antónia Tawny Reserva** balances the sweetness with good acidity and figgy fruit. The two aged tawnies are excellent: the sweet, nutty **Quinta do Porto 10 Year Old** and the oaky, creamy **Duque de Bragança 20 Year Old**. There is a rich, blackcurrant and treacle-flavoured, unfiltered **Ferreira Late Bottled Vintage Porto**. The **Ferreira Vintage** is sweet and gentle, with blackcurrant and treacle flavours, developing to black olive and cedar with bottle-age. The Ferreira style is so gentle, it is hard to believe the wines will have long lives ahead. But they mature magnificently: the oldest we tasted was 1863. It was delicious.

Rua da Carvalhosa 19,
  4400-082 Vila Nova de Gaia
T +351 223 746 106
E ferreira.visitors@aaferreira.pt
W www.sogrape.pt
Visits 10-12.30, 2-6 €2.50/€10

Graham's

You don't even have to walk up the steep Rua Rei Ramiro from the river-front at Gaia – Graham's will whisk you up to their lodge by shuttle. They are extremely well-equipped to welcome visitors, who come in their thousands through the year. Just as well, as this is the only contact the mighty Symington empire has, at present, with the public who buy their wines. There are plans to open up a visitor centre at Quinta dos Malvedos in the Douro, but it hasn't happened yet.

The Graham's Visitor Centre is housed in the enormous Graham's lodge (which also holds 3,500 pipes and many large vats of maturing port). You can watch a short film about Graham's estates in the Douro, and the making and blending of port (in a choice of seven languages), and do a tour round the lodge (six languages). And you finish up with a taste of three Graham's ports, the white, LBV and 10 Year Old Tawny. All of that is for free, as we write, although they are wondering whether to make a charge. If you have an appetite for more, in the Graham's Wine Bar you can taste other ports and DOC Douro wines from Symington Family Estates (SFE): maybe the 'Vintage Tasting' (Graham's 2000, Dow's 1985 and Quinta do Vesúvio 1994, €30), the 'Single Quinta

Vintage Tasting' (Malvedos 1996, Bonfim 1995 and Senhora da Ribeira 1999, €15), the 'Tawny Tasting' (Graham's 30 Anos + 40 Anos, €20) or the 'DOC Douro Tasting' (Chryseia 2004, PostScriptum 2004, Altano Reserva 2003 and Prazo Roriz 2004, €15). There's no food to eat as you sip – unless you arrive in a party and have pre-booked one of the private rooms and ordered a menu. And, of course, you can buy wines, books and other wine-related items in the shop.

W & J Graham (named after the Scottish brothers William and John Graham) was founded in 1820. In 1890, the family built the imposing Gaia lodge, on the site where it still stands today, overlooking the town of Gaia and the city of Porto opposite. They also invested, in the same year, in Quinta dos Malvedos, a fine estate on the north bank of the Douro just west of Tua. They built a house there as their centre of operations up-river – and not just any old house. In an era when most houses of however many bedrooms had only one bathroom, this had seven, and was known for many years by the locals as the *'casa das sete retretes'*, or the 'house of the seven loos'. Although the quality of the Graham's ports never wavered, after the successes of the 19th and early 20th centuries, the company was hit by the generally hard times for the port trade in the 1950s. In 1970, Graham's was sold to another great port family of Scottish origins, the Symingtons, and is now one of the SFE brands.

Within the SFE range, the Graham's ports are made in a relatively, sweet, supple style, but always well-balanced. **Six Grapes Reserve** is laden with spicy, peppery fruit. The aged tawnies are impressive, too, from the raisin and fig-flavoured **Graham's 10 Years Aged Tawny**, through the elegant, nutty **Graham's 20 Years Aged Tawny**, to

the intensity and freshness of the **Graham's 30 Years Aged Tawny**, with its cream, caramel, nut and leather aromas. Or, if you like really old tawny, the **Graham's 40 Years Aged Tawny** is intensely woody and creamy. Most of the **Malvedos** vintage port is made in new stainless steel *lagares* at the quinta, fitted with cooling systems and robotic 'treaders', though some is still foot-trodden. As a 'single quinta' vintage port, it is released in years when **Graham's Vintage** is not declared, and is lighter and more accessible. 1998 was the first year the new robotic *lagares* were used, and the result is a **Malvedos** with lovely blackcurrant fruit and soft, smooth tannins. **Graham's Vintage** is always one of the best vintage ports, sweet, ripe and dense, and capable of living to cedary, poised old age.

Rua Rei Ramiro 514,
    4400-281 Vila Nova de Gaia
T +351 223 776 330
E turismo@symington.com
W www.grahams-port.com
Visits May-Sept 9.30-6 (Sun appt only)
    Oct-Apr Mon-Fri 9.30-1, 2-5.30

Kopke

The lodge may be developed for visitors in the future, but at the moment Kopke has a shop, where you taste and buy their wines. Kopke was established by a German family in 1638, and is another port company that has been bought by the Spanish-owned company Sogevinus. After more than 200 years of Kopke family ownership, the company passed to the Bohane family, who lived in London. The Bohanes sold Kopke in 1953 to Barros Almeida, and it was they who were bought by Sogevinus in June 2006. In recent years, Kopke has had a good reputation, above all for its *colheitas* (single vintage tawnies) and its vintage ports. In 1995, they started producing DOC Douro wines at the modern Quinta de São Luiz winery. The **Kopke Arinto** is a barrel-fermented DOC Douro white, rich, bready and mineral, and the **Kopke Tinto Reserva** a fresh, berry-fruited red, with good acidity. The **Kopke Vintage** is very aromatic with ripe tannins, ageing to rich blackcurrant and cedar. But the glories of the house remain the **Kopke Colheitas**, extraordinarily complex, intense tawnies, with incredible length and subtlety.

Avenida Diogoheite 310-312,
*   4400-111 Vila Nova de Gaia*
T+351 220 109 015
E contact@kopkeports.com
W www.kopkeports.com
Visits May-Oct 10-8 Nov-Apr 10.30-7.30

Messias

Although the headquarters of Caves Messias is in Bairrada, their largest single estate is in the Douro, the Quinta do Cachão. This was named after a huge rock, the Cachão da Valeira, which used to stand in the middle of the river Douro, making the route down to Gaia a nightmare to navigate for *barcos rabelos* laden with pipes of port. In 1907, the rock was blown up, and the passage to Gaia was less dangerous. Quinta do Cachão was created in 1845, and bought by Messias in 1956. It lies about halfway between Taylor's Quinta de Vargellas and the Valeira dam, on the south bank of the river.

The estate has about 200ha, of which half are planted with vines. This has all been replanted by Messias, and the vines are 20 and 8 years old. Everything is planted varietally, with a majority of Tinta Roriz and Touriga Nacional, some Touriga Franca, Tinta Barroca and Tinto Cão, and a little Malvasia Fina and Rabigato for the white wine – because Messias do make characterful DOC Douro wines, as well as port, in a modern winery recently installed at the estate.

The **Quinta do Cachão Touriga Nacional** has lovely floral aromas and bright aromatic fruit. The **Quinta do Cachão Grande Escolha** is even better, with Touriga Franca, Tinta Roriz and Tinta Barroca in the blend, rich and powerful, with intensity and length. Those white vines give one of the most interesting white ports you'll find anywhere, the complex, woody, honeyed **Messias Very Old Port Branco Seco**. The **Messias Vintage** is very sweet and treacley, quite traditional in style. Messias' great strength lies in its *colheitas*. They have been tucking away parcels of wine since they bought Quinta do Cachão in 1956, and the **Messias Colheitas** range from the young, sweet and rich, back to extraordinary nutty, woody, intense poems in port concentration and personality.

You can visit the Messias lodge in Gaia, but only by prior arrangement. They can also organise cellar tours for groups, with a tasting included, for €10 per person.

Rua José Mariani 139,
*   4401-901 Vila Nova de Gaia*
T+351 223 745 770
E portomessias@cavesmessias.pt
W www.cavesmessias.pt
Visits Mon-Fri 9-5 (appt only) €10

Niepoort

It would be a pity to walk past this lodge, but the number is displayed on a tiny plaque fixed to the wall, and there's no other sign the building is anything other than a blank-walled warehouse. Inside it's a treasure-trove. Don't expect smart tasting-rooms and films about the history of port and vineyards in the Douro. This is a working cellar, the office crammed with past samples of wines sent for export

approval, the warehouse space filled with every size of container imaginable, from huge *balseiros* (upright vats) to precious demi-johns. In order to gain entry, you have to make an appointment, but, once inside, you will marvel at the cellars going down into the depths of Gaia, and be given a free tasting of Niepoort ports.

And the Niepoort ports are magnificent (for Niepoort table wines, *see page 101*). The basic **Niepoort Tawny**, **Ruby** and **White** ports are exemplary, and then come two 'introductions to port', the plummy, powerfully fruity **Niepoort Júnior Tinto**, and the nutty, sweet, up-front **Niepoort Sénior Tawny**. **Niepoort LBV** is a step up: excellent, ripe, with dark, blackcurrant and treacle fruit, and capable of ageing several years. The **Niepoort Vintage Ports** are legendary, filled with ripe, black fruits and treacle when young, ageing to cedar and spice complexity. In 1999, Dirk Niepoort created **Secundum**, to offer a more accessible style of vintage port. The Secundum, he muses, is the youthful, charming Mozart to the Vintage's intense, profound Bach. Niepoort are unusual in making superlative aged tawnies (10, 20 and 30 year old) and *colheitas* (tawnies from a single year). Most houses do one or the other. So watch out for the **Niepoort 10 Year Old Tawny**, and indeed its senior brothers, the **20 Year Old** and **30 Year Old**. They go from very good to glorious complexity. Likewise the Niepoort Colheitas, nutty and full of dried fruit flavours in the younger vintages, and extraordinarily complex symphonies of nut, dried fruits, candied citrus peel and spices from the older ones.

Maybe one of Niepoort's secrets is the family succession, not only of the Niepoorts through five generations, but also their master blenders. The Nogueira family has provided four generations of blenders, and the fifth is learning the trade now. As Dirk Niepoort says: 'With port, we know a little bit what we're doing now. With table wines, we're still feeling our way.' Most onlookers would say that the family firm of Niepoort excels in both categories.

Rua de Serpa Pinto 278,
  4400-307 Vila Nova de Gaia
T+351 222 001 028
E info@niepoort-vinhos.com
W www.niepoort-vinhos.com
Visits Mon-Fri 9-12, 2-5 (appt only)

Offley

The company may have been founded in 1737, but it was Joseph James Forrester *(page 86)* who made it successful after he joined in 1831. Forrester was an artist, cartographer and dynamic businessman. He charted the Douro, drew and painted views of it, and became an expert on oidium (powdery mildew, a fungus that attacks vines). For his services to the region he loved, he was made a Baron by the King of Portugal. For many years, Offley owned Quinta da Boavista, 4km down-river from Pinhão on the north bank of the Douro, but the Forrester family finally sold out in 1924. In 1962, Offley was bought by Sandeman, who then bought Quinta da Boavista back again in 1979.

And Boavista has remained the main source of grapes for Offley ports ever since. Sogrape bought Offley in 1997, and with it, Quinta da Boavista. Boavista is a 50ha estate, with 39ha of vineyard. About 25ha are of old mixed vines, the rest varietally planted with Touriga

Franca, Tinta Roriz, Tinta Barroca and Touriga Nacional. The **Offley LBV** is mainly made from Boavista grapes, with dark, berry fruit and firm tannins. **Offley Vintage** is rich and herby (all from Boavista grapes), made in an approachable style. The **Offley Barão de Forrester 10 Anos Old Tawny**, and its siblings the **20 Anos** and **30 Anos**, ascend in quality and concentration from figgy sweetness, through creamy intensity, to woody, cedary complexity.

Offley suggest that you contact them to book visits, but that's only absolutely necessary for larger groups (or to avoid them). The lodge is open all week from March to October. If you want to visit outside these months, get in touch. You may be lucky!

Rua do Choupelo 62,
  4400-088 Vila Nova de Gaia
T+351 223 743 852
E offley.visitors@offley.pt
W www.sogrape.pt
Visits Mar-Oct 10-12.30, 2-6
  €2.50/€8

Quinta do Noval

There is no Quinta do Noval lodge to visit in Gaia, because it burnt down in a fire in 1981. In 1982, the van Zeller family, then the owners, started building a new lodge at the estate, just north of Pinhão. And Quinta do Noval's entire winemaking and maturation operation has been run from there ever since. But there is a shop in Gaia, where you can taste and buy wines. For the rest of the Noval story, *see page 99*.

Avenida Diogo Leite 256,
  4400-111 Vila Nova de Gaia
T+351 223 770 282
E rosario@quintadonoval.pt
W www.quintadonoval.com
Visits Jun-Sep 10-8 Oct-May Mon-Fri 9-5

Ramos Pinto

You can't miss the large yellow-painted Ramos Pinto lodge and museum, right on the river-bank at Gaia. This is one of the most worthwhile visits in Gaia, as Ramos Pinto have carefully preserved the interior of the 1930s offices as a museum. The founder of the business, Adriano Ramos Pinto, and his brother António, started and expanded the business in 1880, in the Belle Époque, the period between the late 19th century and the First World War. They conquered the lucrative Brazilian market, and used beautifully-designed advertisements featuring scantily-clad nymphs to publicise their ports. These shocked (and delighted) contemporary audiences. Many of these are on display at the Casa Ramos Pinto in Gaia.

Ramos Pinto has been as much an innovator in winemaking and viticulture as in marketing. It was at the Ramos Pinto estates that the experiments were done that resulted in the choice of five recommended grape varieties for the Douro in 1981. Ramos Pinto owns two estates in the Cima Corgo, Quinta do Bom Retiro and Quinta da Urtiga, both in the Rio Torto valley, with 65ha of vines between them. They are perfect for port, but not for the table wines José António Ramos Pinto Rosas and his nephew João Nicolau de Almeida wanted to make. So Rosas bought what is now Quinta de Ervamoira *(page 97)* in 1974, then Quinta dos Bons Ares (20ha vineyard) in 1985. These now provide grapes for DOC Douro wines and for ports. In 1990, Ramos Pinto was bought by Champagne Louis Roederer, who have continued to invest in and support the Portuguese management.

Ramos Pinto ports (and unfortified wines) are made only with grapes from their own estates. The **Ramos Pinto Porto LBV** is unfiltered (so may have a sediment), rich and intense, with flavours of cedar and blackcurrant. The single quinta **Quinta de Ervamoira Vintage** has a wonderful gum cistus fragrance, with elegance and richness. **Ramos Pinto Vintage** is incredibly smooth and harmonious, with floral fragrance and cedary, blackcurrant length. Ramos Pinto tawnies are very good, too. The **Quinta de Ervamoira 10 Anos** is nutty and full-bodied. **Quinta do Bom Retiro 20 Anos** is creamy and mature, with length and complexity, and **Ramos Pinto 30 Anos** is elegant and woody, delicate and fragrant.
Avenida Ramos Pinto 400,
4400-266 Vila Nova de Gaia
T +351 223 707 000
E anapoles@ramospinto.pt
W www.ramospinto.pt
Visits Jun-Sep Mon-Sat 10-6 Oct-May
Mon-Fri 9-1, 2-5
Closed public hols

Real Companhia Velha

The lodge of Real Companhia Velha (RCV) is off to the left of the Avenida da República after you've crossed the Dom Luís I Bridge from Porto. It is massive, and covers a huge area. One good way of having a quick look round Porto *and* a visit to the RCV cellars is to take the 'Porto Tripeiro' tour on Diana Tours' mini-train, which will give you a $1^3/_4$ hour tour of the city, including the RCV cellar visit, for €6. Or you can just turn up at the lodge and have a cellar and a tasting of 2 ports for €2.

RCV is one of the most historic port shippers, and was for a long time the sole controller of the quality of Douro wine. *(For the story of RCV, see page 92.)* The company, whose major shareholders are the Silva Reis family, have one of the largest holdings of vineyard land in the Douro, and have consistently been innovators in Douro wine production. Ports are made in a light, easy-going style. The **Royal Oporto LBV** is ripe, sweet and blackcurranty. Best are the sweetly nutty older **Royal Oporto Colheitas** and the dense, aromatic, Touriga-dominated,

Quinta das Carvalhas Vintage (which is still foot-trodden in granite *lagares*).
Rua Azevedo Magalhães 314,
4430-022 Vila Nova de Gaia
T+351 223 775 100
T+351 223 702 546 (for mini-train)
E vera.alheiro@dianatours.pt
W www.dianatours.pt
W www.realcompanhiavelha.pt
Visits Apr-Sep 9.30-7 Oct-Mar Mon-Fri
9.30-1, 2-5 €2/€6 with train

Rozès

It's a steep walk up the Rua Cândido dos Reis, but you'll find a light, airy tasting room when you get there, visits to the cellar, and a shop where you can buy Rozès ports. Rozès is owned by the (mainly Champagne-producing) Vranken company, and left very much to its own devices in the Douro (*see page 90*).

A lot of the Rozès marketing effort is put into the 'Color Collection', a trio of brightly-coloured bottles, white, red and gold. The white is the sweet, nutty **Rozès Reserve White**, with notes of honey and milk chocolate. The red is the **Rozès Reserve Red**, big, ripe and up-front, with red fruit and damson flavours. The gold is the rich, sweet, creamy **Rozès Reserve Gold**, a 10 year-old tawny. Further up the range is the unfiltered **Rozès Late Bottled Vintage**, opulent and thick with raspberry and plum fruit, and notes of dark chocolate and treacle. The **Rozès Vintage** is made in a very accessible style, with blackcurrant and treacle flavours, and smooth tannins, but has the structure and intensity to last.
Rua Cândido dos Reis 526/532,
4400-070 Vila Nova de Gaia
T+351 223 771 680
E rozes@rozes.pt
W www.rozes.pt
Visits Jun-Sept Mon-Fri 10.30-5.30
Oct-May appt only

Sandeman

This is another of the best lodge visits: an excellent display about how port is made, then a film of the Douro and the port wine process. The basic tour costs €2.50 (refunded if you buy any bottles in the shop), and takes you through the ageing cellars and the Port Museum, with a tasting of a red and a white port. The Museum has a marvellous collection of antique wine bottles. You can also book for the '1790 Tour' (after the year George Sandeman left Perth and founded the company, originally in London). This costs €12, and takes in more of the cellars, and a tasting of six ports at the end, including the Sandeman LBV, and aged tawny and Sandeman Vintage.

The company was founded by George Sandeman, and it's good to be able to say that the current Chairman is George Sandeman, eldest son of the seventh generation of the family. The original George Sandeman was the first port shipper to brand his barrels (with a hot iron), in 1805, thus coining 'branding' as a way of differentiating products. His 'Crowsfoot' branding iron, featuring the company's initials, GSC, is on display in the Museum. He started operating in Porto and Jerez (shipping sherry as well as port) in the first decade of the 19th century.

Sandeman continued to innovate through the 19th century, shipping wines under the George Sandeman name, unheard of at the time, when importing merchants bottled wines under their own name, whoever had shipped them. Through the 20th century, the innovations continued, with Sandeman taking advertisements in newspapers, creating the 'Don' image that remains to this day, and increasingly shipping their wines already bottled. In 1980, Sandeman was bought by Seagram, and 22 years later by Sogrape, who still own it today.

The **Sandeman Founder's Reserve** is a rich, plummy style of port, in contrast to the woody, dry **Sandeman Imperial Reserve**. **Sandeman LBV** is quite austere, with firm tannins and sweet, dark fruit. The sweet, velvety, blackcurranty **Vau Vintage** is made to be drunk young (much of it in the US), whereas the **Sandeman Vintage** is dark and rich, the recent vintages especially elegant and intense. The Sandeman aged tawnies are a delight: the **Sandeman 10 Years Old Tawny** is dry and cedary, the **Sandeman 20 Years Old Tawny**, creamily elegant and nutty, the **Sandeman 30 Years Old Tawny**, austere, tangy and intense, and the **Sandeman 40 Years Old Tawny**, woody yet creamy, with great length and complexity.
Largo Miguel Bombarda 3,
4400-222 Vila Nova de Gaia
T+351 223 740 533/34/35
E sandeman.visitors@sandeman.com/
the.don@sandeman.com
W www.sandeman.com
Visits Mar-Oct 10-12.30, 2-6
Nov-Feb Mon-Fri 9.30-12.30, 2-5.30
€2.50/€12

Symington Family Estates

There's a lot to Symington Family Estates (SFE) apart from Graham's. To sum up briefly, two other famous port labels (Dow's and Warre's), one of the most famous single port estates in the Douro (Quinta do Vesuvio), three other port labels (Smith Woodhouse, Gould Campbell and Quarles Harris), and a joint venture at Quinta de Roriz with João van Zeller *(page 93)*. And that's just the ports. In DOC Douro wines, a venture with Bruno Prats, ex-owner of Château Cos d'Estournel (Chryseia and Post-Scriptum), Quinta de Roriz again, and their own label, Altano *(page 89)*. SFE also owns the majority of the Madeira Wine Company *(page 407)*.

All these labels are supported by the largest ownership of planted vineyard in the Douro. If you include the estates SFE owns, those owned by individual members of the Symington clan, and long-term rental and partnerships, SFE's vineyard holdings up to July 2006 were over 600ha. Then they bought the estates, cellars and stock of Cockburn's, taking the total to 950ha, easily the largest total holding for any one group in the Douro.

The first Symington (Andrew James, known as AJ) arrived in Porto only in 1882 to work for the textile side of the Graham's business. But through the woman he married, Beatrice Atkinson, the Symingtons working in SFE today can trace their family back 13 generations, to Walter Maynard, English Consul in Porto from 1659, and port shipper since 1652. It was AJ who really took the family's fortunes forward, moving from textiles to port. He joined Warre's, and was senior partner by 1905. Then, through a share-swap, he also became a partner in Silva & Cozens (who own Dow's). The next generation of Symingtons replanted and developed the company's three quintas in the Douro (Zimbro, Bomfim and Senhora da Ribeira) – this at a time when most port shippers steered well clear of the business of growing grapes and making wine.

After the Second World War, times were hard for the port trade, and some

companies went under. The Symingtons hung on in there, sold one of their quintas (since rebought), and worked hard to keep the port flame burning all over the world. Persistence was rewarded in the 1960s. The family bought the rest of the shares in Warre's in 1961 and, in 1970 bought three more companies, Graham's, Smith Woodhouse and Gould Campbell.

Since then, the Symingtons' progress has been impressive. They have bought quintas up and down the Douro (including the iconic Quinta do Vesuvio), have introduced revolutionary robotic *lagares* in their wineries, and have been one of the most innovative port shippers. In addition, the venture with Bruno Prats has produced two highly-regarded DOC Douro wines, Chryseia and Post-Scriptum, and the knowledge gained from the project has hugely improved the Symingtons' own table wine brand, Altano.

But it is for their ports that the Symingtons are best-known. *(For selections from Graham's see page 135.)* The Dow's range is founded on two estates, Quinta do Bomfim and Quinta Senhora da Ribeira. Made as single-quinta vintages, they are both superb. **Quinta do Bomfim** has a typically herby, austere style, with earthy blackcurrant fruit, and **Quinta Senhora da Ribeira** is more elegant, with fragrant raspberry fruit and stylish chocolatey tannins. **Dow's Vintage** shows the same herbiness of Bomfim, with a richer, more complete expression. Even the **Dow's Trademark Reserve** has the austerity, with spicy, peppery fruit. The **Dow's LBV**, with fruit from Bomfim and Senhora da Ribeira, is rich and intense, with herby fruit and sweet but firm tannins. The Dow's aged tawnies build from the nutty, dryish **Dow's 10 Years Aged Tawny**, through the creamier, rich but quite austere **Dow's 20 Years Aged Tawny** to the

herby, woody, complex **Dow's 30 Years Aged Tawny**.

Warre's, the other major company in the Symington port-folio, has owned Quinta da Cavadinha, in the Pinhão valley, since 1978, and bought Quinta do Bom Retiro Pequeno in 2006. **Warre's Warrior**, its reserve ruby, is port's oldest brand, and a consistently reliable, fruity wine. Even better is the **Warre's Traditional Late Bottled Vintage**, bottled after four years of ageing in oak barrels, then matured for another four or five in bottle before release. This means there is always a sediment, but it gives wonderfully rich blackcurrant fruit, with a herby twist to the finish. **Quinta da Cavadinha** is a stylish, elegant, very aromatic single-quinta vintage, and **Warre's Vintage** has the same glorious aromas, but is richer and longer-lived.

Quinta do Vesuvio, bought by the Symingtons in 1989, is a legendary Douro estate, created by António Bernardo Ferreira in 1923, and made more famous by his son's widow, the great Dona Antónia Adelaide Ferreira. It is a huge estate, with 132ha of planted vineyard and a massive, granite-blocked winery, with enormous *lagares*. Wines here are all foot-trodden, and the only wine released is a vintage port. This has been released every year the Symingtons have owned it, except for two years, 1993 and 2002, when weather conditions were too bad to allow a wine of sufficient quality to be made. **Quinta do Vesuvio Vintage** is a beautiful wine, smooth-textured, aromatic and floral when young, ageing to rich, plummy, complex intensity.

Smith Woodhouse, Gould Campbell and Quarles Harris are lesser-known SFE labels. Among their outstanding wines is the **Smith Woodhouse Traditional Late Bottled Vintage**, a rich, unfiltered LBV, with three years of additional ageing in bottle after its four years in barrel. Both Gould Campbell and Smith Woodhouse are capable of producing very good (and usually reasonably-priced) vintage ports.

Taylor's

This is one of the aristocrats of port. The company has consistently been at the forefront of quality in port production, amongst the first with modern advances such as vertically-planted vineyards and robotically-plunged *lagares*. Now Taylor's is one of the companies most keenly focused on port marketing, with an excellent visitor centre at their cellar in Gaia, as well as the Barão de Fladgate restaurant. So far, however, they are the only famous port company that has chosen not to invest in producing DOC Douro wines.

At the Taylor's visitor centre you will learn about vine-growing, port-making and coopering the barrels, see the cellars, and taste Taylor's Chip Dry white port and Taylor's LBV. There is no charge, but you may be tempted to buy some bottles in the shop, or stop for lunch at the Barão de Fladgate restaurant *(page 145)*, which has magnificent views of Porto.

Taylor's is one of the port shippers in the Fladgate Partnership, a family-owned company still in the hands of the successors of Job Bearsley, the wool merchant who started it in 1692. Job's son, Bartholomew, was the first English port shipper to buy an estate in the Douro, the Lugar das

Lages at Salgueiral. It is still owned by Taylor's – or Taylor, Fladgate & Yeatman, to give the company its full name. The first Taylor joined the company in 1816, the first Fladgate in 1837 and the first Yeatman in 1844. The majority shareholder in Taylor's is now Alistair Robertson, who took over when his uncle, Dick Yeatman, died. Robertson's son-in-law, Adrian Bridge, is now Managing Director, so the family line continues. David Guimaraens, who has followed in his father Bruce's footsteps as the Taylor winemaker, is a descendant of the family that has always worked with Fonseca, another shipper in the Fladgate Partnership.

The most famous of the Taylor's quintas, Quinta de Vargellas, was bought in 1893. It lies in the Douro Superior, roughly opposite Cockburn's Quinta dos Canais, and has recently been increased in size by the purchase of the next-door

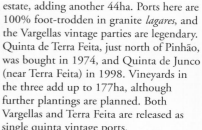

estate, adding another 44ha. Ports here are 100% foot-trodden in granite *lagares*, and the Vargellas vintage parties are legendary. Quinta de Terra Feita, just north of Pinhão, was bought in 1974, and Quinta de Junco (near Terra Feita) in 1998. Vineyards in the three add up to 177ha, although further plantings are planned. Both Vargellas and Terra Feita are released as single quinta vintage ports.

The history of Taylor's has been one of innovation. The company produced the first dry white port, Taylor's Chip Dry, in 1934. More importantly, in 1970, when the port industry was still soldiering on through the tough decades following the Second World War, Taylor's launched their Late Bottled Vintage, a style of wine that caught the imagination of port drinkers all over the world, and went a long way to saving the industry. Taylor's are still the market leaders with their appealing, herby, firm-tannined **Taylor's Late-Bottled Vintage**. Though Taylor's produce very successful aged tawnies, the glory of the house is its vintage ports. **Quinta de Vargellas Vintage** is dark, sweet and intense, full of flavours of blackcurrant and herbs, with smooth, chocolatey tannins. It ages magnificently. Tiny quantities of the rare, expensive **Vargellas Vinha Velha** are made from time to time – 1995, 1997, 2000 and 2004 so far. **Taylor's Vintage** is one of port's great wines, unforthcoming in its youth, but opening to sweet, black-fruited complexity, elegance and length as it matures.

Rua do Choupelo 250,
4400-088 Vila Nova de Gaia
T+351 223 742 800
E turismo.taylor@taylor.pt
W www.taylor.pt
Visits Mon-Fri 10-6 Easter & summer also
open Sat

Wiese & Krohn/Krohn

Yet another port shipper whose name suggests a non-Portuguese origin, Wiese & Krohn was started by two Norwegians in 1865. Theodor Wiese and Dankert Krohn first came to Portugal to trade in *bacalhau* (salt cod) – much of which still comes from Norway's waters – but then realised there was an opportunity in port. Edmund Arnsby, an Englishman, bought Dankert out when the latter retired to Norway, and then took on Edmundo Falcão Carneiro and his brother Frederick as partners. When Arnsby retired in 1933, and Frederick died in 1937, Edmundo bought their shares. His grandson and granddaughter, José and Iolanda, now run the company.

Krohn (the 'Wiese &' has been dropped from the name on bottles) have a lovely estate in the Rio Torto valley, Quinta do Retiro Novo, but do not receive visitors there. This was bought in 1989, and has 14ha of vines, half of them mixed old vines, half recent vineyards planted by variety. They do receive visitors, however, at one of their six lodges in Gaia, with a new visitor centre opened in 2004. Here you can have a look round the cellar, where over 10,000 pipes of port lie maturing peacefully, as well as having a tasting. The cost will depend on what you want to taste

(and they have some fabulous old *colheitas* – the 1900 is still available for sale).

Although Krohn are best known for these *colheitas*, they have recently put a lot of effort into smartening up their table wines. Grapes for these come from their estate, as well as from neighbouring farmers around the villages of Sarzedinho and Valencã do Douro. A smart new winery has been built at Retiro Novo, featuring modern cooling systems and stainless steel robotic *lagares*. The top ports are still foot-trodden in granite *lagares*.

Valtorto DOC Douro is improving every year, the most recent vintage full of aromatic, red fruit flavours, with soft, ripe tannins. The **Krohn LBV** is dark and treacley, with black fruit and cedar notes.

Quinta do Retiro Novo Vintage has elegant black fruit flavours and smooth tannins, made in an accessible style, and drinkable young. The aged tawnies are made in an austere, woody style, with the **Krohn 10 Year Port** fairly dry and nicely nutty, the **Krohn 20 Year Port** taking on flavours of raisin and cream, with a touch of coconut, and the **Krohn 30**

Year Port woody and complex, with creamy, nutty complexity.

Krohn are keen to emphasise that their aged tawnies are very different from their colheitas. Whereas aged tawnies are blends, with continuity of flavour the most important consideration, every colheita is different, a snapshot of what a particular year has given. The young **Krohn Colheita** ports are good wines, vigorous and red-fruit-flavoured, but without the creamy, nutty characters associated with old tawny. It takes about 20 years before the true aged flavours become apparent. The older **Krohn Colheitas** are magnificent wines, with complex flavours, intensity and tremendous length. Seventeen different vintages, back to 1958, are still available to buy.

Rua Serpa Pinto 149,
4400-307 Vila Nova de Gaia
T+351 223 771 720
E wk@krohn.pt
W www.krohn.pt
Visits Summer 10-7 Winter Mon-Fri
10-12, 1-5 Closed Dec & Jan

Eat in Porto and Gaia

Well, we have to start with tripe. Porto's butchers shops and meat markets are full of *tripas*, usually veal tripe, often hanging from hooks, and the locals are so fond of it that they are nicknamed *tripeiros* – tripe-eaters – by the rest of the nation. The most famous dish is *tripas à moda do Porto*, a rich, gooey stew made with dried beans, calves' feet or pigs' trotters, bacon, ham, sausage, chouriço, maybe pigs' ears, chicken, onions, carrots – and tripe, of course – all flavoured with cumin and served with rice. Tripe is also known as *dobrada* meaning literally 'pleated' or 'folded' – once you have seen it you'll see what they mean.

Another local speciality is the *francesinha*, a kind of meaty Welsh rarebit – bread topped with steak, smoked and fresh sausage, then chillied tomato sauce containing beer and brandy, then melted cheese. It can be very basic, or very good. A famous dish that originated in Porto is Bacalhau à Gomes de Sá. You can eat this oven-baked codfish dish anywhere in the country, but it all started here – Gomes de Sá was the son of a 19th century Porto salt-cod merchant, who fell on hard times and had to work as a chef. He layered flaked fish with diced potato, onion, garlic, milk and olive oil, baked it, then added black olives, parsley and chopped hard boiled eggs.

Fresh fish and seafood is of course available in profusion in Porto and Gaia. Just up the coast from Porto, and part of greater Porto, is the industrial and fishing port of Leixões on the estuary of the river Leça, flanked by Matosinhos to the south and the old fishing town of Leça de Palmeira on the northern bank. Matosinhos and Leça are full of fish

restaurants, and very accessible from central Porto by bus or the blue line of the new Metro. Matosinhos restaurants range from smart and expensive to tiny, inexpensive *tasquinhas* and *tascos* – why is it that the southern word *tasca*, meaning little family restaurant, has a sex change up here in the north? Beware of price – fish is often charged by weight. Another great conglomeration of fish restaurants – including some of the Porto area's most modern cooking – is in the wealthy beach suburb of Foz do Douro, as well as in other small towns and villages around the estuary, some of which are accessible by bus or tram. If you are self-catering, there is wonderful fish and seafood in the city markets, but the freshest of all, and the greatest choice, is in Matosinhos or even further north, on the Angeiras beach.

Local fishes include tuna *(atum)*, wreckfish *(cherne)*, swordfish *(espadarte)*, sole *(linguado)*, the meaty sea bream

Above Wine risotto *(arroz de vinho)* in modern dress

Left A delicious fish stew *(parilhada de peixe)*

Right Seasonal steaks of shad *(sável)* and other fish await the grill in Gaia

(goraz), fine-flavoured gilt-head bream *(dourada)*, hake *(pescada)*, firm, meaty and delicious sea bass *(robalo)*, and excellent monkfish *(tamboril)*, often found in risotto as *arroz de tamboril*. The least expensive fishes are the inevitable *sardinhas*, horse mackerel *(carapau)*, and sprats *(espadilhas)*. Fishes mostly come grilled, or in a thick fish and potato stew *(caldeirada de peixe)*. A *Caldeirada do Senhor de Matosinhos* is a festive version, made with the very best fish. Shellfish include prawns *(camarões)*, the big-clawed European or rock lobster *(lavagante)*, the expensive and clawless but delicious spiny lobster *(lagosta)*, the strange but tasty goose-neck barnacles *(percebes)*, octopus *(polvo)*, small squid *(lulas/lulinhas)* and spider crab *(santola)*, which may come stuffed *(santola no carro)* but is better eaten plain. Seafood also comes in a mixed stew called a *cataplana*. There are river fish, too: salmon *(salmão)*, eel-like lamprey *(lampreia)* when in season, with its strong, oily character, often served as a kind of risotto *(arroz)*, and trout *(truta)*, which may be laced with lard or ham *(à moda de Barroso)*.

Non meat-eaters beware: fish dishes here often include meat or meat fat. There is olive oil from the Douro (top ones including CARM, Sardeiro, Vale d'Ondel, Niepoort, Quinta do Crasto, Taylors and Ramos Pinto) but the

northern cooking fats of preference are usually meat dripping, lard and butter. Fish, like meat, tends to be overcooked in traditional restaurants, for British tastes – not helped by steaks being thinly cut. Ask for it rare or lightly cooked *(mal passado)*.

The cities of the Douro estuary have borrowed cooking traditions from all the northern regions, the Minho, Trás-os-Montes, the Douro valley, and the Beiras, and that means plenty of meat to balance the fish. There are excellent free-range calves and kids from the Douro valley – kid risotto *(arroz de cabrito)* is often on the menu – and roast pork in profusion. Expect any bit of the animal to be used – *orelheira* is fried pigs' ears sprinkled with parsley, salt and vinegar, and any dish with *cabidela* in its name has been thickened with blood – not our favourite.

Passing quickly to vegetables, you will probably need to eat soup to clock up five a day. The *caldo verde* – cabbage, potato and chouriço soup – is good here, made from the proper, dark *couve galega* cabbage of the Minho, served with a chunk of the excellent local corn bread – *broa*, or *broa de milho*. There's fruit from the Douro – cherries, citrus fruits, almonds and figs; and from the nearby Beiras, the lovely Queijo da Serra, a great unpasteurised ewe's milk cheese so smooth and runny when young that you have to eat it with a spoon.

Some of Porto's traditional restaurants are very good indeed. But nowadays, like Lisbon and the cosmopolitan Algarve, it has its contemporary restaurants, cooking fine, local ingredients in a modern way. Here is our selection, old and new.

RESTAURANTS – MODERN PORTUGUESE

ALDOAR (PORTO, WEST)

Bull & Bear This fine, contemporary restaurant is the headquarters of one of Portugal's leading chefs, Miguel Castro e Silva, on the ground floor of the modern derivatives market building on the long Avenida da Boavista. Recently renovated, it is starkly elegant, white and red with the odd bit of modern art. Miguel's food is creative and delicious. He champions fresh local ingredients – fish, pig's trotters... all served in light, modern guise, and full of flavour, including spices. The menu changes regularly, as does the *ementa de degustação* (tasting menu). An excellent wine list is strong on the Douro, and has many wines by the glass, some of them unusually fine. Service is attentive. This is not a big restaurant, so do book. A little wine bar alongside serves *petiscos* (page 149).
Avenida da Boavista 3431
T+351 226 107 669
E rest.bullandbear@gmail.com
€50 ♀ *V*
Closed Sat lunch, Sun; lunch on public hols

FOZ DO DOURO (PORTO, COAST)

Cafeína The chef has recently changed in this well-loved restaurant in the streets

behind the Atlantic beach of Foz, but initial reports are good. Cafeína is fun. The clientele is mostly young, and most definitely cool and smart. A 19th century house was gutted and refitted in contemporary sophisticated mode, with rich, dark colours, and soft lighting. Music, often jazz, may be loud. There are two spaces – a bar-café and the restaurant. The wine list is excellent and long, the glasses lovely, and there are lots of wines by the glass, including 'wine flights' – three or four glasses per meal with a linking theme. Service is young and attentive, and you can dine till very late.
Rua do Padrão 100
T+351 226 108 059
E cafeina@mail.pt
W www.cafeina.pt
€30 ♀ *V*
Closed 2 Jan lunch, Easter Sun, 24 Dec din, 25 Dec

Foz Velha Marco Gomes is one of Porto's top chefs, his precise, creative cooking rooted in Portugal, and based on fresh local ingredients. There are two tasting menus with matching wines by the glass. And the menu always offers a vegetarian dish! The wine list is reasonably priced, a good but limited choice. Service is attentive and professional, led by Gomes' other half, Carla Carvalho. The restaurant is on the first floor of a buiding in the oldest part of town around the castle. Walls are red, blue and lilac, the space softly lit at night, brightly sunlit by day, always atmospheric. You should book.
Esplanada do Castelo 141
T+351 226 154 178
E mail@fozvelha.com
W www.fozvelha.com
€35 ♀ *V!*
Closed Sun, Mon lunch

Shis Formerly called Ourigo, this was always a delightful place for a drink or a meal, and now, since summer 2007, they have one of Porto's best chefs: Antonio Vieira, chef until recently at Cafeína. Shis has a big decking terrace, built out on stilts over the beach and the rocks, a glass windbreak facing the Atlantic, and views of the Douro as it pours into the Atlantic. It's a smart, elegant venue, nice even in winter when you can enjoy the views from the calm comfort of the glass and steel cube that houses the main restaurant and bar. A pianist plays Wednesday to Friday. The wine list is short but good, and service is friendly and efficient.
Esplanada do Castelo, Praia do Ourigo
T+351 226 189 593
E info@shisrestaurante.com
W www.netmenu.pt/praiaourigo
€35 ♀ *V*

GAIA (VILA NOVA DE)

Barão de Fladgate Strutting peacocks add to the very English feel of the garden and terrace of the Taylor's restaurant. But the food in the restaurant is modern Portuguese, with the excellent Quinta da Vargellas olive oil in evidence. On the terrace there are also sandwiches and salads, with stunning views over Gaia, the river and Porto. Apart from the 'home-made' ports, the long wine list reaches way outside the company, including some rare bottles.

Caves Taylor's, Rua do Choupelo 250
T+351 223 742 800
E general.office@tresseculos.pt
W www.tresseculos.pt
€30 ♀ *V*
Closed Sun din

LORDELO DO OURO (PORTO, WEST)

Porto Novo On the ground floor of the super-modern Sheraton Porto Hotel *(page 154)* the restaurant is big and of course

modern, with a terrace for summer. Chef Jerónimo Ferreira is a native of Porto, his cooking contemporary Portuguese with influences from his stints in North America, the UK, France, Austria, Holland and Italy, as well as the Algarve, Madeira and Lisbon. Breakfasts are excellent, and there's a stunning buffet lunch on Sundays.
Sheraton Porto Hotel & Spa,
*   Rua Tenente Valadim 146*
T+351 220 404 000
E sheraton.porto@sheraton.com
W www.sheraton.com/porto
€40 ♀ *V* 🛏
Open every day

MATOSINHOS (PORTO, COAST)

Degusto This modern restaurant (with wine bar) has one of the best wine lists in Portugal, many wines served by the glass. It was once Italian, but new chef Vitor Claro (one of Portugal's best young chefs) now creates delicious variations on Portuguese themes. If you have no time or

room for a full meal (though the cuisine here is light and fine), try the excellent *petiscos*. It is vital to book on Fridays and Saturdays. The brilliant Vinhos e Coisas Wine Centre, a sister establishment, is next door *(page 152)*.
Rua Sousa Aroso 540-544
T+351 229 364 363
E degusto@vinhoecoisas.pt
€40 ♀ *V*
Closed Mon lunch, Sun; 1st half Aug

MIRAGAIA (PORTO, WEST)

À Mesa com Bacchus Dining at this tiny, atmospheric restaurant is an interactive experience with chef-owner Mário da Fonte. There is no menu. Mario produces nine to ten courses, creative, modern cooking firmly based in Portuguese traditions, with half a dozen wines from his excellent, Douro-strong list. And he will pop in and out of the kitchen to discuss the food, and life. Open only for dinner, from 8pm – set aside the whole evening. This may be expensive by Portuguese standards, but it is a special experience. The restaurant seats maximum 20 people, and you must book, mentioning any dietary needs. Walk, or come by taxi.
Rua de Miragaia 127
T+351 222 000 896
€50 ♀ *V*
Closed Sun; lunch every day

Sessenta-Setenta Only a few years old, this is one of the city's most innovative restaurants. Part of the ruins of the Convento de Monchique were renovated to create the attractively stark, granite-walled interior. A huge terrace has views far and wide across and along the river.

Francisco Meirelles' cooking is very creative (sometimes too much so), the wine list very good, concentrating on Douro and Alentejo, and service is efficient and friendly. Come by taxi, or on foot down narrow, winding streets, then through the tunnel. Reserve for dinner.
Rua Sobre-o-Douro 1A
T+351 223 406 093
€25-€30 ♀ *V Closed Sun*

RAMALDE (PORTO, WEST)

Poivron Rouge This is the restaurant of the Méridien Park Atlantic Hotel *(page 154)* in Porto's new business district, north-west of centre. The young chef, Victor Matos, is one of Portugal's best, his cooking light and inventive, based on local produce, Portuguese with influences

from elsewhere, and presentation is mouth-watering. The wine list is good if fairly short, and the chef's suggested wine matches with dishes are also available by the glass. Service is excellent. The spacious and relaxed dining room is modern, but the walls are covered with old black and white photos of Porto. A terrace, garden and bar alongside serve lighter meals and snacks.
Le Méridien Park Atlantic, Avenida da
*   Boavista 1466*
T+351 226 072 500
E restaurante.porto@lemeridien.pt
W www.lemeridien-oporto.com
€40 ♀ *V* 🛏
Open every day

RESTAURANTS – GOOD TRADITIONAL PORTUGUESE

BONFIM (PORTO, EAST)

Casa Nanda Friendly little restaurant with huge portions of good local cuisine made from the best ingredients – the tripe here is legendary! Good wines. Tiny, so you must book.
Rua da Alegria 394
T+351 225 370 575
€15-€17.50 ♀
Closed Mon, Sun din; July

Portucale This was an avant-garde restaurant for Porto in the '60s, and little seems to have changed since. Loved locally for its spectacular views and unique style, Portucale is rather expensive, and very old fashioned in its decor and style of service. But the slightly modernised traditional food is very good, the wine list not the

longest, but interesting, with some rarities. On the 13th floor of a 1960s tower block, at the top of the Albergaria Miradouro *(page 153)*, Portucale has three big windows from which you can see most of Porto. A meal of *petiscos* at the bar will cost you €10-€20.
Rua da Alegria 598
T+351 225 370 717
E rest.portucale@miradouro-portucale.com
W www.miradouro-portucale.com
€40 ♀ *V* 🛏 *Open every day*

Rogério do Redondo Large and simply decorated, this is very popular with the locals for its good, traditional northern cooking, including *bacalhau*,

fried fish, seafood, roast kid and veal: high quality raw materials, expertly handled. The adventurous or the sqeamish should note that all kinds of 'interesting bits' of meat and fish appear on the menu – calves feet with beans, cod's liver with cod's liver rice, black pudding, fish cheeks and roe... Wash it all down with good wines, including excellent Vinho Verde.
Rua João António Aguiar 19
T+351 225 379 533
€25 ♀ *V Closed Sun*

Suribachi A vegetarian refuge in this city of fish and meat, 80m east of the Praça da Batalha. Cooking is 'macrobiotic' (wholegrains and vegetables) and inventive: very good vegetarian dishes, salads, even some vegetarian versions of traditional Portuguese dishes. True vegetarians beware – some things contain fish or seafood. It's a smoke-free zone. There's a terrace, and a shop attached.
Rua do Bonfim 135-140
T+351 225 106 700
€15 V! No credit cards Closed Sun

CAMPANHÃ (PORTO, EAST)

Casa Aleixo Good and inexpensive, Casa Aleixo has been here for over half a century, near the Campanhã railway station, east of Porto city centre. It is family-owned, the decor simple but nice, with stone walls, a chequered floor, white tablecloths, and the kitchen open to view. Cooking is conservative but very good:

soups, fish, roasts and traditional dishes, and good Douro wines. Parking is notoriously difficult – come by train or metro!
Rua da Estação 216
T+351 225 370 462
E casaaleixo@sapo.pt
€20-€25 ♀
Closed Sun, public hols; 1 week Jan,
   3 weeks Aug

FOZ DO DOURO (PORTO, COAST)

Oporto Opposite the São João da Foz church, Restaurante-Bar Oporto has good, traditional cooking with an accent on fish, seafood, and game in season. It's a spacious but cosy place with comfortable sofas in the bar whilst you await your table, open fires in winter, and relaxing tones of ochre, olive green – and port wine colour, of course, to match the portraits of historic Porto characters on the walls. The wine list is good.
Largo de Igreja 105-107
T+351 226 100 727
€30 ♀ *Closed Sun; Mon lunch*

GAIA (VILA NOVA DE)

Adega & Presuntaria Transmontana 1 & 2 The owner of these two Gaia restaurants is from Mirandela in Trás-os-Montes, up in the wild north east, a land of meat-eaters. No 1 is more central, no 2 down by the river in the vicinity of the port wine lodges. Both are cosy, rustic restaurants famous for their *petiscos* (series of small dishes). Dine on a series of little portions of ham, sausage, pork, beans, seafood, tripe...
No 1: Rua Cândido dos Reis 132
T+351 223 759 792
€25-€30 ♀ *V Closed Mon*
No 2: Avenida Diogo Leite 80
T+351 223 758 380
€25-€30 ♀ *V Open every day*

GAIA (VILA NOVA DE) *continued*
Ar de Rio A big, modern block on the riverfront by the port lodges, popular with tourists and locals alike for its buzzy atmosphere, spectacular views of river and bridge, and excellent *francesinhas* (cheese, sausage and ham on toast), as well as traditional dishes and grills. Eat in, or out on a covered terrace. In the evening enjoy or avoid the music videos on big screens!
Avenida Diogo Leite 5
T+351 223 701 797
E arderio@mail.telepac.pt
W www.arderio.com
€16 V Closed Christmas

Tromba Rija This is a place to come when you are really hungry. An all-inclusive price introduces you to a huge range of traditional Portuguese fare, through *petiscos* to pudding, served at a buffet.
Avenida Diogo Leite 102
T+351 223 743 762
E reservasgaia@trombarija.com
€25 Closed Mon lunch, Sun din

LEÇA DA PALMEIRA (PORTO, COAST)
Casa de Chá da Boa Nova Down steps to the beach, nestling into the rockscape by the lighthouse, this magical designer building has huge, retractable glass windows looking out to sea, and lots of polished red wood. It's an especially exciting experience if the sea is rough! There is fine fish well cooked, and a good wine list. Leça is a 20 minute drive or longer bus-ride from Porto. For the tea room and bar, *see page 150.*
Avenida da Liberdade
T+351 229 951 785
€25-€30 ♀ V Closed Sun

O Chanquinhas A long-established, traditional manor house restaurant with excellent grilled fish and seafood, good

regional cooking from fine raw materials, and good wines include jugs of house Vinho Verde. Service is friendly and attentive.
Rua de Santana 243
T+351 229 951 884
E chanquinhas@netcabo.pt
W www.chanquinhas.com
€25-€30 ♀ V Closed Sun

LORDELO DO OURO (PORTO, WEST)
Peixes & Companhia 'Fish & Company' is on the first floor of an old building on the riverside, with fine views. Delightfully rustic, the atmospheric dining room has oak beams. Delicious, fresh fish and seafood is cooked simply but very well.
Rua do Ouro 133
T+351 226 185 655
€25 ♀ V Closed Sun

MATOSINHOS (PORTO, COAST)
Dom Zeferino A very simple but excellent fish and seafood restaurant down a side street. Wines are good, mainly Vinho Verde and Douro, service efficient and friendly.
Rua do Godinho 163
T+351 229 372 273
E domzeferino@hotmail.com
€17.50 Open every day

Esplanada Marisqueira Antiga Here by the beach for more than half a century, this smart (very pink) restaurant with its plants and *azulejos* always has an excellent range of fish and seafood, perfectly and

mostly plainly cooked. There are also good fish soups, and *arroz* or *açorda de mariscos* – risotto or a risotto-like dish thickened with bread. A good wine list draws from the Minho and the Douro. There's a pretty terrace *(esplanada)*. It's wise to book.
Rua Roberto Ivens 628
T+351 229 380 660
E esplanadamarisqueira@gmail.com
€35 ♀ Closed Mon

O Gião Meals begin here with a vast variety of inexpensive little starters – *petiscos* or *entradas* – and progresses to copious traditional dishes based on fresh fish and top-class meat. An interesting wine list, reasonably priced, includes some rarities – Gião is owned by TV wine presenter José Silva. Decor is simple, the welcome warm.
Rua Brito e Cunha 640
T+351 229 350 993
E giao2@sapo.pt
€25 ♀ V
Closed Sat lunch, Sun; 3 weeks Aug

Trinca Espinhas A trendy former wine warehouse cooking fine, fresh ingredients, including lots of fish, in a mix of traditional and modern styles. One of the set menus is an interesting series of fish and vegetable skewers.
Avenida Serpa Pinto 283
T+351 229 350 246
€30 ♀ V Closed

Veleiros Small, relaxed family restaurant renowned for its octopus, simply baked fish, and well-cooked traditional dishes. Good wine list.
Rua Almeiriga 2520, Cabo do Mundo
T+351 229 958 531
E marioveleiros@hotmail.com
€25 ♀ V Closed Sun, public hols

RAMALDE (PORTO, WEST)

Degrau Chá Small, elegant, comfortable restaurant with attractive modern decor, the cuisine a combination of traditional and modern, with contemporary presentation.
Rua Alfonso Lopes Vieira 180
T+351 226 098 764
€25 ♀ *Closed Sun; Aug*

RIBEIRA (PORTO)

Alzira An atmospheric little place, narrow with stone walls and a friendly welcome, just off the Ribeira. Good local cuisine includes roasted kid, *bacalhau*, octopus, rabbit, and good *tripas à moda do Porto*.
Viela do Buraco 3
T+351 222 005 004
€30 Closed Mon

Dom Tonho Near the bridge on the main Ribeira drag, the famous Dom Tonho is built into the old city walls. It's a favourite haunt of locals as well as tourists. The decor is quite contemporary, white against granite interior walls. Cooking is good traditional northern, based on excellent, fresh raw materials; seafood is a speciality, along with tripe. The wine list is one of Portugal's best. Window tables have great views. Remember that you have to pay for any of the on-table pre-meal nibbles you decide to eat, which sometimes arrive in unrequested profusion. There's another, much simpler Dom Tonho, same stable, over the water, on the Gaia side.
Cais da Ribeira 13-15
T+351 222 004 307
E porto@dtonho.com W www.dtonho.com
€40-€45 ♀ *V Open every day*

A Grade A real traditional *tasca* in the narrow streets with only four or five tables, and views of the Douro. The food is cooked and served by the owner, always good. Only a few wines, but well chosen.
Rua de São Nicolau 9
T+351 223 321 130
€15 ♀ *V Closed Sun*

Mercearia Good fish and seafood in an atmospheric old restaurant right on the waterfront, with stone walls, old photos, and beams.
Cais da Ribeira 232/3
T+351 222 004 389
€20 V
Apr-Sep open every day Oct-Mar closed Tue

SANTO ILDEFONSO (PORTO, NORTH OF CENTRE)

Paparico Lovely, peaceful, rustic little restaurant, open only for dinner, north of centre. It is run by Yuko (Japanese) and António Cardoso, whose cooking is very good. Portions are big, the menu and wine list short. You must book.
Rua Costa Cabral 2343
T+351 225 400 548
€30 V
Closed Lunch every day; Sun, Mon; Aug

VITÓRIA (PORTO, CENTRE)

Adega Vila Meã An atmospheric, simple, traditional place near the Torre dos Clérigos, with *azulejos*, checked cloths, and on the walls, shawls and mountain walking sticks. Good food with a Trás-os-Montes flavour, and good wines.
Rua dos Caldeireiros 62
T+351 222 082 967
€20 ♀ *V Closed Sun; Aug*

DRINK AND SNACK

ALDOAR (PORTO, WEST)

Bar do Bull & Bear An excellent wine bar, with a changing dozen wines by the glass, a fine list of ports and Moscatels, and very good and varied hot and cold *petiscos*, good cheeses and salads. *Avenida da Boavista 3431 T+351 226 107 669 Open 12 noon-1am Closed Sat lunch, Sun*

BAIXA (PORTO, CENTRE)

Café Guarany One of Porto's famous cafés, dating from the 1930s and re-opened after sensitive renovation in 2003 to the delight of the local people. Historically a haunt of artists, poets and musicians, Guarany is always packed and lively. It's a great place for breakfast, an afternoon cup of coffee, or a quick lunch of well-cooked traditional fare. Guarany was the main indigenous tribe in Brazil in the 17th century – hence the Brazilian decorative touches. There may be live piano music, *fado*, blues... *Avenida dos Aliados 89 Open every day 9am-midnight*

FOZ DO DOURO (PORTO, COAST)

Praia da Luz In the most wonderful situation, right on the beautiful beach between Foz and Matosinhos, this

elegant, modern café, bar and restaurant is a great place for breakfast, or for a drink as you watch the sun set over the Atlantic – wines are good, mainly Douro, Alentejo and Dão. There are white sun shades, tables outside and in, deckchairs, and in the winter open fires and blankets. It's calm by day, lively after dark. At the southern end of the Avenida – parking may be difficult. *Avenida do Brasil/Rua Colonel Raul Perez Open every day 9am-3pm, shorter opening Christmas and New Year*

GAIA (VILA NOVA DE)

Bogani Café With the lights of the Ribeira twinkling across the water, this wonderful, half-covered terrace is the perfect place to watch the sun go down, a glass of tawny port in hand, as you sink into the white, leather-look armchairs. The coffee is seriously good, food pleasant and a bit pricey – soups, sandwiches and salads. There may be live music. Find it at the west end of the new Cais de Gaia, near the wine cellars, with an impressive glass-sheltered interior for cooler weather. *Cais de Gaia Open every day 11am-2am*

LEÇA DA PALMEIRA (PORTO, COAST)

Casa de Chá da Boa Nova A magical tea room and restaurant *(page 148)* built on the rocks right by the sea, a 20-minute drive (or a bus ride) from Porto, across the river from Matosinhos. *Avenida da Liberdade Open Mon-Sat 11am-midnight Closed Sun*

MATOSINHOS (PORTO, COAST)

Degusto Wine Bar An elegant, startlingly modern wine bar with a wine list that ranges broadly and brilliantly across Portugal and the world, many wines served by the glass. Food is light and modern, and there are excellent *petiscos*. It is wise to book on Fridays and Saturdays. *Rua Sousa Aroso 540-544 T+351 229 364 363 E degusto@vinhoecoisas.pt Open Mon-Thu 6-midnight Fri & Sat 6-2am Closed Sun;1st half Aug*

D'Oliva Converted from a warehouse, smartly minimalist, with a beautifully layered wall of schist, this is a huge and popular restaurant and bar, open till very late. Come for *petiscos* (Portuguese and Italian, less fishy than the neighbours), with many Portuguese wines by the glass. *Rua Brito e Cunha 354 Open Mon 8-12.30 Tues-Thu 12.30-3, 8-12.30 Sat 1-4, 8-1 Sun 1-4, 8-midnight Closed Mon lunch*

MASSARELOS (PORTO, WEST)

Solar do Vinho do Porto A wine bar with ports from all the producers in the former wine cellar and stables of the Quinta da Maceirinha, a mansion that otherwise houses the Museu Romântico, an art gallery and museum of furniture. The bar has a lovely rose garden with box hedges, fountains and river views, and an arched, covered terrace with comfortable

easy chairs – a lovely spot for an evening drink. The bar is run by the Instituto dos Vinhos do Douro e Porto, the official wine institute. The wines are selected in an annual tasting, to which each company can submit five wines, from which a maximum of three are chosen. Many are available by the glass, right across the price range, and there's info on tap. The only food is delicious Queijo da Serra, either hard or soft. There is also a shop. *Rua de Entre-Quintas 220 Open Summer Mon-Sat 2-midnight Winter Mon-Thurs 2-10, Fri & Sat 2-midnight Closed Sun, public hols*

RIBEIRA

Vinologia Opened in 2000, this small wine bar is one of the very best places in Porto to taste (and drink) port. The by-the-glass list is huge, port only, and focuses on wines from smaller-scale and lesser-known producers – some that we ourselves had never met. French owner Philippe Duhard and his staff are keen to advise and inform, and the atmosphere is welcoming and lively. You'll spot the yellow-painted façade just by the tunnel that leads to the Dom Luis I Bridge. Inside, the 18th century house has been modernised, with a red brick bar. Food is limited to port-friendly nibbles (apricots,

raisins, chocolate, nuts… depending on the type of port you choose) or the scrumptious, gooey Serra da Estrela cheese with walnut and raisin bread, chocolate pudding, or chocolate-coated dried figs. There's also a shop, selling, of course, port. *Rua São João 46 W www.lamaisonduporto.com Open daily 2-midnight*

SANTO ILDEFONSO (PORTO, NORTH OF CENTRE)

Bufete Fase This *tasco* (or *tasca*) is possibly the best *francesinha* place in town. It has a long bar and four tables at the back, and is run by a husband and wife team who really make you feel at home. (There are also steaks and hot dogs.) *Rua de Santa Catarina 1147 T+351 222 052 118 Closed Sun; public hols*

Café Majestic We always imagined JK Rowling writing Harry Potter in a dingy British café. But in fact she once lived in Porto, and Café Majestic was apparently the magical spot where Harry was born… This would be a fitting place for the venerable Dumbledore to dine amidst the green marble, cherubs, gilded mirrors and chandeliers. He might call in for breakfast, or coffee with delicious cakes – or enjoy a lunchtime *francesinha*. He would certainly have enjoyed a glass of port, or Douro wine. At the back of the main art-deco café is a winter garden, at the front a shaded terrace. *Rua de Santa Catarina 122 Open 9.30-midnight Closed Sun*

Confeitaria do Bolhão Across from the market, dating back to 1896, the front is a busy bread and cake shop, behind which you can have coffee and cakes, or a quick soup or *francesinha* in the friendly café-restaurant, lost in time. *Rua Formosa 339 Open Mon-Sat 8am-9pm*

VITÓRIA (PORTO, CENTRE)

Livraria Lello One of the loveliest places to stop for a cup of coffee or a glass of port is the little café on the gallery of this amazing, 1906-built, neo-Gothic temple to books. There are just four tables, with comfortable chairs, and a small bar that was once a shop counter. Watch the customers browse… *Rua das Carmelitas 144 Open Mon-Fri 10-7.30, Sat 10-7 Closed Sun, public hols except in Dec*

MARKETS, WINE AND FOOD SHOPS

ALDOAR (PORTO, WEST)

Trago Spacious, smart, modern wine shop and deli, just off the Avenida da Boavista on the way out of town, with a big range of Portuguese wines, oils, vinegars, cheeses, jams, chocolates… *Praceta do Professor Egas Moniz 30*

BONFIM (PORTO, EAST)

Mercado do Bolhão The famous food market of Porto is to be transformed (inside only) into a shopping centre below, whilst

upstairs will still be a produce market. Visit while you can – mornings are the best time. The early 20th century ironwork building is bustling and atmospheric, selling excellent bread, dried beans, herbs, olives, fish and seafood, meat (some of it still alive), sausages, cheese, honey, and heaps of fresh fruit and veg – watch vast quantities of cabbage being shredded for caldo verde soup. *Rua da Sá da Bandeira/Rua Formosa Mon-Fri 7-5 (Mon fewer traders) Sat 7-1 Closed Sat pm, Sun*

CEDOFEITA (PORTO, BOAVISTA)

Mercado do Bom Sucesso Bright, attractive and recently renovated 1950s building selling a vast range of fresh fruit, veg, fish, meat. Just south of the Rotunda da Boavista. *Largo Ferreira Lapa/ Rua Caldas Xavier/Praça do Bom Successo Mon-Fri 7-5 Sat 7-1 Closed Sat pm, Sun*

CORDOARIA

Casa Oriental This is an old, unspoilt grocer and greengrocer, near the Torre dos Clérigos, with fruit and veg stalls out on the pavement, top class *bacalhau*, and spices. *Campo dos Mártires de Pátria 111*

Garrafeira Cleriporto Another little shop near the Torre dos Clérigos specialising in ports (including old and rare), plus wines, also including some old vintages, Madeiras and whiskies, Cognacs and old Portuguese *Aguardentes* all at fair prices. *Rua da Assunção 38*

FOZ DO DOURO

Alberto Augusto Leite Here for more than half a century, this is perhaps Porto's best selection of Portuguese wines and port. Huge stocks include some very old vintages. *Rua do Passeio Alegre 868*

Foz do Douro *continued*
Cafeína Fooding House Small, contemporary, elegant deli in the same street as the Cafeína restaurant *(page 145).* Excellent wines from Portugal and abroad, cheeses, charcuterie, oils... *Rua do Padrão 152*

Gaia (Vila Nova de)
Clube Gourmet, El Corte Ingles Department store, deli and fine wine shop. The wine range is large and impressive, including fine and rare as well as some less expensive bottles, with the accent on Portugal. There are also fine cheeses, Portuguese and foreign, oils, charcuterie, hams, fresh truffles... *Avenida República 1435*

Lordelo do Ouro (Porto, west)
Loja da Praça Gourmet High-quality deli and wine shop between the Serralves park and Foz, selling a good range of national and international wines, plus deli products, Portuguese as well as foreign, including fine cheeses, hams and charcuterie, truffles, caviar, coffees, chutneys, olive oils and vinegars. *Praça Dom Afonso V 55*

Massarelos (Porto, west)
Solar do Vinho do Porto There's a shop selling a huge range of ports from all the producers in this 'educational' wine bar *(page 150)* – you can taste before you buy. *Rua de Entre-Quintas 220*

Ramalde (Porto, west)
Garrafeira Tio Pepe Large, smart fine wine shop with especially good ranges of Douro wines and ports, including old and rare, in an industrial estate on the way out to the coast. *Rua Engenheiro Ferreira Dias 51*

Ribeira
AVEPOD – Vinhos de Quinta At the end of an alleyway behind the Pestana Hotel, a retail outlet for 60 smaller producers of Douro wines and port – about 350 different wines, plus wine accessories, olive oils, dried fruit etc: generally below normal retail prices. *Rua Fonte Taurina 89*

Loja Essência do Vinho Attractive shop selling port in the cloister of the Palácio da Bolsa, with a good wine range and a tasting room. *Palácio do Bolsa, Rua Ferreira Borges*

Vinologia Wine shop in a wine bar with a wonderful range of ports from small producers. Taste first in the wine bar *(page 150). Rua São João 46*

Santo Idelfonso (Porto, north of centre)
A Pérola do Bolhão Art deco grocery shop, little changed since 1917, selling wine and all kinds of food including cheese, charcuterie, nuts, chocolates, sweets, canned fish... *Rua Formosa 279*

Matosinhos (Porto, coast)
Vinho & Coisas Wine Centre

A seriously wonderful wine shop with a huge range of excellent bottles from all around the world, including of course Portuguese wines at all price levels. Deli products include chocolates, biscuits and coffee. There are regular wine tastings, and Degusto, a fantastic restaurant and wine bar *(pages 146 and 150). Rua de Sousa Aroso 540-544*

Wine O'Clock One of rapidly-growing group of wine shops with competitive prices, very modern design and a huge range of wines from Portugal and worldwide. On the first floor is an impressive collection of spirits including rare whiskies, Cognacs and Armagnacs, port, and a locked fine wine sanctum. There are tastings on Saturdays. *Rua Sousa Aroso 297*

Vitória (Porto, centre)
Garrafeira do Carmo Some of the best prices in Porto (and Gaia) for a big range of ports is to be found in this pretty little shop, just west of the Natural History Museum. *Rua do Carmo 17*

Sleep in Porto and Gaia

BAIXA (PORTO, CENTRE)

Hotel Infante de Sagres Opened as a hotel mid-20th century and apparently little changed since, this grand, old fashioned hotel is luxurious, friendly and comfortable. The public rooms are resplendent with chandeliers, wrought iron, polished tile floors, wood panelling, and oriental rugs. The location is perfect, just a few metres from Avenida dos Aliados, in the midst of the financial and shopping district. The bedrooms are gradually being renovated.

Praça Dona Filipa de Lencastre 62,
4050-259 Porto
T+351 223 398 500
E bookings@hotelinfantesagres
W www.hotelinfantesagres.pt
€150 🛏64 ✕

BONFIM (PORTO, EAST)

Albergaria Miradouro A pleasantly old-fashioned, comfortable hotel high up in a tile-clad 1960s tower block. It is excellent value, in a slightly run-down residential area off to the north-east of the Mercado do Bolhão, a ten-minute walk from the main tourist areas. This is the highest point in Porto, and the views (the hotel is on floors 10 to 13) are stunning. Corner rooms on the top floor have panoramic views in two directions. Excellent breakfasts are taken in the 13th-floor restaurant, Portucale, which also serves grand and expensive traditional meals *(page 147)*. Hotel staff are friendly and helpful, and parking is included in the price – a considerable advantage in the crowded streets of Porto.

Rua da Alegria 598, 4000-034 Porto
T+351 225 370 717
E alb.miradouro@miradouro-portucale.com
W www.miradouro-portucale.com
€50-€65 🛏30 ♊ ✕

CEDOFEITA (PORTO, CENTRE)

Residencial Brasília Once a large family house, the Brasília is fairly small and very friendly, with a garden and garage, and conveniently central.

Rua Álvares Cabral 221, 4050-041 Porto
T+351 222 006 095
E reservas@residencialbrasiliaporto.com
W www.residencialbrasiliaporto.com
€35-€40 🛏11 ⑤4

FOZ DO DOURO (PORTO, COAST)

Hotel Boa Vista Right by the Castelo de São João da Foz, in the nicest, oldest part of this smart seaside town, the hotel Boa Vista was recently modernised, but is still characterful. Ask for one of the 25 rooms with a sea/river view. Suites have balconies. There is a rooftop swimming pool, bar and restaurant, where you will have breakfast – pleasant food, phenomenal views. The beach is just opposite, buses stop nearby and run four times an hour, once an hour after 9pm, into Porto and Matosinhos. Parking in their private garage is €4 extra.

Esplanada do Castelo 58, Foz do Douro,
4150-196 Porto
T+351 225 320 020
E reserva@hotelboavista.com
W www.hotelboavista.com
€80-€92 🛏67 ⑤4 ✕ 🏊

LAVADORES (GAIA, WEST)

Casa Branca Beach & Golf Hotel Right on the unspoilt Lavadores beach, in a village 7km west of Gaia, Casa Branca doesn't *actually* have a golf course – it organises visits to courses 4km or more away. On site, there is free access for hotel guests to a gym, indoor pool, jacuzzi, sauna and Turkish bath; you pay extra for spa treatments, tennis and squash. Staff are friendly, children welcome, and they offer, externally, various other activities, including paintballing and watersports. Most rooms have Atlantic-view balconies. The windswept exterior looks a little tired, but inside all is spick. The Casa Branca restaurant on the beach has good wines and traditional cooking, and there is also a wine bar. Parking is plentiful, and regular buses, till late, take 40 minutes into town, taxis 20 minutes for €10.

Rua da Bélgica 86, Praia de Lavadores,
  4400-044 Vila Nova de Gaia
T+351 227 727 400
E reservas@casabranca.com
W www.casabranca.com
€140-€250
🛏53 Ⓢ4(4) ♀ ✕ 🏊 ♨ 🏋

Lordelo do Ouro (Porto, Boavista)

Sheraton Porto Hotel & Spa This is currently Porto's most modern hotel, renowned for its fantastic spa, excellent breakfasts, and spectacular Sunday lunch buffets. The hotel restaurant, Porto Novo *(page 146)*, is one of the city's best. Public rooms are spacious and clad in white marble, wood, glass and steel, bedrooms large and comfortable, in chocolate-and-port-coloured hues. Glass lifts are fun, as are the fairy lights on the trees that

surround this modern tower. The Seralves museum and the Casa da Música are not far way, and the beaches of Foz just off to the west. Parking is no problem.

Rua Tenente Valadim 146, 4100-476 Porto
T+351 220 404 000
E reservations.porto@sheraton.com
W www.sheraton.com/porto
€100-€200
🛏242 Ⓢ25 ♀ ✕ 🏊 ♨ 🏋

Ramalde (Porto, west)

Le Méridien Park Atlantic Porto In a smart residential district not far from the Fundação de Serralves and the Casa da Música, on the way out to the beaches of Foz, this hotel is high-rise, modern and elegant. Rooms are big and contemporary, three of the sixteen floors smoke-free. The Poivron Rouge Restaurant *(page 146)* is one of Porto's top eating venues. There is plenty of parking.

Avenida da Boavista 1466,
  4100-114 Porto
T+351 226 072 508
E reservas.porto@lemeridien.pt
W www.lemeridien.com/porto
€237-€357 🛏190 Ⓢ42 ♀ ✕

Ribeira

Hotel da Bolsa Small and modern inside, this hotel is wonderfully central to the tourist action, 100m behind the Ribeira, 50m from the Palácio da Bolsa and the Igreja de São Francisco. Public rooms are small and bedrooms smartly

simple and comfortable. Breakfast is the only meal available, but scores of restaurants lie just beyond the doorstep. They have a deal with a public car park 100m away, €9 for 24 hours.

Rua Ferreira Borges 101, 4050-253 Porto
T+351 222 026 768
E reservas@hoteldabolsa.com
W www.hoteldabolsa.com
€72-€95 🛏30 Ⓢ6(3)

Pestana Porto Hotel This lovely hotel cleverly interconnects six tall, narrow former merchant houses, built partly upon a piece of Porto's medieval city wall. Right down by the river, on the edge of the Ribeira, the Pestana is well run by friendly and helpful staff. Rooms are comfortable and elegant, in rich, peaceful colours. Those that have river views also have balconies. There's an underground public car park 200m away, with special rates for guests, but it may be best to go by taxi, and on foot.

Praça da Ribeira 1, 4050-513 Porto
T+351 223 402 300
E pestana.porto@pestana.com
W www.pestana.com
€193-€289 🛏45 Ⓢ3 ✗

SANTO ILDEFONSO
(PORTO, NORTH OF CENTRE)

Pensão Avenida Friendly, comfortable and central, this 19th century townhouse is close by the São Bento station. It's on the fourth and fifth floors, but there is a lift if all those hills have worn you out.
Avenida dos Aliados 141, 4000-067 Porto
T+351 222 009 551
E pensaoavenida@clix.pt
W www.pensaoavenida.planetaclix.pt
€40 🛏15

Residencial Vera Cruz A characterful, pleasantly old-fashioned hotel in the centre of town, on a busy street just off Avenida dos Aliados. Staff are friendly, the atmosphere relaxed, the rooms spacious. A breakfast room on the eighth floor has a small terrace.
Rua Ramalho Ortigão 14, 4000-407 Porto
T+351 223 323 396
E geral@residencialveracruz.com
W www.residencialveracruz.com
€50 🛏25 Ⓢ5

Residencial Pão de Açucar Stylish as inexpensive hotels go, this big, imposing 1930s building is just west of the Avenida dos Aliados, not far from São Bento station. It is fairly peaceful despite its central location, and delightfully old fashioned. Bedrooms are big and comfortable, and six of the rooms have private terraces. The spiral staircase is amazing. The hotel has no car park, but there's a private one nearby.

Rua do Almada 262, 4050-032 Porto
T+351 222 002 425
E paodeacucar@iol.pt
W www.residencialpaodeacucar.com
€60-€120 🛏38 Ⓢ13

Residencial Castelo Santa Catarina

You can't mistake the Castelo at the top of the Rua Santa Catarina. And if you stay there you'll never forget the curious building, whether you consider it a work of art, or over the top. Surrounded by tall palm trees and a lovely garden with terraces, it is smothered with *azulejos*, right up to the top of its extraordinary crenellated tower. There are more *azulejos* inside, along with art deco and other intricate furnishings, stained glass, chandeliers and bright colours. One of the suites is in the tower.
Staff are friendly and helpful. It's ten minutes' walk down from this (less smart) end of the Rua Santa Catarina to the tourist areas – which, on the positive side, makes for more peaceful nights. The Castelo has its own car park, private, safe and free.

Rua Santa Catarina 1347,
*   4000-457 Porto*
T+351 225 095 599
E porto@castelosantacatarina.com.pt
W www.castelosantacatarina.com.pt
€48-€70 🛏22 Ⓢ3

SÃO FELIX DA MARINHA
(GAIA COAST)

Hotel Solverde Porto Modern and comfortable, right on the beach just north of Espinho, down the Atlantic coast from Gaia. It has an indoor pool, spa and gym, two outdoor heated seawater pools, squash, tennis, mini-golf, volleyball, cycles to rent, playground, playroom, and a children's club for all ages. Rooms with sea views have balconies. The station is nearby; trains to Gaia cost €2.50 return, or it's a 15 minute drive. Staff are very helpful.
Avenida da Liberdade, Sao Felix da
*   Marinha, 4410-154 Vila Nova Gaia*
T+351 227 313 162
E hotelsolverde@solverde.pt
W www.solverdehotel.com
€165-€200
🛏166 Ⓢ8 ✗ ⚓ 🛁 🛖 🔍 🏹

VITÓRIA (PORTO, CENTRE)

Grande Hotel de Paris Even though renovated, this inexpensive hotel is still old fashioned and characterful, with many original features, antiques, and charm. It was once a gentlemen's club. There's a games room, bar, library and grand breakfast room. The garden has shady mature trees, right in the centre of town, by the Torre dos Clérigos. All rooms are different, many quite spacious; the front rooms can be noisy. Staff are helpful.
Rua da Fábrica 27-29, 4050-247 Porto
T+351 222 073 140
E reservas@ghparis.pt
W www.ghparis.pt
€50-€70 🛏42

Beiras

The granite heart of Portugal is a national treasure, all too rarely visited. Mainland Portugal's highest mountain range, the Serra da Estrela, makes a diagonal barrier across the centre of the Beiras, surrounded by yet more mountains stretching out to the Spanish border. These are some of the loveliest landscapes in the Iberian Peninsula, the highest peaks coated white in winter and transformed into a canvas of rock-strewn purple during the springtime blossoming of the heather. Sheep and goat farming has been the main means of survival in the remote uplands, and local shepherds have turned necessity into a gloriously gloopy, creamily flavourome cheese – Queijo da Serra da Estrela – as well as numerous other cheeses. To the east, inhabitants of the fortified villages battled with invaders as well as the environment. The government has helped to restore many of these historic villages *(aldeias históricas)*; in some of them you can stay in scenic comfort. And suddenly these idyllic places are accessible, thanks to new motorways that carve into the craggy interior. These should open up escape routes for the fresh, bright-fruited wines from the Beira Interior, as well.

Another country lies to the west of the Serra da Estrela. The Mondego, Portugal's longest home-grown river, rises in the Serra da Estrela, and winds through the high, forested Dão country, flowing majestically through Coimbra, capital of the Beiras, before entering the sea in a wide estuary at Figueira da Foz. The wine region of Bairrada, with its suckling pig capital of Mealhada, sits centrally upon the hilly coastal stretch, sloping gently down towards flatter, sandier land, and the sea. It's an almost straight coastline of golden surf beaches, broken in the north by long sandbanks and lagoons.

And now we are going to confuse you again. Our chapter is based upon the Vinho Regional area of Beiras, whose boundaries differ slightly from those of the current administrative districts of Aveiro, Coimbra, Viseu, Guarda and Castelo Branco, which make up the old administrative province of Beiras. Many local people (and older books) still think in terms of the officially obsolete regional divisions of Beira Litoral (coastal), Beira Baixa (lower, in the south-east) and Beira Alta (upper). Just think wine, and you'll know where you are.

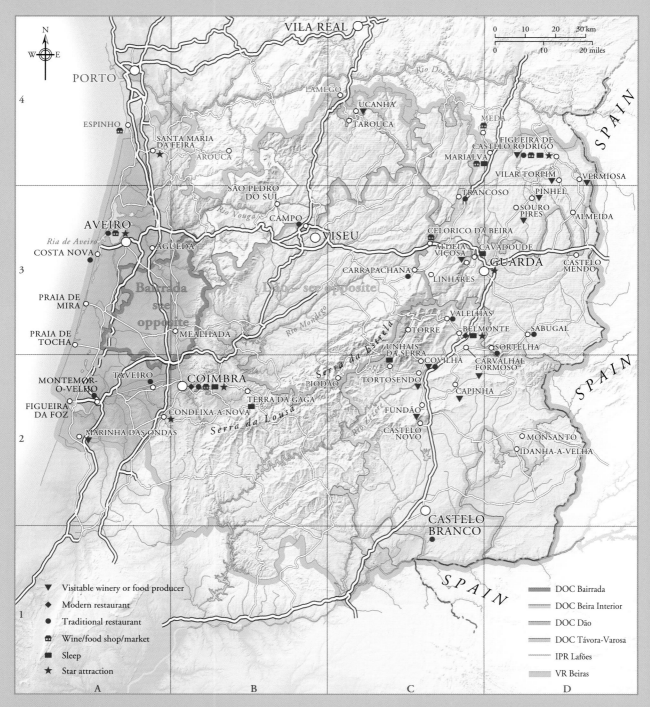

N
W E
S

VILA REAL

4

PORTO

ESPINHO

SANTA MARIA
DA FEIRA

AROUCA

LAMEGO

UCANHA
TAROUCA

MEDA

FIGUEIRA DE
CASTELO RODRIGO

MARIALVA

VILAR TORPIM

VERMIOSA

SÃO PEDRO
DO SUL

TRANCOSO

PINHEL

ALMEIDA

3

Ria de Aveiro

AVEIRO

COSTA NOVA

ÁGUEDA

Rio Vouga

CAMPO

VISEU

SOURO
PIRES

CELORICO DA BEIRA

ALDEIA
VIÇOSA

CAVADOUDE

GUARDA

CASTELO
MENDO

CARRAPACHANA

LINHARES

PRAIA DE
MIRA

Rio Mondego

MEALHADA

VALELHAS

SABUGAL

PRAIA DE
TOCHA

TORRE

BELMONTE

SORTELHA

Serra da Estrela

UNHAIS
DA SERRA

COVILHÃ

CARVALHAL
FORMOSO

TAVEIRO

COIMBRA

PIODÃO

TORTOSENDO

MONTEMOR-
O-VELHO

TERRA DA GAGA

CAPINHA

FIGUEIRA
DA FOZ

CONDEIXA-A-NOVA

Serra da Lousã

FUNDÃO

MARINHA DAS ONDAS

CASTELO
NOVO

MONSANTO

IDANHA-A-VELHA

2

Rio Zêzere

**CASTELO
BRANCO**

1

▼ Visitable winery or food producer

◆ Modern restaurant

● Traditional restaurant

🏬 Wine/food shop/market

■ Sleep

★ Star attraction

DOC Bairrada

DOC Beira Interior

DOC Dão

DOC Távora-Varosa

IPR Lafões

VR Beiras

A   B   C   D

Bairrada
see
opposite

Dão – see opposite

Rio Douro

SPAIN

SPAIN

SPAIN

0   10   20   30 km
0   10   20 miles

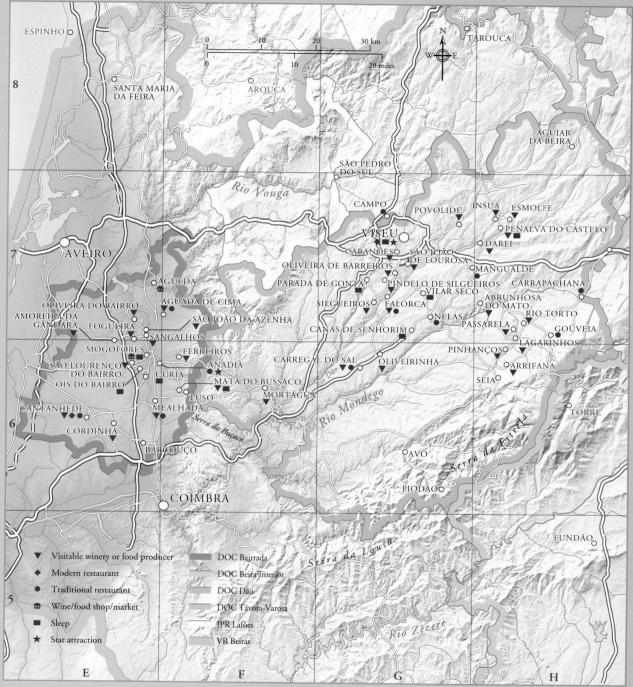

ESPINHO

SANTA MARIA
DA FEIRA

AROUCA

TAROUCA

8

N
W&E
S

0   10   20   30 km
0   10
              20 miles

AGUIAR
DA BEIRA

SÃO PEDRO
DO SUL

Rio Vouga

CAMPO   POVOLIDE   INSUA   ESMOLFE

PENALVA DO CASTELO

VISEU   DAREI

7 AVEIRO

CABANÕES   SÃO JOÃO
              DE LOUROSA

OLIVEIRA DE BARREIROS   MANGUALDE

ÁGUEDA

AGUADA DE CIMA

OLIVEIRA DO BAIRRO

PARADA DE GONTA   PINDELO DE SILGUEIROS   CARRAPACHANA

VILAR SECO

SÃO JOÃO DA AZENHA   SILGUEIROS   FALORCA   ABRUNHOSA
DO MATO   RIO TORTO

AMOREIRA DA
GÂNDARA   FOGUEIRA
              SANGALHOS

NELAS   PASSARELA   GOUVEIA

CANAS DE SENHORIM   LAGARINHOS

MOGOFORES   FERREIROS

PINHANÇOS

SÃO LOURENÇO
DO BAIRRO   CURIA   ANADIA   CARREGAL DO SAL   OLIVEIRINHA
OIS DO BAIRRO   MATA DO BUSSACO   ARRIFANA

SEIA

CANTANHEDE   LUSO   MORTÁGUA   Rio Dão

Rio Mondego

MEALHADA

6 CORDINHÃ   Serra do Buçaco   TORRE

BARCOUÇO

AVÔ

Serra da Estrela

COIMBRA

PIODÃO

Serra da Lousã

FUNDÃO

▼ Visitable winery or food producer   DOC Bairrada
◆ Modern restaurant   DOC Beira Interior
● Traditional restaurant   DOC Dão
🏠 Wine/food shop/market   DOC Távora-Varosa
5   IPR Lafões
■ Sleep   VR Beiras
★ Star attraction

Rio Zêzere

E   F   G   H

Wine in the Beiras

BAIRRADA

Corn and eucalyptus may appear to be the main crop as you drive into sandy, hilly Bairrada. Then comes a flatter part, and suddenly the trees are easily outnumbered by vines grown in yellowish clay-based soils. *Barro* means 'clay', and is probably the origin of the region's name. The main grape here is the Baga, pronounced 'bugger', which is exactly what it can be. When it ripens, it can make some of Portugal's best reds, but all too often in Bairrada's maritime climate, it doesn't. Historically, good years come about three times a decade, not often enough to make a decent living.

This led, in 2003, to a radical change of the DOC rules. As recently as 1991, it had been confirmed that any Bairrada red or rosé had to have a minimum of 50% Baga. No foreign varieties were allowed, and of the three other 'recommended' black grapes, only one was capable of ripening better than Baga. The only bright spots were the inclusion of Preto Mortágua (aka Touriga Nacional) and Alfrocheiro among 'permitted' grapes. Business was bad. Tastes were changing, even within Portugal. The older generation wanted 'proper' red wines, and by 'proper', they meant with plenty of tannin. The frequently unripe tannins of Baga delivered that in abundance for the oldies, but younger Portuguese drinkers (and most of the world's export markets) didn't want to know. Some winemakers abandoned Bairrada, except for a small proportion of their production, and called their wines 'VR Beiras'. Finally it was decided that the DOC rules had to change. Now almost everything is allowed, and red Bairrada has two sets of rules. One allows Cabernet Sauvignon, Merlot, Syrah, Pinot Noir, various Portuguese grapes from other regions, as well as the old permitted Bairrada grapes (although Moreto has been discarded). The other sticks more or less to the old rules (Touriga Nacional and Alfrocheiro have been elevated to 'recommended'), and these wines can be called *'Clássico'*. But not all traditionalist producers choose to put *Clássico* on the label…

This means you have no idea what a bottle of red Bairrada will taste like unless it helps you by announcing grapes on front or back label. Does its producer belong to the traditionalist camp (no de-stemming, fermentation

> **Wine regions**
> DOC Bairrada
> DOC Dão
> DOC Távora-Varosa
> DOC Beira Interior
> IPR Lafões
> Vinho Regional Beiras
>
> **Main local grapes**
> *Red* Baga, Tinta Pinheira (Rufete), Jaen
> *White* Maria Gomes (Fernão Pires), Síria
> *For details of grapes see page 428*

Opposite An array of vine varieties at Campolargo, *page 170*

Left Traditional sparkling wine production

Right Autumn vines

Below New Borges vines in the Dão

DÃO

The cool, dry Dão region is bordered by granite mountains, Caramulo and Buçaco to the west, the ranges of Lapa, Leomil, Nave and Cascalheira to the north, and the Serra da Estrela to the east and south. Much of the DOC area climbs into the foothills of these ranges, and most of the soil is granite, or granite decomposed down to a coarse sand, with some schist in the south-west. Granite soil means high acidity. Higher vineyards mean cooler, slower ripening, and higher acidity. To a lover of wines worth cellaring, this is welcome news. But it does mean Dão wines are not easy to sell in large quantities – which is just as well, really, as the best are in short supply.

with natural yeasts in open *lagares*, ageing in old oak vats) or the modern (French varieties, de-stem, fermentation in closed stainless steel tanks, age in new oak)? Or somewhere in between? Or is it a modern Cabernet Merlot blend with some Touriga Nacional, from the likes of Carlos Campolargo? Or one of Luís Pato's silky Bagas, destemmed and aged in new oak? There are wonderful reds to be had in Bairrada, just a bewildering variety under the label.

The traditionalist camp tends to be advised by Rui Moura Alves, an oenologist who manages to coax extraordinarily complex, long-lived wines from Baga. In the good years, these are firm-tannined but splendid; in lesser ones, they are lean and take a while to be drinkable.

Bairrada is also a white wine region – indeed, some winemakers believe this is where its greatest potential lies. White rules have changed less, though Sauvignon Blanc, Pinot Blanc and Verdelho have crept onto the lists. The traditional combination of Arinto, Bical and Cercial makes wonderful, steely, long-lived wines, and for those with less cellar-space, a Maria Gomes and Chardonnay blend delivers appealingly fragrant and fruity youngsters.

Until the arrival of modern viticulture and winemaking and the new varieties, it was bubbles that buoyed up Bairrada's wine industry. As in France's Champagne region, high-acid, less-ripened grapes can make delightful fizz – even under-ripe Baga can find a home. Muscatty Maria Gomes is the young and frothy cheer leader. Arinto, Bical and Cercial, sometimes in blends with Chardonnay, can develop to steely, toasty maturity.

Much has changed for the better in Dão. The better grape varieties have grown in importance, and the co-operatives have lost their legal stranglehold on production. From the 1950s to the end of the 1980s, growers were allowed to deliver their grapes only to the newly-founded co-operatives, who had to receive everything, good and bad, and were hampered by a lack of modern equipment and knowledge. Only one family had the means to bottle its own wines, Casa de Santar, and a couple of Bairrada-

This is the only remaining IPR (DOC-in-waiting) on the Portuguese mainland, a small region squashed on the wine map between the south of Vinho Verde and the north of Dão. The rules for the Lafões wines (high acidity, low alcohol) and the grapes permitted (Arinto, Cercial, Sercial, Azal Tinto etc) are far more akin to Vinho Verde than to Dão. The region's request to be included in Vinho Verde was rebuffed some time ago. We have never seen any Lafões wines outside the region, and are not convinced that they will make it to DOC.

based merchants, Caves São João and Aliança, somehow managed to continue to sell good Dão wines, bought and blended from the co-ops. The historic reputation of Dão as one of Portugal's highest-quality wine regions was almost shattered.

These restrictions were lifted four years after Portugal joined the European Community in 1986. Sogrape immediately bought an estate, and built a modern winery. Other companies have followed. And many growers have stopped sending their grapes to the co-ops and started making and bottling their own wines. There is now a big divide between growers who sell grapes and those who

make wine. The grape-sellers grow Tinta Roriz and Jaen at high yields; nearly two-thirds deliver to co-ops, a third to big companies. The winemakers grow at least half Touriga Nacional, a fine and lower-yielding variety that can make top wines either by itself or with other good grapes such as Alfrocheiro or Tinta Roriz. Up to the end of the 1990s, there was a lot of Baga in Dão, standing little chance of ripening. Much has been replanted, but some still feeds into the co-ops. In Dão, Touriga Nacional and Alfrocheiro can perform at their very best, making reds of character and intensity, with wonderful perfume and substantial tannins, and always with fresh acidity.

There are good white wines, too. Encruzado is the lead player, supported mainly by Bical, Malvasia Fina and Cercial. But only in the cool vineyards around Tondela are there more white grapes than red.

You can drive for kilometres in the Dão region, often through forest, without seeing a vineyard. Less than 20,000ha are planted with vines in the Dão DOC region, around five per cent of the 386,000ha theoretically available for plantation. Dão wines are losing ground to the easier pleasures of wines from regions such as the Douro and the Alentejo – and that is ironic when the wines of Dão have never been better.

Opposite and left Rock-strewn, mountainous vineyards in the Beira Interior

Right New barrels, new attitudes – there is huge potential to make fine wine in the Beira Interior

TÁVORA-VAROSA

In the mountains to the north-east of Dão, Távora-Varosa's vines (only 4% of the Beiras' total vineyard area) are planted at an average altitude of 550m – perfect cool conditions for growing grapes for sparkling wine grapes. Much of the vintage pops over the 'border' to nearby Lamego (in the Douro chapter), to be made into sparkling wine by Raposeira, the largest fizz producer in Portugal. Half the grapes in the older vineyards are Malvasia Fina, with increasing amounts of Chardonnay and Pinot Noir, both imported almost a century ago. With an admiring eye on the fine Douro reds just to the north, growers have also been planting red varieties for still wines, especially (and probably misguidedly) Touriga Franca, a notoriously late-ripening variety. Soils here are mostly schistous slate like the Douro, or granite, but Távora-Varosa does not have the Douro's ripening power.

BEIRA INTERIOR

Much more mountainous than their western neighbour Dão, the Beira Interior wine areas cover a vast swathe of inland Portugal that includes the Serra da Marofa just south of the Douro region, the eastern slopes of the Serra da Estrela, the Serra da Gardunha, and all the mountains that form a natural border with Spain. Most of those mountains are granite; granite walls border roads, the older houses are built of granite blocks, and vast granite boulders break through the surface of the sparsely-covered fields. Even when you're obviously in a valley, the altitude is probably around 300m.

All this height and granite has its effect on Beira Interior wines. Soil is poor, acidities are high, and alcohol levels can rise as diligent growers wait for tannins to ripen. Many growers do not wait, the co-ops receive unripe grapes, and some are seriously struggling as international wine prices dip. But the potential to produce exciting wines is enormous. Today, Beira Interior is roughly where the rest of Portugal was ten years ago. A few producers (including some co-ops) have taken up modern ways in vineyard and cellar, and they are already outperforming the rest. In the north, the Douro grape varieties have travelled down the Côa valley to dominate vineyards, but in the Beira Interior they are more difficult to ripen. There has been a lot of replanting of vineyards in the southerly Cova da Beira sub-region, and grape quality there is hugely improved. And the area has its own homegrown star, the white grape, Fonte Cal.

163

AMOREIRA DA GÂNDARA E7

Filipa Pato

It's never easy to follow in a famous father's footsteps, in the same line of business, but Filipa Pato has managed it. With a background in chemistry, she worked in wineries in Bordeaux and Argentina before coming home to Portugal. Here she set about identifying the most important factors (grape variety, soil, sunlight, landscape, vine age, pruning...) determining the finished wine. She calls some of her wines 'Ensaios FP' (Filipa Pato's experiments). She is very keen on blends, particularly of wines from the two DOC regions, Bairrada and Dão. In the old days, it was rare that both regions would have good harvests in the same year, so the locals would blend between the two. Likewise, when making sparkling wines, Filipa prefers a blend of white and red grapes.

She uses only Portuguese grapes, and ferments some reds in small, open-topped oak vats, some in stainless steel. Whites are fermented in stainless steel and used oak barrels. The blends for the Ensaios wines vary from year to year (depending

on which region has had a good harvest!). In the best years she makes wines from specific regions, sometimes from single vineyards, which she calls 'Lokal', naming the soil type. So there is 'Lokal Silex' (from flinty soil in Dão) and 'Lokal Calcário' (from the chalky-clay soil of Bairrada). Her latest idea, in association with her father, Luís Pato, is a sweet white, which has qualified as Bairrada. She picked up the idea of using cryoextraction (freezing the grapes to eliminate water content to make sweet wine) whilst doing a vintage at Leeuwin Estate in Western Australia.

The **3b FP Baga Bical Espumante Bruto** is very pale pink, the Baga fermented in used barrels, the Bical in steel, then bottle-fermented. It's a fresh, crisp and creamy fizz, with red fruit flavours. The 2005 **Ensaios FP Branco** is half and half Arinto and Bical, half steel-fermented, and half oak, crisp, lemony and mineral, elegant but accessible. The 2005 **Ensaios FP Tinto** is a blend of Alfrocheiro, Touriga Nacional and Baga, from Dão and Bairrada, full of bright red fruit, with brisk acid and tannins. 2003 **Lokal Calcário Baga** is old-vine Baga, ripe, rich and savoury, with dark fruit, smooth tannins, length and harmony. 2005 **Lokal Calcário Silex** is Touriga Nacional (softened in less ripe years with a little Alfrocheiro), rich and aromatic, with dense, firm tannins and bright raspberry and herb flavours. The new **FLP Bairrada** sweet wine is Sercialinho, Cercial and Maria Gomes, minus some of its water content, steel-fermented to give a sprightly, citrussy, honeyed wine.
Ribeiro da Gândara,
*   3780-017 Amoreira da Gândara*
T +351 231 596 432 / 961 736 945
E filipa@filipapato.net
W www.filipapato.net
Visits appt only
€ variable

Luís Pato To say that Luís Pato has single-handedly forced Bairrada to come to terms with modern winemaking techniques and the world outside its boundaries would be an exaggeration – but not by much. There are other good companies who have made and continue to make good wine in the region, but Luís Pato has been a one-man revolutionary army for at least the last 20 years. Throughout his skirmishes with the authorities, he has continued to make good wine, often bending local rules to a point at which they have later snapped. He is a duck (*pato*, in Portuguese) that walks by himself, whether it's discussing the suitability of new oak for ageing reds, Cabernet Sauvignon as a permitted grape variety, or experimenting with cryoextraction. If you meet him on your visit, in cooler weather he'll probably be wearing his leather jacket ('still a rebel'), and relishes his position as the dissenter of the region. A few years ago, he decided not to submit his wines for approval as Bairradas, but to bottle them instead as VR Beiras, under its much more flexible rules.

He always has a new project to discuss. First came his new winery and reception centre, then the possibility of making a Portuguese wine blended from grapes of different regions, planting a vineyard in Brazil, a new 'Anti-Port' at ten per cent alcohol – a port-like 2008 wine made with concentrated juice; he has all kinds of new ideas for sparkling wines, and is still working on the way forward for red wines

(unoaked and lower alcohol). Having led the way with plantations of French varieties in the region, he has now renounced them, and returned to the natives in his vineyards. Meanwhile, partly thanks to Luís Pato's battles, other Bairrada producers frolic among foreign grapes.

His sparkling wines are very good. Indeed he is beginning to specialise in sparkling, grafting vines over to white varieties and installing new equipment. The **Luís Pato Bruto Maria Gomes** is fresh, light and modern, with a whiff of muscatty fragrance. In 2007 he added a strawberry-fruity **Touriga Nacional** pink fizz. **Luís Pato Casta Baga** is a lovely, dry summer rosé fizz, with gentle red fruit flavours, and the **Luís Pato Vintage Bruto** is toastily complex. From the 2008 vintage, for Christmas 2009, there will be a new single vineyard sparkling wine, mostly Touriga Nacional from the Vinha Formal vineyard, partly fermented in new oak. This will be a *Bairrada* – 'to show what I defended'.

For still wines, Luís has returned to his and Bairrada's roots, Baga for his best 'chalky-clay' vineyards (43ha out of his total 65ha), Touriga Nacional and whites for the sandier others (from which he makes excellent whites and bubbly). And one small vineyard is literally on its roots, a patch of Baga planted direct into sandy soil, not grafted onto rootstock. So far the phylloxera bug has not attacked…

For the majority of his wines, he is reluctant to return into the official Bairrada fold. It is paradoxical that a producer who makes some of the best of the new-wave *clássico* reds in the Bairrada region should not bottle under the Bairrada label, but as VR Beiras. When the local authorities attempted to woo him back, his first

concession, in typical Pato fashion, was to cooperate with his daughter, Filipa, on **FLP**, a wine they have labelled Bairrada, but made in a style historically unfamiliar to Bairrada: a sweet white!

His still rosé, the **Luís Pato Rosé**, is made from Baga, raspberry-fruited, fragrant and creamy. His most serious white, the **Luís Pato Vinha Formal**, is Bical fermented in new oak, rich, oaky and citrussy when young, and softening to steely lemon and greengage as it ages (which it does very well). **João Pato Tinto** is the young, fresh, unoaked red, made of Touriga Nacional, with soft tannins and lovely raspberry fruit. **Trepa** is a new creation, a rich, sinewy blend of Tinto Roriz (TR) from the Douro and Baga from Luís' Vinha Pan, in Bairrada (PA). The **Vinhas Velhas Tinto** is pure Baga, with intense raspberry perfume and soft tannins. **Vinha Pan** is dark and intense, with raspberry and damson flavours, high acidity and firm tannins. **Vinha Barrosa** is dense and fragrant, dark and austere, but lifted by its wonderful fragrance. **Quinta do Ribeirinho Baga Pé Franco** is immense, with sweet, intense raspberry fruit and huge concentration. *Ribeiro da Gândara, 3780-017 Amoreira da Gândara T+351 231 596 432 E contacto@luispato.com W www.luispato.com Visits Mon-Sun appt only €10*

CANTANHEDE E6
Adega Cooperativa de Cantanhede
After a shaky start in 1954, when the co-op found it difficult to persuade growers to join in large numbers, membership has increased from the original 100 to the current 1,400, now farming 1,200ha. This makes it the largest producer of Bairrada DOC wine (which accounts for 60% of the co-op's production). The

winemaker, Frederico Gomes, feels that Bairrada is a region for white and sparkling wines, with excellent quality grapes even if cultivation techniques are very basic. He also thinks the future for under-ripe Baga (of which he sees a great deal) is in sparkling wine. An experimental 2000 Baga bubbly he showed us was rich and savoury, with real character and life.

The Cantanhede co-op also makes good reds. A vertical tasting on our last visit showed that the top reds, even from the first bottled vintages of 1962, 1963 and 1964, are wines of longevity, richness and subtlety. The top reds from Cantanhede undoubtedly contributed to the award of DOC status to Bairrada in 1978.

The white **Cantanhede Bairrada Bical** is bright, crisp and fresh, with a pleasing aroma and good acidity. The top reds, are also very good, the **Marquês de Marialva Baga Reserva** firm-tannined, with rich, berry fruit under the tannin in cooler vintages, rich and fleshy in better ones.

Visits are to the winery, their little wine museum, tasting room and the shop, theoretically free, but it would be a pity not to taste anything, and that will cost €3. *Apartado 4, 3064-909 Cantanhede T+351 031 419 540 E visitors@cantanhede.com W www.cantanhede.com Visits Mon-Fri 9.30-12, 2-5.30 Closed Sep (appt only, 1 week in advance) €3*

CORDINHÃ E6
Quinta de Baixo Eye surgeon João Alberto Póvoa owns this 12ha estate about 5km east of Cantanhede, and makes wines in a traditional, foot-trodden, *lagar*-fermented style. He started bottling the wine in 1990, and takes winemaking

advice from Rui Alves, as do several others of Bairrada's best producers. A 7ha section of the vineyards is new and densely planted, other vines are old. The **Quinta de Baixo Tinto** blend of Baga with 30% Touriga Nacional is rich, ripe and intense, with lots of tannins, but loads of flavour. **Quinta de Baixo Reserva Tinto** has very sweet, ripe fruit, with smoky, inky intensity. **Quinta de Baixo Grande Escolha Tinto** has the 30% Touriga Nacional again, with very high tannins but lots of ripe, dense flavours. The **Quinta de Baixo Garrafeira Tinto**, made just from the old vines, is huge, with very high tannins and alcohol balanced by good acidity. It has concentrated, chewy fruit. These are uncompromising wines that require a lot of patience.
Cordinhã, 3064-909 Cantanhede
T+351 231 429 264
E quinta.baixo@netc.pt
Visits appt only

FERREIROS F6
Caves do Solar do São Domingos

Sparkling wine was what this company started with in 1937, and fizz still forms an important part of their production. It's the sparkling wine cellars that are the principal attraction for the annual 5,000 to 6,000 visitors. But that's not all they make. Caves São Domingos control the production from over 100ha of vineyard in Bairrada, and make red and white Bairrada as well. (They also sell Dão wine made for them in the Dão region.) They overhauled the vineyard and winemaking team in 2004, and modernised their winemaking facilities in 2006. The **São Domingos Bairrada Branco Bruto** is a blend of Bical, Maria Gomes and Arinto, bright, crisp and lemony. **São Domingos Bairrada Prestígio Branco Bruto**, half oak-fermented, is mineral, crisp and creamy, with bready

flavours. **São Domingos Grande Escolha** is a VR Beiras, a blend of Dão and Bairrada, Touriga Nacional, Baga and Tinta Roriz, dense, austere and with high tannins. **Quinta de São Lourenço Bairrada** is a Baga/Touriga Nacional blend, a traditional, high-tannin red with ripe red fruit aromas. **Lopo de Freitas** is named after the company's owner (for the last 40 years) and made only in the best years. It's modern Bairrada, with Baga, Touriga Nacional, Syrah and Cabernet in the blend, rich, dense and fruity, with firm tannins and lots of oak.
Apartado 16, 3781-907 Anadia
T+351 231 512 068
E efreitas@cavessaodomingos.com
W www.cavessaodomingos.com
Visits Mon-Fri 11-3 Sat appt only

FOGUEIRA E7
Quinta das Bágeiras Mário Sérgio Alves Nuno *(on left of picture, with Rui Moura Alves)* progressed from winning second prize in Portugal's Young Farmer of the Year competition in 1989, and second prize again in 1991, to winning Portugal's Farmer of the Year in 2004. He had started working with his father and mother in 1989 on the family vineyards, bottling the 1987 red as his first effort (it won a prize). The project which won the prize in 1991 was for the construction of a cellar to make sparkling wine (at that stage no new cellar had been built in the region for 20 years). The next step is to be a shop and tasting room, which should be finished by the time this book is published. Nuno is a very friendly and likeable producer, justifiably proud of his success, and happy to admit the part played in it by his winemaking consultant, Rui Alves.

Of his production, 40% is red, a little is white and the largest part is sparkling wine. He has 28ha, including some very old vines, both red and white. Winemaking is traditional: fermentation in concrete *lagares* for the reds without destemming, hand-plunged with wooden *macacos*, aged in big oak vats, no new oak. He uses small *lagares* to settle the solids for the whites and sparkling wines.

The **Quinta das Bágeiras Branco Garrafeira** is made from old vines, half Bical, half Maria Gomes, oak vat-fermented, aged on the lees through the winter, then for another year or so in the vat. It's rich and full-bodied, with a lovely, creamy feel and high acidity. There are notes of greengage and pine, length and balance. The sparkling wines are white grapes only, 60% Maria Gomes, 40% Bical. The **Quinta das Bágeiras Super Reserva Bruto Natural** is steel-fermented and has 30 months on the lees. It emerges restrained and delicate, with rich, citrus and mineral character, and high acidity. The **Quinta das Bágeiras Grande Reserva** has five years on the lees, high acidity and greengage fruit, and a chocolatey, creamy, minerality. **Quinta das Bágeiras Tinto Reserva** has 20% of Touriga Nacional in with the Baga, and lovely, bright, cherry fruit and herby, aromatic Touriga character. **Quinta das Bágeiras Tinto Garrafeira** is made from vines nearly 100 years old, rich, intense and voluptuous, with high but supple tannins, and intense, cherry and damson fruit.

Nuno is happy to receive visitors, but only by appointment. He can show you

the vineyard and winery and give you a tasting, and all for free. Then he'll sell you a bottle or two in his new shop.
Fogueira, 3780-523 Sangalhos
T+351 234 742 102
E quintadasbageiras@mail.telepac.pt
Visits appt only

MEALHADA E6

Caves Messias If you happen to meet one of the members of the families who own Caves Messias, don't be surprised if you're handed a business card saying that their name is Messias. Not their family name, their first name. It's a tradition in the family to call at least one of their sons by the name of the founder, Messias. His family name was Baptista, and his direct descendants still hold some of the company's shares; as do another branch, the Vigário family. So far, four generations of the family have worked in the business.

Messias is a large company, that produces and sells wine from all over Portugal. They own estates in Bairrada, Dão and the Douro, and also sell wine from Vinho Verde and the Terras do Sado; and they make sparkling wine and brandy. Of the seven million bottles produced each year, three-quarters are exported, mainly to Brazil.

The cellars are easy to find, right beside the pale yellow Cine-Teatro Messias, off Mealhada's main street. They have a well-practised visitor reception, and will show you the winery and give you a free tasting of their sparkling wine. It's a big and impressive winery, with lots of stainless steel tanks (and some cement ones), a bottle maturation cellar underground, and the sparkling wine cellar at an even lower level. Here they still do *remuage* (the shaking and twisting of the bottles to get the yeast deposit into the neck) by hand, although, as we were told, the four workers

who specialise in this are ageing, and they may have to invest in machines before long.

Messias use canopy management and limit yields in their vineyards to get the results they want. They have also experimented with the grapes they grow in their Bairrada vineyard, Quinta de Valdoeiro. This was originally bought in the 1940s, and has grown by acquisition to its present size of 130ha, 70ha of which are vines. In 1985, they started replanting the vines, with Arinto, Bical, Cercial, Chardonnay and Castelão, later adding Baga and Cabernet Sauvignon. Replanting continued in 1994, with Touriga Nacional and Syrah. Now they reckon they have the right blend for the white Valdoeiro, of Arinto, Bical and Chardonnay. They also bottle a pure Chardonnay, half barrel-fermented, sold only to the Algarve, mostly to British visitors! They make wines from all the red varieties, sometimes as single grapes, sometimes as blends.

The estate in Dão, Quinta do Perredo, is a more recent purchase, bought in 1998, with 20ha of vines. Here Messias have added Touriga Nacional and Alfrocheiro to the grape mix, and have started to use them in the estate's wine (only red). Messias also have an estate in the Douro, Quinta do Cachão, with 110ha of vines, and a lodge in Gaia (*page 136*).

Quinta do Valdoeiro Bairrada Chardonnay is creamy and nicely bready, with fresh acidity. **Quinta do Valdoeiro Bairrada Branco**, with the addition of Arinto and Bical, and less oak flavour, has a good balance between honeyed flavour and crisp minerality. **Quinta do Valdoeiro Bairrada Tinto** has bright raspberry fruit, dense tannins and intensity. **Quinta do Valdoeiro Bairrada Reserva**, half Baga, a

third Touriga Nacional, and the rest Syrah and Cabernet, is definitely a new-style Bairrada, rich, ripe and raspberry-jammy, with firm tannins, good acidity, intensity and length. **Quinta do Perredo Dão** is another modern red, one-third each of Touriga Nacional, Alfrocheiro and Jaen, with lovely damson perfume, smooth tannins, and seductive fruit length. Best of the Messias sparklers is the **Quinta do Valdoeiro Bruto Chardonnay Baga** a faint pink in colour, with lovely aromas of red fruits and chocolate, rich, full-bodied bubbly.
Rua Comendador Messias Baptista 56,
*   3050-361 Mealhada*
T+351 231 200 970
E mail@cavesmessias.pt
W www.cavesmessias.pt
Visits Mon-Fri 11-3 Closed Aug

OLIVEIRA DO BAIRRO E7

Artwine Albano Melo started Maposer in 2002, and changed the name to Artwine in 2006. He has a 5ha estate in Bairrada, and also buys grapes in from other producers. The first year of production was 2003, but the Blaudus wines were not made until the next year. The red wines are foot-crushed and fermented in open wooden *lagares*, but with the stalks removed, so not totally traditional. **Blaudus Espumante Reserva Bruto** is a blend of Arinto, Bical and Maria Gomes, crisp, honeyed and refreshing. Our favourite red is **Blaudus Touriga Nacional Bairrada**, a lovely, herby, aromatic expression of Touriga Nacional, with high tannins and good acidity.
Rua do Bairro Novo,
*   3770-218 Oliveira do Bairro*
T+351 914 217 649
E geral@artwine.pt
W www.artwine.pt
Visits Mon-Fri 10-7 appt only

Caves Aliança Founded in 1927, Aliança is one of the largest wine producers in Portugal, and a member of the G7 group *(page 20)*. It was originally started by an alliance between 11 partners (thus the name – Aliança), and its holdings have grown impressively over its 80 years. In April 2007, the financier Joe Berardo announced he was buying a majority share in the company.

From its base in Bairrada, Aliança has built up a portfolio of branded wines covering most of Portugal. The latest strategy has been to add a range of estates in winemaking regions, use them as regional bases for vinification, and produce a range of top-quality wines from each of them. This has resulted in over 400ha of vineyards, with large estates in the Alentejo, Dão and Douro, as well as in Bairrada. In order to achieve the desired quality, they enlisted the help of Bordeaux oenologists, first Michel Rolland, then (and still) Pascal Chatonnet.

Their most recently-bought estate, Herdade do Barranco, in the Redondo sub-region of the Alentejo, has 50ha of vines at the moment, planted in 2001, but there could be 120ha one day. Quinta da Terrugem is the other Alentejo vineyard, of 60ha near Borba (with less possibility of expansion) and close to the marble quarries (hence the brand 'Alabastro').

Quinta dos Quatro Ventos is the Douro estate, with 45ha of vines, some of them mixed plantings of *vinhas velhas*. Quinta d'Aguiar is out by the Spanish border in the Beira Interior, with 90ha of vines planted in 1999. Closer to home, Quinta da Garrida is Aliança's Dão estate, with 112ha of fairly recently planted vines. And, in Bairrada itself, Quinta das Bacheladas has 5ha and Quinta da Rigodeira 27ha.

Aliança is used to receiving visitors, and offers free tours round the sparkling wine cellar and the brandy store, and a glass of fizz afterwards. If you want a more extensive tasting, give them some notice, and they'll arrange it. The cost will depend on what you want to taste. And they have a wine shop with all their wines available to buy.

Aliança's range is huge, so this is a selection of our favourites. **Galeria Bairrada White** is made from Bical with a tiny amount of barrel-fermentation, lean, honeyed and mineral. **Quinta da Garrida Dão Tinto** has lovely red fruit flavours, with a sweet perfume and firm tannins. The **Quinta da Garrida Dão Reserva** is pure Touriga Nacional, beautifully aromatic, with elegant herby flavour, fresh acidity and firm tannins. **Casa d'Aguiar Tinto** is pure Touriga Nacional as well, with bright, floral perfume, high acidity and ripe, plummy fruit. **Quinta da Rigodeira**

Bairrada Baga has very firm but smooth tannins, and lots of honeyed, malty flavour. **Quinta da Baceladas Bairrada** makes a very different wine, in the modern style, from Merlot and Cabernet Sauvignon, fresh and grassy, with good blackcurrant fruit. **Quinta da Dôna Bairrada** is Baga with some Touriga Nacional, dark and cedary, with malty intensity. **Quinta dos Quatro Ventos Douro Tinto** is smooth and dark-fruited, with black fruit and treacle flavours, and lovely length. **Quinta dos Quatro Ventos Douro Reserva Tinto** is one of the top wines, quite reserved, with bright, ripe black fruit flavours and smooth tannins. **Quinta da Terrugem Alentejo Tinto** has soft, sweet-fruited flavours, with easy tannins. **T Quinta da Terrugem Alentejo Tinto** is another of their top wines, sweet-fruited, ripe and appealing.

Rua do Comércio, Apartado 6,
3781-908 Sangalhos
T +351 234 732 000
E luciana.sardo@caves-alianca.pt
W www.caves-alianca.pt
Visits Mon-Sat 10.30, 11.30, 2.30, 3.30,
4.30 Closed Sun, public hols
Wine shop 10:30-1, 2-6.30

Caves do Freixo An unusual company to find in this selection as they make no wine themselves, neither have they any vineyards. But they do sell good wines. How? The owners of the company, set up in 2001 in a cellar that used to be called Caves Império, employed Rui Moura Alves to hunt down good wines and blend them (if necessary). The brief was to find traditional wines, fermented in *lagares*, with natural yeasts. Just the sort of wine Rui has most time for. He sources similar wines from producers in Dão and the Douro also, which we have not yet tasted. But we have tasted the two Bairrada reds.

The **Império Bairrada Colheita Tinto** comes from three small Bairrada producers, and has malty, rich aromas, high acidity, ripe tannins, and dark, savoury fruit. The **Império Bairrada Reserva Tinto** comes from one grower, whose vines are 45 years old. It's rich and dark, with a faint aroma of tobacco, with richer fruit than the other, but also more tannins and acidity. It needs time. Visits to this company are free, but you must make an appointment.

Rua do Comércio Apartado 115,
3781-908 Sangalhos
T+351 234 730 730
E cavesdofreixo@netvisao.pt
W www.cavesdofreixo.com
Visits Mon-Fri 9-5 appt only Closed Aug

Casa de Saima One of the standard-bearers for the red wines of Bairrada. Graça Maria da Silva Miranda coaxes the best out of her 18ha of vineyards, with the help of the high priest of Bairrada Baga, Rui Moura Alves. Most of the vines are Baga, including 4ha of 70 year old vines (which she uses for her Garrafeira). The white (Maria Gomes, Bical and Cerceal) and rosé (Baga and Touriga Nacional) are steel-fermented, and have no oak maturation. Her best wines are undoubtedly her reds, foot-trodden and fermented with the stalks in *lagares*, then aged in big old oak vats. In hot years such as 2003, the reds are lovely to drink young, though they will keep, too. In cooler years (2002, for instance), they are uncompromising at the start, and need patience, trust and ten years in the cellar.

The **Casa de Saima Reserva Bairrada Tinto** had about one-third Touriga Nacional with the Baga, which adds an aromatic, herby character to the austere Baga fruit. Tannins are well-managed, soft and supportive. **Casa de Saima Garrafeira**

Bairrada Tinto is the really outstanding red, made from the old vines, and pure Baga. It's dark and intense, with high, ripe tannins, and settles down after a few years in bottle to cedary, smoky elegance, kept going by the tannins and high acidity.
Apartado 64, 3781-908 Sangalhos
T+351 234 743 278 / 962 724 499
E gmiranda@iol.pt
Visits Mon-Fri (appt only) Closed Jul-Sep

Sidónio de Sousa Another of Bairrada's small, high-quality producers. Dulcinea Ferreira's father used to deliver the grapes from his small vineyard to the Mogofores co-op. When Sidónio de Sousa and Dulcinea took the estate on, they bought more vineyards and started bottling the wine. Their first bottling won prizes both locally and nationally, and they have built a reputation from there. At present, they have 11ha of vines at Ancas, and 1ha at Sangalhos, and would like a few more. Most of the vines are Baga, with a few Bical and Maria Gomes vines in the old vineyards. There are 2ha of these, nearly 100 years old. The rest are only ten years old. The white grapes go into the production of sparkling wine, most of which, however, is red. De Sousa thinks he may be the only serious producer who sells more red sparkling wine than white! Most of the production is red Bairrada, made from Baga, with a little Merlot he's trialling. Grapes are *lagar*-fermented, and the winemaking consultant is Rui Alves.

The **Sidónio de Sousa Espumante** is crisp, honeyed and citrussy, with lean, dry, powerful flavours. The red fizz, **Sidónia de Sousa Super Reserva Tinto Bruto**, is fascinating, with malty, savoury flavour and firm tannins. It's great with suckling pig. Best of the reds is the **Sidónio de Sousa Bairrada Garrafeira**, made from 90 year old Baga vines, rich, savoury and

malty, with very firm but ripe tannins and lots of smoky intensity. A wine that needs patience, but worth waiting for.
Largo da Vila, 3780-128 Sangalhos
T+351 234 746 121
E vinhos.sidonio@clix.pt
Visits Mon-Sat 10-7 appt only

SÃO JOÃO DA AZENHA

Caves São João Seemingly endless underground tunnels of wine-bins are stacked high with bottles – Caves São João may well hold the largest stock of old unfortified wine in Portugal. And it's good wine. The company is still owned and run by the Costa family, who founded the business in 1920. The brothers José, Manuel and Albano Costa began trading in Douro wines, then Bairrada, still and sparkling, eventually creating the Frei João Bairrada and Porta dos Cavalheiros Dão brands. Brothers Luís and Alberto Costa were in charge when we went 20 years ago, now it's Maria José Palma and her

sister, Maria Gabriel Abrantes, with Luís's son, Manuel José Costa. The company has never owned much land, and has made wonderful wines by buying grapes and wines from local producers. In Bairrada, they buy from growers who farm about 60ha of land; about 40% comes in as wine, the rest as grapes. In Dão, they have to buy it all as wine, as they are not allowed to make and bottle Dão outside the DOC region. But they have a special relationship with one particular Dão estate, who

produce wine under their supervision.

And they do own a Bairrada estate, Quinta do Poço do Lobo, 35ha, bought in 1972. They planted 25ha with vines, but were more adventurous than Bairrada rules allowed in those days. Their grape mix was Baga, Cabernet Sauvignon, Castelão, Arinto and Chardonnay, with Touriga Nacional added in the 1990s, and a little Merlot and Semillon. Up until 2003, the fermentations of the reds were in epoxy-lined concrete vats, but then stainless steel *lagares* and closed steel tanks (both with pneumatic plungers) and rotating steel vats were added. All the basic reds have at least three months in the cellar before release, the *reservas* between one and two years.

They believe that Bairrada has the conditions to make the best white wines in Portugal, and their old whites certainly prove that Bairrada whites can age. They're good young, too, as proved by the crisp, lemon and honey flavours of the **Frei João Branco Bairrada**. As for older whites, we tasted a magnificent **1974 Frei João Branco Reserva**, elegant and creamy, with lovely lemon and floral fragrance. The young **Frei João Tinto** is half Baga, a third Castelão and the rest Touriga Nacional, savoury and malty, with a lovely strawberry, figgy perfume. The old Frei João red *reservas* are vigorous and fragrant, and the latest release **Frei João Reserva Bairrada** is even better, with sweet, intense fruit, bright acidity, firm tannins and herby, vigorous flavours. **Quinta do Poço do Lobo Cabernet**

Sauvignon is a rich, blackcurrant and oak giant, and needs a while in the cellar to soften the very firm tannins.

Caves São João Reserva is a VR Beiras red that makes the transition from Bairrada to Dão, half Baga, with equal parts of Touriga Nacional and Alfrocheiro, and 10% Cabernet Sauvignon, with rich, ripe, strawberry-scented fruit, a hint of herby Touriga, and firm tannins. Then it's into Dão, with the **Porta dos Cavalheiros Reserva Branco** wines amazingly long-lived, like their Bairrada cousins. The young **Porta dos Cavalheiros Reserva Tinto**, equal measures of Touriga Nacional, Tinta Roriz and Alfrocheiro, and a touch of Jaen, is rich and sweet-fruited, with a lovely balance between herby Touriga and strawberry Alfrocheiro, and firm, ripe tannins. The older red *reservas* are elegant and cedary, with firm tannins and high acidity that have kept them alive.

You'll have to pay €5 extra to visit at the weekend, and make an appointment. We'd recommend you go on a weekday, and think about putting what you save towards an old bottle.
São João da Azenha,
   3781-901 Avelãs de Caminho
T +351 234 743 118
E cavessaojoao@mail.telepac.pt
W www.cavessaojoao.pt
Visits 9-6 Sat, Sun appt only
€7.50 Sat & Sun €12.50

São Lourenço do Bairro E6
Campolargo We're not sure if the 110ha vineyard outside Carlos Campolargo's winery is the largest singly-owned vineyard in Bairrada, but if you add this and another 70ha at Quinta do Valle d'Azar, he is probably the largest single grower in

Bairrada. He is emphatically an exponent of Bairrada's new-wave wines, with a bewildering variety of grapes in his vineyards: Baga, Alicante Bouschet, Castelão Nacional, Sousão, Tinta Roriz, Tinta Francisca, Touriga Nacional, Cabernet Sauvignon, Merlot, Petit Verdot, Pinot Noir and Syrah among reds, and Arinto, Bical, Sercial, Sauvignon Blanc and Viognier for whites. Recent plantings in the vineyards have been of white varieties, as Campolargo sees a good future for Bairrada whites.

Although he's a lawyer by profession, Carlos Campolargo is the third generation in a line of winemakers. His father was the one who enlarged the vineyards, starting in the late 1960s. He stopped making wine in the 1990s, and was selling his grapes, mainly to Aliança. Carlos started again in 2000, and built the new winery in 2004. It's a fine building, with a roof covered with nine truckloads of Tagus stones and a lot of rainwater (we hope it springs no leaks). Everything inside is modern and high-tech, with a little stainless steel *lagar* installed because the quantity of Petit Verdot was too small for vats. Now there's enough Petit Verdot for a vat, but he still uses the little *lagar*, because he likes the results.

He wants to find a partner to open a restaurant in the winery, and he intends to build seven rooms. The idea is a small hotel, perhaps more a restaurant with rooms. Meanwhile, he is happy to receive

Bairrada – Wine in the *Beiras*

visitors, and would prefer people to make an appointment. You'll get a tour of estate and winery, and a tasting, and what you pay will depend on what you taste. And there is a lot to taste. His **Borga Bruto** is a blend of Chardonnay and Pinot Noir, amazingly Champagne-like, with notes of

cream, chocolate and red fruits, and bready richness. The **Arinto Madeira Branco** is oaky but well-balanced, with minerality and greengage fruit. The **Campolargo Tinto** is pure Pinot Noir, stylish and quite delicate, with savoury, red fruit flavours. **Magnabaga** (big Baga) has austere, curranty aromas, high tannins and acidity, and rich, baked fruit. **Vinha da Costa** is his Syrah blend (with Tinta Roriz and Merlot), elegant and savoury, with good tannins and red fruit flavours. There is an interesting pair of **Termeão** wines. The label with the white bird in the tree is the second wine, mostly Touriga, with herby, aromatic immediacy, and the red bird label is the top wine, much oakier, but with lovely raspberry and herb length. **Contra a Corrente** is 80% Cabernet and the rest Castelão, smooth and blackcurranty. **Campolargo CC** is half and half Castelão and Cabernet, deep, cedary and ripe, with elegance and perfume. **Valdazar** is sweet, perfumed and easy, with sweet fruit and good structure. **Diga?** is the Petit Verdot,

dark and earthy, with floral perfume.
Malaposta, 3780-294 Anadia
T+351 231 512 383
E geral@campolargovinhos.com
W www.campolargovinhos.com
Visits Mon-Fri 9-1, 2.30-6.30 appt
*   preferred*
€ variable

Colinas de São Lourenço Or San Lorenzo Hills, to give it its export name. This is another of the modern wineries built on the outskirts of São Lourenço do Bairro, owned by Silvio Cerdeira, for 21 years the mayor of Anadia. He had other businesses, including ceramics, but invested in vineyards when he retired, starting with 10ha. Now the company has 62ha, and is aiming for 80ha. It's another company that has embraced the new Bairrada rules wholeheartedly, with about a third of the vineyard planted with French grapes. But there are plenty of Portuguese grapes as well: Baga, Touriga Nacional, Tinta Barroca, Alfrocheiro, Jaen, Bastardo, Tinta Roriz, Arinto and Bical, and Merlot, Syrah, Cabernet Sauvignon, Pinot Noir (two clones, one for sparkling wine), Chardonnay and Sauvignon Blanc. There are also a couple of hectares of old mixed vines. The winery is immaculate, with a vibrating sorting belt, pneumatic plunging tanks, 'flying' vats on hoists to perform the 'rack and return' (délestage in French) method of straining off fermenting juice then pouring it back on top of the cap of skins and pips, and all sorts of different fermenting vats. The company still sells grapes to other companies for sparkling wines, as they

haven't yet got their own fizz production going. But they will one day.

The **Colinas de São Lourenço Chardonnay Arinto Bairrada** is partly oak-fermented, but that doesn't dominate its pleasant, light, honeyed, faintly mineral flavours. The **Colinas de São Lourenço Pinot Noir Touriga Nacional Bairrada Rosé** is creamy and pleasant, just off-dry. The **Colinas de São Lourenço Private Collection Bairrada Tinto** is the top red, made with different blends depending on the vintage, but so far with Baga as a major component, rich and sumptuous, with smooth tannins and lovely perfume.

Visits to the winery and vineyard are free, but if you want to taste, that will cost €7.
Rua Principal, 3780-312 São Lourenço
T+351 231 528 312
E colinaslourenco@mail.telepac.pt
W www.sanlorenzohills.com
Visits Mon-Fri 9-7
€7 (tasting)

Quinta do Encontro This is the latest new winery to be built in the village. It looks out across the vineyard straight at Carlos Campolargo's winery the other side of the valley. Vines have been grown in these vineyards since 1930, and made into wine in a basic winery in Paredes do Bairro, a couple of kilometres to the north. In 2000, the owner, João Paulo Seabra Almeida, formed a partnership with Dão Sul (*page 174*) with the intention of upgrading the quality of the wines made from his vines.

And now there is a new winery, being built when we visited in 2006. Dão Sul is in charge of vineyards and winemaking. There are 25ha of potential vineyard here, of which 10ha are functioning vines at the moment, after some redevelopment and replanting. Most is Baga, with some Touriga Nacional, Merlot, Cabernet Sauvignon, Tinta Roriz and Castelão for the reds, and Bical, Maria Gomes, Arinto and Chardonnay for whites. They have new visitor arrangements, and you can turn up any day of the week, at any time, and someone will look after you. In practice, we'd suggest you get in touch before you go.

The **Quinta do Encontro Bical** is crisp and appley, with lemony acidity and good minerality. **Quinta do Encontro Merlot Baga** is ripe and savoury, with bright raspberry Merlot fruit softening the savoury Baga. And the top wine, **Encontro 1**, is about two-thirds Baga and a third Touriga Nacional, with a dash of Merlot, intense, ripe and rich, with savoury, curranty Baga and bergamot-scented Touriga, the result dense and tannic.

Apartado 246, São Lourenço do Bairro,
*   3781-907 Anadia*
T+351 232 960 140
E daosul@daosul.com
W www.daosul.com
Visits appt preferred
€ variable

DÃO — WINERIES AND WINES

ABRUNHOSA DO MATO H7

Quinta dos Roques About 10km south of Mangualde, this estate has a real family feel. The family is Roques de Oliveira, so 'Quinta dos Roques' was an appropriate name. At the end of the 1970s, the family opted to concentrate on growing grapes. But which varieties? Some of their workers had heard of Cabernet and Chardonnay, and urged them to grow these. But the family decided to stick with

local grapes, and planted mostly Touriga Nacional, with Jaen, Alfrocheiro, Tinto Cão, Tinta Roriz and Rufete as supporting cast. For whites, they chose Encruzado, with some Malvasia Fina, Bical and Cercial. They also decided to stop delivering their grapes to the local co-op, and to make their own wine.

The plan was master-minded by son-in-law Luís Lourenço, enticed away from his career as a maths teacher. A new winery was built, incorporating pneumatic presses and computerised cooling systems alongside the old granite *lagares*, and an airy, spacious tasting room. The business flourished, and in 1997, the family

bought another estate, Quinta das Maias. In crow terms this is about 15km away, or 25km by road. It is much higher, at about 600m altitude (Roques is about 350m). The 40ha of vineyard at Roques date from 1980, and the 35ha at Maias are split between 13ha of old vines and 22ha planted more recently. Quinta dos Roques is open for visitors on weekdays without prior appointment, and by arrangement at weekends. It is possible to visit Quinta das Maias, by appointment only. The €5 charge includes a tour of winery and

vineyards, as well as a generous five-wine tasting session.

Luís brought in Rui Reguinga, the well-known winemaking consultant, to improve the portfolio in 2002. All wines from both estates are made as DOC Dão. The **Quinta dos Roques Encruzado** is two-thirds barrel-fermented, with a rich, bready, lemony flavour touched by tropical fruit. **Quinta das Maias Branco Reserva** is all barrel-fermented and two-thirds Encruzado (plus Malvasia Fina, Verdelho and Barcelo), lean, creamy and citrussy. The single variety **Quinta das Maias Barcelo** (an old local white grape) has a lovely citrus-zest perfume, with subtle, floral notes and minerality. Of the reds, **Quinta dos Roques Tinto** is appealing and easy-drinking, with soft, red-fruit flavours and fresh acidity. **Quinta das Maias Jaen** is soft, voluptuous and seductive, with mulberry perfume. **Quinta dos Roques Touriga Nacional** is herby and aromatic, with firm, smooth tannins and rich, ripe fruit. **Quinta dos Roques Tinto Reserva** is a gloriously harmonious red, with rich, creamy, raspberry fruit and smooth, rich tannins.

Rua Direita 12, Abrunhosa do Mato,
    3530-050 Cunha Baixa
T+351 232 614 500
E quintaroques@vinta.pt
Visits Mon-Fri 9-12.30 Sat 1.30-6 Sun
    appt only Closed last 2 weeks Jul €5

ARRIFANA H6

Quinta da Bica In total, this estate is 100ha, but only 15ha are vineyard. The rest are forest and grazing for sheep whose milk is sold to make *queijo da serra*. The family has owned the estate since the 17th century, and have been bottling their wine

since 1989. The vineyard has been replanted, and the vines are now 25, 10 and 2 years old. They are happy to receive visitors (and to sell them wine), and plan to offer bed and breakfast within a couple of years. The **Quinta da Bica Rosé** is pleasant, with creamy, berry fruit. **Quinta da Bica Tinto** has soft, strawberry

flavours, and smooth tannins. **Quinta da Bica Tinto Reserva** has more Touriga Nacional (aged in new oak), smooth tannins and ripe, savoury, plummy fruit.

Arrifana, 6270-184 Santa Comba de Seia
T+351 238 311 937 / 913 446698
Visits 4-8 appt only
€15 (includes food)

AGUIEIRA

Quinta da Aguieira This is the Borges' Dão estate, which they have owned in its entirety since 2000, having bought the first half in 1995. Vines cover 60ha of the 100ha of land, completely replanted since Borges bought it, with the advice of the distinguished viticulturalist Rogerio de Castro. Borges also buy in grapes for their big Dão brand, Meia Encosta.

Borges was started in 1884, by two brothers, António and Francisco. They were in banking, lotteries, insurance and match production. In 1918 they decided to concentrate on banking and wine, run as independent businesses. The wine company was bought in 1998 by José Maria Vieira, distributor of the Borges wines in Portugal. Originally Borges bought wine to blend, then grapes (to make into wine), and most recently has invested in three estates, Quinta de Simães in the Vinho Verde region *(page 39)*, Quinta da Soalheira in the Douro, and Quinta da Aguieira. The Borges Dão wines are impressive. Even **Meia Encosta Tinto** is fresh and lively, with good raspberry fruit and a touch of oak. **Quinta de São Simão da Aguieira** has lovely red fruit flavours through which herby, aromatic Touriga Nacional shines. We preferred two of the three single variety Borges Dão reds, the bright, elegant, raspberry-scented **Borges Trincadeira** and the bergamot-scented, fresh, appealing **Borges Touriga Nacional**. Top of the Dão range is the **Borges Dão Reserva**, roughly two-thirds Touriga Nacional and one-third Tinta Roriz, with 10% of Trincadeira squeezed in.

Of the Douro wines, the **Borges Douro Branco Reserva** is honeyed, bready and crisp. The **Borges Douro Tinto Reserva** has ripe tannins and good acidity, with good red fruit flavours and a hint of herby aroma. The **Soalheira 10 Anos** tawny

port is a sweet style, with good nutty, creamy flavours, and the **Roncão 20 Anos** is much woodier, with nutty intensity. The **Borges LBV** has lovely black fruit flavours and firm tannins – a serious LBV. The **Borges Vintage Port** is very good, with rich, ripe, aromatic fruit and firm tannins.

CABANÕES G7

UDACA The União das Adegas Cooperativas do Dão is a union of nine co-ops, Penalva, Mangualde, Nelas, São Paio, Vila Nova de Tázem, Ervedal da Beira, Nogueira do Cravo, Santa Comba Dão and Silgueiros. These represent between 50% and 60% of Dão's entire production. UDACA doesn't actually make wine, but blends, ages and sells it. Unlike the co-ops that furnish the wine, UDACA sells everything in bottle. Unlike the traditional co-op, UDACA has no obligation to accept everything brought to it, but chooses the wines it wants to blend and sell. It was one of the few bottlers of wine in the early days: most was sold in bulk to the merchants. **Dão Touriga Nacional** has good bergamot perfume, good acidity and firm tannins. **Irreverente** is a VR Beiras aimed at the younger market, with ripe blackberry fruit, soft tannins and fresh acidity. **Adro da Sé Reserva** is rich and smooth, with blackberry fruit and ripe tannins. **UDACA Garrafeira** has 10 years in bottle (and no oak), and emerges delicate, elegant, floral and savoury, with good length.
Apartado 268, Cabanões, 3501-903 Viseu
T+351 232 467 060
E geral@udaca.pt
W www.udaca.pt
Visits Mon-Fri 9-5.30 €3

CARREGAL DO SAL G6

Dão Sul Much of the new energy in the Dão region has come from Dão Sul. The company is not yet 20 years old, and already it has set new standards of quality by which single estate wines of the region are judged.

Carlos Lucas, chief winemaker and part-owner of Dão Sul *(below)*, does not believe in buying in grapes or wine. The company was started in 1989 by Casimiro Gomes, a viticultural expert, who invited Lucas to join as winemaker. They went to a lawyer to draw up an agreement, and the lawyer also wanted a shareholding. So did the first land-owner they approached. They were the four founding partners. Lucas likes owning or renting estates, keeping control of the whole process, from growing grapes to selling finished wines. As a result of various acquisitions and partnerships, Dão Sul now makes the wines from three estates in Dão, two in the Douro *(page 93)*, and one each in Bairrada *(page 171)*, Estremadura *(page*

265), and the Alentejo (not to mention Brazil).

The Dão wines are made at Quinta de Cabriz, less than 3km south-west of Carregal do Sal, itself about 45km north-east of Coimbra in the valley of the Mondego river. Quinta do Cabriz also has a very good 84-seat restaurant *(page 191)*, and an active programme of wine tourism. They say they're open all the time, every day of the week, and you can just turn up without an appointment. We'd suggest you ring them if you want to visit outside normal office hours, and certainly book if you want to eat in the restaurant. You'll get a tour of the winery and a tasting, and the price will vary depending on what you want to taste. Quinta de Cabriz has a marvellous modern winery, but the Paço de Santar is even better, if you can persuade someone to receive you there. It's a historic manor-house, built in 1609, with a wonderful old cellar where they still make a little wine each year – as an excuse to have a party! There's also a gleaming modern winery where they do the real winemaking. Paço de Santar (owned by Dão Sul) has 34ha of vines, and there are 100ha that belong to the Casa de Santar, owned by the Vasconcellos e Souza family (and rented by Dão Sul). Quinta de Cabriz has 35ha, and the other estate Dão Sul rents, Quinta dos Grilos, has 17ha.

Lucas wants 'to make wines people want to drink'. **Quinta de Cabriz Encruzado** is half fermented in new French barrels, and emerges lean and mineral, with oak notes softening the steeliness. **Paço dos Cunhas de Santar, Vinha do Contador** is entirely oak-fermented, very aromatic, lemony and mineral, with lovely acidity and a rich texture. **Quinta de Cabriz Colheita Seleccionada** is inexpensive and smooth, ripely red-fruited. **Quinta de Cabriz Touriga Nacional** is full of bergamot, raspberry and herby scents, with lovely freshness and firm tannins. **Pedro & Inês Dão** is a lighter, more elegant style, with two-thirds Alfrocheiro and the balance Baga, scented and fragrant. **Casa de Santar Reserva** is much more traditional, dark, rich and intense, with firm tannins and good length. The 'icon' wine from Cabriz is **Four CCCC**, a blend chosen by the four winemakers (three called Carlos, one Casimiro), Touriga Nacional, Tinto Cão, Baga and Trincadeira. It's chocolatey and opulent, with very smooth tannins and fresh acidity.
Apartado 28, 3430-909 Carregal do Sal
T+351 232 960 140
E daosul@daosul.com
W www.daosul.com
Visits every day, no fixed times € variable

DAREI H7

Casa de Darei You could eat and drink well from the products made on the 150ha farm surrounding the lovely, granite-blocked manor house of the little village of Darei. There are apple orchards (particularly the Beiras variety, Bravo de Esmolfe), olive groves that produce olives and oil, sheep whose milk is used to make one of Portugal's most renowned cheeses, the Queijo da Serra, pigs, chickens, and five hectares of vines. Add to this a charming granite house and two flats to rent *(page 205)*, 70ha of forest in which to wander and 2km along the banks of the River Dão, and it seems an ideal place for a restful holiday. Find it just north of the Mangualde exit from the IP5, off the road to Penalva do Castelo.

The estate was bought in 1994 by the Machado Ruivo family, who replanted the vineyards in 1996, and started making and bottling their own wine in 1999. They are very geared up to receiving visitors, and will happily show you round their immaculately-kept cellar and estate, and give you a tasting. There is also a shop where you can buy the wine and other local produce.

Three broad terraces of vines are at about 350m altitude, and benefit from a relatively cool climate. The other vineyard is down by the river, and gives richer, riper fruit. The white **Lagar de Darei** is partly fermented in a small oak vat, part in cement, which gives a creamy softness to the minerally, Encruzado-dominated blend. The red **Lagar de Darei** is a firm, fresh

blend of Touriga Nacional, Jaen, Aragonez and Alfrocheiro. And 2003 is likely to be the first vintage of **Casa de Darei Tinto**, a firm, fragrant blend dominated by Alfrocheiro.

Darei, 3530-000 Mangualde
T +351 232 613 200
E mail@casadedarei.pt
W www.casadedarei.pt
Visits Tue-Sat 9-5 appt only

ESMOLFE H7

Quinta da Vegia João Pedro Araújo has an estate in Vinho Verde country as well, Quinta de SanJoanne *(page 40)*. He used to make red there, but this is the real place for red wine. At 550m above sea level, it's high, bare country, all forest and granite boulders, about 25km east of Viseu and just north of Penalva de Castelo. There are no white grapes here at all in this recently-planted, 20ha vineyard, reclaimed from forest. The new vines (now five years old) are Touriga Nacional, Tinta Roriz and Trincadeira, and João Pedro is using grapes from local, rented vineyards to make his second label, Porta Fronha, until the new vines are up to speed. The current **Porta**

Fronha is mainly Tinta Roriz, with Touriga Nacional and Alfrocheiro, and has lovely, ripe, raspberry fruit and firm tannins. The young **Quinta da Vegia Tinto** is Touriga Nacional and Tinta Roriz, herby and aromatic, with smooth tannins and aromatic, raspberry fruit. A sneak preview of the **Quinta da Vegia Tinto Reserva** shows it is dark and fragrant, with serious tannins, fresh acidity and herby, raspberry fruit. The best here is yet to come.

Esmolfe, 3550-074 Penalva do Castelo
T+ 351 226 09 58 77
E quinta@casadecello.pt
W www.casadecello.pt
Visits appt only €10

ÍNSUA H7

Casa da Ínsua A new era has begun for this historic 18th century house, just west of Penalva do Castelo. The Olazabal family, owners of Casa da Ínsua, signed a 25-year contract in 2004 with VisaBeira Tourism, to develop the house into a 50-bedroom luxury hotel. Visabeira own hotels, restaurants and other leisure and tourism-related businesses in Portugal and Mozambique. They were hoping, when we last visited in 2006, to open the hotel in three years. But already you can visit the winery, the magnificent gardens, the 17th century chapel and the entrance to the house. Or you can take one of the tasting options, either just wines, or wine and *queijo da serra*, plus the tour. It is a beautiful place, well worth seeing.

Casa da Ínsua used to have 400ha, the biggest single estate in Dão, founded on a fortune made in Brazil. Now there are 33ha of vineyard in production, eight hectares of which are newly planted Tinta Roriz and Alfrocheiro. The peculiarity of the Casa da Ínsua vineyards is their Cabernet Sauvignon and Semillon. These are allowed in their Dão wines (as long as they don't exceed 40% of the blend), because they have been there for over 100 years, well before the first modern legislation for Dão was passed in 1993. They also have more Jaen than most Dão vineyards, 'to counter the powerful Cabernet'. Other varieties include Touriga Nacional and Tinta Pinheira for red, and Malvasia Fina and Encruzado for white.

Casa da Ínsua Branco starts fermentation in stainless steel, and finishes in new and used oak. The result is steely and mineral, with hints of honey, cream and citrus. The **Casa da Ínsua Tinto** has bright, blackcurranty fruit, firm tannins and high acidity, and the **Casa da Ínsua Tinto Reserva** has more Touriga Nacional in the blend, which gives an intensely herby, aromatic aspect, with firm tannins and rich fruit.

Ínsua, 3550-126 Penalva do Castelo
T+351 232 642 222
E casadainsua@visabeiraturismo.pt
W www.visabeiraturismo.pt
Vists Apr-Aug Mon-Fri 9-12, 2-6 Sat &
*   Sun 10-11, 2-5 Sep-Mar Mon-Fri*
*   9-12, 2-5 Sat & Sun 10-11, 1-4*
€ variable

LAGARINHOS H7

Quinta da Ponte Pedrinha This estate, in the foothills of the Serra da Estrela just west of Gouveia, has grown grapes for wine for centuries. And, since 1997, the Osório family have been making and bottling their own wines. They have 50ha of vines (out of 200ha for the whole property), and most are for red wines. The 5ha of white grapes make the **Quinta da Ponte Pedrinha Branco**, an excellent, steely, mineral, focussed blend of Encruzado, Cercial and Arinto. **Quinta da Ponte Pedrinha Reserva** is half Touriga Nacional, and most of the rest is Tinta Roriz, with 5% Jaen. It's a ripe, malty wine, with firm tannins and fresh acidity. **Quinta da Ponte Pedrinha Touriga Nacional** is very good, with herby, aromatic, red fruit flavours and soft, easy tannins.

Lagarinhos, 6290-094 Gouveia
T+351 238 485 000 / 965 054 485
Visits Mon-Fri 9-5 Closed Aug

MORTÁGUA F6

Boas Quintas Nuno Cancela de Abreu is a highly respected winemaking consultant who has worked in the Douro, Ribatejo, Alentejo, Estremadura and Terras do Sado. This is his home territory, and where he decided to start his own business in 1991, based at the family house in Mortágua. It is called Boas Quintas ('good estates'), and refers to three patches of vineyard, two in

Mortágua (50km or so south-west of Viseu), and one in Nelas, about 35km to the north-east. These three parcels add up to 10ha, planted in 1991. Half the vines are Touriga Nacional, with smaller amounts of Tinta Roriz and Jaen, Trincadeira, Bastardo and Rufete. The best red wines are bottled as Quinta da Fonte do Ouro Reserva and Quinta da Fonte do Ouro Touriga Nacional. In years when Nuno feels the quality isn't sufficient to bottle under these labels, the wines are released under the Quinta da Giesta label. There are white and rosé Quinta da Giesta wines, as well. The **Quinta da Giesta Touriga Nacional Rosé** is made by bleeding off juice destined for Touriga Nacional red after it has had four hours' skin contact. The **Quinta da Giesta Branco** is fresh and lemony, with hints of honey and flowers. **Quinta da Giesta Tinto** is bright and lively, with high acidity and pleasant, berry fruit. **Quinta da Fonte do Ouro Reserva** has bright, raspberry fruit, high acidity again and a meaty elegance. **Quinta da Fonte do Ouro Touriga Nacional** is our favourite, bright and lively, with flavours of blackcurrant and herbs, firm but ripe tannins, and a rich texture.

Boas Quintas will receive visitors at the winery, and give you a tour and tasting, at no charge. They would prefer people to get in touch before coming.

Rua Dr. João Lopes de Morais 4,
*   3450-153 Mortágua*
T+351 231 921 076 / 7
E wines@boasquintas.com
W www.boasquintas.com
Visits Mon-Sat 10-6 appt preferred

OLIVEIRA DE BARREIROS G7

Quinta da Leira Another small, privately-owned estate making excellent Dão wines under the name Vinha Paz.

Outeiro de Espinho

Quinta dos Carvalhais 20 years ago, when we first went to Dão, very few producers were making wines we wanted to write about. One shining exception in the general gloom was Sogrape. Faced with a legal obligation to buy uninteresting wine from under-funded co-ops, they came up with a typically creative solution. They supplied the co-op in Vila Nova de Tazem with modern equipment and technical support, and bought wine from them – almost as if they had their own winery. When the era of co-op domination ended, Sogrape bought Quinta dos Carvalhais in 1989, and set the standards for the new era of Dão winemaking. They built a new, modern winery in 1990 and replanted the vineyards (now 50ha). In addition, they buy grapes from almost 600 growers, to make the brands such as Grão Vasco, Duque de Viseu and, now, Callabriga. The Carvalhais winery is less shiny than it used to be, but it's still evolving. They use *micro-billes* now for the fermentation of sparkling wines, tiny bubbles of permeable plastic in which the yeast is enclosed for the secondary fermentation in the bottle, so it can be easily eliminated before the wine is prepared for final corking and sale.

The winery at Quinta dos Carvalhais is big, and Sogrape make different ranges of wine there. **Duque de Viseu Branco** is half and half Bical and Encruzado, soft and honeyed, with crisp acidity. **Quinta dos Carvalhais Encruzado** has a touch of Verdelho as well, and is 60% barrel-fermented; it's honeyed, bready and savoury, with lovely acidity and good complexity. **Duque de Viseu Tinto** is soft and easy,

with some Touriga Nacional aromas and firm tannins. **Quinta dos Carvalhais Colheita Tinto** has the same blend as Duque de Viseu (Touriga Nacional, Tinta Roriz and Alfrocheiro), but richer and oakier, with soft tannins and malty intensity. There are three Quinta dos Carvalhais single varietals, the ripe, appealing strawberry-jammy **Quinta dos Carvalhais Alfrocheiro**, the solid, red-fruited **Quinta dos Carvalhais Tinta Roriz**, and the dense, rich, aromatic **Quinta dos Carvalhais Touriga Nacional**. **Quinta dos Carvalhais Reserva** is a blend of Tinto Roriz and Touriga Nacional, rich, oaky and tannic. It needs time. **Callabriga Dão** is another blend, of almost half Touriga Nacional, one third Tinta Roriz and the rest Alfrocheiro, beautifully balanced, with spicy, aromatic, herb and red fruit flavours, and soft tannins.

Surgeon Dr António Canto Moniz inherited the little granite winery from his mother, whose grandmother was Spanish, called de la Paz. The ownership goes back five generations. Dr Canto Moniz's father was also a doctor, and winemaker. There are 12ha of vines, near the family house, immaculately kept, almost all for red wine. Dr Canto Moniz makes white wine only for home consumption. He has a

gloriously minimalist winery, just granite *lagares* and oak barrels. Fermentations are cooled by plaques filled with well water. Five or six men tread the grapes three times a day for three hours at a time. Skins are pressed in the *lagar*, then the wine goes into barrel for between 10 and 20 months. As Dr Canto Moniz says, it's in the vineyards that the work has to be done, including snipping off about half the potential crop in August so the rest can really ripen. The **Vinha Paz Colheita** has soft, easy, strawberry fruit and good length. The **Vinha Paz Reserva** has more Touriga Nacional, giving rich, bright floral aromas and firm tannins, complexity, acidity and great length.
Oliveira de Barreiros,
  São João de Lourosa, 3500-884 Viseu
T +351 937 015 354
E vinhapaz@hotmail.com
Visits appt only

Quinta de Reis Dr Jorge Reis is a gynaecologist with 15ha of 10-year-old vines at his estate 5km south of Viseu. He sells the grapes from 12ha to Sogrape, and makes wine out of the rest. His first vintage in bottle was the 2004. He makes just one wine, 60% of Touriga Nacional, and equal parts of Jaen and Tinta Roriz for the rest. **Vinha de Reis** has ripe plummy aromas, smooth tannins and appealing, perfumed length. He receives visitors by appointment only, and will show you round and give you a free wine tasting.
3500-892 Viseu
T +351 232 441 032 / 914 788 531
E quintadereis@sapo.pt
W www.quintadereis.com
Visits Apr-Oct appt only

OLIVEIRINHA G6

Quinta do Cerrado This used to be apple-country. Vines were planted here only in 1993. Now there are 30ha, of Touriga Nacional, Tinta Roriz, Alfrocheiro, Jaen and Bastardo for the reds, and Encruzado, Bical and Rabo de Ovelha for whites. The winery is all stainless steel, with temperature control and a pneumatic press. The **Dão Cunha Martins Rosé** is Tinta Roriz, bright and aromatic, with

pleasant red berry fruit. The **Quinta do Cerrado Reserva Dão** is herby and easy, with fresh acidity, and the **Lagares do Cerrado Touriga Nacional** is dark and inky, with very firm tannins and some herby aromas.

Oliveirinha, 3430-399 Carregal do Sal
T+351 232 968 224
E uniaocomercial@mail.telepac.pt
W www.quintadocerrado.com
Visits Mon-Fri 9-6 appt only

PASSARELA H7

Casa da Passarela Manuel Santos Lima likes to take things slowly. 'If you go too fast, you miss the details,' he says. He has 40ha of vineyard, all replanted when he took over from his uncle 15 years ago, and other patches of land cleared for when he is ready to plant them. The estate is about 12km from Gouveia, in the foothills of the Serra da Estrela, at about 500m, with very rocky granite soil. He doesn't like the flavours of oak, preferring what he calls 'natural wines'. Maybe one day, when the vines are 25 years old, he might try some

barrels, and use the estate name on the labels. For the time being, they are labelled 'Somontes'. The white label **Somontes** is based on Alfrocheiro, ripe yet bracing, with high acidity and almost a tingle of minerality. The black label **Somontes** has more Touriga Nacional, and perfumed raspberry fruit, refreshing acidity and firm tannins. You can either pay €2.50 to visit the vineyards, or €2.50 for the winery, or have them both, with a tasting, for €5.

Passarela, 6290-093 Lagarinhos
T+351 238 486 312
E passarela@mail.telepac.pt
Visits Feb-Jun Tue, Fri appt only €5

PENALVA DO CASTELO H7

Quinta da Boavista The number of villages in the area with the name 'Tavares' attached give you some idea of how long the Tavares family has lived here. 'For ever', they say. This is a 50ha estate, with 8ha of vines. As well as the vines, they have various little houses to rent, and breed racehorses. João Tavares de Pina, winemaker son of the family, studied in Bordeaux 25 years ago, then worked at Vila Real on yeast selection.

From 2005, there are two versions, both blends, one predominantly Jaen, the other Touriga Nacional. The Jaen-based **Terras de Tavares Tinto** is quite dry, with firm tannins and perfumed strawberry length. The Touriga **Terras de Tavares Tinto** is very aromatic, with bright acidity, firm tannins and lovely bergamot perfume. You can buy the wines at trade prices if you visit, get a free tour of house and estate, and pay for what you open to taste.

3550-059 Penalva do Castelo
T+351 919 858 340
E casatavaradespina@sapo.pt
W www.quintadaboavista.com
Visits appt preferred 🛏

PINDELO DE SILGUEIROS G7

Quinta Vale das Escadinhas A lovely little modern cellar complete with stainless steel vats of different sizes, a peristaltic pump and a good modern, pneumatic press. It's owned by the Figueiredo family, who have 13ha of vines at Quinta da Falorca, from 20 years old to just planted. Most of the vines are Touriga Nacional, with Tinta Roriz, Alfrocheiro, Jaen and Rufete. Before 1964, everything was sold in bulk. Between 1964 and 1999, everything went to co-ops or merchants, as grapes or wine. Then, in 1999, they started selling their own brand. **Quinta da Falorca Rosé** is creamy and almost dry, with rosehip perfume. **Quinta da Falorca Dão Reserva** is soft and aromatic, with ripe, strawberry fruit. **Quinta da Falorca Barricas** is mostly Touriga Nacional, smooth, aromatic and substantial. **e-falorca** is bright and unoaked, with red fruit flavours and bright acidity. **t-nac by Falorca** has rich fruit and smooth tannins, and the **Quinta da Falorca Garrafeira** has glowing aromatic fruit, firm ripe tannins and wonderful bergamot fragrance.

You are welcome at the cellar for a tour and tasting, free of charge, but you must make an appointment.

Pindelo de Silgueiros, 3500-543 Silgueiros
T+351 232 950 099 / 934 824 710
E pedrofigueiredo@qve.pt
Visits Mon-Sat 10-12, 3-6 appt only

PINHANÇOS H6
Quinta de Sães
Combine one passionate and committed winemaker and two mountain vineyards, and you get some of the best red wines in Portugal. Álvaro de Castro has two estates, Quinta de Sães (14ha of vines), where he lives and has the winery, and Quinta da Pellada (30ha of vines), a wind-swept, hill-top vineyard with a lovely old granite house. Álvaro has rebuilt and restored the house. He trained as a civil engineer, but decided he would rather make wine at the family estate. It's about halfway between Seia and Gouveia, in the west of the Dão region, in the foothills of the Serra da Estrela. Pellada is at about 520m altitude, and the soil is very definitely granite-based, with some quartz. With the wind that sweeps through the vineyard, there's hardly time for fungal diseases to damage the vines before they're blown off to the next village. The oldest vines are 38 years old. Quinta de Sães has five of its 14ha in trial plots of Touriga Nacional, Tinta Roriz, Cabernet Sauvignon, Merlot and Syrah, 'just to play with'. Álvaro de Castro swears he'll never make a single variety Cabernet, but does have some 'very nice' Merlot, picked at the beginning of September, at 13.5% potential alcohol.

That's typical of the man, always experimenting, pushing the boundaries, always throwing out ideas, in a light-hearted, even jokey way, but often with a serious intent. On our last visit but one, he suggested that the perfect Dão red would not be made with the traditional grapes, maybe Baga or Syrah might be better. He cited a pure Baga 1970 he remembered, then pulled out his last

bottle to make the point. He himself started making wine only in 1989, after the region's era of co-op domination. Now he works with his daughter Maria, a trained winemaker, and she does the clambering over barrels in the cellar. Álvaro gives the impression of being much more interested to show us barrel samples than finished wines. Along with ideas for the future, work in progress is what fascinates him.

Dão Álvaro de Castro is smooth, dark and plummy, with lovely acidity and good herby flavour. **Quinta de Sães Dão Reserva** is fresh and bracing, with herby fragrance and invigorating tannins. **Quinta da Pellada Dão** may come in different versions. The blend with more *vinhas velhas* (old vines) is rich and voluptuous, and that with more Touriga Nacional richly aromatic, with bright red fruits, good tannins and bracing acidity. **Pape Dão** is made from grapes from Casa da Passarela and Quinta da Pellada (thus the name, 'Pa-Pe'). It starts life very oaky, but quietens to ripe, herby Touriga aromas and dark Baga intensity. **Dado** is a wine Alvaro makes with Dirk Niepoort, a blend of Dão and Douro. As such, it has to be a table wine, with no mention of vintage or varieties. But it's excellent, with the slightly firmer tannins of the Douro, and dense, rich complexity. Álvaro's top red is **Carrocel**, the best he can do each year, which will vary from vintage to vintage, but always be worth trying. Visits are possible, but only if someone is there.

Álvaro, Maria or the cellarmaster will receive you, show you the vineyard and give you a tasting. But do get in touch first!
Pinhanços, 6270-141 Seia
T+351 238 486 133
E quintadapellada@quintadesaes.jazznet.pt
Visits appt only

POVOLIDE G7
Casa dos Gaios Alexandra and Pedro Paraiso both work at Viseu University, but took over the management of this 15ha vineyard about ten years ago. The first thing they did was to replant the vines, so all are relatively young. Anselmo Mendes is their winemaking consultant. They bottle only a Reserva, in an amphora-shaped bottle with a slim base, suitable for female hands (because they believe that women will be more involved in the wine market in future!). **Casa dos Gaios Reserva Tinto** is very ripe, with a treacley aroma, red and black fruit flavours, firm tannins and good length.
3505-243 Povolide
T+351 232 426 878 / 917 245 383
E paraiso@viseudigital.pt
Visits 9.30-7 appt only

RIO TORTO H7
Quinta do Corujão Five generations of António Batista's family have grown grapes here, but it was only in 1996 that he built his own winery; he made his first vintage in 1997. He had replanted the 12ha vineyard in 1990, one hectare of Encruzado and a little Bical for white wine, the rest Touriga Nacional, Jaen, Alfrocheiro, Tinta Roriz, Tinta Amarela and Tinta Pinheira. Fermentations are in steel and *lagares*, and he uses oak barrels to mature his reds. **Quinta do Corujão Branco** is fresh and steely, with flavours of honey and lemon. **Quinta do Corujão**

179

Reserva is aromatic, ripe and lively, with firm tannins and bright acidity. For the **Quinta do Corujão Grande Escolha**, António almost halves the yield by green harvesting in the summer. The result is intense and firm, with raspberry and bergamot aromas, and bright acidity.
Rua do Barreiro 8, Rio Torto,
*   6290-261 Gouveia*
T+351 238 486 495 / 966 444 092
Visits Mon-Fri 10-5 Closed Sep, first half
*   Oct appt only*

SILGUEIROS G7

Quinta do Perdigão José Perdigão is better known as an architect in the Dão region at the moment than as a wine producer. It was he who rebuilt the Solar do Dão in Viseu (magnificently), and he also has a rather elegant stainless steel spittoon to his credit. In 1997, he planted 7ha of red grapes near Silgueiros, 20km south of Viseu, and made his first wine in 1999. He uses no herbicides, and is tempted by biodynamic farming. His **Quinta do Perdigão Rosé** is fresh and aromatic, with lovely acidity. The red **Quinta do Perdigão Colheita** is pleasant, with bright, slightly jammy red fruit. The **Quinta do Perdigão Reserva** is sterner stuff, predominantly Touriga Nacional, with floral aromas, bright fruit and high tannins. The **Quinta do Perdigão Touriga Nacional** is the best, rich and aromatic, with a scent of bergamot, quite oaky, with smooth tannins.

3500-543 Silgueiros, Viseu
T+351 232 421 812 / 919 565 781
E arq.perdigao@mail.telepac.pt
W www.quintadoperdigao.com
Visits appt only
€8 tour, tasting, wine glass

TÁVORA-VAROSA — WINERY AND WINES

UCANHA C4

Murganheira Founded in 1964, just to make sparkling wines, Murganheira diversified into still wines in the 1970s. Acácio Laranjo, the founder and owner until his death, chose 'Murganheira' as the brand name as he had been born in the little village of Murganheira a couple of kilometres from the present cellar near Ucanha. It was he who ordered the construction of the sparkling wine cellar, blasted out of a hill of blue granite, advised by a winemaker from Champagne. After his death, his daughter and son-in-law sold the company to Orlando Lourenço, the present winemaker, and three others. Through various further sales, about half the company is now owned by the Banco Português de Negócios.

The cellar is very impressive, with jagged blue granite walls below ground, a modern winemaking cellar and bottling at ground level, and beautifully-designed, modern offices, lab and reception rooms above, looking out over the surrounding countryside. Of the Murganheira bubblies, **Murganheira Chardonnay Brut** is creamy and buttery, with lemony freshness and good acidity. **Murganheira Cuvée Reserve Especial** (Tinta Roriz and Tinta Barroca) is toasty, with good berry fruit and a rich texture. **Murganheira Grande Reserve** is lean and savoury, with good acidity and toasty length. **Murganheira Vintage Brut** is pure Pinot Noir, honeyed, rich and quite complex. Among the still wines, the **Murganheira Branco Seco Távora-Varosa** is fresh, lemony and appealing, and the **Murganheira Reserva Tinto** is meaty and jammy, with soft tannins and tarry length.
Abadia Velha, 3610-175 Ucanha
T+351 254 671 185
E murganheira.sede@clix.pt
Visits appt only

BEIRA INTERIOR — WINERIES AND WINES

ALDEIA VIÇOSA C3

Quinta de São Lourenço Nuno Soares da Fonseca, a lawyer, has 12ha of vines, just to the east of the Serra da Estrela, about 6km by microlite to Chãos, then another 6km to Guarda. He sold wine in bottle for the first time in 2005, having invested in temperature control equipment and pumps. His **Quinta de São Lourenço Branco** is barrel-fermented mixed old vines, complex if a little oaky, but with good acidity. The **Quinta de São Lourenço Tinto** is from mixed old vines again, with complex berry fruit, firm tannins and highish alcohol and acidity.

Quinta de São Lourenço,
*   Aldeia Viçosa 6300-025, Guarda*
T+351 916 710 277
E informacoes@quintadoministro.com
W www.quintadoministro.com
Visits Mon-Fri 10-6 appt only

CAPINHA C2

Quinta dos Currais José Diogo Tomás bought this estate in 1989, but he comes from a family of winegrowers. He has only been making and selling wine for a few years here: his first vintage was in 2001. The farm has 160ha, but most of that is forest, *quercus robur* (the white oak grown in the USA) and cherry trees (the wood is used for furniture). And he has 30ha of vines, now about 10 years old. It is high country, at about 500m altitude, and 25km south-east of Covilhã. All the wines are DOC Beira Interior. The **Quinta dos Currais Branco Síria** is creamy and lemony, with good acidity. **Quinta dos Currais Colheita Seleccionada** is about half and half Fonte Cal and Arinto, and the 2004 we tasted has a bit more sugar than the winemaker wanted (the fermentation stopped and wouldn't restart), but had rich, honeyed flavours and bright acidity under. The **Quinta dos Currais Tinto**

Reserva is a blend of roughly equal parts of Tinta Roriz, Touriga Nacional and Castelão, rich and intense, with firm tannins and herby black fruit flavours.

6230-145 Capinha
T+351 966 160 978
Visits appt only

CARVALHAL FORMOSO C3

Quinta dos Termos João Carvalho has a textile factory and teaches textile engineering at Covilhã University as well as owning this recently refurbished wine estate just east of Belmonte, in the Cova da Beira sub-region. Quinta dos Termos had been bought in 1945 by his father, who made wine from 6ha of vines and sold it in bulk to local inns. Through the 1980s, the farm was rented out to a lawyer. Looking after the vineyards was not his main priority. João inherited the property when his father died in 1993, and decided to replant the vineyards in 1997. His first vintage was 2001. He still has 3ha of old vines, and 47ha of young ones, mostly red varieties. His goal is to plant 12ha more, maybe partly of an ancient local white variety, Fonte Cal, which he is trying to re-establish as part of a project with Lisbon University.

João is very well-organised, and his vineyards are immaculately kept. His cellar, likewise, is modern and well-equipped, with a fermentation cellar, barrel and bottle storage on the ground floor, underground storage for sparkling wines, and offices, lab and a tasting room upstairs. He offers visits to the winery without notice, to winery and vineyard with a bit of notice, and also wine tastings with local *petiscos*. Tours are free, tastings cost €10. Please give warning if you are five people or more.

Quinta dos Termos Branco is 80% Síria and 20% Fonte Cal, unoaked, but with some maceration before fermentation.

It has surprisingly rich, honeyed aromas, highish acidity, honeyed, mineral flavour, and real concentration and balance. The **Quinta dos Termos Fonte Cal Reserva** has flavours of honey, apple, quince and greengage; it is mineral and steely, with high acidity, wine of real character. **Quinta dos Termos Tinto** is about equal proportions of Tinta Roriz, Alfrocheiro, Touriga Nacional and Trincadeira, big, rich and ripe, with firm tannins and sweet fruit length. **Quinta dos Termos Reserva** is made from the old vines, dark, rich and inky, with high tannins, tight intensity and tarry, savoury length. João also makes single variety red wines, of which the best is the intensely floral and herby **Quinta dos Termos Touriga Nacional**. The sparkling wines are also good, a honeyed, slightly toasty **Quinta dos Termos Fonte Cal Brut**, and a brightly fruity, raspberry-perfumed **Quinta dos Termos Baga Brut**.

Carvalhal Formoso, 6250-161 Belmonte
T+351 275 471 070 / 967 017 494
E quintadostermos@netvisao.pt
Visits Tue-Sat 9-1, 2-6 Closed Aug 1-20
€10 (tasting & food)

COVILHÃ C3

Adega Cooperativa da Covilhã This co-operative makes good modern, easy-drinking wines, but is not in good shape financially at present. We heard mutterings throughout the region. Everyone wants them to win through, but no one quite knows if they will. The wines are good – do go and buy some! The **Piornos Branco** is mostly Síria, with a little Arinto, crisp,

modern and lemony. **Piornos Trincadeira** is dark and serious, with a touch of oak and bright acidity. **Piornos Reserva**, Rufete, Trincadeira and Jaen, is soft and ripe, with rich red fruit flavours. And the **Covilhã Colheita dos Socios** is a lovely, strawberry-fruited red, with good firm tannins, smoky maturity and good length.
Quinta das Poldras, 6200-165 Covilhã
T+351 275 330 750
E contacto@adegacovilha.pt
W www.adegacovilha.pt
Visits Mon-Fri 9-5

Figueira de Castelo Rodrigo D4

Adega Cooperativa de Figueira de Castelo Rodrigo Only just south of the eastern end of the Douro region, this co-op has about 1,000 members, farming 1,200ha. Altitudes are between 500m and 700m, so acidity is never a problem, even in the heat of summer. **Castelo Rodrigo Branco** is mainly Síria and Malvasia Fina, soft and aromatic, with good acidity. **Castelo Rodrigo Tinto** is unoaked Tinta Roriz, Rufete, Marufo and Touriga Franca, with simple, juicy raspberry fruit. There are three single variety reds, a rich, raspberry-jammy **Castelo Rodrigo Alfrocheiro**, a fragrant, aromatic **Castelo Rodrigo Touriga Nacional**, and an austere, herby **Castelo Rodrigo Tinta Roriz**.
Rua Pedro Jacques Magalhães 7,
Apartado 11,
6440-108 Figueira de Castelo Rodrigo
T+351 271 319 220
W www.adegacastelorodrigo.com
Visits Mon-Fri 9-5

Fundão C2

Adega Cooperativa de Fundão
Towards the southern end of the Castelo Branco sub-region, this co-op has about 1,000 members, farming 1,500ha of vineyard. Their vineyards are to the north

and the south of Gardunha mountain, not quite as high as some parts of the Beira Interior, between 300m and 400m altitude. **Cova da Beira Branco** is 40% Arinto and equal parts of Fonte Cal and Síria, crisp, honeyed and characterful. **Cova da Beira Tinto** is about two-thirds Trincadeira, and a mix of other grapes, with bright, slightly baked fruit, firm tannins and high acidity. **Fundamus Prestige Tinto** comes from vineyards south of Gardunha mountain, 60% Aragonez (aka Tinta Roriz) and 40% Jaen, with a year's stay in new oak barrels. It is quite oaky, but has good, sweet-fruited red berry flavour under, and some length.
Rua Cidade da Covilhã, 6230-346 Fundão
T+351 275 752 275
E geral@adegafundao.com
W www.adegafundao.com
Visits Mon-Fri 8.30-6 Sat appt only

Pinhel D3

Adega Cooperativa de Pinhel High-country co-operative with about 2,300 members farming 3,000ha of vineyard, at an average altitude of 500m. Where possible, they are trying to persuade their members to replant late-ripening Touriga Franca with earlier-ripening varieties. One of the best aspects of their wines is that no oak is used, allowing the brightness of the high altitude to shine through unobscured. The **Pinhel DOC Branco** is bright and steely, mostly Síria, with lean, crisp, lemony fruit. The **Pinhel Rosado** is

even better, with attractive berry fruit and good acidity. **Encostas do Côa Tinto** is a VR Beiras (because of the greater flexibility in the rules), a hint rustic, but with good, ripe, red and black fruit flavours. **Varanda do Castelo** is back within the DOC Beira Interior rules, a blend of Rufete and Marufe (a black grape much prized locally as an eating grape), dark, savoury and meaty, with firm tannins, good acidity and a hint of black olive on the finish.
Largo dos Combatentes da Grande Guerra,
6400-348 Pinhel
T+351 271 413 352
E adega-pinhel@mail.telepac.pt
Visits Mon-Fri 9-12 2-5

Souro Pires D3

Rogenda Rui Moura Alves is the consultant winemaker at this estate just south of Pinhel, owned by the parents of one of Portugal's well-known wine critics, João Afonso. Rui has a preference for *lagares,* but there are steel tanks as well, and the wines are of a very high standard. **Rogenda Branco**, made from barrel-fermented Malvasia Fina and Chardonnay, is rich, opulent and oaky, with high acidity, exotic flavours, length and persistence. The **Rogenda Branco Bruto Natural**, Malvasia Fina and Viosinho, is delicate, citrus and greengage-flavoured fizz. **Rogenda Tinto** is Touriga Nacional and Tinta Roriz, elegant and red-fruited, with firm tannins. **Rogenda Reserva**, pure Touriga Nacional, is very aromatic, floral and herby, with high, ripe tannins and lovely acidity.
Souro Pires, 6400-000 Pinhel
T+351 271 412 469
E teresamafonso@iol.pt/madeiraafonso@iol.pt
Visits appt only

TORTOSENDO C2

Almeida Garrett You are more likely to notice this brand-name rather than the company's real name, Sociedade Agrícola da Beira, which shortens to the acronym SABE. The company is owned by the Garrett family, descendants of the romantic poet and freedom fighter Almeida Garrett, who wrote in the first half of the 19th century. The Garrett family settled near Castelo Branco at the beginning of the 19th century, and made wine in the Castelo Branco, Covilhã and Fundão areas. They imported the first Chardonnays into Portugal in the late 19th century. They still grow Chardonnay in their 50ha vineyard, most of which has been replanted recently. They also make sheep's cheeses, olive oil, and have cattle and forests. *(Opposite, Zito Almeida Garrett, current owner.)*

The village of Tortosendo lies at nearly 600m altitude, so there's no problem with acidity in the Almeida Garrett wines! It's a very good range, starting with the unoaked **Entre Serras Chardonnay**, bright and lemony, with acidity that disguises the 15% alcohol. The **Almeida Garrett Chardonnay**, on the other hand, gets the full oak treatment, delicate, bready, creamy and citrussy, with length and balance. The red **Entre Serras** is lightly oaked, too, a blend of Tinta Roriz, Trincadeira and Tinta Barroca, with bright raspberry and damson fruit and firm tannins. **Almeida Garrett Colheita Seleccionada Tinto** has 40% Touriga Nacional in the blend, and you can taste it, bright-fruited, aromatic and herby.

Almeida Garrett Touriga Nacional is lovely, with herby aromas, dense, ripe flavour and good acidity. The **Almeida Garrett Reserva Tinto** is Touriga Nacional, Syrah and Merlot, soft, ripe and savoury, with firm tannins, length and perfume.
Rua Dona Maria Rosália Proença 15,
   6200-758 Tortosendo
T +351 275 951 217 / 275 951 725
E sabesa@mail.telepac.pt
Visits Mon-Fri 8.30-12.30, 2.30-6.30 appt
   only Closed Easter & Christmas €5

VERMIOSA D4

Vinhos Andrade de Almeida Oscar de Almeida started growing grapes over 60 years ago, and his family have continued along the same path. The estate now has 28ha of vines, but has only recently started to make wine. All the grapes used to be delivered to the local co-op, now perhaps one-fifth are made into wine on the estate, in a winery built in 2004. The **Versus Síria Branco** is steely, lean and mineral. **Versus Tinto**, a blend of Tinta Roriz, Touriga Franca, Touriga Nacional and Tinta Barroca, is rich and appealing, with soft, raspberry fruit and firm tannins. A tiny amount of an **Oscar de Almeida Touriga Nacional** has also been made, with ripe, aromatic raspberry fruit, excellent acidity, opulence and balance.
Rua do Chafariz Velho, 6440-261 Vermiosa
T +351 937 771 414
E vinhosandradedealmeida@gmail.com
Visits appt only

VILAR TORPIM

Quinta do Cardo It may be flat land, but Companhia das Quintas' Beira Interior estate is high flat land. In fact, at about 700m altitude, the company believes it to be the highest vineyard in Portugal. The ochre-yellow winery stands in a 169ha estate, of which 80ha are vines, planted in

reddish clay-based soil south of Castelo Rodrigo. It was the second property bought by Miguel Azevedo (in 1999) when he was putting together Companhia das Quintas. As few chemical products are used as possible in the vineyard, and the winery is well-equipped. **Quinta do Cardo Síria** is strongly lemony, brisk and steely. **Quinta do Cardo Rosé** is from a blend of Touriga Nacional, Touriga Franca, Tinta Roriz and Mourisco, herby, ripe-fruited and just off-dry. **Quinta do Cardo Special Selection**, pure Touriga Nacional, is a delight, wonderfully bright, aromatic and herby, with floral intensity. The surprise is the **Quinta do Cardo Bruto**, a sparkling red made from the local grape Mourisco, bright, fresh and creamy with lovely raspberry fruit.
6440-999 Figueira de Castelo Rodrigo
T +351 271 377 131
E cardo@companhiadasquintas.pt
W www.companhiadasquintas.pt

WATCH OUT FOR THESE WINES

Narigudo Tinto, VR Beiras (Uvacasta)

Morpheu Tinto, DOC Beira Interior (Uvacasta)

Quinta de Foz de Arouce

The Osório family has lived here since the 17th century. Foz de Arouce is south of Coimbra, near the foothills of the Serra da Lousã, and sheltered from Atlantic weather by various mountain ranges. João Osório, Conde de Foz de Arouce, is in charge, helped by two sons-in-law, Luís Castro and João Portugal Ramos, both notable wine producers in their own rights. The estate has 15ha of vines, nearly 3ha 70 years old, the rest replanted in 2000 and 2005. The old vines are mostly Baga, and 2ha of white is Cercial. The young vines are a mixture of Baga and Touriga Nacional. Sometimes he has to pick as late as early October, so it's risky, and he lost the 2000 and 2002 vintages. But when the weather holds, he has occasionally seen his old Baga get to 18% potential alcohol! Grapes from the white and the old red vines are crushed in stone *lagares*, then the whites are fermented in old oak and aged in newer oak; the *vinhas velhas* red finishes its fermentation in the *lagares*. Other reds are fermented in steel. He first sold under the Foz de Arouce label in 1988. The **Quinta de Foz de Arouce Branco** is lean, minerally,

lemony and elegant, with a touch of oak. It ages to creamy, toasty minerality. **Quinta de Foz de Arouce Tinto** is young vine Baga, tarry and intense. The really exciting red comes from the old vines, **Quinta de Foz de Arouce Vinhas Velhas de Santa Maria**, old Baga masquerading as Touriga Nacional, with extraordinary perfumes of bergamot and orange peel when young, and dense, ripe tannins, and evolving to complexity, elegance and more perfume with age.

MARINHA DAS ONDAS A2

Quinta dos Cozinheiros A very particular place, 8km from the sea, in the south-western corner of Beiras. The grapes grown (Maria Gomes and Bical for whites, Baga and Touriga Nacional for reds) are more in tune with Bairrada than with other Beiras regions, and the consultant is Luís Pato, one of Bairrada's greatest winemakers. Owner José Mendonça divides his 15ha of vineyard into two soil types, Pliocene and Miocene clays. The Pliocene soil is on a plateau 100m above sea level, and makes light, fresh wines; the Miocene, in a valley, gives richer wines. All the vineyard work is done by hand. The **Quinta dos Cozinheiros Maria Gomes** is light and fresh, with lemony aromas. The **Quinta dos Cozinheiros Branco** has 20% of Bical in with the Maria Gomes, from the richer soil and mostly fermented in older oak, with flavours of toast and marmalade. His top wines are called Utopia. The **Utopia Branco** is the same grape blend as the Branco, fermented in new French oak barrels, discreet, rich and creamy, with bready, subtle flavours. **Quinta dos Cozinheiros Bruto Rosé** is a bubbly made from Baga and Touriga Nacional, crisp and refreshing, with hints of strawberry and herbs. **Quinta dos Cozinheiros Lagar** is mainly old vines (Baga predominant), fermented in *lagares*, tangy, savoury and herby, with high acidity. **Quinta dos Cozinheiros Poerinho** (aka Baga) is dark and intense, with rich berry fruit. **Utopia Tinto** (Baga) is rich and oaky, quite traditional, with length and floral perfume.
3090-769 Marinha das Ondas
T+351 233 950 155
E qtacozinheiros@mail.telepac.pt
W www.quintadoscozinheiros.com
Visits Mon-Fri 10-6 Sat & Sun appt only
€10 (wine and cheese tasting)

Mata do Bussaco F6

Bussaco Palace Hotel This wonderful, extravagantly ornate hotel in the middle of Buçaco Forest (you'll see the spelling variation when you're in the area) has a tradition of making its own wines. They have very little in the way of vines, just two small vineyards near Curia in Bairrada, of 1ha and 2ha respectively, and buy from local producers in both Bairrada and Dão. As the hotel is outside the DOC limits for both regions, it would not legally be possible to make wine labelled as either, even if they wanted to – which, historically, they have not, and they show no sign of changing. The late José dos Santos, General Manager at the hotel for over 40 years, and very much in charge of the cellar, was guarded about his sources of grapes. The wines were very good, red and white, and guests should enjoy them without worrying too much how they had been made. Paulo Mesquita,

the current General Manager, is much more forthcoming. The white wine (roughly equal amounts of Maria Gomes, Bical and Encruzado) is barrel-fermented in new French oak barrels. The red (half and half Baga from Bairrada and Touriga Nacional from Dão) is foot-trodden in stone *lagares*, then aged for two years in the barrels used to ferment the white wine the year before. The **Buçaco Branco Reserva** starts fragrant, creamy and lemony, with a hint of oak, and develops steely complexity and minerality with age. The **Buçaco Tinto Reserva** is rich but restrained at first, with firm tannins and pure-fruited raspberry and damson flavours, then develops savoury, malty, complexity as it ages, with notes of wood and beeswax.

Cellar-visits and tastings are possible only if you are staying at the hotel, or have a reservation for lunch or dinner. The wines are on sale only at the Almeida hotels. They offer three different tastings, the 'Classical', of two young wines, the 'Epic', of two young wines and two older, and the 'Royal', of two young wines and two very old wines.

Mata do Bussaco, 3050-261 Luso
T +351 231 937 970
E bussaco@almeidahotels.com
W www.almeidahotels.com
Visits free to hotel guests and restaurant
*   customers 2 days' notice*
Tastings €12, €24, €35

THE POWER OF PINK – MATEUS & CO

It would be unthinkable to write a book about Portuguese wine and food without including Mateus Rosé. With the exception of port, Mateus is easily Portugal's best-known wine. But in a book organised by regions, it's hard to know where to put it. Mateus Rosé is a wine of no fixed abode, a wine whose roots are in Portugal, but in no particular region. However, most of the juice gathered to make Mateus is fermented at a large Sogrape winery in Bairrada, so in this book we shall make the Beiras its home.

Mateus Rosé was born in tough times during and after World War Two, when the north of Portugal was growing too many grapes that were not really good enough to make port or red wine. But they exactly fitted the recipe for good, low-alcohol rosé. The partners who formed Sogrape were the first to put these grapes to good use. Mateus'

eventual success spawned a host of lookalikes, and these non-regional rosés have played a large part in draining any potential Portuguese wine lake. But Mateus is still out in front, subtly changing its iconic packaging, and creating pink Mateus progeny from other countries. And Mateus still laps up much of the less-ripe Baga from Bairrada, and other varieties from Trás-os-Montes, the Beiras and Douro, while Lancers Rosé does the same for Castelão in Terras do Sado. Through skilled winemaking and modern techniques, pigs' ears turn into purses, and grapes that lacked sun are transformed into a dream of Portuguese summer.

Eat in the Beiras

Some of Portugal's greatest gastronomic experiences await you in the Beiras. Roast suckling pig *(leitão)* can be bought anywhere in Portugal, but Bairrada's is best – if you choose the right restaurant. Queijo da Serra da Estrela is Portugal's most famous and probably most delicious cheese, and its bi-product, ricotta *(requeijão),* is wonderful with *doce de abóbora,* a jam made from the region's plentiful pumpkins. There's all kinds of game in the mountains, wild duck in the marshes around Aveiro. Fish and seafood including excellent mussels down the coast, and trout, eels, elvers and the eel-like lampreys *(lampreias)* in the rivers. As ever, there are local delights for the sweet of tooth.

The best roast suckling pig we've ever eaten was in a little old tractor shed in a field up winding lanes somewhere in Bairrada. It was ridiculously moist and tender, its salty crackling super-thin, crisp and smoky. The worst was fatty and limp, outside Mealhada in a big *leitão* cafeteria that advertised its wares with bright neon piglet signs. We couldn't finish our shared plate.

The small town of Mealhada has become Bairrada's suckling pig capital. It's a one-dish town, with over 50 *leitão* joints along the 3km main drag. Not a good birthplace, if you're a piglet. Some restaurants get through hundreds a day, especially at weekends. People flock from far around, or make a small sortie from the Lisbon-Porto motorway; you can eat it on the spot, or pick up a take-away for a picnic in the woods. Mealhada also stocks the ready-meal shelves of supermarkets all around the country.

So what are their secrets? Their piglets are sometimes, but not always, a cross between the flavourful northern *bisaro* pig and other local breeds. They are typically five to six weeks old, milk-fed by their mothers. Some of the best restaurants employ their own butcher, because *leitão,* they say, is best slaughtered and roasted within the day; and in the meantime it shouldn't be refrigerated. In Mealhada they make a thick paste of crushed garlic, salt and pepper, parsley, bacon, meat juices, lard, olive oil, a bit of white wine and bay leaf, and gently rub the skin with this before stuffing the cavity and sewing it up.

Traditionally the piglets were threaded, whole, onto a wooden pole, but nowadays most poles are stainless steel. The roasting

Left From March onwards, the mountain ewes of the Serra da Estrela concentrate on motherhood – not until late autumn are they milked again for the wonderful gooey cheese

Queijo da Estrela and Other Cheeses

You'll have to visit early in the year to catch the spectacular Queijo da Serra da Estrela at its gooiest. It is made mainly from November to March, from the winter milk of sheep grazing only in the Serra da Estrela. The curdling agent is not animal rennet, but a rennet made by fermenting an extract of a wild mountain thistle, cynara cadunculus. Rules for the production of this DOP (Denominação de Origem Protegida) cheese are very strict, and include a maturation period of at least thirty days. The result is a squat, yellow-rinded cylinder, from which the top is sliced to spoon out the gloopy, whitish-yellow cheese. The paste becomes thicker and darker as the cheese matures and the year progresses. Is it better young or mature? Opinions differ. Many dubious cheeses pretend to be the real thing, and may disappoint – check that it says 'DOP' on the label. And eat it with the local rye bread.

Numerous other sheep and goats cheeses are made in the Serra da Estrela, including soft, white, fresh cheeses. The ricotta made as a bi-product of Queijo da Estrela, Requeijão da Serra da Estrela, also has a DOP. The whey drained from the infant cheese is heated until the proteins coagulate, then the solids are strained off again. Eat requeijão with pumpkin jam *(doce de abóbora)* or honey and cinnamon for breakfast or dessert.

The other Beiras cheeses mentioned in official despatches come mostly from the south-eastern mountains around Castelo Branco. Queijo de Castelo Branco and Queijo Amarelo da Beira Baixa are similar in style to Queijo da Serra da Estrela. Queijo Picante da Beira Baixa is a hard cheese, from goats' or ewes' milk, sharp and powerful with a bit of age. There's one more demarcated cheese south of Coimbra: Rabaçal is small and white, and can be fresh and curdy, or aged, firm and quite strongly flavoured.

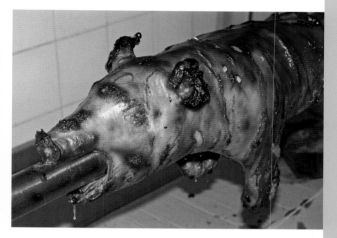

Left A mouthwatering dessert from Púcara restaurant in Viseu, Dão

Above Ready to eat, meltingly tender, crispy *leitão* in the suckling pig capital of Mealhada, in the heart of Bairrada

should be done in a wood-fired oven. Several times during the cooking, the *leitão* is removed from the oven to chill a little. The fat is wiped off with a cloth, and it may be basted with cooling white wine. This apparently adds greatly to the crispiness and elasticity of the skin. Roasting time is between one and a half and two hours. It is done when it achieves the colour of 'toasted hazelnuts', they say. Traditionally it was served with slices of orange, potatoes boiled in their skins, and a simple salad. Most restaurants now serve it with chips.

And what to drink with it? The locals often plump for sparking Bairrada, white or red, but some prefer the local still wines.

Pigs do not have to be small to be beautiful. Full-grown pork is as vital to the Beiras cuisine as anywhere else in Portugal. In bars and as pre-prandial nibbles you'll be served salty strips of pork cracklings *(torresmos)*, and various hams and sausages including black pudding *(morcela)*, often slightly sweetened and containing pumpkin; and the very bready *farinheira* – a sausage containing lots of bread and pumpkin, with pork fat and paprika. Stuffed pig's stomach *(buchos de porco recheados)* appears on lots of menus –

stuffed with pork, breadcrumbs, eggs, wine and lots of onion and garlic. So does pork liver *(iscas)*, and grilled pork fillets *(febras grelhadas)*.

Chanfana is a local stew traditionally of elderly goat but nowadays often kid or lamb, with lots of garlic and red wine. Lamb *(borrego)* and kid *(cabrito)* are often roasted *(assado no forno)*, and roast veal *(vitela assada)* may come coated in rock salt. Game includes rabbit *(coelho)*, hare *(lebre)*, wild boar *(javali)*, and from mid-October to Christmas there's lots of quail, pheasant and partridge.

Corn bread *(broa de milho)* is delicious. Broa or maize polenta are incorporated into many local dishes, such as the *sopa da Beira*, made with ham hock, turnip tops and

cabbage and thickened with maize; or *migas de Lousã*, layered haricot beans, crumbled broa and turnip tops, all moistened with garlicky olive oil. *Bacalhau assado com broa* is oven-roasted with a topping of garlicky *broa* crumbs.

From the coast and the lagoons by Aveiro there's fish and seafood, of course. Mussels may be served on skewers, deep fried then marinated in a clove-scented vinaigrette. Eel stews *(caldeiradas de enguias)* are popular, and octopus rice *(arroz de polvo)*, made with the local rice, onions and olive oil. Lampreys *(lampreias)* cause a stir in the new year, as do elvas, expensive and now almost endangered baby eels *(enguias-bebés* or *meixões)* from autumn to spring.

It can't be Portugal if it doesn't end with something sweet. Consider, if you are self-catering, some wonderful

requeijão with the dark mountain honey *(mel da Serra da Lousã)* – this has also won demarcated status, in the mountains south-east of Coimbra. There are various regional honey cakes. The area around Fundão, Covilhã and Belmonte, over to the east in the Beira Interior, is renowned for its cherries and peaches. Around Esmolfe, east of Viseu in Dão country, they produce a sweet, aromatic little apple called Maçã Bravo de Esmolfe.

But it may not be long before you succumb to the local eggy concoctions. *Tigadela* is a lemony baked custard; *queijadas de Coimbra* are little curd cheese tarts set with the aid of lots of egg yolks; *pastéis de Vouzela* have flaky pastry with a sweet eggy filling; Viseu has its famous egg sweets, and Aveiro its *ovos moles,* syrupy, cooked egg yolks oozing from little boats or barrels. Those we can love, but we draw the line at *lampreia de ovos,* a sweet, curled-up effigy of the blood-sucking fish, made with ground almonds, eggs and yet more egg yolks, lots of sugar, and

chocolate drops for eyes, especially at Christmas.

Above Monday morning market in Tondela brings in farmers and even individuals with excess garden produce

Far left Delicious seafood

Left Yummy dessert from Púcara in Viseu

RESTAURANTS

AGUADA DE CIMA F7

Casa Vidal For local wine producers, this is one of the top places to eat roast suckling pig *(leitão à moda de Bairrada)*. Casa Vidal employs its own butcher, and cooks the meat to meltingly tender, crispy perfection. If you can resist the roast *leitão*, suckling pig also comes in various other ways, and there's roast kid, or goat and red wine stew *(chanfana)*. Though not long, the wine list has some good bottles. In the middle of an elusive little village 10km north of Mealhada, Casa Vidal is partly tiled, with simple, white decor. Don't arrive too late. The piglets may have flown.
Rua das Almas, Almas Areosa
T+351 234 666 353
€15 ♀
Open Tue-Thu lunch only, Fri & Sat lunch & din Closed Mon; Sun Oct-Jun

Fidalgo Good, traditional food includes suckling pig, excellent ham, grills and good home-made puddings in this atmospheric, rustic restaurant. An excellent selection of Bairradas dominates the wine list. There are old brick ovens, an old beamed ceiling, and paraphernalia of domestic and country life for decoration.
Largo Almas Areosa
T+351 234 666 226
€20 ♀ *V*
Closed Sun din

ANADIA (MALPOSTA) F6

Pompeu dos Frangos In this wonderfully old fashioned restaurant, where time stopped at least a century ago, the only thing to order is one of the melt-in-the-mouth *franguinhos* – 21-day-old poussins imbued with a secret marinade and tenderly grilled – with a good Bairrada off the very decent wine list. In the olden coaching days, this was a posting inn on the main Lisbon-Porto road – historic *azulejos* on the interior walls bear witness to the restaurant's former function.
Estrada Nacional 1,
Malaposta
T+351 231 512 653
E carlosaires@pompeu.pt
W www.pompeu.pt
€13 (chicken and wine) ♀

AVEIRO E7

A Barca This small restaurant in a restored old house by the port has won prizes for its cooking, based on the freshest of fish and seafood. The signature dish is clams cooked with white wine, garlic and fresh coriander *(amêijoas à Bulhão Pato)*. It's a light-hearted place with checked table cloths and very friendly, attentive staff. There's a modest but good list of Bairrada wines. Find it opposite the characterful flea market, the Mercado Negro.
Largo José Rabumba 5
T+351 234 426 024
€20 ♀ *V No credit cards*
Closed Sat din, Sun; 2nd half Aug or 1st half Sep

Mercado do Peixe An interesting wine list (fairly priced) accompanies simple, traditional fish and seafood dishes in this

new restaurant in central Aveiro. Decor is smart but minimalist – the main focus is through the big picture windows, down onto the town, and the canal.
Largo do Mercado do Peixe
T+351 234 383 511
E mercadopeixe@hotmail.com
€25-€30 ♀ *V*
Closed Sun din; 24 & 25 Dec, 1 Jan

AVEIRO (COSTA NOVA) E7

Praia de Tubarão A fun sea-side restaurant in one of Costa Nova's typical old white and red striped house, with well-cooked fresh fish and wonderful clams *(amêijoas)*. Other specialities are stews *(caldeiradas)* of fish and eel *(enguias)*. The wine list is good, if a bit short of wines from Bairrada, the nearest region just inland.
T+351 234 369 602
E a.dotubarao@iol.pt
€28 ♀
Closed Mon; 1 week May, Sep, 2nd half Oct

Dóri A very good Portuguese wine list accompanies the seafood at this lagoon-side restaurant. Highlight of the menu is a wet rice dish made with 'swimming crab' *(arroz de navalheira),* and the fried cuttlefish *(chocos fritos)* are delicious. Decor is modern style, with some old pictures of the village, and the terrace overlooks the calm water. A *dóri* was a small cod-fishing boat.
T+351 234 369 017
€20-€25 ♀ *Closed Mon*

BARCOUÇO E6
Manuel Júlio Between Coimbra and the suckling pig capital of Mealhada, a little restaurant whose roast suckling kid *(cabrito)* has been much appreciated by the locals ever since the restaurant was started by the grandparents of the current owners three-quarters of a century ago – but they do excellent roast piglet *(leitão)* as well, and substantial portions of other traditional dishes.
Estrada Nacional 1, Santa Lúzia
T+351 239 913 512
E manuel-julio@mail.telepac.pt
W www.manueljulio.pt
€15-€20 ♀ *V*
Closed Sun din

BELMONTE C3
Convento de Belmonte The Pousada of Belmonte (one of two that do not belong to the main group of *pousadas*) offers light, modern cooking, beautifully executed and presented, based on fine local products including herbs from the garden, and upon local traditions, despite the Brazilain origins of young chef Valdir Lubave. At weekends there are impressive lunchtime buffets, and the mushroom festival runs from October to December. The mushroom ice cream is not to be missed! This is a lovely place to stay *(page*

203) quite apart from the great food.
Serra da Esperança
T+351 275 910 300
E pousadadebelmonte@mail.telepac.pt
W www.pousadas.pt
€25 ♀ 🛏

BELMONTE C3
Quinta da Bica Part of a new golf resort on the outskirts of medieval Belmonte, this new restaurant offers complicated, inventive, modern cooking. The very modern dining room surrounds a glass cube, where the kitchen staff bustle in full view of diners. There's a bar, with beautiful exposed stone walling and stone mosaic floor, and a cosy seating area with log fire. Next project will be a new hotel.
Quinta da Bica, Gaia
T+351 275 431 434
E quinta-da-bica-golf@sapo.pt
€35

CAMPO G7
Santa Luzia This fresh, bright, friendly restaurant serves good local cooking just off the motorway north of Viseu. There is game in season, maybe hare or partridge. For afters, try the delicious ricotta with pumpkin jam *(requeijão com doce de abóbora).* The wine list is strong on local wines, plus wines from the Douro and Alentejo.
Estrada Nacional 2
T+351 232 459325
E santaluzia@restaurante-santaluzia.com
W www.restaurante-santaluzia.com
€18 ♀ *V*
Closed Mon

CANTANHEDE E6
Marquês de Marialva José Carlos Guerra worked for ten years in good restaurants in France before returning to this house on the square in Cantanhede, where he was born, to start up on his own. But it's not a French restaurant. The food here definitely has its heart set in Bairrada, though certain French influences dance around the edges, and charm their way inside. Choose from different set menus, but all  start with a selection of cured ham *(presunto),* charcuterie *(enchidos)* and cheeses, with fruit and nuts, and delicious bread and butter; and they finish with desserts that combine the flair of both nations. Numerous little dining rooms range from golden elegance to rustic, exposed stone walls and beams. Service is attentive. The wine list is, of course, particularly strong on Bairrada, including some venerable bottles. You must book.
Largo de Romal 14
T+351 231 420 010
E marques.marialva@clix.pt
W www.marquesdemarialva.com
€30-€40 ♀ *V!*
Closed Sun din; national hols din

CARRAPACHANA H7

Escorropicha, Ana! The dining room of 'Drink up, Ana!' is the beautifully restored upper room of an old granite house, the exposed stone walls hung with rustic knick-knacks. Downstairs is a village bar. Choose starters from a buffet and move on to hearty mountain dishes such as salt-cod with cabbage and moistened, crumbled corn-bread *(migas de bacalhau)*, or medallions of veal with black pudding *(medalhões de vitela com morcela)*. Service is attentive, the cellar well stocked with regional wines. Find it on the N17 south-west of Celorico da Beira.
Largo da Feira 1
T+351 271 776 691
E geral@escorropichana.com
W www.escorropichana.com
€20 ♀ V
Closed Mon din, Tue

CARREGAL DO SAL G6

Encontrus Probably the most sophisticated restaurant in the Dão region: chef Vítor Sobral's dishes are rooted in tradition, but modern in presentation, raw materials scrupulously sourced. You might choose cheeks of *porco preto* with chestnuts *(bochechas de porco preto com castanhas)*. The wine list has a very good Dão selection. There are two dining rooms and a bar, simply smart. Service is friendly and efficient.
Largo do Jardim Dr Manuel da Costa 3
T+351 232 960 200
E mail@encontrus.com
W www.encontrus.com
€16 ♀ V
Closed Sun din, Mon

Quinta de Cabriz Go-ahead, expanding wine company Dão Sul have a very good restaurant in the visitor reception centre at their Dão estate *(page 174)*. There are

two smart dining rooms serving traditional regional ingredients and dishes with modern touches, well cooked and well presented. There is very good local charcuterie *(enchidos)*. You might choose one of the tasting menus (€40); one of them is based around grape varieties. It's very busy at lunch and weekends.
Antiga Estrada Nacional 234
T+351 232 961 222
E daosul@daosul.com
W www.daosul.com
€25 ♀ V
Open every day

CASTELO BRANCO C2

Praça Velha Just one of the many attractions of Praça Velha is its long wine list and tasting menus with accompanying wine. The setting is intimate, romantic – a converted barn with great stone pillars supporting an old beamed roof, an arch at the end leading to a cosy area where a log fire burns in winter. Excellent charcuterie *(enchidos)*, grilled kid *(cabrito)* and local dishes; Thursday is *cozido* day – boiled meat and veg.
Praça de Camões 17
T+351 272 328 640
E pracavelha@gmail.com
€20-€22 ♀ V
Closed Sun din, Mon

COIMBRA F6

Arcadas da Capela The restaurant of the Hotel Quinta das Lágrimas *(page 203)* is worth a long detour for the creative, Michelin-starred cooking of Albano Lourenço, who

worked with some of the starry chefs of the Algarve. He is backed by Joachim Koerper from Eleven in Lisbon. Dishes are harmoniously and beautifully assembled from fine, seasonal, local raw materials, and fresh herbs and fruit from the garden.

Eat à la carte, or choose one of the two tasting menus. Service is excellent. The restaurant is narrow, flanked by glass-filled arcades, bright and elegant, looking out over the garden and fountain where Pedro and Inês are said to have secretly met *(page 196)*. The wine list is very long and very good, and includes a wine made specially for them by Dão Sul called – Pedro & Inês.
Rua António Augusto Gonçalve, Santa Clara
T+351 239 802 380
E hotelagrimas@mail.telepac.pt
W www.arcadasdacapela.gastronomias.com
€50-€117 ♀ ⇌

A Capella In the historic centre of Coimbra, drink good wine, eat *petiscos*, and soak up the sounds and sentiment of this ancient and modern temple of *fado*. This is a cult place to listen to Portugal's folk music – here in Coimbra only men perform. The Capela de Nossa Senhora da Vitória is a converted medieval chapel, now kitted out with tables downstairs, up in the gallery and outside on an upper terrace.
Capela de Nossa Senhora da Vitória, Largo
*   da Vitória, Rua Corpo de Deus*
T+351 239 833 985
E mail.acapella@gmail.com
€20 inc €10 entrance ♀

A Taberna Small, casually smart restaurant near the football stadium with clean, tiled interior, wood-fired ovens, friendly service and very good northern produce including charcuterie and the local Rabaçal cheese. Try the goat and red wine stew *(chanfana)*.
Rua dos Combatentes da Grande Guerra 86
T+351 239 716 265
E ataberna@portugalmail.pt
€23 V
Closed Sun din, Mon

Zé Manel dos Ossos There are only a few wooden tables in this tiny, simple, atmospheric place hidden down an alleyway. Served with humour, there may be grilled kid or belly of suckling pig, a beany wild boar stew *(feijoada de javali)*, and the boiled pork bones come highly recommended by the locals. Paper towels on the walls bear messages in numerous languages from satisfied customers.
Beco do Forno 12
T+351 239 823 790
€8-€10 No credit cards
Closed Sat din, Sun

COVILHÃ C2

Cozinha da Avó Attractive modern restaurant with a big terrace overlooking the swimming pool of a country club. Well-cooked local fare is accompanied by good wines served in nice glasses.
Clube de Campo, Quinta do Covelo
T+351 275 331 174
E dircom@imb-hotels.com
W www.imb-hotels.com
€18 ♀ *V*
Closed Sun din, Mon

FALORCA G7

O Martelo On benches around the fire in winter, outside in summer, surrounded by locals, start with a bottle of the home-made Dão, some cheese and excellent sausage, black pudding, cured ham and very good bread. This is a welcoming village restaurant, a traditional, solid granite house where kid *(cabritinho)* is a particularly succulent speciality, along with veal cutlets, *bacalhau* or preserved octopus grilled over vine prunings. Portions are substantial. The granite walls are lined with wine bottles, and decorated with boards stuck with customers' cards and appreciative notes. The wine is called Curral da Burra (Female Donkey Enclosure – it sounds better in Portuguese) and

that's the name by which the locals know the restaurant, too. Find it south of Viseu.
Falorca de Silgueiros
T+351 232 958 884
€30 No credit cards

FIGUEIRA DE CASTELO RODRIGO (CASTELO RODRIGO) H7

O Cantinho dos Ávos The beautifully-restored little mountain village of Castelo Rodrigo (south of Figueira de Castelo Rodrigo) is topped by a ruined castle. Up one of its narrow streets, the 'Grandparents' Little Corner' serves good local dishes and home-made sausages *(enchidos)*, accompanied by interesting wines. It is indeed small, but there's plenty of room on the terrace, whence there are fine views over the high plains and mountains.
Rua da Sinagoga 1
T+351 271 312 643
€10 ♀ *V on request No credit cards*
Closed Thurs Oct-Jun; 10 days Oct,
*   1 week May*

GOUVEIA

O Júlio A long-established family restaurant with a simple, comfortable dining room serving Beiras cuisine, lovingly prepared, including game in season and excellent puddings. You can see into the kitchen, with its wood-fired oven. Service is very friendly and helpful, and a good wine list is especially strong on Dão.
Rua do Loureiro 11
T+351 238 498 016
€15 ♀ *V*
Closed Tue; 2nd half Sep

MANGUALDE G7

O Valério An old stone house with a rustic atmosphere, where the good-humoured owner will serve you delicious Beiras dishes, roasts from the wood-fired oven, local charcuterie *(enchidos)* and

Queijo da Serra. The grilled octopus *(polvo grelhado)* is to die for. Wines are from the nearby Dão vineyards. One of the best places to eat in the Beiras.
Rua Combatentes da Grande Guerra
T+351 232 611 955
€10-15 V
Closed Sun; 1st half Sep

MEALHADA A2
Churrascaria Rocha Large roadside restaurant east of Mealhada on the way to Luso selling excellent *leitão* and good sparkling wine, not the most atmospheric, but the favourite of many of the local wine producers.
Fonte Nova
T+351 231 202 357
E churra-rocha@clix.pt
€20
Closed Tue

MEALHADA (PENEIREIRO) A2
Nova Casa dos Leitões A large and simple roadside restaurant popular with local wine people as one of the best places to eat *leitão*. It is conveniently open from 9am till midnight (last orders 11pm), and also does take-away *leitão*, whole or by the kilo. You could also choose *chanfana, rojões* or even a fishy *cataplana*. Some of the wines are home-made, and quite good. Find it just south of Mealhada.
Estrada Nacional 1, Peneireiro, Aguim
T+351 231 518 025
E ncleitoes@portugalmail.pt
€20 ⚲
Closed 25 Dec

NELAS G7
Os Antónios Once the winery of an old manor house, Os Antónios has big oak beams and loads of atmosphere and character. It was recently renovated and is under new management, but the same chef is

producing good, typical, regional cooking, including excellent stone-grilled beef and fine *bacalhau* dishes. There's a tempting wine list, strong on Dão, and including some old wines.
Largo Vasco da Gama 1
T+351 232 949 515
W www.osantonios.com
€15 ⚲ V
Closed Sun din

Bem Haja This *(pictured below)* was a top recommendation from numerous local wine producers for its good list of Dão wines and excellent, somewhat creative local cooking – for example partridge with coffee *(perdiz com café)*. There's roast kid on Sundays, and excellent Queijo da Serra. This used to be a winery (the old wine press is still there to prove it). Two dining rooms are bright and airy, with exposed granite block walls and beams and cheerfully coloured table cloths. There are log fires in winter. 'Bem haja!'

is a greeting to passers-by, something like the 'Eh oop!' of northern England.
Rua da Restauração 5
T+351 232 944 903
E restaurante.bemhaja@gmail.com
W www.bemhaja.cjb.net
€25 ⚲ V

SABUGAL D3
O Robalo 'The Sea Bass' is seriously above sea level, up in the mountains of the Beira Interior. The delightful old building with its exposed beams, granite walls and huge hearth has been in the same family for generations. It specialises in grills, including succulent lamb, kid and river fish, and excellent charcuterie. Wines are local.
Largo do Cinema 4
T+351 271 753 566
E restauranterobalo@hotmail.com
€17.50 V
Closed Sun except in Aug;
*   1st 20 days Oct*

Dom Sancho I
A lovely medieval building within
this wonderfully preserved fortified village.
Up a flight of stone steps, the restaurant
has exposed granite walls and good,
hearty local cooking. Finish with the
delicious ricotta with pumpkin jam
(*requeijão com doce de abóbora*).
Largo do Corro
T+351 271 388 267
E belicha_gomez@hotmail.com
€17 V
Closed Sun din; Mon

TAVEIRO A2

Dom Azeite A wonderful old olive-press
room, complete with museum pieces of
the trade, is the setting for this very special
restaurant, where the menu has become
fishier and more interesting following the
recent change of ownership – while the
quality of the cuisine is as good as ever.
Apart from grilled fish and seafood, there
is a rich fish stew (*cataplana*), goat cooked
in red wine (*chanfana*), wild sea bass
(*robalo*), and a few foreign interlopers such
as paella, or crêpes with mixed berries.
Wines are decent rather than sensational,
best from Bairrada and Dão. Find Taveiro

about 6km downstream from Coimbra,
on the south bank of the Mondego; Dom
Azeite is in the village centre.
Rua dos Combatentes 95
T+351 239 981 010
E domazeite@portugalmail.com
€25 V! Closed Sun din

TRANCOSO C3

Área Benta Modern, fun design in a
lovely old building in a narrow street –
old stone walls, decor in pink tones, and
good, traditional food well cooked. Lots
of Douro producers recommended us to
this place, as well as locals. *Benta* means
holy or blessed.
Rua dos Cavaleiros 30A
T+351 271 817 180
E areabenta@mail.pt
W www.areabenta.pt
€14-€15
Closed Mon, and Sun din in winter

VALELHAS C3

Vallécula One of the best places to eat in
the Beira Interior, a small family restaurant
serving local cuisine based on well-sourced
produce. Find it in the central square of
the village of Valelhas in the eastern folds
of the Serra da Estrela. The stone building
dates from 1642, and members of the same
family have cooked here for generations.
You might choose veal with oyster
mushrooms (*vitela com pleurotas*) or rabbit
with chestnuts (*coelho com castanhas*).
There's a good local wine list.
Praça Dr José de Castro
T+351 275 487 123
€20 ♀ V! No credit cards
Closed 1st half Sep

VISEU G7

Muralha da Sé By the cathedral, a low,
granite building with a garden terrace
and two sunny dining rooms, elegantly

rustic with modern touches. The same
could be said of the cooking, which is a
contemporary take on traditional dishes
and local ingredients, nicely presented.
An excellent wine list ranges around the
world, as well as Portugal, with plenty of
good Dão, of course.
Adro da Sé 24
T+351 232 437 777
E muralha.se@iol.pt
€20 V
Closed Sun din, Mon; 2 weeks Oct

Púcara This attractively modern (*above*)
restaurant on two floors serves stylish
modern cuisine based on local culinary
traditions and excellent local ingredients.
There's also *porco preto*, the flavoursome
pork and ham from the Alentejo. A good
wine list is particularly strong on Dão, but
has good selections, too, from the Douro
and Alentejo. There's a terrace, and a shop
selling oils and some deli products. Mundão
is on the north-eastern edge of Viseu.
Quinta do Catavejo, Lote 44, Mundão
T+351 232 429 174
E geral@pucara.pt
W www.pucara.pt
€20 ♀ V
Closed Sun din, Mon

MARKETS, FOOD AND WINE SHOPS

ÁGUEDA E7

Oficina de Sabores Wine shop with a fine selection of wines from Bairrada and elsewhere in Portugal. *Rua Joaquim Francisco Oliveira 27*

AVEIRO A3

Doce Pimenta Gabriel Vieira's new (early 2007) up-market gourmet food and wine shop in the Vera Cruz quarter of Aveiro sells wines, olive oils, spices, preserved vegetables, biscuits and locally-skimmed sea salt. Clean, white interior, friendly service. *Rua José Estevão 97*

Mercado do Peixe Aveiro's impressive fish market – buy fish and seafood straight from the fishermen who landed them. Now housed in a bright, modern building, it's all over by lunchtime. *Praça do Peixe*

Pastelaria Avenida First-class cakes, pastries, tarts, sweets and Aveiro speciality 'oves moles' ('soft eggs' – mainly egg-yolks and sugar) served in a listed building at the end of the avenue that leads from the station. *Avenida Dr Lourenço Peixinho 84*

Wine O'Clock Modern shop with over 2,000 wines, both Portuguese and foreign, as well as spirits, accessories and deli products. *Cais dos Mercantéis*

CELORICO DA BEIRA C3

Cheese market Cheese is the main draw at Celorica da Beira, a small town nestling at the northern tip of the Serra da Estrela mountains at an altitude of 500 metres. Its popular cheese market held on alternate Fridays attracts traders and cheese-makers from all over the region. A charming old cheese shop in the centre also caters for passing visitors.

FIGUEIRA DE CASTELO RODRIGO (CASTELO RODRIGO) D4

Sabores do Castelo Tea rooms and shop selling wine, jams, olive oils and *doce de abóbora* in the southerly of the two villages. *Rua Praça 18*

COIMBRA B2

Dom Vinho Both wine and customers are treated well in this excellent Coimbra shop in the Santo António dos Olivais part of the city. Not just Portuguese wines but interesting wines from elsewhere. *Rua Armando Sousa 17*

Garrafeira de Celas The spirit of education seeps across from the nearby university into this reasonably-priced wine shop, where tastings and other events are organised for clients. Well-displayed range of wines from all over Portugal, wine accessories, a good selection of vintage and tawny ports and sensible advice. *Rua Bernardo de Albuquerque 64*

ESPINHO A4

Casa Alves Ribeiro We're cheating – Espinho is up in the north-west, just off

the Beiras VR map. Everything from brilliant *bacalhau* to freshly-ground coffee, with a wide selection of wines from cheap to champion. And Riedel glasses to drink them from. *Rua 19 294*

Gaveto A truly amazing selection of Portuguese wines and spirits is only the start of what you will find in this gourmet's treasure-trove. Cheeses, jams, foie gras, patés, oils, vinegars, chutneys, dried herbs, spices, sea salt, tea, coffee, chocolates, rice, truffles, pasta, cookware and hand-painted ceramics are some of the other goodies. *Rua 62 457*

Market, a big one, on Mondays, selling food and other goods.

MOGOFORES (MALAPOSTA) E6

Garrafeira Vogabante A small wine shop in the village of Malaposta east of Mogofores with a good range of Bairrada wines. *Estrada Nacional 1*

MARIALVA D4

Casas do Côro Lovely wine-shop set in this enchanting, well restored village *(aldeia historica)*. Good wines from all over Portugal, at fair prices.

MÊDA C4 **Vinho & Eventos** Just over the 'border' in the Douro chapter, an excellent wine shop and deli *(page 109)*. *Avenida do Parque*

Explore the Beiras

Let's start in the south-west, by Portugal's longest beach, at FIGUEIRA DA FOZ at the mouth of the River Mondego. It's a bustling seaside town, crowded in summer, with a casino, marina and surf. From here, it's a pleasant hour-long drive up the coast road, skirting some spectacular, untamed Atlantic beaches, such as Tocha and Mira, to AVEIRO. Affectionately known as the Venice of Portugal, the city is surrounded by salt-flats, beaches and lagoons and dominated by canals. It was once a prosperous port, but a great storm in 1575 left in its wake a sand bar nearly 50km long between city and Atlantic. Today it is mostly famous for the waterfowl of its lagoons, and its *moliceiros*, the gaily painted, gondola-like fishing boats you'll see parked along the main canal. Built out on the barrier 13km to the west, COSTA NOVA is a pretty seaside and surfing resort with some good fish restaurants, bursting out of their stripily-painted seams on summer weekends.

The wine region of Bairrada sits in the midst of the flat to gently hilly, wooded lowlands just in from the beaches. MEALHADA is the obvious lunch stop for a spot of succulent, crispy *leitão*, advertised on signs all along the main roads into town. Wine-tasting at the local cellars will greatly aid digestion.

Portugal's third city, COIMBRA, is not to be missed. Birthplace of six kings and the seat of Portugal's first university – one of the oldest in the world – it is the region's principal city and was the country's capital under the first Portuguese dynasty, until Lisbon was bestowed the honour in the 13th century. Nowadays it's the students who seem

to dictate affairs, particularly in May when the whole place explodes into colour and song as part of the end-of-academic-year celebrations. The River Mondego twists through the historic city centre.

A short drive southwest of Coimbra across the river lies CONIMBRIGA, a Roman site of impressive proportions and one that in its heyday commanded the great empire's route across the Iberian Peninsula *(see below)*. North of

THE SAD AND GRUESOME TALE OF PEDRO AND INÊS

Coimbra was the setting for Portugal's Romeo and Juliet story from the mid-14th century, featuring Pedro I and Inês de Castro. After the death of his wife, the then Prince Pedro fell in love with Inês, her Spanish lady-in-waiting. Fearful of her influence, King Afonso V had her murdered in Coimbra, unaware that the couple had secretly married in Bragança in order to legitimize their four sons. When Pedro succeeded to the throne in 1357 he took his revenge by murdering two of the three assassins and later exhuming his wife's body to proclaim her queen. He forced all the courtiers and nobles present to pay homage to her crowned corpse and kiss her decomposing hand.

Above Coimbra, on the twisting banks of the River Mondego, main city of the Beiras

Right Aveiro has been called the Venice of Portugal. Its lagoons are a great source of seafood

THERMAL SPAS – A CURE FOR GOUT?

Portugal's spas have traditionally been a serious, therapeutic business, around the thermal springs of the north and centre. The most famous are at Luso and Curia, near the Forest of Buçaco east of Mealhada. CURIA attracts patients suffering from rheumatism, hypertension, gout, kidney ailments and stress. The waters of LUSO rise in the São João spring in the centre of town, where visitors mingle with residents to drink, and fill up their containers. Both centres have on-site accommodation, restaurants and leisure facilities. SÃO PEDRO DO SUL near Viseu claims to be the oldest spa in the country – King Afonso Henriques apparently bathed his wounded leg in its soothing waters after the Battle of Badajoz in the 12th century.

Coimbra at the northernmost tip of the Serra do Buçaco is the big and beautiful Buçaco Forest, encircled by a wall built to exclude temptation for the monks who planted this wonderful landscape of native and exotic trees and shrubs.

VISEU, capital of the Dão country, is high on our list of Portugal's most charming towns. Once you have penetrated the defensive outer ring of confusing roundabouts, Viseu has the distinct feel of a small country town, but is in fact a city of art treasures, palaces and churches. Its soul is the 13th century cathedral at the highest point in the middle of town.

Heading southeast through the forested hills and valleys towards the Serra da Estrela, the scenery becomes mountainous, with high peaks slowly coming into view. In winter, the landscape is draped in white – and draws skiers and tobogganists; in spring the thaw feeds brooks and streams. The Parque Natural da Serra da Estrela covers 1,011sq km – the country's largest protected area. Well over 100km long, it forms a great granite barrier across the region.

Set at the foot of the mountain, SEIA is a light and airy town whose broad streets are lined with shops selling the local ewe's-milk cheese *(Queijo da Serra da Estrela)* and high-quality sheepskin goods. The N339 road then rises steeply to TORRE at the very top of the Serra da Estrela, where a small stone tower marks mainland Portugal's highest point. The onward journey is a roller-coaster ride of hairpin bends and head-spinning views as the road descends sharply to the pretty town of COVILHÃ, a perfect

Left A walk through the fragrant, exotic Mata Nacional do Buçaco, a vast walled forest planted in the 17th century by Carmelite monks

Right Village houses in the Serra da Estrela

ALDEIAS HISTÓRICAS – HISTORIC VILLAGES

In the mid-1990s, the Portuguese government started an initiative to restore some of Portugal's prettiest and most traditional-looking villages as part of a scheme to spread tourism to lesser-known parts of the country. Most of the chosen ones were in the Beiras. Today, the lovely fortified hilltop villages of ALMEIDA, BELMONTE, CASTELO MENDO, CASTELO NOVO, CASTELO RODRIGO, IDANHA-A-VELHA, LINHARES DA BEIRA, MARIALVA, MONSANTO, PIÓDÃO, TRANCOSO and SORTELHA can be appreciated in their full glory. Make a detour to Portugal's eastern edge and the granite village of MONSANTO, seemingly sprouting organically from the hillside. Though besieged more than 20 times, by Moors or Spaniards, it was never taken.

Far left The spectacular waterfall of Fraga da Pena in the Serra da Estrela

Left View from the Belmonte belfry

Right Castelo Rodrigo

base from which to explore. With its steep, narrow streets and spectacular mountain vista, Covilhã is the hub of Portugal's woollen industry. It was already a thriving cloth centre in Moorish times, and today's visitors have plenty of opportunity to shop for gloves, jackets, slippers and other woolly items. Near AVÔ, Fraga da Pena is a wonderful waterfall.

GUARDA, on the north-east flank of the Serra da Estrela, is Portugal's loftiest city and a very tempting stopover. On a 1,075m high plateau, it was founded in 1197. Many parts of the original walls are still standing, including three of the main entrances. It has a fine cathedral.

It's a straight drive down the A23, passing en route the enchanting little town of BELMONTE (birthplace of Pedro Álvares Cabral, discoverer of Brazil) to CASTELO BRANCO. The town occupies a low hill at the centre of flat lands just 18km from the Spanish frontier. Broad avenues and large squares give a pleasing air of prosperity. The town's top attraction is the Jardim Episcopal, an arrangement of little granite statues amidst trimmed boxed hedges and orange trees.

❋ VIEW FROM THE TOP ❋

AGUIAR DA BEIRA Tucked away in the pure granite landscape to the north of the Serra da Estrela, the town is pretty enough, but the views sweeping away to the distant hills of Spain are among the best in Portugal.

CABEÇA DA NEVE The peaks of the Serra do Caramulo, inland from Aveiro, provide head-spinning mountain views, over villages set amidst rock-strewn pastures, and Viseu, far to the east.

CRUZ ALTA More than 500 metres up in the Buçaco Forest, fine views of the ocean. A nearby museum relates the story of Wellington's Battle of Buçaco against the French in 1810.

LINHARES Arrive from Celorico da Beira at the end of the day to watch the sun set over the castle's two splendid towers, with the Serra da Estrela looming behind.

SERRA DA ESTRELA Numerous *miradouros* on the scenic road linking Manteigas and Gouveia.

AVEIRO **Boat trips** From outside the tourist office, take a boat trip around the lagoon. See the salt pans and nature reserve, home to a vast population of birds.

CONDEIXA-A-NOVA **Conímbriga** An easy 15-minute drive south from Coimbra, this sprawling 13-hectare site predates the Romans, who developed it into a thriving military outpost, one of the largest in the Iberian Peninsula. There's much to see, including the baths, villas, patterned pavements and a hot and cold water system. *Site open Mar-15 Sep*

every day 10-8.15 Sep-14 Mar 10-6.15) Museum open Mar-15 Sep Tue-Sun 10-8.15 Sep-14 Mar 10-6.15 Closed 1Jan, Easter, 1 May & 25 Dec.

SANTA MARIA DA FEIRA **Castelo** King of the Beiras castles is this fairytale structure with pointed turrets high on the horizon midway between Aveiro and Porto. Built between the 11th and 15th century, it has been adapted and renovated periodically since. The Great Hall is reached through a sunken gateway and the two parts of the castle are linked by a secret tunnel. Don't miss the lovely chapel outside the west

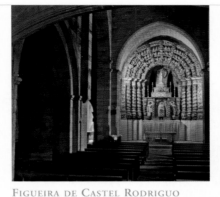

wall. The castle holds a ten-day medieval festival in August. *Open Tue-Sun 9.30-12.30, 2-6 Closed Mon (and sometimes earlier in winter)*

CHURCHES

AVEIRO **Convento de Jesus** Exquisite church with gold rococo interior, dates back to the 15th century and celebrates the life of Saint Joana, daughter of King Afonso V, who died at the convent in 1490. A series of striking paintings depict her entry into the convent through to her death. *Avenida de Santa Joana Princesa Open Tue-Sun 10-5.30 Closed public hols*

COIMBRA **Mosteiro de Santa Cruz** Founded in 1131, the church and monastery of Santa Cruz is historically the most interesting building in the city. It contains the tombs of Portugal's first two kings, Afonso Henriques and his son Sancho I, the lovely two-storey Cloister of Silence and the sacristy with rare paintings. *Praça 8 de Maio Open Mon-Sat 9-noon, 2-5.45, Sun 4-6*

FIGUEIRA DE CASTEL RODRIGUO **Convento d'Aguiar** This ruined Cistercian convent has a fine, austere church with beautiful barrel-vaulted stonework. *Open Tue-Sun 10-7.* Stay at the convent's delightful guest house nearby *(page 205).*

GUARDA **Sé** The city's imposing granite cathedral is austere Gothic, ornamented later with twisted Manueline columns and Renaissance details, including a large and intricate altarpiece. *Praça Luis de Camões Open Tue-Sat 9-12, 2-5*

VISEU **Sé** Behind a solid, twin-towered façade lies an elegantly simple Gothic interior with a fine renaissance double cloister. *Open 8-12, 2-7*

MUSEUMS

ANADIA **Museu do Vinho Bairrada** Six large ground-floor rooms in this new, purpose-built museum exhibit historic wine-making equipment. There's also a wine shop and garden restaurant. *Avenida Eng Tavares da Silva Open Tue-Fri 10-1, 2-6 Sat, Sun & public hols 11-7*

BELMONTE **Museu do Azeite** In this beautiful mountain village, where olive oil is a vital crop, the Museum of Olive Oil exhibits tools of the trade on three floors, with a restaurant and café and grounds – including an olive grove, of course. *Sítio do Chafariz Pequeno Open Wed-Sun 9.30-12.30, 2-6 Closed Mon; 1 May, 25 Dec, 1 Jan*

CARAMULO **Museu do Automóvel** Over 100 vintage vehicles include an 1899 Peugeot (the oldest car in Portugal and still in full working order), an immaculate 1911 Rolls Royce and a rare Bugatti 35B, which in 1931 established a new speed record by breaking the 200 kilometres-per-hour barrier. Motorcycle fans will marvel at the neat set of 1950s Harley Davidsons. *Rua Jean Lurçat 42 Open 10-1, 2-6 (5 in winter) Closed 24 Dec, 25 Dec (am), 1 Jan, Easter Sun (am) & Easter Mon*

VISEU **Museu de Grão Vasco** Alongside the cathedral, a grim-looking former bishops' palace houses the wonderful paintings of the 15th to 16th century Vasco Fernandes (the 'Great Vasco') and his contemporary Gaspar Vaz, amongst others, both from the city. *Largo da Sé Open Tue 2-6 Wed-Sun 10-6 Sun 10-2 Closed public hols*

FAIRS & FESTIVALS

JANUARY SANTA MARIA DA FEIRA **Festa das Fogaceiras** One of the loveliest castles in the region has a festival to match. Long files of young girls dressed in white carry bread and cakes in decorated baskets on their heads, in honour of a vow made by St Sebastian to provide bread for the survivors of an epidemic that struck the town in the 16th century. AVEIRO **Festa de São Gonçalinho** Also with bread as its main theme, the townsfolk let their hair down in honour of the patron saint of fishermen. Those who have prayed for the safe return of a fisherman climb to the top of a chapel and throw down loaves to the hungry crowd below.

FEBRUARY/MARCH **Feiras do Queijo da Serra** Hosted by different towns each year, a fair surrounding the Beiras' annual mountain cheese competition. Cheeses

from perhaps 50 producers, cheese-making demos, with folk dancing and sheep-shearing shows on the side (say *that* after a glass or two of Vinho Regional…)

MAY MONSANTO Festa das Cruzes This event marks the end of a prolonged siege. The desperate townsfolk threw a plump calf over the castle walls to deceive their attackers. Amazingly, it worked! To celebrate, the women of Monsanto climb up to the castle to the sound of tambourines and traditional songs before throwing pots of flowers and an imitation calf made of roses as the older women sing and dance.
COIMBRA **Queima das Fitas** The Burning of the Ribbons is the annual students' bash, a week-long frenzy of partying that starts with a romantic serenade on the steps of the old cathedral, culminating with a

lively parade through the city's streets.
VISEU **Viseu Gourmet** A prestigious new event that is to be repeated, held at the Solar do Vinho do Dão in Viseu. In May 2007, top Portuguese chefs, plus a few foreign ones, spent three days 're-inventing Beiras cuisine', giving demonstrations and also interactive dinners, where participants helped the chef to cook, and then a somelier chose wines to match and explained his choices. There was food and wine matching, a gourmet restaurant manned by the famous chefs, and a Gourmet Food Circus – a finger food dinner with specialities from the Beiras.

JUNE ANADIA Festa do Vinho et da Vinha This Bairrada wine fair attracts thousands of visitors to taste the wines of well over 100 producers to the strains of

local music. Succulent suckling pig and chips from the various cafés and restaurants within the fair will soak up the samples.
CELORICO DA BEIRA **Festa do Santo António** The whole town turns out to celebrate this annual knees-up with a communal picnic down by the river. The place is famous for its cheese, so no prizes for guessing what's in the sandwiches.
FUNDÃO and VILA VELHA DE RÓDÃO Cherry festivals early in the month, with guided tours to cherry orchards and local restaurants pulling out all their cherry recipes.

AUGUST AVEIRO Festa da Ria The city explodes into life once again for the annual Estuary Feast, featuring boat races, folk dancing and a competition for the best-painted *moliceiro* boat.
VISEU **Feira de São Mateus** This month of festivities dates back to 1392 and features plenty of music, folk dancing, handicrafts, much wining and dining and a fair with over 400 exhibitors.

SEPTEMBER NELAS Feira do Vinho do Dão Early in the month, a street fair where Dão wine producers offer wines to taste from stands along the streets.
AGUEDA **Festa do Leitão à Bairrada** The Bairrada Roasted Suckling Pig Festival lasts five days, during which more than 500 piglets may be consumed, along with large quantities of sparkling Bairrada.

DECEMBER VISEU Dão Vinhos e Sabores The first weekend of the month, three days of tastings of Dão wines (40 local producers), wine and food pairing, and cookery demonstrations by top Portuguese chefs, at the Solar do Vinho do Dão. It's an informal event, with live music, where you can chat to the winemakers while you taste. *Rua Dr Aristides de Sousa Mendes, Fontelo*

Sleep in the Beiras

BELMONTE C3
Pousada/Convento de Belmonte
Just over 1km from the town of Belmonte, the former convent nestles discreetly into the hillside. It's a magical place to stay, a stunning renovation and transformation, a sensitive juxtaposition of old and new. Flagstones, pillars, walls and door surrounds are made of huge granite blocks. The bar is in the old sacristy. Spacious rooms have terraces with spectacular views, and vases of mountain flowers decorate the public spaces.
Convento de Belmonte, Serra da Esperança, 6250 Belmonte
T+351 275 910 300
E pousadadebelmonte@mail.telepac.pt
W www.pousadas.pt
€170-€230
🛏23 S 1 ♀ ✕ ⚓

CANAS DE SENHORIM G7
Hotel Urgeiriça
South-west of Nelas, in the centre of Dão country, a renovated but still agreeably old-fashioned hotel set in gardens of mature trees and box-edged flower beds. There's an outdoor pool, tennis court and pool table. It's conveniently 25km from Viseu or the Serra da Estrela.
Urgeiriça, Canas de Senhorim
T+351 232 671 267
E reservas@hotelurgeirica.pt
W www.hotelurgeirica.pt
€80-€90 SC €130
🛏82 S 3 SC 5(2,4&6) ✕ ⚓ ✎

CAVADOUDE C3
Quinta do Pinheiro Delightful, old-fashioned rooms to rent on a sheep farm that makes excellent Queijo da Serra cheese. It's an atmospheric place, with a lovely swimming pool, on the edge of the Serra da Estrela, by the Mondego River. Guarda is only 5km away.
Cavadoude, 6300-080 Guarda
T+351 271 926 162
E qta.pinheiro@mail.telepac.pt
W www.quintadopinheiro.com
€75
🛏3 SC 2(2+2) ✕ ⚓ *Cards Amex only*

COIMBRA (SANTA CLARA) B2
Hotel Quinta das Lágrimas On the site of a medieval royal hunting lodge, the palace *(above)* was built in the 18th century, surrounded by 12ha of botanical gardens and woods. The Arcadas da Capela restaurant is one of the region's best *(page*

191), and breakfasts are excellent. It's a peaceful spot, on the opposite bank and 20 minutes' walk from Coimbra. A big modern spa was recently added, in cubist contrast to the warm, period elegance of the main house. The new building also has a gym, indoor pool, sauna and Turkish bath. Choose between ultra-modern rooms by the spa and garden or classic rooms in the palace *(below)*.

Rua António Augusto Gonçalve, Santa Clara
T+351 239 802 380
E hotelagrimas@mail.telepac.pt
W www.quintadaslagrimas.pt
€142-€169 (garden rooms), €178-€210
   (palace rooms)
🛏49 S 5 ♀ ✕ ⚓ ♨ ⚘ ✎ ✎

CURIA E2

Curia Palace Hotel It's no wonder that this imposing art deco hotel is frequently used as a film set when a grand 1920s ambiance is required. The Curia Palace reopened softly in June 2008 after a three-year closure for renovation. Although now you can click into the new century through internet connections, a conference centre and a modern spa, you will soon be transported back – by a wealth of stained and painted glass, ironwork, painted and carved panelling, original furniture, old clocks and light fittings. A museum area has a quaint old telephone exchange and a barber's shop. A 'mini-clube' may be in operation, with play rooms, safe interior courtyard and tiny children's loos – the hotel is keen to attract families. Outside, 12ha of parkland include formal gardens with resident swans and a small zoo/farm, tennis courts, table tennis, mountain bikes, a 9 hole par 35 golf course, and a large, retro outdoor swimming pool and pool bar to supplement the lovely oval-shaped indoor pool in the spa. There's still some work to be done on the gardens and grounds.
Curia (Tamengos), 3780-541 Anadia
T + 351 231 510 300
E curia@almeidahotels.com
W www.almeidahotels.com
€90-€150
🛏97 ⑤3 ⚲ ✕ ⚓ ♨ ✓

DAŘEI H7

Casa de Darei A lovely 18th century granite manor house just north of Mangualde, set amidst forests, sheep pasture and vines – you can visit the winery even if not resident *(page 175)*.

The Dão river flows through the property, forming a wide lake at this point. The house, long abandoned, has recently been tastefully restored, to provide individual rooms for rent, and self-catering apartments. Room prices include breakfast, which is an optional extra for apartment guests. A shop sells farm produce, including wine.
Lugar de Darei, 3530-107 Mangualde
T +351 232 613 200
E mail@casadedarei.pt
W www.casadedarei.pt
€55-€60, apts €120 & €145
🛏3 ⑤c 2(6&6+2) ⚲ ⚓ *river*
Min nights 2

FIGUEIRA DE CASTELO RODRIGO D4

Hospedaria do Convento Beside the Cistercian Mosteiro de Santa Maria de Aguiar (a national monument), in the Serra da Lousã mountain range, this was a lodging-house for ecclesiastical and noble travellers. An elegant, peaceful, historic building, it has been sensitively converted to offer cosy accommodation with contemporary comfort. Unwind on the tennis court, or in the Turkish bath.
T+351 271 311 819
E geral@hospedariadoconvento.pt
W www.hospedariadoconvento.pt
€65-€85 🛏9 ⑤1 ⚓ ⚲

FIGUEIRA DE CASTELO RODRIGO (CASTELO RODRIGO) D4

Casa da Cisterna Right up in the hills near the Spanish border, just south of the Douro Internacional, there are rooms and an apartment to let in a beautifully restored old house in the narrow streets of a hilltop village. Colourful, tastefully modern interiors blend into the ancient shell. Small, grassy, terraced gardens overlook the village and countryside, and the swimming pool has been created inside an

old cistern. Castelo Rodrigo is just south of Figueira de Castelo Rodrigo.
Rua da Cadeia 7, 6440-031 Castelo Rodrigo
T+351 271 313 515
E casadacisterna@casadacisterna.com
W www.casadacisterna.com
€65-€100
🛏6 ⑤1 ⑤c 1(6) ⚓ *No credit cards*

MARIALVA C4

Casas do Côro Not so long ago, this was a group of abandoned, dilapidated houses nestling beneath an 11th century citadel in one of Portugal's most beautiful mountain villages. We're right up in the north of the northern section of the Beira Interior DOC, just a few kilometres from the boundary of the Douro wine and port regions, surrounded by rocky terrain and wonderful mountain views. The houses have been beautifully renovated and charmingly, luxuriously decorated, with serious modern comforts. There are rooms and a suite to rent as well as whole self-catering cottages with little gardens, kitchens and open fires. All share a pool, jacuzzi and sauna. Breakfasts are excellent, with home-made cakes and bread. Other meals (on request) are also delicious local fare – the olive oil, almonds, pumpkins, fruit and veg will probably be their own, and they make their own charcuterie and sheep's cheese. A deli sells wines, olive oils and local produce. You could also pop over to Mêda, just 5km away but in the Douro chapter, for another excellent wine and food shop *(page 109)*. They will organise walks, mountain biking, hunting, fishing, hot air ballooning, canoeing…
Marialva, 6430-081 Mêda
T+351 271 590 003
E casa-do-coro@assec.pt
W www.assec.pt/casa-do-coro
€125-€135 🛏5 ⑤1 ⑤c 5(4,6,8, all+1) ⚲ ✕ *on request* ⚓ ♨ *jacuzzi*

MATA DO
BUSSACO F6
**Bussaco Palace
Hotel** *(also pictured
on previous full page)*
Staying amidst the
time-worn
splendour of this
Manueline palace
is an unforgettable
experience. Built
in 1907 as a royal
hunting retreat, and a hotel since 1917, it
has marvellous carved, twisted columns,
sweeping staircases and impressive murals,
and is set within peaceful, formal gardens
and the wonderful Forest of Buçaco (yes,
they are a bit confused about the spelling).
Spacious bedrooms range in period design
from 18th century to mid-20th. There's a
faded air, but there are modern amenities
nevertheless, such as high-speed wireless
internet access, and air-con. Breakfasts are
huge; our meal in the palatial dining
room, with its beautiful terrace, was
pleasant. Coimbra and the spa town of
Luso are just nearby.
*Mata Nacional do Bussaco, Luso,
3050-261, Coimbra*
T+351 231 937 970
E bussaco@almeidahotels.com
W www.palacehoteldobussaco.com
€120-€230
🛏58 ⑤4 ♀ ✗ ℃

MOGOFORES E6
Casa de Mogofores There are en-suite
rooms and an apartment to let in this
characterful manor house and its
outbuildings, set in parkland and woods
28km from both Coimbra and Aveiro. It
belongs to the Campolargo family, whose

large and excellent Bairrada wine estate
is in the neighbouring village of São
Lourenço do Bairro *(page 170)*. There is
an indoor heated swimming pool, Turkish
bath and gym.
*Rua Nossa Senhora Auxiliadora, Mogofores,
3780-453 Anadia*
T+351 231 512 448
E geral@casademogofores.com
W www.casademogofores.com
€80
🛏3 ⑤C 3(2+1) ♀ ✗ on request 🏊 ⚡
No credit cards

OIS DO BAIRRO E6
Casa de Ois In the delightful garden of
the home of outstanding winemaker Luis
Pato *(page 164)*, a separate flat has two
double rooms to rent, with two
bathrooms, and a sitting/dining room
with basic cooking facilities. (Guests may
also cook in the old wine cellar, which is
equipped to receive large groups.) From
the small outdoor swimming-pool there

are magnificent views over the vineyards.
Ois is a medieval village 2km from the
spa of Curia.
*Rua de Santo André 39,
3780-502 Ois do Bairro*
T+351 231 528 156
E contacto@luispato.com
W www.luispato.com
€60
🛏2 ♀ 🏊 *No credit cards*

PARADA DE GONTA G7
Quinta dos Três Rios In a wooded
valley in the centre of the Dão region, this
large stone house has views down over a
wide sweep of the River Pavia, its weirs
and waterfalls. It was recently bought by
a British couple, Hugh and Jane Forestier-

Walker, whose son Edward was much
involved in the renovation and creation
of six guest suites, some mansarded at the
top of the house. Their daughter Caroline,
an accomplished pastry chef, cooks
optional evening meals with Portuguese
tendencies (€20 for three courses,
including wine) served communally on
the terrace, or in the kitchen. Wine comes
from their 2ha of vineyards and they
organise two or three-night wine tours in
the region. There are bicycles to borrow.
*Rua Francisco de Oliveira 239, Parada de
Gonta, 3460-391 Tondela*
*T+351 232 959 189/ +44 020 8816
8853/ Skype hughfw54*
E hugh.jane@minola.co.uk
W www.minola.co.uk
€85-€125 ⑤6 ♀ ✗ on request
Min nights 2

PENALVA DO CASTELO H7

Casa Tavares de Pina At Quinta da Boavista, an excellent family wine estate *(page 178)* on the left bank of the River Dão, east of Viseu, there are apartments and rooms to rent in the main house and a separate cottage, which can be rented as a whole unit. The main house is built in traditional granite, cosily decorated and furnished with antiques. Meals other than breakfast (which is included) are very good, but must be ordered. There's a pool in the garden. The family also breed racehorses here, and it is possible to ride – if you dare.
T+351 919 858 340
E casatavaresdepina@sapo.pt
W www.casatavaresdepina.com
€60-€120
🛏2 Ⓢ2 sc 1(4+1) ☿ ✗ on request ⚓
No credit cards

TERRA DA GAGA B2

Casa do Vale do Linteiro Two sweet stone houses to rent in the Serra da Lousã mountains east of Coimbra separated by a stone courtyard. One has been renovated in original 18th century farmhouse style, the other is contemporary. Both have fireplaces and well-equipped kitchens. They share a pool, and forest views. Terra da Gaga is a sunny, hill-top village.

Terra da Gaga, 3200-350 Serpins
T+351 239 404 377
E valelinteiro@portugalmail.pt
W www.valelinteiro.com.
€70-€90
sc *2(4&6)* ⚓
Min nights 2

UNHAIS DA SERRA C2

Hotel and Mountain Spa A smart new mountain spa hotel is due to open in January 2008. This was a popular place to take the 'miracle waters' up to the 1920s – in a glacial valley on the south-east slopes of the Serra da Estrela, at 750m above sea level – the warm thermal springs being reputed to cure all kinds of ailments. Well integrated into the mountainous landscape, the impressive new building has a long, sloping roof, lots of glass and traditional materials. As well as medical spa facilities, it will have a recreational spa with massage, health club and gym, 'dynamic' swimming pools and paddle tennis courts. The buffet restaurant (traditional, modern and healthy) is to be headed by chef Orlando Dias. The wine list will be local, national and international.
Avenida das Termas, Unhais da Serra,
  6215-604 Covilhã
T+351 275 330 406
E dircom@imb-hotels.com
W www.imb-hotels.com
€120 🛏*72* Ⓢ*17* ☿ ✗ ⚓ ♨

VILAR SECO G7

Quinta da Fata South of Viseu in the heart of Dão country, this is a prize-winning wine estate whose imposing 19th century manor house has rooms and apartments to let. There's a secluded pool in the garden, a huge, ancient lime tree, lots of trimmed hedges, a lovely, part-shaded terrace, and vines and forest all around. The house itself has period furniture and lots of character, as do the big, cuddly Serra da Estrela mountain dogs.
Vilar Seco, 3520-225 Nelas
T+351 232 942 332
E quintadafata@sapo.pt
W www.quintadafata.com
€58 🛏*4* Ⓢ*1* sc *2(2+2)* ☿ ⚓
Closed 23-26 Dec
Min nights 3 high season

VISEU G7

Hotel Grão Vasco Conveniently in the very centre of town, this smart, elegant, spacious 1960s building has delightful gardens. Renovated rooms are attractive and comfortable, the quietest ones facing the garden pool. Food in the restaurant is traditional and of high quality.
Rua Gaspar Barreiros, Viseu 3500-032
T+351 232 423 511
E geral@hotelgraovasco.pt
W www.hotelgraovasco.pt
€85 🛏*106* Ⓢ*3* ✗ ⚓

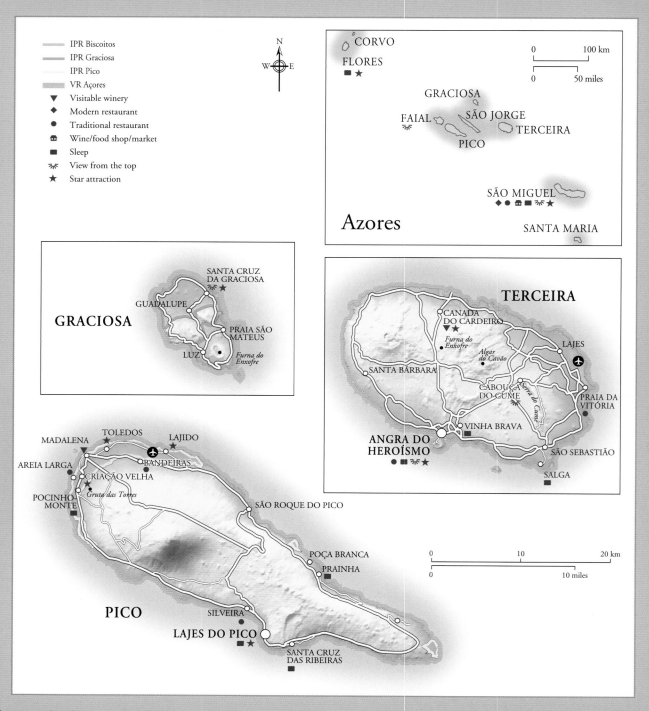

Legend

— IPR Biscoitos
— IPR Graciosa
— IPR Pico
▓ VR Açores
▼ Visitable winery
◆ Modern restaurant
● Traditional restaurant
🏠 Wine/food shop/market
■ Sleep
🌿 View from the top
★ Star attraction

N
W E
S

Azores

CORVO
FLORES
■ ★

0   100 km
0   50 miles

GRACIOSA
FAIAL SÃO JORGE
🌿 PICO TERCEIRA

SÃO MIGUEL
◆ ● 🏠 ■ 🌿 ★

SANTA MARIA

GRACIOSA

SANTA CRUZ
DA GRACIOSA
🌿 ★
GUADALUPE
PRAIA SÃO
MATEUS
LUZ ● *Furna do
Enxofre*

TERCEIRA

CANADA
DO CARDEIRO
▼ ★
*Furna do
Enxofre* ●
*Algar
do Cavão* LAJES
✈
SANTA BÁRBARA
CABOUCA
DO CUME PRAIA DA
VITÓRIA
VINHA BRAVA
ANGRA DO
HEROÍSMO SÃO SEBASTIÃO
● ■ 🌿 ★
SALGA
■

PICO

MADALENA TOLEDOS LAJIDO
★ ★
AREIA LARGA ✈ BANDEIRAS
CRIAÇÃO VELHA
POCINHO *Gruta das Torres*
MONTE
■ SÃO ROQUE DO PICO

POÇA BRANCA
PRAINHA
■

SILVEIRA
LAJES DO PICO
■ ★
SANTA CRUZ
DAS RIBEIRAS
■

0   10   20 km
0   10 miles

Azores

Beneath the beautiful, peaceful islands of the Azores, the earth is in ferment. Out in mid-Atlantic, on the same latitude as Lisbon, this is the meeting point of four tectonic plates. Six of the nine major islands have active volcanoes, there are picturesque crater lakes, smoking fumeroles, bubbling geysers, waterfalls, grottoes, 'beaches' composed of swirls of lava… The last earthquakes were in 1980 and 1998. Black basalt is the building material, and there's plenty of sulphur around to spray the vines!

And moulds must like the climate. You won't be long on the Azores before someone tells you, 'We can have every season in a single day.' Cartfuls of umbrellas always stand at the ready at the little island airports. Kept mild by the Gulf Stream, the islands are the spot where polar and tropical air masses meet. The weather changes with astonishing rapidity. The islanders are walking weather stations, very much aware of wind direction, quick to predict when the island-hopping planes will be able to arrive, or take off. Fog and rain are frequent, and there's a nearly-constant light veil of cloud. But for walkers, cyclists, sailors and nature-lovers, these islands are

fascinating. Every island has a different feel, a different degree of isolation, a different volcanic landscape. Nearly every coastal parish has a natural swimming pool in the rocks, with added steps and hand rails. Off shore there are whales, dolphins, turtles and a wealth of fish.

Blue hydrangeas grow wild beside roads, which may be paved with red or dark grey volcanic grit. Grey dry stone walls divide small, bright green fields, and form patchworks of tiny enclosures to protect the vines. From a distance, stone walls may look like hedges, green from a flourishing cover of mosses, lichen and little ferns. In places, junipers and laurel woods are remnants of the forest that was largely cut down by early settlers.

The islands were discovered in the 15th century, and settled by emigrés from Portugal and Flanders. They brought vines, maize and cattle, and traded with the old and new worlds. Wood was an early commodity, then woad, then internationally-prized wine, and oranges; whaling was important until banned in 1987. Pasture has now replaced most of the vines, and dairy farming vies for the title of top earner with tuna fishing and tourism.

Wine in the Azores

Wine regions
IPR Biscoitos
IPR Graciosa
IPR Pico
Vinho Regional Açores

Main local grapes
Red Merlot, Agronómica
White Arinto, Verdelho, Seara
Nova, Generosa, Rio Grande
For details of grapes see page 428

When you see the conditions in which Azores wine has traditionally been made, you will understand why production is declining. Vines were historically grown in *currais* (known as *curraletas* on the island of Terceira), little 'corrals', or enclosures, bounded by dry stone walls made of volcanic rocks. Some of these are barely two metres wide by three metres long. There is often no soil as such: vines are planted in cracks in the rock. Sometimes a small hole has been hollowed out into which the vine is planted. To do anything mechanically is impossible: this is historic agriculture, centuries old. And there is the added problem of a dwindling (and ageing) work-force.

The reasons for these *currais* were twofold: to shield the vines from winds and sea-spray, and to help along the ripening in this cool, damp climate by surrounding the vines with sun-warmed stones after sunset. Historically, the results were impressive, and the mid-Atlantic position of the Azores certainly helped wine sales through the 16th and 17th centuries, as the fleets of the Discoverers put in to refuel and take on supplies. In the 18th and 19th centuries, Azores wines were well enough known to find markets in North America, Europe, Russia and Brazil. Then, from 1850 onwards, oidium and phylloxera wiped out the Azorean vineyards. Eventually, the European *vitis vinifera* vines were replaced with American vines and hybrids, because they are immune to the insect's attacks. But these gave very inferior wines.

The kind of wines that made the Azores' reputation were the same as those in two of the three present IPRs, Pico (on Pico island) and Biscoitos (on Terceira). These are made from Verdelho, Arinto and Terrantez, the varieties planted before phylloxera struck, grown in *currais*, and usually fortified up to the 16% minimum alcohol required by the IPR rules. The best are made from grapes that have ripened to well over 16% potential alcohol. Graciosa, the other IPR, is an unfortified white wine, also made from the traditional white trio of grapes, with the possible addition of Malvasia Fina and Fernão Pires. IPR wines are usually labelled VLQPRD (for Biscoitos and Pico) and VQPRD (for Graciosa).

Few IPR wines are made now, and the new direction for Azorean wines is very much VR Açores. Despite the arrival in the 1980s of grapes such as Generosa, Seara Nova, Rio Grande, Agronómica, Saborinho and Complexa (none of which lived up to their optimistic names), advances have been made. The early-ripening Merlot has definite potential, even though the Azores climate is more suited to white wine production. New vineyards use more modern viticulture, sometimes training vines along wires. But there are still over four times as many 'American' vines as European *vitis vinifera*. The American vines and their hybrids give *vinho de cheiro*, 'fragrant wine', whose strange, musky, 'animal' smell and flavour is much loved by Azoreans (and Azoreans whose families emigrated to North America in the 19th and early 20th centuries).

WINERIES AND WINES

PICO, MADALENA

Cooperativa Vitivinícola da Ilha do Pico Everyone agrees that the wine quality at this 250 member co-operative has risen since Maria Álvares joined as winemaker. She's almost a local, from the island of Terceira; she studied winemaking on the mainland at Vila Real University, then returned to the Azores. She has modern equipment to make the better wines, pneumatic presses, peristaltic pumps and a new destalker, but not enough for all the production.

The cellar was originally built to make the traditional style of fortified Pico wine, from Verdelho, Arinto and Terrantez, but it soon became apparent that this would not make enough money. Next step was to vinify grapes from the American vines and hybrids. This was successful, and the Pico co-op still has a brand today, Cavaco (lobster), whose red and white versions are in great demand in the Azorean emigrant communities of North America.

Hope for the future is pinned on the unfortified reds and whites, Terras de Lava, Frei Gigante and Basalto, with a small amount of fortified wine still made. Red grapes struggle to ripen, and results with whites are much better. **Terras de Lava Branco** is mostly made of some rather unpromising grapes, with a quarter Verdelho, Arinto and Terrantez, but manages to be fresh and grassy, with a pleasantly creamy feel. **Frei Gigante** is

even better, mainly Arinto, with smaller amounts of Verdelho and Terrantez, high, steely acidity and a rich, creamy texture. **Lajido**, the VLQPRD Pico fortified wine, is a blend of Verdelho, Arinto and Terrantez, matured in oak for three years, quite dry and nutty, with high acidity.
Avenida Padre Nunes da Rosa 29,
  9950-302 Madalena, Pico
T+351 292 622 262
E geral@picowines.net
W www.picowines.net
Visits Mon-Fri 8-12, 1-5 appt only

PICO, VALVERDE

Curral de Atlantis Jorge Böhm (nurseryman and owner of Quinta de Plansel in the Alentejo) bought this 12ha vineyard in 1995. The vines had been abandoned. He cleared out the old *currais*, put down *bagacinha* (very small-sized, sand-like lava 'soil') and planted vines, all trained on wires. So far he has released wines made from Viosinho and Gouveio, and Cabernet Sauvignon and Merlot. As well as winemaking advice from Paulo Laureano, Böhm works with a father and son team who look after the vines, Manuel and Marco de Faria. You can visit Curral de Atlantis, and you will be shown the vineyards and winery, and taste. It's all free, but you do have to give them at least 24 hours' notice.

The winery is housed in a large lean-to, protected from the winds by stout

sheets of plastic and green netting *(above)*. There are steel tanks, an array of oak barrels and an elderly Willmes pneumatic press. Despite the unprepossessing surroundings, the wines are modern and well-made. The **Curral Atlântis Viosinho Gouveio Branco** is lean and appley, with good acidity. **Curral Atlântis Merlot Cabernet Sauvignon** is the best red in the Azores (so far!), with bright, blackcurranty fruit, smooth tannins and a hint of coconutty oak. There is also a very good, nutty, rich, sweet but balanced **Curral de Atlântis Licoroso**, made from Verdelho, Arinto and Terrantez grapes shrivelled on the vine, fermented for 6 to 12 months, then aged in new oak.
9950-365 Madalena, Pico
T+351 292 622 534
Visits Mon-Fri 11-12, 4-6 appt only

TERCEIRA, CANADA DO CARDEIRO
Casa Agrícola Brum This is not just a winery, but a museum as well, the 'Museum of Biscoitos Wine'. Luis Brum, whose family originally came from Flanders but have been on Terceira for 117 years, was the keeper of the sacred flame until he handed over to his two sons in 2006. He opened the museum to the public to celebrate the 100th anniversary of his family's presence on Terceira. It's really worth seeing the collection of different vines just outside the cellar, as well as visiting the fascinating museum. There is no charge for entry at present.

Luís Brum does not believe there's any point making red wine on Terceira: he says there's not enough sun. And he pointedly makes only *vinhos de mesa*, as a protest at his belief that the Terceira government does not support the local wine industry satisfactorily. Despite their lowly title, these wines are some of the best we found in the Azores, made in a small cellar, with up-to-date equipment. The **Donatário Branco**, mainly Verdelho with a touch of Terrantez de Terceira (Arinto), is lemony, fresh and steely, with good acidity and alcohol. **Da Resisténcia**

Branca is pure Verdelho, ripe and creamy, with hints of greengage and honey. **Chico Maria** is the fortified *licoroso*, pure Verdelho again, and made in dry, medium-dry and sweet styles. They are all very good, but the dry version is the best, tangy, nutty and intense, with high acidity.
Canada do Caldeiro,
9760-054 Praia da Vitória, Terceira
T+351 295 908 305/404
E museudovinhocasabrum@hotmail.com
W www.casaagricolabrum.com
Visits Apr-Sep Tue-Sun, Oct-Mar Tue-Sat
10-12, 1.30-5.30 Closed 1 week Sep

Eat in the Azores

Cows' milk is the main product of the Azores, much of it turned into milk powder for export, but also butter and cheese. There are two cheeses with Denominação de Origem Protegida (DOP) classification, both made with unpasteurised milk from cows grazing on natural pasture on the islands after which the cheeses are named. Queijo do Pico, made in flat rounds about 16cm across, is whitish-yellow, smooth and creamy and fairly piquant, at its best in winter and spring. Queijo de São Jorge is a firmer cheese, a descendant of the cheeses made by the early Flemish settlers, yellow, hard or semi-hard; it comes in big, flat rounds weighing 8 to 12 kilos each. When young, its texture is something between young Gouda and Cheddar, but it develops a granular, crumbly texture and a piquant flavour with maturity. Ilha is less regulated, made from pasteurised or unpasteurised milk, hard-crusted, firm and pale yellow, mild to nutty. You may also come across Queijo de São João, a flavoursome cheese with a soft paste and yellow rind.

The Azores' other DOPs are for fruit – pineapple (ananás) and passion fruit (maracujá) São Miguel has some of the world's finest pineapples. They are particularly aromatic, sweet and juicy, introduced long ago from Brazil, and grown in greenhouses on the south coast of São Miguel, around Ponta Delgada, Lagoa and Vila Franca do Campo. One of our recommended hotels *(page 226)* is on an estate that produces pineapples. You will undoubtedly meet on menus the lovely combination of *morcela* (black pudding) *com ananás.*

Apart from black pudding, another pork speciality you may be served as a pre-prandial nibble is salty pork crackling, *(torresmos de porco)*; *torresmos* often arrive on the restaurant table unordered, along with the bread. The succulent Azores beef is exported to Madeira as well as the mainland. On Terceira it is often served in the form of *alcatra* – marinated in wine and then baked in the oven – traditionally in a clay pot but nowadays often enveloped in foil – until meltingly tender. *Alcatra* may also be made with fish. If visiting São Miguel, do make a pilgrimage to the impressive Lagoa das Furnas in the east of the island, to eat the *cozido das furnas* – a meat and/or fish and vegetable stew cooked in the hot earth *(see overleaf).*

The islands' main fish is tuna, line-caught (to spare the many dolphins) from May to October. Small-scale fishermen catch more chub mackerel *(cavala)* than anything else, along with the smaller horse mackerel (known here as *chicharro*, on the mainland as *carapau*), sea bream *(goraz)*,

rock or scorpion fish *(rocaz)*, conger eels *(congros)*, and a kind of hake *(abrótea)*. Fish is often served in soups or rice. Delicious limpets *(lapas)* are in season only from June to September and may be served as a kind of risotto *(arroz de lapas)*. Octopus comes cut up small and stewed with wine, onions and red pepper paste *(polvo guisado com vinho)*. Grilled squid *(lulas grelhadas)* can be delicious but may be rubbery if they are left more than a few moments on the grill. Lobster is very expensive and some is imported.

Vegetables often come in the form of soups: fennel soup *(sopa de funcho)* is popular, and *caldo de couves* is a soup of finely shredded cabbage, olive oil and pureed potato, with a couple of slices of *chouriço* – much like the Minho's *caldo verde*. Many dishes, sweet and savoury, are seasoned with allspice, *pimenta da Jamaica*. And locally-grown sweet potatoes feature strongly.

There are two interesting alternatives to wheat bread: *pão de milho* is a corn bread, finer-textured than the *broa* of northern Portugal; and *massa souvada*, similar to *brioche*, but slightly lighter, part way between bread and cake, made with wheat flour, eggs, a touch of sugar, butter, lemon and nutmeg, raised by yeast. It is really delicious toasted for breakfast, when the sugar slightly caramelises. Traditionally, even though slightly sweet, it is eaten at the *Festas do Espírito Santo (page 224)* with the beef-and-vegetable *Sopa do Espírito Santo*.

On Pico, another sweet, egg-enriched yeast bread is associated with the Festas do Espírito Santo: the *bolo de véspera* is round and flat, with a hole in the middle, decorated with a Holy Ghost symbol. *Fofas* used to appear in Faial and São Miguel only at Carnival time in February, but now these 'sweetie-pies' (aniseed-flavoured choux pastry filled with sweetened, whipped cream) are sold all year. On Graciosa, try the *queijadas*, cinnamon-flavoured, star-shaped cakelets filled with caramel cream.

São Miguel, Furnas
Cozido das Furnas
You'll have to get up early to see the huge pots of *cozido* being lowered into their earthy ovens beside São Miguel's Lagoa das Furnas crater lake – at 6 or 7am. It takes a couple of strong men to carry the pots, full of chicken, beef, or pork with *chouriço*, bacon and black pudding, turnips, sweet potatoes, yams, cauliflower and cabbage; some *cozidos* are made with *bacalhau*. The pots are hermetically sealed, wrapped in sacks or cloth, and lowered on ropes or long metal hooks into the hot ground. Arriving at the spot after a gentle breakfast, all you will see is a series of large 'molehills'. Cooking time is between five and six hours – it will be ready in time for lunch. Try this succulent, filling, one-pot dish in the local restaurants, where it may go under the lengthier title of *cozido nas caldeiras à moda das furnas*. The restaurant of the Terra Nostra Garden Hotel *(page 226)* is our hot tip.

RESTAURANTS

PICO, AREIA LARGA

O Ancoradouro 'The Anchorage' is a cheerful, buzzing restaurant where all kinds of fish, seafood and fishy dishes are brilliantly prepared. Thick basalt walls ward off the winter weather, wide windows looking out towards the island of Faial. Eat in summer on a waterside terrace. There's a good offering of Pico wines, and a safe, middle-of-the road list of wines from the mainland. Perfectly situated for a visit to the curious vineyard *currais*. Just south of Madalena.
Rua João Lima Whitton Terra, Areia Longa
T+351 292 623 490
€20 V
Open summer every day Closed Oct

PICO, BANDEIRAS

O Luís Near the Pico wine co-operative, famous locally for its seafood stew *(caldeirada de peixe)*, well-prepared fresh fish and seafood. There are also pizzas, and some meat dishes.
Avenida Pedro Nunes da Rosa
T+351 292 623 901
€15 V
Closed Oct- early Nov

PICO, SILVEIRA

Hocus Pocus The light, airy restaurant of the Aldeia da Fonte hotel *(page 226)*, near Lajes do Pico on the south coast, is one of Pico's best, and this is the island's top spot for vegetarians. But there is also meat and fish, local and mainland Portuguese dishes, international and even oriental cuisine (Chinese and Japanese). It is very much open to non-residents. The restaurant itself is non-smoking, but active smokers can be served the same menu in the bar. Set in woods and gardens overlooking a beautiful, secluded bay, Hocus Pocus has a pretty terrace for fine weather.

Aldeia da Fonte
T+351 292 679 504
E info@aldeiadafonte.com
W www.aldeiadafonte.com
€30 ♇ *V!*

SÃO MIGUEL, FAJÃ DE BAIXO

Estalagem Senhora da Rosa Just north-east of Ponta Delgada, an elegant but relaxed dining room in a delightful hotel set in fine gardens *(page 226)*. Home-grown vegetables and fruit are a highlight – including their own pineapples. Cooking is good local traditional, with creative touches. Service is friendly and efficient.

Rua Senhora da Rosa 3,
9500-450 Fajã de Baixo, São Miguel
T+351 296 630 100
E senhora.rosa@mail.telepac.pt
W www.estalagemsenhoradarosa.com
€30 V!

SÃO MIGUEL, FURNAS

Restaurant Terra Nostra Garden The fresh, bright dining room of the Terra Nostra Garden Hotel is a good place to try the famous dishes buried and cooked for hours in the hot, volcanic earth – on the menu here is the traditional meat-and-veg *cozido nas caldeiras à moda das furnas,* and a fishy version, *caldeirada de bacalhau nas caldeiras,* as well as other traditional fare. Service is good and friendly, and the wine list is quite good by island standards.

Rua Padre José Botelho 5
T+351 296 549 090
E reservas@bensaude.pt
W www.bensaude.pt
€22 V

SÃO MIGUEL, LAGOA

Borda d'Água A simple restaurant with sea-blue decor, a seaside feel, and excellent fish and seafood, right by the fishing port. Choose your own fish to send to the grill. There's also good local cheese, grilled beef steaks, and wonderful, fresh, juicy pineapple for afters. Lagoa is east of Ponta Delgada.
Largo do Porto 52
T+351 296 912 114
E arruda.oliveira@sapo.pt
€20 Closed Sun

SÃO MIGUEL, LIVRAMENTO

Le Pavillon If mussels are a speciality here, then that's because Roland and Yves, the chef-owners, are Belgian. Simple but classy dishes are based on organic local produce. The short wine list is mainly from continental Portugal. Decor is bold and modern, furniture cuboid. Livramento is a village just east of Ponta Delgada, before Lagoa. Open evenings only; you must book ahead.
Canada Bago das Socas 51
T+351 296 385 738
€25 V
Open din only Closed Mon, Tue;
Christmas and New Year

SÃO MIGUEL, PONTA DELGADA

A Colmeia The restaurant of the Hotel do Colégio *(page 227)* is one of the very top places to eat in the Azores. Cooking by chef Guiomar Correia is creative and modern, based on island traditions and excellent local produce. Miguel Castro e Silva of The Bull & Bear restaurant in Porto was originally consultant chef. The wine list is good, drawn from the islands, Portugal and the world, with a good selection by the glass and well-informed wine service. The atmosphere is gently sophisticated, friendly and relaxed, the decor yellow ochre and wood, with plenty of natural light. This is a popular venue for business lunches as well as hotel guests, so do book ahead, especially in summer. They opened a new wine bar *(right)* in July 2008.
Hotel do Colégio, Travessa do Colégio
T+351 296 306 600
E acolmeia@hoteldocolegio.com
W www.hoteldocolegio.pt
€35 ♀ V! ⌀
Closed lunch at weekends

A Colmeia Grill & Wine Bar New little brother of A Colmeia restaurant *(left)* with sea views, in the new Portas do Mar bar/restaurant/shopping complex. An informal, fun wine bar, excellent value, with a terrace serving traditional grills of top quality local meat and fish, plus a selection of steaks with various sauces. A long menu of *petiscos* and tapas could be your entire meal, or just the beginning. The wine list is good, both local and from the mainland, with numerous wines available by the glass. Eat any time from noon to 1am.
Portas do Mar 2
T +351 296 098 693
E acolmeia@hoteldocolegio.com
€20 ♀ V!

SÃO MIGUEL, RIBEIRA GRANDE

O Ala Bote Come for the sea views and fantastic sunsets from the terrace of this smartly simple restaurant. The *cataplana de cherne* (mixed seafood and stone bass) gets good reviews, along with other seafood, well-cooked local and Portuguese mainland dishes, and the odd classic European dish. There's live music at weekends.
Rua East Providence 68
T+351 296 473 516
E alabote@alabote.net
W www.alabote.net
€20 ♀ V! Closed Tue

SÃO MIGUEL, RIBEIRINHA

O Gato Mia Simple village restaurant in a leafy street, friendly and efficient, with good traditional island cooking and a wine list that is above average for the Azores. *Alcatras* from the owner's native Terceira feature on the menu – beef, kid or rabbit marinated in wine and garlic oven-cooked until meltingly tender. Ribeirinha is in the middle of the north coast of São Miguel.
Rua Fulgêncio Ferreira Marques 13
T+351 296 479 420
E o_gato_mia@hotmail
€19 ♀ V!
Closed Tue; 23-26 Dec

TERCEIRA, ANGRA DO HEROÍSMO

Adega Lusitânia In the city centre, in a former wine store that survived the earthquake of 1980, a rustic restaurant with blue gingham table cloths and a friendly atmosphere. Good local cooking includes fish and seafood, and beef *alcatra*. A good wine list has a good selection from the islands as well as many bottles from mainland Portugal.
Rua de São Pedro 63-65
T+351 295 212 301
€15 ♀ V
Closed Sun; 1 month Dec/Jan

TERCEIRA, PRAIA DA VITÓRIA

O Pescador One of the best places to eat in Terceira, a well-established, friendly restaurant with two big dining rooms, serving very good fish, seafood and fishy dishes, plus meat dishes and good home-made puddings. The wine list is impressive, in island terms, and service is excellent.
Rua Constantino José Cardoso 11
T+351 295 513 495
E reservas@opescador.pt
W www.opescador.pt
€20 ♀ V

WINE AND FOOD SHOPS

SÃO MIGUEL, PONTA DELGADA

O Rei dos Queijos On the right hand side of the market, 'The King of Cheeses' has a spectacular range of island cheeses, plus some wine and deli products. *Rua do Mercado da Graça, São Pedro*

A Vinha A high quality wine shop on two floors with an excellent selection of wines from throughout Portugal, including ports and Madeira. Bottles range from good, everyday wines to fine and rare, magnums and bigger. Service is friendly and knowledgeable. *Avenida Infante Dom Henrique 45*

Explore the Azores

Fly direct, or via Lisbon, or even via Madeira. There are small international airports now on São Miguel, Terceira and Faial, and other islands are linked by local flights or ferries, but not all, especially in winter. It's easy to mistake the Azores for a close little cluster, but the archipelago measures 650km from end to end. On most islands there are cars to hire (book ahead to be sure), as well as inexpensive local buses, and taxis – although at the last count Corvo had only two taxis. Roads are on the whole easy, many recently modernised. For walkers, ancient footpaths are being cleared and signposted.

CORVO The smallest and most northern island has one small town, Vila Nova do Corvo, whose small, white and grey houses and alleyways climb up the hillside. There are no vines. The one road leads past little fields and dry stone walls up to the crater. Corvo is 6.5km long, 4km wide and has just 0.2 % of the total population of the Azores.

FAIAL A small island with a modern feel. It is popular with yachting folk. The capital, Horta, faces the small port of Madalena on Pico island, and a regular ferry plies between. There have always been strong links between Pico and Faial. Faial's fertile interior is topped by the wide and beautiful Caldeira do Cabeço Gordo. 6.3% of the Azores population lives here. It measures 21x14km.

FLORES Occupied by pirates in the early days, Flores is very hilly, very pretty, a walker's paradise, with breathtaking scenery, ravines, waterfalls, water jets, a beautiful crater lake, and yes, lots of flowers, but no vines. 17km long by 12.5km wide, it has just 1.8% of the population of the archipelago.

GRACIOSA A small island subsisting peacefully on cattle farming and traditionally also on viticulture. But with

VOLCANO VOCAB

aquecedor de água geyser, periodically erupting or bubbling hot spring

caldeira caldera, large depression at the top of a volcano formed by explosion or collapse, sometimes containing a pool or lake

cratera crater

enxofre sulphur

fontes termais thermal springs

fumarolas fumeroles – gases escaping though fissures in the earth's surface, including steam, carbon dioxide, carbon monoxide and hydrogen sulphide; coloured sulphur deposits sometimes form around them

fumarolas de lama bubbling mud pools, kept liquid by hot subterranean water

lagoa lagoon, crater lake, which may be coloured by mineral compounds, orange from iron, yellow from sulphur, green from copper.

lajido lava field

lama mud

mistérios swirls of solidified lava down by the sea

nascentes termais thermal springs

vulcão volcano

Above Roads are often paved with striking red volcanic grit

Left Cloud formations ever-changing over Pico's volcano

Right The volcanic shore of the island of Faial

217

subsidies nowadays for cattle pasture, not for vines, and the wine hard to sell, the cows are getting the upper hoof. The main visitor attractions are the spectacular underground lagoon and fumeroles *(page 223)*. Graciosa measures 12.5x8.5km, and has 2.2% of the population.

PICO A wave of cloud breaks over the mountain peak and pours slowly down the slope. Pico is a magically calming place today, but evidence of past energy is all around. Lava and debris from a series of eruptions long ago joined to give one long island. Early settlers used the volcanic stones to build myriad tiny dry stone wall enclosures *(currais)*, thereby killing two birds: clearing the vast numbers of stones, whilst creating shelter for their vines and other crops. The amazing patchwork of vineyards around the north-western tip of the island richly deserve

their status as a UNESCO World Heritage Site. Pico is the most southerly of the central group of islands, windswept, drier than most other islands, warmer, scrubbier and less green, because the volcanic soil is more recent, less decomposed. The different types of lichen are fascinating; a particular variety of heather one to two metres high is protected here, and the island has the biggest collection of the impressive dragon trees in the Azores. Fig trees also grow amidst the vines in the *currais*.

The coast is remarkable for its *mistérios* – swirls of lava flows that extended the island. Divers can explore the underwater lava formations, caves, tunnels and arches; rays arrive around the coast in June. The volcanic peak

Above Pico's volcano, seen from Faial

Left Yachts off Pico, with volcanic backdrop

Right Red lava formations on Pico

Far right Chapel in the *mistérios*

Left The long-ago collapsed coast of São Jorge: the *fajãs*

Right Fajã dos Cubres on São Jorge

Below Peaceful green bay on Santa Maria Island

dominates all, surrounded by little villages, grazing cattle and vines. Quiet little MADALENA is the capital. Moving around the north coast, LAJIDO, by the little airport, has a good natural swimming pool and a fascinating little museum-village by the sea, a tiny cluster of old wineries *(page 223)*. SÃO ROQUE DO PICO is an old fishing town. Just down the coast is another good natural swimming pool, at POÇA BRANCA. Pico's second settlement after Madalena was PRAINHA, on the north-east coast, inland of a large, tree-covered *mistério* and the delightful little **Lagoa do Caiado**. Lajes do Pico on the south coast is the starting point for whale and dolphin-watching trips. As well as the Azores' highest peak (snow-capped in winter), Pico has more volcanic caves than any other Azores island; you can visit the impressive **Gruta das Torres** in CRIAÇÃO VELHA just south of Madalena *(page 223)*. It's a 7km ferry trip across to Horta on Faial, possible on a day trip. Pico measures 42x15.2km, and has 6.4% of the population.

SANTA MARIA is the southernmost island, off to the east, south of the capital island of São Miguel. It is unusual for its sandy beaches, but it also has natural rock pools, with lots of little bays, ideal for watersports; and it has the warmest climate of the archipelago, ranging from 25°C in summer to 12°C in winter. Inland, Santa Maria is very rural, tiny, green, hilly fields and vineyards in the east giving way to a dry, flat plateau in the south-west, where the airport has been built. The island measures 18x9.5km and has just 2.5% of the population.

SÃO JORGE Cheese is São Jorge's claim to fame; the islanders also take great pride in their beef. Long ago, the cliffs of the north coast collapsed; the fallen matter decomposed to form *fajãs*, fertile, low-lying coastal strips which are used for crops and dairy pasture. The lake and undersea cave of the Fajã da Caldeira de Santo Cristo along this coast is the Azores' only source of cockles *(amêijoas)*. Walkers enjoy the north-coast paths. In the

south, you can sometimes watch the sea bubbling from underwater fumeroles in the bay of Velas. Long, thin São Jorge measures 56x8km, and has 4.3% of the population.

SÃO MIGUEL The largest island in the Azores, São Miguel was formed in two volcanic bursts, the eastern part four million years ago, the western part only 500,000 years ago. It became rich in the 18th century on the proceeds of its early orange crop – many grand houses in the capital of Ponta Delgada date from this period. Ponta Delgada is also the capital of the archipelago. The older parts are marked particularly by the grey basalt and white mosaic pavements, sometimes geometric, sometimes incorporating designs such as ships. Roads were laid out in the 19th century in a grid pattern, with gardens and squares. Expansion and modernisation has been rapid in the past two decades: São Miguel has moved into the 21st century ahead of the other islands. Ponta Delgada has the Azores' first university, a new marina, modern hotels around the port, and two new, fast roads. It has some good restaurants, too. More than half the inhabitants of the Azores live on São Miguel, many of them in Ponta Delgada.

São Miguel is a happy hotbed for would-be vulcanologists, who can observe fumaroles, geysers, steaming mineral springs and bubbling mud pools, as well as exploring crater lakes and the rocky coast with its cliffs and grey sandy beaches. Geothermic energy provides a third of the electricity used on the island. At the western tip are the much-photographed crater lakes of Sete Cidades. Towards the eastern end of the island, the wide crater embracing

Above The new marina of Ponta Delgada on São Miguel, the most cosmopolitan of the Azores archipelago

Right The smaller of the Sete Cidades lakes on the island of São Miguel

the spa town of Furnas and the Lagoa das Furnas lake has coloured sulphur geysers, 20 hot springs, a warm, mustard-coloured swimming pool, fabulous tropical gardens planted in the 18th century, and ground in places so hot that you can literally cook your dinner in it. The Terra Nostra Hotel is the cool place to stay, and to eat the famous *cozido*. The Lagoa do Fogo, in the midst of a nature reserve in the centre of the island, is the crater of an extinct volcano; it's a remote, tranquil place, with clear water and beaches great for picnics. Further towards the east coast lie the wooded Serra da Tronqueira mountains and the high Pico da Vara, home of the rare Azores bullfinch.

Roads and green fields of cows are defined by high hedges, sometimes by black dry stone walls. Blue hydrangeas and agapanthus bloom along roadsides, moss, algae and ferns flourish and there are quite a lot of vines, almost all American varieties. São Miguel measures 65x12km, and has 53% of the population.

TERCEIRA This was the third of the islands to be discovered (its name means 'Third' in Portuguese) and was the islands' main administrative centre

Opposite Crater lake on the island of São Jorge

Left One of the ubiquitous *impérios*, shrines to the Holy Spirit

Right Hydrangeas were introduced from Japan

until the 19th century, with the fine bay of ANGRA DO HEROÍSMO the main port. An earthquake devastated three-quarters of the city on New Year's Day, 1980, but the old centre was restored, and four years later was declared a UNESCO World Heritage Site.

The early settlers were faced with countryside scattered with so many rocks and stones that here and there they made vast piles of stones, as well as using the stones to build walls around small, green fields of pasture, and little vine enclosures – called *curraletas* on Terceira, rather than *currais*. The coast is black lava, with natural swimming pools, and Terceira, too, has its crater lakes and fumeroles.

A thousand American soldiers are based in LAJES; they have their own supermarket, to which neither locals nor tourists have access. At festival times, beware the bulls.

Even if you visit at the wrong time to meet a bull in person, films of the *tourada à corda* might while away a stormy hour at the airport (also in Lajes), entertaining you on overhead screens whilst you wait for your island-hopping plane to brave the weather. A bull (with padded horns) runs in the village streets or on the beach, chasing local dare-devils whilst tethered to a very long rope, which is held (or sometimes accidentally dropped) by a team of the dare-devils' mates. Terceira is 29km long, 17.5 wide and has 23.5% of the population – there are said to be more cows than people!

❊ VIEW FROM THE TOP ❊

Serious walkers keen to scale the peaks for the top-most views should note that official permission is sometimes necessary. Here are a few more easily accessible vantage points.

FAIAL **Caldeira do Cabeço Gordo** From the rim of the wide, green crater at the centre of Faial, there are great views of the island, Pico and the ocean.

GRACIOSA, SANTA CRUZ DA GRACIOSA **Furna Maria Encantada** Take a tunnel through the rock for views across Graciosa from a crater edge.

SÃO MIGUEL, SETE CIDADES **Vista do Rei** There are various viewpoints around the rim of the crater lakes of Sete Cidades, but this 'King's View' gives the most famous vista down over the main lakes, the bridge and village. The volcanic peak here erupted in 1440; the ugly black hole reported by the first settlers has turned into a scene of breathtaking beauty.

TERCEIRA, ANGRA DO HEROÍSMO **Monte Brazil** A road leads conveniently to the volcanic crater and nature reserve on the promontory that sticks like a beautiful green wart into the sea off Angra do Heroísmo; there are spectacular views over

two bays, the island and its capital city.

TERCEIRA, CABOUÇO DO CUME On the east of the island, half way along the road over the ridge of the Serra do Cume towards São Sebastião, spectacular views down onto Praia da Vitória and the interior.

BETWEEN MEALS

GRACIOSA **Furna do Enxofre** Steps lead down into a vaulted cavern, a wide, sulphurous lagoon and fumeroles of boiling mud, which emit gases including carbon monoxide and dioxide. Visits are prudently guided, and gas levels carefully monitored. The cave was closed for a while in the summer of 2007 owing to unusually high levels of carbon dioxide. Visit, if you can at lunchtime, when the sun shines in. *Open 11-4*

PICO, CRIAÇÃO VELHA **Gruta das Torres** Don helmet and headlamp for a guided visit down Portugal's longest lava tube, 5,150 metres long and 17 metres high, lit by a natural skylight. An attractive visitor centre gives access to the first part of the cave via a solid rock staircase. Find it south of Madalena. *Open Jun-Sep every day 2.30-5.30 May-Oct Sat & Sun 2.30-5.30*

PICO, LAJIDO **Moinho do Frade** Lovingly restored windmill in the midst of the vineyard *currais* near Lajido. Even if the interior is closed, do climb the steps for the best view down over the *currais* from the mill platform. *Open May-Sep every day 10-6 Oct -Apr Sat 4-5 Sun 3-4*

SÃO MIGUEL **Campo de Golfe das Furnas** A very fine, challenging but peaceful 18-hole golf course with views over the Furnas Valley, clouds and mist permitting. *Achada das Furnas, 9675-000 Furnas T+351 296 584 341* **Campo de**

WHALE WATCHING

PICO, LAJES DO PICO **Espaço Talassa** Half-day whale-watching trips in small boats, with radio tracking. *Rua do Saco T+351 092 672 010*

PICO, MADALENA **Pico-Sport** Based in Madalena but diving also off Faial and São Jorge, this young company offers sensitively-managed whale watching, serious diving including night dives, and the opportunity to discover the wildlife of the underwater lava formations, caves and canyons. *T+351 292 622 980 / 292 623 761*

Golfe da Batalha On the north coast, only ten minutes' drive from Ponta Delgada on the new fast road, a high-class course with fine sea views, passing through volcanic scenery, lush vegetation and woodland. There are plans for a new hotel and spa, with villas and apartments. *Rua do Bom Jesus-Aflitos, 9545-234 Fenais da Luz T+351 296 498 559*

TERCEIRA **Algar do Cavão** The most-visited and most famous of the volcanic caves of the archipelago, right in the centre of Terceira, within the crater of Caldeira Guilherme Moniz. A man-made tunnel

leads to a deep cave and underground lake of clear water. Admire the unique, milky-white stalactites and stalagmites and the impressive natural chimney, green at the top with moss, plants and lichen, which lets in the daylight from 100m above. A possible future UNESCO World Heritage Site. Guided visits. *Open every day mid-Apr-May 3-5.30 Jun 2.30-5.45 Jul & Aug 2-6 Sep 2.30-5.45 1st 2 weeks Oct 3-5.30 Winter visits by special request*

TERCEIRA **Furnas do Enxofre** Near the Algar do Cavão, high in the centre of the island, spiralling hot sulphur fumeroles are surrounded by coloured deposits. They are particularly impressive in the cool temperatures of early morning. There are footpaths and information panels.

MUSEUMS & GALLERIES

FLORES, SANTA CRUZ **Museu das Flores** Home and farm implements and shipwreck finds, displayed in a former Franciscan convent, the Convento da Boaventura. *Largo da Misericórdia Open Tue-Fri 9-12.30, 2-5.30 Closed Sat & Sun; public hols*

GRACIOSA, SANTA CRUZ DA GRACIOSA **Museu Etnográfico da Graciosa** Museum of daily life and farming on Graciosa, with a wine and vineyard section. *Rua das Flores 2 Jun-Sep 9-12.30, 2.30-5.30 Closed public hols Oct-May closed Sat, Sun & public hols*

PICO, LAJIDO **Nucleo Museológico do Lajido** A fascinating cluster of little wine

cellars and tiny houses, which still serve in some cases for winemaking, sometimes just as a place to while away an evening or a Sunday with friends, sometimes as little summer holiday houses. A few have been renovated by wealthy emigrants, back now and then from North America. There's a sturdy basalt chapel, and you can visit a small, working museum-distillery, and see the tracks of ox carts of days gone by, engraved into the lava of the 'beach'.

Pico, Toledos **Museu do Vinho** In a village just north of Madalena, surrounded by vines in currais, and wonderful, ancient dragon trees, this interesting and well-organised wine museum is in various buildings of the former Convento das Carmelitas. *Rua do Carmo Open summer Tue-Fri 9.30-12.30, 2-5.30 Sat & Sun 2-5.30 Open winter Tue-Fri 10-12.30, 2-5 Sat & Sun 2-5 Closed Mon, public hols*

São Miguel, Ponta Delgada
Museu Carlos Machado The Azores' most prestigious museum is housed in the former Convento de Santo André. Exhibits range through geology and mineralogy, viticulture, agriculture, and fishing. There are paintings of life in the archipelago, and a natural history section with stuffed birds and animals. *Rua João Moreira Open May-Sep Tue-Fri 9.30-12.30, 2-5.30 Sat & Sun 2-5.30 Oct-Apr Tue-Fri 10-12, 2-5 Sat & Sun 2-5 Closed Mon, public hols*

Terceira, Canada do Caldeiro
Museu do Vinho dos Biscoitos Lovely little private museum of the island's viticulture and winemaking, created and run by the Brum family, who make some of the island's best wines *(page 212)*. *Casa Agrícola Brum, Canada do Caldeira, Praia da Vitória Open Apr-Sep Tues-Sun Oct-Mar Tue-Sat 10-12, 1.30-5.30*

CHURCHES

São Jorge, Manadas **Igreja de Santa Bárbara** In a south coast fishing village, an 18th century baroque church with beautiful cedarwood ceiling and *azulejos*.

São Miguel, Ponta Delgada **Igreja de São Sebastião** Built in the mid-16th century, the structure is Gothic, the exterior Manueline, and the entrance was modified in Baroque style in the 18th century. Admire the elegant portal in carved limestone, carvings in jacaranda wood, *azulejos*, and gold thread embroidery. *Largo de Matriz*

Terceira, Angra do Heroismo **Igreja de São Gonçalo** 17th century church with gilded, carved altarpiece, *azulejos*, 16th century paintings and cloisters. *Rua Gonçalo V Cabral*

FAIRS & FESTIVALS

March/April-May **Festas do Espírito Santo** The Feasts of the Holy Spirit are hugely important on these religious islands. Emigrants return to celebrate with their families. There are *festas* every Sunday from Easter to Whit Sunday (Pentecost), the day that celebrates the gift of the Holy Spirit to Jesus' disciples. Festivities centre around Holy Spirit Shrines *(Impérios)*, tiny, colourful chapels, of which almost every town and village has one or two. Festivities differ from place to place, but most begin with a *Grande Coroação*, a Great Crowning Ceremony, when a child is crowned emperor of the festivities in the parish church. The culminating Feast of the Holy Spirit is on Whit Sunday, the seventh Sunday after Easter. The local *festas* committee distribute food to all present: *Sopa do Império*, or *Sopa do Espírito Santo*, a soup of beef, vegetables and sometimes mint, accompanied by the sweetish *massa souvada* bread and hybrid wine *(vinho de cheiro)*. There may be bull-running in the streets *(tourada à corda)*, to the end festivities and almost certainly bands, dancing and fireworks.

August São Miguel, Caloura **Festa do Pescador** Fishermen's festival in the third week of the month at the little port of Caloura near Água de Pau in the middle of the south coast. There's a traditional village fair, and lots of fish, especially mackerel *(chicharro)* and black scabbard fish *(espada)*, served with hybrid wine *(vinho de cheiro)* and corn bread *(pão de milho)*.

September Pico, Madalena **Festa das Vindimas** In the second week of September, Madalena's traditional Vintage Festival includes a boat race, the Rota do Verdelho, and lots of wine and food.

Sleep in the Azores

FLORES, ALDEIA DA CUADA

Aldeia da Cuada On a beautiful, peaceful plateau above the sea on the west coast of Flores (Portugal's western-most frontier), this delightful village was abandoned in the 1970s by inhabitants who left for new lives in America. The ten renovated cottages now have modern comforts – kitchen and bathroom and (mostly) one large bedroom. You can't bring a car. Approached along a lane paved with basalt, the village is surrounded by little fields and dry stone walls, backed by mountains. In Fajã Grande 2km away, you can bathe in sea pools, eat out and shop modestly, and all around there's great walking, spectacular scenery, waterfalls, and sea.

Aldeia da Cuada, 9960-070 Flores
T+351 292 590 040
E aldeiacuada@mail.telepac.pt
W www.aldeiadacuada.com
€55-€70
SC *16(2, 4&12) No credit cards*
Min nights summer 3

PICO, LAJES DO PICO

Casa da Arriba Above a lovely bay just outside Lajes do Pico on the south-east coast, this sturdy, two-storey basalt house was built a hundred years ago to store viticultural and agricultural equipment, and has been tastefully converted into a simple, comfortable cottage. It has two bedrooms, bathroom, kitchen and sitting room, and gardens with views of the sea and the volcano.
9930-000 Lajes do Pico
T+351 916 236 780
E casasdopico@hotmail.com
W www.casasdopico.com
€75 SC *1(4) sea*

PICO, POÇINHO-MONTE

Pocinho Bay Enchanting rooms to rent in various converted buildings of a former farm, isolated beside a beautiful bay just south of Madalena on Pico's west coast. Rooms are a designer blend of old features, exposed basalt walls and tasteful, creative, modern touches and comforts, including queen size beds – one each if you so choose. 'Modern spirit with Azorean soul' is how the owners put it – they will be around to prepare breakfast and assist during your stay. There are hills to the back, sea and a natural rock swimming pool to the front, and a lovely, modern fresh water pool near the rooms. Footpaths around the 13ha property lead to various shady (or sheltered) places to relax. Eat at the excellent Ancoradouro restaurant *(page 215)*, 2km away.
Pocinho-Monte, 9950-107Madalena, Pico
T+351 292 628 460
E geral@pocinhobay.com
W www.pocinhobay.com
€125-€140
6 *Closed Jan & Feb*

PICO, PRAINHA

Adegas do Pico A number of delightful little houses to rent, by the week or for shorter stays, cosily converted from small basalt winery buildings *(adegas)* around the fascinating vineyard area of Prainha and Baia das Canas on the north-east coast. There are woods, *mistérios*, and a small lake. All the cottages are right by the sea. The Casa da Vinha (sleeping two) is surrounded by old vineyards and woodland; the Casa do Farol (sleeping up to 7), five metres from the sea with a lovely first floor veranda, is a little grander and less rustic than the other houses.

Rua do Cais 17A,
  9940-355 São Roque do Pico, Pico
T+351 292 642 583
E info@adegasdopico.com
W www.adegasdopico.com
€60-€80
SC *5(2, 2+2, 4, 4+2, 4+3)* ⚊ *sea*
No credit cards

PICO, SANTA CRUZ DAS RIBEIRAS

Casa do Vinho Lovely, tiny white cottage by the sea amidst the *currais* on the south-east coast of Pico. Beautifully converted from a former winery, it has one double-bedded room, bathroom, kitchen, old bread oven and barbecue, and a big covered terrace looking out to sea.

9930-000 Santa Cruz das Ribeiras
T+351 916 236 780
E casasdopico@hotmail.com
W www.casasdopico.com
€50
SC *1(2)* ⚊ *sea*

PICO, SILVEIRA

Aldeia da Fonte An ecologically-minded hotel and restaurant set in woods and gardens overlooking a secluded bay – on the south of the island, a five-minute drive from Lajes do Pico. Six grey basalt buildings amongst the trees have delightful rooms, suites and self-catering and family suites sleeping four, some with open fires. A colony of bats adds to the mood at night. If you so wish, there's yoga and meditation, painting and flower arranging, and all kinds of leisure and sporting activities. Swimming is possible all year round in a natural pool amidst the rocks, and for strong swimmers there's a diving point, and steps lead up from the open sea. The Restaurant Hocus Pocus *(page 215)* is a haven for vegetarians, as well as serving fishy and meaty local and international fare. Both bar and restaurant open onto an attractive terrace.

Silveira, 9930-177 Lajes do Pico, Pico
T+351 292 679 500
E info@aldeiadafonte.com
W www.aldeiadafonte.com
€65-€96
🛏 *16* SC *16(2&4)* ♑ ✕ ⚊ *sea*

SÃO MIGUEL, FURNAS

Terra Nostra Garden Hotel In the centre of the small village of Furnas, within gardens and close to a fascinating volcanic landscape of thermal springs, bubbling geysers and hot earth, this beautifully restored Art Deco hotel (with modern additions) is a peaceful place to stay. Best of the pleasant, simple rooms have balconies overlooking the spectacular

botanic gardens, where peacocks roam. A large, mustard-coloured, earth-heated natural swimming pool is free for guests, and peaceful outside tour-bus hours, and there's a smartly transparent indoor pool. (Bring old swimwear – the sulphurous water will turn it yellow!) Breakfasts are pleasant, and meals positively good in the hotel restaurant *(page 215)*, which serves the local speciality of dishes cooked by being buried for hours in the hot earth. There's a pool table and games room. The Casa do Palácio in the grounds has two 'presidential suites'.

Rua Padre José Jacinto Botelho 5,
  9675-061 Furnas, Sao Miguel
T+351 296 549 090
E reservas@bensaude.pt
W www.bensaude.pt
€145
🛏 *79* S *2* ♑ ✕ ⚊

SÃO MIGUEL, FAJÃ DE BAIXO

Estalagem Senhora da Rosa Just north-east of Ponta Delgada, a delightful hotel, a successful mix of modern and classic decor and furnishings, amidst really beautiful, long-established gardens with shady walks, pineapple greenhouses, orchards and vegetable gardens. A good restaurant serves up-market local food, including home-grown fruit and vegetables. Rooms are in the main house, apartments in a separate building. A new outdoor pool is under construction as we write, and there's a fine snooker room and bar. A minibus service will take you into town, and there's parking.

Rua Senhora da Rosa 3,
  9500-450 Fajã de Baixo, São Miguel

T+351 296 630 100
E senhora.rosa@mail.telepac.pt
W www.estalagemsenhoradarosa.com
€76-€100
🛏27 S 1 SC 10(2+2) ✕ 🛶 by 2008

São Miguel, Ponta Delgada

Hotel do Colégio This lovely old hotel
set just back from the harbour in the centre
of town was built in the 19th century as
a private manor house, but served for
many years as a primary school, known as
'A Colmeia', The Beehive. Parts of it also
housed the town's music academy. Service
is excellent. The best and largest rooms are
in the old part of the building, which is
full of character, atmosphere and original
detail. A Colmeia *(page 216)*, now the
restaurant, has probably the best and most
creative cooking in the Azores, with a
good selection of wines. Breakfasts are
also very good. There's a heated courtyard
pool, health club and gym, Turkish bath
and sauna. The hotel has private parking.
Rua Carvalho Araújo 39,
9500-040 Ponta Delgada, São Miguel
T+351 296 306 600
E reservas@hoteldocolegio.com
W www.hoteldocolegio.pt
€97-€132
🛏55 S 1 ⚲ ✕ 🛶 🏛 ⚟

Terceira, Angra do Heroísmo

Quinta de São Carlos Elegant, late 18th
century mansion within very easy walking
distance of the centre of this beautiful
capital city. It was recently converted into
a guest house by the family who have
owned it for well over 100 years, with
modern comforts, but retaining its style and
antique furnishings. Extensive gardens
include a large outdoor swimming pool.

Caminho do Meio 38, São Carlos,
9700-222 Angra do Heroísmo, Terceira
T+351 295 332 298
E reservas@quintadesaocarlos.com
W www.quintadesaocarlos.com
€75-€105
🛏5 S 1 🛶

Terceira, Salga

Rural Salga A cheerily colourful guest
house by the sea in the south-east corner of
Terceira, in the little village of Salga, just
south of São Sebastião. There's a pretty,
flower-hung courtyard with a shaded area
(below), and a pool in the garden. Five en-
suite rooms all have sea views. The sea is
100m away, and it's seven minutes' walk
to a natural sea pool.
Canada do Funcho 4A, Salga,
9700-644 São Sebastião. Terceira
T+351 295 905 034
E reservas@ ruralsalga.com
W www.ruralsalga.com
€50-€70
🛏3 SC 2(3&4) ✕on request 🛶
No credit cards
Min nights summer 2

Terceira, Vinha Brava

Quinta da Nasce-Água An elegant,
peaceful country house hotel furnished
with antiques beside impressive gardens
3km from the capital, Angra do Heroísmo.
Rooms are large, with mountain views,
breakfasts are good, and staff helpful.
There's an attractive outdoor pool, sauna,
Turkish bath, tennis and golf practice
range (and the island's golf course is
within very easy reach).

Vinha Brava, 9700-236 Angra do
Heroismo, Terceira
T+351 295 628 500
E nasceagua@mail.telepac.pt
W www.quintadanasce-agua.com
€100-€145
🛏14 S 2 ✕ 🛶 ♨ ✓ ⚲

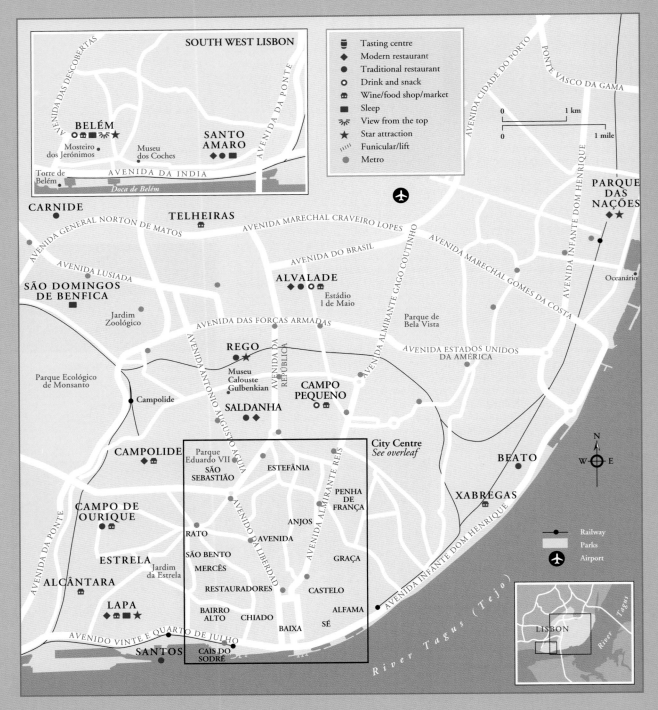

SOUTH WEST LISBON

BELÉM

Mosteiro
dos Jerónimos

Museu
dos Coches

**SANTO
AMARO**

Torre de
Belém

AVENIDA DAS DESCOBERTAS

AVENIDA DA INDIA

AVENIDA DA PONTE

AVENIDA DAS DESCOBERTAS

Doca de Belém

Tasting centre
Modern restaurant
Traditional restaurant
Drink and snack
Wine/food shop/market
Sleep
View from the top
Star attraction
Funicular/lift
Metro

0   1 km
0   1 mile

CARNIDE

TELHEIRAS

AVENIDA GENERAL NORTON DE MATOS

AVENIDA MARECHAL CRAVEIRO LOPES

AVENIDA CIDADE DO PORTO

PONTE VASCO DA GAMA

**PARQUE
DAS
NAÇÕES**

AVENIDA DO BRASIL

AVENIDA LUSIADA

**SÃO DOMINGOS
DE BENFICA**

Jardim
Zoológico

AVENIDA DAS FORÇAS ARMADAS

ALVALADE

Estádio
1 de Maio

AVENIDA ALMIRANTE GAGO COUTINHO

AVENIDA MARECHAL GOMES DA COSTA

Parque de
Bela Vista

AVENIDA INFANTE DOM HENRIQUE

Oceanário

Parque Ecológico
de Monsanto

Campolide

REGO

Museu
Calouste
Gulbenkian

SALDANHA

AVENIDA ANTONIO AUGUSTO AGUIAR

AVENIDA DA REPÚBLICA

**CAMPO
PEQUENO**

AVENIDA ESTADOS UNIDOS
DA AMÉRICA

AVENIDA DA PONTE

CAMPOLIDE

Parque
Eduardo VII

**SÃO
SEBASTIÃO**

ESTEFÂNIA

City Centre
See overleaf

BEATO

AVENIDO DA LIBERDAD

AVENIDA ALMIRANTE REIS

**PENHA
DE
FRANÇA**

XABREGAS

**CAMPO DE
OURIQUE**

RATO

ANJOS

AVENIDA

ESTRELA

Jardim
da Estrela

SÃO BENTO

MERCÊS

GRAÇA

ALCÂNTARA

RESTAURADORES

CASTELO

AVENIDA INFANTE DOM HENRIQUE

LAPA

**BAIRRO
ALTO**

CHIADO

ALFAMA

SÉ

BAIXA

AVENIDO VINTE E QUARTO DE JULHO

SANTOS

**CAIS DO
SODRÉ**

River Tagus (Tejo)

N
W   E
S

Railway
Parks
Airport

LISBON

River Tagus

River Tagus (Tejo)

Lisbon

isbon is several cities wrapped up in one, each of distinctive style and period. The steep, narrow, cobbled streets and little stairways of the Moorish Alfama district are literally a millennium away from the stunning modern architecture of the Parque das Nações, just over to the east. The Baixa, the low-lying town centre, dates from the earthquake of 1755, its shops and cafés ranged with military precision along wide black-and-white-cobbled streets and squares. Lisbon is Portugal's major port, a huge bay 15km from the ocean on the wide estuary of the Tagus, and everywhere from the city's hills there are views across the water. Only a decade ago, warehouses and run-down docks separated most of the city from the riverside. The eastern dockland/industrial area, the Parque das Nações, has since been transformed into a desirable residential and leisure area – it was propelled into the smart new millennium by *Expo '98*, which was hosted here after massive investment. Even the Alcântara docks have been spruced up, their warehouses and sailors' haunts turned into restaurants and clubs.

An unbelievable number of museums delve into every possible topic, from toys and horse-drawn coaches to the local fado music, from *azulejo* tiles to things military, scientific, religious and marine. There are world-class art galleries, opera, rock concerts, night life.

And the food? Lisbon is in the forefront of the Portuguese gastronomic revolution. That's not to say that you won't find plenty of stodgy fare if you simply head into the nearest tourist restaurant or bar. Yet Lisbon has truly gastronomic restaurants if you know where to go. Some are international in style, but an increasing number work inventively with Portuguese ingredients and local culinary traditions, giving them a modern twist. Many Lisbon restaurants have stunning wine lists. And by other European standards, these top restaurants are not expensive. Bars, cafés and cake shops will also tempt you at every corner.

Luckily, Lisbon's hills will get your heart pumping, burn a few calories – and then work up a new appetite. The central districts are sufficiently compact to explore on foot. But there are idler solutions, from the delightful yellow trams, to the efficient metro, or the plentiful, inexpensive taxis. There's a new cable car to whisk you along above the river, and funiculars *(elevadores)* to transport you effortlessly to higher planes.

Explore Lisbon

Our favouite *bairro* (borough) of Lisbon is the Moorish Alfama, just east of centre. The oldest *bairro*, its little cobbled streets, steps and passages spill down the hillside, dilapidated in places, but delightfully atmospheric. There are *tascas* (tiny family-run restaurants), shops, a jumble of small houses and the odd mansion or palace, all spreading over three hills, topped by the massive ruins of the **Castelo de São Jorge** (Saint George's Castle), glowing yellow in the sun. Most of what you now see of the castle is medieval – but remains found on the site date back to the Iron Age. There are lovely little streets within the castle walls. You are never far from the smell of sardines (cooked and raw!) and barbecue smoke. Drinking fountains are a reminder that the *bairro* got its name from the Arabic word for spring, well or fountain – Lisbon was occupied by the Moors from the 8th to the 13th centuries. The Moors clearly chose their spot very well – their old town substantially survived the disastrous earthquake and tsunami of 1755.

Not so the lower town, the Baixa. The daytime heart of the modern city, and one of the main shopping areas, this 'lower town' had to be completely rebuilt after the quake *(see box on page 234)*. The Metro cannot pass under the Baixa as the 18th century town planners rebuilt the district upon a wooden cage to resist future seismic destruction. Straight, parallel streets of imposing, sober buildings were laid out in a grid formation. The wide, pedestrian **Rua Augusta** cuts through the Baixa, paved with mosaics and

Left & above Eating out on warm Lisbon nights

Right The hilltop Castelo de São Jorge

Far right Ornate black and white mosaic paving in the Baixa

Sundays and Mondays Plan these days, *domingo* and *segunda-feira,* with care – many attractions, bars and restaurants are shut, even in the capital!

Meals Lunch happens between 1 and 3pm. Dinner for locals starts around 9pm, though tourists can often be served from 7pm.

Monuments and museums tend to open 10am–12.30pm, 2pm–5pm; many close on Mondays.

Shops usually open 9am–1pm, 3pm–7pm, but are often shut on Saturday afternoons and Sundays.

Transport For cheaper multiple journeys on trams, buses, *elevadores* (lifts), and the Metro, buy a **Cartão Sete Colinas** (Seven Hills Pass) at the Metro stations, or at Carris (tram and bus) kiosks. The card itself costs 50c, and you then digitally load multiple journeys at 75c each, or day passes at €3.50 – note that day passes expire at 1.30am. A **Lisboa Card** is more expensive, but includes all public transport and entry to 27 museums for €11.25 (24 hours) and €23.50 (72 hours). Wind around the streets of the old quarters on **tram no 28** – a lazy and inexpensive way to see the sights and get your bearings – but note that if you break your journey you'll have to pay again. There are other fun and effortless ways to climb the steep hills: the Eiffel Tower-like **Elevador de Santa Justa** with its link recently re-opened over to the Bairro Alto; and three funiculars, **Elevador da Glória** (also recently re-opened, from Restauradores to Bairro Alto), **Elevador da Bica** (from near the Cais do Sodré metro station to the Bairro Alto) and **Elevador do Lavra** (from Avenida to Anjos).

BAIXA Lisboa Welcome Centre

Information is only a fraction of what's on offer in Lisbon's spacious tourist centre. Recently created within the arched and vaulted Pombaline buildings of the Terreiro do Paço, between the Baixa and the river, it also houses exhibitions, a café, and shops including a delicatessen selling cheeses, bread, *chouriço*… The excellent Terreiro do Paço restaurant (separate entrance on the square) is part of the complex.

Terreiro do Paço (Praça do Comércio), corner with Rua do Arsenal
www.visitlisboa.com

lined with shops, restaurants, cafés, and at one end with street vendors' stands. Bisecting streets are often named after the type of tradesmen historically grouped there – shoemakers, silversmiths, goldsmiths – and you'll still find a flush of haberdashers here, ironmongers there, linen shops or stationers grouped together.

Between the main Baixa district and the sea, and still part of the Baixa, is the huge, arcaded Pombaline square **Praça do Comércio** (as it is called on the maps), more often known as **Terreiro do Paço** ('Square of the Palace') – the first royal palace here was destroyed in the earthquake. All the arcaded buildings around the square were the new post-quake palace, used by the royal family until the revolution of 1910, and then by the government. Highlights of the square are the Sala Ogival, offering complimentary tastings from a nationwide range of wines *(opposite)*; the Lisboa Welcome Centre *(left)*; the excellent Terreiro do Paço restaurant *(page 239)* – and a terminal for ferries across to the Setúbal Peninsula.

From the **Praça da Figueira** in the Baixa you can catch trams to just about everywhere, and the railway station lies north-west of the big Rossio square. There are lots of tourist restaurants around here – pick with care.

Just to the north of the Baixa is the lower terminal of the Elevador da Glória, which will hoist you inexpensively up

BAIXA Sala Ogival Lisbon

This is an amazing place that you should not miss – a rather grand, comfortable and welcoming tasting/exhibition centre promoting Portuguese wines. You can taste up to six wines free of charge, from a huge, nationwide selection. The wines of three regions are on taste at any one time. There are also

special wine events on the annual Dia do Vinho (Wine Day) on the first Sunday in July. Sala Ogival is run by the Portuguese wine promotion organisation ViniPortugal, and occupies one of the historic Pombaline buildings on the Terreiro do Paço, next door but one to the Lisboa Welcome Centre *(see page 232).* A calm, cool spot to take a break – and meet some new wines – on a hot, bustling day in the Baixa. *Terreiro do Paço/Praça do Comércio Open Tue to Sat 11am–7pm*

to the BAIRRO ALTO, the 'upper district', to the west of the centre. 'The Bairro', as the locals call it, was built, also on a grid plan, in the late 16th century, and like the Alfama it largely escaped the destruction of 1755. By day the Bairro Alto is quiet and a bit scruffy, decorated with graffiti and washing hanging from balconies. There are steep and narrow cobbled streets, little grocers, book shops, clothes

and shoe shops, hairdressers, tea rooms, and lots of bars and *tascas*, many of which keep their shutters down until the evening. After dark, the Bairro wakes up, and music throbs out into the streets. This is the place to come for lively bars or clubs. The top end can turn a bit wild as the night progresses.

Now for some posher bits: the sophisticated CHIADO district lies between the Bairro Alto and the Baixa. Rua Garrett, its main shopping street, bristles with designer shops. There are smart cafés, theatres, art schools and up-market houses. The area has been carefully restored after a big fire in 1988, which began in the Rua do Carmo, and spread to Rua Garrett. North of the Baixa, the AVENIDA DA LIBERDADE was modelled on the Champs-Élysées in Paris. With its closely-planted trees, it offers shady access to yet more designer shops, amidst hotels, offices and numerous lanes of traffic. Over to the west, the LAPA is a rich residential district dating from the mid-18th century, home of the wealthy, of embassies, diplomats and up-market hotels.

BELÉM, still further to the west, it is a UNESCO World Heritage Site, and a reminder of Portugal's imperial past. It has the feel of a calm, grand seaside resort, with a busy marina, broad promenades, formal gardens and cafés. Belém (Bethlehem in Portuguese) suffered less damage in the earthquake than the Baixa, and has numerous historic buildings, including lots of museums. Grandest amongst them is the Mosteiro dos Jerónimos (Jerónimos Monastery), a stunning 300-metre long building in late

Far left Setting out for an evening in the Bairro Alto

Left The spacious Praça do Rossio is lined with shops and cafés

Right The Torre de Belém, guardian of the harbour

EARTHQUAKE AND TSUNAMI

Lisbon, early in the morning of 1 November 1755, was one of the biggest and most beautiful cities in Europe. It was All Saints Day, and many *Lisboetas* (Lisbon inhabitants) were at mass when the ground began to shake. Three distinct jolts, the second most violent. The quake is now thought to have measured nine on the Richter Scale. It lasted less than ten minutes, opening fissures five metres wide in the Baixa area. Churches collapsed, burying the worshippers. Survivors who rushed to open spaces by the river watched in horrified fascination as the water was sucked out to sea, leaving fish and old shipwrecks stranded in the bay. Forty minutes after the quake, a huge wave returned, followed by two smaller ones. The low-lying town centre (the Baixa) was violently swamped. And then, where the water had not reached, the fires began. They were started by cooking fires and votive candles, and later by looters and arsonists. The town burned for five days. Estimates of the dead range from 60,000 to 100,000. Only 15 per cent of the city's buildings remained.

It was the prime minister, Sebastião de Melo (later to be Marquis of Pombal), who took charge. He used the army to force able-bodied *Lisboetas* to stay, and help in the clear-up. And in the coming months and years he employed military engineers to plan and rebuild the city centre: the Baixa Pombalina. Thus, 'Pombaline' Lisbon is built on a wooden cage, to resist further quakes, with spacious squares and wide, parallel streets arranged in a grid. The buildings are elegant, but more practical and economical than the grand and ornate architecture they replaced.

Gothic/Renaissance style crossed with Manueline *(page 432)* – really worth a visit. Also impressive (especially from the outside) is the Manueline Torre de Belém (Belém Tower) at the water's edge.

Lisbon's other riverside districts have been tourist no-go areas until very recently. The dockland area between ALCÂNTARA by the Ponte 25 de Abril (25 April Bridge) and CAIS DO SODRÉ south of the Bairro Alto used to be a red light area. Now the river front here has been cleaned up, the warehouses converted into cafés, bars, clubs and restaurants (including the excellent VírGula). The big covered food market, the Mercado da Ribeira (officially called the Mercado 24 de Julho), is just by the Cais do Sodré station. But the really serious – and beautiful – dockland development is the modern PARQUE DAS NAÇÕES,

Left Convento do Carmo, memorial to the earthquake

Above The graceful Gare do Oriente

Right Cable cars and the Vasco da Gama bridge

Opposite Café on the top of Elevador de Santa Justa

Lisbon's east end, just before the Ponte Vasco da Gama (Vasco da Gama Bridge). Old warehouses and factories were demolished to make way for a big, well-planned area of distinguished, modern architecture in preparation for *Expo '98*. And now in the second millennium, it really works as a new residential and leisure district. There are apartment blocks, offices, the Vasco da Gama shopping centre, cultural and leisure centres, sculptures, gardens along the river, and sports facilities. The station, the Gare do Oriente is a masterpiece of sweeping steel and glass. This is an entertaining place to come in the day time, with or without children. You can rent bicycles, do water sports, ride high along the shore in the cable car, visit the new interactive science museum, the stunning Oceanarium *(page 236)*, or the parks. By night there's Lisbon's new casino, with its top-class restaurant, Pragma *(page 240)*.

VIEW FROM THE TOP

All over Lisbon's seven hills, you will stumble across panoramic views over the city, the river and the Setúbal Peninsula on the opposite bank. These are some of our favourites:

ALFAMA **Miradouro de Santa Luzia** A small garden with a bougainvillea-laden pergola and wide views over the Alfama, towards the castle and river.

BAIRRO ALTO **Miradouro de São Pedro de Alcântara** A shady spot to take in stunning views of the Castelo, Avenida, Baixa and Bairro Alto. The Elevador da Glória funicular (starting from near Rossio station) will drop you nearby.

BAIXA **Elevador de Santa Justa** High above the Baixa, with great views of the city centre, enjoy a coffee or glass of freshly squeezed orange juice in the tower-top café. A disciple of Eiffel designed this vertical cast iron and filigree lift at the turn of the last century. Queue in Rua de Aurea to go up. From three tiers down below the café, a walkway will take you to the Bairro Alto.

CASTELO **Castelo de São Jorge** From the shady terrace within the castle (open daily 9am–9pm), get a good idea of the layout of the city. Best of all, climb up the Torre de Ulisses (Tower of Ulysses) for a 360 degree view through the telescope. The

viewpoint **Largo das Portas do Sol** is very close to the castle, giving different views over the river and Alfama.

CHIADO **Armazens do Chiado** Great views from this up-market shopping centre in an old department store.

GRAÇA **Largo da Graça** Lovely vistas from under the umbrella pines, near the Castelo; then move on 100 metres to the **Miradouro da Senhora do Monte**, for even better views over almost the whole city and the river to the Setúbal Peninsula.

BELÉM Torre de Belém
In the days of the discoveries and the Portuguese empire, this defensive Manueline/Gothic fortress was buffeted by the waves out in the estuary. The ocean has since receded, leaving the ornate tower (a UNESCO World Heritage Site) jutting out into the water just off the Belém seafront. The exterior has Moroccan and Venetian influences; inside are austere, vaulted rooms – an armoury, living quarters and a prison. In rough weather, dodge the waves as you cross the walkway. It is worth climbing to the top for panoramic views of the estuary and the western part of the city. *Avenida da India Open Oct-Apr 10-5, May-Sep 10-6.30*

PARQUE DAS NAÇÕES Oceanário
This glass building set out over the water is one of the biggest and best sea life centres in Europe. Separate concave glass tanks representing the ecosystems of the world's five oceans are viewable from two levels. *Esplanada Dom Carlos I, Doca dos Olivais Open Oct-Apr 10-6, May-Sep 10-7*

MUSEUMS & GALLERIES

ALFAMA/DOCAS Museu Nacional do Azulejo (The National Tile Museum) Displayed around the cloisters of a 16th century convent (the Convento da Madre de Deus), the huge collection ranges from Moorish tiles to *azulejos*. Highlights are a tile panorama of Lisbon just before the earthquake, and the convent's church, built in the 16th century and stunningly decorated in the 18th century. *Rua da Madre de Deus 4 Open Tue 2-6, Wed-Sun 10-6, Closed Mon, public hols*

BELÉM Museu dos Coches (Coach Museum) In the east wing of the Palácio de Belém, this must be the best collection in the world of horse-drawn carriages. The pink palace is also the President of Portugal's official residence. *Praça Alfonso de Albuquerque Open Tue-Sun 10-6 Closed Mon, public hols.*

CHIADO Museu do Chiado The national museum of contemporary art, 1820 to the present day. *Rua Serpa Pinto 4 Open Tue-Sun 10-6 Closed Mon*

LAPA/DOCAS Museu Nacional de Arte Antiga (Museum of Ancient Art) The 17th century palace that houses the national art collection once belonged to the famous Pombal family. The local name for the museum is Casa das Janelas Verdes or House of the Green Windows – though they are no longer green. This is an impressive collection of 14th to 19th century art, tapestries, ceramics, and exhibits from the former empire. *Rua das Janelas Verdes Open Tue 2-6, Wed-Sun 10-6 Closed Mon, public hols*

REGO Museu Calouste Gulbenkian
North of the Parque Eduardo VII, ranking amongst Europe's finest collections of art and artefacts, this is the bequest of Turkish-American oil millionaire Calouste Gulbenkian, who adopted Portugal as his home during the Second World War. Exhibits are wide-ranging: art, sculpture, rugs, ceramics, jewellery etc from Europe and the East, ancient Egypt, classical Greece and Rome. *Avenida de Berna 45A Open Tue-Sun 10-6 Closed Mon, public hols Free on Sun, €3 Tues-Sat*

REGO Centro de Arte Moderna
The modern art collection of the Calouste Gulbenkian Foundation. *Rua Dr Nicolau de Bettencourt Open Tue-Sun 10-5.45 Closed Mon, public hols*

CHURCHES

ALFAMA Igreja de Santa Engrácia, Panteón Nacional Lisbon's most beautiful and biggest Baroque building took 284 years to complete, from 1682 to1966. *Campo de Santa Clara, São Vicente de Fora Open Tue-Sun 10-5 Closed Mon, public hols*

BAIRRO ALTO Igreja de São Roque 16th century church, simple outside, but on the inside mosaic and jewel pictures look like paintings. *Largo Trinidade Coelho Open 10-5 Closed Mon, public hols*

BELÉM

Mosteiro dos Jerónimos

It is easy to understand how the Jerónimos Monastery took a century to build. Funded by profits of the spice trade, building began in 1501, spanning the Manueline, Gothic and Renaissance styles, with oriental and maritime motifs. The grandest façade overlooks the Tagus estuary – indeed the monastery stood right beside the shore until the shoreline changed. Greatest highlights are the church, the cloisters and the south portal. The church has slender pillars carved to represent palm trees, spreading web-like across the dome; there are similarly ribbed, vaulted ceilings in the sacristy and refectory, beautiful stained glass windows, and the tomb of Vasco da Gama. The West Portal has stunning filigree carving, and the cloisters, on two levels, are elaborately carved with distorted figures hiding amidst vegetation. This is a UNESCO World Heritage Site.

Open Oct-Apr 10-5, May-Sep 10-6.30 Closed Mon, public hols

Fun and feasting – Lisbon's festivals combine serious religion with pagan rites, folk music with rock bands, and generally grilled sardines with free-flowing easy-to-drink Alentejo wine

FAIRS & FESTIVALS

FEBRUARY/MARCH

Carnaval Carnival happens all over Portugal in the period leading up to Lent, but Lisbon's is one of the best. There are processions of floats in the town centre and the Parque das Nações, disguises, dancing, parties, and plenty of wine and food.

JUNE

Festa de Santo António Lisbon explodes into all-night party mode on 13 June, or the nearest weekend, for the Feast of Saint Anthony (a Christian replacement for the summer solstice). People open their houses and sell wine and sardines, or grill sardines in the streets, to be served with boiled potatoes, salad and olive oil on a bread 'plate'. There are competitions between the *bairros* (districts), a parade of the *bairros* down the Avenide da Liberdade, coloured street lights, music, dancing, concerts, street theatre and fireworks. Men give pots of basil to their girlfriends, young people jump over bonfires and singe thistle flowers in the fires to predict their future spouse.

Festas dos Santos Populares (Feast Days of the Popular Saints) More partying and feasting in the second half of the month, especially on 23-24 June for São João (St John) and 28-29 June for São Pedro (St Peter).

NOVEMBER

Encontro com o Vinho e Sabores (Wine and Flavours Experience) Lisbon's big wine and gourmet consumer fair early in November in the Centro de Congressos, just west of the Ponte 25 de Abril (the old bridge). Tastings of wines, cheeses, olive oils, charcuterie etc from over 200 producers, mostly Portuguese.

Festas de São Martinho On Saint Martin's day, 11 November, street vendors sell hot, salted chestnuts in newspaper cones, and you can taste the year's new wine, or *agua pé*, an alcoholic drink made by adding sweet, unfermented grape juice to a bitter wine from the second pressing of the grapes. Later into the night, young *Lisboetas* may start jumping over those bonfires again…

Eat in Lisbon

Although there *has* been a gastronomic revolution in Lisbon in recent years, traditional Portuguese food is still fare of the day in most of Lisbon's restaurants. Being a capital, Lisbon inevitably also has its McDonalds (18!), its pizzas, Chinese restaurants, and, increasingly, restaurants at the finer end offering sushi, fine Italian, Spanish or vaguely international cuisine. But much more importantly, Lisbon now also has restaurants that take a new, modern look at Portuguese cuisine, using fine Portuguese ingredients just that little bit differently. Lisbon today has numerous world-class chefs, who have often returned here after an enlightening spell in kitchens abroad. And there are plenty of gastronomically-minded *Lisboetas* prepared to pay for seriously fine food and wine. Prices may seem high by local standards, but most of Lisbon's finest restaurants are still far less expensive than top-class cuisine in other Western European capitals.

For this book we have focussed on fine *Portuguese* restaurants, or at the very least fine Portuguese fusion, even though our wine friends sometimes pointed us also towards top 'foreign' restaurants. If we want to eat sushi, we might

Right Seasoned customers at the Antiga Confeitaria de Belém
Below left Relaxing with a glass as the sun goes down
Below right In the Pragma restaurant in Casino Lisboa

head for Tokyo some other time… We have also sought out restaurants that do traditional Portuguese food *well*.

Food in Lisbon is influenced not only by the sea, but also quite strongly by the proximity of the simple peasant food of the Alentejo, which can be very filling, and comes in large portions! There are lots of bready dishes, and lots of fish, seafood and steaks. Meat and fish can be over-cooked – you might ask for it *mal passado* (rare) but there is no guarantee… A speciality is *caldeirada rica*, a dense fish soup, and of course *bacalhau* (salt cod) is on the menu everywhere in various guises. If you head for the nearest tourist restaurant, there is a good chance of disappointment. You could on the other hand strike really lucky, whether in an expensive restaurant or in one of the delightfully old fashioned little *tascas* on the way up to the Castelo São Jorge…

Lisboetas eat out a lot – so it is wise to book in good restaurants, especially on busy Friday and Saturday nights, and on Sundays and Mondays, when many restaurants close.

If you have room, there is also much scope in Lisbon for eating between meals. In the autumn and winter, street vendors will sell you hot chestnuts, and the capital is full of pastry shops. Try the Lisbon speciality, *pasteis de nata* – small egg custard tarts in thin flaky pastry, delicious eaten warm from the counter with a sprinkle of cinnamon and icing sugar.

RESTAURANTS – MODERN PORTUGUESE

ALVALADE

Na Ordem Com... Luís Suspiro
A new restaurant, with possibly the finest and most imaginative cooking in Lisbon, by renowned chef Luís Suspiro. Why 'Na Ordem'? The restaurant is within the headquarters of the Portuguese medical association, the Ordem dos Médicos –

but it is open to the public. The decor is elegant (wood, restful autumnal tones), the food sophisticated, seasonal, artistic, playful, exuberant and complicated – a delicious new take on traditional dishes. Various set menus are very reasonably priced. The wine list is long and curiously mixed – some excellent wines, some less so, but prices are fair. You are safe within the *Seleccão de Brancos/Tintos*, the selections by the bottle rather than by the glass.
Avenida Gago Coutinho 151
T+351 218 406 117
E luissuspiro@naordemcomluissuspiro.com
W www.naordemcomluissuspiro
€70 ♀ V Closed Sun

BAIXA

Terreiro do Paço This excellent contemporary Portuguese restaurant was built into one of the stunning vaulted Pombaline buildings in the big square by the sea at the foot of the Baixa – call in

first for a free tasting with the neighbours, the wine promotion centre of Sala Ogival *(page 233)*! 'O Paço' upstairs serves elegant and delicious Portuguese fusion food, with first class ingredients and interesting flavour combinations. The simpler downstairs restaurant opens only in summer, spilling out onto the pavement and serving lighter meals. The list of Portuguese wines is long and good, at fair prices – some less interesting wines in the Alentejo section, however.
Praça do Comércio
T+351 210 312 850
E terreirodopaco@quintadaslagrimas.pt
W www.terreiropaco.com
€50 ♀ V on request
Closed upstairs Sat lunch, all day Sun; downstairs open weekday lunch in summer, closed weekends, totally closed in winter

CAIS DO SODRÉ

VírGula With fine views of the river, the 25 de Abril Bridge and the Cristo Rei statue on the opposite bank, VírGula is a modern, informal-sophisticated restaurant in a converted salt warehouse down near the Mercado da Ribeira. Decor is minimalist, with high ceiling and a network of huge air conditioning steel pipes a major design feature. Candle-lit at night, this is a romantic spot. Sit on the high stools at the long bar to explore the *petiscos* menu – oysters, clams, wonderful ham... In the main restaurant, chef Bertílio Gomes uses fresh, top quality Portuguese products in his creative cuisine, with welcome and attractive use of vegetables. VírGula has an extensive list of very well-chosen wines at all levels, from inexpensive to rare, from Portuguese to Austrian, with a good selection by the glass. By the way, *virgula* means comma, *gula* means gluttony.

Rua Cintura do Porto de Lisboa, 16, Armazém B, Cais de Santos/Cais do Sodré
T+351 213 432 002
E restvirgula@sapo.pt
€45 ♀ V
Closed Sun all year; lunch in Aug

CAMPOLIDE

Eleven Viewed from the outside, this is a pink concrete box at the top of the Parque Eduardo VII. Inside, Eleven is airy, light and modern, and the inventive, accomplished cooking has won a Michelin star. Service is friendly and attentive. Eleven has a superb wine list, both Portuguese and world-wide, with lots of wine by the glass. A lunchtime business menu is excellent value. Why the magic number? There are 11 partners, including chef Joachim Koerper, who commutes between Lisbon and his 2-star restaurant in Spain.
Rua Marquês de Fronteira, Jardim Amália Rodrigues
T+351 213 862 211
E 11@restauranteleven.com
W www.restauranteleven.com
€65-€100 ♀ V on request
Closed Sun

LAPA

York House Hotel The leafy courtyard is a great place to eat outdoors in summer and a welcome escape from the bustle of Lisbon. But do book. This is a popular lunching spot for business people and politicians from the nearby National Assembly. For cooler weather, the dining room has a vaulted ceiling, *azulejos* and cosy alcoves. Food is modern Portuguese.

A good, mostly Portuguese wine list is arranged (unusually for Portugal) according to grape variety.
Rua das Janelas Verdes 32
T+351 213 962 435
E manager@yorkhouselisboa.com
W www.yorkhouselisboa.com
€70-€80 ♀ *V* 🛏

PARQUE DAS NAÇÕES
Pragma Fausto Airoldi A contemporary, elegant restaurant in Casino Lisboa serving creative and modern Portuguese cooking by one of Portugal's top chefs, Fausto Airoldi. Ingredients are top class, kitchen skills backed by the most modern technology. There's an optional degustation menu, with matching wines. The amazing wine list has posh bottles from home and abroad, unusually for Portugal listed with grape varieties, and many fine wines by the glass. Decor is dark – black and reds with white relief.
Casino Lisboa, Alameda dos Oceanos
T+351 961 355 100
E reservas@evolucaogastronomica.com
W www.pragmalx.com
€60 ♀ *V on request – please phone*

SALDANHA
Panorama Talented young chef Henrique Sá Pessoa moved recently from Flores in the Bairro Alto Hotel to the new top-floor gastronomic restaurant of the revamped Sheraton. Time served in London and Australia has made him particularly sympathetic to vegetables: at least two vegetarian starters and two main courses will bring high-class relief to vegetarians adrift in this city of fish and meat. But there is fine fish and meat too – the style is Portuguese with Mediterranean influences. A degustation menu at €45 is particularly good value. The excellent wine list is mostly Portuguese. The view

alone would be worth a visit – from the 27th floor of Lisbon's tallest building – and this is some of the best, most inventive modern cooking in Portugal.
Sheraton Lisboa Hotel & Spa, Rua Latino
* Coelho 1,*
T+351 213 120 000
E sheraton.lisboa@sheraton.com
W www.starwoodhotels.com/sheraton
€50-€55 ♀ *V*

SANTO AMARO
Valle Flor The grand but pretty Valle Flor restaurant is part of the Pestana Carlton Palace Hotel, a former mansion, built for a cocoa millionaire in the early 20th century. This is one of Lisbon's pricier restaurants, but the food and wine are exceptional. The service is friendly, formal and discreet, and Aimé Barroyer's cooking is contemporary, creative Portuguese, with a lightness of touch. There is a very good list of Portuguese wines and numerous wines by the glass.
Hotel Pestana Palace, Rua Jau 54
T+351 213 615 600
E valle-flor@pestana.com
W www.pestana.com
€65-€70 ♀ *V* 🛏

SÃO SEBASTIÃO/MARQUÊS DE POMBAL
Luca Luca used to be very much Italian, but now you might call its cooking fusion with a strong Portuguese theme – even though the two chefs are North Italian and Japanese! It's a cuisine based on fresh produce, flavours and textures. A shortish wine list has good bottles at all price levels, especially Alentejo and Douro. The place is large and minimalist, attractive and friendly, and always full, so book. The kitchen is open to view, a young team cooking for a young clientele. Their 'Tapas Bar' also serves a tempting buffet from 7pm.

Rua Santa Marta 35
T+351 213 150 212
E luca@luca.pt
W www.luca.pt
€30 ♀ *V on request*
Closed Sat lunch, Sun

SÃO SEBASTIÃO
Bocca West of the Praça Marquês de Pombal, this exciting new restaurant and bar opened in 2008. Food is light, modern, inventive, beautifully presented, the wine list not long but very well selected, mostly from Portugal, with more than 60 wines by the glass. It has a smart-informal feel, the design cool and modern. Service is friendly and very professional.
Rua Rodrigo da Fonseca 87D
T +351 213 808 383
E reservas@boca.pt
W www.bocca.pt
Lunch €25 din €50 ♀ *V!*
Closed Sun, Mon, public hols

Varanda, Ritz Four Seasons The plush, formal restaurant of the Ritz Four Seasons Hotel *(page 249)* serves wonderful lunches that attract the city's business community as well as gastronomes. Lunch is a buffet with a bewildering range of dishes. Dinner à la carte is amongst Lisbon's most inventive modern cuisine. Even so, this is a less popular evening venue, except for hotel guests. Occasionally the invention stretches taste-buds a little too far, but their cooking of fish and seafood is deliciously precise. The wine list is very strong on Portuguese wines (not marked up too fiercely), with classics from other countries well represented, too.
Rua Rodrigo da Fonseca 88
T+351 213 811 400
E fsh.lisbon@fourseasons.com
W www.fourseasons.com/lisbon
€70-€100 ♀ *V* 🛏

RESTAURANTS – GOOD TRADITIONAL PORTUGUESE

FADO IN LISBON

Lisbon is one of two epicentres (Coimbra is the other) of *fado*, Portugal's sentimental and often mournful folk music. But *fado* houses can be a terrible tourist rip-off. Even if the music is good, the obligatory food and wine is often bad, and very expensive. However an evening of *fado* is a great way to burrow into Lisbon culture. Watch the locals at the neighbouring tables, and note how they love their national folk music, how they halt their meal to listen attentively, and nostalgically join in with the chorus. You may even feel moved to join in too! Fine *fado* might be sung anywhere from an elegant restaurant to a poky *tasca*, and by anyone from a *fado* star to the local postman. The Alfama may be the best place to stumble upon the really soulful stuff. The more formal *fado* houses usually open between 8 and 8.30pm, the *fado* starts around 9.30, and you can usually stay until 2 or 3am... Here are some useful addresses for *fado* aficionados.

THEORY...

ALFAMA Casa do Fado e da Guitarra Portuguesa An interesting museum where you can hear the music and get to know the famous singers of yesteryear, and learn about the Portuguese guitar – mandolin-shaped,

with six double strings. A well-stocked shop sells a big range of CDs and sheet music *Largo do Chafariz de Dentro 1 Open 10–6 Closed Mon*

...AND PRACTICE

ALCÂNTARA Timpanas An unpretentious place enjoyed by locals. *Rua Gilberto Rola 24*
ALFAMA Clube de Fado Cosy, stylish, historic venue near the cathedral attracting top singers, €7.50 show, €45 meal. *Rua São João da Praça 94 – must book* T+351 218 852 704
Parreirinha de Alfama Very good *fado*, fairly priced. *Beco do Espírito Santo 1*
BAIRRO ALTO O Faia Touristy and expensive but good singers. *Rua da Barroca 54/56*
Adega do Ribatejo Inexpensive and fun, nice tiles. *Rua de Diário de Notícias 23*
A Tasca do Chico A very inexpensive, atmospheric *fado* pub, where even you can sing a solo! *Rua Diário de Noticias 39*
LAPA Senhor Vinho Famous but friendly, €50 including the show, which is genuinely good *fado* – the wines are good too. *Rua do Meio à Lapa 18*

cooked. The wines are good. I de Maio is popular with both locals and tourists – booking avoids the queues.
Rua da Atalaia 8
T+351 213 426 840
€20-€25 ♀ Closed Sat lunch, Sun

Pap'Açorda So trendy that you must book, and relatively expensive, Pap'Açorda serves good traditional Alentejo food with a slightly modern lift. Start with drinks at the marble bar, then move on into the pinks and whites of the smartly buzzing dining rooms, beneath the chandeliers.
Rua da Atalaia 57-59
T +351 213 464 811
€50 Closed Mon lunch, Sun

Terra A delightful vegetarian restaurant in Lisbon! Terra's organic buffet ranges from oriental to Mediterranean to salads and veggy versions of traditional Portuguese dishes. There's even a selection for vegans, plus organic juices, beers and wines. Inside the decor is fresh, with white walls and lots of wood (and it's a no-smoking zone!). A lovely, tree-shaded garden is romantically lit in the evening, and heated when necessary to prolong *ao fresco* dining.
Rua da Palmeira 15, Principe Real
T+351 213 421 407
W www.terra.vg
€20-€24 V including vegan!

ALVALADE

O Poleiro A small, simple restaurant with excellent food and a very good wine list. Well-cooked, traditional dishes often have a flavour of the Minho or Alentejo, and sometimes there will be a little modern twist. Don't be put off by the exterior – inside, O Poleiro (The Perch – bird variety) is cosy and welcoming, all pinks and browns, dark wood and tiles, the walls hung with old street lamps and kitchen

utensils. North of the town centre, up towards the airport, parking is easy.
Rua de Entrecampos 30A
T+351 217 976 265
€27 ♀ V on request
Closed Sun; 2nd half Aug

BAIRRO ALTO

I de Maio A cheerful, simple restaurant with white tiles, gingham table cloths, and simple meat and fish dishes, well

BAIXA

Muni Traditional Portuguese dishes are on the menu of this small, cosy, vaulted restaurant, and they are well cooked. Eat petiscos, good fish and seafood. In season, partridge *(perdiz)* stew is a speciality. Prices are very reasonable, the wine list good.
Rua dos Correeiros 115/117
T+351 213 428 982
€25 ♀ Closed Sat, Sun, public hols; Sep

BEATO

Restaurante d'Avis A snug, rustic restaurant on the way up the river towards the Parque das Nações – a good place to try traditional Alentejo dishes, seafood, and roast baby goat *(cabrito)*.
Rua do Grilo 98
T +351 218 681 354
€27 V Closed Sun; Aug

CAMPO DE OURIQUE

A Tasquinha d'Adelaide A very, very small restaurant (you *must* book) with half-boarded walls, ochre paint and old fashioned pictures. Good, home-made, hearty Transmontano cooking, stunning roast lamb *(cordeiro)*, interesting wine list.
Rua do Patrocinio 70-74
T+351 213 962 239
€30 ♀ Closed Sun, public hols

CARNIDE

O Galito A long-established restaurant next to the Military College, run by a mother and son, serving very good Alentejo fare and excellent wines (loads by the glass). A cheerful place with tiles, wood, white walls and table cloths, and a generally older clientele. Even though a little out of the way in the north-west suburb of Carnide, it is worth booking.
Rua da Fonte 16A
T+351 217 111 088
€25 ♀ Closed Sun, public hols, 1st half Sep

ESTEFÂNIA

Horta dos Brunos A small, atmospheric, unpretentious restaurant east of the Parque Eduardo VII with a top, nationwide wine list at reasonable prices, good glasses, and traditional dishes impressively cooked. Service is attentive, fun and welcoming.
Rua Ilha do Pico 27
T+351 213 153 421
€30 ♀ Closed Sat lunch, Sun, public hols

MERCÊS

Conventual Between the Bairro Alto and Parque Mayer, Conventual is formal, smart and relatively expensive in Portuguese terms. Expect to dine alongside politicians and businessmen, and to drink well – the wine list is long and very good. The food is well-cooked traditional style, based on excellent, fresh ingredients served up in rich sauces. This place was once a convent, hence the name and the religious decor. It's hard to park around this medieval square – come by public transport, and do book.
Praça das Flores 44/45
T+351 213 909 246
€45–€50 ♀ V on request
Closed Sat and Mon lunch; Sun; Aug

REGO

O Polícia Here for over 100 years, this smart-casual restaurant is generally full of Portuguese customers rather than tourists, despite its proximity to the garden of the Fundação Calouste Gulbenkian gallery and museum. Cooking is traditional, from very good ingredients, nicely presented, and the wine list is good, too. There's lots of offal on the menu, along with good meat and fish, sauces are well-flavoured, salads good. Portions are quite big – order modestly, and if you like your steak rare, point this out. There are several dining rooms, some attractively tiled, some wood-panelled, the floors a delightful black and white mosaic, like a Baixa pavement, but smooth.
Rua Marqués Sá da Bandeira 112A
T +351 217 963 505
W www.opolicia.restaunet.pt
€40 ♀ V Closed Sat din, sun, public hols

RESTAURADORES

Bonjardim/Rei dos Frangos Famous for its amazing value, this buzzing little restaurant is down an alley-way between the Praça dos Restauradores and Rua das Portas de Santo Antão. The main restaurant has tables outside, a bar and a really attractive *azulejo*-clad restaurant upstairs. Best options are the huge platefuls of succulently spit-roasted chickens *(frangos)* with chips, good salad and optional piri piri sauce. Fish may disappoint.
Travessa Santo Antão
T+351 213 424 389
€20

Solar dos Presuntos Just north of the Baixa, surrounded by tourist restaurants, this one is in a different league, with good-quality, traditional Portuguese fare and an excellent wine list, including top Portuguese wines and old Madeiras, served in nice glasses. Upstairs is more traditional (run by the father), downstairs more modern (the domain of the son), but everywhere the service is good and jokey. It's a big place, but always buzzing.
Rua das Portas Santo António 150
T+351 213 424 253
E restaurante@solardospresuntos.com
W www.solardospresuntos.com
€35 ♀ V on request
Closed Sun, public hols

SALDANHA

Sessenta Amidst the office buildings to the east of the Parque Eduardo V11, this new restaurant (opened in July 2008) has great food, good wine and wine service, and attractive modern design, highlighted by the startling red water glasses. And it's not expensive. The team came from VírGula *(page 239)* and chef Mario Rua has also worked for several years in France. Traditional dishes are executed with flair, with added French sensitivity, and artistic, modern presentation. The wine list is not long, but very good, and a Verre de Vin machine allows opened

bottles to be preserved under inert gas, so that numerous wines are available by the glass. Lunches are excellent value – the office lunch option of main course, drink and coffee is just €10. In late afternoon and evening, until 7pm, the wine bar serves freshly-prepared *petiscos*. Evenings are more romantic, and *à la carte*.
Rua Tomas Ribeiro 60
T +351 213 526 060
E geral@sesenta.pt
W www.sessenta.pt
Lunch €16 din €30 ⚲ V!
Closed sun

SANTO AMARO
Solar dos Nunes This delightful, cosy, traditional restaurant west of the 25 de Abril Bridge has its roots in the Alentejo. A frieze of *azulejos*, and myriad little pictures, cooking pots and paraphernalia adorn the walls, ceiling and every available perch. The wine list is excellent, the food copious and well cooked. Very popular with the locals, so it's always best to book.
Rua dos Lusíadas 70
T+351 213 647 359
W www.solardosnunes.pt
€30 ⚲ Closed Sun

SANTOS
Tromba Rija By the Santos train station, down by the river and docks, Tromba Rija is a good place to get acquainted with traditional Portuguese dishes, cheeses and puddings without having to battle with a menu. It is excellent value so long as you arrive hungry – eat as much as you want from a huge buffet and then go back for more.
Rua Cintura do Porto de Lisboa 254
T+351 213 971 507
E reservaslisboa@trombarija.com
€39.50 V

DRINK AND SNACK

ALFAMA
Cafeteria DeliDeluxe There's a big choice of enticing wines, with a skimpy mark-up, in the café at the back of this fine deli, opposite the Museu Militar. On a 2,000-strong list, 70% of the wines are Portuguese, and six to a dozen wines are always available by the glass. There's a good, international selection of beers, too. Eat inside or out on the terrace by the river: there are tempting cheeses and charcuterie, salads, toasts, sandwiches, oie gras, *carpaccio*, pastries… It's a perfect place for a weekend breakfast, brunch or light meal. You'd be welcome to join informal tutored tastings on Thursday early evenings. *Avenida Infante D Henrique, Armazém B, Loja 8 Open Mon-Fri 12-10, Sat 10-10, Sun 10-8*

BAIRRO ALTO
Cultura do Chá Lovely, atmospheric café, delicious pastries and cakes, light snacks, and a huge range of teas and infusions. *Rua dos Salgadeiras Open 10-9.30 Closed Sun*

AVENIDA
Enoteca Chafariz do Vinho You'll love this place. The *chafariz* was an 18th century 'cistern', part of the water system of the Águas Livres Aquaduct. Now it is a wine bar, with tables on two levels of a metal structure within the old stone-blocked walls. It has an amazingly good wine list (Portuguese and foreign), with very fair prices, including 14 really interesting wines by the glass – no wonder, as the place is run by one of Portugal's top wine writers, João Paulo Martins. Food tends to be simple – plates of cold meat and cheese, *petiscos*, salads, cheese platters, pasta dishes, plus a few more complex items. You can eat till late – the kitchen is busy until 1pm.
Chafariz da Mãe d'Agua, Rua da Mãe d'Agua à Praça da Alegria
T+351 213 422 079
E clientes@chafarizdovinho.com
W www.chafarizdovinho.com
€28 or less ⚲ V Closed Mon

Pastelaria-Padaria São Roque Rest your legs here after climbing up to the top of the Bairro Alto. This is much more a café than a bread and cake shop, with art deco tiles, gold-painted domed ceiling, grinning Neptunes, full of local people drinking little cups of coffee, chatting and reading the papers. *Rua Dom Pedro V 57 Open 7-7 Closed Sun*

Solar do Vinho do Porto Smart wine bar inside the refurbished Ludovico Palace, at the top of the Elevador da Glória. Run by the Port and Douro Wine Institute, it has the best selection of port in Lisbon, representing all the producers. Drink by the glass or bottle, buy books on port. *Rua de São Pedro de Alcântara 45 Open 11am-midnight Closed Sun*

BAIXA
Confeitaria Nacional Old fashioned pastry shop and café, little changed since it opened in 1829, with a mirrored ceiling and old glass counter. At Christmas, its *bolo rei* is legendary. *Praça da Figueira 18B/C Open Mon-Fri 8-8, Sat 8am-2pm Closed Sun*

BELÉM
Antiga Confeitaria de Belém On the city side of the Jerónimos Monastery, this early 19th century cake shop is famous for its *azulejo*-rich decor, and its Pasteis de Belém, fine flaky pastry tarts with a baked creamy eggy filling, sprinkled with cinnamon and icing sugar. Eat them warm, with coffee, or take them away. *Rua de Belém 84-92 Open 8am-midnight*

CHIADO
Café Brasileira Long, narrow, busy Café Brasileira is in the main drag of smart Chiado shops. Redesigned after a serious neighbourhood fire in 1988, it has grand marble facades and dark decor, evocative paintings, mirrors, marble chequerboard floor and an old clock at the end. Delicious coffee, lots of cakes and pastries, juices, soft drinks and spirits. There are tables outside as well. *Rua Garrett 120 Open 8am-2am every day*

MAGNÓLIA CAFÉ FINE FOOD
A small chain of airy, contemporary café-delicatessens, also take-away. Relief is on hand for vegetarians – there are great salads and tempting natural juices. A good place for a cup of coffee, or breakfast, or a delicious afternoon pastry. Deli products are also for sale.
ALVALADE *Avenida de Roma 17 Open Mon-Fri 8-8; Sat, Sun, public hols 10-8*
CAMPO PEQUENO *Campo Pequeno 2 Open Mon-Fri 8am till late, weekends 10am till late*
SÃO SEBASTIÃO *Centro Comercial Saldanha Residence, Loja 0.06, Avenida Fontes Perreira de Melo 42E. Open 10am-11pm*

Cervejaria da Trinidade Unimpressive on the outside, beautiful within, this beer hall is not far from the Elevador de Santa Justa. Dating from 1836, once a convent, then a brewery, it's now a 'Historical Cultural Monument'. Admire the vaulted ceilings and buxom representations of the four seasons in the main hall. There's a courtyard terrace for summer. Have a coffee, or a beer and *petiscos* – and there are a few desirable wines. *Rua Nova da Trinidade 20C Open every day 10am–2am*

MARKETS, WINE AND FOOD SHOPS

ALFAMA/DOCAS
DeliDeluxe New, modern deli near Santa Apolónia station in former dockland area, opposite the Museu Militar. Excellent cheese, charcuterie, oils, vinegars, dried mushrooms, fresh veg, teas, coffees, jams, and a huge range of Portuguese and foreign wines. At the back is a lovely café/wine bar, with terrace on the river *(page 243)*. *Avenida Infante D Henrique, Armazém B, Loja 8*

BAIRRO ALTO
Mercearia da Atalaia A beautiful new deli and wine shop that only *looks* expensive. Good wines, from inexpensive to fine, many of them organic, all with tasting notes in English and Portuguese. *Rua da Atalaia 64A*

BAIXA
Adivinho – Aromatíssimo Comércio de Vinhos A great range of wines – stored in perfect conditions in an attractive shop

(inside, at least) under Pombaline ceiling arches. Loads of information and advice on hand, and wines from all over the country, plus accessories, including fine glasses. *Travessa do Almada 24*

Casa Macário Small, characterful old shop with a very good selection of wine and port, not rarities, but well chosen, including wines at modest prices. *Rua Augusta 272/276*

Garrafeira Nacional A long-established wine shop in a street parallel to the Rua Augusta, with a very good selection of Portuguese wines, as well as whiskies, at fair prices, too. There are old and rare wines, fine ports and Madeiras, and well-chosen bottles at more modest prices. The oldest bottles are kept in a lovely brick-arched 'museum'. *Rua de Santa Justa 18*

Manuel Tavares On a street running between Rossio and Praça da Figuera. There is quite a good set of wines and ports, excellent cheeses, good charcuterie, nuts, dried fruits and chocolate. *Rua da Betesga 1A/1B*

BELÉM
Coisas do Arco do Vinho Smart, serious wine shop, one of Portugal's best, inside the Belém Cultural Centre, with a huge range of wines, including old and rare. Interesting wine accessories, and deli foods. *Centro Cultural de Belém, Rua Bartolomeu Dias, Loja 7/8*

CAIS DO SODRÉ
Mercado da Ribeira The huge covered market down by the port has it all: fruit, veg, fish and seafood, meat and chicken, eggs, snails, charcuterie, ham, cheese, olives, pulses, herbs, nuts, bread, flowers… It is open early morning to noon. (Note that on maps it is called Mercado de 24 Julho.) *Avenida 24 Julho Open Mon-Sat 7am-1pm Closed Sun*

CAMPO DE OURIQUE
Garrafeira do Campo d'Ourique Wine and spirits shop north of the Basilica da Estrela, crammed with bottles, brimming with advice. *Rua Tomás da Anunciação 29A*

Loja Portugal Rural North of the Basilica da Estrela, this airy, modern shop has produce from all over Portugal, breads, cheese, charcuterie, oil, vinegar, fruit and veg. Linked to ProRegiões, an organisation promoting the regions, it's a good place to find wines from lesser-known producers. *Rua Saraiva de Carvalho 115*

CAMPO PEQUENO
Magnólia Fine Food A shop-only version of the small chain of Magnólia Cafés. Smart and modern, with up-market cakes, sweets and tempting deli products. *Largo do Campo Pequeno 4*

Venha à Vinha Garrafeira Serious, attractively modern wine shop with a good range of Portuguese wines. *Avenida João XXI 72B, Galeria Via Veneto, Loja 30*

CAMPOLIDE
Wine O'Clock Modern shop with a huge and impressive range of wines at competitive prices, from everyday to fine and rare, plus a fascinating collection of whiskies, Cognacs and Armagnacs. They organise tutored tastings, and are keen to advise. *Rua Joshua Benoliel 2B*

CHIADO
Santos Ramalho, Rei do Bacalhau A delightfully old fashioned shop just south of the Museu do Chiado. Admire the different types of *bacalhau* laid out on cardboard, sacks of all kinds of dried beans and lentils, sausage skins tied up with pink ribbon, ranks of tinned sardines and other seafood – great aperitif nibbles to take home. *Rua do Arsenal 56-58*

LOJA DO VINHO (AGROVINHOS)
Four wine shops in Lisbon selling a range of good Portuguese wines from all over the country, plus port and spirits, as well as charcuterie, oils, honeys, jams etc.
ALCÂNTARA *Rua Fradesso da Silveira*
LAPA *Rua da Lapa 58/60*
SÃO BENTO *Praça das Flores 11*
XABREGAS *Rua de Xabregas 38.*

GRAÇA

Feira da Ladra The 'Thieves' Fair' or flea market on the edge of the Alfama is a kind of jumble sale, but it includes food – fish and veg – as well as antiques, second hand clothes and bric-a-brac. *Campo de Santa Clara Tue and Sat only, 7.30am-1pm*

LAPA

VinoDivino Small and elegant, this was a butcher's shop in the 19th century, and retains old features. An ever-changing range of wines, including fine and rare. *Rua da Lapa 65-67*

RATO

Garrafeira Internacional By the Parque Mayer, this shop is linked to Companhia Agricola do Sanguinhal in Bombarral *(page 260)*. It sells their wines and wines from other Portuguese producers, at all prices, also a few foreign wines, and deli products. *Rua da Escola Politécnica 15*

SÃO SEBASTIÃO

Club do Gourmet, El Corte Inglés Probably Lisbon's best deli *(right)*, this food hall in a department store to the east of the Parque Eduardo VII is fully priced, but has a huge and tempting range of fine wines, both Portuguese and foreign, oils, vinegars and charcuterie, cheeses, and other deli products. Their range of cured hams (Portuguese *presunto* and Spanish *jamon*) is mouth-wateringly impressive. *Avenida António Augusto de Aguiar 31*

TELHEIRAS

Oil & Vinegar Modern deli and health food shop on a busy street west of the university. Also books, and good wines. *Centro Commercial Colombo, Avenida Lusíada*

Wine & Flavours Telheiras is a suburban residential/university area, but well worth the detour for these tempting deli products and extensive range of well-chosen wines from Portugal and beyond. Fizz is a speciality. *Rua Projecto Simões Reposo 11*

Sleep in Lisbon

AVENIDA

Hotel Britania

On a street parallel to Avenida da Liberdade, this recently restored hotel still maintains its 1940s marble-rich, art deco style. Spacious rooms, calm elegance, comfort – and friendly staff.

Rua Rodrigues Sampaio 17, 1150-278 Lisboa
T +351 213 155 016
E britania.hotel@heritage.pt
W www.heritage.pt
€195-€223 🛏33 ⑤ 1

BAIRRO ALTO

Bairro Alto Hotel

This is an absolutely lovely place, a calm, relaxed hotel, contemporary and elegant. The 18th century building is very centrally placed on the borders of the Bairro Alto and Chiado. Each floor is themed in a different colour – Bordeaux, blue, yellow and white. Rooms are modern with good bathrooms and fine views. In the Flores restaurant, the chef has changed since our visit, but the style is modern Portugese, some of the combinations perhaps rather over-adventurous. The wine list is short but has a good selection. Lighter meals are served on the delightful terrace, overlooking the city.

Praça Luis de Camões 8, 1200-243 Lisboa
T +351 213 408 288
E info@bairroaltohotel.com
W www.bairroaltohotel.com
€250-€380 🛏55 ⑤4 ♀ ✕ ⚙ ✗

BAIXA

Lisboa Tejo Hotel

A fairly inexpensive place to stay right in the centre of the Baixa. Decor is modern and very bright, the rooms comfortable. There's an Arabic well within the hotel.

Rua dos Condes de Monsanto 2,
*   1100-159 Lisboa*
T +351 218 866 182
E hotellisboatejo@evidenciagrupo.com
W www.evidenciahoteis.com
€85-€120 🛏58 ⑤4

Pensão Residencial Gerês

Though a little tired on the outside, inside this place is delightful – old fashioned, with traditional tiles, white walls and simple decor. All rooms have bathrooms, even if sometimes small, and though no breakfast is available, there is a huge choice of delicious breakfasts to be had in nearby cafés and cake shops. Very central – just round the corner from the Rossio.

Calçada do Garcia 6, 1150-168 Lisboa
T +351 218 810 497
E info@pensãogeres.com
W www.cb2web.com/geres
€55-€60 🛏18

BELÉM

Jerónimos 8

A 'design hotel' immediately to the east of the great Jerónimos Monastery, well connected by tram, bus and train to the city centre. (Buy your Sete Colinas travel card from the nearby newsagent.) Breakfast is definitely a high point – good orange juice, smoked salmon, good ham and *requeijão*, perfectly cooked scrambled egg and sausage, tasty jams including (very typical in Portugal) tomato jam and pumpkin jam, both flavoured with cinnamon. Design is angular, minimalist, with sculptures and modern art, wood, marble, glass, red, browns, beiges and

white. Room numbers are woven into the corridor carpets! A wine bar serves good modern snacks, with a good, fairly-priced but short wine list. Staff are very friendly, helpful and efficient.

Rua dos Jerónimos 8, 1400-211 Lisboa
T +351 213 600 900
E jeronimos8@almeidahotels.com
W www.jeronimos8.com
€125-€280 🛏61 ⑤4 ♀ ✕

CASTELO

Antiga Casa do Castelo

Within the Castelo São Jorge walls, a small, delightfully decorated weekend apartment for two. Occasionally available for longer stays – the owners normally use it during the week.

Rua do Espírito Santo 2, 1100-224 Lisboa
T +351 245 964 006 (rarely manned,
*   best to email)*
E antigacasa@yourhomeinlisbon.com
*   or antigacasa@sapo.pt*
W www.yourhomeinlisbon.com
€255 3 nights, €550 week – min 3 nights
🆂🅲 1(2-3)
Usually available only at weekends

Casa Costa do Castelo

Great views and great value. You need to be fit and healthy – not just for the walk up the hill (there's always the tram no 28) but also for the stairs – this is a renovated family house just below the Castelo São Jorge. There are four rooms with a view and an apartment to let on the 4th and attic floors. There's a sitting room for guests to share, and garden and orchard terraces with stunning views. Organic breakfasts.

Costa do Costelo 54, 1100-179 Lisboa
T +351 218 822 678
E castelo.reservation@c-c-castelo.com
W www.c-c-castelo.com
€75-€95 🛏4 🆂🅲 1(4) *No credit cards*

Palacio Belmonte

Just by the Castelo, this 15th century palace, spared by the earthquake, was latterly semi-abandoned until beautifully and sensitively restored a few years ago – ancient brick, whitewashed walls, *azulejos*, broad-planked wooden floors. You will feel like a private guest, rarely seeing your fellow inhabitants or even the staff, though they are there when required. Emerge from your secluded suite to relax in libraries, studies and comfortable drawing rooms, enjoy the views from little terraces and comfortable indoor nooks and crannies, explore the staircases, the garden with outdoor pool. The chef will prepare food to be served in suites or garden.
Páteo Dom Fradique 14, 1100-624 Lisboa
T+351 218 816 600
E office@palaciobelmonte.com
W www.palaciobelmonte.com
€450-€1,200 ⑤ *11* ✗*room service* 🏊

Solar do Castelo

A smart, welcoming, comfortable hotel within the Castelo walls, in an 18th century mansion built on the site of the royal palace kitchens. There is a lovely mix of modern with ancient: marble and

wood, tiles and textiles give a contemporary touch within the old building, and you can inspect the ruins in the garden. Breakfast is in the secluded patio. This is a car-free zone, so travel light.
Rua das Cozinhas 2 (ao Castelo),
1100-181 Lisboa
T+351 218 806 050
E solar.castelo@heritage.pt
W www. heritage.pt
€238-€273 🛏*14*

CHIADO
Lisboa Regency

Part of the redeveloped Armazéns do Chiado, in the heart of this smart *bairro*, this small, relaxing, trendy hotel has creative 'fusion' decor, Portuguese and oriental art, subtle, warm colours and attractive lighting, by nature and design. There are great views from the bar and roof terrace over the city centre and river estuary.
Rua Nova de Almada 114,
1200-290 Lisboa
T+351 213 256 100
E regencychiado@madeiraregency.pt
W www.regency-hotels-resorts.com
€173-€252 🛏*38* ⑤*2* ✗*bar snacks*

GRAÇA
Albergaria Senhora do Monte

A small, reasonably-priced no-nonsense *pensão* down a little street near the Castelo de São Jorge, perched high over Lisbon. Take the lift to the top floor for stunning views from the restaurant, bar and terrace – a wonderful place to have breakfast. Splash out just a little on a 'junior suite' for a private terrace.
Calçada do Monte 39, 1170-250 Lisboa
T+351 218 866 002
E senhoradomonte@hotmail.com
W www.senhoramonte.blogspot.com
€95-€120 🛏*28*

LAPA
As Janelas Verdes

Just beside the Museu Nacional de Arte Antiga, between the Lapa and docks, this is a cheerful, peaceful boutique hotel, formerly an 18th century aristocratic town house. The clientele tends to be cultured, and not so young. A spiral staircase leads up to plush, comfortable rooms, a library, and a peaceful patio garden with flowers, fountain and fine views of the river and the city.
Rua das Janelas Verdes 47, 1200-690 Lisboa
T+351 213 968 143
E janelasverdes@heritage.pt
W www.heritage.pt
€218-€263 🛏*29* ✗*room service*

Lapa Palace Hotel

Even if you can't afford a room here, you could settle for the coffee shop, and imagine that you're in residence. This 18th century palace is one of Portugal's finest hotels. Rooms are luxurious. All is elegance and marble, with frescoes, *azulejos*, flowery drapes, an impressive spa, and a fine Italian restaurant. The palace is surrounded by a peaceful tropical garden, with waterfalls and a heated swimming pool.
Rua do Pau da Bandeira 4, 1249-021 Lisboa
T+351 213 949 494
E info@lapa-palace.com
W www.lapa-palace.com
€325-€2,500
🛏*109* ⑤*20* 🍷 ✗ 🏊 ♨ 🤸

York House

First a convent, then a military hospital, York House was turned into a guest house by two Yorkshire women in 1880, and has kept the name. This is a comfortable, luxurious place to stay, recently refurbished in tasteful, contemporary style, the lovely colours blending in with the historic features. The restaurant and bar open onto a secluded, leafy courtyard, serving good, modern cuisine and serious wines *(page 239)* – though breakfast may impress less than other meals. Note that there are 49 steps up from street level to reception, and no lift. Book well in advance.
Rua das Janelas Verdes 32, 1200-691 Lisboa
T+351 213 949 494
E manager@yorkhouselisboa.com
W www.yorkhouselisboa.com
€120-€240 🛏32 ♀ ✕

RATO
Casa de São Mamede

Built in the mid-18th for a Lisbon magistrate, this friendly, old fashioned hotel is furnished with antiques and boasts a tiled dining room, nice wooden floors, and spacious rooms with air conditioning. On a busy street three minutes from the Rato metro station, ten minutes north of the Bairro Alto.
Rua da Escola Politécnica 159,
1250-100 Lisboa
T+351 213 963 166
W www.saomamede.web.pt
€70-€85 🛏28

SANTO AMARO
Vila Galé Ópera

A big, new, affordable hotel with lots of facilities down by the 25 de Abril Bridge, convenient for Belém and the restaurants of the dock area. Common areas of the hotel are imaginatively decorated on an operatic theme *(below)*. Rooms are spacious. The restaurant has its own Alentejo wine range, Santa Vitória, which is very good *(page 338)*.
Travessa do Conde da Ponte,
1300-141 Lisboa
T+351 213 605 400
E opera@villagale.pt
www.vilagale.pt/hoteis/opera
€76 🛏243 §16 ♀ ✕ 🏊 ⚜

SÃO DOMINGOS DE BENFICA
Quinta Nova da Conceição

In the suburbs towards the north of the city, just west of the Jardim Zoológico (Lisbon Zoo), this 18th century mansion has spacious common areas, a breakfast room tiled with azulejos, interesting furniture and quirky decor. Outside there are big grounds, a pool and tennis.
Rua Cidade de Rabat 5, 1500-158 Lisboa
T+351 217 780 091
E qtnovaconceicao@netcabo.pt
€155 🛏3 🏊 ♀

SÃO SEBASTIÃO/MARQUÊS DE POMBAL
Ritz Four Seasons

Just to the west of the Praça Marquês de Pombal at the top of the Avenida, this is one of Lisbon's top hotels, elegant, charming, comfortable and contemporary. It's very grand, and just the sort of place where you can play at politician-spotting, as they gather together in besuited groups in the lobby, bars and restaurants. Bedrooms are spacious, and most have terraces with spectacular views. There are artworks galore, a magnificent pool, and a spa with all the usual massages, exfoliating rubs, even Ayurvedic treatments. The gym and 400 metre running track are up on the roof, with Lisbon and the river Tagus to inspire you as you jog or pump iron. All kinds of business facilities are available, from pagers to translation services. The breakfast buffet in the Varanda restaurant *(page 240)* seems unsurpassable – until you see the lunch buffet...
Rua Rodrigo da Fonseca 88, 1099-039 Lisboa
T+351 213 811 423
E fsh.lisbon@fourseasons.com
W www.fourseasons.com/lisbon
€315-€497
🛏262 §20 ♀ ✕ 🏊 ⚜ ✻

Lisboa and the Ribatejo

Lisboa and the Ribatejo have in common their proximity to Lisbon, and to water, in one case the ocean, in the other the wide valley of the River Tagus. Having long discussed joining together as a single VR region, they decided in late 2007 to remain unwed. However, the former Estremadura VR region took on the name Lisboa, the name that a united region might have taken.

The two regions share proximity to Lisbon, but they are very different. The south of the Lisboa VR extends Lisbon's sophistication in a westerly direction. In a matter of minutes, Lisboetas can be on the championship golf courses, the smart beach of Cascais, the breath-taking surfing beach of Guincho, in little resorts up the beach-and-dune-strung western coast – or in the luxuriant hills of the Parque Natural de Sintra-Cascais. Cascais, a little fishing village 40 years ago, has all but engulfed Estoril, which back then was its senior neighbour. Large hotels and palatial residences line parts of the coast, and some of the best restaurants in the country are here to feed the inhabitants and visitors. The palaces of Sintra and, to the north, the monasteries of Alcobaça, Batalha and Tomar

(in the Ribatejo, *pictured left*) are amongst Portugal's finest monuments. Fatima ranks for the Roman Catholic Church amongst its holiest shrines.

Driving out of Lisbon to the north, you are soon in a lush, rolling landscape of vines and orchards. In the wind-swept Lisboa VR, old hilltop windmills have been supplemented by ranks of modern wind turbines. North of Leiria, a beautiful, ancient pine forest runs along peaceful beaches, and between Batalha, Rio Maior and Alcacena, the limestone range of the Parque Natural das Serras de Aire e Candeeiros offers scenic walking amidst its gorse and olives, dry stone walls, plateaux, valleys and peaks.

The Ribatejo (literally 'the bank of the Tagus') is friendly and rural, the land of the magnificent Lusitano horse, and of fighting bulls, an expanse of watery grassland, willows, rice fields, leafy vineyards and productive fields of strawberries, melons, tomatoes and other vegetables. Each winter the scenery turns grey as the Tagus bursts its banks, restoring its vivid colours in spring when the crops sprout forth. Away from the river plain, the Ribatejo rises into hills of olive groves, orchards and ever more vineyards.

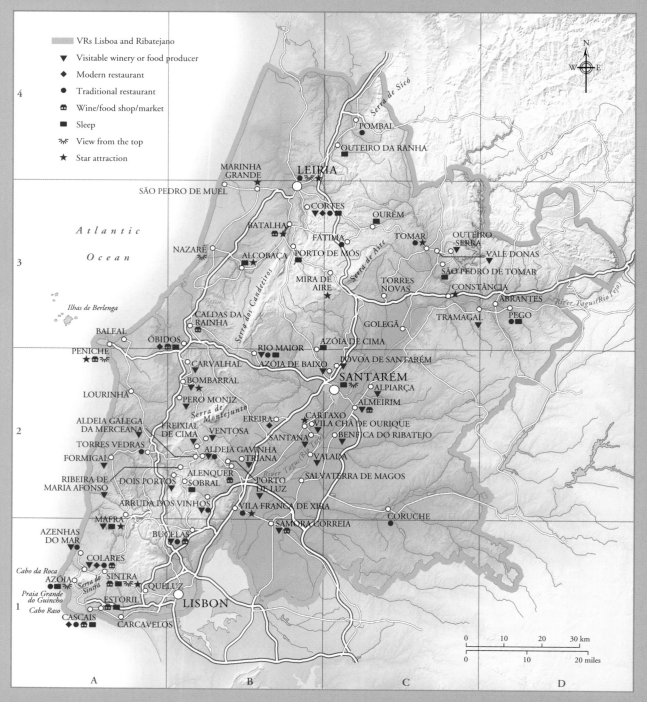

VRs Lisboa and Ribatejano

▼ Visitable winery or food producer
◆ Modern restaurant
● Traditional restaurant
🏠 Wine/food shop/market
■ Sleep
🎋 View from the top
★ Star attraction

4

N
W E
S

3

Atlantic

Ocean

Ilhas de Berlenga

2

1

POMBAL

OUTEIRO DA RANHA

MARINHA
GRANDE

LEIRIA

Serra de Sicó

SÃO PEDRO DE MUEL

CORTES

OURÉM

BATALHA

FÁTIMA

TOMAR

OUTEIRO-
SERRA

NAZARÉ

ALCOBAÇA

PORTO DE MÓS

VALE DONAS

Serra de Aire

SÃO PEDRO DE TOMAR

MIRA DE
AIRE

CONSTÂNCIA

TORRES
NOVAS

ABRANTES

River Tagus (Rio Tejo)

CALDAS DA
RAINHA

GOLEGÃ

TRAMAGAL

PEGO

Serra dos Candeeiros

BALEAL

ÓBIDOS

RIO MAIOR

AZÓIA DE CIMA

PENICHE

CARVALHAL

AZÓIA DE BAIXO

PÓVOA DE SANTARÉM

SANTARÉM

LOURINHÃ

BOMBARRAL

ALPIARÇA

PERO MONIZ

*Serra de
Montejunto*

ALMEIRIM

ALDEIA GALEGA
DA MERCEANA

FREIXIAL
DE CIMA

VENTOSA

EREIRA

CARTAXO

SANTANA

VILA CHÃ DE OURIQUE

TORRES VEDRAS

ALDEIA GAVINHA

TRIANA

BENFICA DO RIBATEJO

FORMIGAL

VALAIDA

River Tagus (Rio Tejo)

RIBEIRA DE
MARIA AFONSO

DOIS PORTOS

ALENQUER

SOBRAL

PORTO
DE LUZ

SALVATERRA DE MAGOS

ARRUDA DOS VINHOS

VILA FRANCA DE XIRA

MAFRA

SAMORA CORREIA

CORUCHE

AZENHAS
DO MAR

BUCELAS

Cabo da Roca

COLARES

AZÓIA

SINTRA

*Praia Grande
do Guincho*

QUELUZ

*Serra de
Sintra*

ESTORIL

LISBON

Cabo Raso

CASCAIS

CARCAVELOS

0   10   20   30 km

0   10   20 miles

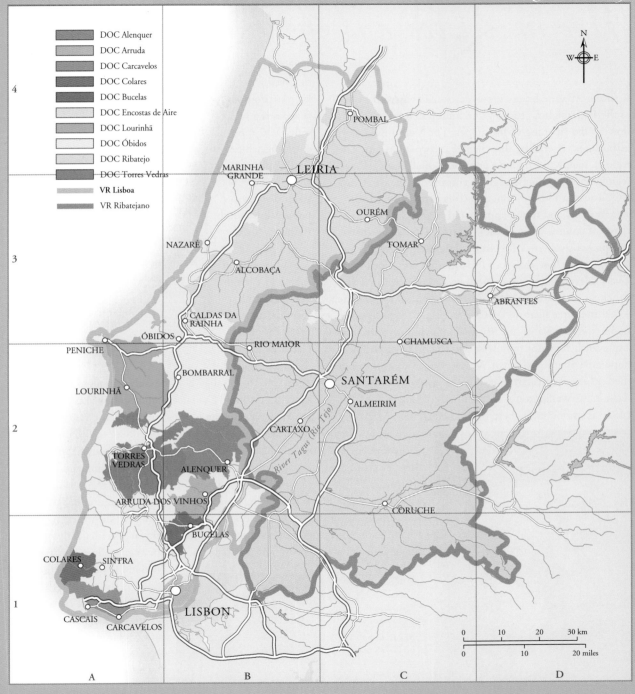

	DOC Alenquer
	DOC Arruda
	DOC Carcavelos
	DOC Colares
	DOC Bucelas
	DOC Encostas de Aire
	DOC Lourinhã
	DOC Óbidos
	DOC Ribatejo
	DOC Torres Vedras
	VR Lisboa
	VR Ribatejano

POMBAL

LEIRIA

MARINHA GRANDE

OURÉM

TOMAR

NAZARÉ

ALCOBAÇA

ABRANTES

CALDAS DA RAINHA

ÓBIDOS

RIO MAIOR

CHAMUSCA

PENICHE

BOMBARRAL

LOURINHÃ

SANTARÉM

ALMEIRIM

CARTAXO

River Tagus (Rio Tejo)

TORRES VEDRAS

ALENQUER

ARRUDA DOS VINHOS

CORUCHE

BUCELAS

COLARES

SINTRA

LISBON

CASCAIS

CARCAVELOS

0   10   20   30 km
0   10   20 miles

Wine in Lisboa and the Ribatejo

LISBOA

A strong Atlantic breeze blows across the vineyard slopes of the Estremadura, turning the hilltop windmills, and slowing the ripening of the grapes. The Vinho Regional Lisboa area covered by this chapter incorporates nine DOC regions, making it the most confusing of all Portugal's wine regions for the non-Portuguese consumer. The three tiny DOCs nearest Lisbon – Bucelas, Colares and Carcavelos – were famous and much appreciated in the past. But in terms of volume at least, these historic DOCs have been comprehensively overthrown by the newer arrivals. Much wine is made here that is of little interest to serious wine lovers. Nevertheless, some producers in this region make delicious, characterful wines. You just need to know which.

Of the three historic DOCs, Bucelas, a 25km seagull's flight from the Baixa in Lisbon, is enjoying something of a revival. It may not have re-scaled the dizzy height of popularity it enjoyed when Wellington's army was camped there in the Peninsular War, but Bucelas wine (known as 'Lisbon' to Wellington – according to old silver decanter labels) is undoubtedly better than it was then. Most was probably fortified in those days. Now it's crisp, dry, mineral white, based on a minimum of 75% Arinto, with Sercial and Rabo de Ovelha to keep it company. Bucelas is a white-only DOC (and sparkling white).

The other two are in a sorry state. Colares, famous for its red Ramisco vines grown in sand, is now supported to a large extent by a charitable foundation *(page 266)*, and Carcavelos is in imminent danger of disappearing altogether, the only current winemakers being a priest and a small research station. Locals have kinder words for the priest's wine than the research station's. Both DOCs have the problem of urban crawl, with land prices for development so far outstripping yields for agricultural land that it makes no financial sense to carry on growing grapes. In addition, Colares is lumbered with a main grape whose historic reputation is hard to justify. The Ramisco ripens with great difficulty. It is grown nowhere else. Historically, it was blended with Molar, an earlier-ripening grape that made softer wine.

Madeira winemakers say Molar is the same as their Tinta Negra (not especially reassuring). Clonal research into Molar is underway, but the sand is slipping away in the hourglass, and the results

Left Planting vines in the sandy vineyards of Colares demands huge effort for scant reward

Right and *opposite* A windswept, rolling landscape of neat vines, carefully tended

Wine regions
DOC Alenquer
DOC Arruda
DOC Bucelas
DOC Carcavelos
DOC Colares
DOC Encostas de Aire
DOC Lourinhã (brandy only)
DOC Óbidos
DOC Torres Vedras
Vinho Regional Lisboa

Main local grapes
Red Castelão, Santarém (Santareno)
White Malvasia Rei, Fernão Pires, Vital, Seara Nova, Alicante Branco
For details of grapes see page 428

are also areas where soil and climate really lead to wines of specific identity and quality. Take Alenquer. One local winemaker compared the Alenquer weather with that of Bordeaux. No one here would ever need to boost

may come too late. White Colares, based on Malvasia, is a better bet. Even the winemaker at the local co-op believes Colares is a region for whites rather than reds.

Carcavelos, a favourite wine of the Marquês de Pombal, has almost gone. It is nearly always sweet. The rules for its production allow for it to be unfortified or fortified, and made either as a red, a white, or from a mix of red and white grapes. Castelão and Preto Martinho are the main red grapes, Galego Dourado, Arinto, Ratinho (yes, that does mean 'little rat') the main whites. One estate, Quinta do Peso, has stopped making wine, though it still has 3ha of grapes. They now go to the priest. The Seminário de Caparide itself has another 5ha, and there are bits and pieces elsewhere. There are still bottles available in shops, but they won't last forever. Soon the only way to taste Carcavelos will be to study for the priesthood at the Caparide seminary!

These three DOCs are drips compared to the huge amount of wine made in the rest of the Lisboa VR area. Big does not always mean bad, however. Yes, there are producers struggling to turn unripe grapes into decent wine, and yes, those are usually co-operatives. But there

acidity. Up close to the hills in the west of the area, the cooling wind is even stronger. But that makes for wines of balance and freshness – red and white, though reds have the edge. And local rules were relaxed in 2002 to allow grapes such as Chardonnay, Sauvignon Blanc, Cabernet Sauvignon, Syrah and Touriga Franca to become 'authorised' varieties (a change also made in Arruda and Torres Vedras). Despite this relatively relaxed attitude to DOC regulations, many of the best wines in Alenquer are made as VR Lisboa. In Óbidos, too, north of Alenquer, the cool, near-coastal weather can give good, crisp whites, light, elegant reds and some of Portugal's best sparkling wines.

In Torres Vedras, weather depends on the distance from the coast and which side of the hills vineyards are planted. The failure of the Torres Vedras co-op in 2003 demonstrated that growers in this part of Portugal cannot get away with delivering grapes of low quality to their co-op. Maximum permitted yields are set at levels at which it is almost impossible to ripen grapes, and too many growers opt for quantity not quality. Arruda is a warmer region, further from the coast, and dominated by its co-op; it makes better wine than many. Encostas de Aire is the most northerly (and largest) of the DOC regions in this area, recently swelled by the inclusion of Alcobaça (which never made it from IPR to DOC status). It is best known for fresh, lowish-alcohol whites. In Lourinhã, right by the coast, the wines are even lighter, and the DOC is only for brandy.

Lisboa is the fourth largest VR region in Portugal, in terms of vines planted, and the country's third largest wine producer. But it makes more basic table wine *(vinho de mesa)* than any other region. Grapes for *vinho de mesa* probably do not even earn enough to cover the costs of growing them. This area does produce the second highest amount of *vinho regional* in the country (after the Alentejo). But the amount of wine it registers as DOC is tiny – only the Algarve, Madeira and the Azores make less. The time has surely come to do away with the complication of nine different DOCs in the region. The three historic DOCs will wither or hang on. The rest would be better off as Lisboa DOC.

RIBATEJO

The Ribatejo has about the same vineyard area as the Estremadura, but, compared to its coastal neighbour, makes 40% less wine. Most of the vineyards are on the wide, flat river valley of the River Tagus *(Tejo)*. The name 'Ribatejo' itself means 'bank of the Tejo'. This fertile river plain is known as the *lezíria*. All kinds of crops thrive in the rich, alluvial soil. As you drive across it – often

> **Wine regions**
> DOC Ribatejo
> Vinho Regional Ribatejana
>
> **Main local grapes**
> *Red* Castelão, Trincadeira
> *White* Fernão Pires, Alicante Branco
>
> *For details of grapes see page 428*

very slowly, behind a tractor or even a herd of goats – you may pass fields of maize, cabbage, cereals, tomatoes, melons, green peppers and potatoes, as well as vineyards. One wine producer told us he had wanted to increase his estate by buying neighbouring patches of *lezíria* land. No one wanted to sell, because agriculture is too profitable here. Dig down a few metres, and you'll find all the water you need. You get very good yields.

But if it's grapes you're growing, and you want to make good wine, you don't want huge yields, and other parts of the region have soils more suited to wine production. The best area is the *charneca*, the sandy-soiled land off the

southern side of the river to the east of Muge, Almeirim and Salvaterra de Magos. On this south-eastern side, the Ribatejo borders on the Alentejo, and the weather becomes hotter and drier – more likely to ripen grapes. Big estates in the area such as Quinta da Alorna have moved their vines back from the fertile river soils into the poorer soils of the *charneca*, as priorities have changed from quantity to quality. North of the Tejo is the *bairro*, a name that reflects the predominantly clay soils (as in the wine region Bairrada). Here the land rises towards the foothills of the Serra dos Candeeiros near Rio Major, and the Serra de Aire near Torres Novas and Tomar. But in Rio Maior rainfall increases as Atlantic weather sweeps in through the gap between the Serra de Montejunto and the Serra dos Candeeiros.

Down by the riverside, the fertile soils have made matters more difficult for quality-minded producers. The Margaride estate has to snip off many of the developing bunches in the summer to avoid huge yields. Growers who deliver their grapes to the large co-ops that produce most of the Ribatejo's wine are probably less conscientious. Most are elderly, set in their ways, and think more is better. Deliver more grapes, and you earn more money – except that if you can't sell the end product for a decent price, it means less money in the long run. The Almeirim co-op is

in dire straits, but, as the second largest co-op in Portugal, locals think it is too big to be allowed to go under. The fact they produce mostly white wine may be their salvation, as the enthusiastic country-wide planting of red wine vines may mean a shortage of whites before long. But three-quarters of their production is sold in bulk, and of the bottled quarter, half is basic table wine. No wonder they're losing money.

There's nothing wrong with the Ribatejo, or its soils, of whichever type. But there's no money in basic wine any more. Good growers and producers, making good wines, make good profits. Others do not. Nowhere is this truer than in the Ribatejo.

Far left The wide River Tagus, flowing through the Ribatejo towards Lisbon – Ribatejo means 'bank of the Tagus'

Left In the sandy-soiled *charneca*, grapes ripen better than in the *leziria*

Left A neat expanse of vineyard, flat and fertile

Above A stunning winery created by Joao Portugal Ramos (page 268)

Right Flood plains, green and productive

ALDEIA GALEGA DA MERCEANA B2

Casa Santos Lima From his front lawn, north-west of Alenquer, José Oliveira da Silva can see his great-grandfather's estate. Many estates in Portugal are decimated by inheritance law, but he still owns these 280ha, of which 180ha are planted with vines. His grandfather exported in barrel, but it wasn't until José sold his first wines in bottle in 1996, that the name of the estate became visible in the outside world. Or perhaps we should say 'names', as José believes in giving his customers lots of brands to choose from. Apart from the various brands he has thought up (Palha-Canas, Portuga, 4Uvas, Eximius), he uses the names of the individual farms on the estate: Quinta da Boavista, Quinta das Setencostas, Quinta de Bons-Ventos, Quinta da Espiga, Quinta das Amoras, Quinta do Vale Perdido, Quinta do Espírito Santo and Quinta do Figo. The estate supplies 95% of José's grape needs, and he buys the last bits and pieces from neighbours whose vineyard work he

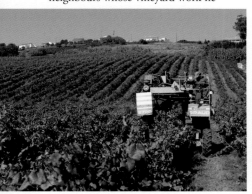

trusts. Most of his grapes are machine-harvested; the vineyards are at most ten minutes from the winery. But he still picks Chardonnay, Touriga Nacional and Touriga Franca by hand.

95% of José's production is exported, and he tries to add one new market every year, to 'spread the risk', he says, his 23-year career in banking momentarily re-surfacing. Norway and Belgium buy a lot of wine in bag-in-box. He is happy to receive visitors, but only by appointment as he travels a lot. You'll see the estate and winery, and taste. The cost will depend on what you taste and the number of people.

Although he is in the DOC region of Alenquer, he sells all his wines except Quinta de Setencostas as VR Lisboa. Why? More flexible rules on grape varieties. And there are a lot of different grapes in his vineyards: Arinto, Fernão Pires, Moscatel, Rabo-de-Ovelha, Seara Nova, Vital, Chardonnay and Sauvignon Blanc for whites, and (deep breath) Alfrocheiro, Camarate, Castelão, Preto Martinho, Sousão, Tinta Barroca, Tinta Miúda, Tinta Roriz, Tinto Cão, Touriga Franca, Touriga Nacional, Trincadeira, Alicante-Bouschet, Cabernet Sauvignon, Caladoc, Merlot, Pinot Noir and Syrah for reds.

Of the huge range, these are our favourites: **Casa Santos Lima Moscatel** is dry, and typically crisp and floral, with aromas of lemon and lavender. **Quinta do Espírito Santo Tinto**, a blend of late-picked Castelão and Tinta Roriz, is rich and ripe, with flavours of dried fruit and chocolate, and good acidity to support the 15% alcohol. **Quinta das Setencostas Tinto**, one of José's few DOC Alenquer wines, has rich, blackberry fruit, firm tannins and a touch of oak. **Palha-Canas Tinto** ('my wine from Douro grapes') is Touriga Nacional, Touriga Franca, Tinta Roriz, Castelão and Camarate, with high

tannins and dark, mulberry and damson fruit. **Casa Santos Lima Camarate** has the traditional figgy intensity of Camarate, with firm tannins and high acidity. **Casa Santos Lima Sousão** is dense, ripe and sweet-fruited, **Casa Santos Lima Alicante Bouschet** is very aromatic, with mulberry and strawberry fruit, and **Casa Santos Lima Syrah Castelão** is malty and red-fruited, with rich tannins. **Casa Santos Lima Pinot Noir Touriga Nacional** is a surprisingly successful combination, malty and savoury, with smooth tannins. **Casa Santos Lima Touriga Nacional** is fresh and herby, with dense, sweet fruit and firm tannins. **Touriz**, his top red, is a blend of the two Tourigas and Tinta Roriz, rich, dense and black-fruited, with firm tannins and a touch of oak – a wine to keep.

Quinta da Boavista, 2580-081 Aldeia Galega da Merceana
T +351 263 760 621 / 263 769 093
E casasantoslima@mail.telepac.pt
W www.casasantoslima.com
Visits Mon-Sat 9-6 appt only
€variable

Quinta de Chocapalha Paulo and Alice Tavares da Silva bought this estate in 1987. He had been in the navy, and retired when they bought the farm. Of the 40ha of vines, some were in poor condition, and had to be grubbed up, especially the Tinta Miúda and Camarate. They now have 45ha of good vineyard, and would like to take this to 50ha. The rest of the estate has apples and pears (Pera Rocha, a good local variety). Paulo's first idea was to deliver his grapes to the local co-op (Merceana). They would make reasonable wine there, and he could mature it. He even spent four years as Director of the co-op. But when his daughter Sandra Tavares da Silva *(above*

right and pages 94 and 103) had qualified as a winemaker and had a bit of experience working for Cristiano van Zeller in the Douro, Paulo and Alice resurrected the old winery at Chocapalha, and put her in charge of winemaking. (She still lives and works in the Douro as well.) Their winery is very small, but they are planning a new one, to be ready for the 2008 harvest. In their old winery, they had room to process only about a third of their grapes. The rest they had to sell. The new winery will take the entire crop.

The Tavares da Silva will receive you hospitably and show you the cellar and vineyards. And, if there are more than six of you, you'll have to pay something for a tasting. Fewer than that, it's free.

Quinta de Chocapalha is a charming house that seems to have grown organically round a central courtyard, with the cellar

and barrels housed in old buildings probably originally intended for carts and horses. The new winery is to be set into the side of the hill overlooking the vineyards. For various reasons, partly flexibility of grape varieties, all the wines are labelled as VR Lisboa. **Quinta de Chocapalha Branco** is a Chardonnay, Arinto and Vital blend, the Chardonnay oak-fermented. It has flavours of honey, almonds and cream, and a lovely minerality. **Quinta de Chocapalha Tinto** is about two-thirds

Tinta Roriz and a third Touriga Nacional, with little additions of Cabernet Sauvignon and Syrah. The fruit is rich and solid, with herby Touriga aromas and firm tannins. The **Quinta de Chocapalha Cabernet Sauvignon** needs a warm year to ripen fully, but when it does the flavour is rich blackcurrant, with smooth, velvety tannins and a hint of grass. **Chocapalha** is the top wine, a Touriga Nacional Tinta Roriz blend, very herby and aromatic, with dense, smooth tannins, length and elegance.
Casa Agrícola das Mimosas, 2580-081
Aldeia Galega da Merceana
T+351 263 769 317
E chocapalha@mail.telepac.pt
W www.wonderfulland.com/wonder2006
/wine/chocapalha/indexwine.htm
Visits Mon-Fri 9-6 appt only

ALDEIA GAVINHA B2

Quinta da Cortezia Just to the north-west of Alenquer, this is a family business owned by Miguel Reis Catarino with his three sisters. Of a little over 100ha, 34ha are forest, the rest vines. Most of the vines are for red wines, and Miguel has opted to plant mostly Portuguese varieties, except for 2ha of Chardonnay and 3ha of Merlot. They use only the estate grapes for the Cortezia wines. Because he travels to promote the wines, and consults elsewhere, he is helped by his niece, Madalena Biancard. Either may receive you for a visit to the cellar and a free tasting, but you have to book.

Vineyard work is the basis of a good wine, he says. Although he trained at Montpellier, he has always had a 'New World' approach. He believes in using gravity, and works with a fork-lift, lifting rather than pumping. The winery is 100 years old, but the old cement vats have an inner epoxy lining and stainless steel fittings, and there are also new 'tronco-

conic', sawn-off-cone-shaped steel vats. He ferments his whites in the cement vats, cooled.

Of 13 different parcels of vineyard, the largest, at 15.5ha, is Cortezia. All have drainage ditches or underground pipes: excess water can be a problem this close to the ocean. He allows weeds to grow between rows in wet years to regulate water, mowing them in dry ones. Elegance and natural acidity is his aim – wines that reflect the natural conditions of Alenquer.

There are two ranges, Quinta da Cortezia for the top-quality wines, and Vinha Conchas at a 'more competitive' price. **Vinha Conchas Branco** is a blend of Fernão Pires and Arinto, with a little Seara Nova, crisp and faintly Muscatty, with good acidity. **Quinta da Cortezia Branco** is almost all Arinto, with touches of Chardonnay and Fernão Pires, flinty and mineral, with steely acidity and clean, lean lines. **Quinta da Cortezia Rosé** is pure Touriga Nacional, creamy, dry and herby. On to the reds: **Vinha Conchas Tinto** is an easy-drinking blend, full of soft, ripe fruit. **Vinha Conchas Special Selection** is even better, with juicy fruit and herby elegance and balance. **Quinta da Cortezia Touriga Nacional** is complex and herby, with tobacco and cherry flavours, fresh acidity and lovely length. **Quinta da Cortezia Reserva** improves with bottle-age, from youthful austerity to ripe, raspberry and cherry fruit, with elegance and balance.
2580-101 Aldeia Gavinha
T+351 263 769 238
E qc@quintadacortezia.com
W www.quintadacortezia.com
Visits Mon-Fri 9-8 appt only

Adega Cooperativa de Arruda dos Vinhos Arruda is about 40km north of Lisbon, north of Bucelas and south of Alenquer. The co-op dominates local wine production, just as it did when we visited 20 years ago. It has about 1,100 members, farming 1,600ha of vines. Red is their main business, but the **Comenda de Santiago Branco**, a VR Lisboa, is citrussy, steely and crisp. **Moinhos do Céu Touriga Nacional Rosé** is also good, herby, creamy and dry. **Comenda de Santiago Tinto** has bright, raspberry fruit and slightly obvious oak. **Extre-Madura Tinto** is not only a fun name, but also a good blend of Syrah and Touriga Franca, malty and restrained, with raspberry length. **Lote 44 Tinto**, a Syrah, Touriga Nacional and Aragonez blend, has pleasant, blackcurrant and blackberry flavours and good acidity.

The co-op wine shop is open from Monday to Saturday. They also offer winery and vineyard tours by prior appointment.
Vale Quente, 2630-162 Arruda dos Vinhos
T+351 263 975 125
E geral@adegaarruda.com
W www.adegaarruda.com
Visits Mon-Fri 9-12.30, 1.30-6 appt only
Sat 9.30-12.30, 1.30-5 appt only

Companhia Agricola do Sanguinhal
The Pereira de Fonseca family owns three estates: Quinta do Sanguinhal (22ha of vines), Quinta das Cerejeiras (13ha) and Quinta de São Francisco (50ha); all the wines are made at Quinta de São Francisco. In the Óbidos DOC, the vines are very influenced by cool Atlantic weather. This is more obviously white wine country than red, although the proportion of reds to whites in the region has risen from very little to nearly a third in the last 20 years. In the Sanguinhal vineyards, under a quarter of the grapes are white. Most of the wines are made as VR Estremadura, a mere four (out of 20) as DOC Óbidos. Quinta das Cerejeiras has a lovely old winemaking cellar, now used as a space for functions, with original *lagares*, screw presses and old wooden vats. This is probably where you will be received, prior to a tour and tasting.

The white wines are good, and inventive. Of the wines we tasted, the **Cerejeiras Colheita Seleccionada Branco** is a lemony, aromatic blend of Moscatel and Arinto, with good acidity and a hint of marmalade. **Quinta de São Francisco Branco** (one of the DOC Óbidos wines) is a blend of Vital, Fernão Pires and Arinto, honeyed and mineral on the nose, with a full-bodied texture, acidity and minerality. **Cerejeiras Colheita Seleccionada Rosé** is light and crisp, with a faint rose-hip perfume. **Quinta de São Francisco Tinto** is another DOC Óbidos wine, the best of the grapes from the estate, with richness, complexity, and cherry and plum fruit. The Sanguinhal single variety wines are good; a ripe, pruney **Sanguinhal Aragonez** and a cherry and herb-perfumed, firm-

Adega Beira-Mar António Bernardino Paulo da Silva has been in the business over 60 years. He is an extraordinarily vital, passionate man, thin and bird-like, who talks at breakneck speed and uses his hands eloquently to illustrate his many stories. He's vague on the matter of succession: he has no children, just nephews who are not very interested in the business. He's vague on where his wines come from, too. He buys wine, blends and matures it. He used to buy grapes, as well, but the little *adega* by the sea is not really equipped for fermentation. The *adega* stretches back a surprisingly long way from the road and seafront. It stores a million litres of wine in tanks, and 50,000 bottles in the cellar. The Ramisco wine is all made at the Adega Regional, the co-op. The rest comes from a cellar at Ramalhal, near Torres Vedras. The **Colares Chitas Tinto** has high acidity, with cherry fruit and wood overtones, light and elegant. The **Casal da Azenha Tinto** is a VR Lisboa, made of Castelão and Tinta Miúda to mimic a Colares; it's a light wine with high acidity and some cherry fruit. **Ribamar Garrafeira** is another VR Estremadura, light, savoury and elegant, with notes of cherry, spice and wood. **Colares Chitas Branco** is pleasant, lightly Muscatty, with good acidity, but less characterful then the reds. Unfortunately, Senhor da Silva is not able to receive visitors.
Avenida Luís Augusto Colares 70/74,
2705-106 Colares
T+351 219 292 036

tannined **Sanguinhal Touriga Nacional** are our favourites. Best for us among the reds is the complex, elegant **Quinta das Cerejeiras Reserva**, mature and perfumed, with cherry, wood and tobacco notes. The **Quinta de São Francisco Vinho Licoroso** is from a solera started 20 years ago, nutty, creamy and rich, with a hint of orange-peel.

Quinta das Cerejeiras, Apartado 5,
* 2544-909 Bombarral*
T+351 262 609 190
E info@vinhos-sanguinhal.pt
W www.vinhos-sanguinhal.pt
Visits Mon-Fri appt only € variable

BUCELAS B1

Caves Velhas This was the company that kept the flame burning for Bucelas wines through the 1950s, 1960s and 1970s. And, before you wonder later on, 'Bucellas' is an old brand owned by Caves Velhas, not a misspelling! The company is part of a larger group that also includes Caves Dom Teodósio *(page 272)* in the Ribatejo. In fact, many of the wines made here when we first visited 20 years ago are now made in the Ribatejo. Production in Bucelas is now limited to Bucelas wines and some brandies. The basic **Caves Velhas Bucellas** is 90% Arinto, creamy, fresh, lemony and above all, mineral. The **Caves Velhas**

Bucellas Arinto is all Arinto, half picked early, half late. It has more perfume than the basic **Bucellas**, citrus, with a creamy feel and bracing acidity. There's a single estate Bucelas, **Quinta da Boição**, from a 30ha vineyard, made from late-picked Arinto and aged in new oak. It's slightly reminiscent of good traditional white Rioja, oaky, with hints of toffee and banana, and crisp acidity. **Caves Velhas Bucelas Garrafeira** (yes, one 'l' this time) is steel-fermented, then aged in bottle for several years before release. It develops creamy, nutty, sherry-like notes, still with the high acidity – a glance back to wines of a different era.

Caves Velhas have a shop in the village where you can buy all the company's wines. They are also happy to receive visitors, but you must make an appointment. You can see the winery, and the in-house cooperage, and taste some wines.

Rua Professor Egas Moniz, 2670-653 Bucelas
T+351 219 687 330
E relacoes.publicas@cavesvelhas.pt
W www.cavesvelhas.pt
Visits Mon-Fri 10-1, 2-5 appt only
€1.25 wine tasting, €3.75 with snacks

Quinta da Murta On a typically sloping hill a couple of kilometres north of the little town of Bucelas, the winery and house are surrounded by 13ha of immaculately-kept vines, 11ha of white, 2ha of red. Francisco Castelo Branco owns and runs the estate and its new,

temperature-controlled winery, with the help of Mário Soares Franco. The white vines are about 13 years old; the Touriga Nacional vines were planted in 2001. Most of the white grapes go into the **Quinta da Murta Bucelas**, all Arinto except a dash of Rabo de Ovelha, which has three or four hours' skin contact before fermentation, and is then fermented in steel at low temperatures. It has lovely, almost peachy aromas, with high, citrussy acidity and real minerality. We preferred this to the oak-fermented version, **Quinta da Murta Bucelas**, a little too oaky for us, though creamy in texture with good citric intensity. The **Quinta da Murta Tinto** is all Touriga Nacional (but young vines), with perfumed raspberry fruit, very firm tannins and good length.

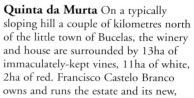

It's wise to make an appointment, though there should be someone there during the working week, and you can tour the vineyard and winery, and taste. Francisco also rents out his house, and is negotiating the possibility of building a small hotel and more houses to rent.

Casal do Mato, Apartado 736,
  2671-601 Bucelas
T+351 219 680 820
E qmurtasoaresfranco@kanguru.pt
W www.quintadamurta.pt
Visits Mon-Fri 10-6 appt preferred,
  Sat & Sun appt only € variable

BUCELAS B1 *(continued)*

Quinta da Romeira On our research questionnaire sent to wine producers, hoping to provoke a few historical anecdotes, we asked if the Duke of Wellington had ever stayed the night. One port producer thought that maybe the Bishop of Norwich had called in, but otherwise we drew a blank. Except here. Yes, the Duke of Wellington did stay here. In fact he used this *quinta* as his headquarters during the Peninsular War campaign, and became very fond of the local wine. Based on the present offerings, we can quite understand (although we suspect Quinta da Romeira's wines are probably somewhat better than they were two centuries ago). The very gracious old house on the estate, painted deep pink with white trimmings, dates from 1703, with major improvements since.

This is the first estate (*quinta*) bought by Miguel Melo Azevedo and his co-investors in 1999 when they started Companhia das Quintas. The business now owns six *quintas*, a large company in Bairrada and a distribution business. It is one of the most exciting and growing wine businesses in Portugal, and is run from here. Miguel is an ex-investment banker, and he and his colleagues are always on the lookout for other estates to add to their portfolio. So far, they have this estate, Quinta do Cardo in the Beira Interior *(page 183)*, Quinta da Cova da Barca (source of the Fronteira brand) in the Douro, Quinta da Farizoa in the Alentejo, Quinta de Pegos Claros in Palmela *(page 307)*, and, their latest purchase, Quinta de Pancas in Alenquer *(page 266)*. Caves Borlido in Bairrada is the large-volume company, mainly producing sparkling wines. And the distribution business, Espírito do Vinho, sells the wines.

Quinta da Romeira has 78ha of vines, mostly white, although 14ha are red, mostly Touriga Nacional, with some Cabernet Sauvignon and Merlot. It is very much a front-runner in the Bucelas region, with 46ha dedicated to Arinto, the area's main grape, and the balance of white Sercial and Rabo de Ovelha. They make various Bucelas wines. **Prova Régia** is steel-fermented after a little maceration on the grape-skins to give added flavour, steely and crisp, with a creamy feel. **Morgado de Santa Catherina** is fermented in new French oak barrels, but retains the Bucelas minerality. It is rich and ripe, but not too oaky, with a creamy texture and lovely acidity, length and balance. **Quinta da Romeira Chardonnay & Arinto** has to be VR Lisboa (as Chardonnay is not permitted under the DOC rules). The Chardonnay element is oak-fermented, and the creamy, bready aspect of that blends very well with the steely Arinto. They also try to make a sweet white each year (also VR Lisboa), from botrytis-affected grapes. **Quinta da Romeira Colheita Tardia** is a blend of Arinto and Sercial, with honeyed, creamy, botrytis aromas and sweetness softening the steely character. Calhandriz is a VR Lisboa brand used for more experimental wines, not necessarily from the estate's grapes. **Calhandriz Rosé** is young and berry-fruited, with a hint of sweetness. **Calhandriz Cabernet & Touriga** actually has about 60% Touriga Nacional, blackcurrant and bright-fruited, with firm tannins and herby length.

2670-678 Bucelas
T+351 219 687 380
E frodrigues@companhiadasquintas.pt
W www.companhiadasquintas.pt
Visits appt only Mon-Fri 10-4, Sat group

CARVALHAL B2

Quinta dos Loridos If you'd like to invite a few friends to a very grand place for the weekend, this could be the perfect answer. The staff reckon it would be less expensive than staying in a hotel. We're not sure, but it would certainly be more impressive. Quinta dos Loridos is a magnificent 16th century manor house, built by a wealthy family of Italian bankers, made even wealthier by the spice trade, and doing business in the nearby city of Óbidos. It was bought by António Avillez in 1989, to add to his portfolio of estates in what was then J P Vinhos. His

Quinta dos Pesos This is a lovely old house and farm, right in the middle of a hugely expensive and built-up coastal area west of Lisbon. The owner died in 2003, and his heirs have not yet agreed on the future of this farm. Although the farm has 22ha, there are only 3ha of vines, but these are precious in the context of the fast-disappearing Carcavelos appellation. Both red and white varieties are blended in the final wine, Rabo de Ovelha, Arinto, Galego Dourado and Boal for the whites, and Castelão and Espadeiro Tinto for reds. The first vintage made was 1987. Whites and reds are fermented separately, then blended, and alcohol (made from the estate's own wine) is added at 77%. Some of the wine is in bottle, the older unbottled vintages kept in barrels, in a large cellar, and some younger vintages held in stainless steel tanks. The current **Quinta dos Pesos Carcavelos** vintage was 1991 when we visited, dark and treacley, with strong overtones of marmalade, nuts, dried fruits and caramel. Acidity is good, and needs to be to balance the 20% alcohol. The bottle has a strikingly inappropriate sky-blue label, but at least it's easy to spot if you see it in a shop!

intention was to build a cellar for sparkling wines, to take advantage of the cool, maritime climate (less than 20km from the sea). And Quinta dos Loridos has become one of the best bubbly producers in Portugal. The estate now belongs to Bacalhôa Vinhos de Portugal *(page 304)*, and house, gardens and cellar have been extensively restored. A recent addition has been the largest Buddhist garden in Europe!

There are 30ha of vines, half white, half red. The varieties planted are a real mixture, many planted just as an experiment. Pinot Noir was abandoned,

but Castelão, Tinta Roriz and Merlot are working well, as are Chardonnay, Arinto, Alvarinho and Viognier. The latest experiments are with non-sparkling wines, Alvarinho, Castelão and Merlot. But fizz makes up the most important part of the production. Some are part-fermented in old oak barrels, and all the *remuage* (daily twisting of the bottles to get rid of the yeast deposit) is done by hand.

The **Loridos Extra Bruto** is three-quarters Castelão and a quarter Fernão Pires, an easy-drinking, honeyed, slightly aromatic bubbly. **Loridos Chardonnay Branco de Brancos Extra Brut** is pure Chardonnay, half fermented in used oak barrels, and with three years on the yeast lees. It's rich and toasty, with notes of tropical fruit, honey and nuts. The **Quinta dos Loridos Alvarinho** is partly oak-fermented, creamy and crisp, with aromatic complexity. The **Quinta dos Loridos Merlot** has red fruit aromas, a hint of oak, and an almost floral brightness. The **Quinta dos Loridos Castelão** needs time to develop in bottle. It is rich and dense, with perfumed cherry length.
Carvalhal, 2540-480 Bombarral
T+351 262 605 240
E quintadosloridos@bacalhoa.pt
W www.bacalhoa.pt
Visits Mon-Fri 9-6 appt only 🛏

COLARES A1

Adega Regional de Colares Until 1994, the ARC made all the wine in the region. Growers would bring their grapes, and take away the appropriate proportion of wine if they wanted to age and sell it themselves. And it was pretty austere stuff, needing decades of ageing before it was drinkable. Now that has changed, and there are two makers and bottlers of wine in Colares, the ARC and Fundação Stanley Ho. The ARC has much better equipment

than it had 20 years ago, temperature-controlled stainless steel vats, for example. But they are down to 12ha of grapes coming from the traditional sandy soils, and 45ha of hard, clay soil *(chão rijo)*. And it's only the grapes from sandy soils that can make the Colares DOC wines. Francisco Figueiredo, the ARC winemaker, is considering what to do. He would like to see the return of the Molar (Madeira's Tinta Negra), the early-ripening traditional red grape of the region, and research is being done to find the best clones. Meanwhile, the ARC has been kept going by hiring itself out as a space for events. It's a wonderful 19th century building, with large old vats and lots of candle-light for maximum atmosphere. At one end, a lovely old-fashioned shop is open normal shop hours during the week, and on Saturdays in August and September. The reds are still hard going, inherently under-ripe, but the whites are good – the climate is better for them. The **Colares Malvasia Branco** is herby and citrussy when young, with high acidity, minerality and notes of lavender and candied fruits.
Alameda Coronel Linhares de Lima 32,
* Banzão, 2705-351 Colares*
T+351 219 291 210
E adegadecolares@sapo.pt
Visits Mon-Fri 9-1, 2-6 tastings & guided
* tours appt only € variable*

Vidigal Wines António Lopes, owner of Vidigal, is a big exporter of Portuguese wines to Scandinavia, taking pride in value for money, and making wine to a price for export markets. And they're good wines, worth looking out for. Vidigal makes wines from local Lisboa grapes under various labels, 'Vidigal' (our favourites are the single-variety Reservas, especially the rich, smooth **Vidigal Reserva Aragonês** and super-ripe, opulent **Vidigal Reserva Merlot**), 'Reserve dos Amigos', 'Trauma' (yes, really, with a couple of Vinhos Verdes, as well) and '**Brutalis**' (a very intense, blackcurrant and treacle blend of Alicante Bouschet and Cabernet Sauvignon). Lopes and his team also make wines from the Ribatejo, Douro, Beiras and Alentejo. **Hot Spot** (a reference to global warming's possible effect in the Alentejo) is an attractive, easy VR Alentejo red made from Aragonez (this is the 'official' spelling). Vidigal are happy to receive visitors by prior appointment during normal office hours.

Quinta da Batarra 230, Cortes,
*   2410-847 Leiria*
T +351 244 819 480
E info@cavesvidigal.pt
W www.cavesvidigal.pt
Visits appt only

DOIS PORTOS B2

Adega Cooperativa de Dois Portos
This co-op in the centre of the Torres Vedras region started making wine in 1964 with 188 members. They now have about 400, farming 800ha, and make 70% red wine. They employ João Melícias' company as winemaking consultants, and reward their members with higher prices for good grapes, picked at the right sugar levels. **Marco Velho Branco** DOC **Torres Vedras** is crisp, fresh and lemony, with steely acidity. **Monte Judeu Tinto Aragonez** is a VR

Lisboa, full of dark, rich, red fruit, with firm tannins and lots of flavour. **Monte Judeu Tinto Alicante Bouschet** is big, rich and spicy, with super-ripe mulberry fruit, and hints of clove and vanilla.
Avenida 25 de Abril 76,
*   2565-206 Dois Portos*
T+351 261 712 150
E acdportos@sapo.pt
W www.acdportos.com
Visits appt only

FORMIGAL A2

Sociedade Vitivinícola do Formigal
Only 5km from the ocean, Sociedade Vitivinícola do Formigal was formed in 2001 to sell wines made by the dos Santos family. Three generations of the family have made wine, for about 50 years. The brothers Pedro and Nuno dos Santos are now in charge of about 50ha of vineyard. They sell all their wines as VR Lisboa. **Maria** is a red made from Tinta Roriz and the two Tourigas, with firm tannins, blackberry fruit and some Touriga Nacional aroma. **Telha d'Ouro** is another red, this time with some Caladoc added, with pleasant black fruit flavours, and firm tannins. **Vinha da Cátedra** is their top wine, 80% Touriga Nacional, the rest Touriga Franca, herby, oaky, dark and tannic. It needs time in bottle.
Largo José Maria dos Santos 2, Formigal,
*   2560-200 São Pedro da Cadeira*
T+351 261 857 292
E info@formigalwines.com
W www.vitivinicolaformigal.pt
Visits appt only

FREIXIAL DE CIMA B2

Quinta do Monte d'Oiro José Bento dos Santos is fanatical about flavours, how to create and combine them. A good trait in a wine producer, you might think, and we'd agree. He is also one of the two best

non-professional chefs we've ever come across (the other is a Luxemburgisch investment banker, since you ask), and the kitchen at his winery is equipped to the very highest professional standard. José is an ex-metal trader, who was always fascinated by food and cooking, and decided he would like a wine estate. He was struck by the similarities between the soils and the Mistral-like summer wind of the Alenquer area and the Rhône Valley, and thought this place might be suitable for Syrah. He bought Quinta do Monte d'Oiro in 1986, ripped out the existing vines, and planted wheat and alfalfa. In 1992, he planted 2.75ha of Syrah and Cinsaut (influenced by Serge Hochar in Lebanon). He waited five years, and picked the first grapes from this Vinha Nora vineyard in 1997, adding another 12.3ha of Touriga Nacional, Touriga Franca, Tinta Roriz, Petit Verdot, Viognier and more Syrah in 1998. In 2001, he built a new winery. The old one is now a splendid barrel cellar. He is thinking of going back to concrete vats for the Syrah.

For it is Syrah that fascinates José, and for which he is best known. Nonetheless, he and his winemaker Graça Gonçalves have accepted that Portuguese varieties also have a lot to offer. His flagships, Vinha da Nora and Quinta do Monte d'Oiro, may be almost all Syrah, but he also makes Têmpera, a Tinta Roriz red, and Aurius, 60% Touriga Nacional. And there's Madrigal, a white made from Viognier. Well, you can't imagine a serious gourmet without a white to complement the sea langoustine with vanilla mayonnaise, fried fennel and wild asparagus, now can you? That was the first course of eight that he and a friend, Nuno Diniz, had cooked for the meal after our tasting.

Madrigal is big and rich, but with lovely apricot aroma and flavour, and

good balancing acidity. **Vinha da Nora Reserva**, Syrah with a dash of Cinsaut, is smooth and oaky, with raspberry-jammy fruit and good length. The **Quinta do Monte d'Oiro Reserva** is a big leap up, sporting a whiff of Viognier, smooth and cultivated, with dense, ripe tannins, lots of oak and good raspberry length. The top Syrah, declared only twice so far, is **Quinta do Monte d'Oiro Homenagem a António Carqueijeiro**, named in memory of a dear friend of José's. It has a small percentage of Viognier again, massively rich and oaky when young, ageing to wonderful, smoky, honeyed complexity, with notes of red fruits, cherry, fig and leather. **Têmpera** (a reference to smithing, as well as to the Tinta Roriz/Tempranillo) is fascinating, with complex flavours of raspberry and mushroom, firm tannins and savoury, elegant length. **Aurius**, mainly Touriga Nacional, with 15% each of Syrah and Tinta Roriz and 10% Petit Verdot, shows the Touriga clearly, with terrific aromatic expression, firm ripe tannins, and earthy length.

Wine tourism is not really José's chosen path, but he is prepared to receive visitors by appointment. What he is keen to do in the future is 'exclusive gastronomic events'. If they're anything like our dinner they will be fantastic. Watch the website!
Freixial de Cima, 2580-404 Ventosa
T+351 263 766 060
E geral@quintadomontedoiro.com
W www.quintadomontedoiro.com
Visits Mon-Fri 9-6 appt only
€ variable

MAFRA (GRADIL) A2

Quinta de Sant'Ana James and Ann Frost bought this historic wine estate *(above)* from Ann's parents in 1992 and started restoring some of the houses on the estate to rent *(page 296)*. The first vines were planted in 1999. It's cool climate country, and they find it easier to ripen whites than reds on their 10ha of vines. The original vines are Aragonez, Castelão and Fernão Pires, followed in 2005 by Touriga Nacional, Sauvignon Blanc and Merlot, and in 2007 by Pinot Noir, Alvarinho and Riesling (a nod to Ann's German ancestors, perhaps). They could sell their wines as DOC Torres Vedras, but choose to use VR Lisboa.

Their **Quinta de Sant'Ana Sauvignon Blanc** is crisp, elegant and restrained, and the **Quinta de Sant'Ana Branco**, a blend of Fernão Pires and Sauvignon Blanc, is peachy, delicately aromatic, and ripe. The **Quinta de Sant'Ana Rosé** is fresh and herby. The reds are good, too, until recently based on the older Aragonez and Castelão, and now beginning to incorporate wines from the younger plantings. Barrel samples of unblended Touriga Nacional look very promising.
Gradil, 2665-113 Mafra
T +351 261 161 224
E ann@quintadesantana.com
W www.quintadesantana.com
Visits 9-5 appt only

PÊRO MONIZ B2

Quinta do Gradil The story goes that this magnificent 110ha estate *(below)* once belonged to the famous Marquês de Pombal, the man responsible for demarcating the Douro region and rebuilding Lisbon after the earthquake of 1755. Apparently he bought it for a close female friend... After centuries belonging to the same family, it was sold to the Gomes Vieira family, who

in 2002 entered into a partnership with Dão Sul, the thrusting Dão owners of Quinta de Cabriz *(page 174)*. The estate is about 10km south of Bombarral. It has 78ha of vines on fertile red soil, most of it clay-based, with the exception of one sandier patch which has irrigation to help it through dry summers. The Gomes Vieiras have done a lot of replanting, pulling up Vital and Fernão Pires vines, and replacing them with Arinto, Chardonnay, Tinta Roriz, Touriga Nacional, Touriga Franca, Tinta Barroca, Cabernet, Merlot, Syrah, Caladoc and Alicante Bouschet. Barley is planted between the rows to combat erosion. There is a modern, well-equipped winery, all temperature-controlled, with pneumatic presses. The intention is to produce more reds than whites, with some top-quality wines and a large amount of cheap and cheerful. All the wines are sold as VR Estremadura. We liked the **Berço do Infante Tinto**, mostly Tinta Roriz, and full of red fruit flavour, with soft tannins. **Quinta do Gradil Tinto** is a much more serious red, a blend of Touriga Nacional, Syrah and Alicante Bouschet, with lovely, herby Touriga aromas and firm tannins, and dense, blackcurrant and blackberry fruit.
2550-073 Pêro Moniz, Cadaval
T+ 351 262 770 000
E gradil@daosul.com
W www.daosul.com
Visits Mon-Fri 9-6 appt only
€variable

PORTO DE LUZ B2

Quinta de Pancas This used to be one of the most go-ahead estates in Alenquer. Two decades ago, they had Cabernet Sauvignon and Chardonnay in their vineyards and were making good, innovative wines. But more recently things had been difficult. They were refinanced in 2002,

Fundação Oriente As the name suggests, this is a charitable foundation (with huge resources, originally from a licence to operate gambling in Macau). It initiates and supports 'cultural, educational, artistic, philanthropic and social actions, predominantly in Portugal and Macau'. Its causes include art exhibitions, music, publishing, dance, educational exchanges, a huge range of activities. The Foundation's involvement with the wines of Colares began in 1999, when they were contacted by Sintra local government officials, who were worried that the largest vineyard in Colares was about to be bought by property developers. The region's main source of grapes would have been bulldozed. Fundação Oriente saw the danger, and bought the vineyard to preserve the viticultural heritage of Colares. Another charitable body set up by Stanley Ho, one of the trustees of Fundação Oriente, already owned another smaller estate in Colares, and a winery, where all the wine is now made. Unfortunately, this is very small, and they have not been able to get planning permission to enlarge it to receive visitors. But you can look through the wire netting at the vineyard in Azenhas do Mar, and see the vines trained along wires, rather than along the sandy soil in the traditional way.

It has not been easy. They had to replant the Ramisco vineyard, and 2004 was their first vintage of red Colares. They have also planted a small area, again of sandy soil, with Malvasia and Arinto, and have just produced their first vintage of white Colares. They estimate that they are now responsible for perhaps 75% of the production of Colares, and that this will increase as the vines develop. The **Colares MJC Ramisco Tinto 2005**, the first vintage from the new vines, is streets better than the 2004 (and it was a very warm year, which may have helped). It's ripe, sweet-fruited, still with characteristically firm tannins, but with enough cherry and herb flavour to carry them. The **Colares MJC Branco** is faintly scented, with pleasantly aromatic lemon and honey notes, tangy acidity and good length.

Fundação Stanley Ho also makes a savoury, slightly grassy, just off-dry **Stanley Ho Rosé** from Aragonez and Pinot Noir at the winery in Colares. They have another winery in the Terras do Sado, where the best wine is the herby, bright **Stanley Ho Tinto**, a VR Terras do Sado, with fresh acidity and rich, intense fruit.

and the Perestrello Guimarães family were bought out in 2006 by Companhia das Quintas, *(page 262, Quinta da Romeira in Bucelas)*. This should provide a firm base and welcome finance for this lovely estate to move forward again. It's a beautiful old house, much changed over the years, but still with some 16th century elements inside. The estate is about 75ha, of which 44ha are vines. Most of the grapes have been machine-harvested in the past, as no vineyard is more than ten minutes from the winery.

Pancas certainly has the potential to produce some of the best wines in the region again. Of the wines currently

available, we liked the smoky, ripe-fruited, creamy **Quinta de Pancas Aragonez**, the dense, herby, aromatic, raspberry-fruited **Quinta de Pancas Touriga Nacional**, and the rich, herby, firm-tannined **Quinta de Pancas Reserva Especial**.

Quinta de Pancas is 2km north-west of Alenquer, a right-hand turn off the road to Ventosa. You must book to visit, for a tour of the cellar and vineyards, and a free tasting.
Porto de Luz, 2580-354 Alenquer
T+351 219 687 380
E cgalvao@companhiadasquintas.pt
W www.quintadepancas.pt
Visits Mon-Fri 10-4 appt only

RIBEIRA DE MARIA AFONSO B2

Agrovitis The highly experienced winemaker João Melícias is the linchpin in this partnership. It was started in 1989 between four growers in the Torres Vedras area. Now they are down to two, with 42ha between them. One of the wineries is at Casa da Ribeira, a well-restored 17th century house (hired out for weddings and large parties). João Melícias also runs a wine consulting business, and has another winery 3km away, in São Domingos de Carmões. All their wines are sold as VR Estremadura, because they have vineyards in Torres Vedras and Alenquer, although both wineries are in Torres Vedras. João considers the brands more important to the company than individual DOC names. There are three brands, Foros for the basic level of wines, then Casa de Ribeira, and Fonte das Moças as the top line.

Fonte das Moças Branco is half and half Arinto and Fernão Pires, with a short stay in new French oak barrels, lean and mineral, with good acidity and an aromatic note from the Fernão Pires. **Casa da Ribeira Touriga Nacional** is quite oaky, with lovely red fruit and herb perfume, firm tannins and good acidity. **Fonte das**

Moças Tinto, one-third each of Touriga Nacional, Aragonez and Syrah, has sweeter, richer fruit, dense and soft, though with enough tannin to last.
Largo da Ribeira, Ribeira de Maria Afonso, 2565-199 Dois Portos
T +351 261 712 129 / 917 252 263
E info@casadaribeira.com
W www.casadaribeira.com
Visits appt only

TRIANA B2

Quinta do Carneiro António Domingues is in the hotel business, with hotels in Lisbon and Brazil, as well as interests in real estate and construction. He decided to pull up some of the 44ha of vines, and replant with Syrah, Alicante Bouschet and more Touriga Nacional. These are now four years old. In addition he has 12 year-old Tinta Roriz, Touriga Nacional, Trincadeira, Castelão and Tinta Barroca. His white varieties are Fernão Pires, Arinto, Jampal and Pinot Grigio. The estate lies in a relatively flat part of the region, about 3km to the north-east of Alenquer, where the weather is hotter, with less wind, and wines have riper flavours than most others in Alenquer. Fermentations are in temperature-controlled tanks outside the winery, and inside there's a barrel-storage cellar and another with steel tanks for blending and storage. Vinhas do Carneiro is the least expensive line, a VR Estremadura. The **Vinhas do Carneiro Branco** is crisp and mineral, with a touch of greengage, and the **Vinhas do Carneiro Tinto** has ripe cherry and raspberry fruit, with smooth tannins. **Quinta do Carneiro Branco** is DOC Alenquer, a blend of Fernão Pires and barrel-fermented Arinto, gentle and creamy, with candied, banana and citrus flavours. **Quinta do Carneiro Tinto** is also DOC Alenquer, a richly perfumed

blend of Castelão, Trincadeira and Cabernet, with firm tannins, lively cherry and raspberry fruit and tobacco length. Pactus wines are all VR Estremadura. Our favourite is the **Pactus Touriga Nacional**, dense, syrupy and herby, with ripe tannins, raspberry and damson fruit and good acidity. **Quinta do Carneiro Reserva** is also VR Estremadura, because of its grape blend, half Touriga Nacional, and equal parts of Cabernet and Tinta Barroca. It's big, ripe and dense-fruited, with herby, aromatic Touriga, rich tannins and good complexity.
Triana, Camarnal, 2580-376 Alenquer
T +351 263 711 372
E quintacarneiro@sapo.pt
Visits Mon-Fri 9-6 appt only Min 10 people €5

WATCH OUT FOR THESE WINES

Quinta da Bela Vista Carcavelos
Confraria Moscatel (Adega Cooperativa de Cadaval)
Vidigal Aragonez Reserva (Caves Vidigal)
Carvoeira Aragonez Alicante Bouschet (Adega Cooperativa de Carvoeira)
Syrah Reserva (Adega Cooperativa de Labrugeira)

ALMEIRIM C2

Casa Agrícola Herdeiros de Dom Luís Margaride This is an absolutely classic *lezíria* estate, named after Dom Luís José Braamcamp de Mello Breyner Cardoso de Menezes, Conde de Margaride. Known locally as 'Luís de Margaride', he was born in 1903, in Santarém. The estate is still run by the Cardoso de Menezes family, thus the name of the company, 'Heirs of Dom Luís Margaride'. Luís Manoel and Hermano Cardoso de Menezes are the current owners of the wine company, with 56ha of vineyard. For neighbours, they have brother, sisters and cousins with 400ha more, farming eucalyptus and cattle, amongst other things. All the vines were replanted between 1999 and 2002, with white varieties Fernão Pires, Trincadeira das Pratas, Arinto and Chardonnay, and reds Baga, Castelão, Trincadeira, Cabernet Sauvignon, Touriga Nacional, Touriga Franca, Aragonez, Pinot Noir, Merlot, Alicante Bouschet and Syrah.

The winery seems to have changed little from when we visited it 20 years ago (when the company was definitely among the best producers in the region). It's a long, white building, dwarfed by the hundreds of hectares of flat farmland that surround it. In fact, there are perfectly good stainless steel tanks, and the equipment necessary to make good wines. What matters more is the vineyard, and Luís is happy to admit they have to do a 'green harvest' (snipping off bunches during the summer) in order to keep yields down and to ensure grapes ripen properly. Even so, the final harvest is always generous.

Dom Hermano Clássico Branco is DOC Ribatejo, half and half Fernão Pires and Chardonnay, lean, steely, refreshing, and aromatic. **Dom Hermano Clássico Tinto** is also DOC Ribatejo, half Castelão and equal parts of Merlot and Syrah, dark and damsony, with rich fruit and firm tannins. **Dom Hermano Touriga Franca**, a VR Ribatejano, is dark and intense, with malty, syrupy fruit and a lovely texture. **Dom Hermano Touriga Nacional** is another VR, with floral, bright, herby aromas, balance, length and perfume. An older vintage of **Dom Hermano Castelão** had a more traditional, dried fruit flavour, with firm tannins, length and complexity.
Quinta do Casal do Monteiro, Estrada Municipal 1, Km 3, 2080-201 Almeirim
T +351 243 592 413/4
E email@margarides.com
W www.margarides.com
Visits Mon-Fri 10-12, 3-5
  Sat 12-5 appt only

Falua You don't expect to find a Portuguese winery on an industrial estate. There are some, but it's often a temporary arrangement while another winery is being built in a more appealing place. This industrial estate is not where João Ramos expected his winery to be. The idea was to rent the block while waiting for planning permission to be granted for a more desirable location, then move. But the permission never came, so the winery has stayed. It's unprepossessing from the outside, a two storey, dove-grey, boxlike building. Inside, it's one of the most modern wineries in Europe. Because they started from scratch, everything was planned. The idea was to build everything on one level, and use the height of the building to do the cooling. They open windows in the top of the dark barrel-ageing cellar at night, and the hot air escapes. Humidity control is also simple: a man wets the floors three times a week. Apart from these simple solutions, everything is highly sophisticated. João, his brother-in-law Luís de Castro, who runs Falua, and their team of winemakers, have the choice of using conventional steel vats for fermentations, rotary tanks (like giant horizontal washing machines), 'tronco-conic' vats (shaped like a sawn-off cone) or newish oak vats. Pipes carrying cold water, compressed air and nitrogen run through the whole winery. (They make their own nitrogen, by the way, from the air.) The bottling line is spotless, and can bottle under vacuum or nitrogen. And the whole winery has a system of 'cleaning in place'

to minimise impact on the local environment. Where they can, they recycle water. They receive visitors, but only by appointment.

Their own 65ha of vines supply a third of their needs. The rest are bought from six or seven growers whose vineyards they supervise through the year. About a third of the grapes are machine-picked. Before they arrive at the winery, they are chilled in a refrigeration chamber belonging to a nearby strawberry grower (he doesn't need it at that time of year). The basic Ribatejo table wines are called Tâmara. Tagus Creek is a brand shared between the two J Portugal Ramos wineries, in Alentejo and Ribatejo. João and Luís showed us five from Ribatejo, all VRs. **Tagus Creek Fernão Pires Chardonnay** is crisp and aromatic, with honeyed flavour and bright acidity. **Tagus Creek Shiraz Touriga Nacional Rosé** has lovely rosehip perfume, and herby Touriga flavour softened by sweet Shiraz fruit. **Tagus Creek Shiraz Trincadeira Tinto** is dangerously drinkable, all juicy strawberry and raspberry fruit and soft tannins. **Tagus Creek Cabernet Aragonez** has dark fruit, firm tannins and good length. **Tagus Creek Reserve Cabernet Touriga Nacional** (half and half) has intense, raspberry and damson fruit, herby notes, and rich, smooth tannins. Conde de Vimioso is the top line, also VR Ribatejano. **Conde de Vimioso Tinto** is herby and aromatic, with raspberry Aragonez and Trincadeira, and a touch of oak. **Conde de Vimioso Reserva**, again VR, has a majority of Touriga Nacional, and shows this with wonderful herby aroma and flavour, supported by rich fruit and strong oak.

Zona Industrial Lote 56, 2080-221 Almeirim
T+351 243 594 280
E falua@falua.net
W www.falua.net
Visits Mon-Fri 9-1, 2-6 appt only

Fiuza Ribatejo meets New World! This is a partnership started in 1994 between the Fiuza family and Peter Bright, an Australian winemaker who has lived in Portugal for over 25 years, involved in many innovative projects. The company has 120ha, and half are planted with non-Portuguese varieties. All are mechanically-harvested, most in cool night temperatures. The winery has all the right equipment, a juice-chiller, pneumatic press, and lots of stainless steel tanks and barrels. Oak is about half French, half American, as Peter likes the flavours of American oak with Cabernet. **Fiuza Sauvignon** comes from limestone soils to the north of the Tejo, and is lean and fresh, with flavours of lemon and passion fruit. Half of **Fiuza Chardonnay** finishes fermentation in barrel, and it's creamy, honeyed, fresh and mineral. A barrel-sample of **Fiuza Touriga Nacional** is bright, herby and sweet-fruited on the nose and palate. Both the meaty, red-berry-fruited **Fiuza Merlot** and the firm-tannined, blackcurranty **Fiuza Cabernet** age well, too. **Três Castas** (the three varieties are Aragonez, Touriga Nacional and Cabernet) is dark-fruited and oaky, with high acidity. **Fiuza Premium** is a complex blend, with good herby fruit and notes of leather and tobacco. Peter Bright also makes three pleasant Ribatejo wines, **Bright Pink**, **Bright White** and **Bright Red**, packaged in aluminium bottles, aimed at drinkers in their 20s and 30s, available in 25cl as well as 75cl sizes.

Travessa do Vareta 11, 2080-184 Almeirim
T+351 243 597 491
E fiuzabright@mail.telepac.pt
Visits Mon-Fri 9-5

Quinta da Alorna This 2,800ha estate has been family-owned since 1723, but not by the same family. It was named by Dom Pedro de Almeida, owner of the estate and Viceroy of India, after he had conquered Fort Alorna. It changed hands in 1920, and has been owned by the Lopo de Carvalho family since then. Management of the vineyard and winery is in the hands of the very experienced and capable Nuno Cancela de Abreu. There are 220ha of vineyard (as well as 1,900ha of pine, eucalyptus and cork-oak forest and 500ha of mixed agriculture). The estate produces all its own grapes, and makes 1.2 million bottles of wine a year. In the 1960s, they had 700ha of vines near the river, but pulled them up and replanted in the poor, sandy soils of the *charneca* 15 to 18 years ago. Now they have Fernão Pires, Arinto, Chardonnay and Trincadeira das Pratas (a local Ribatejo grape) for whites, and Castelão, Cabernet Sauvignon, Syrah, Alicante Bouschet, Tinta Miúda, Tinta Roriz, Trincadeira and Touriga Nacional for reds. Chardonnay and Arinto are hand-picked, the rest by machine.

Two large 1950s-built sheds house the winemaking, including temperature-controlled stainless steel tanks, installed in 2000, and barrel ageing.

The **Quinta da Alorna Branco** is half and half Fernão Pires and Arinto, Muscatty, crisp and off-dry. **Quinta da Alorna Branco Reserva** is much more serious, a lovely blend of steely Arinto and rich, savoury, barrel-fermented Chardonnay. **Quinta da Alorna Rosé Touriga Nacional** is another winner, with red fruit and rosehip perfume and just off-dry. **Quinta da Alorna Reserva Touriga Nacional Cabernet Sauvignon** has herby, intense spicy fruit, blackcurrants and blackberries, notes of liquorice, and firm tannins. Most of the top wines are made as VRs, to allow more freedom with grape blends. A curiosity is **Alorna Licoroso**, a fortified Fernão Pires, light, very sweet and creamy, with notes of coffee, nuts and fennel.

There's an attractive estate shop, selling oil and vinegar as well as the wine, open every day except Monday.

Km 73, N118, 2080-023 Almeirim
T +351 243 570 700
E geral@alorna.pt
W www.alorna.pt
Visits Mon-Fri 10-12, 3-5 Sat & Sun
    appt only
Wine shop Tue-Sat 10–12:30, 2–6:30
    Sun & public hols 10-12.30, 2-6

ALPIARÇA C2

Pinhal da Torre The Saturnino Cunha family own two estates, Quinta de São João (with 19ha of vineyard) and Quinta do Alqueve (with 36ha). Both are down on the *lezíria*, but the family take care not to let the vines over-produce, by green-harvesting in the summer. There is a magnificent 1947-built winery, still used for storing wine, but that may be transformed into a restaurant, wine-shop and tasting room before long. Most of the wines the company makes are red, and the **Quinta do Alqueve Tradicional** is a blend of Touriga Nacional, Trincadeira, Tinta Roriz and Castelão, 60% foot-trodden in *lagares*, with mature, cedar and tobacco notes, some cherry fruit and high acid and tannins. It's a VR Ribatejano, as is the **Quinta do Alqueve Touriga Nacional Syrah**, which has ripe, raspberry aromas, high acidity, firm tannins, flavours of red fruit, black cherry and tobacco, and good length.

Quinta de São João, 2090-201 Alpiarça
T +351 243 559 700
E geral@pinhaldatorre.com
W www.pinhaldatorre.com
Visits 9-6 appt only

Quinta da Lagoalva de Cima This is another huge estate down by the riverside, on which vines take up only 45ha of the 5,500ha. The rest is cork and eucalyptus forest, 400 cows, 1,200 sheep, cereals and a Lusitano horse stud. The Campilho family, the owners, have grand plans for the large yellow and white-painted house. They might build a restaurant, or even convert it into a country hotel, with good food, wines, equestrian activities and other attractions. For the time being, there's a shop that sells their wines, and they are happy to organise visits. A tasting of the basic trio of wines is free. More than that you pay for. Other businesses they run include the Baskin-Robbins ice-cream concession in Portugal, golf course building, and selling irrigation systems.

Diogo Campilho is in charge of the vineyards and winemaking, assisted by the ubiquitous oenologist Rui Reguinga. Diogo studied winemaking at Vila Real University, then worked for three years in Australia's Hunter Valley. Maybe that's where he got the idea of picking at night. All the whites are night-harvested, and some of the reds. The vineyard has the usual Ribatejo grapes, Fernão Pires, Arinto and Chardonnay for whites, plus Sauvignon Blanc, Verdelho, Viognier and Alvarinho. Reds have Tannat and Syrah as well as Cabernet Sauvignon, Tinta Roriz, Alfrocheiro and Touriga Nacional. A new winery was built in 2002.

All the wines are VR Ribatejano. **Quinta da Lagoalva Rosé** is mostly early-picked Touriga Nacional, with Alvarelhão and Cabernet, pleasant, strawberry-fruited and off-dry. **Quinta da Lagoalva Reserva Tinto** is Syrah, Cabernet and Alfrocheiro, soft and smooth, with plum and strawberry flavours and vanilla perfume. **Quinta Lagoalva de Cima Tinto** is Touriga Nacional and Tinta Roriz, with rich,

raspberry fruit, herby Touriga perfume, and lovely acidity. **Lagoalva de Cima Alfrocheiro** is dark and restrained, with damsony fruit and firm, ripe tannins. **Lagoalva de Cima Syrah** is dark, firm, rich, with smoky, raspberry and damson fruit.

Lagoalva de Cima, 2090-222 Alpiarça
T +351 243 559 070
E geral@lagoalva.pt
W www.lagoalva.pt
Visits Mon-Fri 9-1, 2-6 Sat & Sun appt only

BENFICA DO RIBATEJO C2

Adega Cooperativa de Benfica do Ribatejo This co-op, 10km downstream from Almeirim, has about 400 members, and draws on grapes from the sandy *charneca* soils as well as from the alluvial ones by the river. They are happy to receive visitors, but may not speak much except Portuguese. Their **Prova Real Branco** is a VR Ribatejano made from early-picked Fernão Pires, crisp, bright, aromatic and steely. **Prova Real Tinto** is Castelão and Aragonez, with pleasing, soft, strawberry fruit. Best we tasted is the **Quinta da Charneca Tinto**, a DOC Ribatejo of Castelão and Trincadeira, with perfumed red fruit and a touch of oak.

EN 118, km 64, 2980-321 Benfica do
    Ribatejo
T +351 243 589 279/249
E adegacoopbenfica@mail.telepac.pt
Visits Mon-Fri 8.30-12.30, 2-6

Quinta do Casal Branco José Lobo de Vasconcellos' family arrived here in 1775. The 1,000ha estate is on the south bank of the Tejo, just a few kilometres down-river from Almeirim. Much of the property is on alluvial soil, but there is also sandy, *charneca* soil further back from the river, and this is where José has his 140ha of vines, 70% for red wines. The oldest part of the winery dates from 1817, but José

had a grant from the EU in 1998, and, after long delays over planning permission, renovated the old winery in 2003. The old *lagares* are now covered with epoxy-resin, and have built-in cooling. Some of the old cement vats have modern, computerised pump-over systems. There is a new bottling line, and a newly insulated roof. José has turned a 19th century winery into something useful for the 21st.

The 40-year-old vines have been retrained to be machine-harvested. José took out some white vines, and replaced them with reds and different whites (such as Sauvignon, Verdelho, Gouveio and Arinto). 40% of the red grapes are still Castelão, some 80 years old, some 40.

And he has plans to convert some old workers' cottages into rooms and houses to rent. There is already a very well-appointed tourism reception centre, with a shop where you can buy all sorts of wines not otherwise available in Portugal. (90% of sales are export.) The estate also has a famous Lusitano horse stud, and cattle.

Over all the white vines are Fernão Pires, and the **Quinta do Casal Branco** is lean, lemony and aromatic, with notes of lavender and citrus. **Falcoaria Branco** is half fermented in oak barrels, rich, creamy, tangy and faintly Muscatty. The Cork Grove is another label (yes, there are cork-oaks on the estate). Our favourites here are the creamy, herby, just off-dry **The Cork Grove Rosé**, the bright, herby, raspberry-fruited **The Cork Grove Castelão Touriga**

Nacional, and the inky, sweet-fruited **The Cork Grove Castelão Alicante Bouschet**. **Quinta do Casal Branco Tinto** is savoury, ripe and appealing, with notes of cherry and tobacco, and some tannin. **Capucho Merlot** is soft and appealing, with good, herby/grassy flavours. **Capucho Cabernet** is ripe and smoky, with blackcurrant fruit and chocolate flavours. **Capucho Petit Verdot** has rich, dried fruit aromas, and dark treacley fruit. Best of the lot is the red **Falcoaria Reserva**, a DOC Ribatejo, mainly Castelão from old vines, with some old Alicante Bouschet and Trincadeira. It's interesting, complex red, with sweet fruit, firm tannins, acidity, length and balance.
2080-362 Benfica do Ribatejo
T+351 243 592 412
E wines@casalbranco.com
W www.casalbranco.com
Visits10-6 appt preferred Closed 25 Dec

OUTEIRO-SERRA C3

Encosta do Sobral This estate may be only 15km north of the Tejo, but it's nearly 300m higher, and in completely different, schistous soil. Encosta do Sobral is 8km from Tomar, with 70ha of vines. It belongs to the Sereno family, who have made wine there for several generations. Until 1999, they had only 20ha of vines, and sold off wine surplus to their needs in bulk. Then they replanted, added 50ha, and a new winery in 2001. **Encosta do Sobral Branco** is floral, bright and citrussy, with Fernão Pires and Malvasia aromas tempered by Arinto steel. Red **Encosta do Sobral Reserva** is Touriga

Nacional plus 10% Touriga Franca, matured for a year in new French oak barrels. It has lovely Touriga aromas, herby and intense flavour. **Encosta do Sobral Reserva Cabernet Sauvignon** is oaky, with aromas of spice and dried fruits. The reds both have good acidity and firm tannins.
Outeiro-Serra, 2300-251 Tomar
T+351 213 851 880
E geral@encostadosobral.com
W www.encostadosobral.com
Visits appt only

PÓVOA DE SANTARÉM C2

Quinta da Ribeirinha The Cândido family has three farms, in the clay and chalk soils of the *bairro*, north of the Tejo. In total, there are 95ha, of which 40ha are vines. They also grow olives and sell their own olive oil. Joaquim Cândido's father started the business in the 1950s, and grew grapes. Joaquim is a neurologist, and never intended to become a full-time farmer. However, his two children are happy to run the estate. Mariana came to work in the business in 2003, after a degree in economics. Rui joined in 2004, having studied biochemistry. The first wines had been released in 1996, under the Rapadas label. Mariana and Rui have added another label, Vale de Lobos, the name of one of their farms (Quinta da Ribeirinha and Terra da Vinha being the other two).

The Cândidos receive visitors in an old olive mill at the front of the winery, in use until about ten years ago. It's a lovely room, old machinery still in place, with a kitchen at one end and a glassed-over well at the other. There's lots of art on the walls, and bottles, jars of preserves, dried gourds and other decorations. As well as a tour round the winery, they offer a tasting of their wines, plus some of the other products from the farm.

Vale de Lobos Branco is a DOC Ribatejo made from Fernão Pires, honeyed, ripe and citrussy, with good acidity and fragrance. They also make a bubbly, **Vale de Lobos Espumante Branco**, again DOC Ribatejo, mostly Fernão Pires again, with toasty, lemony flavour and good acidity. Apparently, roast kid is the dish to eat with their sparkling red, the medium-dry, strawberry-jammy, refreshing **Vale de Lobos Tinto Espumante**. The Rapadas wines are all less expensive, and VR Ribatejano. **Rapadas Tinto** is very easy-drinking, with up-front, red fruit flavours and soft tannins. **Vale de Lobos Tinto**, DOC Ribatejo again, has warm, generous cherry and strawberry fruit, with a whiff of farmyard, and good length. **Vale de Lobos Syrah**, from young vines, is soft, malty and ripe, with rich, raspberry-jammy fruit and smooth tannins. We tasted a range of barrel samples of young single-variety wines, of which the star was a herby, aromatic, raspberry-fruited Touriga Nacional.

Rua Bispo D. António de Mendonça 17,
2000-533 Póvoa de Santarém
T+351 243 428 200 / 963 958 414
E marianacandido@quintadaribeirinha.com
W www.quintadaribeirinha.com
Visits Tue-Sun 10-12, 1-7 Sun appt only
€5 wine & food tasting

RIO MAIOR B2

Caves Dom Teodósio João Teodósio Barbosa started dealing in agricultural products in 1924, and set up this wine and spirit company 20 years later. Its headquarters are in Rio Maior, conveniently placed for the IP6 road that runs between Caldas da Rainha and Santarém. It's a company that has evolved from buying and selling wine, brandy and other drinks to buying wine estates as well. These estates are all in the Ribatejo. In 1980, they bought Quinta de Almargem, and Quinta de São

João Batista and Quinta da Faia in 1987. The Barbosa family sold the company to Cruz & Companhia in 1996, and in 2001, Caves Velhas became part of the group. As well as the operation in Bucelas *(page 261)*, Caves Velhas brought with them another Ribatejo estate, Quinta do Bairro Falcão.

The Bucelas wine and some brandies are still made at Caves Velhas, but all the Dom Teodósio wines are made or bottled in the Ribatejo. Quinta de São João Batista is a 120ha property, with 90ha of vineyard. There is a large pale pink house in need of a fresh coat of paint, and a grand old winery. Dom Teodósio would like to build a new winery, but planning permission has so far been denied because of the proximity to a Natural Reserve, the Paúl de Boquilobo, an important migration point for heron and other water-fowl. Almost everything is machine-picked here – easy on the flat land – except a few hectares of old vines. 95% of the production is red. You can visit, but need to give them at least three days' notice. A tasting will be easier at the Rio Maior headquarters.

Serradayres Branco, a VR Ribatejano, is pure Fernão Pires, lemony, fragrant and bright. The **Serradayres Tinto Garrafeira** is the other we liked in this range, smooth and mature, with flavours of cherry and tobacco. Casaleiro is a brand that comes in many versions, single-variety and blends. **Casaleiro Rosé** is a blend of half-and-half Castelão and Trincadeira, easy and appealing, with soft, strawberry fruit. **Casaleiro Tinto Reserva**, mostly Castelão, has dark, rich, cherry and plum fruit and a whiff of American oak. We also tasted various young Casaleiro Reservas. **Casaleiro Reserva Touriga Nacional Syrah** is jammy and herby, with rich, red fruit flavours and firm tannins. **Casaleiro Reserva Syrah** is bright and berry-fruited, with balance and

length. **CDT Vindima** is a young red, Castelão with a little Syrah, with dense, cherry fruit and some residual sugar. **Quinta de São João Batista Tinto** is Castelão, with nicely maturing notes of tobacco and cedar, and ripe, soft, red fruit. A younger version had half Alicante Bouschet added, which gave it a sweeter, syrupy intensity. **Quinta de São João Batista Tinto Reserva**, Castelão again, has ripe, red fruit flavours and some oak. The top red is **Quinta de São João Batista Reserva Pisa a Pé**, a foot-trodden blend of Castelão and Trincadeira, with intense, dried fruit flavours and firm tannins.

Over lunch, we tasted some Dom Teodósio wines from other regions. Our favourites were **Cardeal Dão Reserva**, dark, smoky, piney and aromatic, with smooth tannins. The **Fernão Duque Dão Reserva** is mostly Touriga Nacional, aromatic, elegant and austere, with high acidity, firm tannins and good length. **Romeira Tinto** is a Palmela DOC red (Castelão again), red-fruited, aromatic, light and smooth, with a lovely fresh finish.

Rua Mariano de Carvalho Apartado 4,
2040-998 Rio Maior
T+351 243 999 070
E caves@domteodosio.com
W www.domteodosio.com
Visits Mon-Sat 10-5 appt only (3 days' notice)

Samora Correia B1

Companhia das Lezírias By the marshlands of the Tagus estuary, this is the largest agricultural estate in Portugal, with 48,000ha! It belongs to the Portuguese state, having been founded in 1836, sold to fund wars against the French, and returned to state ownership in the 1974 revolution. The 20,000ha of cork are the world's largest cork plantation. There are 1,000ha of rice, as well as cereals, eucalyptus, 4,000 cattle, Lusitano horses, olive trees, and 130ha of vines. Plantings have changed from principally Castelão, Alicante Bouschet, Fernão Pires and Trincadeira das Pratas when estate manager Frederico Falcão arrived in 2001. Now Touriga Nacional, more Cabernet Sauvignon, Malbec and Tannat have been added, and Moscatel, Sauvignon, Verdelho and more Alvarinho for whites. A new winery will be ready for the 2008 harvest. At the moment, reds are better than whites. **Catapereiro Escolha** is fresh, fruity and good value. The DOC **Companhia das Lezírias Tinto**, a blend of Castelão, Alicante Bouschet, Touriga Nacional and Cabernet Sauvignon, is rich, herby and firm. The berry-fruited, dark **Alicante Bouschet** is the best single varietal. **Patriarcal** (Touriga Nacional and Cabernet Sauvignon) has rich, blackberry fruit and oregano fragrance. A special wine, **Companhia das Lezírias 170 Aniversário**, is inky-smooth and powerful, and the **Companhia das Lezírias Reserva**, another Touriga Nacional/Cabernet blend, is serious, substantial and intense.

Adega de Catapereiro, EN 118, 2135-318
  Samora Correia
T +351 212 349 016
E lezirias.vinhos@cl.pt
W www.cl.pt
Visits appt only
€ variable

Santana B2

Quinta da Fonte Bela You can see the tall chimney of the distillery that used to operate at Fonte Bela from a long way across the flat lands of the *lezíria*. Now the storks use it as a convenient nesting location in spring, and stay till the young family is ready to fly off at the end of summer. This massive winery shows how large the *lezíria* wine estates were. It was bought by DFJ Vinhos in 1998, to serve as a headquarters, production centre and cellar. The vineyards of the estate belong to another company.

DFJ was the creation of three men, Dino Ventura (super-salesman), Fausto Ferraz (the business brains) and José Neiva Correia, one of Portugal's top winemakers. Dino and Fausto had been successful selling Portuguese wine made by José and other producers all over Europe, and this was to be their joint venture. It worked well, and is still working, though Dino died a few years ago, and Fausto is no longer involved. The new 'D' is Duarte Carvalho e Silva, owner of vineyard land in the Ribatejo and José's present partner in the project. José has always aimed to make Portuguese grape varieties and their flavours accessible to drinkers in other countries. His style of wine is not thick with the tannin the older Portuguese wine-lovers admire, but easy-drinking and, importantly, not too expensive. Some of the wines sold by DFJ he makes, others he blends. Duarte and José have vineyards in Ribatejo and Lisboa respectively, and the company also buys from other growers and co-ops. DFJ sells wine from these two regions, as well as others from the Douro, Dão, Bairrada, Beiras, Terras do Sado, Alentejo and Algarve.

The top two wines from Ribatejo and Lisboa are made as DOC. Others are made as VRs, enabling José to experiment with varieties not traditionally grown in the region. At his family estate, Quinta do Porto Franco, in particular, there are 230ha of vines, growing a range from Alvarinho (very successfully) to Alicante Bouschet (less so).

DFJ has a huge range of wines, so we'll pick our favourites, starting with the local ones. **Segada Tinto** is VR Ribatejano, half and half Castelão and Trincadeira, with spicy, ripe, berry fruit and good tannins. The **Grand'Arte Trincadeira** is another VR Ribatejano, with lovely, aromatic, raspberry fruit and firm tannins. From Lisboa, **Manta Preta** is half and half Touriga Nacional and Tinta Roriz, dense, aromatic and herby, with gentle tannins and some complexity. Another half and half wine is **DFJ Touriga Nacional Touriga Franca**, also a VR Lisboa, herby and firm-tannined, with hints of liquorice and chocolate. **Grand'Arte Touriga Nacional** looked to be a winner, with rich fruit and firm tannins, but was tasting dumb from recent bottling. **Grand'Arte Alvarinho** is lovely, crisp, lemony, aromatic but restrained. **Pink Elephant Rosé** is a new wine, developed with José's UK importer, creamy, well-balanced, fresh, and just off-dry. Last of the VR Lisboa wines is **Grand'Arte Touriga Nacional Rosé**, herby and crisp, with aromatic berry fruit. **Francos Reserva** is a DOC Lisboa from José's family estate, Touriga Nacional, Touriga Franca and Alicante Bouschet, bright, ripe and herby, with dense tannins, a touch of oak and good length.

Santana, 2070-512 Valada, Cartaxo
T +351 243 704 701/5
E info@dfjvinhos.com
W www.dfjvinhos.com
Visits Mon-Fri 10-4 appt only

TRAMAGAL C3

Quinta do Casal da Coelheira The Rodrigues family make more red than white from their 64ha of vineyard on the south bank of the river. **Casal da Coelheira Chardonnay** is honeyed and intense, with high acidity. The **Casal da Coelheira Reserva** is a Ribatejo DOC, dark and very ripe, with high tannin and acidity. **Casal da Coelheira Mythos** is sweetly spicy, with syrupy Alicante Bouschet fruit, length and intensity.
EN 118 1331, 2205-645 Tramagal
T+351 241 897 219
E geral@casaldacoelheira.pt
W www.casaldacoelheira.pt
Visits appt only €5

VALE DONAS C3

Quinta do Cavalinho The Costa family has been selling its own wines since 1993. Quinta do Cavalinho's total area is 30ha, with 19ha of vines in the chalky-clay soils of the Tomar region, the rest forest. They have recently planted Chardonnay, Sauvignon, Syrah and Cabernet Sauvignon, to join the traditional varieties. Touriga Nacional is next on the list to be planted. VR Ribatejano wines are sold as 'Solar dos Costas'. All the rest are DOC Ribatejo. **Quinta do Cavalinho Branco** is stainless steel-fermented Fernão Pires, very perfumed, peachy and floral, with lively acidity and a creamy feel. **Quinta do Cavalinho Colheita Seleccionada Tinto**, a blend of Castelão

and Aragonez, is herby and restrained, with firm, ripe tannins and a note of oak flavour. **Herdade dos Templários Garrafeira** is mainly Castelão, with 20% each of Aragonez and Alicante Bouschet, dark, syrupy and savoury, with blackberry and treacle flavours, highish acidity, good tannins and length.
2300-608 Tomar
T+351 249 311 630
E geral@quintadocavalinho.com
W www.quintadocavalinho.com
Visits Mon-Fri 8.30-5.30 appt only
€ variable

VILA CHÃ DE OURIQUE B2

Quinta do Falcão This estate used to belong to Inês Monteiro's family but had become subdivided. It was bought back by Joaquim and Inês Monteiro in 1988, who also bought most of the estate of Quinta da Fonte Bela (the other part of which is owned by DFJ Vinhos). Between the two estates, they own 200ha, much of it devoted to breeding show-jumping horses. They also have 35ha of vineyard, and make the wines at Fonte Bela. So, if you want to visit the winery, go to Fonte Bela (you can do two wineries with one visit, if you decide to go to DFJ as well). They will also receive visitors at Falcão.

Most of the vines are young, 12 years old at Falcão and four at Fonte Bela. **Quinta do Falcão Tinto** is a VR Ribatejo, half Touriga Nacional, the balance equal parts of Castelão and Cabernet, rich and syrupy, with good, herby Touriga Nacional aromas, raspberry fruit and very firm tannins. **Quinta do Falcão Reserva** is a Ribatejo DOC, mostly Castelão with 20% of Cabernet, very appealing, with ripe, cherry and strawberry fruit, good acidity and firm tannins. **Paço dos Falcões Reserva** is back to VR, half and half Touriga Nacional and Syrah, with smoky, malty

notes from the Syrah, raspberry fruit and smooth, firm tannins.
2070-653 Vila Chã de Ourique, Cartaxo
T+351 243 789 428/225
E quintafalcão@iol.pt
W www.quintadofalcao.pt
Visits Mon-Sat appt only €20

Vale d'Algares This is the dream of Alejandro and Sónia Martins, of horses, hospitality and wine. Since 2001 they have bought four farms here, have an equestrian centre and eventing course amidst cork oaks, 31ha of vineyard (30ha more to come) and a magnificent winery. They plan a huge indoor arena and a 5-star spa hotel, to open early in 2010. The winery is dramatically modern, hidden within an old one. Pedro Pereira Gonçalves, the winemaker, makes two ranges of wines, the simpler one called 'Guarda Rios' (Kingfisher). **Guarda Rios Branco** is a VR blend of barrel-fermented Chardonnay, Sauvignon, Alvarinho and Fernão Pires, complex, aromatic and harmonious; there's an off-dry, fragrant **Guarda Rios Rosé**, and a big, smooth, Shiraz-dominated **Guarda Rios Tinto**. **Vale d'Algares Branco**, a steely, rich Viognier, is the first wine of the top range.
Rua Colonel Lopes Mateus 13, 2070-641
Vila Chã de Ourique
T +351 243 709 321
E geral@quatroancoras.com
W www.valedalgares.com
Visits appt only

WATCH OUT FOR THESE WINES

Ninfa (JTM Barbosa)
Paço d'Aviz Clássico Tinto (Talhão)
Padre Pedro Reserva Tinto (Casa Cadaval)
Quinta da Atela Tinto
Quinta dos Patudos Tinto

Eat in Lisboa and the Ribatejo

LISBOA

Much silver crosses the palms of restaurateurs on the Costa de Prata – the Silver Coast west of Lisbon. The many top-class restaurants, and the many fishy beach restaurants, can rely upon a steady trade from the capital, from the wealthy residents of Cascais, Sintra and Estoril, not to mention holidaying visitors from elsewhere. This coast has the country's most productive fish and seafood farms, centred around Foz do Arelho and the Lagoa de Óbidos, a lagoon 5km from the lovely town of Óbidos. There are delicious crabs and mussels, and clams and cockles are to die for. Do try the *amêijoas à Bulhão Pato* – clams quickly steamed in their shells, with garlic, olive oil, lemon juice and lots of coriander leaf; the dish was created in honour of Bulhão Pato, poet, writer, translator and scholar of the late 19th, early 20th century. Much money is splashed on lobsters – in simple restaurants usually best eaten plain: it always seems a pity to drown them in sauce, or bury them in a baked dish, where they may end up over-cooked.

Anyway, better a perfect sardine than a loused-up lobster. Cascais claims to have the best sardines in the world. Pre-prandial nibbles around here are likely to include sardine or sardine roe pâté to spread on your bread. Peniche is the main fishing port, bringing in amongst other fishes flavoursome sea bream *(pargo)*, delicious sea bass *(robalo – which is also farmed)*, and grey mullet *(tainha)*, the least exciting of the three. There's eel and conger eel.

Oily fish is sometimes prepared as an *escabeche,* fried and then dressed with vinaigrette and lots of parsley. Fish stew, *caldeirada rica de peixe,* has all kinds of fish, with onions, garlic, tomatoes, piri piri, green pepper, and fresh herbs if you're lucky. Fish and seafood also appears regularly in soups – s*opa de peixe* or *sopa de mariscos.*

Apart from fish, simple beach restaurants sell a lot of *frango à piri-piri* – grilled chicken with hot chilli sauce. Best of the local meats is partridge, when in season.

There's a traditional tendency to deep fry. With an eye on the waistline and some bad experiences behind us, we do our best to avoid the local *ovos verdes* – butter-stuffed boiled eggs, floured and deep fried, as well as the deep-fried cod fritters *(pataniscas de bacalhau)*, and 'little fish of the garden' *(peixinhos da horta)*, deep-fried battered green beans!

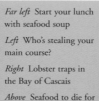

Far left Start your lunch with seafood soup

Left Who's stealing your main course?

Right Lobster traps in the Bay of Cascais

Above Seafood to die for

275

FRUIT BOWL

Fruit-growing is big business in the north of the Lisboa VR region. The Leiria district grows 80 per cent of Portugal's pears, many of them a big, sweet, juicy, aromatic variety called Pêra Rocha. Harvested in September to October, they keep well, unlike most other varieties of pear. The original tree was discovered in Sintra, in the garden of a Senhor António Rocha; now Portugal has thousands of hectares of the variety. Leiria also grows a third of Portugal's apples, and a fifth of its peaches, mostly yellow-fleshed varieties. There are also delicious figs, and pine nuts from the pine forests.

The Ribatejo grows the sweetest and most delicious melons of various different varieties, including the white *melão branco do Ribatejo* and the rough-skinned, dark green *casca de carvalho*, both rugby-shaped; the round *meloa* – the Canteloupe – is also very good. Strawberries are another important crop on the Ribatejo's riverside *lezíria*, and vineyards are cropped for the table as well as for wine.

The calories do not stop there. The Lisboa area will tempt you with numerous famous sweets and pastries, very delicious and fortunately rather small. 'Breezes of the Lis' *(Brisas do Lis)* were invented and named in the 1930s after the river that runs through the heart of Leiria, in the north of the region. They are luminously yellow thanks to the numerous egg yolks mixed with sugar and ground almonds; they are baked in tiny flat rounds, then sugar-glazed. Bite-size *Queijadas de Sintra* have a pastry case and a filling of curd cheese, ground almonds, egg

yolks, sugar, flour, coconut and cinnamon. Torres Vedras and Ericeira have their *pastéis de feijão* – pastry filled with sugar, a paste of haricot beans, ground almonds, lots of eggs and extra egg yolks, and sprinkled with icing sugar. Walnuts are the new ingredient in the *Nozes de Cascais*, which are coated in crunchy caramel. And that's not all, but the waistband is bulging, so let's move on inland to the Ribatejo…

QUINTA VALE DE LOBOS

Olives are planted on the higher, drier land of the Ribatejo, and the region has one of Portugal's best olive oil producers. You can visit, tour the groves and learn about growing olives and making olive oil. It is also possible to book a tasting, for an extra charge. There must be at least six of you, and you must make a prior appointment.

It's a historic family estate, run by Verónica and Joaquim Santos Lima. On a simple tour you will learn about varieties of olive, pruning, picking and pressing, and you can buy the prize-winning oils at the new shop. Tutored tastings aim to equip you with the insider skills to recognise and describe a good olive oil. They include demonstrations of olive oil faults: for example off-flavours that creep in when the picked olives sit around for a few days before processing, so that those at the bottom of the pile begin to ferment.

Quinta Vale de Lobos was a pioneer back in 1867 of fine extra virgin olive oil production in Portugal, Joachim's grandfather having imported equipment from Italy. Joaquim himself also pioneered semi-intensive planting in rows, which permits speedy machine harvesting, day and night, and choice of the ideal harvesting moment. Apart from the 200-year-old

groves of the local Galega variety, 13ha were planted semi-intensively 20 years ago, and the Santos Limas have recently planted thousands of new trees, over 80ha, in an even more intensive way, in modern rows with drip irrigation. The new trees were in full production for the 2007 harvest: it takes only three to seven years for a modern tree to bear a good crop (depending on variety and rainfall), compared with more than ten years in the olden days.

At Vale de Lobos, they keep their yields very low, pick directly from the tree (many producers pick up fallen olives), and process immediately. If the olive press is full, they stop picking. The olives are pressed, and the paste is mixed with cold water and beaten to release the droplets of oil. Friction can cause temperatures to rise at this point, and it is vital to control the temperature if the flavoursome, volatile components of the oil are to be retained. The oil is finally extracted by a gentle centrifuge. The estate is not easy to find – 6km north of Santarém. Look out for the white wall on each side of the driveway. *Azoia de Baixo, 2005-097 Santarém T+351 243 429 264 E valedelobos@mail.telepac.pt W www.valedelobos.com*

RIBATEJO

You won't do much slimming in the Ribatejo either! The Ribatejanos also have a liking for the stodgy, bready dishes most associated with the Alentejo, such as *açorda*, made with dense corn bread. They grow rice *(arroz)* on the *lezíria*, the flat land by the river, and dishes may come with rice, potatoes *and* bread. Food in the Ribatejo is traditionally rustic, but it has the great advantage of loads of wonderful fresh fruit and vegetables grown on the alluvial plains, as well as fish from the Tagus, and plenty of meat – those bulls don't *only* fight. And amidst all this traditional cooking, the Ribatejo harbours the home base restaurant of one of Portugal's most creative and

accomplished chefs, Luís Suspiro, at the restaurant Condestável in Ereira, west of Tomar.

In the traditional restaurants, vegetable soups and stews are popular and delicious – but vegetarians should not get too excited. Vegetable dishes will almost certainly be laced with *chouriço*, bacon or blood sausage, and may perhaps be lent a gooey consistency by the odd pig's ear. Non-vegetarians should relish the green bean soups, and the famous *sopa de pedra*, a chunky, catch-all soup whose ingredients include pulses, potatoes, garlic, coriander, ham, sausage and, yes, pigs' ears. *Favas com chouriço* are an oniony, garlicky, meaty, broad bean stew. Tomatoes abound in the low-lying fields – tomato rice *(arroz de tomate)* is on many menus, and anything might come with a garlicky tomato sauce. *Magusto* is a cabbage dish with corn bread crumbs, beans and olive oil.

River fish include delicious Tagus eels, and shad *(sável)*, often served as a moist, bready *açorda* or a risotto *(arroz)*. As elsewhere, *bacalhau* is much in evidence. With the Alentejo just off to the east and south, *porco preto*, the delicious pork and ham of the Alentejo black pigs, features on many of the best menus. Beef is an important part of the diet, and you'll find lots of roast kid *(cabrito assado)*, usually cooked with garlicky roast potatoes.

Amongst delicious goat and sheep's cheeses, the best known is from the rocky, hilly country around Tomar. The tiny Queijo de Tomar is bit like the Rabaçal of the Beiras, usually eaten fresh but sometimes mature, hard and nutty, the mature ones often sold in olive oil.

Tomar is also famous for its *Fatias*. A *fatia* is a slice, and the slices in question are of course rich and sweet. The recipe we were given demanded nothing more, nothing

less than 24 egg yolks and 1 kilo of sugar, to be beaten for ages, baked in a *bain marie*, sliced up small, and then dunked in hot sugar syrup. Santarém has its *celestes,* very small, very sweet, full of ground almonds and eggs. *Delícias de batata* contain potato along with almonds and egg yolks. *Cavacas da Rainha* are little flat sponge cakes glazed with sugar syrup. And the *really* famous eggy invention of the Ribatejo, made now in households and *doçarias* all around the country? *Fios de ovos* are sweet strands of egg that look like soft, bright yellow noodles. They are eaten neat, or incorporated into other desserts. If you fancy a go, beat together two whole eggs with ten more egg yolks, and pipe the mix in a thin stream into simmering sugar syrup, fishing it out before it sets too hard. It's a skilful job, frustrating for the novice, and one in which Ribatejo housewives take especial pride.

Below Fishing on the river in the Ribatejo

Right Cascais claims to have the world's best sardines, the small ones being most highly prized – eat them with grilled peppers and potatoes

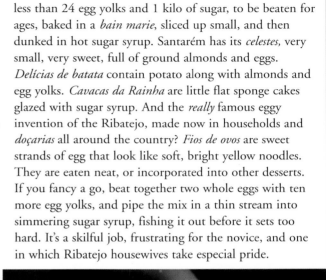

ABRANTES D3

A Cascata Good-quality, regional fare, with fish soup, clams with coriander and garlic *(Bulhão Pato)*, or local charcuterie *(enchidos)* to start, and lots of beef, roast kid, a choice of *bacalhau* dishes, prawn *feijoada*, duck risotto and others to go on with. A good choice of sweet dishes to finish.
Rua Manuel Lopes Valente Júnior 19
T+351 241 361 011
€20
Closed Sun din, Mon

ALDEIA GAVINHA B2

Adega Vila Verde A simple village restaurant west of Alenquer, recommended by local wine producers, where you will eat copiously and well. The hot home-made bread is brilliant, and comes with olives, *escabeche* of mackerel, egg salad, octopus salad, oil and vinegar. Then it could be *bacalhau*, fish risotto, grilled squid or grouper. Or a huge veal chop, or delicious Alentejo pork *(porco preto)*. There are plenty of good local wines to choose from, even a nip of *bagaço* fire-water to finish you off.
Estrada Nacional 9
T+351 263 760 574
€18 ♀ No credit cards
Closed Mon

ARRUDA DOS VINHOS B2

O Fuso You can see that this used to be a wine cellar, with the *lagares* and the old

screw for the wine-press. Their speciality is cooking huge servings of meat over a wood fire, particularly rib of beef, but they also turn their hand to *bacalhau*. And you might have started with black pudding risotto or grilled *chouriço*. It's not really a restaurant for vegetarians. The wine selection is predominantly local.
Rua Cândido dos Reis 94
T+351 263 975 121
€20
Closed 24 Dec din

AZENHAS DO MAR A1

Piscinas das Azenhas do Mar By the sea near Colares, this is a place for people-watching on a hot summer's lunchtime, or for a sunset romantic evening for two: provided, that is, your chosen one loves fish and seafood. The location is wonderful, tucked under the little cliff-top village of Azenhas do Mar. It's a glass-fronted 1950s cabin on stilts – not beautiful in itself. But the setting is amazing, above a seawater swimming pool, cliffs opposite, and the ocean stretching to the horizon. The seafood and fish is excellent: for starters maybe grilled limpets *(lapas)*, dressed crab, fish soup, strange but delicious goose-neck barnacles *(percebes)*; then plainly grilled, super-fresh fish. The wines are adequate rather than amazing.
Azenhas do Mar
T+351 219 280 739
E azenhas-do-mar@sapo.pt
W www.azenhasdomar.com
€35-€40 V

AZÓIA A1

O Casarão A big, professionally-run place, serving hundreds of customers in a smart but rustic atmosphere. Most of the dishes are traditional, such as brochettes of squid with prawns, duck risotto and *rojões à portuguesa* (roast chunks of pork

in a tomato sauce). But some are slight variants: the veal comes with mushrooms, the slices of pork with succulent chestnuts.
Estrada Nacional 19,
    Cruzamento da Azóia
T+351 244 871 080
E info@ocasarao.pt
W www.ocasarao.pt
€25
Closed Mon

Refúgio da Roca Much recommended for the quality of its plainly-grilled fish and seafood, this pleasantly rustic restaurant offers a friendly welcome. Skewered meat is an alternative, also skilfully grilled. There's a good selection of wines, not just local. Start with fish soup, perhaps, or

clams, or baby squid. Then move on to something from the grill, and finish with some Sintra cheesecake, rice pudding or *farófias*, a Portuguese version of the French *îles flottantes*.
Estrada do Cabo da Roca
T+351 219 290 898
E rrroca@sapo.pt
W www.refugiodaroca.com
€25-€30 ♀ V
Closed Tue

AZÓIA (PRAIA DA ADRAGA) A1

Restaurante da Adraga You could order a steak if you really wanted meat, but fish and seafood are what this down-to-earth beachside restaurant is known for. The bright yellow restaurant, decorated inside with a maritime theme, has been run by the same family for four generations, so they must be getting it right. Try to reserve a table by the window, and enjoy the super-fresh fish and seafood, the friendly service and a bottle of wine from the small selection. And have a walk along the beach afterwards.
T+351 219 280 028
€30

BUCELAS B1

Barrete Saloio This bar and restaurant, highly recommended by several local wine producers, made a point of its rusticity by changing its name from 'Pensão Frutuoso Inácio' to the present 'Bumpkin's Cap'. Decor is a blend of crazily-paved pillars and tiled walls. But everyone loves the food, the welcoming atmosphere and the well-stocked cellar. Specialities include grilled squid *(lulas ao aguilho)* and veal chops *(costeleta de novilho)*, and if you're a *bacalhau* fan, you can have it in five different ways.

Rua Luís de Camões 28
T+351 219 694 004
E barretesaloio@netcabo.pt
W www.barretesaloio.eu
€12-€20 ♀ *V*
Closed Mon din, Tue; Aug

CASCAIS A1

100 Maneiras Estalagem Villa Albatroz was built in 1903, with delightful views over the bay of Cascais, by Luísa, Duchess of Palmela for her friend, the writer Maria Amélia Vaz de Carvalho. 100 Maneiras (Cem Maneiras) has been the restaurant there for nearly ten years. It is one of the best in Portugal (and prices reflect this), where chef Ljubomir Stanisic cooks inventive and exquisitely presented dishes, drawing on the finest ingredients. As you'd expect – with the quay where local fishermen still land their catches right by the hotel – fish and seafood are much in evidence. (There are delightful views over the bay of Cascais.) Starters, meat and desserts also show lightness of touch, imagination and artistic flair. The wine list is excellent (and advice likewise), with a wide range from abroad as well as the best of Portugal, and a big selection by the glass. Decor is stylishly modern but restful, tablecloths black. You must book.
Rua Fernando Tomás 1
T+351 214 835 394
E geral@100maneiras.com
W www.100maneiras.com
€60 ♀ *V* 🛏
Closed Sun din, Mon

Enoteca Wine Bar de Cascais This is a young enterprise (started in 2002), but already they have had to move to double their space. It's a light, airy, modern room, one wall taken up with wine bottle display. Wine is the focus here, with more than 400 wines available, about 50 by the glass. But the food is good as well, with Portuguese dishes such as *bacalhau com migas* (crumbs), sirloin with potato gratin, and black pork with spinach and corn bread. Or you could try one of the tasting menus, of starters or main courses. Or there are salads, soups, and platters of ham, *enchidos* or cheeses, and puds various, including one of our favourites, ricotta with *doce de abóbora* (pumkin jam). There's a sushi bar, too!
Rua Visconde da Luz 17
T+351 214 822 328 / 962 596 609
E enoteca_cascais@hotmail.com
W www.enoteca@guiadacidade.com
€35-€40 ♀ *V*

Fortaleza do Guincho A fortress originally built to repel invaders has now succumbed to the skills of French chefs,

and welcomes visitors from all over the world. Vincent Farges is the young head chef; he has worked in France and Greece, so the cooking has an international note, while faithful to the best Portuguese ingredients. Here, of course, these include wonderful local fish and seafood, as well as meltingly tender beef and Pyrenean lamb. Dishes such as poached skate with aromatic herbs, crispy potatoes with young vegetables and garlic purée *(raia escalfada com aromáticos, batata estaladiça*

com pequenos legumes e puré de alho) give an idea of Farges's attitude to contrasting textures and delicate flavours. And if you like an exotic finale, your dreams should come true with the likes of coconut and mango crust, roasted exotic fruits skewer, exotic sherbet and peppered mango sauce *(crocante de côco e manga, espetada de frutos exóticos assada, sorvete das ilhas com molho de manga apimentada)*. It will come as no surprise that the wine list is very good indeed.
Estrada do Guincho
T+351 214 870 491
E restaurante@guinchotel.pt
W www.guinchotel.pt
€70 ♟ *V* 🛏

CASCAIS A1 *(continued)*

Porto de Santa Maria It wouldn't really make sense to order meat. They say this is the best fish and seafood in and around Lisbon. Fish baked in salt and fish baked in a bread crust are two of the specialities. The restaurant is housed in a pavilion right over the beach, looking out over the sands and the Atlantic. You will eat the freshest fish and *mariscos*, perfectly cooked, and accompanied by a large and well-chosen selection of Portuguese and 'foreign' wines.
Estrada do Guincho
T+351 214 879 450
W www.portosantamaria.com
€75 ♟ *V*
Closed Mon

CASCAIS (PAREDE) A1

Os Prazeres da Carne A vegetarian could find a meal here, by careful selection, and fish-eaters will find plenty to keep them happy, too. But, as you might expect from a restaurant called 'The Pleasures of Meat', there is a lot of meat on the menu. The 'Divine Pleasures'

are mostly prawns and salmon cooked in various ways, and the 'Pleasures of the Flesh' (an alternative translation) are, well, flesh: mostly beef from Argentina. It's a lovely location, perched above a bay to the west of Cascais, attached to the Casa da Guia. Admire the view from the large windows or the open balcony. They describe their style of cooking as 'Brazilian nouvelle cuisine'. The wine list is not long, but it is well-selected, mostly reds.
Casa de São José da Guia,
  Estrada do Guincho
T+351 214 843 334
E prazeres_da_carne@hotmail.com
W www.prazeresdacarne.com
€25-€30 ♟ *V*
Closed Mon lunch

COLARES A1

Colares Velho If you're desperate for a decent cup of tea, Colares Velho also describes itself as a 'Salão de Chá' ('tea room'). We'd probably opt for lunch or dinner, to make the most of the older vintages of Colares on the list. It's in the middle of Colares, in what used to be a grocer's shop, and it still has a part that sells various gourmet goodies, so you can eat well, then do some shopping. It's a light, attractive room, still supported by the slender columns that must have held up the old shop, and the atmosphere is friendly, the service good. The food is creative, with good use of fresh ingredients and a readiness to cater for vegetarians (spinach risotto with walnuts is just one of their inventive suggestions). We're told the kitchen team has just changed (July 2007), so let's hope things have gone from good to even better.
Largo Dr Carlos França 1-4
T+351 219 292 406
€35 ♟ *V!*
Closed Mon, Tue

CORTES C2

Restaurante Casa da Nora There are two strands to the food served in this beautifully restored restaurant just south of Leiria, traditional and modern. Part used to be an olive-oil press, and there are numerous graphic references to this, in drawings on the cream-painted walls, and old implements linked with olive oil, including the old water-wheel used to provide the power. Some of the walls are bare brick, others stone. You have to decide whether to opt for the traditional menu or the *criativa* (creative). Both have good dishes, and people single out the fish soup with coriander, the octopus roasted in olive oil and the chicken cabidela. The 'creative' menu offers goat's cheese with cashews, pears and salad, rack of lamb with rosemary risotto, Gorgonzola, pear and chestnut risotto. And it changes with the seasons.
Largo Poeta José Marques da Cruz 8
T+351 244 891 189
E geral@casadanora.com
W www.casadanora.com
€30 V 🛏
Closed Sun din, Mon

CORUCHE (MONTE DA BARCA) C2

Restaurante Sal e Brasas Here in Portuguese bull-fighting country, down in the south of the Ribatejo, what would the speciality be but grilled beef? (Not that they kill the bulls, but there are a lot of cattle around.) There are good *petiscos*, and meltingly delicious *porco preto* – this is, after all, not far from the cork forests of the Alentejo, and the black pigs. Add rice pudding *(arroz doce)* and a wine list surprisingly strong on Douro reds, and you'll have a good meal. If you're not vegetarian, that is.
Cruzamento do Monte da Barca
T+351 243 618 319
€25 ♀ *No credit cards*
Closed Mon

EREIRA B2

Condestável You might be forgiven for wondering if you had been relocated into a Scottish baronial castle as you gaze round at the wild boars' and stags' heads, crossed swords, hunting horns and other medieval trappings that adorn the stone walls of this extraordinary restaurant, just west of the IP1/E80 motorway as it passes Cartaxo. Extraordinary, because in this setting you will find some of the finest and most modern cooking in Portugal. Luís Suspiro, owner and chef, also has a highly-regarded restaurant in Lisbon (Na Ordem…com Luís Suspiro, *page 240*). His methods are modern (vacuum-packed, low-temperature, slow cooking, for instance), but he is not just a slave to culinary fashion. The menu changes with the seasons, and his imagination. He uses the best ingredients, local if possible: organic extra-virgin olive oil, Alentejo black pig, the best and freshest fish, herbs, vegetables and fruit. Bread is made on the premises. The wine-cellar is up to the standard of a top restaurant. Everything is

done, as he puts it, 'with much soul, care, expertise and love'.
T+351 243 719 786
E geral@condestaveldeluissuspiro.net
W www.condestaveldeluissuspiro.net
€75 ♀ *V*
Closed Sun din, Mon

FÁTIMA C3

Tia Alice If you think exposed stone walls, bare beams and a wooden roof will necessarily mean rustic cooking, you're in for a surprise here. Yes, it is traditional, but at the highest possible level. The cooking is still led by the redoubtable Alice Marto and her younger relations. Dishes such as salt cod in a white sauce, baked in the oven *(bacalhau gratinado)*, duck with rice *(arroz de pato)* and even simple roast chicken (on Saturdays) are delicious. Other classics are fish risotto with sea-bass and monkfish *(arroz de peixe com robalo e tamboril)*, goat simmered for

seven hours in red wine *(chanfana)*, and roast veal. Honey cake *(bolo de noz)* is the preferred pud. The wine list is well chosen, by Alice's son, Nuno, who also gives good suggestions for food matching. It *has* been whispered that some pilgrims come to Fátima just to eat here…
Rua do Adro 152
T+351 249 531 737
E tialice@mail.telepac.pt
€30 ♀ *V*
Closed Sun din, Mon; Jul

LEIRIA (MARRAZES) B3

Tromba Rija Marrazes is barely out of Leiria, on the N1 towards Pombal. This is the original, which has sprouted offspring in Lisbon and Vila Nova de Gaia. It's a place you will not make the most of if you are not hungry. The name, which means 'pig's snout', originates in the *feijoada* that gave birth to this restaurant, whose main meat ingredient was, er, pig's head. It's a long story, which started in a butcher's shop and ended with three very well-known restaurants. This one has bare stone walls with arched niches storing the wines, and tables that groan under somewhere between 50 and 80 dishes. Hot, cold, salads, sausages various, fish, seafood, meats, vegetables – you think of a Portuguese dish, it's probably there. And the beauty of it all is that you help yourself. No language problems, no kids saying 'there's nothing I like on the menu'. Then there are selections of cheeses, and puds. And a very good wine-list. They should really offer somewhere to lie down afterwards…
Rua Professor Portelas 22, Marrazes
T+351 244 852 277
E elisabete@trombarija.com
W www.trombarija.com
€30-€32.50 ♀ *V*
Closed Sun din, Mon lunch

fillet with *farinheira* cream and chestnut purée. The lower ground floor room is bright and airily decorated, and looks out onto the small garden and the city walls. A splendid platter of seafood or fish soup might start your meal, and you can choose safely between dishes based on fresh local fish or tender meat (duck with wild rice risotto, perhaps). The wine list is particularly strong on Estremadura wines.

Óbidos B3

Cozinha das Raínhas Food in this elegant and secluded hotel right inside the city wall of Óbidos has the same understated quality as the accommodation *(page 296)*. It's traditional, but served and presented with modern flair, combining good local ingredients in ways that sometimes surprise with their invention, such as black pork

Rua Padre Nunes Tavares 6
T+351 262 955 360
E reservas@senhorasrainhas.com
W www.senhorasrainhas.com
€35 ♀ V 🛏
Closed 24 Dec din, 25 Dec lunch

Pombal C4

Manjar do Marquês Just off the N1 (that's the *old* main road) as it passes Pombal, this is a large, friendly restaurant and bar, that has been serving traditional Portuguese cooking for over 20 years. Fish fillets with *arroz de tomate* is one of their best-loved dishes. Good *pasteis* and *pataniscas de bacalhau*, roast kid and pork dishes (such as *rojões com migas e morcela de arroz* – chunks of roast pork with fried 'crumbs' and black pudding risotto. The wine-list is good, varied, and reasonably priced.
EN 1 km 151

T+351 236 200 960 / 917 292 830
E paulo@manjardomarques.com
W www.manjardomarques.com
€20 ♀
Closed Sun din; 2nd half July

Rio Maior B2

Restaurante Cantinho da Serra This simple but excellent restaurant looks out over the road to the west of Rio Maior, and is probably the best place to eat in the vicinity. (And it's very close to the fascinating inland salt-pans – *salinas* – of Rio Maior.) We have heard good reports of the kid cooked in red wine, of the snail *feijoada*, of the rabbit casserole and, if you're very hungry, you may wish to order these. But, once you have made the most of the sensational *petiscos*, you may not have room for anything else, except, of course, the platter of varied sweet dishes – the usual Portuguese egg and sugar confections, chocolate mousse, fruit cooked in red wine, and other delights. The *petiscos* are worth the journey. Broad beans and chouriço, pork crackling, cheeses various, enchidos various, stuffed eggs, migas (cubes of broa with cabbage, garlic, olive oil), black pudding, pig's cheek, scrambled eggs with farinheira, octopus salad, cod's roes with tomato salad, it's almost endless. And that's why we didn't have a main course. The selection of wines is wider than local.

Estrada Nacional 1, Alto da Serra
T+351 243 991 367
€20
Closed Mon; July

TOMAR (ALGARVIAS) C3

Chico Elias This is a very popular restaurant, and although it can seat over 100 people, you have to book. According to local legend, the creative brainwaves of Maria do Céu Simões started to vibrate one day when she was left with more snails than she needed to serve by themselves, so she incorporated them into a *feijoada* (bean dish). This was a resounding success, and she has gone on to create several dishes that have become favourites with her customers. Rabbit cooked in a pumpkin, *bacalhau* with pork, and fricassé of eels are some of the most popular. She uses a wood-fired oven, and many of the dishes take 24 hours to prepare. You might finish with some of the local sweet specialities, such as *Fatias de Tomar, doce de feijão com abóbora* (made with haricot beans and pumpkin, but sweet), or *pêras bêbadas* when the local pear trees are producing, cooked in local wine.
Rua Principal 70, Algarvias
T+351 249 311 067
€30 No credit cards
Closed Sun din, Tue; 1st half Sep

TORRES VEDRAS A2

Trás d'Orelha A welcome ray of gastronomic light in Torres Vedras, Trás d'Orelha has a good local wine list (plus some good wines from the Alentejo and Douro) and good, hearty food, mostly traditional Portuguese. Clams or mussels (plain or à Bulhão Pato), lamprey (when in season), black pudding risotto, *cabidela* of duck, lamb stew, roast kid, wild boar, partridge, hare or pheasant (in season), even some fresh fish dishes. (And there's

not a *bacalhau* dish in sight on the current menu!) Heads of stags gone by gaze down rather reproachfully as you eat. The peculiar-sounding restaurant name 'Behind the Ear' is a colloquial expression meaning 'very good'; it refers to the between-friends-and-family Portuguese congratulatory gesture of ear-tweaking!
Rua da Paz 9, Catefica
T+351 261 326 018
W www.trasdorelha.jaleca.net
€20 ♀ V on request
Closed Sun din, Mon; 2nd half Aug

VENTOSA (ATALAIA) B2

Páteo Velho Housed in an old farmhouse, Páteo Velho is now about ten years old, and very popular with locals. It's a rather barn-like room, with simple but pleasant decor, sometimes spreading outside onto the patio. You could start with mixed charcuterie, rocket salad with *presunto* (cured ham), or wild pigeon pie, then continue with roast leg of pork with roast potatoes, *cataplana* of fish, or duck risotto, and finish with pumpkin cake *(toucinho do céu)*. Wash it all down with decent local wines.
Rua 25 de Abril 25, Atalaia
T+351 263 760 466
E maria.a.veloso@vodafone.pt
W www.pateovelho.com
€18-€20 V
Closed Sun din, 2nd half Aug

VENTOSA (LABRUGEIRA) B2

Senhora Tasca It's something of a surprise to find such an adventurous cooking style out here in a small village 12km north-west of Alenquer. The starters are typical, *bacalhau* fritters, scrambled eggs with *farinheira* (a sort of bready sausage), fried mushrooms, beans with chouriço. The duck risotto, however, comes with dates and pine kernels, the

pork fillet with plums and orange, and the beef casserole with 'drunken pears'. By the time you reach the 'three chocolate bavaroise with mint cream', we hope you'll be won over, as are many of the local wine producers. There is a good wine list.
Rua Comendador António Máximo Lopes
*   de Carvalho 25, Labrugeira*
T+351 263 779 205
€25 ♀ V on request
Closed Sun din, Mon; 1st half Aug

VILA FRANCA DE XIRA B2

O Recanto do Ti Pedro (Residencial Flora) It's not an inspiring building – late 1950s, a bit box-like. But the restaurant in this hotel is the best you'll find around. The cooking is modern traditional, not too different to worry the regulars, but sufficiently so to provide welcome variety for travellers. Yes, you'll probably find dishes such as clams with coriander and garlic *(à Bulhão Pato)*, grilled prawns, veal chop – and very well-executed, too. But there are also river fish dishes, and meat dishes with appropriate but slightly unusual sauces. There's a very good wine selection, and lots of good puds.

Rua Noel Perdigão,12
T+351 263 271 272
E residencial.flora@mail.telepac.pt
W www.flora.com.sapo.pt
€20-€25 ♀ 🍴
Closed Sun; mid-Aug-mid-Sep

ALENQUER B2

Real Celeiro *Rua Serpa Pinto 81* and **Quer Vinho e Queijo** *Largo Espírito Santo 2* are two good wine shops in the little town of Alenquer, the commercial centre of Estremadura's most successful wine region.

ALMEIRIM C2

Quinta da Alorna You can just drop in to this appealing roadside wine shop opposite the entrance to Quinta da Alorna. Inside, you'll find deep pink walls with stencilled vine-leaves, and all their wines, together with a few other local products. *Km 73, N118*

BATALHA B3

Vinho em Qualquer Circunstância Is it a shop? Is it a bar? Is it a club? It's all of these, a bar for 16 years, reinvented as a shop/bar/club, encouraging the drinking of good wine, in any circumstances (always in moderation!). Members of the club on the first floor can store up to 24 bottles of wines in their own mini-cellar. We passers-by can buy excellent bottles, and stop for a quick glass and a snack. *Estrada de Fátima 15*

BUCELAS B1

Enoteca Caves Velhas We bet most wine-shops wish they had this much space. Caves Velhas, just round the corner from this posh new shop, are able to display all their wares on handsome shelves and free-standing units. Not just their own wares, either, but selections of non-Portuguese wine and brandies they distribute, and wine accessories. *Rua Dom Afonso Henriques 1*

CALDAS DA RAINHA B3

Estado Líquido *Rua Dr Lionel Cardoso 14* and **Garrafeira Capinha** *Rua Dr Francisco Sá Carneiro 11* are two highly recommended wineshops in Caldas da Rainha.

CASCAIS A1

Cabaz Tinto is a tiny wine-shop specialising in top-quality wines from single estates. *Rua Frederico Arouca 97*

Garrafeira FAH An excellent selection of wine, ports and oils at this shop 300m from the seafront in Cascais. *Rua Visconde da Luz 3*

Market The main covered market sells fish, meat, fruit and veg. *Open Mon-Sat 9-5* Within the Mercado building, a separate Mercado Saloio (Farmers' Market) sells country bread, cheese, charcuterie *(enchidos)*, flowers and more fruit and veg. *Wed-Sat 7-1*

Vinhos à Solta no Dão Wine-shop-cum-winebar on the ground floor of the Casa da Guia. Wide selection of good wines from all over Portugal, and a terrace where you can enjoy them by the glass or bottle, with *petiscos. Avenida Nossa Senhora do Cabo 101*

COLARES A1

Adega Regional de Colares Wonderful old-fashioned wine shop at one end of the Adega Regional building just east of centre in Colares. Worth visiting even if you're not a great fan of Colares wine! *Alameda Coronel Linhares de Lima 32, Banzão*

Ribeirinha de Colares This is the kind of deli-cum-restaurant every neighbourhood should have. They seem to work non-stop, serving lunches and dinners at those times of day, and doing coffees and snacks in between. And they also sell a wide range of excellent cheeses, charcuterie, pastries, pasta, teas, coffees, jams, frozen dishes and a small list of wines (including, of course, Colares) *Avenida Bombeiros Voluntários 71*

ÓBIDOS B3

Casa dos Sabores d'Óbidos This is a coffee house, a cake-shop and a wine-shop rolled into one. A decent array of wines, particularly ports, and also Ginginha (a liqueur made from sour cherries), which you can drink out of a chocolate cup, then eat the cup. *Rua Direita 66*

PENICHE A3

Market Very good fish, flower and vegetable market in the Mercado Municipal. Local fishermen also set out the day's catch at very reasonable prices. *Rua Arquitecto Paulino Montez Mon-Fri 7-2 Sat 6.30-2*

Tasca do Joel The former waiting room for this small restaurant has been turned into a wine and food shop with a very good selection of wines (particularly Douro and Alentejo) as well as an array of hams, patés, oils and other goodies. *Rua do Lapadusso 73*

SAMORA CORREIA B1

Cave Mestre A light, airy shop with wines well-displayed on pale wood shelving. A good wine list, with oils, vinegars, glasses and other accessories. *Azinhaga do Brejo 1*

SINTRA A1

Bar do Binho Quirky shop and wine bar specialising in port (including some ancient vintages) and fine Portuguese cheeses. You can buy by the bottle or by the glass, or take the wines away. *Praça da República 2*

Clube Gourmet, El Corte Inglês As ever, a large selection of wines and spirits from the major European countries as well as Portugal's finest. *Beloura Shopping, Floor 1, Shop C18*

Com Corpo e Alma About halfway between Sintra and Alcabideche, this is a beautiful new wine shop (the owners are architects) selling wines, glasses, cigars, oils, vinegars, chocolates, wine books and wine accessories. They also organise interesting tastings. *Beloura Alpha Mall, Shop 4, Viela da Beloura nº 6, Quinta da Beloura*

Confeitaria Piriquita This is one of the most famous sources of *queijadas de Sintra*, close to the Sintra Palace. They also make *travesseiros* (pillows), of sweet, stuffed pastry, of course. *Rua des Padrias 1*

Pastelaria Sapa Local lore has it that Maria Sapa was the first person to bake the little cheesecake tarts *(queijadas)* for which Sintra is now famous. The premises are now protected by royal decree (though we're not sure how that works in a republic). *Volta do Duche 12*

Explore Lisboa and the Ribatejo

Far left The Bay of Cascais, once upon a time a fishing village

Left Uncrowded for once – the wide beach at Nazaré, and Sintra's unique Pena Palace

West of the capital along the coast, the elegant, cosmopolitan but rather sedate resort of ESTORIL has one of Europe's biggest casinos, a palm-strung promenade around the sandy bay, parks and mansions. CASCAIS is moments away, a fashionable, pretty seaside town upon a fine, broad, sandy beach, with bars, clubs and restaurants. It is also a wealthy commuter town, removed from the bustle of Lisbon, just twenty minutes away. Its western side has kept something of the feel of the fishing village it once was – indeed it is still a fishing port, with bobbing boats and afternoon fish auctions on the beach. Just round the Cabo Raso cape, the Praia do Guincho is probably Portugal's best surfing beach, a breathtaking stretch of pale sand backed by dunes and pines. Beyond its bay is the great rocky promontory of Cabo da Roca, mainland Europe's most westerly point.

Visitors to this windy headland can buy a certificate from the cliff-top tourist office to testify that they've been to the place where 'the land ends and the sea begins'!

Pretty seaside villages lie ahead up the coast, but winelovers may be drawn inland to admire the valiant vines growing in the sand dune vineyards of COLARES. And from here, we head up into the hills to fairy-tale SINTRA. With fine views over the ocean, extravagant palaces, royal and aristocratic summer retreats, mansions and exotic gardens nestle amidst lush green vegetation, on hills and in wooded valleys. The small historic centre of Sintra, a UNESCO World Heritage Site, gets very crowded in summer. The verdant Parque Natural de Sintra-Cascais stretches from here to the coast

Up the coast again, ERICEIRA is a fun place in summer, with old whitewashed houses and steps leading down to good little surfing beaches. PENICHE is a busy fishing port (sardines and lobsters are a speciality) surrounded by a modern high-rise sprawl, but the centre is beautiful, relaxed and atmospheric, the large harbour overlooked by a star-shaped 16th century fort. Now a great headland, it was once an island before the channel silted up in the

Left The Parque de Monserrate, just west of Sintra, 30ha of wild and tended garden

Right Guincho, a stunning surfing beach, caught napping here in a moment of calm

FÁTIMA – VISIONS AND PILGRIMAGE

It was 13 May 1917, and the First World War was raging, but three young children – Lúcia (10), Francisco (9) and Jacinta (7) – were out tending their sheep in the hills around Fátima. And suddenly they saw the figure of the Virgin Mary standing on the branch of an oak tree overlooking the Cova d'Iria spring. Her message was of peace and salvation, according to Lúcia, who was the only one to hear what she said. The 'lady of light' went on to predict the emergence of communism in Russia and the attempt on Pope John Paul's life in 1981. She appeared to the children on the same day every month until 13 October, when she performed the Miracle of the Sun for 70,000 believers and sceptics who turned out to witness the sun spin in the sky before zig-zagging its way towards earth – and back again. Both Francisco and Jacinta died shortly after (which she also predicted) in the great Spanish flu epidemic of 1919, but Lúcia passed away in February 2005 at the ripe old age of 97. A little chapel marks the site of the apparitions; the bullet extracted from Pope John Paul 11 is lodged in the crown of the Virgin's statue. Pilgrims visit all year round (four million people visit the site each year, and there are several masses a day) but the great influx is on the nights of 12 May and 12 October, when thousands gather to celebrate mass in the vast square in front of the neoclassic basilica. To accommodate the thousands, a new, very expensive and highly controversial modern church is due to open in October 2007, to the south-west of the square. A low, round building, sleek and simple and reached by a walkway (some have unkindly compared it to a ping-pong bat or a football stadium), it has a slatted roof to let natural sunlight into the vast interior.

Left The Parque Dom Carlos in the spa town of Caldas da Rainha

Right A curious gargoil watches over the monastery at Batalha, one of the region's World Heritage Sites

16th century. From here you can catch a boat to the rocky BERLENGA ISLANDS with their seabird sanctuary and exciting snorkelling. Around the Peniche headland, the sheltered bay by the village of BALEAL has become a surfing kindergarten, its gentle swells and min-crests perfect for beginners. There are shoals of surfing schools.

On up the coast, the large and crowded seaside resort of NAZARÉ has a centre of narrow streets leading to a wide beach where fish still dries on old wooden racks. North from here, an ancient pine forest, the Pinhal de Leiria, lines the coast. Planted originally to halt erosion as well as to provide wood for ships, it's a beautiful, peaceful walk or picnic, with some quieter beaches, the nicest being SÃO PEDRO DE MUE.

Inland, LEIRIA is the centre of hilly orchard and vineyard country. The town itself is attractive and quiet, dominated by an imposing medieval castle on a wooded hill, with pretty cobbled streets and squares in the old quarter, threaded through by the River Lis.

BATALHA and ALCOBAÇA are obligatory cultural stops, two of Portugal's most beautiful monuments. The Mosteiro da Batalha and the Mosteiro de Santa Maria de Alcobaça *(overleaf)* are both UNESCO World Heritage Sites.

FÁTIMA, to the southeast of Leiria, is one of the most important pilgrimage centres of the Roman Catholic Church. It is the site where three shepherd children had repeated visions of, and messages from, the Virgin Mary early last century *(see opposite)*. Besides the carparks, the many hotels and souvenir shops, the town itself consists

mainly of a vast square (twice the size of St Peter's in Rome), a large white basilica containing the tombs of the three seers, and the large, new and much maligned Igreja da Santissima Trindade.

CALDAS DA RAINHA is a once grand, now faded spa town, treating patients rather than pampering tourists. You should not miss the walled medieval town of ÓBIDOS. Walk the ramparts of the hilltop castle (now a *pousada* hotel) and round the town walls for drop-dead views (barriers are not much in evidence) of windmills, vineyards and surrounding farmlands, while down in the residential area below, narrow cobblestone streets are lined with whitewashed houses and terracotta roofs. In spring and summer the whole town bursts into the colours of geraniums, morning glories and bougainvillaea. The town and castle were rebuilt by King Dinis when he gave the whole town to his wife Isabel as a wedding present in 1282. Queens of Portugal have owned it ever since.

Now we head east, on the new motorway to SANTARÉM, the capital of the Ribatejo. Once a strategic fortress town, it is now a busy agricultural centre where many of the

region's most important fairs and markets take place; the ten-day fair in June is Portugal's most important, and includes bull-running, bull fights and equestrian events. There are fine churches and mansions, a pedestrianised centre whose mosaic pavements include images of the famous bulls. A meandering drive south through the low-lying meadows of the *lezíria*, winds up in CORUCHE, a remote, attractive little town.

Highlight of the northern Ribatejo is TOMAR, a charming little town whose old part on the west bank of the River Nabão has medieval buildings and twisting, cobbled streets and the extraordinary hilltop Convento de Cristo, another Unesco World Heritage Site. It was home of the Knights Templar of recent *Da Vinci Code* fame,

Above The medieval monastery at Alcobaca

Left Obidos castle, a wedding present truly fit for a queen

Right Torre das Cabacas in Santarem; and Obidos

Left The eighth century Castelo dos Mouros, the Moorish Castle, dominates the old town of Sintra. Walk up through the woods for spectacular views from the battlements

whose Order was founded during the First Crusade to keep open the pilgrim routes to the Holy Land.

It's a very short and pleasant drive south to the whitewashed town of CONSTÂNCIA, one of the prettiest places in the area, at the confluence of the Zêzere and Tagus rivers. It was once a Roman town, but its great claim to fame is as the birthplace of the great 16th century poet, Luís Vaz de Camões.

Above the River Tagus, to the west, ABRANTES is another charming town of former strategic importance. It was here that King João I gathered his army before marching to victory at Aljubarrota against the forces of Castile in the 14th century, thus preserving Portugal's independence from Spain.

☀ VIEW FROM THE TOP ☀

AZÓIA **Cabo da Roca** Jutting out from the Serra de Sintra, 18km west of the town, Cape Roca is the westernmost tip of Europe, with fine views of the coast and out to the ocean. A lighthouse, monument and tourist shop mark the spot.

LEIRIA **Castelo** The town's dramatic hilltop castle provides one of the best views in the region, including the famous Pinhal de Leiria, the long coastal pine forest planted by successive kings in the 13th and 14th centuries.

NAZARÉ **Miradouro do Sítio** Reached by funicular from just north of the tourist office, this belvedere looms 110 metres above the town and affords breathtaking views down the coast. *Jul & Aug 7am-2am Sep-Jun 7am-midnight*

SANTARÉM **Jardim das Portas do Sol** Part of the citadel walls from Moorish times, the Gates of the Sun open onto lovely gardens that overlook the Tagus and great plains of the Ribatejo in the distance.

SINTRA **Palácio da Pena** Perched high on the ridge of the Serra de Sintra, the gardens and terraces of this amazing 19th century palace afford tremendous views over the entire Lisbon Coast, with the capital visible when the weather is clear. *Estrada da Pena Open Jun 10-5.30, Jul-15 Sep 10-7, 16 Sep-30 Jun 10-5.30 Closed Mon*

CONSTÂNCIA **Castelo de Almourol** Set majestically on an islet in the middle of the River Tagus, this is a fairy-tale castle of Walt Disney proportions. It was built on the site of a Roman fortress in 1171 by the Grand Master of the Templars, Gauldim Pais. Oh, and it has a ghost as well, that of a Moorish prince who died of love for his captor's daughter, although there are many local variations to this theme! There may be a ferry across, and once there, entrance is free.

LEIRIA **Pinhal de Leiria** Covering some 12,000 hectares, this is one of the oldest state forests in the world. Many of the original trees were brought in from the Landes area of France. Begun in the reign of King Afonso III (1248-1279), it was subsequently developed by King Dinis to curb the spread of the sand dunes which were gradually being blown inland by the strong ocean gusts. The forest later provided a good source of timber for the building of caravels and other types of early seafaring vessel during the Age of Discovery in the 15th and 16th centuries. There are good paths for walking, and picnic and camping places.

MAFRA **Palácio Nacional** Visible from miles around, this enormous and extravagant baroque palace and monastery *(above)* was built during the reign of King João V in one of Portugal's most prosperous periods. The story goes that Franciscan monks managed to persuade the king that his wife would produce a long-awaited heir if he built them a monastery - and magically the first of the royal brood was born soon after. There's much to see, in particular the magnificent library with over 40,000 books in gold embossed leather bindings. *Open Wed-Mon 10-5 Closed Tue Sun free*

MIRA DE AIRE **Grutas de Mira de Aire** These magnificent caves are the largest of many to be found in the 40,000ha Parque Natural das Serras de Aire e Candeeiros. Filled with the most splendid stalagmites and stalactites, it's an underground world of lakes and waterfalls descending 110 metres through a succession of tunnels and walkways, culminating with a spectacular light and water show. *Open Apr & May 9.30-6 Jun & Sep 9.30-7 Jul & Aug 9.30-8.30 Oct-Mar 9.30-5.30*

PENICHE **Ilhas das Berlengas** An archipelago of extraordinary red rock formations 12km out to sea, with spectacular crags, caverns, coves and grottoes. From Peniche, it takes about an hour to reach the largest island, Berlenga Grande, a protected nature reserve with nesting sites for seabirds. It also has a 17th century fort.

VILA FRANCA DE XIRA (POVOS) **Centro Equestre da Lezíria Grande** 3km south of Vila Franca de Xira, this well-organised equestrian centre is very much the hub of the Lusitano horse-breeding region. The Lusitano is a pure-breed horse, very hardy and exceptionally skilled at anticipating his rider's next move. From the battlefield to the bullring, the animal has more than earned his credentials over the centuries, and today can be admired in this most natural of habitats. *Estrada Nacional 1, Povos T+351 263 285 160*

SINTRA **Palácio Nacional** In the main square, dominating the town, this strange but very striking royal palace is a mixture of Moorish, Gothic and Manueline architecture. The central part was built by King João I in the 16th century on the site of a 13th century castle. Highlights include the best collection of Moorish-designed *mudejar* tiles in the country and the Sala dos Cisnes (Swan Room) with its lovely ceiling adorned with 27 gold swans.

MUSEUMS
ALCOBAÇA **Museu Nacional do Vinho** The National Wine Museum has several sections demonstrating white and red wine production over the years, use of barrels, vats and huge old clay Ali-Baba fermentation pots, even an old fashioned tavern. The old winery that houses the collection of over 10,000 exhibits was built in 1875 as a private enterprise, but became a co-operative and was brought up to date in 1948. They began to collect old winemaking equipment in 1968, and when the co-op moved to modern premises in 1976, the building became a museum. *Rua de Leiria, Olival Fechado Open Mon-Fri 9-12.30, 2-5.30 Closed Sat, Sun, public hols*

BOMBARRAL Museu da Companhia Agrícola do Sanguinhal On the fringe of the Estremadura and Ribatejo regions. A tiny museum in a historic winery. *Quinta das Cerejeiras T+351 262 609 190/198 E info@vinhos-sanguinhal.pt*

CARTAXO Museu Rural e do Vinho Much more than a showcase for Ribatejo wines, this recently smartened-up museum in the sports and cultural centre covers a variety of themes such as olive oil production, bull and horse breeding and the traditionally-dressed Ribatejo cowboy known locally as the *campino*. There's also a reconstruction of an old tavern. *Quinta das Pratas, Avenida 25 de Abril Open Tue-Fri 10.30-12.30, 3-5.30 Sat, Sun & public hols 9.30-12.30, 3-5.30 Closed Mon*

MARINHA GRANDE Museu do Vidro Housed in a magnificent palace, the museum gives a good insight into glass-making, important in the town for the past 250 years. The Royal Glass Factory (Real Fábrica de Vidros) was founded in 1748 and run by Englishmen until 1826. It was then given to the state and became one of the country's main producers of glass and fine crystal. *Palácio Stephens Open Tue-Sun 10-6 (7 in summer) Closed Easter, 25 Dec, 1 Jan*

SINTRA Museu do Brinquedo Unusual museum that started as a small, private collection of toys and now houses more than 40,000 exhibits, ranging from lead soldiers and rag dolls to rare colouring books and tin cars. In the shop you can buy collectors' items and antique toys, while another part of the building caters for the restoration of pieces donated to or acquired by the museum. *Rua Visconde de Monserrate Open Tue-Sun 10-6 Closed Mon*

TOMAR Museu dos Fósforos The town has many major attractions, but the most curious must surely be the Match Museum boasting Europe's (if not the world's) largest collection: over 2 million of the striking little objects contained in 43,000 boxes from 122 different countries, some dating back to the early 19th century. What makes this unique museum even more appealing is its peaceful location in the cloisters of a 17th century convent. *Convento de São Francisco Open Wed-Sun Summer Wed-Sun 10-7 Winter 12-5 Closed Mon, Tue, 25 Dec Free*

CHURCHES

ALCOBAÇA Mosteiro de Santa Maria de Alcobaça Vast Gothic abbey built to mark a famous military victory in 1147 when Portugal's first king, Afonso Henriques, took Santarém from the Moors. In gratitude, he vowed to establish a monastery of impressive proportions. The result was one of Europe's finest medieval monuments. Dominating the town in the main square, the church was finished in 1223 and features a soaring nave 110m in length which today maintains its Cistercian austerity, overpowering in its simplicity. Don't miss the grand kitchen, two-storey Cloister of Silence and the tombs of the 'dead queen' Inês de Castro and her royal lover, King Pedro I. *Open Apr-Sep 9-7 Oct-Mar 9-5*

BATALHA Mosteiro de Santa Maria da Vitória Just 20km north-east of Alcobaça stands an equally impressive abbey, the finest example of Gothic architecture in Portugal, founded in the late 14th century to mark another famous triumph, this time King João I's defeat of the Castilians in the Battle of Aljubarrota. Highlights include the Royal Cloister, the Chapter House with its star-vaulted ceiling, and the Founder's Chapel, with the tombs of King João I and his English wife Philippa of Lancaster, along with their most famous son, Henry the Navigator. The world's longest-standing diplomatic union, the Treaty of Windsor, was signed here between Portugal and England on 9 May, 1386. *Open Apr-Sep 9-6 Oct-Mar 9-5 Sun free*

TOMAR Convento de Cristo This important 12th century church dates back to the days of the Reconquest when the Moors were on the run and Portugal was in the process of becoming a nation. The nucleus is the 16-sided Charola, the original Templar church inspired by the Holy Sepulchre in Jerusalem. Tomar became the headquarters of the Order of Christ in Portugal, and this building, with its central octagon of altars, reflects the Order's wealth at the time. Henry the Navigator later added the Gothic cloister and King Manuel I built the church and chapter house in the Manueline style, loaded with symbols of Portugal's new empire in the East. *Open Jun-Sep 9-6.30 Oct-May 9-5.30 Sun free*

FAIRS & FESTIVALS

FEBRUARY ÓBIDOS Festival de Chocolate de Óbidos There's chocolate around every corner of the narrow, cobbled streets of Obidos for the annual ten days of the Chocolate Festival, previously in November, but scheduled for 14 to 24 February in 2008. Admire the amazing chocolate sculptures, observe competitions between chocolatiers and pastry chefs, or take part in chocolate-based cookery classes. There are children's classes too. And, of course, indulge.

MARCH SALVATERRA DE MAGOS **Mês da Enguia** On the south bank of the Tagus not far before it widens into the estuary, Salvaterra de Magos celebrates its month-long Eel Festival, with special eel dishes in all the restaurants.

EASTER MONDAY CONSTÂNCIA **Festa da Senhora da Boa Viagem** A colourful feast dedicated to local fishermen and boatmen who bring their vessels to the edge of town to be blessed. An impressive firework display lights up the night sky and at dinner time the nearby fairground becomes a mass of people huddling around charcoal stoves.

APRIL/MAY CARTAXO **Festa do Vinho** At the turn of the month, this is a fun, local affair with producers' stands, local food and music.

JUNE ÓBIDOS **Mercado Medieval de Óbidos** Popular event early in the month with lots of atmosphere, food and wine. SANTARÉM **Feira Nacional da Agricultura** Portugal's biggest agricultural fair, also known as the **Feira do Ribatejo**, is a nine-day event. It traditionally starts on the first Friday of the month and includes horse shows, riding competitions, bull fights and displays of bull herding and folk dancing, *fado* and folk singing. On-site restaurants give visitors the chance to taste the food and wines of the region. The **Festival Nacional do Vinho do Ribatejo**, with tastings and events, is part of the fair. Finding a hotel during the *Feira* will not be easy.

JULY VILA FRANCA DE XIRA **Festa do Colete Encarnado** One of Portugal's biggest bullfighting festivals, the famous Feast of the Red Waistcoat is so-named because of the traditional costume of the Ribatejo herdsmen. On the eve of the festa, wild bulls run through the streets, galloping freely at tremendous speed, scattering revellers as they go.
TOMAR **Festa dos Tabuleiros** The mother of all festivals *(above)*, with the town emblazoned with brightly-coloured paper flowers, this spectacular ten-day street party consumes the entire region once every four years (the next one is scheduled for 2011). The centuries-old celebration is one of the oldest and most popular cultural and religious events in the Iberian Peninsula. The hightlight is the march of the *tabuleiros*, a lively afternoon parade of young girls in dazzling white dresses carrying tall trays of bread and paper flowers above their heads. The next day, oxen are slaughtered, and families are given meat and bread.

AUGUST BATALHA **Festa de Nossa Senhora da Vitória** Running parallel with the annual fair, the Feast of Our Lady of Victory celebrates Portugal's impressive victory in the Battle of Aljubarrota in 1385. Much of the action takes place in front of the town's magnificent 14th century monastery, recently trumpeted as one of the Seven Wonders of Portugal.

SEPTEMBER NAZARÉ **Romaria** Dedicated to Our Lady of Nazaré, the lively annual festival begins in the second week of the month with townsfolk parading through the streets carrying a statue of the Virgin from the parish church down to the sea. The statue is said to have been brought from Nazareth in the Holy Land by a pilgrim in the 4th century, hence the town's name.

OCTOBER ABRANTES **Feira Nacional de Doçaria Tradicional** Now shifted from June to the last weekend in October, the National Fair of Traditional Sweets and Desserts offers sweet wares from 30 or so exhibitors from all over Portugal, including the islands,

OCTOBER/NOVEMBER SANTARÉM **Festival de Gastronomia** Launched in the early 1980s to showcase the best of Ribatejan cuisine, this important two-week food and wine festival has blossomed into an international event with its own purpose-built venue conveniently located in the centre of town. You can sample food and wine from all over Portugal, Madeira and the Azores. Each day a different region cooks in the central restaurant, and there's local wine, cheeses and other food and crafts on sale.

NOVEMBER GOLEGÃ **Feira Nacional do Cavalo** The great horse fair held every year on the Feast of São Martinho is one of the region's biggest events. Much more than a local affair, top horse breeders and dealers from all over the country, many dressed in traditional costume, bring their best animals for sale. It's also an agricultural fair where farmers buy and sell livestock in preparation for the coming year.

Sleep in Lisboa and the Ribatejo

ALCOBAÇA B3

Hotel Santa Maria Just in front of the abbey, a simple but charming hotel with friendly, attentive staff. Rooms are large, and breakfasts good. It's only five minutes' walk to the wine museum!
Rua Dr Francisco Zagalo 20,
* 2460-041 Alcobaça*
T+351 262 590 160
E hotel.santa.maria@mail.telepac.pt
W www.hotelsantamaria.pt
€40-€60 🛏 *83* Ⓢ *2*

Casa do Vale There's something very intimate and rather bohemian about the decor in this country house. It was purpose-built not so long ago, but has already nestled its way in amongst the hills and vineyards as if it had been here for ever. Decorative herbs in the kitchen, basketweave furniture, rugs and throws, hanging shells, modern art and beautiful use of colour: it would be hard not to relax at the Casa do Vale. A large pool stretches to the terrace edge, with views of the valley, fruit trees and vines, and hammocks beckon here and there. On request, Helen will cook barbecues, or meals: Portuguese, Italian or modern style.
Travessa dos Guedes Reis, Cela,
* 2460-355 Alcobaça*
T+351 919 384 292/ 262 500 243
E helenguedesreis@hotmail.com
W www.casadovale.net
€75-€85
🛏 *3* ✕ *on request* ⚓ *No credit cards*

AZÓIA A1

Quinta do Rio Touro A charming jumble of red-roofed, white-walled houses peeps out from the lush vegetation. The 3ha organic farm lies within walking distance of the village of Azóia, in the little valley of the River Touro. The Cabo da Roca, Europe's eastern-most point, is

only 5km away, Sintra, Estoril and Cascais nearby. It belongs to former diplomats Maria Gabriela and Fernando Reino, who restored the land and its buildings, and now grow limes and other fruit trees alongside delightful gardens and pine woods, and have filled their house with memories of their world-wide postings. There are three suites in the main house, two in the guest house, the Casa das Hortas, 100m away amidst the crops, and another house has just been completed. Suites can house a couple, or families of three or four. Relax in the long pool, on the secluded patio with sea views, or amidst the books in the library.
Caminho do Rio Touro, Azóia,
* 2705-001 Colares*
T+351 219 292 862
E info@quinta-riotouro.com
W www.quinta-riotouro.com
€120-€200 🛏 *6* Ⓢ *2* ⚓
Min nights 2 or 3

AZÓIA DE CIMA B2/3

A Nossa Casa In a village north of Santarém in the Ribatejo, an attractive, cosy house dating from the early 20th century, furnished with antiques. Rooms are comfortable and elegant, and there are open fires in the common areas in winter.
Rua Maria do Rosário Tainha,
* 2025-452 Azóia de Cima*
T+351 243 479 118/ 964 067 007
E casqueiroachete@gmail.com
€55 🛏 *5* *No credit cards*

CASCAIS A1

Casa da Pérgola A historic Cascais mansion with wood-panelled and stucco ceilings, *azulejos,* marble or polished wood floors, antiques and paintings and pretty colours. There are ten comfortable en-suite rooms to rent, with joint use of a guest sitting room and dining room and the rampant, flowery garden. It's two minutes' walk to the beach, and you're right in the centre of town.
Avenida Valbom 13, 2750-508 Cascais
T+351 214 840 040
E pergolahouse@vizzavi.pt
W www.pergolahouse.com
€80-€129
🛏 *10* *No credit cards Closed Dec-Feb*

CASCAIS A1 *(continued)*
Fortaleza do Guincho Perched dramatically on a cliff above the crashing surf and wide, sandy beach, this isolated fortress was originally built to spot invaders. The views (from every room) are still superb – many rooms have glazed balconies. The sturdy, once-grey building has been painted yellow, and well-designed comforts have been installed within. The formal restaurant *(page 281)* is very highly-rated, and breakfasts are very good.
Estrada do Guincho, Cascais 2750-642
T+351 214 870 491
E reservations@guinchotel.pt
W www.guinchotel.pt
€180-€280 🛏*24* Ⓢ*3* ⚥ ✗ ⚓*sea*

CORTES
Casa da Nora A former farmhouse by the side of the River Liz, in a village just south of Leiria, with seven modern guest rooms. It's a characterful little hotel, with a pretty garden and courtyard. A very good restaurant offers a choice of creative cuisine or good traditional Portuguese *(page 282)*. They sometimes run cookery courses.
Largo Poeta José Marques da Cruz 8,
*   Cortes, 2410-847 Leiria*
T+351 244 891 189
E geral@casadanora.com
W www.casadanora.com
€75-€95 🛏*7* ✗ ⚓

ESTORIL A1
Hotel Palácio Estoril This grand, historic hotel on the seafront has been newly refurbished. Rooms are plush, bathrooms spacious. There are magnificent, mature gardens to the rear, and it's a 200m walk to the beach. A new spa is due to open during 2008.
Rua Particular, 2769-504 Estoril
T+351 214 680 400
E info@hotelestorilpalace.pt
W www.palacioestorilhotel.com
€200-€350 🛏*129* Ⓢ*32* ✗ ⚓

MAFRA (GRADIL) A2
Quinta de Sant'Ana This enchanting wine quinta *(page 265)* is half an hour from Lisbon, nestling just over the hill from the great palace of Mafra amidst vineyards and eucalyptus woods, orchards and paddocks. The family is German/English, the atmosphere nevertheless as Portuguese as you could wish. There are various houses to rent, all deep ochre yellow on the outside, beautifully furnished and decorated in bright, fresh colours within. Spacious Casa Marreco is modern yet mellow, set apart on a hilltop with great views, a lovely terrace and its own garden and pool. The other two houses are within the mature gardens by the main house, and share its pool (and trampoline). Casa da Adega was once a distillery, next to the winery, small and cosy with a secluded cobbled courtyard shaded by olive trees. Casa do Caseiro is the old lodge beside the main family house *(above right)*, charmingly rustic. All are child-friendly. There's an old chapel, and a former theatre and below it a converted olive press and terrace, which are used now for weddings and events. You can buy the *quinta's* delicious wine, fruit and vegetables, honey, *marmalada* and jams.

Gradil, 2665-113 Mafra
T +351 261 961 224
E ann@quintadesantana.com
W www.quintadesantana.com
Adega €516-935, Caseiro €562-956,
*   Marreco €1,052-2,042 per week*
ⓈⒸ*3(4+2, 6+1, 8+2)* ⚥ ✗*on request* ⚓
No credit cards

ÓBIDOS B3
Casa das Senhoras Rainhas A very special little hotel right by the city walls, beautifully renovated in a style that is modern but in keeping with the spirit of the old building.
Staff are friendly and helpful. You'll be keen to get out of your comfortable bed, because breakfast is delicious and beautifully

presented, on the terrace or in the cheery yellow dining room. Meals in the restaurant are very good, too *(page 284)*. Don't bring too much luggage – parking is difficult in little Óbidos, and you may have to trundle your suitcase some way over cobbles.
Rua Padre Nunes Tavares 6,
*   2510-102 Óbidos*
T+351 262 955 360
E info@senhorasrainhas.com
W www.senhorasrainhas.com
€144-€186 🛏*10* ⚥ ✗

OURÉM C3

Casa Alta Should you wish to visit the shrine at nearby Fátima, Father Mariani will provide transport free of change. High up by the castle, this is a wonderful medieval house, with luxuriously appointed rooms and bathrooms, and breath-taking views. The house was completely renovated in 2003. Catherine of Bragança spent her last night here before leaving for England to marry Charles II. Outside, a sweet crazy-paved terraced garden has a swimming pool. All faiths can worship together in

the chapel. There's English-style breakfast, and meals on request, at a communal table.
Castelo de Ourém, 2490-000 Ourém
T+351 249 543 515
E casa.alta@gmail.com
W www.casaaltaroyallodge.com
€95 (small) €150 (standard)
🛏3 ✗ *No credit cards*

Pousada Conde de Ourém It's the location of this pousada that is so wonderful, within the walled streets of hilltop, medieval Ourém, just below the castle. Two medieval houses and a former hospital have been converted to form accommodation around a pretty courtyard. Inside, décor is simple and surprisingly modern. Food is not the strong point.

Largo João Manso, Castelos,
2490-481 Ourem
T+351 249 540 920
E recepcao.ourem@pousadas.pt
W www.pousadas.pt
€108-€216
🛏30 ✗ ≈

Quinta da Alcaidaria-Mor Just outside Ourém on the road to Tomar, there are rooms to let in a smart and cosy country house with antiques, ancestral paintings, fine wood-panelled ceilings and open fires. It was built 300 years ago for the king's personal physician. It's a friendly place with large en-suite bedrooms, a pool in the garden, and peaceful farmland round about.
2490-799 Ourem
T+351 249 542 231
E geral@quintaalcaidaria-mor.pt
W www.quintaalcaidaria-mor.pt
€90-€115 SC €125
🛏6 [SC] 4(4+2) ✗*on request* ≈
No credit cards

OUTEIRO DA RANHA C4

Casa do Vale do Papo In the sturdy, rocky countryside of the Serra de Sicó, about 8km south-east of Pombal, there are three en-suite guest rooms in a collection of white and stone farm buildings, which in parts are very old indeed. The rooms have been simply and tastefully renovated, incorporating and highlighting historic features, with the addition of smart, modern woodwork. Guests have use of a kitchen, dining room, sitting room with fireplace, and a patio with barbecue. There's a pool, and a rocky, lawned garden. In high season it is rented only as a whole house, but individual rooms can be rented out of season.
Rua Ferreira Gomes 1, Outeiro da Ranha,
3100-766 Pombal
T+351 236 217 663/ 917 509 371
E info@casadovale.com
W www.casadovale.com
€70 🛏3 ≈ *No credit cards*
Min nights 7 in high season

PEGO D3

Quinta de Coalhos In an *Alice in Wonderland* castle *(above)*, complete with turrets and pinnacles, fountain and knight in stony armour, there are three colourful rooms and one suite to rent. The house was built in a curious mix of styles in the early years of the 20th century by a doctor-vet with a passionate interest in sculpture and painting. It has been renovated over the past 20 years by Maria

Isabel and José Alberti. Guests share a sitting room with huge open fire, and an ornate swimming pool in the gardens.
Lugar de Coalhos, Estrada Nacional 118, Pego, 2205-306 Abrantes
T+351 241 833 294 / 967 018 436
E quintadecoalhos@mail.telepac.pt
W www.quintadecoalhos.com
€90-€100
🛏3 ⑤1 ♀ ✗ *on request* ⇌
No credit cards
Min nights 2, or 1 at higher rate

PORTO DE MÓS B3
Quinta de Rio Alcaide This beautiful stone house was once a water-driven

paper mill, amidst pine forest on the slopes of the Parque Natural das Serras de Aire e Candeeiros. There are en-suite rooms and various cottages and converted farm buildings to let, including an old windmill. A swimming pool and small lake in the garden are fed by a natural spring, and a river runs through the property. Rooms are elegantly rustic, tastefully and cosily decorated; one has an open fireplace. There are horses.
T+351 244 402 124
E rioalcaide@mail.telepac.pt
€48-€50 ⓈⒸ *€40-€145*
🛏3 ⓈⒸ *8(2+1, 2+2, 4+2, 6+2)* ⇌
No credit cards

RIO MAIOR B2
Casa do Foral In the centre of Rio Maior, this ivy-clad house has spacious guest rooms and a modern relaxation area with snooker, dining room, bar and sofas. The hosts' sitting room has a beautiful panel of *azulejos* at which you should peek. Wine lovers will find a friend – Carlos Madeira is passionate about wine, and has converted an ancient fruit store, buried a cool eight metres deep in his garden, into a fabulous wine cellar. Rio Maior is just 3km from the hills of the natural park.
Rua da Boavista 10, 2040-302 Rio Maior
T+351 243 992 610
E info@urbilazer.com or moinhoforal@hotmail.com
W www.casadoforal.com
€65 🛏6 ♀ ⇌

SANTARÉM C2
Casa da Alcáçova What a privilege to be able to stay in a manor house within the ramparts of Santarém's hilltop castle! You could not wish for finer views, down over the *lezíria,* the Ribatejo's green and fertile river plains. Eight guest rooms are plush and classic in design. There's a pool beside the medieval walls, a small gym, and the remains of a Roman temple. Breakfasts are very good.
Largo da Alcáçova 3, Portas do Sol, 2000-110 Santarém
T+351 243 304 030
E info@alcacova.com

W www.alcacova.com
€125-€175
🛏7 ⑤1 ♀ ✗*on request* ⇌

SÃO PEDRO DE TOMAR C3
Quinta do Troviscal A very special place overlooking the Castelo de Bode dam, where there are rooms and a renovated cottage to rent. Beyond the lawn, the bank drops steeply to the water, where a small rowing boat is moored on the floating jetty – no motor boats are allowed to disturb the peace. Rooms are decorated with perfect simplicity. There's freshly-squeezed orange juice and home-made jam for breakfast. Across the cobbled walkway from the main house, the Casa dos Monstros (Monster House) was named by the owners' children because once upon a time it was abandoned, trees growing from its windows. Now it's a delightful holiday cottage. The owners are on hand, and as friendly as their horses and labradors.
Castelo de Bode, 2300-186 São Pedro
T+351 249 371 318 / 917 333 456.
E vera@troviscal.com
W www.troviscal.com
€85-1€20 ⓈⒸ *€150-€200*
🛏2 ⑤1 ⓈⒸ *1(4+2+2children)*
⇌ *in reservoir*
Min nights 3 (cottage 7) in high season

SINTRA A1

Lawrence's Hotel Said to be the oldest hotel in Portugal (1764), just a few minutes' walk from the centre of Sintra, the charming Lawrence's has a good restaurant. It is small, luxuriously and tastefully decorated and furnished; all rooms have king sized beds. It has a wooded garden, delightful, cosy public rooms, and lots of little corners to sit and read or relax. Staff are very helpful.

Rua Consigliéri Pedroso 38-40,
* 2710-550 Sintra*
T+351 219 105 500
E geral@lawrenceshotel.com
W www.lawrenceshotel.com
€201-€307
🛏11 ⑤5 ✗

SINTRA (LINHÓ) A1

Penha Longa Hotel & Golf Resort
A large, luxurious, brightly decorated modern hotel with attentive service in a beautiful location in the southern Sintra hills *(below)*. This was the site of a 14th century monastery, then a royal palace in the 17th and 18th centuries. The views are spectacular. There are five restaurants, the Arola is very good, with nice wine. Surrounding the hotel are gardens, tennis courts and a running track, adult and children's pools, an 18-hole championship golf course and a less demanding 9-hole course. There are squash courts, and a new spa.

Estrada da Lagoa Azul, Linhó,
* 2714 -511 Sintra*
T+351 219 249 011
E resort@penhalonga.com
W www.penhalonga.com €
€350
🛏150 ⑤44 ♀ ✗ ⚓ ♨ 🏋 ✒ ✎

SINTRA A1

Quinta da Capela A magical place, a small hotel in a ducal manor that was rebuilt after the great Lisbon earthquake. The small chapel *(Capela)* survived – it has a domed and ribbed Manueline ceiling, and *azulejos* cover the walls; a mass is usually held there on Sundays. In the woods outside Sintra, near the Monserrate palace, the quinta has beautiful gardens with box-edged lawns and mature trees. Bedrooms are charming and comfortable, the drawing room/library a restful spot to unwind. There's a small gym and sauna, and a little pool hidden in the garden.

Estrada Velha de Colares, 2710-502 Sintra
T+351 219 290 170
E quintadacapela@hotmail.com
W www.quintadacapela.com
€140 🛏5 ⑤2 ⑤ᶜ2(4) ⚓ 🏋

SOBRAL B2

Quinta Salvador do Mundo Only 30 minutes from Lisbon but set amidst peaceful countryside with sweeping views, this old stone farmhouse has been lovingly restored, and comfortably furnished with antiques. Relax on the long veranda or cobbled terrace, or in the garden, and dine in the shadow of an old wine press. There's a swimming pool with a view, and a pool table.

T+351 261 942 880
E quintasalvador@ip.pt
W www.quintasalvador.com
€105-€130
🛏9 ✗*on request, min 12 people* ⚓
No credit cards
Closed Nov-Feb
Min nights 2

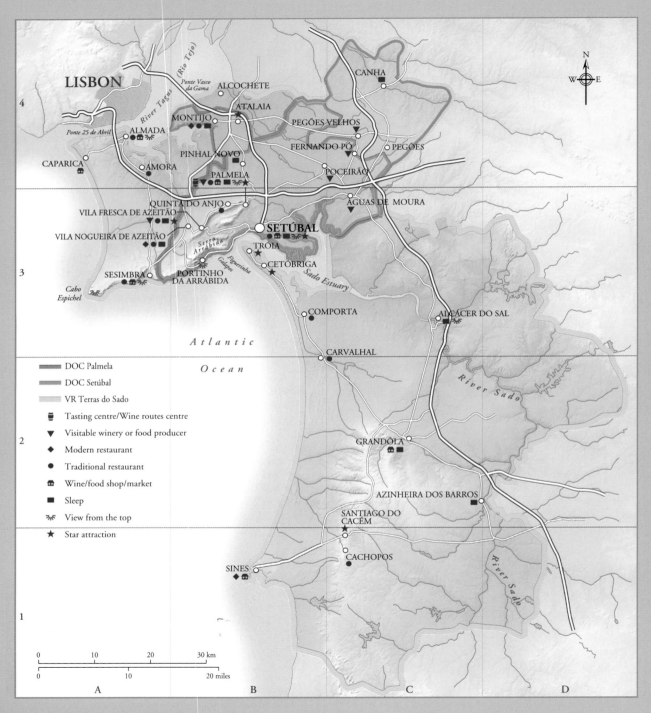

LISBON

Rio Tejo

Ponte Vasco da Gama

ALCOCHETE

CANHA

ATALAIA

PEGÕES VELHOS

MONTIJO

Ponte 25 de Abril

ALMADA

FERNANDO PÓ

PEGÕES

PINHAL NOVO

CAPARICA

AMORA

PALMELA

POCEIRÃO

QUINTA DO ANJO

ÁGUAS DE MOURA

VILA FRESCA DE AZEITÃO

SETÚBAL

VILA NOGUEIRA DE AZEITÃO

Serra da Arrábida

TRÓIA

Figuerinha Galápos

CETÓBRIGA

SESIMBRA

PORTINHO DA ARRÁBIDA

Sado Estuary

Cabo Espichel

COMPORTA

ALCÁCER DO SAL

Atlantic

CARVALHAL

Ocean

River Sado

DOC Palmela

DOC Setúbal

VR Terras do Sado

Tasting centre/Wine routes centre

GRANDÔLA

Visitable winery or food producer

Modern restaurant

AZINHEIRA DOS BARROS

Traditional restaurant

Wine/food shop/market

SANTIAGO DO CACÉM

Sleep

View from the top

Star attraction

SINES

CACHOPOS

River Sado

N
W E

0   10   20   30 km

0   10   20 miles

A   B   C   D

Terras do Sado

You can see the northern shore of the Setúbal Peninsula from Lisbon across the River Tagus, with the impressive figure of Cristo-Rei (Christ the King) dominating the shoreline. For years, the only way across was the ferry, or the 25 de Abril Bridge, with horrific jams at peak hours. Since 1998, the Vasco da Gama bridge has changed all that. With its six lanes of traffic, it spans an impressive 17.2km (making it the longest bridge in Europe), crossing from 6km north of Lisbon centre to link up with the motorway down to Setúbal town. These days, Lisbon folk flood here for weekends on the 'Costa Azul', or for a night out in a good restaurant. Many even commute daily into the city. You'll definitely bump into more Portuguese than foreign tourists.

Join the exodus from Lisbon, or make this your base. Though the beaches are busy, there is great surfing down the Atlantic coast, as well as calm, child-friendly, diver-friendly coves in the south. There is good fishing, scuba diving, riding, and some top golf courses. Explore the quiet streets of Palmela and Sesimbra, and the busy working port of Setúbal.

Escape to the east, to the wildlife-rich Nature Reserves of the Sado and Tagus Estuaries – two of the richest areas for wetland birds in Portugal, and places of pilgrimage for bird-lovers from all over the world. Or to the Arrábida Natural Park, a range of limestone hills towering over the southern coast, where well-charted walks criss-cross the unspoiled woodlands, dairy sheep graze in the hillside meadows, and Moscatel vines produce grapes for the famous sweet Setúbal wine.

Wine grapes have been grown here for centuries, by the Phoenicians, the Romans, the Arabs... The two wine DOCs are Setúbal and Palmela, as well as an increasingly successful Vinho Regional, Terras do Sado. The gooey Azeitão cheeses are renowned throughout Portugal. There are fish markets to die for, and some very good seafood restaurants, merging into meatier fare the nearer you get to the Alentejo.

This chapter covers the Setúbal peninsula and also takes a large bite into the Alentejo, down the coast towards Sines, and inland towards the source of the River Sado near Ourique. This, the Setúbal *concelho* (county), is the area in which Vinho Regional Terras do Sado may be made.

Wine in the Terras do Sado

The Terras do Sado's proximity to Lisbon means that houses are a more profitable crop than vines these days. But vineyards are still very important in local agriculture. Two grapes dominate the Setúbal peninsula DOCs, white Moscatel and red Castelão. **DOC Setúbal** is the famous, historic wine of the region – a sweet, fortified wine made mostly from Muscat grapes grown in the centre and south of the peninsula, around the towns of Palmela, Setúbal and Sesimbra. Many of the vines grow on the limestone slopes of the Arrábida Natural Park. Until the EU took an interest, these wines had been known as 'Moscatel de Setúbal' for nearly a century. According to local rules, a minimum of 67 per cent Moscatel grapes in the blend would suffice. That wasn't enough for the EU, which stipulates a minimum of 85 per cent if a wine is to be labelled as being from one grape. You will still find some labelled **Moscatel de Setúbal** and **Moscatel Roxo** (a red member of the Muscat family), if they have the required 85 per cent Moscatel grapes. But others have dropped the 'Moscatel de' from their labels. The best, most aromatic Muscat of Alexandria grapes come from the cooler, north-facing Arrábida vineyards perched high above the rocky coast.

Wine regions
DOC Palmela
DOC Setúbal
Vinho Regional Terras do Sado

Main local grapes
Red Castelão
White Moscatel

For details of grapes see page 428

The grapes are fermented in contact with their flavour-rich skins, and alcoholic fermentation is stopped by adding grape brandy. Then the wines macerate on the skins for three to four months, before spending at least two years maturing in oak barrels or vats. Most Setúbal is sold soon after this minimum maturing period, when it's fresh and lively, often with flavours of orange, lemon and flowers. However, there are **aged Setúbal Moscatels**, made in very limited quantities, mostly by the two best-

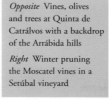

Opposite Vines, olives and trees at Quinta de Catrálvos with a backdrop of the Arrábida hills

Right Winter pruning the Moscatel vines in a Setúbal vineyard

known producers on the peninsula, José Maria da Fonseca and Bacalhôa Vinhos de Portugal. These can be very complex wines, and are well worth seeking out: they are some of the finest fortified Muscats in the world. Both companies also produce small quantities of the rose-scented, fortified **Moscatel Roxo**.

DOC Palmela covers most of the same area as that of Setúbal, and extends up to the north coast of the peninsula as well, around the town of Montijo, and further north-east, to take in Pegões. It comes in both red and white versions, though there's far more red, mostly made from Castelão. The red Castelão grape ripens more effectively here than anywhere else in Portugal. In fact, in most of Portugal this is a grape in retreat, as growers pull it up or graft it over to other varieties, complaining how hard it is to ripen. But on the warm, sandy soils around the town of Palmela in the eastern part of the Setúbal peninsula and the land immediately further east, with plenty of sun but cooled by Atlantic breezes, Castelão attains a balance that

combines complex red fruit flavours with brisk acidity and ripe tannins.

Red Palmela has to be at least 67 per cent Castelão, with help from Alfrocheiro, Bastardo, Cabernet Sauvignon and Trincadeira. Since 75 per cent of the vines planted in the entire Terras do Sado are Castelão, red Palmela is usually more than 67 per cent! **White Palmela** is mostly made from Fernão Pires, with some Moscatel in the Arrábida part of the DOC.

There's a very flexible choice of grapes for the **Vinho Regional Terras do Sado** wines (as is often the way with VR). Terras do Sado is the name given to the Vinho Regional region that includes the whole of the Setúbal peninsula together with a large stretch of land further south. Soils, altitude and inclination to the sun vary enormously. Even though the vineyards bordering on the VR Alentejano region offer some of the best conditions in Portugal for the Castelão red grape, a vast array of grapes from other countries and areas of Portugal is permitted for VR. The local rules have not included Sangiovese and Nebbiolo for reds, and Chenin Blanc and Silvaner for whites, but that might change. Apart from those, just about every grape from Alvarinho to Zinfandel is being planted. Go-ahead producers take full advantage of this. Syrah, Tannat and Touriga Nacional are already making good wines.

PALMELA

Casa Mãe da Rota de Vinhos da Península de Setúbal e Costa Azul

Let's hope you won't need to ask your way to this delightful and helpful place! A tasting room and 'Wine Routes' information centre, in a former winery, it provides an easy opportunity to 'taste around' the region. It offers maps, good suggested routes, a wonderful website (currently only in Portuguese), and can set up appointments for you to visit the ten participating wineries. There are exhibitions, and you can buy wines here too.

Largo de São João
T+351 212 334 398
E rotavinhos.psetubal@mail.
telepac.pt
W www.rotavinhospsetubal.com
Open Mon-Sat 10-1, 2-5.30
Closed Sun, public hols

ÁGUAS DE MOURA C3

Hero do Castanheiro Monte do
Castanheiro and the vineyards that
surround it were given to Artur Oliveira's
grandfather by Artur's great grandfather.
The company, which started selling wines
in bottle only in 1998, makes mainly red
wines in a traditional style, using *lagares* for
fermentation and French and American oak
for maturing the wines. The family owns
about 13ha of vines, 90 per cent of which
are Castelão. The other ten per cent are
Fernão Pires, the traditional white variety
of the region. Most vines are 35 years old,
with smaller amounts replanted more
recently. Artur Oliveira makes the wines,
assisted by oenologist António Saramago,
known for his adherence to traditional
methods. They make complex, traditional
reds, which evolve well in bottle.
Monte do Castanheiro, PO Box 34,
*   2965-999 Águas de Moura*
T+351 265 913 250
E info@herodocastanheiro.pt
W www.herodocastanheiro.pt
Wine-shop Mon-Fri 9-12.30, 1.30-6
*   Sat 10-4*
Visits appt only
Wine & food tastings (gps only) from €15

AZEITÃO B3

Bacalhôa Vinhos de Portugal This
is the headquarters of one of Portugal's
largest wine producers, Bacalhôa Vinhos de
Portugal. The company is mostly owned
by one of Portugal's wealthiest men, Joe
Berardo, a great patron of the modern
arts, whose love for the decorative arts is
evident at all the wineries in the group.
The Azeitão winery is thoroughly modern,
and the mix between art and wine makes it
really worth a visit. As you drive in off the
E4/N10, you see a vast, white, hexagonal
umbrella structure, covering offices, ware-
housing and ageing cellars. Just in front of

the entrance are some ancient olives,
rescued from under a proposed dam and
transplanted here. Off to the right is a
late-20th century temple to wine – a
circular arrangement of gleaming stainless
steel tanks, rising through four concentric
circles to the tallest in the middle.

You walk in past some copies of soldiers
from Emperor Qin's famous terracotta
army. The visit starts with a viewing of the
largest collection of *azulejo* tiles in Portugal,
the earliest from 15th century Spain. Then
you will go to the Moscatel ageing cellar,
a semi-circular ex-greenhouse, in which
the barrels of sweet Moscatel sit in the
baking sun (which accelerates the process
of ageing). After that, it's off to see two
million bottles of red wine ageing in the
red wine cellar, and a quick visit to the
two bottling lines.

Outside, you'll be shown the gleaming
steel vinification tanks. A quick look at
the 5ha of vineyards near the winery comes
next, followed by a tour of the Japanese
garden, decorated with sculptures by the
renowned sculptor Nizuma, and featuring
a persimmon tree directly descended from
one that survived the atomic bomb on
Nagasaki. Your winetasting will be in the
shop, your last stop on the tour, and the
standard pair of wines includes a red,
Serras de Azeitão and the sweet white
JP Moscatel de Setúbal. Do try it, even
if you don't normally drink sweet wines.

João Pires & Filhos Lda, as the company
was known originally, started back in the
Algarve as a small business dealing in bulk
wine in 1922. It moved to the Setúbal
peninsula in 1966, but it was the arrival
of António Francisco d'Avillez as majority
shareholder in 1972 that set the company
on its present course, to become one of
Portugal's largest producers and exporters
of wine in bottle.

Avillez decided that selling wine in
bottle was the way forward. He created
**Tinto da Ânfora, Má Partilha, Catarina,
Cova da Ursa** and **Quinta da Bacalhôa**, all
brands you will still see in the range. Peter
Bright *(page 269)* was his winemaker, a
young Australian who had arrived in
Portugal in 1974 and liked the country
and its grapes.

Avillez also started building wineries in
different wine regions. As well as his base
on the Setúbal peninsula, he had estates in
Alentejo (Herdade das Ânforas, *page 325*),
Vinho Verde, Bairrada and Carcavelos. He
bought Quinta dos Loridos, in Carvalhal,
near Óbidos, a specialist producer of
sparkling wines *(page 262)*. Then the
Berardo family got involved, and were
majority shareholders by 1998. This was
also the first year JP Vinhos (the new
name) made its wines at the new winery
at Quinta da Bassaqueira. Quinta da
Bacalhôa was added to the portfolio in
2000. The Palacio da Bacalhôa *(page 317)*

is a wonderfully restored historic house, dating from the first half of the 16th century. It also has a vineyard of Cabernet Sauvignon and Merlot, from which the first bottled wine was sold in 1979.

In 2005, JP Vinhos changed its name to Bacalhôa Vinhos de Portugal (BVDP). Joe Berardo is also a shareholder in Quinta do Carmo in the Alentejo *(page 332)*, Henriques & Henriques in Madeira *(page 404)*, Sogrape and, most recently, Caves Aliança.

The wines made by the Bacalhôa Vinhos de Portugal team from all three of the wineries are very reliable. We deal here with the ones that originate in the Terras do Sado. **Catarina** is an excellent value, inexpensive lightly oaked white blend of Fernão Pires and Chardonnay, which develops surprisingly well with a touch of bottle age. **Cova da Ursa** is a barrel-fermented Chardonnay – probably Portugal's best straight Chardonnay. **Quinta da Bacalhôa** is a blackcurrant Cabernet Sauvignon, softened by 10% Merlot, and **Palácio da Bacalhôa** is a rich but elegant, complex Cabernet-based wine, with about a third of Merlot and a dash of Petit Verdot. **Só Touriga Nacional** is a gloriously aromatic solo Touriga Nacional. All of these are VR Terras do Sado. The DOC Palmela **Private Selection Palmela** is a lovely example of a more traditional style of red from the Castelão grape.

Then there are the Moscatel wines. Even the basic **JP Moscatel** is good, and the older versions are increasingly complex, delicious and, of course, expensive. The **1983 20 year old Moscatel** is fresh yet wonderfully complex, with aromas of orange peel, old wood, nuts and flowers. But not as floral as the **Moscatel Roxo** (red Muscat), delicate and complex, with rose-petal aromas.

Quinta da Bassaqueira, Estrada Nacional 10, Vila Nogueira de Azeitão, 2925-901 Azeitão
T +351 212 198 060
E info@bacalhoa.pt
W www.bacalhoa.pt
Visits Mon-Thu 9-6, Fri 9-12.30 (appt only) Sat/Sun min 25 people
Cost €2
Wine shop Mon-Sat 9.30-6
E lojadovinho@bacalhoa.pt

José Maria da Fonseca You have two options if you want to visit José Maria da Fonseca (JMF) at their home base in Azeitão. Either you can go to the historic Manor House Museum, still used for wine ageing but otherwise serving as a visitor reception centre, or to their new FSF winery, very close to the Bacalhôa winery.

The Manor House Museum is a lovely 19th century building, restored in 1923, and home to the Soares Franco family until 1974. Here you'll learn about the history of the company, take a walk in the gardens behind the house, and visit three of the old cellars. Then you'll taste a couple of JMF wines, one of their famous Muscats and one other. You can order what JMF call a 'special tasting', with more wines, even some food, for which there is a charge, the price depending on what you have.

That's probably a better option than visiting the modern FSF winery (named after Fernando Soares Franco, father of António and Domingos Soares Franco, who currently run JMF.) This is a large, modern winery, refurbished and re-opened by JMF in 2001, with over 400 vats as well as lagars for foot-treading grapes during fermentation. (It has the same address, Quinta da Bassaqueira, as the Bacalhôa winery, as they used to form part of the same estate.)

The company was started in 1834 by José Maria da Fonseca, a young maths graduate from the Dão region, who had settled in the Setúbal Peninsula. He was ahead of his time, and opted to sell wine in bottle rather than barrel, as was more usual at the time. Periquita was his first big brand (and still the JMF wine with the greatest world-wide reputation). He also sold Setúbal Moscatel, and Palmela

Superior. After his death in 1884, the firm prospered, selling to Brazil, until the world-wide recession of the 1920s. They had to sell off some vineyards to keep going, and it was not till António Porto Soares Franco created two rosés, Faisca in 1937, and Lancers in 1944, that JMF regained its old momentum.

JMF has since been very successful, creating more brands such as **BSE** (yes, really – it stands for Branco Seco Especial – 'Special Dry White'), **Terras Altas** (from Dão) and **Pasmados**, and launching special red wines from the Setúbal peninsula vineyards as Garrafeiras, identified with initials, **RA** ('região Algeruz' – Vinha Grande de Algeruz is JMF's biggest vineyard in the region), **CO** ('clara de ovo' – clarified with egg-white) and **TE** ('tinto especial' – special red). Now, António and Domingos Soares Franco, the sixth generation of the family in the business, have launched a range of very posh wines,

305

including the excellent, complex **Hexagon** (six generations of family, six grapes – Touriga Nacional, Syrah, Trincadeira, Tinto Cão, Touriga Franca and Tannat), the dark, smooth **FSF** (in tribute to Fernando Soares Franco – Syrah, Trincadeira and Tannat, foot-trodden and lagar-fermented), the dense, rich **Domini Plus** from the Douro and the three Garrafeira wines, now just known by their 'code' initials. **RA** and **CO** are pure Castelão, and **TE** blends in Cabernet Sauvignon as well.

Fortified Muscats remain a particular speciality of JMF. These rise from a fresh, orangey, young **Moscatel**, through a complex, nutty **20 year-old**, up to the light, floral **DSF Private Selection** (with Armagnac used for the fortification) and finally up to the **20 year-old Moscatel Roxo** (a rare red variety of Muscat) and the fabulous **Trilogia** (a blend of 1900, 1934 and 1965 vintages).

JMF now own about 800 hectares of vineyard (including 72 hectares of the **José de Sousa Rosado e Fernandes** Alentejo estate – *page 337*). **Periquita**, their most popular brand, is a good value everyday red (**Periquita Clássico** is even better). **BSE**, despite the unfortunate name, is good, crisp, modern white, a blend of Fernão Pires, Antão Vaz and Arinto. **Albis** is a good, off-dry white, fragrant with Moscatel. **Quinta de Camarate** red, from

the Soares Franco's home estate, is a soft, herby blend of Touriga Nacional, Castelão and Aragonez. Any of the wines in the **DSF Private Collection** is worth trying: the **Syrah Rosé** is delicious!

Quinta da Bassaqueira, Estrada Nacional 10, Vila Nogueira de Azeitão, 2925-511 Azeitão
T+351 212 198 940
E enoturismo@jmfonseca.pt
W www.jmf.pt
Visits Mon-Sun 10-12, 2-5.30 appt only
Manor House Museum & Wine Shop, 11-13 Rua José Augusto Coelho, Vila Nogueira de Azeitão, 2925-942 Azeitão
T+351 212 198 959
Wine shop 10-1, 2-6.30 Closed public hols

FERNANDO PÓ C4

Casa Ermelinda Freitas This is the only winery in the Freitas family (out of four) that sells in bottle. Ermelinda has been succeeded by her only daughter, Leonora. The Freitas family has been growing grapes and making wine in the Terras do Sado for four generations, but it was only in 1997 that they began to bottle their wines. Since 1998, the consultant oenologist has been Jaime Quendera.

Casa Ermelinda Freitas is very keen on receiving visitors, and has built a swanky new shop (selling their wines and a selection of home-made jams), a tasting room and a big room for receptions that can seat up to 400 people. (So bring some friends!) The visit is free, but you will pay for the wines you want to taste. You will see all their new vinification equipment, including squat, steel vats (the neighbours said they looked like frogs) with stainless steel screens inside, whose height can be adjusted to keep the cap of skins and pips submerged under the fermenting liquid. They also have a new ageing cellar (more

American oak than French) and bottling-line. The whole winery is insulated against the summer heat.

There are 130ha of vineyard, about 100ha of Castelão and 5ha Fernão Pires, with a little Moscatel. The other 30ha were planted in 2001 and 2002 with Touriga Nacional, Alicante Bouschet, Trincadeira, Syrah and Aragonez for reds, and Arinto, Chardonnay and Sauvignon Blanc for whites. The **Terras do Pó** ('land of dust') wines (red and white) are simple, fruity and well-made, and the **Terras do Pó Reserva** red is richer, with more tannin. Barrel samples of Touriga Nacional look promising. 40ha of the Castelão vines are 50 years old or more. These go into two superior wines, **Quinta da Mimosa** and **Leo d'Honor**. **Quinta da Mimosa** has concentration and poise, and ages brilliantly. **Leo d'Honor** is made from late-picked grapes off 60 year-old vines and produced in limited quantities, with five weeks maceration on the skins, is very rich, with substantial tannins. A small amount of rich, toffeed **Moscatel de Setúbal** is also made.

Fernando Pó, 1695-621 Águas de Moura
T+351 265 995 171
E geral@casaermelinda.com
W www.casaermelinda.com
Wine shop Mon-Fri 10-6
Visits & tastings appt only

PALMELA B4

Adega Cooperativa de Palmela Founded in the co-operative glory-days of 1955 with about 50 members, this co-op now has over 400 members, and makes over 5 million litres of wine a year, much of which is sold in bottle. About 60% of all the grapes processed in Palmela come here. Red wines make up the bulk of the production. The small quantity of white wines made are mostly blends of Fernão

Pires and Moscatel. Most of the red wine is Palmela DOC, the top label being **Villa Palma**. **Vale dos Barris** is their superior brand for VR Terras do Sado wines. They make a little Moscatel and brandy.
Palmela Gare, 2950-401 Palmela
T+351 212 337 020
E adegacoopalmela@mail.telepac.pt
W www.acpalmela.pt
Wine shop & tours Mon-Fri 9-5 Sat/Sun
*   appt only*

PEGÕES VELHOS C4
Sociedade Agrícola de Pegos Claros
This is a close neighbour of the Santo Isidro co-operative, based on the sandy soils on the border between Palmela and the Alentejo. Founded in 1920, it became part of the Companhia das Quintas group in 2004. Of 600ha of vineyard, 50ha are more than 30 years old, and another 30ha recently planted exclusively with Castelão. The grapes are fermented in open lagars and trodden by foot. After this, the wine stays in large oak barrels for a year, and is then bottled, but not sold until it's at least three years old. The estate makes one DOC Palmela red, **Pegos Claros**, in a traditional style, with intense, jammy, figgy flavours, firm tannins and good acidity.
2985-153 Pegões Velhos
T+351 265 896 221
Visits Mon-Fri 10-4 appt only
Wine shop Mon-Fri 8-12, 1-5
*   Sat/Sun appt only*

Cooperativa Agrícola de Santo Isidro de Pegões
The story of the Santo Isidro de Pegões co-operative began when José Rovisco Pais, a beer baron, gave his land in Pegões to the Lisbon State Hospitals in the mid-1950s. The government 'colonised' this land, sharing it between farmworkers, supervising its plantation, and establishing the co-operative in 1958.

There were 204 houses in the Pegões 'colony', each with 16ha of land, 4ha each for vines, trees, cereals and vegetables.

The co-operative was taken over during the 1974 Portuguese revolution, but returned to the farmers by the government in 1980. Now, there are about 1,000ha of vineyard, divided between 140 members, some with more land than others. There's been a lot of investment since 1987: a computerised, temperature-controlled, modern winery, with 90 stainless steel vats, pneumatic presses, 1,600 oak barrels and modern bottling-lines.

Pegões co-op is geared up to receive visitors on weekdays. They will show you the winery, and take you on a trip round the vineyards if you have come by car. Then you can taste some of the wines before you buy.

Most of the red grapes are Castelão, from the very particular, ancient sandy soils of the region. Two labels are used for Palmela DOC wines only, **Fontanário de Pegões** and **Rovisco Pais**, both meaty and dense, with firm tannins that need some bottle-ageing. Not wines for an impromptu picnic! All their other wines are VR Terras do Sado, giving Jaime Quendera and his winemaking team the flexibility to blend in such grapes as Chardonnay, Pinot Blanc, Syrah and Alicante Bouschet. There are also several single-variety red wines, made from Alicante Bouschet, Aragonez, Cabernet Sauvignon, Syrah,

Trincadeira and Touriga Nacional. None of the wines is less than well-made. Top of the red range is the **Adega de Pegões Colheita Seleccionada**, a rich, dense blend of Cabernet, Shiraz, Trincadeira and Touriga Nacional. Their best white is the good-value **Stella Blanco dry Muscat**.
1 Rua Pereira Caldas, 2985-158 Pegões
*   Velhos*
T+351 265 898 860
E geral@cooppegoes.pt
W www.cooppegoes.pt
Wine shop Mon-Fri 9-12, 2-5
*   Sat/Sun appt only*

POCEIRÃO C4
Herdade do Carvalho All the vines on this estate's 20ha were uprooted in 2000 and replanted with Aragonês, Trincadeira, Merlot, Syrah, Cabernet Sauvignon and Castelão. Their wines are made at the modern *adega* of Quinta de Catralvos, supervised by the experienced oenologist Nuno Cancela de Abreu. Eduardo and Nuno Kol de Carvalho, the brothers who own the estate, are modernists, and opt for controlled-temperature steel tanks for fermentation, with a bit of barrel-ageing to polish.

They sell a lot of their grapes, and make only two wines, a rosé and a red. The red **Domingos Damasceno de Carvalho**, a VR wine made from Aragones, Syrah, Cabernet Sauvignon and Merlot, is rich and plummy, with really ripe fruit and tannins.

Herdade de Carvalho are prepared to receive visitors at Quinta de Catralvos or at their vineyard, and to give you a tasting.
Rua Domingos Damasceno de Carvalho,
2965 Poçeirão
T+351 919 538 240
E scg@sota.pt
W www.damasceno.net
Visits appt only

Eat in the Terras do Sado

Being sandwiched between Lisbon and the Alentejo, the Setúbal Peninsula borrows from the food traditions of both. As well as these influences, there are abundant fish and seafood from the surrounding ocean and estuaries, and one of Portugal's most delicious and distinctive cheeses, *Queijo de Azeitão*.

The cosmopolitan cuisine of Lisbon has also crossed the Tagus. There are a few top-class modern Portuguese restaurants, good enough to draw the gastronomes out of the city. And everything from hamburgers to Chinese restaurants has also emigrated over the river to join the simpler dishes based on fish, beans, pork and locally-grown vegetables. Meanwhile, Alentejo cuisine has come here, too, accompanying Alentejanos as they are drawn to the prospects of better jobs in or near Portugal's capital. So in some restaurants of the Terras do Sado you can find bread-based Alentejo country dishes. There's *açorda*, a thick bread soup with seafood or meat, garlic and often egg yolks; and *migas*, a drier, fattier dish of fried breadcrumbs,

QUEIJO DE AZEITÃO

Azeitão cheese is a gastronomic highlight of the peninsula. Made from unpasteurised sheep's milk, these delicious cheeses are runny inside, and best eaten by removing a 'lid' and scooping out the gooey cheese with a spoon. They can also be left to mature longer, becoming drier, flatter, firm and chewy. The offical 'DOP' production areas are around Setúbal, Sesimbra and Palmela. The sheep graze on the verdant, lower pastures of the Arrábida mountains.

Quiejo de Azeitão was modelled on the mountain sheep's cheeses of the Beiras by Gaspar Henriques de Paiva, who came to farm in the peninsula about 1830. Missing the mountain cheese *(queijo da serra)* of his homeland, he shipped down a shepherd and went into production. Instead of rennet, he used extract of cardoon (a type of wild thistle) We now know that the thistle flowers contain an enzyme that curdles milk – it is still used today. The curd is filled into small, round, muslin-lined moulds, and matured for a couple of weeks at between 10 and 12°C, washed daily with brine. The fermentation inside the cheese (which has by now formed a yellow rind) takes place in a drying room, for approximately ten days at a slightly higher temperature. The minimum legal time between the sheep being milked and the sale of the cheese is 21 days, but some cheeses are left much longer to achieve extra piquancy.

AZEITÃO
Museu do Queijo de Azeitão

Although many producers sell direct, EU regulations make it difficult for members of the public to visit commercial cheese dairies. So this museum, incorporated into a dairy farm, is the best place to find out more about Azeitão cheese. You can turn up without an appointment for a guided tour of the museum, located in the 18th century blue-and-white courtyard of an organic farm. (English, French and Spanish spoken, as well as Portuguese, and a guided visit costs €1.) Exhibits span the past 100 years of cheesemaking. With prior appointment, and subject to numbers, you may be able to see demos of traditional cheesemaking, or even play at being a hands-on cheesemaker – a

cheesemaking demo costs €7.50-€10, depending on numbers. Apart from dairy sheep, the farm has organic eggs, vegetables and fruit, which it sells in its grocery shop, along with honey, bread and biscuits.

Quinta Velha-Queijeira, 2925-000 Azeitão
T+351 212 191 125
E geral@quintavelhaonline.com
W quintavelhaonline.com
Visits Spring and summer 10-7, winter 10-1, 3-6.30
Cheesemaking demo appt only
No credit cards

garlic, chillies, seafood or meat. Further inland you may find interesting meat stews, maybe hare stew (*lebrada*) or partridge (*perdiz estufada*). You'll meet a lot of beans and bean stews (*feijoas* and *feijoadas*) – rabbit (*coelho*) cooked with beans is a Palmela speciality.

But fresh fish is the highlight. At the local fish markets and restaurants, look out especially for oysters (*ostras*), cultivated in the estuaries, and delicious red mullet (*salmonete*) – Setúbal-style red mullet is cooked with fermented fish, a culinary remnant of Roman occupation, but it comes in other guises, too. There is gilt head bream (*dourada*), scabbard fish (*peixe espada*), and swordfish (*espadarte*) – the latter cooked as steaks or smoked – and plenty of crab, prawns, clams and mussels. Setúbal is famous for its sardines, as well as mackerel (*cavala*) and eels (*enguias*), maybe cooked with rice and peppers. Seafood soups and *Caldeirada à Fragateira* (fish and seafood stew, often with potato) and are on most menus.

Setúbal has olive groves and orchards. In the autumn you can eat the Muscat grapes, and pears (*pêras*) cooked in Moscatel wine. Try the local honey, made by bees foraging amongst the herbs and maquis of the Arrábida hills. There are locally harvested pine nuts, incorporated into savoury as well as sweet dishes and cakes. The Sado Estuary is a land of rice, used in all kinds of ways in the local cuisine – in the seafood risotto-like *arroz de mariscos*, or sweet rice puddings made with creamy sheep's milk. Try the sheep's butter, and lovely small fresh sheep's cheeses, as well as the unctuous, semi-soft Queijo de Azeitão.

Far left Winter ploughing the rice fields around Acácer do Sal

Left Tending the characterful honey from the Arrábida hills

Right A seafood paradise

ALMADA A4

Ponto Final A simple, casual, rustic white house by the waterside, with a terrace and great views across to Lisbon. (Ferries bring city customers across from the Terreiro do Paço or Cais do Sodré.) Good, traditional food including Alentejo dishes, and Alentejo wines.
Cais do Gingal 72, Cacilhas
T+351 212 760 743
€20
Closed Tue; 20 Dec-20 Jan

AMORA A4

Palácio do Vinho An amazing wine selection is the first attraction of this simple family restaurant, which is off the tourist track, not far from the 25 de Abril Bridge. But the food is good too, excellent raw materials including fine hams and pork products from the *porco preto*, the Alentejo black pig, as well as fresh fish and seafood. There is suckling pig *(leitão)* and kid *(cabrito)*. The wine list focuses on small producers, and is particularly impressive in the Alentejo section, good on local wines and stronger on reds than whites.
Estrada Nacional 10, Cruz de Pau
T+351 212 245 110
W www.palaciodovinho.pt
€25 ♀
Closed 2 weeks Jun, 2 weeks Oct

AZEITÃO (VILA FRESCA DE) B3

Pé do Vinho A newish restaurant in a narrow ex-warehouse, part modern, part rustic, with richly coloured walls, and interesting exhibitions of art, photographs, prints etc. Do visit the loo, inside an old wine vat! Food is good traditional, and the very descriptive wine list is almost limited to the wines of J M da Fonseca and Bacalhôa. There are some interesting Moscatels to end the meal.

Rua dos Trabalhadores da Empresa
Setúbalense 10
T+351 212 188 048
E pedevinhorest@hotmail.com
€25-€30 ♀
Closed Mon

AZEITÃO (VILA NOGUEIRA DE) B3

O Azeitão After a visit to the José Maria da Fonseca winery, this is just nearby. Brothers António and João Amaral turn fresh, local produce into Portuguese dishes with international influences. It's a cosily rural, brown-hued place, with gingham table cloths, and an array of old farm implements and domestic utensils on walls and shelves. Wines come from four Azeitão producers. If you book for Wednesday you're lucky – it's fado night.
Praça da República 8
T+351 212 188 310
E joao.amaral@iol.pt
W www.restauranteazeitao.com
€25 V
Closed Thu & Sun din; 1st half Jan,
2nd half Oct

Quinta de Catralvos An inventive, modern take on local fresh produce from internationally renowned chef Luís Baena, who draws gastronomes out from Lisbon. Dishes are small and beautiful, and the idea is to taste several different dishes –

maybe eight or ten – in the same meal. A short but interesting wine list includes wines made on the quinta. Smart, simply elegant dining room. There are guest rooms, and cookery courses, lasting from one to several days.
Estrada Nacional 379
T+351 212 197 610
E geral@quintadecatralvos.com
W www.quintadecatralvos.com
€45 V 🛏
Closed Mon, Tue-Thu din, Sun

CACHOPOS C1

A Escola This friendly, attractive, airy restaurant was once the primary school of the village of Cachopos. The menu is chalked on the old blackboard – hearty Alentejo dishes, strong on meat and game as well as fish, and the wines are from the Alentejo, too. Dine amidst appreciative, nostalgic locals, white walls, high arches, and a touch of chintz in the table cloths. Cachopos is on the main road along the south bank of the Sado estuary, between Alcácer do Sal and Comporta.
Estrada Nacional 253
T+351 265 612 816
W www.saboresdosado.com
€18-€20 Closed Mon; last 3 weeks Oct

COMPORTA B3

Ilha do Arroz A really delightful bar-restaurant in the dunes at the top of the long, secluded Carvalhal beach. Thirty metres from the water's edge, you have fine views over the Arrábida mountains. An atmospheric place, with modern decor, bright colours, and different areas – sit at tables, flop on the sofas… Chef José Guerreiro's menu includes tempting salads as well as seafood. 15km south of Troia, 26km from Alcácer do Sal.
Praia de Comporta
T+351 265 490 510
E ilhadoarroz@iol.pt
Closed Tue; annual winter hols variable
V

Museu do Arroz Recently done up, the 'Museum of Rice' is in an old rice factory. The decor is a mix of rustic and modern

– you could choose to eat in a sushi lounge, and there are indeed some museum exhibits relating to the production of rice. You won't be surprised to find plenty of rice dishes on the menu, also steaks, and lots of wonderfully fresh fish and seafood.
Estrada Nacional
T+351 265 497 555
E museudoarroz@sapo.pt
€30 V
Closed Mon; often Jan

MONTIJO B4

Girassol An attractive, quite elegant roadside restaurant 2km outside Montijo in the direction of Sarilhos Grandes. Service is good and friendly, and everything is home-made, from good ingredients: expect game in season, eel, *porco preto* (excellent black pig pork products), roast kid, and tempting home-made puddings.
EN11 Broega-Sarilhos Grandes
T+351 212 891 820
€15-€20 V on request
Closed Tue

Nobre Expensive by local standards, but excellent. Justa and José Nobre offer a modern interpretation of traditional dishes – they were three times winner of the Concurso (Competition) da Gastronomia de Lisboa and indeed can be considered almost a Lisbon restaurant, being just 20 minutes over the bridge from the city. The wine list is well chosen, and the service top class. The dining space is light, airy and very spacious, with white and lime table cloths a design feature.
Avenida de Olivença, near Praça de Touros
T+351 212 317 511
E nobremontijo@sapo.pt
€30 V
Closed Tue; 2nd half Aug

PALMELA B3

Retiro Azul An inexpensive but attractive restaurant near the bus station, a favourite of local wine producers, serving good seafood and regional dishes. Good service.
Largo do Chafariz Dona Maria
T+351 212 350 021
€20 Closed Wed

QUINTA DO ANJO B3

Alcanena Cosy, rustic restaurant in a converted old winery, with very tasty traditional food and a good selection of wines. Choose between the covered terrace and restaurant (with menu), or a separate room offering a buffet with a huge selection of Portuguese dishes and salads, cheeses, charcuterie and tempting puddings.
Rua Venâncio Costa Lima 99
T+351 212 870 150
E alcanena@clix.pt
€20 ♀ Closed Wed; 2 weeks Jun

SESIMBRA A3

Pedra Alta Cosy and rustic inside, adorned with photos ancient and modern, and a big terrace with sunshades when the weather is good. Traditional Portuguese dishes and lots of fish displayed fresh to choose for the grill.
Largo de Bombaldes 13-15
T+351 212 231 791
E pedra.alta@clix.pt
€30-€35 V Open every day

Ribamar From the white, shady terrace you have a lovely outlook across the beach to the sea and fishing boats making for the harbour. Inside, the decor is simple, creamy-white, pink tablecloths, arches. Ribamar takes a modern approach to Portuguese cooking, offering a great range of fresh fish and seafood. The wine list is extensive.
Avenida dos Náufragos 29
T +351 212 234 853
E ribamar@ribamar.com.pt or
    anthel.lda@clix.pt
W www.ribamar.com.pt
€30-€35 ♀ V
Open every day

Setúbal B3
Poço das Fontaínhas In the pretty Poço das Fontaínhas quarter of the town, near the Troia ferry embarkation point, this friendly, fun restaurant is a bit hard to find. There are tables tucked into a

pavement space, and more in the blue interior. Eat seafood, really fresh grilled fish or meat, and good home-made puddings.
Rua das Fontaínhas
T+351 265 534 807
W www.saboresdosado.com
€20
Closed Mon

Verde e Branco Simple, lively, fun restaurant, very popular with locals, serving grilled fish and meat.
Rua Dona Maria Baptista 33
T+351 265 526 546
€15 No credit cards
Closed Mon, public hols; Aug

Xica-Bia Romantic, brick-vaulted restaurant serving Alentejo-style fish, meat and game, and sweet, gooey puddings.
Avenida Luísa Todi
T+351 265 522 559
E xicabia@xicabia.pt
W www.xicabia.pt
€20 V on request
Closed Sun; 1st 2 weeks Aug

Sines B1
Restaurante Trinca Espinhas Right down in the south of the Terras do Sado, friendly Trinca Espinhas offers good cooking with plenty of grilled fresh fish and seafood, modern Portuguese with occasional international elements. It is decorated on a sea theme, model seagulls suspended overhead, deep sea blue paint-work, bleached, slatted wooden tables, a cosy area with wicker chairs and cushions for drinks and coffee. Watch, hear and smell the sea, especially on the terrace.
Praia de São Torpes
T+351 269 636 379
E lamagalhaes@vodafone.pt
€25
Closed Thu; Nov

Markets and Food Shops

Almada A4 Garrafeira d'Almada Just this side of the bridge, good range of Portuguese wine, port, whisky, *aguardente* and wine accessories.
Avenida Egas Moniz 2A

Azeitão B3 Market First Sunday of the month
Caparica A4 Fish market Daily
Grândola C2 Market Second Monday of the month
Palmela B3 Market Second Sunday of the month
Mercado Anual The annual Christmas market on 8 December
Sesimbra A3 Covered market By the port, fantastic fish.
Fish auction On the beach
Setúbal B3 Mercado do Livramento Wonderful art deco covered market with three big halls – admire the azulejos inside, depicting regional scenes: wine and olive harvest, the salt trade… Great source of all types of food, wonderful for fish.
Avenida Luisa Todi
Sines B1 Market First Thursday of the month

Explore the Terras do Sado

Building is big business these days in the Setúbal Peninsula, so it's lucky that conservation areas and nature reserves exclude developers from large chunks of beautiful countryside. Some of Portugal's finest scenery is to be found in the hilly **Parque Natural da Arrábida** along the peninsula's south coast. There are spectacular limestone cliffs, rocky outcrops, streams, Mediterranean maquis, thickets, cork woods, pine and eucalyptus forests, orchards…and meadows where sheep graze on mountain plants and herbs, providing milk for the famous Azeitão cheese. And on certain slopes you will see Moscatel vines, their grapes destined for the sweet Setúbal wines, as well as for the table. Intrepid explorers might be lucky to spot rare wildlife – such as wildcats, pole cats, eagle owls or peregrine falcons. The Arrábida coast has lovely coves and beaches, white cliffs and caves. Sadly, forest fires have devastated some woodland areas of Arrábida in recent years, but there are still great walks.

Roads down to the Arrábida beaches are often steep and narrow. The quaint fishing port of SESIMBRA is no exception. It may be easier to reach on a weekday and out of the holiday season, because Lisbon people flock here – and it has to be said that nowadays apartment blocks on the hillsides slightly mar the view. Within the town are *more* charming narrow, winding streets, full of tourist cafés and bars. The calm bay is protected by the Arrábida

Bottom left Winter-pruned vineyards, with Arrábida backdrop

Right Convento da Arrábida

Below View from the Arrábida hills to Troia

mountains, its sandy beach good for kids, snorkelling and diving. This is also a good starting point for deep sea fishing. The fishing harbour is west of the main town – follow the promenade and the late afternoon sun to watch the fish auction. You can buy the freshest of fish from little stalls by the side of the road.

Leave the car at the top when you visit PORTINHO DA ARRÁBIDA, half way between Sesimbra and Setúbal. This is another lovely white sheltered beach, and a sweet little village over-looked by an old monastery up on the hills. From here, visit the sea cave of **Lapa de Santa Margarida**, and see evidence of ancient human habitation. Further to the east again, the

GALAPOS beach is good for scuba diving, and the FIGUEIRINHA beach a windsurfers' hang-out.

The eastern, inland end of the **Tagus Estuary** to the north and the **Sado Estuary** to the south of the peninsula are both nature reserves, with salt marshes, mudflats and lagoons that attract a huge range of waterfowl, including migrating flamingos, storks, egrets and herons. Storks nest on rooftops. Look out for otters, too, and hundreds of species of butterflies. Exploring the Sado estuary by boat you may meet dolphins – boat trips start from the big, busy industrial port of SETÚBAL. Portugal's third biggest port is a working town rather than a tourist showcase, but you will enjoy the harbour with its cargo, fishing and pleasure boats, the unspoilt back streets, and the excellent food market near the port. The 16th century Forte de São Filipe dominates the town, now partly a pousada. Don't miss the the beautiful Igreja de Jesus (Convent of Jesus) and its museum, and the Roman remains of a fish condiment factory under a glass panel in the floor of the tourist office.

Opposite Setúbal is the long, thin peninsula of TROIA. The Transado ferry from Setúbal to Troia is the quickest way over to the unspoilt marshlands, dunes and beaches to the south of the estuary. There are two crossings an hour, less often early and late – allow 40 minutes. Troia, at the tip of the peninsula, has some high-rise tourist flats, but as you drive down there are lovely beaches on the Atlantic side of the road, fishing villages on the protected eastern side, and villas, and a championship golf course. In Troia, and CETÓBRIGA out in the marshes, ruins of Roman fish factories are worth a detour. The main town here amidst the marshes and rice paddies is historic ALCÁCER DO SAL, with its twisting narrow streets and steps, and whitewashed houses, overlooked by a 12th century castle turned *pousada* (hotel). And everywhere around there are rice paddies. Visit the nearby unspoilt fishing villages of Lagoa and CARVALHAL.

North of Setúbal, PALMELA is visible from miles around, high on the north-east edge of the Arrábida hills – especially when the hilltop Castelo (castle) is floodlit at night. The Castelo de Palmela is now also also a pousada.

Above Storks in the belfry

Left A fishing boat and lobster pots

Right A thatched pile of sea salt, extracted from the salt flats near the town of Alcácer do Sal

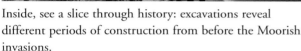

Left The busy industrial and fishing port of Setúbal, and rice fields in the winter

Right The whitewashed houses of Alcácer do Sal reflected in the estuary of the River Sado

Inside, see a slice through history: excavations reveal different periods of construction from before the Moorish invasions.

There is a lot of tourist development down the west coast of the peninsula, the **Costa da Caparica**. CAPARICA is a fishing-cum-tourist village with beach bars, restaurants, and all-night beach cafés, a fun place in summer with good surfing. A little train runs down this coast along the dunes in the summer, 18 stops servicing different expanses

of beach. Further south is a nudist beach, and a huge eco-tourism project is under construction.

The north coast is a dormitory for Lisbon. It is worth visiting ALCOCHETE in the north east of the peninsula, looking out over the salt marshes and estuary. This little town has also been invaded by the builders since the new bridge, but it is still a pretty place, surrounded by salt pans and piles of drying salt, and visited by migrating flamingos in spring and autumn.

❈ VIEW FROM THE TOP ❈

ALCÁCER DO SAL Climb up for a drink at the Pousada de Dom Afonso II for fine views over the rooftops (complete with storks' nests), river and rice fields.

ALMADA **Cristo Rei** You can take a lift (€4) to the terrace of the 82m-high pedestal on which stands the Statue of Christ the King, facing Lisbon on the north bank of the estuary. Great views of the city.

ARRÁBIDA Spectacular views across the bay of Setúbal, and over towards Lisbon, from the Estrada da Escarpa, the road that meanders along the Arrábida crest and mountainside. Look especially for the *miradouro* (viewpoint) above the Convento da Arrábida.

CABO ESPICHEL It's a 100m drop straight down to the sea. So beware as you gaze out from the edge of these windswept cliffs. Here on the barren south-west tip of the Setúbal Peninsula, there's a lighthouse, the Baroque Santuário de Nossa Senhora do Cabo church, and some little lodgings for pilgrims.

PALMELA From the keep of the Castelo de Palmela, take in lovely views over the Serra de Arrábida. On a fine day you can even see Lisbon.

SESIMBRA View the coast from the ramparts of the Moorish castle above the town.

SETÚBAL Stay, or call in for a drink at the hilltop-fort Pousada of Castelo de São Filipe, with spectacular 360° vistas over city and estuary, and the Alentejo plains in the hazy distance.

AZEITÃO (VILA FRESCA DE) São Simão Arte Azulejos Studio-factory and shop, traditional hand-made, hand-painted tiles, also hand-painted dishes and panels. Outstanding amongst local tile producers. *Rua Almirante Reis 86, Vila Fresca de Azeitão Open every day 9-9*

PALMELA Campo de Golf do Montado Play a round of golf amidst the Moscatel vines at this championship-grade, 18-hole, par 72. *Apartado 40, Algeruz 2951-901 Palmela T+351 213 300 541 E geral@golfdomontado.com.pt W www.golfdomontado.com.pt*

SANTIAGO DE CACÉM Miróbriga Roman remains Inland from Sines, just outside Santiago, an old Roman settlement is still being excavated: a well-preserved Roman road, and vestiges of a bridge, stairways, baths, inns, houses and a temple. *Just off N120 Open Tue to Sat 9-12.30, 2-5.30 Sun 9-12, 2-5.30*

SETÚBAL Roman fish condiment factory See the remains under the glass floor of the tourist office.
Dolphin watching Boat trips run by Vertigem Azul. It is worth booking. *Edifízio Marina Deck, Rua Praia da Saúde 13, Loja 11 T+351 265 238 000 W www.vertigemazul.com*
Sailing galleon trips from TroiaCruze. *Rua das Barrocas 34 T+351 265 228 486*

TROIA Troia and Cetóbriga/Caetobriga In Troia itself, visit impressive ruins of Roman baths, houses, religious buildings and fish factories. There's more evidence of Roman fish factories on the lagoon side of the peninsula at Cetóbriga: beside the tourist office are ruins of Roman fish salting tanks of the 1st to 5th century. *Closed lunch, Sun pm, public hols*

VILA NOVA DE SANTO ANDRÉ Badoca Safari Park Between Santiago do Cacém and Sines, this large and excellent safari park has more than 420 animals, from giraffes to gnus, tigers and zebras, with fun activities on the side for children, and a restaurant serving Azamor wines – the complex belongs to the producers *(page 328). Herdade da Badoca T+351 269 708 850 E badoca@badoca.com W www.badoca.com Open Feb-Mar Mon-Fri 10-5 Sat/Sun 9.30-6 Apr-May, Sep-Oct 9.30-7 Jun-Sep 9am-10pm*

CHURCHES
PALMELA Igreja de São Pedro Main claim to fame of the Church of St Peter: the 18th century blue and white *azulejos* that completely cover walls, depicting the life of St Peter. This church is the focal point of the religious part of Palmela's wine harvest festival. Grapes are blessed and ceremonially crushed here in the square in front of the church by foot in a large tank before the thanksgiving mass. *Largo do Município*

SETÚBAL Igreja de Jesus The gorgeous salmon-coloured Azeitão limestone strikes the tone in this beautiful late-15th century church of the early Manueline/Gothic style *(page 432).* Salmon-toned candy-twist columns, arches, door and window frames, and the ribbed vault of the chancel, are offset by simple white walls, with high-

lights of green and white *azulejos*. Find it north of the old town. Right next door is the Museu Municipal *(see below).Praça Miguel Bombarda Closed Mon*

MUSEUMS
ATALAIA Museu Agrícola da Atalaia Near Montijo, a museum of wine and olive oil production, set amidst orchard and vegetable garden. *Open Mon-Fri 9-5.30 Closed Sat, Sun, public hols*

SETÚBAL Museu Regional de Arqueologia e Etnografia The Museum of Archaeology and Ethnography has an eclectic mix of local archaeological finds and memories of local life and industries: fishing, salt manufacture, cork, lace, weaving, spinning, and traditional costumes. *Avenida Luisa Todi 162 Open Tue-Sat 9-12.30, 2-5.30 Closed Sun, Mon, (also Sat in Aug)*
Museu Municipal Just beside the Igreja de Jesus, this museum is particularly famous for the 'Setúbal Primitives', a collection of 16th century Portuguese paintings, amongst the most important works of renaissance art in Portugal. Other exhibits include Moorish kitchen equipment found during the excavation of Palmela Castle. *Praça Miguel Bombarda Open Tue-Sat 9-12, 1.30-5.30 Closed Mon, Sun, public hols*

VILA FRESCA DE AZEITÃO
Quinta da Bacalhôa

Garden lovers will enjoy a visit to Quinta da Bacalhôa. The garden was commissioned, along with the palace, by Brás de Albuquerque, son of Portugal's first Viceroy to the Indies. Formal and geometric, all green, no flowers, it has Indian and Italian influences, with swirls of manicured box hedges, a great reflecting pool, and orange grove and vineyards beyond. The 16th century Palácio was built as Albuquerque's country retreat, in a blend of Italian Renaissance, Indian and Moorish styles. There is a wonderful collection of *azulejos*. After falling into disrepair at the beginning of the 20th century, the Palácio was painstakingly restored by an American, Orlena Scoville, through the 1940s. She also planted Cabernet Sauvignon and Merlot, from which the first bottled wine was sold in 1979. The vineyards surrounding the palace and gardens are still the source of the famous Quinta da Bacalhôa wines, but the wines are made five minutes down the road at the modern winery of Bacalhôa Vinhos de Portugal *(page 304)*. You can buy the wines at the palace, and arrange to taste them here, by appointment. Allow about an hour for the visit.
*Estrada Nacional 10, Vila Fresca de Azeitão T+351 212 198 060
E palaciodabacalhoa@bacalhoa.pt
Open Mon-Sat 9-6 Closed Sun, public hols*

FAIRS & FESTIVALS

FEBRUARY FERNANDO PÓ (PALMELA) Mostra de Vinhos da Marateca e Poceirão Three-day wine-fair, open to the public, where 30 or more local producers show their wines.

APRIL QUINTA DO ANJO (between PALMELA and AZEITÃO) **Festival do Queijo, Pão e Vinho** Small-scale cheese, bread and wine festival at the end of April, where two dozen or more producers offer products for tastings, including the new wines; sheep shearing, Azeitão cheese-making, and you could even join the locals on organised walks. **ALCOCHETE Círio dos Marítimos de Alcochete** 500-year-old fishermen's festival on Easter Saturday, Sunday and Monday, with a special mass, donkey processions and great festivities, with plenty of food and wine, on Saturday night.

MAY AZEITÃO Feira-Festa dos Frutos e Sabores da Arrábida Four-day food fair in May with stalls and tastings of wine, traditional sweets, bread, cheese, events organised by Slow Food, as well as horse shows, music, and organised walks and cycle rides.

JUNE ALCÁCER DO SAL PIMEL Towards the end of June, a four-day annual fair for the sweet-toothed. 100 exhibitors bring their pine nuts, honey and waist-expanding quantities of delicious eggy cakes and sweets. Competitions for the best products, bull fights, horses, rock concerts, activities for children.

JUNE/JULY MONTIJO Festa de São Pedro End of June, early July, the centuries-old Feast of Saint Peter, patron saint of fishermen, involves a procession on the river, the blessing of the fishing

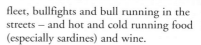

fleet, bullfights and bull running in the streets – and hot and cold running food (especially sardines) and wine.

AUGUST ALCOCHETE Festas do Barrete Verde e das Salinas With its climax on the night of the second Saturday of the month, the 'Festival of Green Cap and Salt-Pans' celebrates salt-panning and bullfights, all wrapped up in a folk festival. After a water procession, there are open-air feasts for the whole town, and revelry late into the *Noite da Sardinha Assada* – the Night of the Grilled Sardine! **ALCOCHETE** 400-year-old fishermen's festival, Sanctuary of Nossa Senhora da Atalaia **GRÂNDOLA Feira de Agosto** Big craft and food fair the last weekend of the month, with musical events and festivities.

SEPTEMBER PALMELA Festa das Vindimas The annual wine harvest festival is a big event, attracting 100,000 visitors in the five days leading up to the second Sunday in September. Major processions, grape pressing ceremony, tastings of dry wines and sweet Moscatels, tastings of Azeitão cheese, illuminations, fairground, sheep-shearing, concerts, sports events, all culminating in spectacular fireworks on the last night. **MONTIJO Mostra de Produtos Regionais** (Regional Produce Fair).

NOVEMBER QUINTA DO ANJO Festa das Sopas e Petiscos A 'Festival of Soups and Petiscos', near the start of the month.

Sleep in the Terras do Sado

ALCÁCER DO SAL C3

Pousada de Dom Afonso II Once a Moorish fort, then a medieval castle, then a convent, now this is one of the most stunning pousadas, with big, comfortable rooms and public spaces, and elegant decor that reflects all the periods of the castle's history, including the present day. From rooms, terraces and battlements, there are stunning views over the rice fields. The terrace restaurant is hot on rice dishes!
7580-123 Alcácer do Sal
T+351 265 613070
E recepcaodafonso@pousadas.pt
W www.pousadas.pt
€170-€230 🛏33 Ⓢ2 ✗ 🛶

AZEITÃO B3

Quinta da Arrábida Two pretty little white self-catering houses in a lovely, mature, landscaped garden with fine swimming pool and a backdrop of the Arrábida mountains.
Casais da Serra, 2925-318 Azeitão
T+351 914 161 190
E reserv@quintadaarrabida.com
W www.quintadaarrabida.com
€70-€120 🛏3 Ⓢ2(2&4) 🛶
Min 2 nights No credit cards

Quinta de Catralvos Elegant, modern bedrooms in a complex that includes a winery, a fine restaurant *(see 'Eat')* and a banqueting suite, all set amidst an expanse of vines. Renowned chef Luís

Baena runs cookery courses here. Conveniently central in the Setúbal Peninsula, with views of the Arrábida hills.
EN 379 2925-708 Azeitão
T+351 212 197 610
E geral@quintadecatralvos.com
W www.quintadecatralvos.com
€90 🛏5 Ⓨ⒳🛶

Quinta de Santo Amaro Apartment in a large farmhouse, comfortable, homely and attractive, with open fires, nice garden, and excellent breakfasts with home-made bread and home-grown oranges. Can be rented as separate rooms.
Aldeia da Piedade, 2925-375 Azeitão
T+351 212 189 230
€90 per room, €255 whole apt
🛏3 or Ⓢ1(6) 🛶 ⚲
Min 3 nights No credit cards

AZEITÃO (VILA FRESCA DE) B3

Estalagem Quinta das Torres The *Torres* are four towers at the corners of this delightful 16th century manor house, each of which is a room with its own long, crenellated roof-top terrace. There are fine *azulejos* in the dining room, and antiques everywhere. A fountain plays in the central courtyard, where walls are draped in wisteria and other climbing plants. The house is set amidst beautiful gardens, olive groves and citrus orchards, and fronted by a large water tank with gazebo.
Vila Nogueira de Azeitão, 2925-601 Azeitão
T+351 212 180 001
E quinta.torres@mail.telepac.pt
W www.quintadastorres.net
€70-€85 🛏10 Ⓢ2(4) ✗

AZINHEIRA DOS BARROS C2

Herdade das Sesmarias dos Nobres This is amazing value, south of Grândola off the N259, a simple but attractive low-built house amidst olives, cork oaks, pines

and eucalyptus, with pasture for horses and sheep. Enjoy a garden with pool, optional regional meals or wine tastings, and air-conditioning.
7570-003 Azinheira dos Barros
T+351 269 594 104
E sesmariasdn@gmail.com
W www.sesmariasdosnobres.com
€45-€50 (less if you stay longer)
🛏8 ✗ 🛶 ♨ ❄ *No credit cards*

CANHA C4

Monte da Charca Within a working Terras do Sado vineyard, a collection of traditional farm buildings have been

converted into lovely, fresh, well-designed holiday accommodation, all air-conditioned. There is the option of spending a day or more working in the vineyard – pruning, summer trimming, harvesting… Working togs are provided, breakfast and lunch with the regular workers, then dinner from the high quality restaurant Quinta de Catralvos *(page 310)*. Enjoy the pool, fishing, kayaking, or borrow the bikes to explore the farm's cycle tracks. Good breakfasts.
Olho de Bode de Cima, Quinta das
   Marianas, Canha, 2985-000 Pegões
T+ 351 212 197 610
E geral@quintadecatralvos.com
W www.montedacharca.com,
   www.quintadecatralvos.com
€65-€130 🛏3 Ⓢ5(3&4) Ⓢ1(4)
   ✗*on request* 🛶

GRÂNDOLA C2

Monte Cabeço do Ouro A very friendly reception, and optional horsey activities await you at this rural house and cottage. Decor and furnishings are simple but comfortable. On the edge of town, within 10km of lovely beaches and the Sado estuary and nature reserve.
7570-909 Grândola
T+351 269 451 292
E ant.menezes@clix.pt
W www.secretspaces.net
€60-€75 🛏 *6* [S] *1* [SC] *3(4)* ✗ *on request* 🏊 ♨ 💆 *jacuzzi*
Min 2 nights

MONTIJO B4

Tryp Montijo Parque A pleasant, inexpensive, modern hotel with spacious rooms and garage parking, close to the new Vasco da Gama Bridge.
Avenida João 23, 2870-159 Montijo
T+351 212 326 600
E tryp.montijo.parque@solmeliaportugal.com
W www.trypmontijoparque.solmelia.com
€50 🛏 *84* ✗

PALMELA B3

Pousada Castelo de Palmela Nestling together on this hilltop are the remains of centuries: once a fortress, then a monastery, damaged in the great earthquake, abandoned for ages after the extinction of religious orders. Palmela Castle was first renovated as a pousada in 1979. It was recently modernised, to the highest of standards. Rooms are delightfully, austerely comfortable. An elegant restaurant in the cloisters leads to a terrace with awesome views.
2950-317 Palmela
T+351 212 351 226
E recepcao.palmela@pousadas.pt
W www.pousadas.pt
€150-€210 🛏 *24* [S] *4* ✗

PINHAL NOVO B4
(between MONTIJO and PALMELA)

Palácio de Rio Frio In the early part of the 20th century, the huge estate surrounding this formal manor house included the world's biggest vineyard, as well as extensive cork forests. Now much reduced, the estate grows rice and sunflowers, the house offers luxurious yet reasonably priced accommodation amidst its elegant, formal furnishings and decor. Highlights are the stunning *azulejos* by Jorge Colaço, especially in the dining room, where they depict the viticultural year of a century ago. Swim in the lovely garden, walk in the woods…
Rio Frio, 2955-014 Pinhal Novo
T+351 212 319 701
E lupi@hotmail.com
€110-€120 🛏 *4* [S] *1* 🏊 *No credit cards*
Min 2 nights   Closed Christmas

SETÚBAL B3

Há Mar ao Luar Called literally 'There's Sea by the Light of the Moon' this is a magical, secluded spot right by the sea, amidst its own gardens and the greenery of the lower slopes of the Arrábida hills. Whether you stay in the hundred-year-old windmill, the *cabana* on the beach or the two apartments within the low, coral-pink main building, accommodation here is welcoming and cosy, the decor quirkily maritime, the colours warm. There's a lovely pool in the garden, and stunning views over the Troia Peninsula and the Sado Estuary. Self-catering. You will need a car.
Alto de São Filipe, 2900-300 Setúbal
T+351 265 220 901
E hamaraoluar@iol.pt
W www.hamaraoluar.com
€75-€120 [S] *2(2/4)* [SC] *4(2/4)* 🏊
Min nights 2 (weekends), 5 (Jun-Sep)
No credit cards

Pousada Castelo de São Filipe Luxurious hotel in a late 16th century fort, the entrance an arch in the old wall. You will stay in gold-green, air-conditioned comfort in the former governor's house, or the guard house, and enjoy magnificent views of the city and estuary from the front terrace and restaurant. Ask to be taken down to the dungeons, to see the cells, military escape routes and instruments of torture; ask also to see the lovely baroque chapel, totally lined with *azulejos*. You will need a car.
Forte de São Filipe, 2900-300 Setúbal
T+351 265 550 070
E recepcao.sfilipe@pousadas.pt
W www.pousadas.pt
€150-€252 🛏 *15* [S] *1* ✗

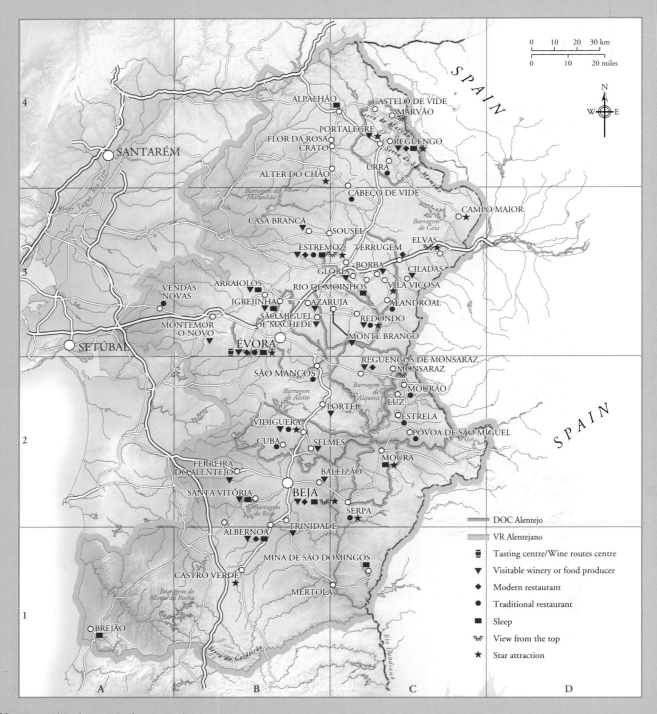

0   10   20   30 km

0   10   20 miles

S P A I N

N
W   E
S

4

SANTARÉM

ALPALHÃO

CASTELO DE VIDE
MARVÃO

PORTALEGRE
FLOR DA ROSA
CRATO

REGUENGO

ALTER DO CHÃO

URRA

CABEÇO DE VIDE

Barragem de
Maranhão

Barragem
de Caia

CAMPO MAIOR

CASA BRANCA

SOUSEL

3

ESTREMOZ   TERRUGEM

ELVAS

BORBA

GLÓRIA

CILADAS

River Tagus
Rio Tejo

VENDAS
NOVAS

ARRAIOLOS

RIO DE MOINHOS

VILA VIÇOSA

IGREJINHA

AZARUJA

ALANDROAL

SÃO MIGUEL
DE MACHEDE

REDONDO

MONTEMOR
-O-NOVO

ÉVORA

MONTE BRANCO

SETÚBAL

SÃO MANÇOS

REGUENGOS DE MONSARAZ
MONSARAZ

Barragem
de Alvito

Barragem
de Alqueva

MOURÃO

LUZ

PORTEL

ESTRELA

2

VIDIGUERA

PÓVOA DE SÃO MIGUEL

CUBA

SELMES

FERREIRA
DO ALENTEJO

MOURA

SANTA VITÓRIA

BALEIZÃO

BEJA

Barragem
do Roxo

SERPA

ALBERNOA

TRINIDADE

CASTRO VERDE

MINA DE SÃO DOMINGOS

Barragem do
Monte da Rocha

MÉRTOLA

1

BREJÃO

Serra do Caldeirão

Rio Guadiana

S P A I N

DOC Alentejo

VR Alentejano

Tasting centre/Wine routes centre

Visitable winery or food producer

Modern restaurant

Traditional restaurant

Sleep

View from the top

Star attraction

A   **B**   **C**   **D**

Alentejo

The Alentejo covers about a third of Portugal, yet has only one-twentieth of the country's population. The pace of life is understandably slow, given the blistering heat of summer and surprisingly cold winters. The long frontier with Spain required the main towns to be heavily fortified. These stand out on the undulating landscape, built on positions from which Romans, Moors and medieval monarchs could see their attackers coming. All these rulers have left their architectural legacies.

Outside the main towns, tiny villages sit low to the parched earth, and local residents follow a way of life that has changed little for generations. In the far north, the Parque Natural de São Mamede has the highest mountains south of the River Tagus, and lush green vegetation unlike anything else in the region, including vines, chestnuts, cherries and corn, as well as olives, pines and eucalyptus.

Heading south, vast plains stretch to the horizon. Around the fortified city of Estremoz, quarries of pink marble echo the reddish soil. South as far as Évora, cork oaks predominate over cereals. After wheat, cork is the Alentejo's most important crop, the spongy bark harvested from tree trunks once a decade. Évora, summer residence of kings and nobles from the late Middle Ages onwards, floats in a sea of cork forests and vines. It's a fascinating city, with winding narrow streets, monuments, squares, cafés and some excellent restaurants.

South again, battalions of olives start marching across the landscape, with a few cork oaks on the hillier parts. Then, in Vidigueira, it's back to vines, and livestock: Alentejano cattle, sheep for cheese and wool, and black pigs *(porco preto)*, which range free, feeding on the acorns before providing some of Portugal's finest pork and ham.

Despite a coastline of dramatic cliffs and, golden dunes, Algarve-style tourism has not arrived here, nor have tourist-related conveniences. So ensure your tank is always full of petrol, and take your Portuguese dictionary. The new airport at Beja, due to take off in 2008, will open the lower Alentejo to international visitors. Alqueva Reservoir – the largest man-made lake in Europe – is already changing not only the climate but the local way of life, with watersports and burgeoning hotels. Enjoy the Alentejo now, before it changes for ever.

Wine in the Alentejo

Alentejo wines are very popular in Portugal – they account for nearly half of all domestic sales. Taste any of the good ones, especially the reds, and you'll see why. The reds have an easy-drinking, generous nature that reflects the ease of ripening grapes in the south of Portugal. Whites are less easy to get right, precisely because of the southern heat.

The Alentejo occupies much of the south-eastern half of the country, down as far as the Algarve. It's a region of rolling plains, hills and even mountains in the north-eastern corner. You might think it would be too hot for vines, and, in summer, it *is* very hot, with temperatures often climbing to 40°C. But not everywhere. As ever, in higher places (and there are some in the Alentejo) at least the nights are cool, allowing the vines some respite.

This vast area has eight different sub-regions to the DOC, corresponding to the old IPR (Indicação de Proveniência Regulamentada) regions of Portalegre, Borba, Redondo, Évora, Reguengos, Granja-Amareleja, Moura and Vidigueira. The one region that is dramatically different from the others is Portalegre, perched in the foothills of the granite mountain of São Mamede in the north-east, its vineyards at higher (and hence cooler) altitudes than most of the rest. Portalegre also has relatively high rainfall for the Alentejo. The central region includes Borba, Évora, Redondo, and Reguengos de Monsaraz. Soils vary. Borba and Évora have red, chalky soils, often with marble chips (there are big marble quarries nearby). Redondo has more granite and schist in its soils, and Reguengos has granite with some chalk. All these areas are hot, but not as hot as those in the southern regions, Granja-Amareleja, Moura and Vidigueira, which have predominantly limestone soils. Clay is a frequent subsoil throughout the Alentejo, which at least makes for some water retention through the baking hot summers.

The northern Portuguese traditionally view the *Alentejanos* either as lazy folk, prone to sleeping in the sun, or as natural rebels – a tendency thought maybe to have developed through resistance to the owners of the traditionally large estates. Maybe it's this revolutionary

> **Wine regions**
> DOC Alentejo
> Vinho Regional Alentejano
> **Main local grapes**
> *Red* Aragonez, Trincadeira, Castelão
> *White* Roupeiro (Síria)
> *For details of grapes see page 428*

> ### ÉVORA
> **Rota dos Vinhos do Alentejo**
> The Alentejo has a well-organised and wide-ranging system of *Rotas dos Vinhos* (wine routes), coordinated from this centre in Évora. Here you can find out from the friendly and well-informed staff about the three different sections of the Rota dos Vinhos, the northern São Mamede Route, the central Historic Route, and the southern Guadiana Route. You can also buy bottles here from all the wine producers who participate in the Rota do Vinhos. *Praça Joaquim António de Aguiar 20-21 Open Mon-Sat 9-1, 2-6 Closed Sun, public hols T+351 266 746 609 / 266 746 498*

nature that has made the Alentejo such a hotbed of new wines in the last few years. Some producers, with no wineries of their own, are developing new wines in wineries belonging to their neighbours.

DOC Alentejo wines can be made only from permitted grape varieties, and only within these eight sub-regions – and indeed not in all parts of the sub-regions. Some areas of sub-regions are considered unsuitable for producing DOC wines. (Now why, one might ask, did they classify them as DOC in the first place?) Any wine not made within the hallowed lands of DOC Alentejo goes by the name of Vinho Regional Alentejano, and may be made from a long list of grapes, including such unlikely candidates as Pinot Noir and Gewurztraminer. As is frequently the way, even wines *within* the DOC confines often use the VR description, because of greater flexibility in the rules.

Some producers print the sub-region names on labels, but most have realised that 'Alentejo' is a more powerful brand than the names of the individual sub-regions. With the expansion of planting in the south of the Alentejo, some excellent wines are now being made in areas outside the DOC regions. Whether these southern vineyards will become too hot in years to come is a worrying question.

It's already difficult for white wines. Grapes planted here are chosen for their ability to survive the summer, rather than for their aromatic qualities. Best is probably Antão Vaz, which combines good acidity with some tropical fruit. Most widespread is Roupeiro (or Síria), which delivers acidity. Vidigueira has a historic reputation for good whites, but most sensible growers in the southern Alentejo have now realised that the climate is much better for reds. Reds are indeed a more obvious choice throughout the Alentejo, with Aragonez the most planted grape, then Trincadeira and Castelão. Moreto and Castelão, which used both to be prized for their ability to retain acidity, are now being superseded by varieties that ripen fully. Trincadeira is widely grown, and makes some of its best wines here, as long as the weather stays dry. (There's a rot problem in wet weather.) Grapes on the up are Syrah and Alicante Bouschet.

Although most wineries now have totally modern equipment, you will still see some of the old clay *ânforas*, in which wine used to be made. These days they are mainly for decoration. A few wineries still use them for some of their fermentations – but they have an unfortunate tendency to explode if the pressure inside rises too high! Most of the Alentejo takes an immaculately modern, stainless steel approach.

Opposite Portalegre
Above Night harvesting
Far left José de Sousa's historic fermentation jars
Left Picking grapes for the Portalegre co-operative
Right Quinta do Rego

ALBERNOA B2

Herdade da Malhadinha Nova The Soares brothers, João (and his wife Rita) and Paulo (and his partner Margareta), have come to wine production with their eyes wide open. The family runs a chain of wine shops, and they distribute wines to hotels and restaurants in the Algarve, so they know about selling wine. They bought the estate south of Beja in 1998, and had to refurbish it completely. Now its 200ha are home to cork oaks, olive trees, black pigs, Alentejo pure-breed cattle, and 27ha of vines. They produced their first wine in 2003, and won three trophies in the International Wine Challenge in 2005.

In the brand new winery, everything is light and bright, pale wood, steel, glass and transparent plastic. It is built on a hill, and operates by gravity. Grapes pass under watchful eyes on sorting tables before being processed. White grapes are pressed outside, then the juice flows down to tanks. Red grapes go straight to the tanks. The winemaking team when we visited for the 2006 vintage was young (including seven young winemakers studying at various universities), all wearing Malhadinha Nova t-shirts, and all enjoying the modern jazz that vibrated through the building. The very experienced Luis Duarte is the consultant winemaker, and Iain Reynolds Richardson, the consultant viticulturalist.

The labels are designed by João and Rita's children, featuring a caterpillar, a palm-print and a Friesian cow. The range starts with the Monte da Peceguina wines. The **Monte da Peceguina Branco** is about two-thirds Antão Vaz, and equal parts of Roupeiro (Síria) and Arinto. The Arinto starts its fermentation in new oak, which gives the wine a lovely creamy texture, as well as bright acidity and notes of honey and toast. The **Monte da Peceguina Rosé** is off-dry, rose hippy and appealing. The **Monte da Peceguina Tinto** is soft, smooth, ripe and jammy. **Aragonês da Peceguina**, is oaky, sweet-fruited and long, with chocolate and berry flavours. **Pequeno João**, named after João and Rita's son, born in 2004, will be different each year. The 2004 we tasted was an almost syrupy-ripe blend of Cabernet Sauvignon and Aragonez, with very smooth tannins. **Marias de Malhadinha** is a special blend of Aragonez, Cabernet Sauvignon, Alicante Bouschet, Touriga Nacional and Syrah, rich, dense, tannic and discreet. The top wines are named after the estate. **Malhadinha Branco** is barrel-fermented Antão Vaz, full-bodied and toasty, with creamy length. The **Malhadinha Tinto** is a blend of Aragonez, Alicante Bouschet and Cabernet Sauvignon, thick and syrupy, with firm tannins and treacley richness.

Albernoa, 7800-601 Beja
T+351 284 965 210
E reservas@malhadinhanova.pt
W www.malhadinhanova.pt
Visits 9-7 appt preferred
€6 / €10 / €20 (inc lunch)

Herdade dos Grous A few years ago, no one thought that good wine could come from the hot country around Beja, but now there are five or six interesting producers. In 2004, the German company that owns Herdade dos Grous (*grous* means stork, by the way) invited one of southern Portugal's busiest consultant oenologists, Luís Duarte, to manage the estate. Now he keeps an eye on 50ha of olive trees, the 98ha reservoir and 200ha of mixed farming (including Alentejo cattle, Merino sheep and horses), as well as the 70ha of vines.

There is also a very good restaurant and a wine-bar *(page 345)* and 24 rooms for rent *(page 359)*. And you can take a tour round the vineyards and cellar and taste some wines. The winery (built in 2005) is modern and well equipped, with robotically-plunged steel *lagares*, conical vats and a beautiful barrel cellar, its roof supported by pillars clad with schist stones from the vineyard.

There are only 9ha of white vines, and the **Herdade dos Grous Branco** is a blend of Antão Vaz, Arinto and Roupeiro, honeyed and mineral, with a hint of oak. **Herdade dos Grous Tinto** has Aragonez, Alicante Bouschet, Touriga Nacional and Syrah, and is ripe, rich and smooth. The **Herdade dos Grous Reserva** is excellent, rich, sexy and syrupy, with dense, ripe tannins and very good length. We also tasted the **Herdade dos Grous 23 Barricas**, so named because the minimum volume for a wine in a local wine competition was 5,000 litres – just over 22 barrels. This is a blend of Touriga Nacional and Syrah, aromatic and seductive with rich Syrah fruit fleshing out the Touriga perfume.

Albernoa, 7800-601 Beja
T+351 284 960 000
E herdadedosgrous@vilavitaparc.com
W www.herdadedosgrous.com
Visits 12 & 4 Wine shop 9.30-6.30

ARRAIOLOS B3

Herdade das Ânforas This is the Alentejo outpost of José Berardo's Bacalhôa Vinhos de Portugal empire. JP Vinhos had been making wine in the Alentejo since 1979 – Tinto da Ânfora is one of Portugal's best-known Alentejo brands. But the winery was down in Moura, in the south of the Alentejo, whereas most of the grapes came from the north and east. So in 1995, the winery was relocated to an ex-ceramics factory in Arraiolos, just north of Évora. This had been built in 1923, and had been used for drying and de-husking rice after the ceramics business closed. Now the old ovens have been cleaned and are used for storing the wine bottles.

The working part of the winery is very modern, but Bacalhôa has respected the integrity of the pottery with the brick walls and arches restored, and *ânforas* as part of the decorations. All the grapes used in the wines come from Bacalhôa-owned vineyards, in Arraiolos, Borba and Arronches (just south of Portalegre). The majority of vines are of the traditional Alentejo varieties, Aragonez, Trincadeira, Alfrocheiro and Alicante Bouschet, with extra options from more recent vineyards of Touriga Nacional, Syrah and Cabernet Sauvignon. Small stainless steel tanks allow different varieties and parcels to be kept separate, and there are robotic *lagares* for some special batches.

Monte das Ânforas Tinto is bright and lively, with good fruit and gentle tannins. **Tinto da Ânfora** is the big brand, easy and seductive, with glowing fruit and good balance. The big brother is **2003 Tinto da Ânfora Grande Escolha**, rich, dense and firm-tannined, with lovely mulberry fruit, fresh acidity and good length. **Dogma** is the most recent addition to the portfolio, deliberately made fruity and modern to win over new markets, with fresh, damson fruit and a hint of oak.

EN 4, Lugar da Cerâmica, 7040-613 Arraiolos
T+351 266 499 182
E herdadedasanforas@bacalhoa.pt
W www.bacalhoa.com
Visits Mon-Thu 9-6, Fri 9-12, Sat & Sun appt only
€2.50 / €7.50 (depending on wines)

AZARUJA B3

Herdade Paço de Camões The Pinsent family is not quite as thoroughly British as it seems. Clare Pinsent was born a Reynolds, of the same family that owns Herdade de Mouchão, with a long history in the cork industry of the Alentejo. Their farm, Paço de Camões, half way between Évora and Estremoz, has 720ha, mainly of cork oaks, and since 2001 they also have 7.7ha of vines. These were planted by Iain Reynolds Richardson, their cousin and a respected viticultural consultant. There's Syrah, Alicante Bouschet, Alfrocheiro, Aragonez, Trincadeira, Touriga Nacional, Tinta Miuda, Tinta Caiada, and almost a hectare of Viognier. The first vintage was 2003.

The wines are made in a converted olive oil press-house, with half-metre-thick walls and modern insulation covering roof and doors. There's an array of small stainless steel tanks inside, and all winemaking is done by gravity, using a forklift truck instead of pumping.

The wines are named after the most famous poems written by Luís Camões, Os Lusiadas. The best known of these is the tenth verse, or *canto décimo*. **Canto X** (or **Canto Décimo**) is about half Syrah, with roughly equal parts of Tinta Miuda, Alfrocheiro and Alicante Bouschet. It's rich, dense, mineral red, with lovely tannins, and flavours of black fruits, treacle and fennel. **Canto V** (or **Canto Quinto**) is the white, an oaky, apricotty Viognier. The white **Zéfyro** is also Viognier, peachy and fresh.

The winery is visitable, but by appointment. You can have a tour of the estate and cellar, and a free tasting. There is also a small farmhouse available to rent between the cork oaks and the vineyards.
Azaruja, 7005-131 Évora
T+351 266 977 474
E pinsent@btinternet.com
Visits Mar-Sep Mon-Fri 9-6 Oct-Feb Mon-Fri 9-4 appt only 🛏

BALEIZÃO B2

Encosta do Guadiana The Ferrão Castel Branco family has been on this estate east of Beja since the beginning of the 20th century, growing olive trees and cereals. They started planting vines only in 1998, and continued until 2001. The estate now has 110ha of vines (as well as 1,000ha of olive trees). Only red grapes are grown at Monte Paço do Conde, and white grapes are bought in from Vidigueira. The main varieties are Aragonez, Trincadeira, Touriga Nacional, Castelão, Alicante Bouschet, Cabernet Sauvignon,

Syrah and Merlot. Grapes are picked by machine, at night and in the early hours of the morning, to avoid the very high daytime temperatures.

The winery is housed in an old barn, fully equipped with air-conditioning, cooling systems, and all the latest winemaking equipment. Rui Reguinga is the winemaking consultant. The **Herdade Paço do Conde Branco** is a crisp, steely blend of Antão Vaz and Arinto. **Herdade Paço do Conde Rosé** is just off-dry, fresh and grassy. The **Herdade Paço do Conde Tinto** is ripe and treacley, with baked berry fruit and gentle tannins, and the **Herdade Paço do Conde Tinto Reserva**, with 80% Touriga Nacional in the blend, is richly aromatic, with smooth tannins and bright fruit.

A processing plant for all the olives produced on the estate is near completion, and Paço do Conde already sells an olive oil. There will soon be a roadside shop selling all the products from the estate. Meanwhile, you can visit the estate, see the winery and have a tasting during the week, although it's advisable to get in touch before you go. At weekends booking is essential. Prices will vary according to what you want to taste.

Monte Paço do Conde, Baleizão, 7800-611 Beja
T+351 284 924 416
E geral@encostadoguadiana,com
W www.encostadoguadiana.com
Visits Mon-Fri 8-5 appt pref Sat & Sun appt only
€ variable

BORBA C3

Adega Cooperativa de Borba For a co-op that was founded in 1955, the oldest in the Alentejo, this is a very modern winery. There has been a big programme of reinvestment over the last four years, and the results are impressive – stainless steel *lagares*, with steel mesh 'plungers', pneumatic pumps, a vacuum filter: very much 'new world' techniques for Portugal. And the wines are terrific, too, making the most of Borba's position and soils to make reds that rank Borba as one of the top co-ops in Portugal. Almost three-quarters of the grapes delivered to the co-op are for red wines.

Adega Cooperativa de Borba (ACB) has 320 members farming about 2,200ha. One viticulturalist works for ACB all year round, and three others help when required. Most grapes are picked by hand – there are a couple of growers who have machines, and they hire them to others, but that adds up to only about 15%. Grapes are meticulously analysed when they arrive at the winery, for nitrogen and potassium as well as the other usual parameters of sugar, acidity, etc.

Best of the ACB whites is undoubtedly the **Montes Claros Reserva Branco**, a blend of local grapes such as Roupeiro, Antão Vaz, Arinto and Perrum, with some

barrel fermentation, rich, and bready, with good acidity and length. The **adegaborba.pt Rosé** is fresh, modern and appealing, made from Aragonez. There is a good range of single- and two-variety reds, as well. Our pick are **Tinta Caiada & Pinot Noir**, light, savoury and elegant; the **Syrah Touriga Nacional**, aromatic, malty and dark-fruited; the **Syrah**, ripe, malty and raspberry-fruited; and the **Touriga Nacional**, aromatic and intense, with good length. **Montes Claros Reserva Tinto** (made in years when no 'cork label' ACB Reserva is released) is treacley and rich, with firm tannins. The **Adega Cooperativa Borba Cork Label Reserva** also has rich, cherry and damson fruit, with a shade more intensity and complexity. The **ACB Garrafeira** is made in the traditional style, savoury and complex, still with freshness and length. The **Cinquentenário Grande Escolha 2003** was a one-off bottling, to celebrate the 50th anniversary of the ACB. It's very good, young, rich and dense, with plenty of potential, a blend of Cabernet Sauvignon, Alicante Bouschet and Syrah – definitely looking forwards rather than back.

Largo Gago Coutinho e Sacadura Cabral 25, Apartado 20, 7151-913 Borba
T+351 268 891 660
E geral@adegaborba.pt
W www.adegaborba.pt
Visits Mon-Sat 9-6 appt preferred

Quinta do Zambujeiro Owned by Emil Strickler, a Swiss industrialist who lives and works in Singapore, Quinta do Zambujeiro is probably the nearest the Alentejo has to a garage wine. OK, there are 30ha of vines, but yields are low, the work in vineyard and cellar scrupulous, and the price high (about €60, if you can find it). Strickler found Portugal by accident, when looking for a golfing holiday in Greece. Instead he was recommended the Algarve, came, and loved it. He bought a house, and discovered the south of Portugal. In 1998, he bought Quinta do Zambujeiro.

Strickler is a stickler for quality, and has no time for the mediocre. He is aiming for the best, and is certainly prepared to spend his money, whether it's on hand-picking the small yield that remains on his vines after thinning the crop in the summer, or buying the best French oak barrels. Unsurprisingly, with such ripe grapes, his wines come out at high alcohol levels – 15% is the average.

There are three levels of wine, and the more expensive the wine, the lower the yield from the vines. **Monte do Castanheiro** is mainly Trincadeira, with Aragonez, Castelão, Alicante Bouschet and Cabernet Sauvignon as well, very ripe and rich, but with good acidity. Next up is **Terra do Zambujeiro**, roughly equal parts of Trincadeira and Aragonez, with the rest made up of Alicante Bouschet and Castelão. It has wonderfully seductive plum and mulberry fruit, with soft tannins. Top wine is **Zambujeiro**, a blend in which Touriga Nacional dominates the Alicante Bouschet, Aragonez and Cabernet Sauvignon, very rich-fruited, with firm

tannins and terrific, sweet raspberry and herb length. These are wines for lovers of big reds!

Monte do Zambujeiro, Rio de Moinhos,
7150-343 Borba
T+351 268 801 431
E qzambujeiro@iol.pt
W www.zambujeiro.com
Visits Mon-Fri 9-1,2.30-5.30 appt
preferred €8

CASA BRANCA B3

Herdade do Mouchão This 900ha estate north-west of Estremoz has been in the Reynolds family since the late 19th century, and making wine in the same *adega* since 1901. The Reynolds family was in the cork business. It is a marvellous example of a traditional Alentejo property, mostly cork oaks and olive trees, with sheep and black pigs as well, making a small amount of wine in a careful, considered way, with Paulo Laureano as consultant. There are 38ha of vines, mostly Alicante Bouschet, a variety despised in its native France, but able to make exciting, intense wines in the Alentejo.

The Alicante Bouschet vines are mostly in the 10ha Vinha das Carrapetras, along with some Trincadeira, about 2m lower than the rest of the estate, in deep, rich soil with some clay, which retains moisture even through the hottest of summers. The rest of the vineyards have a fairly standard Alentejo blend of Trincadeira, Aragonez, and Castelão for reds, and a little Antão Vaz, Arinto and Perrum for whites. The high-

ceilinged winery stays quite cool through the day, after windows have been opened at 6am to let in fresh air. (They are closed at 9am, to stop hot air entering.) Grapes come into the winery through windows above the *lagares*, and have a cold maceration before fermentation – the winery has a modern refrigeration system. Reds are not destalked. The fragrant, strawberry-fruited, treacley **Dom Rafael Tinto** is fermented partly in *lagares*, partly in some recently-bought French oak vats. It then spends 18 months in vats or used barrels before bottling. The mineral, faintly tropically-fruity **Dom Rafael Branco** is unoaked, and bottled fresh. **Mouchão** is a blend of Alicante Bouschet and Trincadeira, fermented in *lagares*, and aged for two years in old vats, with 20% spending one year in new barrels, to give more elegance. Then it has a couple of years in bottle before being sold. It is dark, rich, intense wine, undoubtedly one of the Alentejo's best, with serious, ripe tannins, notes of treacle, mint and blackcurrant, and terrific length and staying power. The top wine is **Mouchão Tonel 3-4**, released only in the best years, immense, intense and powerful, with alcohol matched by acidity and dense, inky tannins, a monumental expression of what Alicante Bouschet can do (with a little help from Trincadeira).

Mouchão's small team is not really used to receiving visitors. But they have said that with sufficient warning, they could. So, visits are strictly by appointment, but if you're anywhere near Estremoz, it would be a real shame not to go to Mouchão.

Casa Branca, 7470-153 Sousel
T+351 268 539 228
E mouchao@mouchaowine.pt
Visits appt only

CILADAS C3

Azamor Alison and Joaquim Luiz Gomes are a dynamic couple – she is English, he is Portuguese. They met while both were studying for MBAs in London. Originally, they bought this 260ha estate south of Elvas by the Spanish border as a second home and a place where Joaquim could breed Lusitano horses, after he had sold his stockbroking company. They also planted 20,000 cork oaks. Joaquim has now started other business ventures, including Badoca Safari Park *(page 316)*, and left Alison to look after the wine side. She started planting vines in 2000, and

Azamor had its first harvest in 2003. The 27ha now include Touriga Nacional, Touriga Franca, Trincadeira, Alicante Bouschet, Syrah, Mourvèdre, Merlot and Petit Verdot.

There are actually two farms, Zambujal and Rego. The vineyard, house and horses are on Herdade de Rego, the winery and olive trees, on Herdade de Zambujal. Alison did an oenology course at the Catholic University of Porto, and has been using a Barossa winemaker, Tim Smith, as consultant since 2005. He, of course, is very familiar with Syrah/Shiraz. The winery is in what used to be the Zambujal farmhouse, and has been well-stocked with modern stainless steel and expensive French oak barrels.

The wines have come on fast from the first two vintages. **Azamor Tinto** is now a lovely blend of about a third Syrah, with Touriga Nacional, Touriga Franca, Merlot, Mourvèdre and Petit Verdot, with richness, complexity and a perfumed finish. There is also a single-variety **Azamor Petit Verdot**, dense and ripe, with rich tannins and sweet raspberry fruit. Finally, **Azamor Selected Vines** unites Alicante Bouschet, Syrah and Trincadeira, to make a dark-fruited, treacley wine, with firm tannins. This is a very interesting trio, and only in the third year of bottling. There's more to come!

Herdade do Zambujal, Ciladas, 7160-101 Vila Viçosa
T+351 217 998 094
E info@azamor.com
W www.azamor.com
Visits appt only

ESTREMOZ C3

Dona Maria This lovely house dates from 1718, and the old winery is about 150 years old. The chapel on the end of the house was dedicated to Nossa Senhora do Carmo (Our Lady of Carmel), after which the house is named – Quinta do Carmo. The name of the wine comes from another story: that King John V of Portugal gave the house and estate to a courtesan with whom he was madly in love. Her name? Dona Maria. Wine has been made on the estate for over a century, but it was only in 1988 that Júlio Bastos, the owner, decided to sell under his own Quinta do Carmo brand. Four years later, he sold half the business to Domaines Barons de Rothschild, the Lafite side of the family (DBR). A new winemaking cellar was built at another property, Herdade das Carvalhas, and the action moved away from Quinta do Carmo and its historic cellar. In 1999, Bastos decided to sell the other half of the Quinta do Carmo business, and start again at the old house. In 2000, he sold 45% to José Berardo, of Bacalhôa Vinhos de Portugal, and the balance to DBR, to give them control.

This is the reason for the dual use of 'Quinta do Carmo'. The old house is called Quinta do Carmo, but Bastos cannot use that name for the wine, as the brand now belongs to DBR. So 'Dona Maria' it is. When we visited, the new winery was roughly half-finished. There were modern concrete vats, and a stainless steel basket press. Most of the steel vats were yet to come. But it still had (and still has) the magnificent pink marble *lagares*, now equipped with coolers like long, low radiators.

When the vineyard is fully planted, there will be 72ha, 62ha of red varieties and 10ha of white. Of these, the older vines near the Dom Martinho estate are the company's real treasure, with nearly 9ha of old Alicante Bouschet – or something like it! – as well as Aragonez and Trincadeira.

Júlio and Isabel Bastos are keen to welcome visitors and sell them wines. There's a tasting room and a shop, and tours of the winery and tastings are offered. If you want to taste more expensive wines you'll be asked to pay accordingly. Meals can be organised for groups. It's always better to make an appointment.

Dona Maria Branco is a blend of Roupeiro, Arinto and Antão Vaz, rich, full-bodied and characterful. **Dona Maria Tinto** (Alicante Bouschet, Aragonez, Syrah and Cabernet Sauvignon) is ripe and syrupy, with smooth tannins and fresh fruit. **Amantis** is a more modern blend, with equal parts of Syrah, Petit Verdot and Cabernet Sauvignon, and 10% Touriga Nacional, dense, ripe and smooth, with good acidity, rich structure and lovely length. **Dona Maria Reserva** is a blend of older vines, foot-trodden in the marble *lagares*, and aged in new French oak, with lots of fruit, firm tannins and great length. There is one other wine, the **JB Bastos Garrafeira**, from the oldest vines, dense and richly blackberry-fruity, with great structure and fabulous length.
Quinta do Carmo, 7100-055 Estremoz
T +351 268 339 150
E donamaria@donamaria.pt
W www.donamaria.pt
Visits 9-6 (closed Aug 1-15) appt preferred
Food gps only, appt only

J Portugal Ramos When we first met João Portugal Ramos (JPR), he was one of the most widely sought-after consultant winemakers in Portugal. He made the reputations of Quinta do Carmo *(page 332)* and the co-ops at Santo Isidro de Pegões *(page 307)* and Portalegre *(page 334)*. He had a winemaking consultancy company, Consulvinus, and he and his team worked in the Douro, Dão, Beiras, Lisboa, Ribatejo, Terras do Sado and Alentejo. After years of working for others, he decided the time had come to start his own wine business. He bought a vineyard outside Estremoz, not far from Borba, in 1989, planted it the next year, and made his first wine a couple of years later. He built his first winery in 1997, Monte da Caldeira, outside Estremoz, and expanded it in 2000. He also has a winery in Ribatejo, Falua *(page 268)*, and has announced his intention to start another in the Douro.

He's still constantly innovating, and insisted that we visit the winery on our second visit in 2006, as he had changed lots of things. He had. There were 14 new French oak vats for fermentation, and a new epoxy resin floor (the old schist one was too difficult to clean). He explained that the (incredibly expensive) French oak vats would work out cheaper than buying 500 new barrels each year, even if he renewed the vats every six years. Most of the fermentations are now done in the modern, 2000-built winery, with the

1997 winery used mostly for storage and maturation. Despite all the modern equipment, some of JPR's top wines are still trodden by foot in large marble *lagares*.

JPR's vineyard holdings have grown, too, from that first 10ha vineyard, to about 140ha, with another 200ha under contract. The best plots are picked by hand, but most are picked by machine. Grapes arrive at the winery by refrigerated truck, and are then loaded into stationary trucks to chill down further before pressing. The Roupeiro, Rabo de Ovelha and Perrum white varieties that JPR has been using for years have now been supplemented by new plantings of grapes such as Sauvignon Blanc, Verdelho and Viognier.

The result of this very modern approach to vineyard and cellar is that even the basic Loios range is good. The **Loios Branco** is bright, aromatic and fresh, the **Loios Tinto**, ripe and gluggable. Next up the quality ladder, the large-volume **Marquês de Borba Branco**, is bright, lemony and steely, the **Marquês de Borba Tinto**, ripe and berry-fruited, with a touch of oak. The range of single-variety wines is impressive. **João Portugal Ramos Antão Vaz** makes the most of the Alentejo's best white grape, lemony, mineral and rich-textured from barrel-fermentation. **João Portugal Ramos Trincadeira** has bright, aromatic, red fruit flavours and good length. **João Portugal Ramos Aragonês** (the Alentejo spelling) is minty and herby, with raspberry fruit and firm tannins. **João Portugal Ramos Tinta Caiada** is malty, generous, with floral length. The dense, figgy, tannic **João Portugal Ramos**

Syrah needs time in bottle. **Vila Santa** is a blend of Aragonez, Trincadeira, Cabernet Sauvignon and Alicante Bouschet, spicy, complex and intense, with notes of dried fruit as well as fresh. The single-vineyard **Quinta da Viçosa** is a blend that varies according to the year, but always reflects well on the young vines of this 40ha estate. Top of the range is the **Marquês de Borba Reserva**, a dark, smooth, harmonious blend, dense and sweet-fruited, that ages brilliantly.

The shop is open from Monday to Saturday, and tours of the winery are free (but do book in advance). Tastings vary in price, depending on the wines. The more substantial tastings are available only for groups of ten people or more.
Monte da Caldeira, 7100-149 Estremoz
T+351 268 339 910
E jportugalramos@mail.telepac.pt
W www.jportugalramos.com
Visits Mon-Sat 9-6 tours appt only
€5.50 / €11 / €14.50
✗ *by prior arrangement*

ESTREMOZ C3 *(continued)*

Monte Seis Reis 2003 was the first vintage for this very tourism-oriented estate just north of Estremoz. The winery was built the following year. The company was started by Helder de Almeida, who made his money in the packaging business. There are about 50ha of vineyard, mainly planted with red grapes, a mix of Portuguese and international varieties,

Aragonez, Trincadeira, Castelão, Tinta Caiada, Alicante Bouschet, Touriga Nacional, Syrah and Cabernet Sauvignon. The winery is modern, and the winemaker is Luis Carvalho.

Monte Seis Reis offers an excellent tour, with a multi-media presentation on the region and why the estate is named after six monarchs (five kings and one queen), an exhibition about the grape harvest and a tour of the cellars. There is also an art gallery that has temporary exhibitions. And you will get a free tasting of three wines. If you want to taste more, or have some nibbles, you will pay modest prices.

The **Boa Memória Branco** is Antão Vaz, partly fermented in new French oak, rich, buttery and oaky, with good balancing acidity and length. **Monte Seis Reis Rosé** is quite dark, verging on a light red, very drinkable, with lively, bright, berry fruit. **Boa Memória Tinto** is figgy and jammy, with very ripe berry fruit flavours. **Bolonhês** is an Aragonez, Alicante Bouschet, Trincadeira and Tinta Caiada blend, treacley, with red berry fruit, smooth tannins and a hint of oak. The **Monte Seis Reis Tinta Caiada** has lovely soft raspberry fruit and some tannin, and the **Monte Seis Reis Reserva** is the pick of the range, partly fermented in *lagares*, with rich, dried fruit, spice and chocolate flavours, smooth tannins and complexity.
Herdade dos Casarões, Santa Maria,
7100-078 Estremoz
T+351 268 322 221
E loja@seisreis.com
W www.seisreis.com
Visits Winter 9-1, 2-6 Summer 10-1, 2-7
appt preferred Closed 25 Dec & 1 Jan
✗ *by prior arrangement*

Quinta da Esperança Another fairly new enterprise, just north of Estremoz, started by José Castro Duarte and his wife Joana, together with winemaker Miguel Reis Catarino of Quinta da Cortezia in Estremadura *(page 259)*. José bought the estate in 1993, having gained invaluable experience on irrigation whilst growing tomatoes for the Israeli government. He planted 25ha in 1994, and has planted another 75ha since. He sold his grapes until 2001, when he released his first Encostas de Estremoz wines.

The **Terras de Estremoz Tinto** is the lightest of the reds, a blend of Aragonez, Cabernet Sauvignon and Trincadeira, easy, gentle and attractive. **Encostas de Estremoz Touriga Nacional** is herby and aromatic, with dense and powerful tannins.

Encostas de Estremoz Quinta da Esperança is dark, rich and intense, with a hint of treacle, mostly Touriga Nacional, with some Trincadeira and Alicante Bouschet.

Quinta da Esperança has a wine shop where you can taste before buying, Staff will also organise a tour round the winery (and the estate, with enough notice), but they do need warning, and you'll pay for what you taste.
Santa Maria, 7100-145 Estremoz
T+351 268 333 795
E geral@encostasdeestremoz.com
W www.encostasdeestremoz.com
Visits 9-7 appt only

Quinta do Mouro Miguel António de Orduña Viegas Louro was not born into wine. He trained as a dentist. Then he went to Madrid after the 1974 Revolution, where he studied medicine, making money in his spare time from selling antiques. When he returned to Portugal after the Revolution, he decided to buy an estate, marry and settle down (the alternative he rejected was to buy a Porsche Turbo Quattro). He found Quinta do Mouro, and succeeded in buying it on the second attempt. His wine training came from his friend Paulo Lourenço, an influential Alentejo wine figure. After Miguel Louro nearly died from hepatitis caught from oysters, he would have lunch with Paulo every Wednesday. Paulo would drink the wine and explain it, but Miguel would just smell it. After many such lunches, the day Miguel recognised the wine just by smelling it, Paulo pronounced him ready to run a winery.

Quinta do Mouro had 18ha when Miguel bought it in 1979. Now it has 50ha, with 22ha of vines – and horses, which Louro breeds for show-jumping. The oldest vines are 17 years old, with younger plantings from six years ago. The soil is almost all schistous, and the vines are unirrigated. Yields are low, and partly limited by starlings and magpies! His son Luís, a qualified winemaker, also helps, and the consultant oenologist is Luís

Duarte. Equipment is very modern, with shallow stainless steel *lagares* for foot treading the grapes, then deeper ones for the actual fermentation, plunged with *macacos* (literally, 'monkeys', but meaning long poles with wooden cross-pieces at the end, to ram down the cap of skins and stalks). There is also a steel net for submerging the cap during fermentation.

Quinta do Mouro does not produce white wine. The grapes planted are the traditional Trincadeira, Aragonez and Alicante Bouschet, plus Touriga Nacional, Cabernet Sauvignon, Syrah and Merlot. The second wine is **Casa dos Zagalos**, a sweet-fruited, easy red. **Quinta do Mouro** is incredibly consistent, always with bright, fresh acidity, aromatic red fruit flavours and well-handled tannins. Vintages so far made have aged very well. Recently, Miguel has experimented with two other wines, the dense, rich, oaky but aromatic **Quinta do Mouro Gold Label**, and the aromatic, seductive, beautifully-textured **Quinta do Mouro Touriga Nacional**.

Luís Louro, Miguel's son, makes a very open, immediate, mulberry-fruited red called **Alento**, from 14ha of young vines he has rented near Évora.
Quinta do Mouro, 7100-056 Estremoz
T+351 268 332 259
E quintadomouro@sapo.pt
Visits appt only

ÉVORA B3
Fundação Eugénio de Almeida This charitable foundation was started in 1963 by Vasco Maria Eugénio de Almeida, who farmed a huge estate around Évora. He had no children. His family had owned the land since the late 18th century (parts of the old, ex-Carthusian monks' wine *adega* date from 1776). He decided the foundation should benefit the spiritual, cultural and educational needs of the people of Évora, helping with the upkeep of churches, giving money to the University of Évora and to local schools, and generally supporting the community. Part of the 6,200ha estate which Eugénio de Almeida gave to the foundation was vineyard. The estate also has Alentejo and Charolais cattle, cork-forests, woods, cereals and 200ha of olives.

The Fundação Eugénio de Almeida (FEA) receives visitors to the winery, but not the estate. And they need about a week's notice. But the old cellars themselves are worth the visit, and you will be given a free tasting. The winery is a mix of old and new, with ancient *ânforas*, cement vats lined with epoxy resin, and stainless steel vats. Grapes are hand-picked by locals, and three-quarters of the wine made is red. None of the whites is fermented or aged in oak.

FEA has one of the best-known labels in Portugal, Pêra-Manca. It's an illustration by an early-20th century painter, Alfredo Roque Gameiro. FEA acquired the brand, and its striking label, in 1987. Since the first vintage of the red in 1990, they have made a red and a white, the red only in the best years. The **Vinho Pêra-Manca Branco** is rich, tangy and full-bodied, made of Antão Vaz and Arinto, aged for six months on the lees. The **Vinho Pêra-Manca Tinto** is one of the Alentejo's classics, rich and complex, with thick

fruit, structure and length, a blend of Trincadeira and Aragonez. Pick of the inexpensive EA range is the **EA Rosé**, a serious, creamy, dry rosé, about half Grenache, half Castelão. The **Cerca Nova Branco** is crisp and citrussy, the **Cerca Nova Tinto**, smooth and cherry-scented. A definite step up is the **Foral de Évora Branco**, lean, mineral and steely, and the **Foral de Évora Tinto** is rich, jammy and ripe. The **Cartuxa Branco** is creamy, rich and mouth-filling, the **Cartuxa Tinto**, smooth, complex and satisfying. In the years between the red Pêra-Manca vintages, a very good **Cartuxa Reserva** is made.

Adega da Cartuxa, Páteo de São Miguel,
*   Apartado 2001, 7001-901 Évora*
T +351 266 748 380
E dir.com@fea-evora.com.pt
W www.cartuxa.pt
Visits Mon-Fri; public hols appt only, min
*   5 days' notice Closed 15 Aug-31 Oct*

FERREIRA DO ALENTEJO B2

Herdade do Pinheiro The Sylvestre Ferreira family has owned Herdade do Pinheiro for more than 50 years. It was António Francisco Sylvestre Ferreira, grandfather of the current proprietors, who started the company. He grew grapes, 400ha for table, 90ha for wine, and eventually started making wine. He never bottled this, but sold it in bulk to merchants and other companies. In the 1990s, he re-equipped the winery with stainless steel tanks, pneumatic presses and new oak barrels for maturing the wines. It was after his death that his grand-children, Ana Sylvestre Ferreira Bicó and Miguel Sylvestre Ferreira, decided to start bottling and selling their wine, in 2000. The estate now has 110ha of vineyard.

The **Herdade do Pinheiro** has rich, raspberry fruit and good acidity, with very smooth tannins despite a month's maceration on the skins. The **Herdade do Pinheiro Reserva** adds an extra dimension of dried fruit as well as the fresh, with dense, creamy tannins.

Apartado 15, 7900-909 Ferreira do Alentejo
T +351 284 732 453
E geral@herdadedopinheiro.com.pt
W www.herdadedopinheiro.com.pt
Visits Mon-Fri 9-6 appt only

GLÓRIA C3

Quinta do Carmo Domaines Barons de Rothschild (DBR) bought just under half this estate from the Bastos family in 1992, then returned in 2000 for enough shares to make them majority owners. In February 2008, DBR sold their shares to their minority partner, José Berardo, of Bacalhôa Vinhos de Portugal. It is a magnificent 1,000ha estate, just south of Estremoz, mostly on deep, rich, chalky-clay soils. When DBR took over, the idea was to plant vines in the best areas, on slopes. The total is now up to 150ha, half at Herdade das Carvalhas (to the south of Estremoz), and half at Dom Martinho (to the north). After planting 33ha of Portuguese grape varieties with drip irrigation, DBR felt the resulting blend lacked something, so they planted Syrah and Cabernet Sauvignon, the Cabernet for tannin structure, and the Syrah for mid-palate richness. It's a big change from the situation they inherited in 1997, when almost all the vines were Alicante Bouschet. The white varieties (Antão Vaz and Roupeiro) are planted on yellow clay and schist soils, with marble stones. The reds are on the clay and limestone soils. Whites are hand-harvested, reds mostly picked by machine, with the exception of young vines and some varieties.

There are still 350ha of cork oaks, and 100ha of olive-trees as well. In fact, Quinta do Carmo will soon be releasing its own brand of olive oil. Otherwise, all the work has gone into changing the vineyards and building a new winery. Reds are fermented in stainless steel, then the Quinta do Carmo wines are aged in barrel (the second wine, Dom Martinho, is unoaked). Everything is temperature-controlled. The result has been a move away from the dark, firm, savoury wines made before the arrival of the Rothschilds, towards a sweeter, more fruit-driven style.

Quinta do Carmo Branco is fresh, bright and easy, a blend of Roupeiro, Arinto, Antão Vaz and Fernão Pires (they abandoned Perrum, finding it didn't ripen properly or give acidity). **Dom Martinho Tinto** (there is no white Dom Martinho) is fresh-fruited and easy-drinking, with a definite whiff of generous Alentejo character. **Quinta do Carmo** is ripe-fruited, with firm tannins and a touch of oak, and **Quinta do Carmo Reserva** has more oak, and is made in a more complex, sophisticated style, with smooth tannins, length and intensity.

Herdade das Carvalhas, Glória, 7100-040
*   Estremoz*
T +351 268 337 320
E nroque@quintadocarmo.pt
W www.quintadocarmo.pt
Visits Mon-Fri 10-5.30 appt only
*   Closed 20 Jul-15 Aug & Christmas*
€5 / €10

Herdade do Peso Sogrape launched their first Alentejo brand, the inexpensive Vinha do Monte, in 1991. Its success (and the success of Alentejo wines in general) persuaded the directors that they should establish a firmer foothold south of Lisbon. A year

later, they entered into a contract with the owners of Herdade do Peso, near Vidigueira, to supply them with grapes. In 1997, Sogrape bought the 465ha estate. The next year, they started building a modern winery. The first 40ha were planted according to the directives of the local authorities, with local grapes, Castelão, Alfrocheiro, Moreto, Aragonez and Trincadeira. Not all of these were successful, and Sogrape favoured Aragonez in the next 70ha they planted, and added Syrah and Alicante Bouschet. They will probably replace the Castelão and Moreto, and have plans to plant another 50ha with more Syrah, Touriga Nacional, Petit Verdot and Cabernet Sauvignon, as well as some Antão Vaz, Arinto and Chardonnay for white wines. The total will end up at 160ha. The rest of the estate consists of a 20ha reservoir, and olive groves.

Sogrape does not have facilities to receive visitors at Herdade do Peso, but it's worth watching for their range of wines in shops and restaurants. **Vinha do Monte Branco**, a recent addition to the range, and made from local growers' grapes, is crisp and fresh. **Vinha do Monte Tinto** is soft and easy, with pleasing red fruit flavours. The **Herdade do Peso Colheita** is rich-fruited and oaky, with good length. There are obvious possibilities for single variety wines, though so far the only one generally available has been the dark, intense, oaky **Herdade do Peso Aragonês**. Top of the line is the rich, oaky, sweet-fruited **Herdade do Peso Reserva**, with firm tannins and good ageing potential. There are plans for an Herdade do Peso 'icon' wine before long.

Herdade do Peso also makes the Alentejo wines in the Grão Vasco, Pena de Pato and Callabriga ranges. The choice of Aragonez as the main grape in the vineyards is particularly important for Callabriga, as this is the variety common to all the Callabriga range. The **Callabriga Alentejo** has ripe red fruit flavours, with a hint of Alicante Bouschet treacle, and the **Callabriga Alentejo Reserva** has rich, spicy red fruit, with firm tannins, good acidity and length.

Igrejinha B3

Herdade dos Coelheiros Of this estate's 800ha, 500ha are cork oaks, and another 70ha walnuts. And there are 38ha of vines, more than twice as many as there were when Teresa Leal's parents, Joaquim and Leonilde Silveira, bought the estate in 1980. Herdade dos Coelheiros (so named because of the large numbers of rabbits on

the estate) used to be a traditional Alentejo property, with cork oaks and cereals. The wine side was Joaquim Silveira's hobby, but he was away working in Lisbon most of the time. Teresa's mother ran the estate, and, when she died in 2002, Teresa gave up her job in her father's company, and came to the Alentejo. She is keen to develop the tourism side of the business, and has

refurbished nine rooms to rent *(page 361)*, as well as organising hunting, fishing, bird-watching, clay-pigeon shooting, canoeing and cycling as activities for visitors and people wanting a day out in the country. She was about to try keeping black pigs when we visited in 2006.

Herdade dos Coelheiros does receive visitors, but with a stipulation that there should be at least eight in the group, with appropriate notice. If you were staying at the estate, however, you might find them open to persuasion.

The family rebuilt the winery in 2005, installing modern stainless steel equipment. The **Tapada de Coelheiros Branco** is a pleasant, tangy blend of Roupeiro, Chardonnay and Arinto, the Chardonnay barrel-fermented. The result is peachy, with notes of tropical fruit and oak. The **Tapada de Coelheiros Chardonnay** is entirely barrel-fermented, elegant and creamy, with tropical fruit and citrus flavours. Their inexpensive red, **Vinha da Tapada**, has red berry fruit and gentle tannins. **Tapada de Coelheiros Tinto** is much more powerful, a blend of Cabernet Sauvignon, Trincadeira and Aragonez, with dark, mulberry fruit, firm tannins and good length.

Monte dos Coelheiros, Igrejinha, 7040-202 Arraiolos
T +351 266 470 000
E herdadecoelheiros@sahc.pt
W www.herdadecoelheiros.pt
Visits appt only

MONTEMOR-O-NOVO B3

Quinta de Plansel Jörg Böhm's relationship with Portugal had a rocky start: his boat sank off the coast of Lisbon when he was a student. But, having got to know the country, first he started importing wines into Germany, then became interested in studying Portuguese native grapes. Eventually, he started a nursery business in 1981, Plansel Viveiros, selling vines in the Alentejo. This still runs parallel to the wine business, and has become one of the largest vine (and olive sapling) nurseries in Portugal. Böhm has been the first provider of some of the great grapes of the north to the growers of the Alentejo.

In 1997, Böhm's winemaker daughter, Dorina Lindemann, started making wines from 60ha of vines at Quinta de Plansel, in Montemor-o-Novo, west of Évora. (Her husband, Thomas Lindemann, works in the vine nursery side of the business.) Red wines account for 80% of production, and Böhm and his daughter know exactly which clones of what varieties they have planted in their vineyard, as they supplied the vines.

Marquês de Montemor Tinto is a soft but robust red wine, with rich, berry fruit. **Plansel Touriga Franca Colheita Seleccionada** has quite evident oak with perfumed, floral fruit under. It needs time to settle into balance. **Dorina Lindemann Aragonez Touriga Nacional Reserva** is the best – it's a rich, smooth and complex

wine, aromatic and spicy, with good length and structure.

They are happy to receive visitors, without charge, and show them the nursery and cellar, and give a tasting. But you must get in touch to make an appointment. To find the estate, go to Montemor-o-Novo and ask for the German man at Quinta de São Jorge (the old name of the estate). They assure us the locals will point you in the right direction!

Böhm also has an interest in Curral de Atlantis, a company making some of the best wines in the Azores *(page 211)*.

Quinta de São Jorge, Apartado 2,
7051-909 Montemor-o-Novo
T+351 266 899 260
E dorina.lindemann@sapo.pt
W www.plansel.eu
Visits Mon-Fri 8-6 appt only

PORTALEGRE C4

Adega Cooperativa de Portalegre
Quality, not quantity, is what counts at this modestly-sized co-op in the north-east of the Alentejo. It was founded in 1955, and 263 members now farm just 750ha of vineyard. The co-op bought Quinta da Cabaça in 2005. (Usually it's the other way round, with struggling co-ops being bought by private companies). The estate has added 20ha more vineyard, and they have buildings they could develop one day.

All the vineyards are influenced by the proximity of São Mamede mountain, just to the north-east, so night-time temperatures are cooler than in the rest of the Alentejo, and allow the grapes respite from the hot summer days. There are grapes from newer vineyards at around 300m, but the best grapes, from older, lower-yielding vines, come from 500 to 600m altitude. The higher, more northerly vineyards are on granitic soils, and the

lower vineyards around Arronches and Monforte are more schistous. The old-vine grapes are used for DOC wines, and the grapes from newer, lower vineyards go into the VR wines. Unlike some Portuguese co-ops, Portalegre sells all its wine in bottle or bag-in-box (not bulk), because it can, and it gets decent prices to pass on to its members.

The range starts with the Aramenha and Terras de Baco VR wines, then climbs to Conventual. The name commemorates the number of convents to be found in the Portalegre region, and carries a picture on the label of the São Bernardo Convent in Portalegre. The **Conventual Branco** is a blend of Arinto, Fernão Pires and Roupeiro (aka Síria), bright and steely, with a hint of Muscatty aroma. **Conventual Tinto** is about a third each of Aragonez, Trincadeira and Alicante Bouschet, with appealing, easy red fruit flavours. The **Reserva Conventual** is a definite step up, with a third of the grapes from old vines. It also has a little Syrah and Cabernet Sauvignon in with the Portuguese varieties. The result is a dark, rich, intense red, with fresh acidity and some complexity. Above this is the **Portalegre DOC**, all from old high-country vines, mainly Aragonez and Trincadeira, but with 10% each of Alicante Bouschet and Grand Noir. This is complex, dense and treacley, with firm tannins and blackberry and black plum length. Top wine is the **Meio Século 50 Portalegre**, made to celebrate the 50th anniversary of the co-op's foundation, dark, rich and savoury, with dense tannins and very good length. The Reserva Conventual and Portalegre DOC are both wines that would get even better if kept. The Meio Século needs years.

Apartado 126, Tebaida, Ribeiro do Baco,
*   7301–901 Portalegre*
T+351 245 300 530
E jmarmelo@adegaportalegre.pt
W www.adegaportalegre.pt
Visits Mon-Sat 9.30-11.30, 3-5 appt only
€7.50/€30 (with food)

Monte da Penha Francisco Fino, his
wife Verónica and their three daughters
came back from England in 1994, when
he sold the textile company he had been
running. His grandfather had planted the
vines at Tapada do Chaves, and Fino had
been in and around vines and wines since
he was a boy. In fact, he had planted 12ha
of vines, including 2ha of white grapes, at
Monte da Penha, his own property just
outside Portalegre, in 1987, and the grapes
from those vines had been used in Tapada
do Chaves. When Tapada do Chaves was
sold in 1998, the Fino family decided to
start their own wine, from the vines at
Monte da Penha. In 1999, 10ha more were
planted, just of red grapes. The vineyards
are at 450 to 600m altitude, on granite
soils, like the whole of the Portalegre
region. They finished work on the cellar
in 2004, and now have everything in
place except a bottling line (and a mobile
bottler comes to do that). The tasting
room has a slate table top, with chalk and
an eraser for those who forgot their pens
and note-pads.

The **Monte da Penha Reserva Branco**,
made from about one-third each Fernão
Pires, Arinto and Roupeiro (with a dash
of Trincadeira das Pratas), varies according
to the weather of the year. Cooler years
give fresh, herby, aromatic wines. Hotter
years give rich, creamy wines, still with a
mineral backbone. The **Montefino Reserva
Tinto** is made in a deliberately modern
style, including Touriga Nacional, ripe
and easy, with smooth tannins and a hint

of herby aroma. **Monte da Penha Reserva
Tinto** is mostly Trincadeira, with Aragonês,
Alicante Bouschet and a hint of Moreto,
savoury, with rich fruit and lovely length
and balance. Above that is **Monte da
Penha Fino Reserva Tinto**, full of dried
fruit intensity, with bright acid and firm
tannins. Lastly, **Monte da Penha Gerações**
is a wonderful blend, with herby aromas,
dense tannins, intensity and length. It
needs time in bottle.
Monte da Penha, 7300-498 Portalegre
T+351 245 208 342
E comercial@montedapenha.com
W www.montedapenha.com
Visits 9-6 appt only €7. / €9

PORTEL B2

Herdade do Meio João Pombo has been
in the travel business for over 20 years, so
he knows how to receive visitors. The
estate is open all year (except Christmas
Day and New Year's Day), and you can
expect a tour of the vineyards and cellars,
with a tasting of the less expensive wines
at the end. Should you wish to taste more
expensive wines, there will be an
appropriate charge.

Pombo owns 23ha of vineyards, but
also draws on grapes from another 120ha
nearby, supplying year-round viticultural
advice.

The **Egoísta Branco** is crisp and
rounded, with a touch of oak. The **Egoísta
Tinto** has smooth, ripe fruit, with bright
acidity and soft tannins. **Herdade do Meio
Tinto** is dark and rich, with raspberry and
treacle flavours and firm tannins. The **HDM
Cabernet Syrah** is ripely blackcurrany,
with syrupy, malty fruit and smooth
tannins. The **HDM Syrah** is smooth-
tannined and malty, with strong oak
flavour.
Apartado 17, 7220-999 Portel
T+351 266 667 300

E sandra.valeriano.hm@herdadedomeio.pt
W www.herdadedomeio.pt
Visits Mon-Fri 9-5 appt preferred; Sat &
*   Sun appt only Closed 25 Dec & 1 Jan*

REDONDO C3
Adega Cooperativa de Redondo
With an annual production of 14 to 15
million bottles a year, the Adega
Cooperativa de Redondo (ACR) is one of
the largest producers in the Alentejo.
Porta da Ravessa, their biggest brand, sold
over 8 million bottles in Portugal in 2005.
ACR's 300 or so members farm about
3,000ha of vineyard. Redondo lies south
of the Serra de Ossa, and about 30km
west of the Spanish border. It's definitely
red rather than white wine country,
although they have a good, barrel-
fermented, tangy **ACR Chardonnay**.
Their Anta da Serra wines are named after
a famous group of local Neolithic
standing stones about 8km from
Redondo. The **Anta da Serra Branco** is
pleasant, mineral with a dash of Muscatty
Fernão Pires. The **Anta da Serra Tinto** is
very fruity, with fresh, perfumed red fruit
flavours and a hint of treacley Alicante
Bouschet. There are good single-variety
and dual-variety wines, a vigorous,
blackcurranty, slightly rustic **ACR
Aragonês Cabernet Sauvignon**, a rich-
textured, bright-fruited **ACR Trincadeira
Merlot**, and a perfumed, aromatic **ACR
Touriga Nacional**. The **Reserva ACR** is
figgy and dark, with cherry and damson
fruit, and good grainy tannins. The **ACR
50 Anos Garrafeira** is rich, smooth and
berry-fruity, with firm tannins.
Estrada de Évora, 7170-999 Redondo
T+351 266 989 100
E enoturismo@acr.com.pt
W www.acr.com.pt
Visits Mon-Fri 9-5 Sat, Sun & public hols
*   appt only €5-€10*

335

REDONDO C3 *(continued)*

Roquevale Carlos Roque do Vale's grandparents owned a winery in Torres Vedras, where he had his first tastes of hands-on winemaking. Later, he studied food engineering at Beja university, and started Roquevale in 1983. He was president of the local Redondo co-op from 1979 to 1989, and sold the grapes from the family vineyards to the co-op. Then he and his wife set up their own wine business, starting with a small winery, then building a bigger one. Now their daughter Joana, a qualified winemaker, is in charge of the wines, and works on exports.

Roquevale is a successful company because they keep their costs down, and don't rely only on expensive wines to make their profits. It makes for headaches at harvest, as Joana has to use every fermentation vat eight or nine times. But, as she says, they sell everything they make. And the 2.5 million litres they now produce is more than eight times what they made in 1989. They have 185ha of vineyard, 40ha of white varieties near the winery (Roupeiro, Fernão Pires, Arinto and Rabo de Ovelha), and the rest red at Madeira Nova de Cima (Aragonez, Trincadeira, Alfrocheiro, Castelão, Alicante Bouschet, Tinta Caiada, Touriga Nacional, Touriga Franca and Cabernet Sauvignon). They used to have a lot of Castelão and Moreto, but have removed the Moreto, and the Castelão will probably follow soon, to be replaced by more Touriga Nacional.

The wines have changed, too. When Roquevale started, there were three brands, Terras do Xisto, Redondo and Tinto da Talha, all made to be drunk young. Joana added a Grande Escolha to the Tinto da Talha range, and created the company's

top range, Roquevale. They also still make wine for other companies. The winery is modern, with a stainless steel, pneumatically-plunged *lagar* and a brand new wooden basket press, as well as the expected array of steel tanks. The underground barrel cellar has an impressive line of old *ânforas* at one end.

Among the Roquevale whites, best by far is the **Roquevale Branco**, half barrel-fermented, full-bodied, oaky and bright. Best of the Terras do Xisto range is the attractive **Terras do Xisto Rosé**, with fresh, berry fruit. The basic **Tinto da Talha** is good, with bright, red fruit flavours, and a hint of tannin. More ambitious is the **Tinto da Talha Grande Escolha**, a blend of Syrah and Touriga Nacional, with firm tannins and bright, aromatic, herby raspberry fruit. The **Roquevale Reserva** is a step up, very typically Alentejo, rich, ripe and dense, with a lovely texture and good, dried fruit and raspberry length.
Herdade do Monte Branco, Apartado 87,
7170-999 Redondo
T +351 266 989 290
E joana@roquevale.pt
W www.roquevale.pt
Visits 9-5 appt only €7.50

REGUENGO C4

Quinta do Centro Richard Mayson has long had a dream. He has spent much of his life in and observing Portugal, has married into an Anglo-Portuguese family, and has written five books about Portugal and its wines. He has always longed to have a place of his own in Portugal, and it's not surprising that the chosen place has vines. He has gone into partnership with Rui Reguinga, one of southern Portugal's top winemaking consultants, who has spent his life till now working for other people. So it's the realisation of a dream for both of them. No wonder they

called the project 'Sonho Lusitano' (Lusitanian Dream).

The estate is up in the hills above Portalegre, at about 500m altitude, and on poor, rocky but well-drained soil, mingling clay with granite and schist. There are about 6ha of 20 year-old vines, and 6.5ha of young plantations. The old vines have Trincadeira, Alicante Bouschet, Grand Noir and Aragonez, with a small amount of Cabernet Sauvignon. Touriga Nacional, Syrah and a small quantity of Viognier were planted in 2006. A winery has just been finished, as we write this, to be ready for the 2007 harvest.

Mayson is converting an old *adega* into two small houses for his family and visiting winemakers. There are four other houses on the estate (which totals just over 20ha) which will eventually be refurbished for tourist lets. They're not ready yet, though. Reguinga and Mayson will do their best to receive visitors. But it absolutely has to be by appointment and may not always be possible.

The aim, eventually, is to make three wines. The only one that exists so far is what will be the second wine, **Pedra Basta** ('enough stones') red, dark, rich and intense, with dense, stony tannins, real mountain wine. There will be two more expensive wines, the top one only produced

in exceptional years. It's a project we shall watch with great interest.
Reguengo, 7300-401 Portalegre
T+351 968 632 567
E richardmayson@btinternet.com
Visits Mon-Fri 9-6 appt only

REGUENGOS DE MONSARAZ C2

Herdade do Esporão This large wine estate 3km outside Reguengos de Monsaraz is one of the best organised for wine visitors in the whole of Portugal. There are different options for tours and tastings, trips round the vineyards, an excellent restaurant, Galeria *(page 349)*, and a good shop.

First records of Esporão date from 1267, and the estate still has a tower (which appears on their labels) that was probably built in the second half of the 15th century. The estate was bought in 1973 by Finagra, a company set up by Joaquim Bandeira and José Roquette. At that time it had just over 400ha of vineyard. One year later, it was nationalized following the 1974 Revolution. By the time Finagra got it back, in 1984, the vineyards were in poor shape, and needed a lot of reorganisation and work. For the first three harvests, Finagra sold the estate's grapes to the Reguengos co-op, but started work on a new cellar in 1987. The first Esporão wines were from the 1989 vintage, from a new winery, with a red wine maturation cellar dug into the hill.

Australian winemaker David Baverstock has been in charge of the wines for 15 years. After ten years' service, he persuaded the Roquette family (now the majority owners) to build a new white

winemaking cellar, and now he has a small-scale winery as well, in which he makes the top Esporão wines. These days the Esporão vineyards add up to 650ha, with contracts with local growers for another 500ha. It's a big operation, and needs to be, as Monte Velho (made from Esporão grapes) is the biggest wine brand on the domestic market.

In 1997, Finagra bought an ex-olive co-op press in Serpa in south east of the Alentejo, south of Vila de Moura, and they now have a very good range of Esporão olive oils *(page 343)*, made from olives supplied by growers around Moura. The latest acquisition has been a couple of cheese-making companies in Serpa, in 2000. So the Esporão shop has other home-made goodies apart from wine. They also run courses on wine, and on matching wine with food. And the Historical Centre in the beautifully-restored tower, not far from the winery, has an excellent exhibition about Perdigões, the largest Copper Age settlement in Portugal and one of the largest in the Iberian Peninsula. There are many Bronze Age artefacts in the display, associated with cooking and farming, hunting and funerals.

Even the two **Monte Velho** wines are good: the white is crisp, floral and citrussy, the red easy and juicy-fruited. The range of single-variety wines is very good: the tropical-fruited, floral **Esporão Verdelho**, the bright, herby **Esporão Touriga Nacional**, the dark, ultra-ripe, soft **Esporão Trincadeira**, the perfumed, sweet-fruited **Esporão Aragonês**, the dense, inky **Esporão Alicante Bouschet** and the raspberry-fruited, elegant **Esporão Syrah**. The **Esporão Reserva Branco** is oaky but balanced, complex and bright-fruited, and the **Esporão Reserva Tinto** is dense, ripe, spicy and thick-fruited. The **Esporão Private Selection Garrafeira Tinto** is huge, rich and soft-tannined, with dense fruit and good acidity. Finally the **Torre de Esporão** is very oaky, but with aromatic, herby Touriga Nacional perfume and notes of fig and red berry.
Apartado 31,
7200-999 Reguengos de Monsaraz
T+351 266 509 280
E enotur@esporao.com
W www.esporao.com
Visits 10-6 appt preferred
Closed 25 & 25 Dec
€2.50/€10

José de Sousa Rosado e Fernandes
José Maria da Fonseca (JMF) have only one base outside their Terras do Sado heartland, and that is in the eastern Alentejo. The winery is José de Sousa Rosado e Fernandes, and the vineyard is Monte da Ribeira. The Soares Francos took their time to find the right estate. We first visited in 1987, the year after they had bought it. The *adega* was in a pretty chaotic state, with dodgy-looking amphorae tethered to the walls by green plastic string. But they had the vineyard, 65ha of it, planted in 1952, 1953, 1954, 1962 and 1974. The vines are Aragonez, Trincadeira and Grand

Noir (like Alicante Bouschet, a red-fleshed, red-juiced grape). All are irrigated, from five wells within the vineyard. A circle of granite boulders rings the vineyard, and another stands on a rise in the ground towards the centre, marking an ancient Celtic burial site. All the posts supporting the wires for the vines are of granite.

Today the winery is immaculate. You enter through a room in which there stands a 4m menhir, with a small exhibition of pottery and stone implements, all found when cultivating the vineyard. The amphorae fermentation cellar is awe-inspiring. You look down from the *lagares* onto 120 amphorae, standing on small raised platforms in ordered rows, beautifully lit in the Romanesque, brick-arched cellar. There is also a modern, 44-vat stainless steel winery where the basic José de Sousa wine is made, as well as Montado red and white wines, first made in 1991.

It's a really worthwhile visit, but do make an appointment. There are guided tours and tastings, and you can buy.

Montado Branco is clean, lemony and modern. The red version, **Montado Tinto**, is soft and ripe, with gentle tannins and appealing fruit. The **José de Sousa Reserva** is rich and ripe, with smooth, dense tannins – quite a modern Alentejo red. The Jose de Sousa Mayor is what used to be known as the Garrafeira. But, as the Garrafeira became more modern, the local tasting authorities would not allow the term '*garrafeira*' to be used. So **José de Sousa Mayor** was invented, a firm, rich, challenging red, dense and complex.

Rua de Mourão 1, 7200-291 Reguengos de
  Monsaraz
T+351 212 198 940 / 266 502 729
E enoturismo@jmfonseca.pt
W www.jmf.pt
Visits Mon-Fri 8-12, 2-5 or by appt only
€1.80(€2.14 Sat & Sun)/€3(€4 Sat & Sun)

SANTA VITÓRIA B2

Casa Santa Vitória The idea that a hotel chain should own a wine estate seems strange until you realise that the winery is actually part of one of the hotel complexes *(page 361)*, and the wine made there is served in every one of the 18 hotels. The next surprise is that the wine is very good. South-west of Beja, it's a substantial estate, with 102ha of vines (and 90ha of olive trees – yes, they have their own olive oil, too). 95ha are planted with red grape varieties, Touriga Nacional, Trincadeira, Aragonez, Cabernet Sauvignon, Syrah, Merlot, Alfrocheiro, Tinta Caiada and Alicante Bouschet, and 7ha with white, Roupeiro, Antão Vaz, Arinto and Chardonnay. The top wines are hand-picked, the rest by machine. Similarly, the top reds are foot-trodden in *lagares*, the rest fermented in steel tanks – although some of the tanks have robotic plungers, and others are very modern and conically-shaped. Most of the oak barrels Santa Vitória uses are French (more subtle, more expensive), only 30% American. The impressive winery was completed in 2004, on three levels, gravity fed.

The **Santa Vitória Branco** is an unoaked blend of Antão Vaz, Roupeiro and Chardonnay, honeyed, fresh and crisp. **Santa Vitória Rosé** has bright, raspberry fruit and a candied, creamy texture – dangerously drinkable! **Santa Vitória Tinto** is rich-textured and ripe, with malty, red fruit flavours and ripe tannins. **Santa Vitória Branco Reserva**, Chardonnay and Arinto, is creamy, ripe, rich, with lovely tropical fruit. **Santa**

Vitória Reserva is full of spicy, red berry fruit, ripe and quite complex. **Inevitável**, is big, ripe and dense, with firm tannins well-covered by rich fruit and **Santa Vitória Touriga Nacional** is brilliantly aromatic with soft, rich tannins.

The free tour doesn't include the cellar, but if you're staying at the hotel, you might be able to persuade them.

Herdade da Malhada, 7800-730 Santa
  Vitória
T+351 284 970 170
E info@santavitoria.pt
W www.santavitoria.pt
Visits 11-1, 4-6 appt preferred
€7.50 (min 10 people)

SÃO MIGUEL DE MACHEDE B3

Herdade São Miguel It's not just vines and cork oaks on Alexandre Relvas' 175ha estate north-east of Évora. You'll find rare breeds of donkeys and horses as well, from Mirandela and Gerês respectively. Relvas is a very successful businessman and politician (Secretary of State for Tourism between 1991 and 1995), who bought the estate in 1997, and planted 35ha of vines in 2001. There are now 85ha of vineyard and 97ha of cork oaks, and a winery built in 2003. Everything is new, in vineyard

and cellar, with viticultural techniques that avoid damage to friendly insects. First grapes to be planted were Aragonez, Trincadeira and Alicante Bouschet. Cabernet Sauvignon was added later.

The wines are very successful for such a young enterprise. Probably having the experienced Luís Duarte as consultant helps. The easy-drinking, raspberry-fruited **Montinho São Miguel** is a blend of Aragonez, Trincadeira and Cabernet Sauvignon. The **Herdade de São Miguel** is made from 40% Aragonez, 30% Trincadeira, and equal parts of Cabernet Sauvignon and Alicante Bouschet, soft, smooth and syrupy, with a touch of ripe tannin. The **Aragonês de São Miguel dos Descobridores** is full of soft, ripe berry fruit, with a long raspberry perfume. Finally, the **Herdade São Miguel Reserva** is about one-third each of Aragonez, Cabernet Sauvignon and Alicante Bouschet, made in a more international style, with more oak than the others, ripe and smooth, with plenty of treacley Alicante Bouschet flavour.

Herdade da Pimenta, São Miguel de Machede, Évora
T+351 266 988 034
E nuno.franco@herdadesaomiguel.com
W www.herdadesaomiguel.com
Visits appt only

SELMES B2

Cortes de Cima Carrie Jorgensen's great-grandfather emigrated from the Azores to New York in 1888. One century later, Carrie and her Danish-born husband, Hans Kristian Jorgensen, arrived in Portugal in search of a new life. They had met in Malaysia, where Hans worked as chief engineer for a plantation company, growing palm oil, coconut oil, cocoa and tea. They looked in California, Bordeaux and Galicia, before settling at this 365ha

estate near Vidigueira. Here they have raised children, olives, cereals and vines. When the Jorgensens arrived there were no vines at Cortes de Cima. Now there are 105ha, including those planted on a long-term-leased neighbouring vineyard. They also have 50ha of cork trees, 50ha of olives, 100ha of cereals and plenty of fruit and veg.

After taking advice from Harold P Olmo, Professor of Viticulture at the University of California at Davis, they decided to plant red wine grapes, although Vidigueira is traditionally a white wine area. They also consulted Richard Smart about their viticulture, and he advised a much higher vine-training system than the local rules permitted. Nothing daunted, the Jorgensens planted red vines, trained them according to Smart's advice, and have been making very good wine since their first harvest in 1996. Hans is in charge of vineyard and wine (assisted by a French winemaker), Carrie supervises everything else.

Cortes de Cima is open to visitors, but they need notice. You can buy the Cortes de Cima olive oils and wines, and taste.

All the Cortes de Cima wines are VRs: the Jorgensens don't believe in the restrictions imposed by DOC regulations. **Chaminé** is their inexpensive red, soft, bright and easy. There are various single-variety wines, a rich, malty **Syrah Cortes de Cima**, a bright, appealing **Trincadeira Cortes de Cima** and a syrupy, intense, aromatic **Touriga Nacional Cortes de Cima. Cortes de Cima** is a blend, principally of Aragonez and Syrah, ripe, smooth and aromatic. Now that Syrah is accepted as a grape for VR, **Incógnito Cortes de Cima** no longer has to hide its identity. 'Incognito' is out in the open, is used for the top Syrah wine, which is smooth, perfumed and intense, dense and

complex. The **Cortes de Cima Reserva** is the top red, perfumed and syrupy, with dense tannins and great length.

Selmes, 7960-189 Vidigueira
T+351 284 460 060
E wine@cortesdecima.pt
W www.cortesdecima.pt
Visits Mon-Fri 9-5 appt only Closed Aug,
24 Dec-1 Jan

TRINDADE B2

Herdade da Mingorra The owner and hands-on boss at this estate is Henrique Uva (Henry Grape, in English). His great-grandfather was the man who collected the taxes on wine for the king, and earned the name in this royal service. It's a big estate, 1,400ha, and the Uva family have been growing grapes there for at least 30 years. Until 2004, Uva sold the grapes to Esporão *(page 337)*. Then he built a

winery, in close co-operation with his consultant oenologist, Pedro Hipólito. It's big, as it has to be to receive grapes from 135ha of vines, and has all sorts of modern equipment, such as pneumatic plungers for the stainless steel lagares, cone-shaped steel vats, a plunging system inside the red fermentation vats, and micro-oxygenation.

Mingorra's vineyards give it a big advantage. 60ha of these are probably the oldest varietally planted vineyards in the

Alentejo, about 30 years old, with another 35ha 20 years old. The estate also has 150ha of olive trees (no olive oil – yet), and grows sugar beet and wheat. There is also a lot of forest, and hunting, a happy hunting ground. They have plans to start receiving visitors in another year or so.

Most of the Mingorra wine is red. The old vines are the ones you would expect to find in the Alentejo, Trincadeira, Aragonez, Alfrocheiro and Castelão, with some Alicante Bouschet and Merlot. The younger vines include Cabernet Sauvignon, Touriga Nacional and Syrah. The white vines are mostly Antão Vaz, with, more recently, Arinto, Verdelho, Semillon, Alvarinho and Viognier. The **Alfaraz Reserva Branco** is straight Antão Vaz, fermented in new French oak barrels, and aged in them for another six months. It's rich, bready and intense, and needs at least another year in bottle. **Alfaraz Tinto** is very Cabernet-dominated, with treacly richness coming from Alicante Bouschet, and good acidity. **Alfaraz Merlot** is ripe and plummy, with firm tannins and a juicy-fruited finish. **Alfaraz Reserva Tinto** is rich, syrupy and intense, dominated by the Alicante Bouschet in the blend. Finally, **Vinhas da Ira** is the wine made

from old vines, dark and wild, with intensity and smooth tannins – a very exciting wine.
Trindade, 7800-761 Beja
T +351 284 952 004
E geral@mingorra.com
W www.mingorra.com
Visits 8-7 appt only, 3 days' notice

VIDIGUEIRA B2

Paulo Laureano Vinus This business used to be Eborae Vitis & Vinum. It has recently had a change of name, reflecting the fact that Paulo Laureano and his wife Teresa now have substantial vineyards of their own, 10ha near Évora, and another 75ha recently bought with the new winery at Vidigueira. That Laureano is a very good winemaker is in no doubt: he is the consultant behind the Mouchão wines, and has received all sorts of awards and plaudits. Now it's time to see what he can do on his own account. He is a devoted supporter of Portuguese grape varieties, and believes that they are one of the most important points of difference for Portuguese wines on export markets. Indeed, the old vines, many of relatively obscure Portuguese varieties, were one of the attractions of the Vidigueira estate. In

this Portuguese-only enclave, interloper Alicante Bouschet, a reject in its own country, France, is an honorary refugee. If you want to visit the winery, you must make an appointment in advance.

We haven't tasted all his wines, but enough to know they're worth looking out for. His **Dolium Reserva** is a blend of Aragonez and Cabernet Sauvignon, smooth, ripe and oaky, with sweet, fragrant length. He also has a barrel-fermented Antão Vaz, **Paulo Laureano Reserve Branco**, citrussy and soft, with lovely, toasty length. His **Paulo Laureano Premium** is less expensive, dense and rich, but accessible. The **Paulo Laureano Reserva** is dense and structured, with high tannins, and dark, rich, serious fruit.
Monte Novo da Lisboa, Apartado 8, 7960-909 Vidigueira
T +351 284 437 060
E luisavr@eborae.pt
Visits Mon-Fri 9-5 appt only

WATCH OUT FOR THESE WINES

Some Alentejo wineries are not open to visitors – or not yet, at any rate. This is a list of wines we have tasted and liked. We hope you enjoy them as well!

Red
Sexy Rosé, **Sexy Tinto** and **Preta** red (Fitapreta)
Quinta da Terrugem (Aliança)
Pontual Reserva (PLC – Companhia de Vinhos do Alandroal)

Monte dos Cabaços Tinto (Monte dos Cabaços)
Borba Reserva (Sovibor)
Monte das Servas (Herdade das Servas)
Alento (Luís Louro)
Terrenus Reserva (Rui Reguinga)
Farizoa (Caves Velhas)
Lapa dos Gaivões and Valle do Junco (João Teodósio Barbosa)
Altas Quintas (Altas Quintas)

Eat in the Alentejo

An hour or two of driving through the Alentejo shows why this cuisine is based upon bread. Cornfields stretch to horizon after horizon. Wheat is the main bread-earner, as well as the staple. This was a land of tough, calorie-hungry labourers, short of money to spend on protein. There were also potatoes and rice, but good, firm, solid bread was the filler, cooked in dishes, as well as alongside. Though such poverty has passed, the *Alentejanos* still love and promote their bread-based dishes.

First style of bread dish is the *açorda,* a bread soup, at its simplest a wet mush of slices or cubes of bread with eggs, garlic, coriander or pennyroyal (*poejo,* a mint-like herb), olive oil and stock – the quality of the stock makes a huge difference. Nowadays meat or fish is often added, as it would have been on celebration days of old. *Migas* (meaning crumbs) are fried bread, sometimes truly crumbs, sometimes slices of bread fried generally in lard or bacon fat, accompanied by sausage, pork and bacon.

Pork is top meat. The Alentejo is of course famous for the meat, ham and charcuterie of its black pigs – *porco preto (see overleaf).* Every scrap of offal is prized. Pigs' ears are a delicacy we have not yet learned to appreciate… but tongues and trotters are another matter. At carnival time, there are delicious *pezinhos de porco de coentrada,* a gooey stew of trotters, garlic, onions and leaf coriander. *Batatas bêbedas* are spare ribs with potatoes, cooked in wine, red pepper, bay leaves, parsley and garlic. Pork also comes mixed with clams in Portugal's most famous pork dish, *porco à Alentejana,* or *lombo de porco com amêijoas*: cubes of marinated pork braised with onion, garlic, tomatoes, sweet peppers, chilli or piri-piri, to which clams in their shells and chopped coriander are added in the final moments. *Xerém,* a cornmeal porridge, also combines seafood with pork.

Charcuterie is made everywhere, but the ones with Denominacão de Origem Protegida (DOP) status are from around Portalegre, Borba and

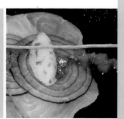

Above and left In the restaurant of the Hotel da Cartuxa, Évora, loin of pork Alentejo-style, with green asparagus *migas,* and *carne de porco à Alentejana*

Right At Divinus, Évora

PORCO PRETO — THE 'OLIVE TREE ON LEGS'

The black pig of the Alentejo is recognised by chefs and gastronomes throughout Portugal and beyond as very special meat: not only the fresh meat, but also the charcuterie *(enchidos)* and the wonderful, rich, flavourful ham *(presunto)*. The *porco preto* is apparently descended from a wild boar of Iberian or Roman origin with a particular genetic capacity for laying down fine streaks of intramuscular fat. These marblings give the meat its unctuous consistency and unique flavour. Dark of skin, the pigs usually also have dark trotters at the end of their long, thin legs.

The black pigs run free for much of their lives, 14 to 16 months, in the Alentejo cork groves, opening and eating the fallen acorns, as well as grass, herbs and roots. There's no shortage of fodder — the Alentejo has 400,000ha of holm oak, and 725,000ha of cork oak forests. The best and most expensive hams *(presuntos)*, classified as 'Bolota', are from pigs that were slaughtered directly after this life of free foraging. The acorns *(bolotas)* are rich in oleic acid, a beneficial, cholesterol-busting fatty acid found also in olive oil. And the flavoursome fat of these black pigs contains between 50 and 60% oleic acid — the porco preto is 'an olive tree on four legs', according to one nutritionist. Nowadays, some Alentejo pigs have a diet in their last months supplemented with grain or other feed. 'Recebo' on the label indicates a partially grain-fed pig. These hams are still good, if less deeply delicious.

The top, acorn-fed hams have the classification of DOP (Denominação de Origem Protegida): Presunto do Alentejo, Paleta do Alentejo, and Presunto de Barrancos (a town in the mountains by the Spanish border whose cool climate is especially suited to the production of fine hams). *Presunto* is ham from the back legs, *paleta* from the forelegs. *Presunto serrano* simply means that the pig was raised in the mountains. *Pata negra* (black foot), incidentally, is not an official term, though it is often used for the black, aristocratic, acorn-eating pigs, some but not all of which have black feet. Confusingly, another, lesser breed also with black feet is also called *pata negra*...

CHEESES OF THE ALENTEJO

Of many delicious Alentejo goat and sheep's cheeses, **Serpa** is the best known. It's a Serra-type cheese, curdled with thistle rennet, lusciously buttery when young in late winter or spring, maturing to a stronger flavour, semi-dry and nutty. The milk should come from the wide Serpa region, the southern third of the Alentejo, but the cheese doesn't have to be made in Serpa. **Nisa** is a pale, pure sheep's cheese from the north, again thistle-curdled, made in a wide area around Portalegre and Nisa. **Mestiço de Toloso** comes from the same area, but is softer, with a wrinkly skin. **Évora** is a small, crumbly ewe's milk cheese, sometimes with a splash of goat, pale yellow, semi-hard to hard. All are curdled with rennet made from local wild thistles. From the whey, farmers make *requeijão*, a delicious, creamy ricotta. Try it for breakfast with the local honey cake, *bolo podre*.

Above An appetising *sopa de cação*, dog fish soup, from the Hotel da Cartuxa in Evora. Dogfish is a mini-member of the shark family, very popular on Alentejo menus

Beja, along with the very fine hams *(presuntos)* from the hills of Barrancos by the Spanish border.

Lamb and kid stews are popular, chickens are much in evidence. *Arroz de cabidela* is not a native Alentejo dish, but appears a lot on menus; it's chicken cooked with rice in wine, garlic, onion, olive oil, *chouriço*, a splash of vinegar and finished with the chicken's blood. *Empadas de galinha,* little, round pies of chicken, bacon and *chouriço*, garlicky and herby, are a speciality of Évora.

From mid-October to Christmas, game is the treat: lots of quail, pheasant, red-legged partridge. The Alentejo is famous for its wild boar *(javali)*, which, like the black pig, becomes fatter and particularly flavourful on a diet of acorns. Its hams *(presunto de javali)* can be very special. You will certainly meet hare *(lebre)* and rabbit *(coelho)*. Snails *(caracóis)* are popular too.

Apart from lamprey (in season early in the year) and eel stews, *bacalhau* is as present here as anywhere in Portugal, but perhaps the most common fish dish is *sopa de cação* – dog fish bread soup. Dogfish is a very small member of the shark family, meaty but not very exciting in flavour – the flavour comes from garlic, olive oil and coriander leaf or pennyroyal. By the coast

OLIVES AND OILS

Around Elvas and Campo Maior in the north-east Alentejo is one of Portugal's most important olive-growing regions. Our favourite extra virgin oils of the Alentejo are Cortes de Cima, Casa Aragão, Quinta das Marvalhas, Quinta da Urze, Quinta Calábria, and Esporão, whose interesting single variety oils are outshone by the more complex blend, the excellent Private Selection.

and increasingly inland, there are the usual excellent sardines, octopus, cuttlefish, squid stuffed with ham and sausage, *cataplana* (borrowed from the Algarve) and mixed fish soups and stews. Fish may be served as a side dish to the ever popular *gaspacho*.

Spanish *gazpacho* is whizzed up in a liquidiser. The Alentejo version, with its welcome ice cubes, keeps its tomatoes, cucumbers and peppers in cubes; they add chunks of bread (of course), or pour the cold soup over a slice of bread in the bowl. Gaspacho sometimes has slices of ham or *chouriço*. Herbs are used in traditional Alentejo cooking more than in some other parts of Portugal – pennyroyal *(poejo)*, coriander leaf *(coentros)*, and oregano *(orégãos)*, which grows wild. Bay leaves flavour sauces, and appear on skewers, between fish or meat, and there's thyme and mint. Wild asparagus may come fried, with scrambled eggs. *Massa de pimentão* flavours many dishes, and this paste of roasted red peppers, garlic and olive oil also arrives as a nibble, to spread on your pre-prandial

bread. Chestnuts are important ingredients, especially around Marvão in the far north-east.

The Alentejo has great fruit from expanses of orange groves and orchards. The plums of Elvas are a treasure. Portalegre has lovely black cherries and small, aromatic, super-sweet Bravo de Esmolfe apples. For pudding, *tecolameco* is a rich, sweet orange and almond cake from Portalegre, *bolo podre* is a very sweet honey cake, dense and yeast-risen, flavoured with lemon and cinnamon, and *sericaia* is a very sweet, egg-and-sugar, cinnamon-flavoured pudding, often served with poached Elvas plums *(ameixas de Elvas)*.

A couple of decades ago, the Alentejo could boast only a tiny handful of interesting restaurants, and a plethora of rustic taverns. Travellers in the Alentejo today, selecting restaurants with care, can expect a much more gastronomic experience. Many chefs are taking the Alentejan traditions in new, creative, lighter directions. In Evora especially, you will be spoilt for choice.

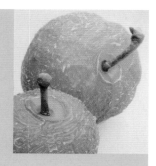

ELVAS PLUMS

The Rainha Claudia Verde greengage, the famous *Ameixa de Elvas,* has a unique, tangy flavour, its sweetness and acidity in wonderful balance. The first trees were apparently brought from Goa to a convent in Elvas, where the nuns developed the technique of sugaring, drying and so preserving these very special fruits. The Portuguese consider them a great Christmas treat (and so do we). They are also served poached in syrup, often as an accompaniment to *sericaia (left).*

RESTAURANTS

ALANDROAL   C3

A Maria The decor here contrives to suggest that you're eating outside, walls painted typical *monte* white, edged with the familiar deep yellow and blue. The sky-blue ceiling adds to the illusion. The only difference is that in here, in summer, it's blissfully cool. There's no illusion in the food, however, which is typically and skilfully Alentejan. Just don't eat too many of the delicious *petiscos!* These might be chicken pie, rabbit or chickpea salads, little mackerel in *escabeche*, or dogfish soup. After that you might order *migas* with pork, roast lamb, baked pig's trotters, bean stew with duck and turnips. There's a good wine list. But you really should leave room for some of the best sweet dishes, all sorts of almondy, figgy, eggy delights.
Rua João de Deus 12
T+351 268 431 143
€25 ♀ *V*
Closed Mon (except public hols); 2nd half Aug

ALBERNÔA   B2

Herdade da Maladinha Nova Alongside the winery *(page 324)*, down the drive from the hotel *(page 359)*, a smart, modern restaurant with terrace offers the accomplished cooking of Artur Carneiro. Alentejo cuisine in light, modern guise and well-judged portions. Enjoy good Alentejo bread, and straight from the farm, olives and olive oil, vegetables, meat and hams.
T+351 284 965 210,
E reservas@maladinhanova.pt
W www.maladinhanova.pt
€45 ♀ *V!* 🍴 *Closed Sun, Mon; Jan*

Herdade dos Grous A lovely, airy restaurant with pale yellow walls and tastefully repro dark wooden furniture. The cooking is 'modern Alentejo', in touch with its roots, but elegantly presented, incorporating ingredients and herbs you'd rarely see in traditional kitchens. Local produce is used wherever possible, even from this wine estate's own farm. Results are delicious, from the hot bread with olive oil and garlic to the assortment of belt-straining sweet dishes. The restaurant is open for lunch all week and also in the evenings at weekends and holidays. A very pleasant wine bar also serves daytime snacks. You can visit the wine estate *(page 324),* and there's a shop where you can buy the estate's wines, amongst other goodies. Or stay here *(page 359)*.
T+351 284 960 000
E herdadedosgrous@vilavitaparc.com
W www.vilavitahotels.com
€25 ♀ 🍴
Closed Restaurant din Mon-Thu Wine bar
   din Sun-Thu

BEJA   B2

Pousada de São Francisco We feel the food has probably improved since there were nuns dining in the magnificent, white-walled, vaulted refectory at this 13th century convent, now beautifully restored as a hotel. The kitchen offers a modern interpretation of Alentejo food,

artistically presented. Familiar themes and ingredients are much on display – *porco preto, presunto*, dogfish, Alentejo Mertolenga beef, and the rest. But the *migas* might look like a delicate dumpling alongside carefully arranged meat, or the soup garnished with fresh herbs and sprinkled with local extra-virgin olive oil. A good wine list is mainly Alentejo.
Largo Dom Nuno Álvares Pereira
T+351 284 313 580
E recepcao.sfrancisco@pousadas.pt
W www.pousadas.pt
€35 🍴

CABEÇO DE VIDE (FRONTEIRA)   C4

Restaurante Rolo There's something rather romantic about an alternative use for a railway station. Trains may no longer rattle through, carrying people or cargo to other places, but something remains, something of the air of impermanence, of possibilities uncharted. Rolo set up in the ex goods-shed of this little station some years ago. The old station is now an inn with 18 rooms, for those who want to travel no further, at least for the night. And the restaurant is known for its buffets and grills. For the first course, help yourself from a selection of 40 different *petiscos* – hams, *enchidos*, vegetable dishes and salads. Then on to grills, beef, pork, lamb, and maybe game. If you've room, there's another buffet of desserts.
Antiga Estação da CP
T+351 245 638 030
E geral@estalagemrainhadleonor.com
W www.estalagemrainhadleonor.com
€25 V 🍴 *Closed Mon*

CUBA B2

Adega da Lua An old winery *(adega)* has been turned into this attractive little restaurant, with appealing touches of blue on tables and windows, and room for about 45 customers. Linger at the little bar for drinks and *petiscos*. Soups may be dogfish, or tomato with fish. Meat comes next, with lamb taking pride of place up here in the hills. There will also be pork, served perhaps with *migas*, or plainly roast.
Travessa das Francas 1
T+351 284 412 200
W www.adegadalua.com
€20 No credit cards
Closed Mon; Aug

ESTREMOZ C3

Adega do Isaías With large, clay, amphora-shaped fermentation jars lining the walls, there's no mistaking that this was once a winery *(adega)*. Trestle tables with checked cloths complete the rustic feel, and the traditional menu is excellent value, mainly tasty meat grills and roasts. Good bread and olives start the meal. You might choose *migas* with pork, duck risotto, or *bacalhau* with prawns. Drink a jug of home-made wine, or choose from a good Alentejo list.
Rua do Almeida 21
T+351 268 322 318
€15-€20 ♀ V No credit cards
Closed Sun, public hols; 2nd & 3rd week
Aug

Cadeia Gratings for chairbacks and bars at the windows will remind you that this was a prison from the 16th century onwards; but the prisoners

would have been much cheered by the white, orange and scarlet designer decor. The food strikes an authentically Alentejo note, with a modern presentation to match the atmosphere. There are substantial soups, toasted sheep's cheese with oregano, marinated mushrooms, and *enchidos*, hot and cold. There will certainly be some *porco preto*, maybe lamb and chicken. And of course there are puddings, and a decent wine-list. A bright upstairs bar in red and white used to be the women's jail, and the jailer's flat. Escape there for coffee, perhaps.
Rua Rainha Santa Isabel
T+351 268 323 400
E cadeiaquinhentista@sapo.pt
W www.acadeiaquinhentista.com
€25-€30 ♀ V! Closed 24 Dec

Pousada Rainha Santa Isabel The restaurant of this historic *pousada (page 360)* is in a wonderful, high-arched hall. On Saturday evening and Sunday lunch, they offer a magnificent 'Royal Buffet', with every sort of Alentejo dish, hot and cold. Otherwise, the long menu offers mainly Alentejo dishes, and decent wines. Soups could be tomato or bean; then *açorda* with pork, wild asparagus and mushrooms in pastry, or salads various. Fish might include dogfish in coriander sauce, *bacalhau* with pennyroyal, stuffed crab or monkfish with clams and coriander. Then there is usually roast lamb, pork stuffed with pigs' trotters and coriander, rabbit with green peppers, and game dishes in season. A good selection of cheeses, and tooth-defying sweet dishes round off the meal in style.

Largo Dom Dinis Castelo de Estremoz
T+351 268 332 075
E recepcao.staisabel@pousadas.pt
W www.pousadas.pt
€35 V ⊟

São Rosas Near the *pousada,* this white-walled restaurant has typical Alentejan cooking, but at a very high level, with touches of creativity and sophistication – yet very fair prices. Starters are straightforward - they could be *enchidos,* roast *farinheira* or *chouriço*. The tomato soup with fish is very popular. Then it's probably best to choose meat, dishes such as sautéed loin of pork with broccoli *migas*, roast pork with plums, chickpea stew, or wild pigeon. There are Alentejo cheeses and a terrific selection of sweet dishes, regional and international. The wine list is excellent.
Largo de Dom Dinis, 11, Estremoz
T+351 268 333 345
€40 ♀
Closed Mon; 1st half Jan,1st half Jul

ÉVORA B3

Divinus Leaving Évora on the A6 towards Estremoz, watch out for the sign to the Convento do Espinheiro hotel, up a track to the left. If you miss it, you'll see it as you pass, an impressive white building, lit up at night. They have various restaurants, but the top one is this, Divinus, in the beautifully-restored wine cellar, not cheap, but excellent. Cooking, though by no means divorced from Alentejo roots, is distinctly modern, polished and elegant. You

might start with a changing selection of *petiscos*, purslane soup with egg and sheep's cheese, or dogfish soup with pennyroyal, then move on to *bacalhau*, pork, lamb or beef dishes, the meat all from special Alentejo breeds. Fish comes fresh from the coast each day. Or, you can opt for the 'Mediterranean' menu and the likes of scallops, foie gras and other exotica. Desserts are delicious works of art. The wine list is very good.
Convento do Espinheiro
T+351 266 788 200
E reservations@conventodoespinheiro.com
W www.conventodoespinheiro.com
€55 ♀ *V* 🛏

Fialho Tucked down a little passage off the Praça Joaquim António de Aguiar, Fialho is one of the temples of traditional Alentejan cooking. It is run by two of the sons of founder Manuel Fialho, Gabriel and Amor, and has expanded over its nearly 60 years from a little neighbourhood diner to the famous restaurant it is today. They serve classic Alentejo dishes such as dogfish soup (*sopa de cação*), lamb stew, pork with *migas*, hare risotto and *açorda de bacalhau*, but have also rediscovered old dishes such as royal bean and game stew, and purslane soup. The wine list is excellent, the sweet dishes exemplary, the atmosphere unstuffy, and the decoration of the restaurant plain, with antlers and plates hung on white walls.
Travessa das Mascarenhas 16
T+351 266 703 079
E restaurante_fialho@iol.pt
W www.restaurantefialho.com
€40 ♀

Hotel da Cartuxa There are many tempting places to eat in Évora, but one of the best is Cerca Nova, the spacious ground-floor restaurant of this very comfortable, centrally-placed hotel *(page 360)*. The cooking and presentation here are superb. The chef António Nobre forages further than the Alentejo for his ingredients and dishes, although there may be a good selection of typical salads as a starter, or asparagus with grilled, garlicky prawns, or grilled goat's cheese on onion. Local main courses might include sautéed octopus with *batata à murro*, crushed olive oil-roasted potatoes, dogfish in a tomato and onion sauce with 'straw' potatoes (finely shredded, then deep-fried), *porco preto* served à Alentejana (in a sauce with onions, peppers and clams), or chicken and rice *cabidela*. Their joint programmes with Esporão winery *(page 337)* include dinner, a winery visit, tastings and a cookery class. *Pictured below.*
Travessa da Palmeira 4-6
T+351 266 739 300
E comercial@hoteldacartuxa.com
W www.hoteldacartuxa.com
€30 V 🛏

Luar de Janeiro 'By the Light of the January Moon' is tiny; it can barely fit in 30 diners, which makes for a pleasant intimacy between staff and customers. Decor is restrained: wood panelling below, white above. Starters are delicious and plentiful: there may be melon and sheep's cheese, *presunto*, *pataniscas de bacalhau*, fried octopus. The quality of the fish is superb – in daily from Setúbal. We ate scrumptiously fresh red mullet (*salmonete*), served with rice with clams, and could have had pig's trotters with coriander, lamb stew or hare risotto. Sweet dishes look tempting (*sericaia* with greengages, *morgados*, made from figs and almonds). A short wine list has exemplary bottles, mostly from the Alentejo.
Travessa do Janeiro 13
T+351 266 749 114
€30 ♀ *V*
Closed Thu, 1st half Jul

Taberna Típica Quarta Feira
A delightful little restaurant in the centre of Évora, where the welcome is friendly and the menu verbal – in numerous languages. There's one wine, one veg (green and whatever is seasonal), dressed with garlic and olive oil, one fish dish plus maybe dogfish soup. The variety is in the meat, pork, lamb, beef or veal, and one dish of the day, which could be partridge or hare in season.
Rua do Inverno 16/18
T+351 266 707 530
W www.evora.net/ restaurantequartafeira
€20-€25
No credit cards
Closed Sun, public hols

Tasquinha do Oliveira There's not a lot of room to move in the small but perfectly formed Tasquina do Oliveira. The ceiling is low-arched, the white walls dotted with glazed earthenware dishes, appreciative articles and other memorabilia, and six tables are laid with white cloths. You'll be greeted by *petiscos* various, perhaps chickpea salad with *bacalhau*, butter beans with sausage, spinach soufflé, salt cod fritters *(patiscas de bacalhau)*, asparagus with scrambled eggs, artichokes with ham, pig's ears with coriander... you pay for what you eat, so do send back unwanted arrivals. And don't nibble too much, because the main dishes are fantastic: hare with beans and turnips, wild boar with apple sauce, wild pigeon risotto, as well as immaculate versions of the Alentejo classics. A list of 150 wines includes some pricy ones. This is one of Évora's more expensive restaurants, but many gastronomes would vote it the best.
Rua Cândido dos Reis 45A
T+351 266 744 841
€40 ♀
Closed Sun, public hols, 1st half Aug

Taverna Squeezed into two rooms of the former convent of Santa Marta, Taverna has been beautifully restored, but there's not much room for anything (including wine!). Luís and Rosario Dias run the place. As usual in the Alentejo, she cooks, and he looks after the customers and wines. You might start with some *petiscos*, chickpeas with *bacalhau*, olives, mushrooms, sheep's cheese or *paio* (a smoked pork sausage); then move on to *migas*, flavoured with asparagus and local, paprika-flavoured pork, or beef spare ribs, cooked slowly in red wine and honey, or pork with potatoes and clams, flavoured with red pepper and coriander leaves. Try to save a

space for some *sericaia*, an eggy cinnamon-flavoured flan, served with greengages. The wine list is small, but well chosen.
Travessa de Sta Marta 5
T+351 266 700 747
E id_pt@aeiou.pt
W www.id.netpower.pt/taverna
€15-€20 ♀ *V*
Closed Mon

MOURÃO C2

Adega Velha This very typical, small, cosy restaurant squeezes in 40 customers. Walls are white-painted, with arches, a tall dresser full of decorative dishes and other memorabilia, and huge clay wine amphorae. Food here is reliable and inexpensive. You might start with grilled liver sausage, rabbit in coriander sauce, oil-marinated sheep's cheese or scrambled eggs with wild asparagus, and go on to lamb stew, roast pork, or hare with bean stew. The locals

will probably be singing, so be sure to have a song or two up your sleeve.
Rua Dr Joaquim José de Vasconcelos Gusmão 13
T+351 266 586 443
€20 V No credit cards
Closed Sun din, Mon

PÓVOA DE SÃO MIGUEL C2

Sabores da Estrela By the shore of the new Alqueva dam *(below)*, this is a lovely spot, with a safe area for children to play. A balcony with tables and chairs affords a superb view of what the locals call 'The Great Lake'. Dishes are familiar, starters such as octopus salad, garlic mushrooms, gaspacho and brawn *(cabeça de Xara)* with pig's ear. (Hmm, maybe not.) Then there's dogfish soup, purslane soup with cheese and egg, pumpkin soup with *bacalhau*, lamb stew, risotto of cabbage with pig's tongue, or of duck with sausage and tomato. Finally, there are enough sweet dishes to send everyone away happy, even the children. (Did they eat up their nice ear?)
Rua Nova de Moura 3, Estrela
T+351 285 915 000
E saboresdaestrela@sapo.pt
W www.saboresdaestrela.com
€20-€25 V No Amex
Closed Mon, Tue lunch

REDONDO C3

O Chana do Bernardino The best kind of traditional Alentejo restaurant, now in bigger premises, with a terrace for summer. It is still vital to book. There's no fixed menu: everything is seasonal, including game. *Petiscos* are generous, maybe olives, roasted peppers, marinated sheep's cheese, pig's liver grilled with garlic, coriander, oil and vinegar, or grilled *farinheira*. Main dishes will almost certainly include *porco preto* in some form, and maybe lamb stew, bean stew with grilled entrecote, perhaps *bacalhau*. There will be fresh fruit or *sericaia* to finish. The wine list is mainly local, a good selection. Prices are very reasonable – no wonder it's popular.
Aldeia da Serra d'Ossa
T+351 266 909 414
€20-€25 ♀ No credit cards
Closed Mon; 24 Dec din, 25 Dec

Enoteca do Redondo This is more of a wine bar than a restaurant, and has a very good selection of wine. In the old town granary, very well-restored, with a stone-flagged floor and brick walls, it is hung with local artists' works. They have a good selection of cheeses, ham, bread, olives and charcuterie *(enchidos)*.
Rua do Castelo
T+351 266 909 100
E museudovinho@cm-redondo.pt
€15 ♀
Closed Mon

REGUENGOS DE MONSARAZ C2

Galeria Júlia Vinagre, ex-owner and creator of A Bolota Castanha at Terrugem *(below)*, runs this very good restaurant at the Herdade do Esporão winery *(page 337)*. It was built to evoke the low arches of traditional Alentejan architecture. Tables have differently-coloured cloths, decorated with flowers. The food chimes in well with the wines – modern and very well-made. All the wines are Esporão, and they are very good. There are Alentejan themes, of course, and good use of local ingredients, but the style of cooking and presentation would grace any restaurant in Lisbon or London. Nibbles are delicious, then choose from seven soups, from tomato with quails' eggs to chestnut. Starters include mixed *enchidos*, even *foie gras*, served with grapes and apple. But at the main course the kitchen really gets into its stride, with a wonderful chickpea stew, thick with other veg and sausages, preserved suckling-pig with olive oil potato purée, and pork medallions cooked in the Esporão sweet wine. Everything is delicious – too bad there have to be ten of you before they will consider letting you in for dinner. But a lunch in the restaurant, after your tour round the cellar, will make your visit to Esporão really unforgettable.
Herdade do Esporão
T+351 266 509 280
E enotur@esporao.com
W www.esporao.com
€50 ♀ V
Closed public hols

REGUENGO C4

Tomba Lobos Fine food comes as a great surprise in this small, unassuming place high above Portalegre amidst rocky vineyards. Chef José Júlio Vintém pushes boundaries, inventing new blends of traditional flavours. *Bacalhau* fishcakes with asparagus, loin of lamb with eight mushrooms, pork tarts with chickpeas are among the regular dishes. Leave room for a bewilderingly tempting selection of desserts. The wine list is very good, majoring on Alentejo and Douro.
Bairro da Pedra Basta 16
T+351 245 331 214 / 965 416 630
E tombalobos@gmail.com
W www.wonderfulland.com/tombalobos

Explore the Alentejo

Let's start in the north of this vast region. CASTELO DE VIDE lies on the edge of the Parque Natural de São Mamede. A very pretty little town, it has picture-postcard cottages, fountains, flowers and groves of olive and chestnut trees. Its buildings span centuries, from Gothic doorways to 17th century tiles in the small chapel of Nossa Senhora da Alegria. The Jewish quarter at the foot of the castle walls has cobbled streets and a synagogue. Castelo de Vide is also well-known for its thermal waters, said to relieve hypertension, hepatitis and diabetes.

Driving south-east through the Natural Park we find MARVÃO, perched on one of the area's highest peaks (865m). From the main square you get a feeling for the inner town: narrow streets with little whitewashed houses, flowers tumbling through the wrought iron balcony railings. On Rua Espírito Santo, the street leading to the castle, you will find the former Governor's House and some particularly impressive balustrades from the 17th century. The castle and fortifications date from the 13th

Below Marvão, stunning views from one of the Alentejo's highest peaks

Right Castelo de Vide, amidst the olive groves, in the north-east, on the edge of the Parque Natural de São Mamede

century, and include a Torre de Menagem, the main watchtower rising above the other buildings. From the approach road to Marvão and from the castle battlements, there are spectacular views across the Natural Park. Marvão is the heart of the Alentejo's chestnut-growing region – vast areas of sweet chestnut woods surround the town.

From here we make our way to PORTALEGRE, the largest city in this cluster, fabulous views all the way. Unlike other towns in the Alentejo, Portalegre has not been dependent upon agriculture. Instead, it made its fortunes from carpets and even silk factories in the 16th and 17th centuries. The way in, Rua 1 de Maio, follows the old city walls, and you can go through one of the old city gates to the main squares. On Rua 19 de Junho, leading from the main cathedral square to the Museu José Régio *(see below),* there are houses dating back to the 17th and 18th centuries.

Due east of Portalegre is CRATO, base of the Order of Hospitallers, who received vast areas of land in the region from King Sancho II around 1232. Known later as the Order of Malta, they moved in 1356 to nearby FLOR DA ROSA, where the fortress-monastery can still be seen. The original castle-monastery in Crato was razed to the ground by Spanish invaders in 1662, so only vestiges remain. South of Crato is ALTER DO CHÃO, originally built – and then destroyed – by the Romans. The Palácio do Álamo is a lovely building, housing the tourist office, an art gallery and a library. Nearby is the former Royal Stud, where by Royal Command, a pure line of Lusitania horses was bred.

ALQUEVA – EUROPE'S LARGEST RESERVOIR

Plans for a dam and reservoir in the region of ALQUEVA in the lower Alentejo were first mooted in the 1950s, but it was only in 1995 that work finally began. In 2002 the sluices closed and in 2004 the hydro-electricity power plant started to operate. With a surface area of some 250km², a length of around 85kms and a lakeside of approximately 1,200km (1,000 of which are on Portuguese territory and the remainder in Spain), Alqueva is the largest artificial lake in Europe. At the bottom is a complete village, whose inhabitants were re-housed in a newly-built community called LUZ (light).

Alqueva attracts millions of visitors per year. Most are day trippers, but as tourism facilities increase, the length of stay is likely to rise. The nearest towns are PORTEL, REGUENGOS DE MONSARAZ, MOURÃO and MOURA. At ESTRELA, right on the water, boat trips, sailing, fishing and swimming are already up and running.

Water has always been a major issue for the Alentejo, and Alqueva was planned to alleviate the desperate shortages and droughts. Its location and surface area are, however, having other side effects, as the local winemakers are discovering. The moisture levels in the atmosphere have risen and this could be affecting the vines which traditionally have had to fight hard and put down long roots in the harsh Alentejo climate.

Major developers are already targeting Alqueva and various residential and tourism projects are well under way. Within the next few years this will be a significant tourist attraction, although the local authorities have promised to control the level and type of development. This, with the new airport at Beja (due to open in 2008), will change the face and the economic profile of the lower Alentejo for ever.

Next important stop southward is the lovely city of ESTREMOZ, a perfect base for exploring this interesting central section of the region. Few cities have as many stories to tell as Estremoz about the bloody history of Portugal. Strategically positioned on a hilltop, it had clear views of approaching enemy forces from fortifications and castles, which along with churches still dominate the city. It actually has two lines of fortifications, the first dating from the 13th and the second added during the War of Restoration of Independence (1640-48), when the city was the headquarters of the army under Nuno Álvares Pereira. The castle is now a *pousada*, one of the most beautiful in Portugal *(page 346 and 360)*.

The city has sprawled way beyond its original boundaries, but the old town itself spreads down the hill from the castle, pretty little streets with shops selling local produce: wine, marble and pottery. Estremoz produces prized pink marble – even today, marble is an important industry. The city's pottery is also well-known for its distinctively red colour and its figures representing daily life through the ages.

East of Estremoz, virtually on the Spanish border, ELVAS is most exciting to us for its local delicacy, the scrumptious sugared greengages. It has also been one of the most important military towns in Portuguese history, pivotal in battles throughout the ages. No surprise, then, that the castle and fortifications still dominate the town. The castle was originally built by the Moors, and added to through the centuries. Its 17th century Torre de Menagem gives views over the city and to the Spanish frontier. The Elvas aqueduct, the Aqueducto de Amoreira, is particularly impressive. Designed by Francisco de Arruda and built between 1498 and 1622, it still functions today, its 843 arches stretching for over 7.5km, some of them over 30m high. In the heart of the old town, around the Largo de Santa Clara, you can see signs of Moorish architecture (a doorway flanked by two towers topped by a verandah), and the old town pillory.

The town of BORBA is fiercely proud of its royal charter, dating back to the birth of Portugal itself. The story goes that, centuries ago, the mayors of Borba and Estremoz agreed not to compete with each other in the promotion of their two most valuable products: marble and wine. Estremoz chose marble, and Borba chose wine – which could be why it now has one of the best-organised wine co-operatives in the country. It could also explain why the castle is built of marble, and the main streets are paved with it. Borba is a spacious and wealthy town with a huge main square centred upon a large white marble fountain erected by Queen Maria in the 18th century.

Just south of Borba is the town of VILA VIÇOSA, former country seat of the Royal family of Bragança and still showing all the signs of its privileged past. Pause at the entrance to the city. Notice the famous Porta dos Nós – Gate of Knots – which symbolizes the power of the Bragança family, and the other Porta do Nó which commemorates the Restoration of Independence in 1640. These gates open onto the beautiful Terreiro do Paço (Palace Square) and the impressive Palácio Ducal. When the monarchy was overturned, in 1910, Vila Viçosa lost its patronage and its considerable wealth. The castle dates back to the 13th century and was restored for the War of Restoration. Today it houses the Archaeological Museum. Its walls still enclose the old town with its small houses and narrow streets. The Porta de Évora faces west and dominates the wide avenue leading to the town. The Largo de Nuno Álvares Pereira, named after the soldier boy hero, contains, as well as the castle, the church of Nossa Senhora da Conceição and the town's unique pillory, decorated with rough-hewn frogs at its base and topped with an open spherical distaff, decorated with carved garlands; it stands some 8m high and is a national

Right The early 14th century castle of Arraiolos, a town famous for its beautifully-patterned wool carpets
Below Vast, rolling fields of wheat or vines stretch to the horizon

monument as well as being the symbol of the town.

To the south-west of Estremoz is the town of ARRAIOLOS, famous for its carpets. It all started as a cottage industry, using local wool and a particular cross stitch to make tapestries, but quickly grew into a major industry. Original designs were taken from classical Persian and Indian themes of nature. Nowadays, the designs are much more varied, but the predominant colours are still yellow and blue. In some of the workshops, you can see women making and repairing these valuable carpets.

Let us head south now. Notice the landscape. Crops of wheat or vines stretch as far as the eye can see, monotone blankets of green, gold or brown, depending on the season. They say that there is no shelter from the sun in the Alentejo, and here it is true: a few cork oaks break the flatness, but even they seem out of place. Elsewhere, hectares of cork oak and olive trees grow in regimented rows, while prized black pigs snuffle under the oak trees in search of acorns. The fires of recent years devastated both crops and livestock, and it is taking time for small farmers to start the production cycle over again.

Manor houses, called *montes*, are set in the heart of

STRIPPING THE CORK

Cork is the bark of a type of oak, *quercus suber*. Half of all the world's cork comes from Portugal – most of that from the Alentejo. This bark can be stripped from the tree (once every nine years) without damaging the tree itself. Cork has a cellular structure that contains a high proportion of air (which is why cork floats), and an elasticity that makes it highly resilient. You can compress cork and watch it spring back to its original size when you release the pressure. Cork oaks are grown in widely spaced forests in central and southern Portugal, and provide a habitat for many different birds and animals. They also provide much of the food for the Alentejan *porco preto* (black pig), which loves nothing more than the acorns that fall in the autumn.

A cork oak is not ready to have its first harvest of cork taken till it is 20 to 25 years old. It really is a tree you plant not for yourself, or for your children, as one grower in the Alentejo told us, but for your grandchildren and their children after them. Skilled men climb the trees (it is not considered a job for women as there might be a danger people on the ground could see up their skirts!) and make a vertical cut down the bark. Then they lever it away from the tree in as large a piece as possible. Smaller pieces fetch less money. It dries on the ground for a few months, then is taken to the cork factories to be boiled to kill any remaining wildlife. The corks are punched out of the sheets, bleached or otherwise treated, graded on appearance, bagged and sold.

Right The beautiful little town of Monsaraz stands on a hill overlooking the River Guadiana

Below Step quietly in the 13th century castle of Beja, a town awakening to the modern world

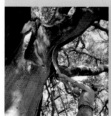

sprawling estates, while workers' cottages are spread around the land in small clusters. The classic bright blue around the doors and windows is meant to keep the devil at bay. This and the other common hues of yellow/ochre and pink/maroon are made from natural minerals.

From Évora, we head south-east towards the Spanish frontier once more. The small town of REGUENGOS DE MONSARAZ has found fame as the home of the Herdade de Esporão, probably the best-known of the Alentejo wines *(page 337)*. It is a typical neat, tidy town, where life revolves around the square, dominated by the church, with banks and coffee shops in equal number! Continue on to MONSARAZ, a beautiful little town where time seems to have stopped. Up on a hill overlooking the River Guadiana and its fertile valley, with Spain not so far beyond, it's a historic place where a steady stream of civilizations have left their mark, including Celts, Romans, Visigoths and Moors. The old stone walls enclose an imposing 14th century castle and clusters of whitewashed cottages lining narrow, cobbled streets. Rua Dereita is especially well preserved: all the houses here date from the 16th and 17th century, their façades flanked by external staircases and featuring ornate iron balconies.

Now we head for the lower part of the Alentejo, whose main city is BEJA. Like Évora, it was important to the Romans, who called it Pax Julia, and later to the Moors. Typically set on a hill with strong fortifications, its castle dates back to the 13th century, upon Roman foundations. In and around the city are many remnants of its rich past, in architecture, monuments and impressive buildings. Nowadays Beja buzzes to a new beat, with retail parks on

ÉVORA

The city of Évora is the administrative capital of the Alentejo and a UNESCO World Heritage site. Évora is fascinating and delightful. Today it manages to combine a rich history and cultural base with all that goes with a large, thriving university. The city's ring road follows the old city walls, which are still intact, and you enter through one of the four principal gates. It helps to get your bearings if you remember you are encircled and that the aqueduct enters the city from the north-west! Parking is always a problem: it would be easier to park outside the walls and walk in. In any case, walking will give you a better feel for this lovely city, and work up an appetite for one of its many excellent restaurants. The Aqueducto da Água de Prata (Aqueduct of Silver Water) was built between 1531 and 1537, and stretches for some 8kms. Outside the city walls, its soaring arches march over the roads whilst inside the city houses have been built beneath them.

Évora was an important Roman city: they called it Liberalitas Julia and built a temple; several of its Corinthian columns are largely intact today *(above)*. It was also occupied for some 500 years by the Moors, who were expelled only in 1165. The fact that the city walls are still intact says much for their strength, while the castle and churches inside testify to the importance and wealth of the city. The main buildings and monuments of Évora are clustered in the centre, close to the Roman temple. Here the former convent of Loios has been converted to a popular Pousada – the rooms are still called cells – and, to the other side, is the beautiful Paço dos Duques de Cadaval (Palace of Dukes de Cadaval).

The Praça do Giraldo, named after the soldier who freed the city from the Moors, has long been a popular venue for live entertainment. In days gone by, the entertainment might have been the decapitation of a nobleman, but nowadays it is more likely to be street theatre or live music! Notice here the 18th century marble fountain and Igreja de Santo António, dating from the 16th century. From here you can explore the surrounding streets, some of which are pedestrianised. You could easily be in an English shire county town with shops selling top-quality products for the 'hunting, fishing, shooting' set, as well as designer objects for the home and family. The university *(below)* is housed in a building that was once a Jesuit school, and which dates back to the 16th century .

Throughout the city you will come across pretty little squares with interesting features, be they Moorish architecture or imposing houses from the 16th and 17th centuries, when the city was at its zenith.

Left The Castelo de Mértola, high above the quiet riverside town

Right The Pulo do Lobo (Wolf's Leap), source of the Guadiana, between Mértola and Serpa, an area rich in wildife

the bypass and a new airport being built on the former military base. This will undoubtedly open up the whole Alentejo to a fresh audience. Whether the sleepy Alentejo is ready for package holidays and cheap airlines remains to be seen!

To the north-west of Beja, crossing the River Guadiana once more along the way, is MOURA. Legend has it that Salúquia, daughter of the Moorish Governor's daughter, was waiting one fateful day for her lover. The lover and his party had been attacked and killed by the Portuguese, who then dressed in the Arab clothes and persuaded the girl to lower the drawbridge and let them in. Grieving for her lover and in shame at having been deceived, she threw herself from the castle tower. The part of the town called **Mouraria** recalls the period of Moorish rule. Its straight streets and low houses are decorated with attractive *azulejos* and distinctive chimneys. The town is known for its mineral water, rich in bicarbonates, apparently good for rheumatics. The popular fizzy mineral water Água do Castelo is sourced from the Fonte de Pisões-Moura, close to the town.

Head south now and into SERPA. Yet another walled town set on a hill, Serpa dates back at least to 400BC. The town's aqueduct, which in part runs along the top of the town walls, dates from Roman times. Serpa's castle was built by the Moors and added to through the centuries. It houses an interesting archaeological museum. You cannot leave Serpa without trying its famous cheese, strong and creamy, with a glass of good, red Alentejo wine!

MÉRTOLA, to the south, is a very pretty whitewashed town with steep, often narrow, streets. Its fortress castle, originally Moorish, dominates the town. Located alongside the River Guadiana, it was formerly an active fluvial trading centre, sending fruit and locally-mined minerals to Europe and north Africa. Today there are restaurants overlooking the river, and pleasure boats ply their trade. The Moors, who held sway here for many generations, left beautiful architecture around the town: its main church is built on the remains of a mosque and you can still see the *mihrab,* or prayer niche, facing Mecca. Mértola is a paradise for archaeologists: digs have uncovered several important sites around the town, telling the story of Roman, Islamic and Christian eras.

CASTRO VERDE (its name literally means green castle or fortification) is actually very white. The cottages, the spring flowers, even the storks who nest atop the chimney and telegraph poles – all are specks of white in this otherwise golden-brown plain. South of Castro Verde is the historic town of ALMODÔVAR, where the plains and cork plantations of the Alentejo meet the Serra do Caldeirão mountains and, thence, the Algarve.

In a region that is largely flat, apart from the Natural Park of São Mamede, the views come from the *torres de menagem*, or watch towers, from the castles that protected the towns and cities.

BEJA **Castelo** The *torre de menagem* of the main castle, complete with battlements and narrow walkways. is now the symbol of the city of Beja. The top floor, up a steep spiral staircase, offers wonderful views of the Alentejo plains.

ELVAS **Castelo** See what generations of soldiers saw from the castle battlements as they prepared for war!

ESTREMOZ **Torre de Menagem** Also called Torre das Três Coroas (Tower of Three Crowns) or Torre dos Três Reis (Tower of Three Kings). Standing 27m high, it is within the castle which is now a pousada. The 13th century castle itself is on a hill dominating the plain. The 138 steps up the tower are rewarded by a spectacular view across the Alentejo. Entrance via the pousada.

MARVÃO The road leading to Marvão gives stunning views over the mountains of São Mamede, as does its *torre de menagem.*

MONSARAZ **Castelo** Views from the castle across the River Guadiana into Spain.

BETWEEN MEALS

ALTER DO CHÃO **Coudelaria de Alter** Close to the town, the Royal Stud stud was established in 1748. Nowadays you can visit the stables to see the pure-bred Lusitanias, the royal coach collection, and even watch a falconer at work. *Coutada de Ameiro Open Tue–Fri 9.30–5.30 Sat & Sun 10.30-5 Closed Mon and public hols*

BEJA **Ruinas Romanas de Pizões** It is thought that the Roman ruins at Pizões were part of a farm estate from the 1st to 4th century. You can explore the remains of a luxurious villa with a series of rooms including bath-houses. South-west of Beja. *Open Tue 1.30-5.30 Wed-Fri 9-12, 1.30-5.30 Sat & Sun 9-12, 1.30-5 Closed Mon, Tue am*

ELVAS **Barragem da Caia** This large reservoir north of the town is the perfect place to beat the summer heat. You can fish (with a licence), swim and indulge in non-motorised water-sports.

ÉVORA **Paço dos Duques de Cadaval** The Palace of the Dukes de Cadaval was originally built in the 14th century, but the façade was re-done in the 17th century. The architecture is a mix of Moorish and Manueline, and its north tower was originally part of the walls of the city. There is also an art gallery. *Open Tue-Sun 10-12.30, 2-5 Closed Mon*

University building, built in 1551-1559 as a Jesuit school. An austere, cloistered building set around a central courtyard, with beautifully decorated tiles in the refectory and classrooms. *Mon-Fri 8-7*

REGUENGO **Parque Natural de São Mamede** Stretching from Marvão and Portalegre to the Spanish border, the park covers over 3,500 hectares and boasts the highest mountains south of the River Tagus. The mountains of Castelo de Vide, Fria, Marvão and São Mamede shape this dramatic landscape. Rich and fertile, the area produces chestnuts, cork and olives, as well as grain. Various walking routes are marked, ranging from 8km to 18km, with starting points in Marvão, Portalegre and Arronches. It is a treasure trove for bird-watchers and nature-lovers. Take a compass and a weatherproof jacket – the weather can change quickly!

VIDIGUEIRA **Roman ruins at São Cucufate** Impressive ruins of a Roman temple and a 3rd century villa, clearly that of an important person. The two-storey construction has a series of arches supporting the upper floor: very unusual in the Iberian Peninsula. 2km outside Vila de Frades on the road to Alvito.

Open Summer Tue 3-6 Wed-Sun 9.30-1, 3-6 Winter Tue 2-5 Wed-Sun 9-12.30, 2-5 Closed Mon, Tue am, public hols

VILA VIÇOSA Paço Ducal Work started on the royal hunting palace of the Dukes of Bragança in 1501 and was completed in the 18th century. The Italian Renaissance style façade is completely covered in local marble. Each of the three floors is in a different classical style; Doric, Ionic and Corinthian. Fifty rooms are open to the public. Don't miss the fine kitchen, and priceless collections of art, books and porcelain. There are painted tiles from the 17th century, portraits, Arraiolos carpets, the former quarters of King Carlos I and Queen Amélia, and a lovely chapel. The 2,000 hectare park is home to animals including deer and wild boar, and there are various delightful water features. *Terreiro do Paço Open Mon-Fri 10-1, 2.30-5.30 Sat & Sun 9.30-1,2.30-6 Closed Mon, Tue am Apr-Sept*

MUSEUMS & GALLERIES

CAMPO MAIOR Museu do Café In the main factory of leading coffee company Delta, this museum traces the history and production of coffee. One of the very few museums dedicated to coffee on the Iberian Peninsula. *Herdade das Argamassas (on the road from Campo Maior to Degolados) Open Mon-Fri 9.30-1, 2.30-6.30*

MOURA Museu do Azeite Olive oil was to Moura what port wine is to Porto. At one time a whole street was dedicated to processing olives. This museum is housed in a former *lagar,* or press, and exhibits traditional machines and techniques. *Lagar de Varas do Fojo, Rua São João de Deus Open Winter 9.30-12.30, 2.30-5.30 Summer 10-1, 4-7*

PORTALEGRE Museu José Régio One of Portugal's better-known poets, José Régio, amassed a fascinating collection of items of everyday rural life during his 34 years in this lovely house: furniture, metalwork and pottery, as well as important items of sacred art and figures of Christ. The poet died in 1969 and this house-museum was opened in 1971. *Rua José Régio Open Tue-Sun 9.30-12.30, 2-6 Closed Mon & public hols*

Museu Municipal Museum displaying a wealth of religious history, including a collection of sacred art, as well as a notable collection of contemporary Portuguese paintings. Also *azulejos* from the 17th to 20th centuries. *Rua Maria José da Rosa Open Tue-Sun 9.30-12.30, 2-6 Closed Mon & public hols*

Museu de Tapeçarias de Portalegre Museum of the traditional art of tapestry and carpet-making, one of the most important local industries. *Rua da Figueira 9 Open Tue-Sun 9.30-1,2.30-6 Closed Mon & public hols*

REDONDO Museu Regional do Vinho do Alentejo Within the local tourist office, a display of winemaking equipment, static and video displays and, of course, samples of the product on sale. *Praça da República Open Apr–Oct Tue-Fri 10-8 Nov-Mar Tue-Fri 10-6 Closed Mon*

SERPA Museu do Relógio The museum of clocks is based in the former Convento do Mosteirinho, a beautiful Manueline building dating from the 16th century, where it spreads its 1,700 exhibits over ten spacious rooms. There is also a library, bar and garden to relax in – if you have the time! *Praça da República Open Tues-Fri 2-5 Sat, Sun & public hols 10-5 Closed Mon*

CHURCHES

BEJA Igreja de Santo Amaro The original church dates back to the end of the 5th century, the era of the Visigoths. A fine example of Paleo-Christian architecture, it is also home to the Visigoth exhibition of the Beja Regional Museum. Not so long ago, the townspeople used to bake cakes in the shape of limbs and leave them in the church, seeking the saint's protection for their own limbs. *Largo de Santo Amaro Open Tue-Sun 9.45-1, 2-5.15*

CASTRO VERDE Basílica Real An imposing building in the heart of town. Its beautiful altar is covered in gold leaf and rich *azulejos* from the 18th century depicting the Battle of Ourique. A sacred art collection includes the relic of the head of São Fabião. *Praça do Município Open Jan-May, Oct-Dec 9.30-1, 2-5.30 June-Sep 10-1, 2-6 Closed Mon & Tue*

ELVAS Igreja de Nossa Senhora dos Aflitos This was originally a Templar church, built in the 16th century and octagonal in shape. A candidate for the title of prettiest church in Portugal, its striking yellow and blue painted tiles were added to the interior in the 18th century. *Largo de Santa Clara*

ESTREMOZ Alongside the castle, now a *pousada,* is the **Chapel of Rainha Santa Isabel,** the Saint-Queen. Her husband, King Dinis, disapproved of her distributing bread to the poor. He caught her one day with loaves in her gathered-up aprons, and challenged her. When the Queen let the aprons drop, out fell not loaves of bread but armfuls of roses. The chapel is beautifully decorated on the inside with *azulejos* depicting stories of the sainted Queen's life, including this 'miracle of the roses'.

357

ÉVORA **Sé** Built between 1186 and 1204 in Romanesque-Gothic style, this is the longest cathedral in Portugal. Its austere exterior is pink granite, but the interior is a treasure of architectural styles and ornate finishes. It also houses an impressive museum of Sacred Art. *Largo do Marquês de Marialva Open every day 9-12.30, 2-5*

Igreja de São Francisco A strange and fascinating church, both outside and in. Battlements, minarets and gargoyles feature on the front, while the main door is topped by a pelican, emblem of King João II. Inside is a somewhat macabre Capela dos Ossos, a chapel of bones, built in the 16th century, with bones of over 5,000 bodies taken from local convents totally covering the walls and pillars. *Praça 1 de Maio Open every day 9-12, 2.30-5.30*

PORTALEGRE **Sé** Work started on this magnificent cathedral in 1556 but it was considered complete only in the 18th century, after many alterations and extensions. Predominantly Renaissance in style with Baroque influence, the interior contains an important collection of Mannerist art, beautiful carvings with gold leaf, and excellent examples of *azulejos* from the 16th to 18th centuries. *Praça do Município*

FAIRS & FESTIVALS

JANUARY ÉVORA **Rota dos Sabores Tradicionais** Restaurants in the city co-operate to promote traditional dishes alongside their normal menus.

FEBRUARY SERPA **Feira do Queijo do Alentejo** All shapes, sizes and smells come together for three days of cheese tasting

FEBRUARY SERPA REGION **Semana Gastronómica do Porco** A whole week dedicated to Portugal's most popular meat – prized black pigs as well as the usual pinkies.

MARCH VIDIGUEIRA **Mostra de Pão e Doçaria Tradicional** A three-day festival of bread and sweet stuff near the end of the month. *Largo Frei António das Chagas*

MARCH/APRIL ARRAIOLOS and SERPA (March), REGUENGOS DE MONSARAZ (May) **Semana Gastronómica do Borrego** Springtime is lamb time, and various towns celebrate with meat dishes washed down by lots of local red wine.

APRIL BARRANCOS **Feira de Presuntos e Enchidos** Mid-month, a fair promoting the wonderful local hams and charcuterie. There are tastings, music and dancing.
ESTREMOZ **FIAPE** Agricultural, wine, food and craft fair at the end of the month, featuring a cookery competition between local restaurants.

APRIL/MAY BEJA **Ovibeja** Big annual agricultural and food fair. Taste local wines and cheeses, watch horse and cart slaloms, and admire a lot of sheep. *Parque de Feiras e Exposições*

MAY MOURA **Feira do Bovino Mertolengo/Olivomoura** A two-fold country fair in honour of the local breed of cow, along with olive oil.

JUNE VIDIGUEIRA **Cortes de Cima Summer Concerts** The beautiful winery hosts a series of events: dance, classical concerts, theatre – accompanied by the delicious wines. *T+351 284 460 060*

JULY BEJA **Semana Gastronómica do Gaspacho e Tomatada** How many ways can you serve tomatoes? Find out in this week dedicated to that lovely soup and at least 57 other varieties of tomato dish.

JULY/AUGUST REDONDO **Festas Floridas** For ten days every two years (next one 2009), streets are decked with flowers, days and nights filled with live music, sporting events, craft exhibitions, eating and drnking.

JULY/AUGUST ARRONCHES and MARVÃO (July), CRATO (August) **Feira de Artesanato & Gastronomia** Local crafts, foods and wines, continuing well into the night, with music and dancing.

SEPTEMBER ELVAS **Festa de São Mateus** A ten-day food and wine fair starting from the 16th with a big, religious street procession on the 20th.

NOVEMBER MARVÃO **Festa do Castanheiro/Feira da Castanha** Chestnuts take pride of place here. Wood carvings and woven baskets are proudly displayed alongside a wide assortment of dishes and, of course, the nuts themselves.

DECEMBER MORA **Mostra Gastronómica de Caça** Mid-hunting season, this is the place to sample (or buy if you are self-catering) wild fowl, rabbit, wild boar and venison.

Sleep in the Alentejo

ALBERNÔA B2

Herdade da Malhadinha Nova Country House and Spa A very special experience awaits you at the heart of the Maladinha Nova wine estate *(page 324)*. From the outside, this small hotel looks like a well-kept white and blue farmouse. Inside is an elegant, relaxing blend of antique-contemporary design. Beds are big and very comfortable, rooms look out across hayfields and vineyards to distant cork oaks. There's an outdoor pool in the garden, and another in the spa with its lovely curved slate wall.

Service is most attentive. Delicious breakfasts at a huge, square, communal table include excellent cheeses, divine home-grown ham, chouriço and jams, melon juice, and home-picked orange juice. The restaurant beside the winery *(page 344)* serves a blend of modern and traditional cooking, based on fine products from the farm. Maladinha Nova organises themed weeks and weekends (cooking, photography, painting, wine…) and there is also riding, trekking, mountain or quad biking, fishing and hunting (and conference facilities).
T+351 284 965 210
E info@malhadinhanova.pt
W www.malhadinhanova.pt
€800 for two nights, all inclusive
🛏8 [S]2 ♀ ✗ 🚣 ♨ *Min nights 2*

Herdade dos Grous You can stay in guest rooms, each with its own open fireplace, on this large country estate near Beja. Apart from wines *(page 324)*, there are olive groves and cork oaks, pasture for local and rare breeds of cattle and sheep, a stud farm with horses to ride, gardens, and a huge lake where you can canoe, row or fish. The adventurous might like to try the high ropes courses, available for different levels of skill. The wine bar and restaurant offer the good wines of the estate, and home-grown and local produce in appetising modern-Alentejan style *(page 345)*.
Albernôa, 7800-601 Beja
T +351 284 960 000
E herdadedosgrous@vilavitaparc.com
W www.herdadedosgrous.com
€125 🛏12 [S]12 ♀ ✗

ALPALHÃO C4

Quinta dos Ribeiros There are rooms and excellent guest facilities on this 70ha working farm, which grows olives, almonds, cherries, plums, apples and pears, as well as vines and woodland. Rooms are in the main house, suites in a converted granary and warehouse. The former cow-shed is now home to a bar, and various outhouses have become changing rooms, showers and a sauna, by the pool. There are mountain bikes to borrow, and a mini-golf course. Find it 25km north-west of Portalegre.
T+351 245 745 100
E info@quintadosribeiros.com
W www.quintadosribeiros.com
€80-€90 (room) €90-130 (suite)
🛏5 [S]3(2 & 2+2) ✗ 🚣 *No credit cards Min nights 7 in high season*

ARRAIOLOS B3

Pousada Nossa Senhora Assunção
This beautifully-restored 16th century convent sits in a valley looking out over the Alentejo hills just north of Évora. It's close to Arraiolos, the old fortified town famous for its carpet-making. This impressive building, its church towering above the rest, is edged in grey granite to contrast with typically white-painted walls. Inside, decor has been kept simple (some say spartan) and rooms are functional rather than beautiful. Activities include tennis and a swimming pool, although many say that the peace and quiet are the best thing about the hotel. The hotel restaurant serves modern Alentejan food.
T+351 266 419 340 / 266 419 365
E recepcao.assuncao@pousadas.pt
W www.pousadas.pt
€170-€230 🛏30 [S]2 ♀ ✗ 🚣 ♞

BEJA B2

Pousada de São Francisco This really is like sleeping in a museum, with creature comforts added. Rooms are larger than in many monastic *pousadas*, delightfully converted. Dating from the mid-13th century (and sufficiently far from the epicentre not to be damaged in the 1755 earthquake), it was converted into a *pousada* only 15 years ago. Public areas are

magnificent; the restaurant is in the former refectory, and the Chapter House with its painted ceiling is a sitting area, the Gothic-vaulted chapel a quiet space. A swimming pool graces a spacious garden, and the restaurant is probably the best in Beja.
Largo Nuno Álvares Pereira
T+351 284 313 580
E recepcao.sfrancisco@pousadas.pt
W www.pousadas.pt
€150-€230 🛏34 [S]1 ✗ 🚣 ♞

BREJÃO A1

Cerro da Fontinha Lovely converted farm buildings by the coast, typically low and white with blue trimmings. The village of Brejão, three minutes' drive away, is just to the north of the border with the Algarve, and within the Parque Natural da Costa Vicentina, with views of the Monchique mountains and the sea. A tall eucalyptus wood shelters the garden from the prevailing winds. The cottages are agreeably simple and rustic, with wood-burning stoves for winter. You can borrow fishing tackle and an inflatable boat, and fish or swim in the lake. There are also mountain bikes.
Brejão, 7630-575 São Teotónio
T+351 282 949 083
E info@cerrodafontinha.com
W www.cerrodafontinha.com
€60-€120
SC *6(2, 2+2, 4+2)* ✕ *on request* ⚓ *in lake*
No credit cards
Min nights 7 high season, 2 low season

ESTREMOZ C3

Pousada Rainha Santa Isabel This was the palace that King Dom Dinis built for his wife, Queen Santa Isabel. She would not be disappointed today with the new interior of the turreted building. And she would surely be impressed by the weekend 'Royal Buffets' in the atmospheric, high-arched dining hall *(page 346)*. Public rooms are luxurious, bedrooms and bathrooms sometimes a bit small, their grandeur a little faded. But staff are friendly and very heplful, and there are great views from the battlements and gardens down over the town and the surrounding farmland.
Largo Dom Dinis Castelo de Estremoz
T+351 268 332 075
E recepcao.staisabel@pousadas.pt
W www.pousadas.pt
€150-€230 🛏 *32* S *1* ✕ ⚓

ÉVORA B3

Hotel da Cartuxa A long, low, white building on two floors near the heart of Évora *(pictured above)*. At the back, a shady terrace overlooks lawned gardens, a delicious pool, and a stretch of the 14th century city walls. Upstairs rooms have small balconies with city or garden views. There's an excellent restaurant *(page 347)*. Colours are restful, public areas spacious, smart and elegant. Staff are extremely friendly, cheerful and efficient, and there is limited parking in the basement.
Travessa da Palmeira 4-6
T+351 266 739 300
E comercial@hoteldacartuxa.com
W www.hoteldacartuxa.com
€86-€160 🛏 *85* S *6* ✕ ⚓

Convento do Espinheiro This is a truly heavenly hotel, barely outside Évora in a large, white former convent, beautifully converted. Peaceful, elegant and comfortable, it can be full but still feel calm and private. The top restaurant, Divinus, is particularly special *(page 346)*. Breakfasts are very good, and rooms delightful, whether in the old convent or the new wing. Outside, within 8ha of gardens and grounds, there's a large church, tennis courts, and one outdoor pool spilling down into another; and a lovely indoor pool, along with a spa, jacuzzi and gym. A free shuttle service takes you to and from central Évora.
Quinta Convento Espinheiro,
T+351 266 788 200
E reservations@conv entodoespinheiro.com
W www.conventodoe spinheiro.com
€215-€275
🛏 *53* S *6* ♈ ✕ ⚓ ♨ ⚕ ☾

Residencial Riviera Friendly and helpful staff, incredibly central location, clean and pleasantly decorated rooms, all these make this modest hotel great value.

There's even a bit of excavated Roman wall in the reception. Apparently, room 211 is the one to ask for – a little more expensive, but lots more space!
Rua do 5 de Outubro 47-49
T+351 266 737 210
E res.riviera@mail.telepac.pt
W www.riviera-evora.com
€65-€75 🛏 *21*

IGREJINHA B3

Herdade dos Coelheiros This large family estate, producing excellent wines *(page 333)*, olives and walnuts as well as cork, has comfortable guest rooms in a long, low building in front of the vines. Relax on the long, covered terrace or by the pool with its shady trees. Teresa Leal is at hand to make your stay a happy one; on request, she will organise all kinds of country pursuits.
7040-202 Igrejinha
T+351 266 470 000
E info@herdadecoelheiros.pt
W www.herdadecoelheiros.pt
€70 🛏9 S 1 SC 1 ♀ ✗*on request* 🏊
   No credit cards

MINA DE SÃO DOMINGOS C1

Estalagem de São Domingos A fascinating and historic house in a mining village, converted into a luxury inn. It was built as the head office of the British mining company, in a late Victorian style, and has been creatively and stylishly adapted. There is an attractive outdoor pool and a restaurant (though we have mixed reports). You can visit the old mines (no longer in use) or just relax on the 'beach' by the nearby river.
Rua Doutor Vargas, 7750-171 Mina de
   São Domingos
T+351 286 640 000
E recepcao@hotelsaodomingos.com
W www.hotelsaodomingos.com
€132-€176 🛏31 ✗ 🏊 🏃

MOURA C2

Hotel de Moura A lovely hotel in a beautiful building dating back to the mid-17th century, a convent for 200 years, then a manor house, and since 1900, a hotel. There are all sorts of activities – staff will arrange ballooning, sailing on the Alqueva dam, riding, cycling, fishing...

Praha Gago Coutinho, 1, Moura
7860-010, Portugal
T+351 285 251 090
E reservas@hoteldemoura.com
W www.hoteldemoura.com
€45-€57 🛏35 SC 2(2 & 2+2) ✗ 🏊
   No credit cards

REGUENGO C4

Quinta Azenha do Ramalho A wonderful retreat 3km south of southern Portugal's highest mountain, São Mamede. You'd be 8km from the nearest shops, in the village of Alegrete, and 21km from the magical village of Marvão. The house is beautifully equipped, with four bedrooms (one with double bed) and two bathrooms, proper kitchen, veranda and barbecue. The loudest sounds will be birdsong, distant goat bells, the soothing gurgle of the adjoining mountain stream – and maybe your children trying to kill each other. You will need a car.
Vale Lourenço, São Mamede
T+44 7837 448 436
E info@azenhadoramalho.com
W www.azenhadoramalho.com
€300 (4 people, 3 nights, low season) –
   €1,540 (8 people, 7 nights, high season)
SC *1(8) No credit cards*

Quinta da Dourada A beautifully decorated group of four apartments and two rooms on a 7ha estate in the Parque Natural de São Mamede. Each sleeps two, and the apartments have kitchenettes and sitting rooms. There's a lovely outside pool, mountain bikes to borrow, and the Apartadura dam to explore.
Ribeira de Niza
T+351 245 203 487 / 937 218 654
E quintadadourado@iol.pt
W www.quintadadourada.com
€65 (room), €80 (apartment)
🛏2 SC 4(2) 🏊 *Min nights variable*

RIO DE MOINHOS C3

Aldeia de São Gregório This is an extraordinary project, an entire (small) village, 8km south-west of Borba, redeveloped as guest accommodation. The houses date from the late 15th century, and had not been significantly altered until ten years ago. Over the centuries, there was a gradual drift away to towns, and the last inhabitants left in the 1980s. In 1998, the village was bought, and all the houses have been sensitively renovated, faithful to their original construction and style, but with modern comforts. One of the other village houses is now a breakfast restaurant for all guests, and there is a shared pool.
T+351 912 244 110
E saogregorio@iol.pt
W www.sgregorio.com
€70-€160 SC 10 (2,3,4,5) 🏊

SANTA VITÓRIA B2

Hotel Clube de Campo Vila Galé You don't have to have young children to stay here – but they would love it. There's a little open-plan zoo, and all sorts of outdoor activities – fishing, paintball, riding lessons, pedal boats, canoeing, mini-golf, tennis, cycling, quadbikes, jeep safaris... Clube de Campo means Country Club, and country this certainly is – right in the centre of 1,620ha of cereals, cows, olives and vines. You can visit the Santa Vitória Winery *(page 338)*, which provides an excellent range of wines for the traditional-style restaurant. The olive oil is good, too. The gym and spa have vineyard views. Bright blue and yellow rooms are simple but comfortable.
Herdade de Figueirinha
T+351 284 970 100
E campo.reservas@vilagale.pt
W www.vilagale.pt
€200 🛏78 S 3 ♀ ✗ 🏊 🎾 🌐

Algarve

ook laterally, and you will discover a number of different Algarves. The south-western tip and the whole of the west coast – the Costa Vicentina – is a nature reserve of remote, wild beaches, where the surfing is some of Europe's best. The south-eastern coast is strung with peaceful, warm lagoons, rich with seafood and wildlife, protected from the Atlantic by islands of dunes and sandbanks – and from further excessive tourist development by the status of natural park or nature reserve. By the time you reach the pretty River Guadiana along the Spanish border, you will have left most of the tourists way behind. The northern Algarve has rolling hills or even mountains, largely unvisited. To the north-west, the Monchique mountains are clothed in forests. Picturesque, cooling, reservoirs in the foothills came with the damming of various rivers to provide water for agriculture, golf courses and the tourists. And between the mountains, the hills and the coast is a wide, agricultural strip known as the Barrocal, with citrus, avocado and almond groves, figs, apricots, greenhouses and market gardens.

Of course, most tourists fly in to the bull's eye of Faro, and spread out onto the central-southern stretch of beautiful beaches, golf courses and resorts, some exclusive, some less so… We head there, too, because many of Portugal's most gastronomic restaurants are to be found amidst the modern villas; some of the most exciting restaurant wine lists are here, too – although local wine production is very limited. Undistinguished Algarve vines have been grubbed up with the help of EU subsidies, the land given over to other crops, including villas. One of the Algarve's four wine DOCs currently hardly produces any wine at all! But there's also a tiny handful of good estates.

Like the remaining vines, the residents and tourists here bask in a delicious climate, summer excesses cooled by Atlantic breezes, never a frost in the shortest of winters. July to mid-September is the high season, when the population is swelled from 350,000 people to over a million by half of all Portugal's tourists. But the warm weather continues late into autumn, and this is a great time to visit, when accommodation prices fall – and restaurants have time to lavish on fewer guests. Or visit in the spring – as early as January and February to catch the almond blossom and the yellow mimosa, March for the orange blossom, and from April onwards, if you head for the hills, wild flowers in extraordinary profusion.

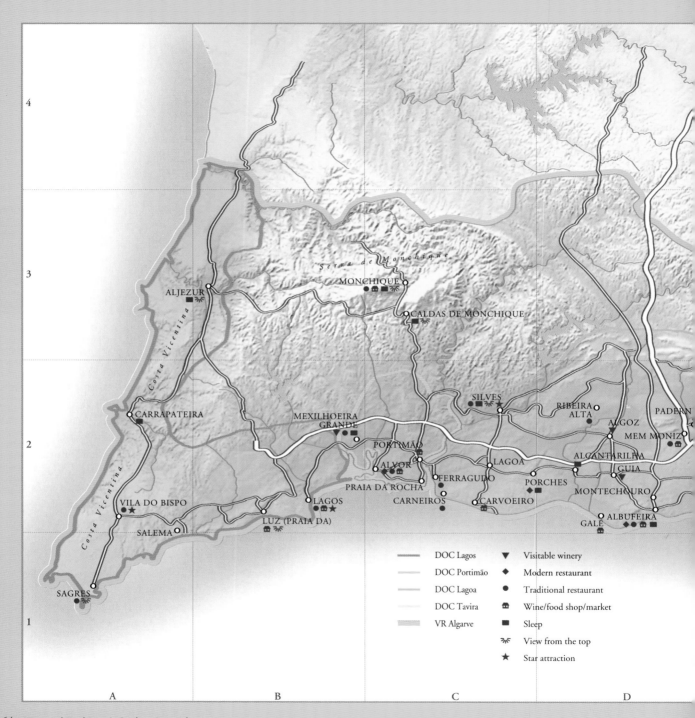

4

3

Serra de Monchique

MONCHIQUE

CALDAS DE MONCHIQUE

ALJEZUR

Costa Vicentina

CARRAPATEIRA

MEXILHOEIRA GRANDE

SILVES

RIBEIRA ALTA

ALGOZ

PADERN

MEM MONIZ

2

PORTIMÃO

ALVOR

LAGOA

ALCANTARILHA

GUIA

PRAIA DA ROCHA

FERRAGUDO

PORCHES

MONTECHOURO

CARNEIROS

CARVOEIRO

Costa Vicentina

VILA DO BISPO

LAGOS

LUZ (PRAIA DA)

GALÉ

ALBUFEIRA

SALEMA

SAGRES

1

A   B   C   D

▬▬	DOC Lagos	▼ Visitable winery
▬▬	DOC Portimão	◆ Modern restaurant
▬▬	DOC Lagoa	● Traditional restaurant
▬▬	DOC Tavira	⌂ Wine/food shop/market
▓▓	VR Algarve	■ Sleep
		𝄐 View from the top
		★ Star attraction

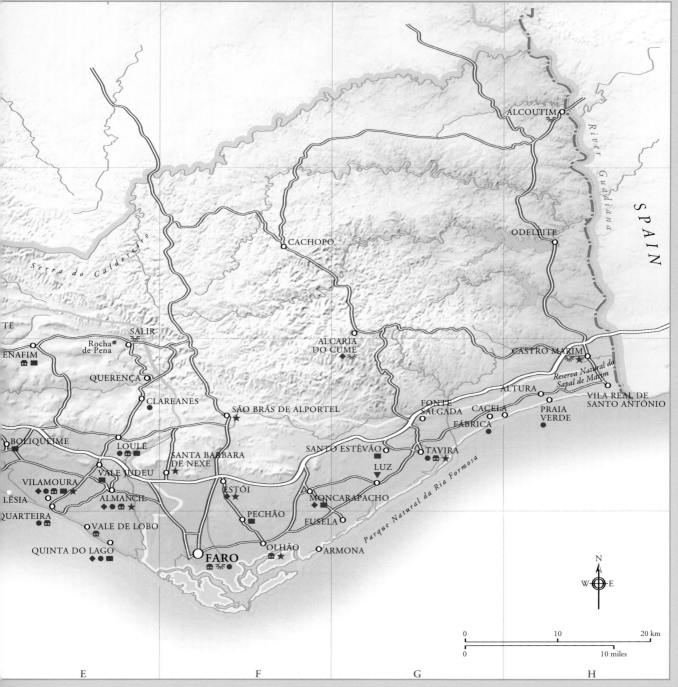

SPAIN

River Guadiana

ALCOUTIM

ODELEITE

CACHOPO

Serra do Caldeireiro

ALCARIA
DO CUME

CASTRO MARIM

*Reserva Natural do
Sapal de Marim*

TE

SALIR

Rocha
de Pena

ENAFIM

QUERENÇA

CLAREANES

SÃO BRÁS DE ALPORTEL

FONTE
SALGADA

ALTURA

CACELA

PRAIA
VERDE

VILA REAL DE
SANTO ANTÓNIO

FÁBRICA

BOLIQUEIME

LOULÉ

SANTA BARBARA
DE NEXE

SANTO ESTÊVÃO

TAVIRA

VILAMOURA

VALE JUDEU

LUZ

LESIA

ALMANCIL

ESTÓI

QUARTEIRA

VALE DE LOBO

PECHÃO

MONCARAPACHO

FUSELA

QUINTA DO LAGO

OLHÃO

ARMONA

FARO

Parque Natural da Ria Formosa

N
W   E
S

0   10   20 km

0   10 miles

E   F   G   H

Wine in the Algarve

The word 'Algarve' conjures up an image of beaches and sea, of holidays and golf-courses, of a coastline popular for its gentle Mediterranean climate. You don't think of it as a place that makes wine. But then, neither do you think of the Algarve as an agricultural landscape, but much of it is. The prime holiday territory stretches back 5km from the south coast, perhaps a bit more in some places. Most hotels, restaurants, night-life and villa developments are crowded into the central coastal strip. Retreat further inland, and development thins out. You find yourself in a landscape of citrus orchards, groves of avocado and almond trees, and, here and there, vines.

Of course, a land-owner will make much more money building villas and hotels on his land, but the Algarve has established an enviable equilibrium. Those who want hectic night-life, bars galore and beach restaurants (including some exceptional ones) can find them by the coast. Those who prefer a quieter holiday, enjoying a rural landscape and staying among the fields and orchards that produce the fresh orange juice for breakfast, the avocados for salads and the almonds for nibbles before a meal can find those

pleasures, too. And there is a growing desire, here on the edge of a country that is fiercely proud of its wines, to make good wines as well.

The mild, sunny climate of the Algarve is easier on the vine than the baking heat just a little further north. Even in summer, the temperature rarely goes much above 30°C, and never falls to freezing in winter. The Algarve is sheltered from northerly weather by mountains, so most climatic influences come from the south, including hot winds that keep the region's rainfall down, and accelerate ripening as harvest approaches. The traditional grapes of the region are sensible rather than inspired – whites that keep their acidity and reds that do well in a warm, dry climate. The most-planted grape is the Negra Mole ('soft black'), a variety as uninspiring as its name. Next comes Castelão, still successful in the Terras do Sado, but a grape in retreat elsewhere in Portugal. The three main white grapes,

Wine regions
DOC Lagos
DOC Portimão
DOC Lagoa
DOC Tavira
Vinho Regional Algarve

Main local grapes
The following are the most-grown of the permitted grapes, but the better wines are made from international and more prestigious Portuguese varieties.
Red Negra Mole, Castelão
White Roupeiro (Síria), Bual Branco (Malvasia Fina), Manteudo
For details of grapes see page 428

Above Clay jars, the traditional fermentation vessels of the Algarve

Left Chilled white with seafood, Gigi's (page 380)

Right Vineyards by Tavira's lagoons

Opposite Lunch by Lagos Bay at Búzio (page 374)

Roupeiro (Síria), Bual Branco (Malvasia Fina) and Manteúdo, can, with skill, make crisp, refreshing wine.

These grapes made up most of what was delivered to Algarve wine co-ops. No wonder there is only one co-operative still operating, at Lagoa, making adequate but unexceptional wines. Privately-owned Algarve wineries are looking far more promising, partly because they have planted more interesting grapes. It's probably only a matter of time before there are even more good Algarve wines. We have listed four producers, all making good to excellent wines. There are others who will probably qualify for inclusion before too long.

At the moment, the Algarve has four separate DOCs, Lagos, Portimão, Lagoa and Tavira. Tavira currently makes hardly any wine and must surely be due for pruning from the list... From the four winemakers listed, we tasted only one wine that was bottled under a DOC label. All the rest were VR Algarve, making use of more flexible VR regulations, more creative with grape blends than DOC. And, frankly, for most potential customers, 'Algarve' is a stronger brand than any of the local DOCs. Given the reorganisation happening in other Portuguese wine regions, we suspect it may not be long before the four current DOCs become sub-regions of a new Algarve DOC region.

ALGOZ D2

Quinta do Barranco Longo Rui Virgínia is passionate about winemaking in the Algarve, and saddened by the urban development he sees all around. For him, the perfect backdrop to his winery is the orange grove, and the vines. He started tending the citrus plantations at Quinta do Barranco Longo in 1997, and bought more land, for vines, in 1999. His vineyard lies 11km from the coast, on a high ridge, the soil a rich red with chalky, limestone under (strikingly reminiscent of Coonawarra in South Australia). At first he planted 12ha of vines and 1ha of citrus, then another 3ha of vineyard in 2007. When we visited, he was rebuilding his winery. It had evolved over the previous six years in a slightly haphazard way, from micro-fermentations in two small vats, with a small stainless steel basket press.

The idea eventually is to have a restaurant, tasting room and shop at Barranco Longo, and offer tours of the vines and orange groves. At the moment, Rui offers tours and tastings, but you have to make an appointment in advance. The cost will depend on what you want to taste. All his wines are VR Algarve, as that gives him more freedom in his blends than he would have if making the local DOC Lagoa. His white, **Quinta do Barranco Longo Branco**, is a fresh,

creamy, mineral blend of Arinto and Chardonnay. His **Quinta do Barranco Longo Rosé** is a serious pink, half and half Touriga Nacional and Aragonez, herby, aromatic and full-bodied, off-dry, but well-balanced by good acidity. **Quinta do Barranco Longo Touriga Nacional** red is underpinned by aromatic, herby intensity, with firm tannins and brisk acidity. The **Quinta do Barranco Longo Reserva** promises well from the barrel sample we tasted, full of rich, ripe fruit.
Apartado 156, 8365-907 Algoz
T+351 966 039 571
E quintadobarrancolongo@mail.telepac.pt
Visits Mon-Fri 10-12, 4-6
Closed last week Aug; Sep (appt only)

GUIA D2

Adega do Cantor As you might imagine, Sir Cliff Richard's venture in the Algarve welcomes visitors. He and his partners – two generations of the Birch family (Nigel and Lesley, Max and Michelle) – were thinking of doubling the size of the shop when we visited. Already they receive a daunting 10,000 visitors per year. The wines are well made, and Adega do Cantor (Winery of the Singer) has driven the renaissance of a comatose wine scene in the Algarve.

The original plan had been to grow fig trees, but Sir Cliff changed his mind, and planted 8ha of Syrah, Trincadeira, Aragonez and Mourvèdre at Quinta do Moinho in 1997 and 1998. He himself has been a regular visitor to the Algarve for 40 years. The Birch family joined the project in 2001, with two other vineyards, Quinta do Miradouro (owned by Nigel and Lesley), which has 10ha of Syrah, Aragonez and Alicante Bouschet, and Val do Sobreiro (Max and Michelle), with 3ha of Syrah and 3ha of Gouveio. They have now cemented a partnership with

another neighbour, who has 3ha of Viognier. In total, about half their grapes are of Portuguese varieties, half 'international', which means none of their wines are DOC Lagoa, but all VR Algarve.

The aim was to debunk the myth that Algarve was good only for beaches. Max did a two-year course in winemaking at Plumpton College in Sussex, and the partners enlisted the consulting help of David Baverstock, chief winemaker at Esporão in the Alentejo. The first wine was made in 2003 (Max Birch is happy to admit that the 2004 was much better). The little winery is immaculate, with robotic plungers and stainless steel *lagares*. That, too, is to be expanded, to double production, although the partners have no desire to grow too large.

The **Vida Nova Rosé** is off-dry, crisp and creamy, with rose-hip perfume and berry fruit. **Vida Nova Tinto** is mostly Syrah, with some Aragonez, Trincadeira and Alicante Bouschet; it has firm tannins and rich, raspberry fruit. **Vida Nova Reserva** is a blend of Syrah and Aragonez, matured in new oak barrels, big, ripe and malty. The first whites were unimpressive, but the **2006 Vida Nova Verdelho Viognier** is a huge improvement, with crisp acidity balancing exotic fruit – perfect with *piri-piri* chicken! In time, there are plans

to release single varietal reds and whites.
Quinta do Miradouro, Apartado 5008,
Álamos, 8200-443 Guia, Albufeira
T+351 289 571 606 / 289 572 666
E adegadocantor@mail.telepac.pt
W www.winesvidanova.com
Shop Mon-Fri 10-1, 2-5 Closed 24 Dec-2
Jan
Visits appt only €7.50

LUZ G2

Quinta das Correias This farm has
been in the Correia family for 200 years,
but diminished in size over the generations
through inheritance divisions and sales.
The estate is now 6ha, of which 5ha are

planted with vines. Carlos Silva e Sousa,
a lawyer and local politician, has revived
the vineyard and winemaking in the
coastal region of Fuseta, whose wines were
famous at the end of the 19th century.
He replanted his vines in 2000: Castelão,
Cabernet Sauvignon, Touriga Nacional
and Aragonez. Everything is small-scale,
and the original farm building now
houses the winery. The first wine made
(now sold out) was called Balsa, and will
be produced only in the best years. Fuzeta
is a VR Algarve, a pleasant, quite alcoholic
blend of Castelão, Cabernet Sauvignon
and Aragonez, with flavours of dried fruits.
His Terras da Luz Tinto is a Tavira DOC,
oaky and tannic, made from Castelão
and Touriga Nacional, and one of the
rare examples of that elusive creature,
a Tavira DOC.

8800-102 Luz de Tavira
T+351 918 621 595
E carlosses@iol.pt
Visits Mon-Sat 5-6 Closed Sun €variable

MEXILHOEIRA GRANDE B2

Quinta do Morgado da Torre This
160ha estate has been in João O'Neill
Mendes's family since 1865. Once there
were 100ha of vineyards. Now there are
only 23ha, mostly red grapes. The rest of
the estate is planted with cereals, cork
oaks, and citrus, almond and carob trees.
Visitors are welcomed at the farm, and
there are plans to build a wine hotel,
offering treatments with extracts of grape-
seed and other wine products.

Morgado da Torre joined the Portimão
co-op when it opened in 1955. Previously
the family had sold their wine in 5-litre
demijohns to locals. In the latter half of
the 1980s, times became tougher, workers
were moving from agriculture to tourism,
and the EU offered subsidies to grub up
vines. In common with many producers
around them, Morgado da Torre pulled
up vines. In 1995, they planted new
vineyards. But three years later the
Portimão co-op closed. So the Mendes
family decided to build their own winery,
and start selling wine again, the first non-
co-op Algarve wine producer of the
modern era.

The vineyard is run along sustainable
lines, using as few chemical treatments
as possible, and only organic fertiliser.
It seems a very traditional winery at first
sight – then you realise the old *ânforas*
(Ali Baba-type wine fermenters) are
principally there for show and used only
for some fermentations. Most wines are
fermented in stainless steel vats, with
temperature control, the reds aged in oak
barrels. There are four options for visits.
You can have a tour of the cellar followed
by a short tasting for free. For groups,
Morgado da Torre offer three further
possibilities, at different prices: a tour of
the farm and vineyards, followed by a
tasting; or the tour, a more extensive
tasting and a buffet of cheeses and cold
meats; or you can do the tour and tasting,
then go off for a meal at a local restaurant,
Solar de Farelo, accompanied by Morgado
da Torre wines. There is a shop at the
estate selling the wines as well as local
agricultural produce.

Morgado da Torre's white wine, **Alvor**,
is a bright, refreshing blend of Arinto and
Síria. They also have a soft, appealing,
rosehippy (and virtually dry) **Alvor Syrah
Rosé**. These are both VRs, as is the red
Alvor Vinha da Barradinha, a rich, ripe,
treacley, red-fruited blend of Touriga
Nacional, Syrah, Cabernet Sauvignon and
Trincadeira. **Tapada da Torre Tinto** is a
Portimão DOC red, a very ripe, firm-
tannined blend of Cabernet Sauvignon,
Syrah, Trincadeira and Alicante Bouschet.
Mexilhoeira Grande, 8500-156 Portimão
T+351 282 476 866 / 918 580 064
E qmt@sapo.pt
Visits Mon-Sat 2-6 (appt only)

Eat in the Algarve

Almost more than anywhere else in Portugal, a bit of insider knowledge is vital to find the best places to eat in the Algarve – there are so many restaurants, of all kinds, at all levels of cuisine from basic international tourist fodder to very straightforward grilled chicken or pork chop, *bacalhau* or sardines; from bad or good traditional Algarve cooking to top-class, world standard modern gastronomy. We drew up our shortlist by eating as many meals ourselves as we could fit in, and consulting local wine producers, Algarve-loving restaurateurs and wine producers from elsewhere, food writers and restaurant critics…

Far left Sweet artistry at Henrique Leis in Almancil *(page 374)*

Left & right Shellfish, fish and a fine selection of vegetables on sale at Apolónia supermarket, also in Almancil

The three zones of the Algarve – coast, Barrocal and the northern hills – each have their own ingredients to add to the Algarve cooking pot. Everyone associates the Algarve first of all with fantastic fresh fish and seafood, but away from the shore, fruit and vegetables are big business. The coastal strip was always the most fertile. Now production is focussed in the poorer land of the Barrocal, between the coast and the mountains. Lemons, tangerines and oranges provide important local flavours, almonds and figs make their way mostly into sweet concoctions *(see overleaf)*, and the salad and vegetable crops give a greener hue to the cuisine here than in most parts of Portugal. Sweet potatoes are a delight, and used in puddings and sweets as well as savoury dishes. There are pomegranates, pears, cherries, even bananas. Vast expanses of greenhouses grow tomatoes.

In the hills and mountains, mid-October to Christmas is the game season – hare, partridge, quail, pheasant, wild boar… which also makes its way down to the coast, along with pork and chicken, and kid *(cabrito)*. *Queijo da cabra do Algarve*, the local goat's cheese, can be good: fresh or mature. Try the mountain honey, too. The north-western mountains of Monchique, high and cool, are renowned for cured hams *(presunto)* and *chouriço*.

But fish rules. The warm, shallow waters of the eastern lagoons are a shellfish paradise that supplies much of Portugal, and beyond, as well as the beach restaurants of the Algarve coast. Clams are to die for. If you are self-

MEDRONHO OF MONCHIQUE

It's on every menu, in every bar and supermarket, and just in case you didn't buy a bottle before, it may be the last possible purchase before the departure lounge in Faro airport… This strong and significant local tipple is a clear spirit distilled from a fruit wine made from the vaguely strawberry-looking fruit of the *arbutus unedo*, the 'strawberry tree'. It's an attractive shrub that grows wild in particular profusion in the mountains of Monchique. Some *medronhos* are sold young, some aged. When sweetened with honey it goes by the name of *melosa*. Some is distilled surreptitiously for home consumption. Drink it as cold as possible, in very small glasses and in cautious quantities!

THE SALT HARVEST

No wonder that fish baked in salt is one of the Algarve's specialities – the eastern marshes around the Ria Formosa and Sapal do Castro Marim are Portugal's main source of top quality salt. It's an ancient process. Sluice gates are opened to let the sea water into the salt pans. Under the summer sun, fragile flakes of salt crystallise on the surface of the brine. Between May and October, this *flor de sal* (flower of salt), the highest quality salt, is gradually skimmed off and sun-dried. *Sal tradicional*, bigger, coarser crystals, precipitates to the bottom of the salt pans, and is hand-raked out to be sun-dried in piles. At the end of the season, the remaining salt precipitate is collected mechanically, to be sold as *sal do mar*. The Algarve also has industrial salt producers. At Loulé, inland from the centre of the southern coast, there are salt mines in underground galleries.

catering, go hunting. You'll see people scanning the wet sand for two tiny holes, a thumb's width apart. Digging down should yield a clam. They need a couple of days in salt water to shed their sand before the briefest of cooking. The most common family of clams are the lovely *ameijoas*, all a succulent treat, but none quite as special as *conquilhas*. Small cockles (*berbigões*) are wonderful here, too. Oysters are farmed in the lagoons, as well as off-shore. There is octopus with big, fat, juicy, warty tentacles; *lulas recheadas*, squid stuffed with ham, onions, tomato and garlic, are an Algarve speciality, and the baby cuttlefish (*choquinhos*) are

not to be missed. Nor are the expensive big red prawns (*carabineiros*), and the weird goose-neck barnacles (*perceves*), a particular speciality of Aljezur, up the western coast. (For help naming and identifying seafood and fish, *see pages 436-7*.)

Sardines are plentiful off the coast, and at the cheapest, snackiest level these are much more fun than horse mackerel (*carapau*). Sardine paste (*pasta de sardinha*) often arrives as a restaurant nibble to spread on bread. Tuna (*atum*) used to pass the southern coast in huge numbers on their way to spawn in the Mediterranean. They were caught especially from the eastern port of Olhão, where they were then canned. Overfishing in the 1960s meant that few mature females were left to spawn, so tuna, though still popular here, now arrives from afar. It may be

Above right A lamb dish at Vila Joya *(page 373)*

Left Two fishes at Gigi's beach restaurant *(page 380)* and squid at Casa do Lago *(page 379)*

Right Dinner at the Old Coach House *(page 375)*

served in thick steaks *(bifes)* or sometimes in the local salad *estopeta de atum* – flaked tuna with raw onion, tomato and green peppers in vinaigrette.

Mixed seafood, meat and vegetables are frequently cooked and served in a *cataplana*, a kind of domed metal cooking vessel *(below)* that is now used all around Portugal, although it originated here. Fish and seafood also comes in stews *(caldeiradas)*, soups, risottos and broths, often liberally sprinkled with coriander.

Snails *(caracois)* creep onto menus from May to July, usually flavoured with garlic and oregano. Chicken piri piri came from Mozambique to restaurants the length of this coast – marinated in very strongly chillied olive oil, grilled or roasted. *Prato de grão is* a local stew of chickpeas with garlic, tomato and cumin. Gaspacho in the Algarve is typically cucumber-free and less puréed here than in Spain, a crunchy, cold soup of tomato, garlic, green peppers and onions. There's *xerém*, a cornmeal porridge dish of Arab origin with pork and cockles; and Algarve cooks also claim to have invented the famous *carne de porco á alentejana* – 'Alentejo-style' pork with clams – the tale goes that fish-fed Algarve pigs needed clams to disguise their fishy flavour.

A love of sweet things is a lasting legacy of the long Arab occupation of the south of Portugal. It was the Arabs who brought almonds *(amêndoas)*, a vital ingredient in most of the Algarve's cakes and little sweets. Figs are the other main feature, along with egg yolks, and lots of sugar syrup, or honey from the northern hills. You will meet *doces de amêndoa* everywhere in the Algarve: little sweets made by boiling ground almonds with sugar to form a paste, flavoured perhaps with lemon or orange flower water, which is then fashioned into shapes of animals, fish or fruit, and blushed with vegetable colouring. Unusually for Portugal these are normally egg-free.

Each town seems to have its highly calorific speciality. The western town of Lagos was the origin of the super-sweet *Bolos de Dom Rodrigo*, but you'll find them now right across the region, wrapped in their little foil parcels to contain the syrup. They are small balls of egg threads *(fios de ovos* – made by pouring a thin stream of egg into hot sugar syrup) stuffed with a soft, sweet paste of egg yolks, ground almonds, sugar and cinnamon, all briefly cooked again in sugar syrup, and sprinkled with cinnamon. *Queijo de figo* (fig cheese), sometimes called *morgado de figo*, is a cooked paste of dried figs, ground or grated almonds, cocoa or grated chocolate, lemon zest and cinnamon, shaped into little sweets or used to stuff dried figs: *figos cheios* (filled) or *figos recheados* (stuffed). The *morgados de Silves* are big cakes, eggy marzipan stuffed with *ovos moles* (a thick, milk-free custard) and *fios de ovos* (egg threads), all coated in royal icing. The small *morgados de Portimão* are similar, with the addition to the filling of sweetened spaghetti marrow *(chila)*. Aljezur, up in the north-west of the Algarve, is famous for its *pastéis de batata doce de Aljezur*, based on the local sweet potatoes. They are a Christmas speciality – very thin pastry made with a little of the local fruit brandy, *medronho*, filled with mashed sweet potato mixed with a little orange juice and orange and lemon zest, crushed almond and cinnamon.

RESTAURANTS – MODERN PORTUGUESE

ALBUFEIRA (PRAIA DA GALÉ) D2

Vila Joya This is one of Portugal's finest restaurants, richly deserving its two Michelin stars. Austrian chef Dieter Koschina, here for more than 16 years, presents new five-course menus every evening, intricate combinations of flavours and textures, lightly and precisely cooked. White-clad waiters glide, sommeliers in matching black tunics are well acquainted with the very extensive list of fine wines, mostly from Portugal. The elegant, arched dining room manages to be exclusive and formal yet friendly, relaxed and romantic, with cliff-top sea views by day, and a terrace and garden for fine weather. Since the hotel residents almost always dine here, it is vital to book ahead (or to stay) – it may be easier to book for lunch than for dinner.
Praia da Galé
T+351 289 591 795
E info@vilajoya.com
W www.vilajoya.com
€90 ♀ V ⛱
Open every day

ALCARIA DO CUME G3

Mesa do Cume Half way up to Cachopo from Tavira, in a beautiful spot up in the hills, 'Table on the Top' was opened in March 2007 by a Dutch couple, Teun van der Geest and Maria Kleinbeernink. The colourful, modern dining room and flowery terrace have spectacular views over the hills and the distant sea. Their cooking is a healthy antidote to stodgy fare, with good use of vegetables, inventive vegetarian dishes always on the menu, and interesting salads as starters or light lunchtime meals. Pork is *porco preto*, fine quality meat from the Alentejo, and all meat is well sourced.

The wine list is short and eclectic, but reasonably priced. Conveniently for hill walkers and even four-wheeled explorers, they serve meals from noon right through to late afternoon. Also snacks, pancakes, toasted sandwiches. Open for dinner Friday only – but phone to check
Alcaria do Cume 814
T+351 281 326 144/ 351 912 725 745
E mesa.do.cume@sapo.pt
www.mesadocume.com
€17 V!
Closed Mon & Tues; din variable

ALMANCIL E2

Amadeus Just west of Almancil on the road to Quarteira, Amadeus was only three years old when it won its Michelin star in 2006. The Mozart connection is Salzburger chef and owner Siegfried Danler-Heinemann, whose menu changes daily, depending on local markets; his cooking is creative but not over-complicated or extravagant. Faced with a wine list that is quite extraordinarily good worldwide, we would focus on some of the wonderful bottles from Portugal. Star billing goes to Douro reds. The house wines are perhaps less reliably exciting. The dining room is romantic pale yellow. Or eat in warm weather on the arched, covered terrace overlooking the garden.
Estrada Almancil-Quarteira, Escanxinas
T+351 289 399 134
E info@amadeus.hm
W www.amadeus.hm
€60 ♀ V
Closed Tue; lunch every day; Jan & Feb

Ermitage The elegant Ermitage has been here for years – indeed under the previous ownership it had a Michelin star. A new team is now cooking modern Mediterranean/Portuguese fare, accompanied by an excellent wine selection, Portuguese as well as international. In an old farmhouse, recently renovated, it has classic decor, with golden walls, mirrors, fires in winter, and a lovely terrace and garden. Open

only for dinner, and frequented more by up-market tourists than by local gastronomes. Find it 3km outside Almancil, towards Vale do Lobo.
Estrada Almancil
T+351 289 355 271
E info@ermitage-algarve.com
W www.ermitage-algarve.com
€70 ♀ V
Open din only Closed Mon Sep-May;
1st 2 weeks Dec; Jan & Feb

ALMANCIL E2 *(continued)*

Henrique Leis Brazilian chef Henrique Leis draws upon experience in France, Italy and Germany in his creative, complicated, assured cooking, which has won him a Michelin star – adding the odd exotic touch from home. The restaurant is relaxed, rustic-elegant, with old beams, modern art, cosy autumnal tones, and open fires in winter. The excellent wine list ranges across Portugal's best, plus fine wines from elsewhere. Previously open for dinner only, it now also serves a more modestly-priced lunch. Find it near Almancil railway station, north of town, on the road to Loulé.
T+351 289 393 438
E henriqueleis@iol.pt
€70 ♀ V
Closed Sun; end Nov-end Dec

Jardim do Vale North of the Almancil railway station, Jardim do Vale has a strong French accent – chef Joël Jouin was one of the first French chefs to settle in the Algarve. Based on the best local ingredients, dishes tend to be sauce-driven. There's a wonderful wine collection, with a bin end list for additional gems. Service is excellent, and there's a lovely garden in summer.
Vale Formoso, Almancil
T+351 289 393 444
€50 ♀ V
Closed Sun; mid-Nov to 27 Dec (approx)

Nelitos On the road out to Vale do Lobo, this fairly new restaurant has one of the region's best and longest wine lists, with good selections from as far away as Australia, as well as Portugal. Manuel Teixeira is Portuguese, but has a background in Italian restaurants in London, and his cooking has strong Italian influences. Pasta features strongly, and good use is made of local fish and

seafood. Dishes are more international than Portuguese. Service is very good. It's a modern setting, with light touches of shocking pink, large outdoor terraces, and open fires in winter.
Estrada de Vale do Lobo, Escanxinas
T+351 289 358 111
E info@nelitos.com
W www.nelitos.com
€40-€50 ♀ V
Open din only every day Closed Mid-Nov-
28 Dec

Pequeno Mundo A beautiful restaurant with a warm welcome and excellent food in an old villa just west of Almancil centre. Gothic-style arches, calm, dusky pinks and creams have a traditional but light and airy feel. There's a pretty courtyard and terrace for summer evenings, and a cosy fire in winter. Chef Guy Doré blends flavours of the south of France with Portuguese elements and fine local produce, in a modern-conservative style: consistently some of the Algarve's best cooking. The wine list is excellent, as is service of both wine and food. Book well ahead, especially in the summer.
Perreiras de Almancil
T+351 289 399 866
€70-€75 ♀ V
Open din only Closed Sun; Dec & Jan

Vincent Dutch chef Vincent Nas won Michelin stars for his cooking at São Gabriel and the Ermitage before taking over and renovating this converted farmhouse. His cooking is creative in an understated way, accomplished, with Italian influences. The wine list and service are excellent. It's a beautiful, atmospheric place, relatively informal, with a lovely, leafy terrace for warm summer nights – Vincent does dinner only. Find it on the road to Quarteira, just outside Almancil.
Estrada da Fonte Santa
T+351 289 399 093
E rest.vincent@sapo.pt
€75-€80 ♀ V
Closed lunch every day; Sun; winter also
Mon; 2-3 weeks Nov-Dec

ALVOR C2

O Búzio At a fabulous vantage point looking out over the Lagos Bay from a cliff-top south of Portimão, O Búzio has great views from its covered terraces.

Cooking by the new Spanish chef is good, with strong modern Mediterranean influences. The well-chosen wine list is long. Parking can be difficult in summer.
Aldeamento da Prainha, Praia dos Três Irmãos
T+351 282 458 772
E gilbertogato@restaurantebuzio.com
W www.restaurantebuzio.com
€45 ♀ *V*
Open every day Closed 1-2 months Nov-Feb

ESTÓI F2

The Old Coach House Restaurant

The cosy, luxuriously pink restaurant of the Monte do Casal country house hotel offers a very international, modern menu, European with occasional dashes of Thai. You might be in England… Cooking is of a high standard. Vegetarians will be happy here – at lunch times there is a complete menu of complex, interesting vegetarian dishes, and evening à la carte menus also offer tempting veggie options. A good wine list favours the Alentejo, and Portugal, with some tempting bottles at fair prices. Degustation menus changing daily can be taken with accompanying wines. There are log fires in winter, a terrace with a posh fountain for summer. Find it just east of Estói on the road to Tavira. Booking is essential – the restaurant is small, and occupied mainly by hotel residents.

Monte do Casal, Cerro do Lobo
T+351 289 991 503
E montedocasal@mail.telepac.pt
W www.montedocasal.pt
€40-€50 ♀ *V!* 🍴
Open every day

MONCARAPACHO F2

Orangerie The seriously good restaurant of the Vila Monte Hotel *(page 392)* – just ten minutes from the coast, half way between Faro and Tavira – is very much open to non-residents. Wines are good, and the cooking is creative, modern and beautifully presented, using home-grown fruit, vegetables and herbs from the gardens

and estate surrounding the hotel, as well as fresh fish and seafood from Olhão, and game and other local produce from the Algarve's hinterland; most ingredients are organic. There is a special vegetarian menu! Menus are created jointly by chef Ricardo Ferreira and consultant chef Albano Lourenzo from the famous Arcadas da Capela da Quinta das Lágrimas, in Coimbra. The bright, airy, spacious dining room, modern in design, opens onto a terrace and lovely gardens, with views of the sea, and orange groves. Service is professional, friendly and attentive.
Sítio dos Caliços
T+351 289 790 790
E info@vilamonte.com
W www.vilamonte.com
€60 ♀ *V!* 🍴
Open dinner only every day

PORCHES C2

O Leão de Porches 'The Lion of Porches' has been established for decades in this characterful, early 18th century house in the old centre of Porches (just to the east of Lagoa). But it was taken over in 2005 by a Dutch couple, chef Peter Uerelst and his wife Bianca Salden, whose cooking – and wine list – are now worthy of the backdrop. Eat in the charmingly elegant interior, or in summer in a courtyard under lemon trees and hibiscus flowers. Cooking is not-too-complicated, classic French/Belgian, from local ingredients, artistically presented on hand-painted plates and bowls – Porches is renowned for its pottery workshops. Lobster and other seafood feature strongly, as well as fish and meat. The new, well-balanced wine list is drawn exclusively from Portugal.
Rua da Igreja
T+351 282 381 384
€50 ♀ *V*
Open Din only Closed Wed; last week Nov,
1st 2 weeks Dec; last 2 weeks Jan, 1st
week Feb

QUINTA DO LAGO E1

Casa Velha There's interesting, creative cooking and a wonderful wine list in this atmospheric ex-farmhouse down by the Ria Formosa (not far from the footbridge across to the dunes). Yannick Guichaoua used to run the kitchen here some years ago, then returned to the Périgord to open a restaurant there. Back since early 2006 as chef/owner of Casa Velha along with his wife, Céline, his food is French-influenced international, based on fine local produce. The traditional, single-storey house has been beautifully restored, smart French style within, in restful autumnal tones, with changing picture exhibitions on the walls. For summer

there is a flowery patio with Moorish-style fountain, and log fires in winter.
6th roundabout heading south, Quinta do Lago
T+351 289 394 983
E yannick.guichaoua@sapo.pt
W www.restaurante-casavelha.com
€70 ♀ *V*
Open din only Closed Sun; end Nov to pre-Christmas, end Jan to end Feb

QUINTA DO LAGO (VALVERDE) E1

Florian One of the Algarve's gastronomic highlights, run by a Dutch couple (Peter and Karen), Portuguese ingredients cooked with international flair. Decor is simply elegant, restful, muted yellows and browns and soft lighting. For summer evenings (Florian does dinner only) there's an attractive terrace and garden. The all-Portuguese wine list is strongest on Alentejo

in the reds, with a good selection of whites from all over. Find it tucked away in Valverde, to the north of Quinta do Lago.
Valverde
T+351 289 396 674
E karenmirande@yahoo.co.uk
W www.florianrestaurant.com
€60 V
Open din only Closed Thu; 28 Nov-19 Jan

QUINTA DO LAGO/VALE DO LOBO E1

São Gabriel Long established in this former ambassador's villa, Swiss-owned São Gabriel has earned a Michelin star. Young German chef Jens Rittmeyer came via Villa Joya, and cooks with an inventive, light and airy touch, with good use of vegetables, and herbs from the garden. Eat on warm nights under huge blue parasols. There are occasional blue touches in the elegant interior, too, a modern match for the antique *azulejos*. The wine list is excellent, with numerous wines by the glass. During the summer, the Thai Garden, with its own Thai kitchen team, offers a fragrant alternative – same opening times. There are two villas for rent in the lovely big gardens *(page 393)*.
Estrada Quinta do Lago
T+351 289 394 521

E restaurante@sao-gabriel.com
W www.sao-gabriel.com ♀ *V* 🛏
€90 (€40 in Thai Garden)
Closed lunch; Mon; Jan & Feb

VILAMOURA E2

Willie's Now proud owner of a Michelin star, German chef Willie Würger (previously chef at São Gabriel) opened here in 2001, by the Pinhal golf course in a smart, residential part of Vilamoura. A vision of golden elegance, the restaurant also has a nice garden terrace, and is relaxed and friendly. Willie is one of the Algarve's top chefs, his cooking classic with German, French and Italian influences, and based on top class, seasonal local produce. The wine list is shortish but well-chosen and fairly-priced, though the Portuguese selection easily outclasses the foreigners. Stick with whites from Douro, Vinho Verde and Bairrada, reds from Douro, Dão and Palmela, and Alentejo of whichever colour, and you'll drink very well.
Rua do Brazil 2
T+351 289 380 849
W www.willies-restaurante.com
€60-€80 ♀ *V*
Closed Wed; 7 Dec-10 Feb

RESTAURANTS – GOOD TRADITIONAL PORTUGUESE

ALBUFEIRA D2

Os Salgados One of the Algarve's best beach restaurants. Fish and seafood is superbly fresh and well cooked, service slick, friendly and attentive.
Praia dos Salgados
T+351 289 592 179
E jcatuna@sapo.pt
€45
Open every day Closed Dec & Jan

ALBUFEIRA (PRAIA DE S. RAFAEL) D2

São Rafael Attractive, modern beach restaurant, with beautiful, well-cooked fish and seafood, and a good wine list, including several interesting wines by the glass.
Praia de São Rafael
T+351 289 540 300
€25 ♀
Open every day Feb-Oct Closed Nov-Jan

ALMANCIL E2

Casa do Campo A smartly cosy Algarve farmhouse, with tree-hung terrace, open fires, live guitar, good, old-style food, and well chosen wines.
Sítio dos Barros de Almancil 200
T+351 289 399 109
€55 ♀ *V*
Open din only Closed Sun; 1st week Sep; 6 Jan to 6 Feb (approx)

A Quinta This is a perfect spot for lunch, on the first steps of the hills just north of Almancil railway station, with fine views of the coastline from Faro to Vilamoura. The dining room in the old farm house is large and bright, rustic but elegant, and there's a lovely terrace. The cooking is good, drawing from the traditional Portuguese repertoire with international touches. Prices are reasonable, and daily specials are great value. The wine list is Portuguese, not long, but well chosen and fairly priced. Booking is essential as A Quinta is popular with everyone, tourists and residents, including the local business community.
Vale Formoso, Almancil
T+351 289 393 357
€40-€45 ♀ V
Closed Sun & Mon; 1 week pre-Christmas to end Jan

ALVOR C2

Ábabuja Converted from two fishermen's cottages right by the new waterfront in this small town just to the west of Portimão, Ábabuja has fishy decor, and the terrace is a place to watch the world go by. Cooking is local, simple but accomplished, and very good value. Very busy in the summer.
Rua da Ribeira 11
T+351 282 458 979
€25 ♀ V
Open every day Closed Jan

CANEIROS C2

Rei das Praias One of the region's best fish restaurants, 'King of the Beaches' nestles between the cliffs by the entrance to this beautiful little beach between Ferragudo and Carvoeiro, east of Portimão. The wine list is excellent, and a huge range of seafood and fish are beautifully cooked and well presented. There are fine views of the beach and sea, as the restaurant perches upon criss-cross stilts high above the sand, open to the sea, with covered terraces. Or eat with toes in sand, on designer tables down below on the beach.
Praia dos Caneiros
T+351 282 461 006
E luis-martinho@iol.pt
W www.reidaspraias.com
€30 ♀ V
Closed Oct-Apr Mon; 10-26 Dec

CLAREANES E2

Monte da Eira Accomplished regional cooking, a good wine list and a genuine welcome in an old white farm building *(above)* on the road north from Loulé to Querença. There's a simple elegance to the whitewashed interior, and the pretty terrace beside the threshing floor *(eira)*. In winter there are log fires.
T+351 289 438 129
E monte.da.eira@sapo.pt
€20-€25 ♀ V No credit cards
Closed Sun din, Mon; 2nd half Nov, 1st week Dec

FÁBRICA E2

O Costa Simple restaurant in a very beautiful spot near the lagoon, half way between Tavira and the Spanish border. All kinds of seafood, fried and grilled, *cataplana, arroz de mariscos*, as well as good beef and *porco preto*. A fishy set lunch is good value.
Sítio da Fábrica, Cacela Velha
T+351 281 951 467
€25-€30
Open every day Closed Dec

FARO (ILHA DE) F1

Camané This sophisticated seafood restaurant has a delightful terrace right on Faro beach, with views over the lagoon, and the airport just moments away. Cooking is excellent, the wine list impressive, and the service friendly and efficient.
Praia de Faro
T+351 289 817 539
E res.camane@iol.pt
€40 ♀ V
Closed Mon; 2 weeks May

Faz Gostos Economist-turned restaurateur Duval Pestana has been beset by difficult circumstances, which have forced him to move first from Olhão, then to Castro Marim, and thence, in September 2008, to Faro. Star of the kitchen is Pestana's mother, Elisabete. She uses the best of local produce in traditional Algarve dishes, including meltingly tender leg of suckling lamb, as well as seafood and fresh fish, simply but excellently cooked. A very good wine selection lives up to her cooking.
Near the cathedral!
T+351 961 624 575
E fazgostos@sapo.pt
€50 ♀ V
Closed Lunch in summer

FERRAGUDO C2

O Sueste There are fine views across to Portimão from this atmospheric fish restaurant in an ancient salt warehouse at the end of the fisherman's quay. Good fishy *petiscos*, grilled fish, seafood and *cataplanas* are accompanied by quite good wines. There are historic arches, *azulejos*, matching blue-checked cloths, and brick walls tastefully encrusted with scenes of the sea. O Sueste does not accept reservations, so arrive early, as this is a very popular place.

Rua da Ribeira 91
T+351 282 461 592
E amadeu.sueste@gmail.com
€30-€35
Closed Mon; Jan

LAGOS (MEIA PRAIA) B2

São Roque A lively, airy, beautifully designed seafood cabin at the western end of the Meia Praia. All is shiny new wood, down to the sea-green-painted tables and chairs. Opening out to the sea and surrounded by a terrace, it offers a huge range of fresh fish and seafood, plus a few meat dishes. And there's a playground to keep children happy while parents pick at shells.

Urbanização de São Roque, Meia Praia
T+351 282 792 101
€30
Open Jul-Sep every day
Closed Oct-Jun Mon

LOULÉ E2

Casa Paixanito Just north of Loulé on the road to Querença, this bright, cosily smart restaurant has a very good wine list (with loads by the glass) and a wide choice of excellent *petiscos* (little dishes), which include, as well as seafood and fine ham, items for the brave, such as black pudding with apple, veal tongue, pig's ears, and snails. The piped music gets mixed reviews, but the atmosphere is good, service excellent. Ochre walls are covered with old framed ads.
Olho de Água, Estrada Loulé-Querença
T+351 289 412 775
E paixanito@sapo.pt
€40 ♀ V
Open Jul & Aug din only, Sep-Jun all day

MEM MONIZ D2

Veneza Wine is the big draw here: one of the best lists in the Algarve spans Portugal, Spain and Italy, at very reasonable prices. The wines are also available in the shop *(page 383)*. The *petiscos* are also famous hereabouts. It's an informal, family-run restaurant, rather refectory-like, converted from a simple village house. The menu offers traditional inland Algarve cuisine (plus *porco preto* – excellent Alentejo pork, ham and charcuterie), and culminates in a boggling array of Algarve puddings, tarts and cakes. Mem Moniz is just south of Paderne, very near the motorway junction.
Mem Moniz
T+351 289 367 129
€30 ♀ V No credit cards
Closed Mon din, Tue; 2nd half Oct

MEXILHOEIRA GRANDE B2

Adega Vila Lisa Come here (if you can book) not just for a meal, but for a unique experience... Artist José Vila began cooking for friends in this unassuming village house over 20 years ago. Long tables and benches mean that you will certainly commune with your fellow diners – from village folk to the famous – as well as with Vila himself, who presides from the kitchen. There is no menu. A fixed price brings a series of traditional dishes, cooked with flair from top local ingredients, accompanied by the house wine and a small selection of Alentejo wines. Vila is also highly respected in the contemporary art world, and his latest pictures adorn the walls. There is no sign outside. Opening hours are limited, especially in winter.
Rua Francisco Bivar 52
T+351 282 968 478
€30 No credit cards
Open Jul-Sep every day din only;
*   Oct-Jun Fri & Sat din only*

MONCHIQUE B3

Albergaria Bica-Boa Very good vegetarian and non-vegetarian regional cooking, in large portions, up in the wooded hills just north of town. Eat out on the terraces. There are also simple, comfortable rooms *(page 392)*.
Estrada de Lisboa 266, 8550 Monchique
T+351 282 912 271
E bica-boa@sapo.pt
€15-€25 ♀ V! ⨳
Open every day

Charrete A charmingly old-fashioned, inexpensive, rustic restaurant that was once a grocer's shop, in the centre of the old town. Characterful, regional cooking includes some seafood but lots of meat, including *cabrito*, as well as vegetable

dishes. The very sweet lemon and cinnamon-flavoured honey pudding has won prizes. The wine list is surprisingly excellent.
Rua Dr Samora Gil 30-34
T+351 282 912 142
€20 ♀ V
Closed Wed

MONCHIQUE (FÓIA) B3
Jardim das Oliveiras Half way up from Monchique to Fóia, this is a great place to enjoy mountain food with some good wines – as well as the views from this lofty spot. The *jardim* (garden) is an olive grove. Inside, various brightly whitewashed spaces have fireplaces or wood-burning stoves for winter, and checked curtains and country bric-a-brac give a rustic feel. A huge wood-fired oven turns out roasts and other mountain meat dishes. There is good ham and charcuterie, local vegetables, and scrumptious home-made cakes, pastries and puddings.
Sítio do Porto Escuro, Fóia
T+351 282 912 874
E restaurante@jardimdasoliveiras.com
W www.jardimdasoliveiras.com
€25-€30 ♀ V
Open every day

PADERNE D2
Moiras Encantadas This traditional, arched barn on Paderne's main street is indeed an enchanting place, its regional, traditional dishes prepared with great care and concern for quality. Tasting menus offer remarkable value. There are some good wines. Paderne is inland, just to the east of the A2 and north of the A22.
Rua Miguel Bombarda 2
T+351 289 368 797
€20 V
Open Jul & Aug every day;
Closed Sep-Jun Sun; 2nd half Jan

PRAIA VERDE H2
Pezinhos n'Areia In a magical spot on one of the last beaches before the Spanish border, 'Little Feet in the Sand' is separated from the beach only by decking, coconut matting umbrellas providing shade. It's a friendly place with appetising *petiscos*, fish and seafood, and well-cooked traditional dishes, including tempting local sweet things to end the meal. The wines are quite good, cocktails a focal point. Opening hours are 10am-9pm in winter, 11am-2am in summer.
Praia Verde, Castro Marim
T+351 281 513 195
E geral@pezinhosnareia.com
W www.pezinhosnareia.com
€25-€30 ♀ V No credit cards
Open Summer every day
Closed Winter din; 10 Dec-15 Feb

QUARTEIRA E2
O Jacinto A simple, relaxed seafood restaurant serving very good grilled fish and perfectly, plainly-cooked seafood. The dining rooms are a pleasant mix of white and wood. Service is friendly and efficient, and there are some nice wines.
Costa Mar 2, Avenida Sá Carneiro
T+351 289 301 887
E jacinto.noel@iol.pt
€20-€25
Closed Mon

Jorge do Peixe Jorge Silva used to have a little restaurant by the Quarteira market, but moved recently to larger premises at the Quinta do Romão resort. Fish (as in 'George of the Fish') is the main attraction, but there are always two vegetarian and four meat dishes. There follow *doces conventuais*, traditional Algarve puddings, and little almond sweets offered as petits fours to end the meal. A good wine selection comes mostly

from the Alentejo, though the house wines are from the Douro. The decor is modern, very square tables and chairs and a clever 'rough sea' effect in crazy walling.
Quinta da Romão
T+351 289 301 481
€20-€25 ♀ V!
Closed Sun; Jan

QUINTA DO LAGO/VALE DO LOBO E1
O Alambique A very friendly, rustic restaurant with terrace, tucked away behind Restaurant São Gabriel, off the road between Vale do Lobo and Quinta do Lago. Excellent fish and seafood, regional and international dishes, and always a vegetarian option.
Estrada Quinta do Lago-Corgo da Zorra
T+351 289 394 579
€40 V! Closed Sun; 2 weeks Dec

QUINTA DO LAGO E1
Casa do Lago With views through its glass walls over both the lagoons of the Ria Formosa in Quinta do Lago, this is a smart, fun place to lunch, or to watch the sun go down. Cooking is good, fish-based Portuguese, and the wines are well chosen.
Quinta do Lago
T+351 289 394 911
E quintadolago@mail.telepac.pt
W www.quintadolago.com
€70 ♀ V
Open every day Closed 24 Dec din, 25 Dec lunch

QUINTA DO LAGO (P DO ANCÃO) E1

Dois Passos It's worth the walk along the beach from Vale do Lobo, or from Quinta do Lago – this famous beach restaurant in the dunes at the western limit of the Ria Formosa has excellent seafood and fish, simply but very well cooked, and tempting *petiscos*. There's a good wine list, too, and lovely views of sea, dunes and lagoon from the covered terrace. Open for lunch only, and only in the beach season.
Praia do Ancão
T+351 289 396 435
€40-€45 ♀ *V*
Open lunch only Mar-Nov every day Closed
Feb & Nov Wed; Dec-Jan

QUINTA DO LAGO (PRAIA) E1

Gigi Praia This is one of our favourite places to eat in the Algarve, indeed in the whole of Portugal. The genial Gigi and his wife Leonore preside over this relaxed seafood restaurant, perched in the dunes across the long footbridge over the Ria Formosa at Quinto do Lago (just visible on the aerial photo, above). Gigi is a regular early bird at the Quarteira fish market, selecting the best and most interesting of the day's catch. He then cooks, popping out from behind the counter to chat or help his friendly staff deliver the plates of mouth-watering seafood. Superbly cooked vegetables, as well as the freshest of salads and herbs, come from local farms. We loved the sweet onions, the most delicious waxy potatoes, and the long beans and carrots, done to crunchy-cooked perfection. Wines are very well chosen, and there's always a wine of the week at a reduced price. Gigi's love of Italian opera shows in the music that accompanies his cooking. Inside you feel you're on a boat, outside, eat under yellow sunshades, with great

views over the lagoon. As beach restaurants go, this must be amongst the most expensive, but then this is a very special place, where you will rub shoulders with politicians, European aristocracy and captains of industry. In season you must book.
Praia da Quinta do Lago
T+351 964 045 178
E gigirestaurante@gmail.com
€40-€50 ♀ *V*
Open Mar-Nov every day, lunch only
Closed Dec-Feb

RIBEIRA ALTA D2

Quinta da Ribeira Good, old fashioned cooking of the Algarve hinterland in a small Barrocal village east of the A2 motorway. A simple, informal restaurant with good *petiscos* and main dishes, some of which have to be ordered in advance. Outside meal-times, there are home-made almond cakes, ice creams and teas.
Sítio da Ribeira Alta
T+351 282 575 714
E ribalta@mail.pt
€15-€20 V No credit cards
Closed Tue; a few days at New Year

SAGRES A1

Mar à Vista Set back and above the beach, to the east of Sagres, this is a restaurant with really fabulous views. It is decorated with nets and other fishing paraphernalia, and unsurprisingly specialises in fish and seafood, in traditional dishes or simply cooked. Try the local oysters, cultivated off-shore, or the curious *perceves*. The wine list is also very good.
Sítio da Mareta
T+351 282 624 247
E maravistasagres@hotmail.com
€20 ♀ *V Closed Wed; 15 Nov-26 Dec*

Vila Velha
A smart, cosy, friendly, rustic restaurant with a well-chosen wine list, serving good, traditional cooking plus the odd international dish and vegetarian options, and tasty

home-made puddings and cakes. Look for a pretty townhouse, pink where the Algarve blue should be, on the way up to the *pousada* from the centre of town.
Rua Patrão António Faustino
T+351 282 624 788
€25 ♀ *V! No Amex*
Open din only Closed Mon; Jan;
1st 3 weeks Feb

SILVES C2

O Barradas A converted country farmhouse, O Barradas is bright and relaxed, simply smart, but with a country feel, and a cosy fire in winter. It's a long-established family business, run by wine enthusiast Luís Pequeno, whose German wife Andrea takes a gently creative approach

to traditional local cooking, specialising in high quality meat and fish. There is excellent Mirandesa veal and beef from the north of Portugal, and very good lamb from the Alentejo. Baked fish is a highlight. Wines are very well selected, particularly strong in the Alentejo but drawn from around the country. They are usefully arranged in the list by style, and knowledgeably served. You can eat outdoors in the covered terrace in warm weather, when it's best to book. Find it just south of Silves railway station, on the way to Lagoa.
Venda Nova, Palmeirinha
T+351 282 443 308
€30 ♀ *V*
Open din only Closed Wed; Jan

Café Inglês Characterful café-restaurant in a lovely setting high above Silves, by the steps below the castle, right behind the cathedral. The main dining room has a bar and a cosy fire in winter. There's an outdoor sitting area where live music adds to the fun atmosphere on Friday and Saturday evenings and Sunday afternoons. There are panoramic views from the rooftop terrace. Food is simple international, including pizzas, seafood, fish, steaks and salads. Wines are sound: we would recommend the inexpensive house red and white Castelo d'Alba.
Rua do Castelo 11, Escadas do Castelo
T+351 282 442 585
E cafeingles@gmail.com
€15-€30 V Closed Mon din

TAVIRA (SANTA LUZIA) G2

Capelo There's excellent seafood and fish in this pleasant, bright, gently old-fashioned place by the lagoon in the village of Santa Luzia, just to the west of Tavira. Select your meal from the live aquarium, or the displays of fish and meat. There are good home-made desserts, and some good wines.
Santa Luzia
T+351 281 381 670
€30-€35 ♀
Closed Wed; Jan

TAVIRA (CABANAS) G2

Grelha Peixe A light-hearted restaurant by the lagoon, just east of Tavira, offering grilled fish or meat: there's wonderful pork from the Alentejo *(porco preto)*, or veal steaks *(posta mirandesa)*. Nibble on very good sheep's cheese while you wait. There are good wines at fair prices. The bar is a boat, and wine racks around the walls are disguised as yachts and a lighthouse...
Rua Comandante Henrique Tenreiro
T+351 281 370 491
€18 ♀ *V*
Closed Thu; Nov

VILA DO BISPO A2

Café Correia Out here in the wild west, you're in the land of no credit cards, and no booking. So you may have to queue for a table in this tiny, unassuming place, unless, sensibly, you visit out of season. Don't be deceived by appearances. The first surprise is the very good selection of wines, including some venerable reds. And the good, homely cooking (west coast seafood and country fare) has won prizes.
Rua 1° de Maio 4
T+351 282 639 127
€35 ♀ *No credit cards Closed Sat*

Eira do Mel A charmingly simple restaurant in an old farm building, whitewashed walls setting off country artefacts and gingham table cloths. This is country cooking, but of a very high standard indeed – local, traditional ingredients beautifully cooked and presented, often in an innovative way. Top class, locally-sourced vegetables include very good sweet potatoes, and apart from local fish and seafood, there are interesting meat options such as wild boar, rabbit or lamb. *Caldeiradas* and *cataplanas* (both mixed fish and seafood dishes) are a speciality, sometimes unusually composed, cross-dressing meat with fish: there may, for example, be sea prawns with *porco ibérico*. The wine list is very well chosen. The atmosphere is friendly and relaxed, service efficient. Not far from the restaurant, you can admire a number of ancient threshing floors *(eiras)* – hence the name.
Estrada do Castelejo
T+351 282 639 016
E eiradomel@sapo.pt
W www.eiradomel.com
€30 ♀ *V*
Closed Sat except in Aug; 1 week around Christmas

VILAMOURA E2

O Cesteiro Top class fish and seafood is on display: you take your pick and have it weighed as you arrive. It's a simple, fresh, rustic restaurant on the first floor of the Vilamarina building, with a terrace overlooking the Vilamoura Marina. The wines are good.
Edifício Vilamarina, Loja 84,
*   Estrada da Falésia*
T+351 289 312 961
E restaurante-cesteiro@sapo.pt
€40 ♀ *V*
Closed Mon; Dec

ALMANCIL E2

Adega Algarvia Cool and airy, all wood and brick and modern vaulted ceilings, this is a wonderful place to browse for excellent wines from all over Portugal, from everyday to fine and rare. But there is also a seriously stunning range from the rest of the world, with a special emphasis on France and Italy. Adega Algarvia are Portuguese importers and agents for many top names in the wine world. You may even forget the beach… *Estrada Vale do Lobo, Sítio da Rabona*

Apolónia Extraordinarily high quality family-run supermarket with an excellent wine selection, very good charcuterie, fresh fish, meat, splendid cheeses, bakery, top quality local fruit and veg as well imported products you might otherwise not find in these parts – such as the fine display of tropical fruits pictured below. You can order special items, maybe roast

suckling pig. Their new store, in Galé to the west of Albufeira, opened in June 2008. *Avenida 5 de Outubro T+351 289 351 440 Open Mon-Sat 8-8 Public hols 8-1 Closed Sun*

Garrafeira César Leite Good wine shop. *Rua da República 139*

BENAFIM E2

Quinta do Freixo Organic farm shop in the countryside north west of Loulé selling home-made, additive-free jams (apricot, pumpkin, quince etc), honey, home-grown herbs and herb teas, and traditional sweets based on their own old variety of figs. Stay on the farm *(page 390). Benafim*

FARO F1

Garrafeira Rui A sensational collection of wines from all over Portugal is tidily and skilfully crammed into this shop, along with a spectacular selection of port and Madeira. You will find good wines for reasonable prices, as well as most of portugal's really top wines. There are also spirits, excellent cheeses, and pastries. *Praça Ferreira de Almeida 28*

Mercado Municipal The spacious food market on the ground floor of the new Faro market building finally opened in February 2007, vastly overdue and over-budget. The ground floor is a feast of fruit, vegetables and fish. *Rua Mouzinho de Albuquerque 17 Open Mon-Sat 6-3*

GALÉ D2

Apolónia Long-awaited, the new branch of this extraordinary supermarket opened in June 2008, as big and beautiful as the one in Almancil. It is open every day. *Vale Rabelho, Urbanização Setobra, Lote 53.*

GARRAFEIRA SOARES

Thirteen well-etablished, quality-conscious wine shops spread along the Algarve coast, owned by the Soares family of the Herdade de Malhadinha Nova winery in the Alentejo *(page 324)*. Shelves, displays and baskets are brimming with bottles at keen prices from all over Portugal, plus some good foreign wines, and spirits.

ALBUFEIRA *Rua Alexandre Herculano 13, Areias de São João; Avenida da Liberdade 48; Avenida Francisco Sá Carneiro 32, Oura; Avenida Francisco Sá Carneiro 100, Monte Choro; Largo Engenheiro Duarte Pacheco 7; Rua Candido dos Reis 34*

ALVOR *Rua Marquês do Pombal 59*

CARVOEIRO *Praça da Praia do Carvoeiro*

PORTIMÃO *Rua Afonso de Albuquerque, Praia da Rocha; Avenida Tomás Cabreira, Edifício Varandas da Rocha, Loja 22*

VALE DO LOBO *Vale do Lobo Shopping*

VILAMOURA *Avenida da Marina, Edifício Marina Plaza, Loja 17; Marina de Vilamoura, Edifício Marina Plaza, Loja 28*

LAGOS B2
Fish market Excellent covered fish market on the waterfront, also some meat and loads of fruit and veg. Saturday fruit and veg market.

LOULÉ E2
Mercado Municipal On Saturday morning in a building with Moorish influences.

LUZ (PRAIA DA) B2
Supermercado Baptista Family-run supermarket west of Lagos with a very good wine section, strong on port. Good deli and veg, and fresh meat includes free range and *porco preto*. *Urbanização Montes da Luz, Lote 58, Praia da Luz*

MEM MONIZ D2
Garrafeira Veneza One of Portugal's best wine shops is to be found in this village south of Paderne, near the meeting of the motorways, with the Veneza restaurant *(page 378)* attached and indeed its tables sometimes spilling over into the shop. Owner Manuel Janeiro has assembled a vast selection of wines from Portugal and abroad. *Mem Moniz, Estrada de Albufeira*

MONCHIQUE C3
Farmers' market On the third Friday of every month

OLHÃO F1
Mercado Municipal Excellent morning fish market in the red brick, turreted market hall – this is one of the Algarve's main fishing ports, as well as being beside the lagoons of the Ria Formosa, source of wonderful clams, oysters and other seafood. Also fruit, veg, spices, flowers etc. *Avenida 5 de Outubro. Farmers' market along the quay on Saturdays.*

PORTIMÃO C2
Casco Garrafeira Good wine shop *Rua João de Deus 24*

QUARTEIRA E2
Fish market One of the two best in the Algarve, along with Olhão, for fish and shellfish, often sold by very small-scale fishermen.

SILVES (FIGUEIRINHA) C2
Quinta da Figueirinha Organic farm shop open Thurdays only to non-residents, in the Barrocal, inland near Silves. From their own and other local organic farms they sell oranges, other fruit and vegetables, carob bread, marzipan sweets and liqueurs (the apricot one is good). *Figueirinha, 8300-028 Silves Open Thu only 9-12, 3-5*

TAVIRA G2
Market and fish auction New covered market by the riverside, Monday to Saturday. Adventurous cooks might buy octopus direct from the fishing boats, on the beach.

Explore the Algarve

Not just to be contrary, but because they are our favourite bits, we're going to start from the edges, and work in towards the airport. Up in the north east, by the **River Guadiana** at the border with Spain, ALCOUTIM is a small village of traditional white houses with nesting storks, overlooked by a medieval castle. The ferry to Spain is €1. It's a quiet and pretty drive down along the river through unspoilt villages to the small, fortified border town of CASTRO MARIM at the mouth of the river. The **Reserva Natural do Sapal de Castro Marim** *(page 388)* has marshes, salt pans, flamingos, white storks and other water birds, resident and migrating. Further down the estuary is VILA REAL DE SANTO ANTÓNIO, a riverside port built like the Baixa district of Lisbon on a grid pattern by Pombal after the earthquake and massive tidal wave of 1755 destroyed the town.

Another Natural Park begins just west of Vila Real, and hugs the coast for 60km, right round and past the airport.

The **Parque Natural da Ria Formosa** is indeed beautiful. Long spits and islands of flat, sandy beach and dunes separate the Atlantic from the mainland. In between are lagoons (fresh or salt-water) channels, marshes, salt pans and wildlife. Tourism at the eastern end is of a gentler kind. CACELA VELHA and FÁBRICA at the beginning of the Ria Formosa still have the feel of old Algarve villages, small, pretty and quiet, with traditional white and blue houses. You can hire fishing boats to cross the lagoon between the two. TAVIRA is touristic but not overwhelmed. It's a good base for visiting the eastern Algarve, with fascinating streets to explore, some good restaurants and places to stay. The Moorish quarter on the hilltop around the Castelo survived the earthquake, as did some of the grander buildings of the 16th to the 18th century that line the River Gilão. It's a town of many gilded churches, built with the wealth from the former trade in tuna. Fishing boats deliver to the daily market. The **Ilha de Tavira** across the lagoon is a relatively secluded sand bar beach 11km long. You can hire fishing boats to cross, or go by ferry. Strike up into the hills from here towards Cachopo for brilliant scenery and views.

GUADIANA RIVER TRIPS

From Vila Real de Santo António, between April and October, two companies run day trips up the river, including lunch, for around €30 or €40, with reductions for children.
Riosul goes as far as Odeleite. *T+351 281 510 200*
Turismar goes right up to Alcoutim. *T+351 281 956 634*

Far left A never-ending job: mending fishing nets in the Algarve sun

Left The lighthouse and spectacular cliffs at the Cabo do São Vicente

Right Rooftops in Tavira

OLHÃO is a busy, working fishing port with docks and fish canning factories, as well as narrow, cobbled, pedestrianised streets that attract a lot of tourists. It has one of the Algarve's best fish markets. From the eastern end of the quay you can take ferries or water taxis to the sand bar beaches of the **Ilha da Culatra** and **Ilha da Armona**. FARO still has a historic centre with winding, cobbled streets and remnants of city walls, despite a history of wars and earthquakes. Beyond are wide streets, parks, pedestrianised shopping areas. The Ria Formosa fans out wider around Faro. Many of the islands are submerged at high tide, but you can swim under the flightpath off the long, thin Isla de Faro. Here we are at the airport, so leap to stage left.

Out on the western coast of the Algarve, the scenery is quite different. Wild, secluded surfing beaches are backed by grey cliffs sometimes flecked or streaked with red. Some beaches are reached only by hardy surfers down long unmade tracks amidst the marshes or through the rocky, scrubby heath and farmland, sometimes hilly. Since 1995, the whole of this coast has also been a Natural Park, with a name almost as long as its 120km line of shore: the **Parque Natural do Sudoeste Alentejano e Costa Vicentina**. Rarely more than 6km wide, the Natural Park stretches right up the Alentejo coast to Sines at the tip of the Terras do Sado. It's another habitat of many bird species, as well as sea otters and amazing wild flowers in spring.

Up in the north west of the Algarve, old ALJEZUR is an ancient white town of Moorish origins with the remains of a 10th century castle and some fantastic surfing beaches. CARRAPATEIRA, half way down the coast, is also a surfer-centre, an unspoiled village with two fine, windswept beaches. Land's end is the wild and always windy **Cabo de São Vicente** (Cape of Saint Vincent) with its powerful lighthouse and views. Around the tip is SAGRES, with a little fishing harbour and more good surfing beaches. Warm currents give Sagres mild winters, but the constant winds make for chillier summers than in most of the region. Now we're heading for the tourist strip, but SALEMA is lovely, still a quiet fishing village.

Tourism begins to rule on the approach to LAGOS, and the first clutch of golf courses is also ahead. On the western side of a big bay, Lagos was the Algarve's capital at the time of the earthquake, and is still an important seaside town, still a fishing port, but crowded with tourists. The coast from here eastwards is spectacular, eroded cliffs, sea stacks, rocks and grottoes in shades of red and ochre. PORTIMÃO (the Romans' Portus Magnus) is a large, tourist-filled harbour town on the estuary of the River Arade. FERRAGUDO, an old fishing village, is being developed but still attractive. Heading for ALBUFEIRA, high on delightful

Left Sea stacks, cliff remnants in the bay, and the castle of Lagos

Right The Vilamoura Marina by night

Overleaf The beautiful hills of Monchique

cliffs, we're in package land – but Joy awaits you on the outskirts *(page 373)*, and there are some good wine shops *(page 382-3)*. VILAMOURA is all villas, hotels and major golf, plus some important Roman remains at Cerro da Vila. QUARTEIRA has a lovely beach topped with high-rise, low cost tourist accommodation, but between here and the airport the coast becomes rather more exclusive.

VALE DO LOBO is a young person's up-market suburbia by the sea. Beach, bars and clubbing are the focal points (or golf, if that youthful moment has passed). Shops and restaurants are right on the spot, the accent is Surrey or Chelsea, and well-off young families return year after year. Villas nudge right up to the edge of the golf course. Erosion of the spectacular red cliffs is also eroding the prices of the sea view villas. A small and elegant side-step to the east takes us to the first lagoons of the Parque Natural da Ria Formosa at QUINTA DO LAGO. Beautiful, tranquil and secure, and spread over 700ha, Quinta do Lago has exclusive properties along the lagoon-side golf course, a top hotel, secluded villas to rent, and appropriately selective places to

eat. Backing it all is ALMANCIL, an inland village-turned-suburbia with the famous, unmissable church of São Lourenço and the adjoining museum; and, in and around, an extraordinary number of fine restaurants drawing their customers from the wealthy tourists and residents down by the sea. The planes are overhead, and we're back to the airport again.

So let's head inland. Driving north out of Faro, you meet the coastal motorway at ESTÓI, site of a Roman villa and soon an intriguing new *pousada* in an abandoned palace *(pages 388 and 391)*. Drive under the motorway and you're in the Barrocal, the hilly, sometimes scrubby, generally agricultural limestone strip before the serious hills begin. SÃO BRAS DE ALPORTEL is a provincial town amidst pretty valleys and citrus groves. LOULÉ to the west, north of Almancil, is a market town with narrow, cobbled streets, traditional, filigree chimneys and a ruined Moorish castle, surrounded by almond-clad hills. It was once the heart of the copper industry – the *cataplana* is said to have been invented here. There are good footpaths for walking around the hills, valleys and pretty white villages – head for SALIR, with its ruined castle, and ALTE, famous for its fountains and the Queda do Vigário waterfall.

Over to the west, on the once navigable River Arade, SILVES was the Algarve's capital in Moorish times, and more important than Lisbon in the Middle Ages. The town's red

WALKING THE VIA ALGARVIANA

In the last couple of years, a well-signed footpath has been established right across the interior of the Algarve from Alcoutim to Sagres through Silves and Monchique, with information in English and German.
Alto de São Domingos 14, 8100-756 Loulé
T+351 289 412 959
E viaalgarviana@vialgarviana.org
W www.viaalgarviana.org

earthquake trade in cork and dried fruit. The surrounding hills with their orange and lemon groves are a pretty place to stay and explore.

Top tourist destinations up in the hills are the small hillside market town of MONCHIQUE in the north west and the renovated hot spa of CALDAS DE MONCHIQUE just below it *(page 391)*, both nestling in the cork oak, pine and eucalyptus forests of the **Serra de Monchique**. Bus tours come here (but they don't stray far into the lovely countryside) and locals drive up on Sunday to admire the views and fill up their water containers. Atlantic rains and a multitude of springs keep Monchique green, but fires have devastated some parts of the woodland in recent years. Monchique is still a traditional place with old houses and narrow, winding streets, and cake shops for the tourists.

sandstone castle is considered the finest Moorish monument in Portugal. There are Moorish narrow streets and stairways, but the many merchant houses date from affluent post-

VIEW FROM THE TOP

ALCARIA DO CUME Village off the road between Cachopo and Tavira, with lovely views of surrounding mountains and the distant sea.
ALCOUTIM **Castelo** Views from the castle across the river to Spain, and over surrounding hills. Entry of €2.60 includes a good little archaeological museum *Open 9-1, 2-5*
ALJEZUR **Castelo** Look out towards America from the ruins of the castle walls.
CALDAS DE MONCHIQUE The *miradouro* (vantage point) above the spa complex has fine forest and mountain views.
CASTRO MARIM From the Castelo, pretend you're a Knight Templar, scowling across the River Guadiana to Spain; the modern view takes in the bridge, and the marshes and salt pans of the nature reserve. *Open Apr-Oct 8-7 Nov-Mar 9-5 Free*
FARO **Sé** Wonderful views of the sea, coast, and the resident storks from the cathedral's square bell-tower *(right)*.
LUZ (PRAIA DA) **Miradouro da Atalaia** High above the sea, east of Lagos, great coastal views.
MONCHIQUE (FÓIA) The highest point in the Algarve, with great hill views all around, even as far as Cabo de São Vicente.
SAGRES **Cabo São Vicente** Five kilometres west of Sagres, bleak, high and windswept, often cold even in summer, the

grey cliffs of the famous south-western cape look out to the Americas. The lighthouse, said to be visible for 90 nautical km, may sometimes be open for visits, offering an even loftier view.
SALIR **Rocha de Pena** This limestone escarpment up in the Serra do Caldeirão north of Querença has views south to the sea, north to the hills.
SILVES **Castelo** From the red sandstone Castelo ramparts, views over the town and surrounding citrus groves to the mountains. *Open every day Summer 9-7, winter 9-6*

CASTRO MARIM **Castro Marim Sapal** Right over by the Spanish border, a wetland reserve where you can observe the saltpans and wild waterfowl from paths along the dykes. (*Sapal* means marsh.) There's an old tidal mill, and tuna fishing boat, and remains of Roman fish-salting tanks. Get maps from the office just north of town. *Sapal de Venta Moínhos Open Mon-Fri 9-12.30, 2-5.30*

ESTÓI **Milreu Roman ruins** Maybe a private villa, maybe public baths, maybe both at different periods, the remains were found under a farmyard half a century ago. They date from the first or second century, with third century alterations. You can see mosaic floors and the remains of the baths, a wine press, temple garden and mausoleums. *Open Tue-Sun Apr-Sep 9.30-12.30, 2-6 Oct-Mar 9.30-12.30, 2-5 Closed Mon; Easter Sun, 1 May, 25 Dec*

OLHÃO **Quinta de Marim** Environmental park 3km east of town, a refuge and breeding centre for injured and rare birds amidst marshes, lagoons, pines and dunes. Watch out for the Mediterranean chameleon, Europe's only. There's a watermill, and some more Roman fish-salting tanks. *Open every day Closed 1 Jan 25 Dec*

VILAMOURA **Cerro da Vila** A very important archaeological site on the north side of the Vilamoura marina, this was a big Roman bathing complex, later converted into a factory for the production of fermented fish condiment. *Open May-Oct 10-1, 4-9 Nov-Apr 9.30-12.30, 2-6.*

MUSEUMS

SILVES **Museu de Arqueologia** A well-presented museum with exhibits spanning Roman and Moorish times, including a rare and impressive Moorish well. *Rua da Porta de Loulé Open Mon-Sat 9-6 Closed Sun, public hols* **Museu da Cortiça** The Cork Museum, in one wing of a former cork factory, has won prizes. Displays explain (also in English) the process of stripping cork bark and transforming it into wine corks and other items. *Fábrica do Ingles, Rua Gregório Mascarenhas Open Summer times variable – phone to check T+351 282 440 480 2nd week Sep-Dec, Feb-mid-July Tue-Sat 9.30-12.45, 2-5.30 Closed Sun & Mon except high season*

SÃO BRÁS DE ALPORTEL **Museu Etnográfico do Trajo Algárvio** Rural museum of 19th and 20th century Algarve costume, mule carts, ox wagons and carriages, agricultural implements, cork-related items, and religious sculptures. It's housed in the mansion and farm buildings of a late 19th century cork magnate. *Rua Dr José Dias Sancho 61 Open Mon-Fri 10-1, 2-5 Sat, Sun & public hols 2-5 €1*

CHURCHES

ALMANCIL **Igreja de São Lourenço** One of the Algarve's finest churches, and one of Portugal's finest displays of *azulejos*. Admire the beautiful floor-to-cupola juxtaposition of Rococo gilding and *azulejos* depicting the life of the saint. Romanesque with Baroque additions, it survived the 1755 earthquake. *Rua da Igreja, São Lourenço Open Mon 2.30-5 Tues-Sat 10-1, 2.30-5 Closed Sun, Mon am*

ALTE **Igreja de Nossa Senhora da Assunção** This pretty inland village has one of Portugal's most beautiful churches; 16th century *azulejos* from Seville cover the interior. *Rua do Prior 5*

LAGOS **Igreja de Santo António** Small, baroque church full of gilt-work, azulejos and paintings. *Rua General Alberto da Silveira Open Tue-Sun 9.30-12.30, 2-5 Closed Mon, public hols €2*

SANTA BÁRBARA DE NEIXE **Igreja Matriz** The church of this tiny village between Loulé and Estói is one of the Algarve's most beautiful, 15th century, with the typical twisted columns of the Manueline period.

TAVIRA **Igreja do Carmo** In the oldest part of town, this church dating from the late 18th century is simple outside, stunning Baroque gilt inside. *Largo do Carmo* **Igreja da Misericórdia** Fine Renaissance church with *azulejos* depicting biblical scenes. *Travessa da Fonte*

VILA DO BISPO **Nossa Senhora da Conceição** On the main square, the town's main church has 18th century blue and white *azulejos* combined with Baroque gilt carving, and a painted wooden ceiling.

FAIRS & FESTIVALS

JANUARY QUERENÇA **Festa das Chouriças** At the 'festival of sausages' (which have undergone a strange gender change in this inland village!), you can taste loads of different kinds at stands set up around the church square. There's a mass in the church, a street procession, music and dancing, and a sausage auction.

FEB/MAR LOULÉ **Carnaval** Towns all over Portugal celebrate Carnival before

GOLF

More than 30 golf courses have rolled out across the Algarve's coastal strip since the first one appeared at Penina in the mid-1960s. Six of them are in Vilamoura. They are all in the American style with lakes and ponds (without the alligators, as far as we know) – and glorious sea views. The golfing peak (mainly northern Europeans) is in February, when prices are fuelled by wealthy Swedes and Germans.

The best courses (according to our golf gurus – we looked, but don't play) are around the **Quinta do Lago** estate (3 x 18 holes, plus a new course under construction), the star being **San Lorenzo**, beautifully designed, with glorious views of the Ria Formosa. Those around Vale do Lobo are perhaps least challenging, although the spectacular cliff-top hole on the **Royal Course** must be the most photographed in Portugal, and the **Vale do Lobo** course has a nice clubhouse and restaurant. Amongst several courses at Vilamoura, the **Old Course** to the north of town is classically-styled amidst lovely mature trees; it has a very good clubhouse. There's a fun nine-hole

course, **Pine Cliffs (Sheraton Hotel)**, with some spectacular sea views and tumbling cliffs; and **Victoria**, west of Vilamoura, has a good club house and restaurant. Grandfather of them all, **Penina** is inland north of Portimão on an old rice plantation; the Penina Hotel is very good and has good food. Other favourites are **Quinta da Ria**, right over in the Ria Formosa to the east of Tavira, with great mountain as well as sea views, lakes, olive and carob trees, and good club house; and its more challenging twin, **Quinta de Cima**; **Palmares**, half way between Lagos and Portimão, with breathtaking views of the Alvor estuary; and **Vila Sol**, to the east of Vilamoura, which has a good hotel.

Easter, but the lively, historic market town of Loulé does it with particular flair. Eat and drink with the crowds, join the three-day street party, and watch the parades. **Portimão** is also a good place to party at Carnival time.

MARCH MONCHIQUE Feira dos Enchidos Tradicionais Monchique, in the cool, high north-western mountains, has ideal natural conditions for making hams and charcuterie, and many small producers. The 'Traditional Sausage Festival' is a good time to taste a range, along with the local spirit, *medronho*, traditional sweets and cakes, mountain honey and liqueurs. There's mountain music and folk dancing.

APRIL ALJEZUR Festival do Percebe The 'Festival of the Goose Barnacle' used to

happen in the autumn, but now these curious crustaceans can't be caught from mid-September to mid-December because of declining numbers.

MAY MONCHIQUE Festa do M The May Day mountain 'Festival of the M', when Monchique celebrates numerous products beginning with that letter: *medronho* (white spirit made from arbutus fruits), *melosa* (*medronho* sweetened with honey), *mel* (honey) and *bolos de Maio*, cakes made with honey, maize and wheat flour and olive oil, and flavoured with coffee, chocolate, lemon zest and cinnamon.

JUNE LAGOA Semana da Gastronomia Portuguesa For Portuguese Gastronomy Week, a dozen or so chefs converge on Lagoa from all over Portugal – a major

event, backed by music and craft exhibitions. **TAVIRA Festa da Cidade** Party in flowery streets and eat sardines (all night if you so choose) on Saint John's Eve (23-24 June).

JULY MONCHIQUE Feira do Presunto First weekend of the month, the 'Cured Ham Fair' is a chance to pig out on the high-quality hams of this upland town, as well as tasting its sweets, cakes, jams, *medronho* spirit and characterful honeys from bees foraging in the rosemary, heather, orange blossom and arbutus flowers of the surrounding mountains. **LAGOS Festa da Arte Doce** Sweet-making festival, last weekend of the month – traditional confections of almonds, figs, egg yolks and lots and lots of sugar *(see page 372)*.

AUGUST PORTIMÃO Festa da Sardinha A big tourist attraction for the first ten days of the month, tons of sardines, plus other fishy food, sweet stuff, crafts and musical events. **QUARTEIRA Festa da Sardinha** More sardines, a shorter, two-day festival, mid-month. **OLHÃO Festival do Marisco** Big seafood festival in the second week of the month, in the Jardim Patrão Joaquim Lopes. Hundreds of stalls, music and folk dancing. The third weekend of August is Olhão's Orange Festival, **Feira da Laranja**.

OCTOBER ALJEZUR Festival da Batata-Doce This small town right up the western coast is famous for its sweet potatoes, which appear in many local dishes, both savoury and sweet. Apart from food and wine, there's folklore, craft and music at this autumn festival. **ALMANCIL Quinzena Gastronómica de Almancil** Gastronomic Fortnight where local restaurants take part in competitions, along with festivities, music and *cataplanas*.

Sleep in the Algarve

ALBUFEIRA D2

Vila Joya Joy Jung came to this small, Moorish-style 'palace' as a baby – her parents bought it as a family home, then turned it into a hotel in 1982. Everywhere there are arches and fluid architectural lines, modern elegance and squishy soft furnishings. Spacious rooms and suites all have terraces with fabulous sea views. Prices include delicious breakfasts and dinner for two in Portugal's only Michelin two-star restaurant *(page 373)*. Terraces then gardens with pools run down to the sea, with steps down eroded cliffs to a perfect, quiet beach. There's an extraordinary spa, and a gym.
Praia da Galé, Apartado 120,
*   8200-902 Albufeira*
T+351 289 591 795
E info@vilajoya.com
W www.vilajoya.de
€390-€450 inc breakfast and dinner for 2
🛏12 S 8 ⚲ ✕ ⚓ ♨ ⚲

ALCANTARILHA D2

Hotel Capela das Artes Classified as a national monument, this lovely, family-run hotel centres on a stately home, Quinta da Cruz, built between the 15th and 18th centuries, with a beautiful chapel. New buildings have been harmoniously added to the old – even the big salt-water outdoor swimming pool somehow looks as if it belongs in the rural setting. There are three jacuzzis, a bar with terrace in the former stables, relatively simple, comfortable rooms all with terrace or balcony, even an art gallery with changing exhibits. Find it inland, between Lagoa and Albufeira, where tourists are near, but far.

Quinta da Cruz, Estrada Nacional 125,
*   Apartado 101, 8365-908 Alcantarilha*
T+351 282 320 200
E admin@capeladasartes.com
W www.capeladasartes.com
€90-€120
🛏 29 ✕ ⚓ *jacuzzis*
Closed Dec, Jan, 1st week Feb
Min nights 2

ALJEZUR B3

Quinta do Lago Silencioso Right up in the north west of the Algarve, in the Natural Park, this is a magical place. Although purpose-built not so long ago (to high ecological standards), the attractive, low building already blends in with its surroundings, lovely (organic) gardens and a large, natural lake, overlooked from the flower-hung terrace.

You can swim in the lake, boat upon it, fish, and then barbecue your catch on the waterside. There are bikes for children and adults, and quiet places to sit, read and contemplate. Breakfast is on the terrace whenever possible, and includes home-grown fruit.
Monte da Bagagem, 8670-158 Aljezur
T+351 282 998 507
E info@quintadolagosilencioso.com
W www.quintadolagosilencioso.com
€60-€80
S 3 SC 1(2+2) ⚓ *No credit cards*
Closed Jan
Min nights 2 off-season, 7 in summer

BENAFIM E2

Casa d'Alvada This delightful rural B&B is on the Algarve's biggest farm, Quinta do Freixo, just between the northern mountains and the agricultural Barrocal, north-west of Faro and Loulé. The pretty, unspoilt village of Alte is just nearby. The guest rooms are in long, low farm buildings, comfortable, rustic rooms with old-fashioned furniture. Good breakfasts include home-made bread, honey and jams. There's a lovely old bar, a pool and olive trees in the garden. The farm, still a family business, has 1,000 rare breed sheep (soon to be organic), bees for honey, cereals, and trees including figs, citrus, olives, pines and cork oaks. The long, twisting, tree-lined lake is for irrigation, but is an attraction for house-guests, too. A restaurant at the end of the lake serves rustic local cuisine, including game bred and shot on the farm. Guests might choose to watch or even help with farm work – picking grapes, shearing sheep, jam-making – or, well togged up in bee suits, join an educational trip to the hives. There's also snooker, ping-pong, clay pigeon shooting, and mountain bikes. The shop sells farm produce *(page 382)*.

*Quinta do Freixo, Benafim,
  8100-352 Loulé*
T+351 289 472 185
E geral@quintadofreixo.org
W www.quintadofreixo.org
€51-€62 (suites €62-€74)
🛏8 Ⓢ2 ✗ ⚓ *No credit cards*
Closed Jan
Min nights Normally 1, Aug min 7

BOLIQUEIME E2

Quinta da Cebola Vermelha An old
farmhouse, elegantly restored, in the
countryside just north-west of Boliqueime,
south of the A22 right in the centre of the
southern Algarve. Rooms are spacious,
tastefully, sometimes wittily decorated,
with terraces, there's a shared sitting room
with open fire and comfortable sofas, a
big outdoor salt-water pool and breakfast
tables amidst the orange trees. Breakfasts
are excellent, as are other meals, available
three days a week – the Dutch owners
were once in the restaurant business.
Campina, 8100-908 Boliqueime
T+351 289 363 680
E info@quintadacebolavermelha.com
W www.quintadacebolavermelha.com
€105
🛏6 ♇ ✗*set dinner 3x week €29.50* ⚓
Closed Jan (usually)

CALDAS DE MONCHIQUE C3

**Villa Termal das Caldas de
Monchique** Famous from Roman times,
this spa was a summer haunt in recent
centuries of the wealthy and aristocratic;
having fallen out of favour in the late
20th century, it reopened, refreshed and
refurbished, in 2001. The spa 'village' has
four hotels and a house with self-catering
apartments, plus restaurants and a wine
bar. On the small central square, the
Estalagem Dom Lourenço is small, cosy
and delightfully old fashioned; Hotel

ESTÓI

Pousada do Palácio de Estói Near
the Roman ruins of Milreu, just south
of the A22 north of Faro, this
spectacular and once-abandoned
Rococo building is now being turned
into a *pousada*, due to open in late
2008. The extravagant pink palace
will have 49 rooms, three suites,
restaurant, bar, spa, swimming pool,
tennis court, conference falilities and
extensive gardens. Watch out for it on
the web site *www.pousadas.pt*.

Central is also small, in 19th century style
but fresh and bright; Hotel Dom Carlos is
a big, modern conversion, a touch more
luxurious; and the modern Hotel Termal
contains the spa, with facilities for the
disabled. The spa is used in the morning
for medical purposes. In the afternoon
you can enjoy almost every conceivable
form of spa therapy, including coffee
treatments, wine and choco-therapy (all
external), and immersion in the waters,
said to be beneficial for respiratory and
musculo-skeletal complaints. There's also
a gym, a lovely garden pool, and forest all
around. Tour coaches invade by day, and
at the bottom of the complex near the spa
there's a bottling plant, but evenings are
quiet.
8550-232 Monchique
T+351 282 910 910
E reservas@monchiquetermas.com
W www.monchiquetermas.com
€90-€130 (€130-€160 Dom Carlos appts)
🛏12(Estalagem), 🛏3(Central),
🛏18(Dom Carlos), 🛏40(Termal)
Ⓢ*10(2+2)* ✗ ⚓ ♨ ✻ ⚲

CARRAPATEIRA A2

Monte Velho A long, low, blue-and-
white building set high amidst the western
hills, renovated and redecorated inside
with audacious colours. A terrace runs
along the front, with stunning views of
hills all around, and fields where donkeys
graze. The sea and glorious, deserted

surfing beaches are just nearby, or you can
walk, cycle or even ride the donkeys along
the paths of the Natural Park.
*No address: 4km south of Carrapateira,
  near Vilarinha!*
T+351 282 973 207
E montevelho.carrapateira@sapo.pt
€90-€100 (Suites €100-€120)
🛏2 Ⓢ7 ⚓*(lake)*
Min nights July & Aug 7

Pensão das Dunas An attractively
renovated old farm house, white with
characteristically blue windows, on the
beach side of the village – the sea is quite
accessible at this point on the west coast.
Nice, simple rooms, sharing bathroom,
sea views, pretty courtyard shaded by palm
trees.
Rua da Padaria 9
T+351 282 973 118
€34-€39 Ⓢ*€35-€40*
🛏*4(shared bathroom)* Ⓢ*6(2+1)*
No credit cards
Closed 1 or 2 weeks Dec/Jan
Min nights 2

FALÉSIA E2

**Hotel Sheraton Pine Cliffs and
Resort** Between Albufeira and Quarteira,
this large, smart enclave on the clifftop
above the Falésia beach has a high class
hotel plus well-equipped, up-market self-
catering apartments and villas. Families
with children of all ages might particularly
appreciate the facilities – a 'Kids' Club'
(6 months to 12 years) has its own pools
and 18-hole mini-golf, and all kinds of
alluring activities. You might not feel the
need to stray off campus – except, maybe,
to eat out: some of the Algarve's top
restaurants are conveniently nearby. A lift
and footpaths take you down the red cliffs
to the virtually private beach, where in
summer a multitude of watersports are

offered, with tuition if required. There's an outdoor pool, three indoor pools, a health club, a busy gym, tennis courts with optional coaches, a nine-hole golf course with optional academy, games rooms, restaurants and shops…
Praia da Falésia, 8200-912 Albufeira
T+351 289 500 100
E sheraton.algarve@starwoodhotels.com
W www.pinecliffs.com
€300-€370
🛏 *215* S *33* SC *A wide choice of appartments, town houses and villas*
♀ ✕ 🛶 ☕ 🏖 ✵ ⁝⁄ ✎

LOULÉ E2
Casa da Luz A comfortable, attractive new villa for up to seven people within the smallholding of Quinta Santa Luzia, in the hills just north of Loulé. There are lovely gardens, and a variety of trees – fig, almond, lemon, carob… It has a pool (sometimes shared with the hosts), terraces, including a large roof terrace, an open fire for cooler months, and air conditioning.
Quinta Santa Luzia, Cruz da Assumada,
Caixa Postal 330-A, 8100-296 Loulé
T+351 289 413 252
E bianca@quintasantaluzia.com
W www.quintasantaluzia.com/en-start.html
€350-€995 per week
SC *1(7)* 🛶 *No credit cards*
Min nights 3

MEXILHOEIRA GRANDE B2
Casa da Palmeirinha A delightful aristocratic country house in an untouristic village inland from Alvor – the Alvor bird sanctuary and nature reserve is just nearby. Dating from the 16th century, the house has been completely restored. Rooms are simple but comfortable. Guests share a dining room, sitting room, terraces and barbecue. There are lovely gardens, an inner courtyard and large swimming pool. They offer no meals other than breakfast, but you can use the family kitchen to make hot drinks and cold food, and the village has the interesting Vila Lisa restaurant *(page 378)*.
Rua da Igreja 1, Mexilhoeira Grande,
8500-132 Portimão
T+351 282 969 277
E josejudice@mail.telepac.pt
€50-€80
🛏 *5* 🛶 *No credit cards*
Min nights usually 2

MONCARAPACHO F2
Vila Monte A discreet, comfortable hotel and exotic spa set in beautiful grounds and gardens in the countryside half way between Faro and Tavira. There's a Moorish feel to the decor with its columns and arches, and many original works of art. Comfortable rooms have recently been renovated, and all have terraces or balconies, with views of the sea, or almond groves. Apart from three pools and a tennis court, there are putting and driving facilities for golfers – and a resident golf tutor. The Orangerie restaurant is good, too *(page 375)*.
Sítio dos Caliços, 8700-069 Moncarapacho
T+351 289 790 790
E info@vilamonte.com
W www.vilamonte.com
€133-€375
🛏 *26* S *29* ♀ ✕ 🛶 ☕ ✎

MONCHIQUE C3
Albergaria Bica-Boa Optional massage, Reiki and meditation might transport you to the mountains of Tibet… This western-Algarvian mountain inn and restaurant is in a beautiful, wooded, peaceful spot, nestling amidst mature trees on a valley side, ideal for anyone who loves walking – and for vegetarians, as Bica-Boa is run by Buddhist Susan Cassidy, whose vegetarian food attracts both locals and travellers *(page 378)*. Breakfasts are also good, served in the garden or on the terraces when the weather is fine. There are just four twin rooms (tastefully simple, traditional and comfortable) so book well ahead. Bica means water jet or spring, by the way, so Bica-Boa is Good-Spring. Find it half a kilometre outside town, on the Lisbon road.
Estrada de Lisboa, N 266,
8550-427 Monchique
T+351 282 912 271
E bica-boa@sapo.pt
€55-€65
🛏 *4* ✕ *V!* 🛶

PECHÃO F1
Quinta dos Poetas, Hotel Rural A newly built hotel in a quiet, country setting with lovely views, north-west of the busy fishing port of Olhao. Large, pleasant rooms all have balconies, and there are spa facilities, a small gym and a games room, as well as a fine outdoor pool and five holes of pitch and putt to practice your golf. Staff are friendly and attentive.
Pechão, 8701-905 Olhão
T+351 289 990 990
E recep@quintadospoetas.com
W www.quintadospoetas.com
€85-€140
🛏 *22* ✕ 🛶 ☕ ✵

PORCHES D2

Vila Vita Parc A top class, cliff-top hotel complex with every pampering and sporting facility you might wish – for you and for your children. The hotel is Moorish-style set in attractive gardens. There are numerous pools, jaccuzis, sauna, health and fitness, beauty and spa, nine restaurants, tennis, mini-golf, warersports, fishing... A crèche and Kids' Park keep children happy, if required. And steps lead down to a private beach. The Vila Vita is owned by the same (German) company that owns the Herdade dos Grous wine estate in the Alentejo *(page 324)*.
Alporchinhos, 8400-450 Porches
T+351 282 310 100
E reservas@vilavitaparc.com
W www.vilavitaparc.com
€185-€485
🛏96 ⑤86 ⚲ ✕ 🏊 ♨ 🏇 🚲 ⚲

QUINTA DO LAGO E1

Hotel da Quinta do Lago Behind the golf course, dunes and lagoon of exclusive Quinta do Lago *(right)*, discreet amidst its private hills and pine forests, the Hotel da Quinta do Lago is extremely luxurious. Relax in the health club with

all kinds of spa facilities, or the outdoor jacuzzi with ocean view. Swim in indoor and outdoor pools or the lagoon. There are stables, tennis, watersports, glorious golf, and jogging paths. Breakfasts are wonderful, there are two good restaurants, or cross the footbridge to Gigi's *(page 380)* for stunning seafood.
8135-024 Almancil
T+351 289 350 350
E info@quintadolagohotel.com
W www.quintadolagohotel.com
€207-€552 (suites €552-€1,873, royal suite €1,750-€3,180)
🛏132 ⑤9 ⚲ ✕ 🏊 ♨ 🏇 ⚲

QUINTA DO LAGO/VALE DO LOBO E1

Hacienda & Villa São Gabriel Within the lovely gardens of the Michelin-starred São Gabriel restaurant *(page 376)* are two villas with elegant, spacious accommodation, maid service, secluded terraces, barbecues and pools to die for. Conveniently located for many of the Algarve's best restaurants.
T+351 289 394 521
E restaurante@sao-gabriel.com
W www.sao-gabriel.com
€520-€1,300 / €900-€1,950
ⓈⒸ*2(2+2&4)* ⚲ ✕ 🏊
Closed Jan & Feb
Min nights 7

SANTO ESTEVÃO G2

O Pequeno Castelo In a lovely, rural family home, two B&B rooms plus two self-catering apartments with private terrace and sea views. Surrounded by fruit trees just outside the little, untouristy village of Santo Estevão, 6km west of Tavira. There's a pool in the garden *(above)*, and your polyglot hosts will cook evening meals on request – local or international style, vegetarian or vegan.
Poço das Bruxas, Santo Estevão, 8801-902 Tavira
T+351 281 961 692
E pequenocastelo@hotmail.com
W www.pequenocastelo.com
€40-€50
🛏2 ⑤1 ⓈⒸ*2(5&2)* ✕*on request V!* 🏊
Credit cards through Paypal
Min nights 3 in high season

SILVES C2

Casa das Oliveiras In the peaceful hills between Silves and Lagoa, this is a welcoming, comfortable guest house, away from it all but within easy reach of the coast. Bedrooms are spacious, all with en suite bathrooms. One has its own private terrace. Guests share a sitting room with dining area, and a large terrace with pool. Breakfasts are substantial; no other meals available, but there are local restaurants, and you are welcome to cook in the kitchenette. The owners are proficient in numerous languages, and keen to help.

Montes da Vala, 8300-044 Silves
T+351 282 342 115
E contact@casa-das-oliveiras.com
W www.casa-das-oliveiras.com
€40-€60
🛏5 ≈ *No credit cards*
Closed very occasionally in winter

SILVES C2 *(continued)*

Quinta da Alegria Spacious and modern, with many comforts (and rented as a whole house) Quinta da Alegria is in the hills five minutes' drive from Silves. The house is set in 13ha of farmland, recently planted with citrus and avocado trees. Guests are presented with seasonal produce grown on the farm. There's a covered terrace and a barbecue area converted from a former bread oven and pigsty! Air-conditioned throughout, the house has five double or twin bedrooms, open-plan sitting and dining rooms both with wood-burning stoves, a well-equipped kitchen, maid and garden service. Outside, enjoy the championship tennis court, and a large swimming pool, which can be heated at an extra cost, and a shaded games area with table tennis and table football. It's five minutes to the nearest golf courses, 12 minutes to the nearest beach.

Figueiral, 8300-000 Silves
T+351 282 443 822 (house)
T+44 1483 205 309 (reservations)
E philr@farleygreen.net
€2,000-€4,500
🆂 *1(10+2 max)* 🍷 ✕ *on request* ≈ ⚲
No credit cards

Quinta da Figueirinha *(above)* On an organic farm in the Barrocal, inland, near Silves, various long, low, white farm buildings have been converted into 11 attractive self-catering apartments with shady terraces and shared pools. The farm produces mainly oranges, but the farm shop (open every day for residents) sells organic fruit and vegetables, carob bread and other home baked bread, home-made marzipan sweets, jams and liqueurs, and organic wine from a producer in Lagos. There's a library, a computer with internet access, and farm tours. You can opt for lunch and/or dinner, and brunch on

Sundays, vegetarian or not, in the restaurant.

Figueirinha, 8300-028 Silves
T+351 282 440 700
E qdf@qdf.pt
W www.qdf.pt
€72-€120 (6 people), €56-€88 (4),
€30-€60 (2)
🆂 *2(6), 4(4), 5(2)* ✕ *V!* ≈
No credit cards
Min nights 7; last minute short bookings

TAVIRA G2

Pousada Convento da Graça/ Pousada de Tavira This ex-convent, ex-army hospital opened in 2006, beautifully restored. It is built around a central cloister, with a modern restaurant in the old convent refectory. The central staircase leads to very well-designed, modern rooms, all with their own balcony. It is very centrally located in the 'museum zone' of this beautiful, historic city, with its Moorish remains. The Pousada boasts a 'wide range of indoor and outdoor facilities'.

Rua Dom Paio Peres
Correia,
8800-407 Tavira
T+351 281 329 040
E recepcao.conventograca
@pousadas.pt
W www.pousadas.pt
€150-€230

🛏*30* 🆂*6* ✕ ≈

Tavira Inn A characterful, comfortable town house on the river bank ten minutes' walk from the town centre, with spacious rooms, artistic decor, a fine outdoor pool and a jazz bar. Humourful, helpful owner Sebastião Bastos is keen to make your holiday a perfect one.
Rua Chefe António Afonso 39,
    8800-251 Tavira
T+351 917 356 623
E bookings@tavira-inn.com
W www.tavira-inn.com
€50-€100, no breakfast
🛏5 ≋ *No credit cards*
Closed end Oct-1 Mar
Min nights 2

Vila Galé Albacora *(below)* Hotels in the Vila Galé chain are always good value; this is one of their most characterful, converted from a former tuna fishing village in the peaceful setting of the Ria Formosa. Fishermen's houses, low buildings in ochre or white, have become guest rooms, each with its own shrub-defined terrace. The village chapel has been restored, and the former school now houses a children's club, offering children's activities free of charge in the summer. There are outdoor, indoor and children's pools, garden, gym and spa facilities. There's even a museum of tuna fishing on site! Breakfast buffets are good, as is the hotel's own Alentejo wine range, Santa Vitória *(page 338)*. The hotel ferry will take you over to the lovely, quiet beaches of the Ilha da Tavira, just across the lagoon, and a shuttle bus runs the 2km into town. All around are salt pans, marshes, and wading birds – come in April when the flamingos pass through. (Note that there is another Vila Galé hotel in the centre of Tavira, also nice, but not to be confused with this one.)
Rua Quatro Águas, 8800-901 Tavira
T+351 281 380 800
E albacora@vilagale.pt
W www.vilagale.pt
€70-€215
🛏157 Ⓢ5 ♀ ✕ ≋ ♨ 🤸

VALE JUDEU E2
The Garden Cottages In the village of Vale Judeu, just north of Quarteira, and within easy reach of many of the Algarve's best restaurants, this quiet little complex was once a wine estate. The old press-house, winery, stables and other farm buildings have been tastefully converted in modern-rustic style into holiday cottages for two, plus one newly built, tucked into private areas of the pretty walled gardens, amongst the fruit trees, or by the farmhouse. There's a large shared swimming pool, and all the cottages have private patios and barbecues.
Vale Judeu, 8100-292 Loulé
T+44 (0)1462 817377 (UK)
E debbie@rmlboyes.fsnet.co.uk
W www.algarvegardencottages.co.uk
€200-€500 (per cottage per week)
Ⓢ𝖼7(2) ≋
Min nights summer 7, winter 3

VILAMOURA E2
Vila Sol Spa and Golf An excellent golf hotel with very good breakfast buffets and six restaurants including the renowned l'Olive, where German chef Tell Wagner produces excellent international and Mediterranean cuisine from fine local ingredients (and the wine list is very good). It's a curvaceous modern building in large grounds with lakes and waterfalls as well as the golf course, which offers three levels of difficulty. There is a world-class spa, indoor and outdoor swimming pools, a small but well-stocked gym, tennis, a crèche and a children's club. From June onwards, a free shuttle will take you to the long stretch of white beach, and another runs the ten minutes to and from the lively town of Vilamoura in the evenings. The apartments of Vila Sol Village are 1km away but share the hotel facilities.
Alto dos Morgadinhos,
    8125-307 Vilamoura
T+351 289 320 375
E reservations@vilasol.pt
W www.vilasol.pt
€185-€380 Suites €610-€1,050
🛏189 Ⓢ54 𝖲𝖢45 ♀ ✕ ≋ ♨ 🤸 ✒ ⛳

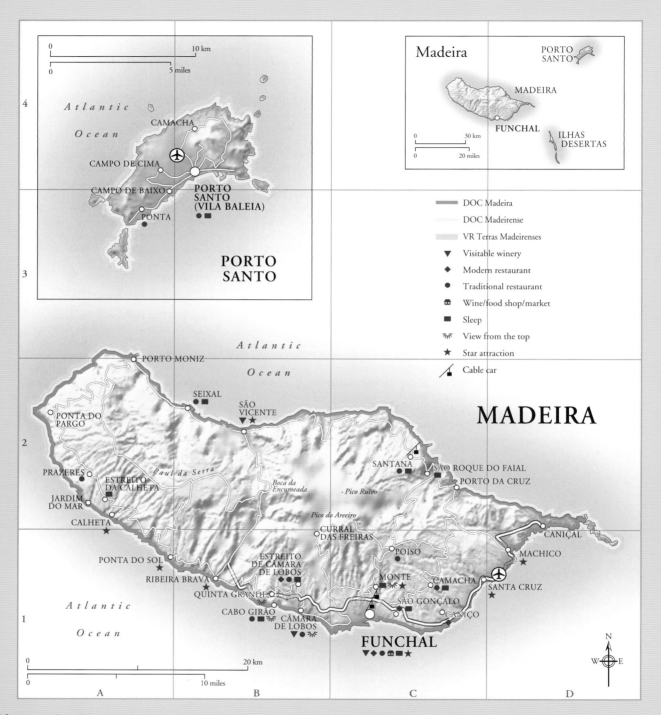

4

0   10 km
0   5 miles

Atlantic

Ocean

CAMACHA

CAMPO DE CIMA ✈

CAMPO DE BAIXO

PONTA

PORTO SANTO (VILA BALEIA)
● ■

3

PORTO SANTO

Madeira

PORTO SANTO

MADEIRA

FUNCHAL

ILHAS DESERTAS

0   30 km
0   20 miles

━━━ DOC Madeira
──── DOC Madeirense
━━━ VR Terras Madeirenses
▼ Visitable winery
◆ Modern restaurant
● Traditional restaurant
⌂ Wine/food shop/market
■ Sleep
❈ View from the top
★ Star attraction
╱▪ Cable car

Atlantic

Ocean

PORTO MONIZ

SEIXAL
■ ●

SÃO VICENTE
▼ ★

MADEIRA

2

PONTA DO PARGO

Paul da Serra

Boca da Encumeada

· *Pico Ruivo*

SANTANA
● ■

SÃO ROQUE DO FAIAL ■
PORTO DA CRUZ

PRAZERES

ESTREITO DA CALHETA

JARDIM DO MAR

CALHETA ★

Pico do Areeiro

CURRAL DAS FREIRAS

POISO ●

CANIÇAL

MACHICO

PONTA DO SOL ★

RIBEIRA BRAVA ●

ESTREITO DE CÂMARA DE LOBOS
◆ ■

QUINTA GRANDE

CABO GIRÃO
■ ●

CÂMARA DE LOBOS
▼ ❈

MONTE ★
■

SÃO GONÇALO
■

CAMACHA

SANTA CRUZ ✈
★

CANIÇO
●

1

Atlantic

Ocean

0   20 km
0   10 miles

FUNCHAL
▼ ◆ ● ⌂ ■ ★

N
W ✦ E
S

| | A | B | C | D |

Madeira

Closer to Morocco than to Lisbon, the volcanic island of Madeira was discovered and claimed by Portugal in the 15th century. It narrowly escaped becoming an English colony 200 years later. When Catherine of Bragança married Charles II of England, the story goes that Madeira was to be part of the dowry. But the scribe who copied the contract was Madeiran, and by a slip of the quill... The English were, however, granted special rights to settle and trading privileges, and their interests in the wine trade flourished.

The island, especially its capital, Funchal, still attracts a lot of British visitors, historically of the genteel, wealthy, retired variety, but the profile is slowly widening. The climate is agreeable all year round; the southern ocean warms the winters, breezes cool the summers. July and August are normally dry, but otherwise clouds build up mid-mountain by noon – it may be sunny on the southern coast, sunny on the peaks, but misty by your hillside hotel pool. Never fear – after a short burst of rain, the sun will be back by evening.

Most tourists stay around the spreading south coast port-resort of Funchal. Indeed, half the local population lives in Funchal, and most of the rest live within sight of the sunny, fertile southern coast. Madeira is small (only 56km at widest east to west, and 23km north to south) but even by the new roads – still wiggly and often steep – exploration takes longer than you might imagine. Modern life is penetrating rapidly into the interior and around the once isolated coasts. EU grants have helped finance an 'expressway' along much of the southern coast, as well as road improvements that have replaced with modern tunnels the old barrier-free, cliff-hanging hairpin bends.

Beyond Funchal, the whole island offers spectacular, wild scenery, even from the roads. Mountains run east-west, with side ridges, ravines and green valleys branching out to the coasts. There are woods of ancient laurels (laurisilva), sweet chestnut and eucalyptus. Springs, waterfalls and rain on the central moorland plateau feed an astonishing network of irrigation channels (levadas), flanked by footpaths, a well-shod walker's paradise. Terraces hewn long ago into the steepest of hillsides are still green with crops, sub-tropical by the sea, temperate in the higher reaches: bananas and other fruit, vegetables, flowers and grapes.

Wine in Madeira

Madeira makes two types of wine, one that has been world-renowned for over 300 years, the other a fledgling industry just beginning to establish itself. The fortified DOC Madeira is of course the famous one. The unfortified wines, DOC (or VQPRD, the term used most on labels) Madeirense and VR Terras Madeirenses, have increased fourfold over the last five years, but are still in their infancy, struggling to gain acceptance, even on the island.

Let's look first at Madeira, the fortified wine, which has contributed most to the ups and downs of the economy of the island. In the modern winemaking world, few would back a wine that is made from what most winemakers would call seriously under-ripe grapes, a wine that is deliberately heated and oxidised as part of the maturation process, and that has to spend a minimum of 20 years in barrel before it can be labelled 'Vintage'. But this is one of

those examples where traditional winemaking techniques, evolved through circumstances, have something to teach winemakers of the 21st century. It could be argued, indeed,

Wine regions
DOC Madeira
DOC/VQPRD Madeirense
VR Terras Madeirenses

Main local grapes
Red Tinta Negra, Complexa, Deliciosa
White Sercial, Verdelho, Boal, Malvasia, Terrantez
For details of grapes see page 428

that to update viticulture and winemaking too far would compromise the identity and quality of this amazing wine.

Madeira and its sandy-soiled neighbour, Porto Santo, lie about 880km off the west coast of Morocco on a similar latitude to Casablanca, and, on the other side of the Atlantic, to the Dominican Republic. The very mild climate is influenced by the Gulf Stream, not too hot in summer (22°C average) or too cold in winter (16°C). Whatever is planted in Madeira's rich, volcanic soil grows with almost indecent vigour. Lush terraces of vines, bananas, tomatoes and kiwi fruits grow rampant in the high-acid soils of the volcanic slopes. The moist, warm climate makes Madeira a paradise for exotic flowers, which grow in profusion.

But the very factors that encourage vigour and vegetation pose problems for vines. Fog and humidity encourage fungal diseases, particularly as most vines are trained on pergolas, and grape-bunches are not as well ventilated as they could be with more open training methods. Yields are high, and most grapes struggle to reach 10 or 11% potential alcohol. The governing body of Madeira wine, the Instituto do Vinho, Bordado e Artesanato da Madeira (IVBAM), has recently raised the minimum level of potential alcohol acceptable for any grapes destined for wine on the island to 9%. (At the

MADEIRA'S GRAPES

Sercial High-acid white grape, traditionally grown at higher altitudes, and made into the driest style of Madeira *(top)*

Verdelho White grape with good acidity (also very good for unfortified wines), usually made medium-dry *(second down)*

Boal/Bual Malvasia Fina on the mainland, a white grape traditionally made into medium-sweet Madeira *(third down)*

Malvasia/Malvazia Two types of Malvasia are grown on Madeira. The traditional, higher-quality one is Malvasia Cândida; the more widely planted is Malvasia de São Jorge *(fourth down)*

Terrantez Known in the Douro as Folgasão, this is a high-acid white grape that had nearly disappeared from Madeiran vineyards. It is now making a limited comeback. Terrantez makes intense, piercing wine of great character, sometimes dry, sometimes medium-dry.

Tinta Negra A red grape, the most widely-planted variety on Madeira, accounting for almost all the wine produced in the younger styles, and used also for colheita Madeiras *(bottom)*

taste. The other factor was fortification: the addition of brandy to the young wine enormously improved its stability. The idea may have come from port shippers, no one is sure, but was widely used by the mid-18th century.

By the end of the 18th century, shippers had realised that they could short-cut the effects of the sea voyage, with the same results, by heating the young wine in their cellars on the island. Some built cellars with glass roofs, so that the sun could heat the barrels during the day. Eventually, they started heating the wines with stoves, a process known as *estufagem*, and discovered it took only three months to get the effects of four or five years of exposure of a wine to sunlight. As always, some overstepped the mark, overheated, and produced wines with burnt, baked flavours.

Through all these changes, the island had developed a dependence on the rising exports of Madeira wine. Apart from crops the islanders grew to feed themselves, wine was a virtual monoculture. Exports rose through the 18th century, first to Brazil, then the West Indies, then Britain. But success brought imitation 'Madeira', less well-made, from other places. Recession after the Napoleonic Wars meant fewer exports and hard times. There was a failure of the Madeira potato crop, the islanders' main staple. In the mid-19th century, the first of the two vine plagues arrived in Madeira: oidium, a fungal disease that attacks leaves, grapes and vines, devastated the vineyards. Then, in 1872, phylloxera arrived. This vine-root-eating louse had munched its way through the wine regions of

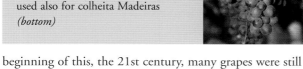

beginning of this, the 21st century, many grapes were still being picked at 7% potential alcohol.)

But high-acid, low alcohol grapes have been one of the factors in the staying power of Madeira's wines. There are two others. One was the discovery, around the end of the 17th century, that shipping young Madeira wine across the Equator, or to the West Indies, actually improved the

Left Terraced vineyards in the hills above Câmara de Lobos

Right Ricardo Freitas, winemaker at Barbeitos, has spearheaded a move to modern, 'single harvest' wines

Europe, and a cure was not found for several years. Times were hard, and many islanders emigrated, to Venezuela and South Africa. Others just abandoned their vineyards.

It has been a long struggle back. The solution for phylloxera, grafting the European vines onto impervious American rootstock, has left Madeira with a legacy of American vines, or hybrids of American vines. Although these probably saved the industry, they are no longer wanted, as they give wine with a strange, disagreeably perfumed smell and taste. So IVBAM regularly offers subsidies (always fully subscribed) to replace them with European varieties. They are no longer permitted in Madeira wine or the unfortified VQPRD and VR wines. But there are still nearly 1,400ha of *americano* vines growing on Madeira. Islanders keep the American varieties (particularly Isabella) for table grapes, apparently, but it might be as well to avoid wine from unlabelled bottles in bars.

The other big change in the island's grapes has been the emerging dominance of red grapes, particularly Tinta Negra. This variety was originally brought to Porto Santo as suitable for the sandy soils there (its original home is sandy Colares *(page 254)*, where it is known as Molar).

LODGE & LABEL LANGUAGE

Americano Ungrafted vine (also known as 'direct-producer', as it's planted directly into the soil, not grafted onto a rootstock) from one of the American vine families, or a crossing with one of these. Or wine made from these vines. Avoid!

Canteiro The process of ageing Madeira in wooden barrels and vats, traditionally starting at higher temperatures on upper floors, and progressing to cooler conditions later.

Colheita/single harvest Madeira made from white grapes or Tinta Negra (which may or may not have had *estufagem*) matured in wood for at least five years before bottling and sale.

Estufa Heating system to speed the ageing of Madeira.

Estufagem The process of heating Madeira in an *estufa*.

Vinho de canteiro Wine that has been aged in the *canteiro* system, released a minimum of 36 months after the last addition of alcohol.

Vinho de estufagem The youngest category of Madeira, which can be released for sale a minimum of 12 months after the estufagem, and not before 31 October of the second year after the harvest.

Vintage/Frasqueira/Garrafeira Madeira made from one of the traditional grape varieties (not Tinta Negra), aged in wooden barrel and vat for a minimum of 20 years before bottling, then another 24 months in bottle before sale.

planting licences for Tinta Negra are being issued, and IVBAM is trying to persuade growers to plant more vines for white grapes.

The number of shippers has declined over the centuries, partly through business failures, partly consolidation. There are now only six shippers exporting Madeira, and a handful of others who sell only on the island, mainly to visitors. Only Henriques & Henriques of the exporters owns much vineyard, so there is considerable competition for the grapes grown by almost 1,300 growers. Câmara de Lobos is the main vineyard area, supplying 60% of the

It grows even better on Madeira, and gives much better yields than the 'noble' white grapes, Sercial, Verdelho, Boal, Malvasia and Terrantez. Of the 420ha of European vines planted on Madeira, 84% are Tinta Negra. (There are other red varieties, Complexa and Deliciosa, which make wine a lot less exciting than their names imply.) Malvasia and Boal make up most of the whites. Almost all the Malvasia is Malvasia de São Jorge, not the traditional Malvasia Cândida (said to be much finer). Unfortunately, some growers of white varieties have changed to red, because they couldn't get high enough prices from the shippers to compensate for the lower yields, but now no

grapes. There are also vineyards in nearby Estreito de Câmara de Lobos, and going west, in Campanário and Arco de Calheta. Limited plantings are to be spotted most of the way along the south-east and north coasts of the island, with the greatest concentration in the north around São Vicente (also the site of the government-owned winery, made available to growers who want to make unfortified wines). Most vines are planted at between 200 and 300m altitude. Below that, soil is too expensive, but above 300m, vineyards are expanding.

Most growers have other jobs, which usually earn them their living – viticulture is a weekend hobby. But younger members of the family don't want to look after the land. Plots are often very subdivided, by Napoleonic rules of succession, in which land is divided equally between children. One grower may tend 15 tiny plots of vineyard. And white grapes in particular are often delivered to the shippers' wineries in pathetically small quantities. The supply of already scarce white grapes is made worse by the

Opposite (left to right) Mammoth maturation at Madeira Wine Company, and the tasting room, Quinta do Furão Hotel

Above Old-style trellised grapes

Right Terraced hillside

In the last stages of *canteiro* ageing, some of the oldest wines are transferred from oak or chestnut vats to glass demi-johns, seen here here below the vats in the Barbeito cellars

DOC/VQPRD MADEIRENSE AND VINHO REGIONAL TERRAS MADEIRENSES

The islanders don't actually drink a lot of Madeira, but they do like a glass of unfortified wine with their food. And there are a lot of tourists who want to buy wine as well. To avoid importing all this from mainland Portugal, the Government built a winery in São Vicente, where anyone can take their grapes to make DOC/VQPRD or VR wine, and in 1999 they created new VQPRD/DOC rules; VR rules followed in 2004. Both sets of rules allow wine to be made from grapes grown anywhere on the islands of Madeira and Porto Santo. A team of winemakers is based at São Vicente, with all the necessary equipment to make wine. If a producer wants different yeasts, or to make the wine differently, he has to provide the yeasts or the expertise.

As a result, the production of unfortified wines has increased by over 400% in the last five years. There are plenty of new plantations, none of them very big. All the long-established Madeira grapes are included, plus an array of international grapes, of which the most unexpected is an obscure German grape called Arnsburger (recommended by a German consultant), which makes very neutral-tasting wine. Otherwise, Chardonnay, Sauvignon Blanc, Chenin, Cabernet Sauvignon, Merlot, Syrah, they're all there, together with Alvarinho, Aragonez, Touriga Nacional, Touriga Franca and Tinta Barroca from the mainland.

It's a bit early to judge, but most of the first efforts are unconvincing, with a few honorable exceptions. The best wines come from small producers, although some of the big Madeira shippers have tried as well. Apart from the style of the wines, the main problem is that the local wines look very expensive on a restaurant wine list, and you have to really *want* to buy them. Nothing except the fruit is produced on the island, so bottles, labels, corks and winemaking materials must be imported, which makes home-grown wine much more expensive. And people are entitled to wonder whether that extra expense is worthwhile.

increasing interest in producing unfortified wines on the island. Producers of unfortified wines are prepared to pay more than the Madeira shippers, particularly for Verdelho (which makes good unfortified wine).

The problem has been addressed for many years by using Tinta Negra to make the less expensive Madeiras. Before Portugal joined the EU, and rules were tightened, there were young three-year-old Madeiras labelled 'Sercial', 'Verdelho', 'Boal' and 'Malmsey' that had probably seen none of these grapes, and were made almost entirely from Tinta Negra. These are now labelled 'Dry', 'Medium-Dry', 'Medium-Sweet' and 'Sweet', without pretence. And the reputation of Tinta Negra has risen as it has been shown that it can make wines of three, five, even ten years that show complexity and intensity.

So how has this become possible? Firstly winemaking has improved enormously. Secondly, as in the Douro, shippers can now choose the brandy they use for stopping the fermentation and taking the alcohol level up to the 17% at which most Madeiras are aged. Then, modern *estufagem* is much gentler, and better-controlled, than in the old days. *Estufagem* certainly saves time (and money), speeding up the ageing process by between five and ten years. But old heaters often went up to 55°C, which was too hot, and gave the wine burnt flavours. Modern *estufas* are kept between 45 and 51°, their temperatures controlled by computer, for about three months. Producers say this is equivalent to four years in *canteiro*.

Canteiro is the term used for Madeiras aged in barrels, with no heat other than the sun. The name comes from the word for a stone window surround or lintel, which was used as a support to stop barrels rolling around the floor. The stone bearers gave way to wood, but the name stuck.

While ageing, the young wines start on the hot, upper floors of a lodge, and come down to lower floors when they have been through the first stages of maturation, and need to develop more slowly. Here they may be stored in larger vats, sometimes made from Brazilian satinwood, much less porous than oak. Satinwood was the old 'stainless steel', and renovated satinwood vats gleam bright yellow in some of the older lodges.

Some Tinta Negra is aged in *canteiro*, and goes into 10 and 15 year-old blends. Wine from white grapes is always aged in *canteiro*, lest its delicate flavours be spoiled by the *estufagem* crash course in heating and ageing. The new

style of age-dated wine, single-harvest or *colheita*, is sometimes sold without a specified grape variety. In those cases, you can be pretty sure the wine is Tinta Negra, and it's often very good.

There is a financial incentive, provided by EU subsidies, to age Madeiras for at least five years (known as *poseima*). If, on your visit to a lodge, you see serried ranks of barrels with official-looking seals on them, you'll know they are earning 14.6 cents per litre per year (or €73 per 500 litre barrel) to hang on in there for a minimum of five years. Subsidies are also available to convert vineyards, buy

alcohol and rectified grape must (to sweeten wines) and to export.

And the island's exporters need all the help they can get, because in 2002 the export rules changed. With a few exceptions, Madeira may now be exported only in bottle. The idea was to prevent fraud (Madeira had seen too much of that in the 18th and 19th centuries), but the immediate effect was to reduce exports sharply. About 60% of Madeira used to be sold in bulk, and this is down to less than 25%. The only circumstances in which Madeira may now be shipped in bulk are if it is going to a very tightly regulated market (such as Switzerland) or if it is 'denatured' before it leaves the island. Much Madeira destined to end its life as *sauce au madère* in French kitchens leaves with 10gm of salt per litre, and some pepper, before it is shipped. It's undrinkable, but still useful in the sauce!

And bottled Madeiras have never been better. The new *colheita* single harvest style means that shippers are able to sell Madeira with a harvest date on the label without having to wait 20 years. The young wines are fresher and cleaner than they used to be, and vintage Madeiras are as good as ever, wines of intense, piercing power, complexity and longevity. Will better viticulture (leading to riper grapes) affect the ageing of the more recent generation of vintage wines? It's too early to tell. But it's worth burying a bottle or two of great old vintage Madeira safely amongst your clothes on your return journey. It's a rare example of a wine that will not spoil after you've opened it. You can enjoy it for months to come. Or even years.

Left Canteiro wines ageing in barrel at Justino Henriques, warmed only by the sunshine

Right Barrels of Tinta Negra wine undergoing the statutory five-year *poseima* maturation

CÂMARA DE LOBOS B1

Henriques & Henriques With 15ha, Henriques & Henriques is the only Madeira shipper to own significant vineyards. Indeed, their aptly named 10ha Quinta Grande (Big Estate) is the largest single vineyard on the island. The Henriques family had been the largest landowners in Câmara de Lobos since the 15th century. The company, founded in 1850, still belongs to the descendants of the partners who joined between 1937 and 1946, the Jardim, Pereira and Cossart families, plus 20% held by José Berardo, of Bacalhôa Vinhos de Portugal.

In 1992, Henriques & Henriques built a modern winery and warehouse just outside Câmara de Lobos. This is where they receive visits. You can turn up here without prior notice, and you will be given a tour of the maturation cellars, including the large glass-walled one that exposes the barrels to the warmth of the sun to speed the ageing process. You can taste some of the basic wines without charge, but will be asked to pay to taste anything from the 10 Years Old range and above. You can also arrange a visit to Quinta Grande (which was planted in 1995), but this has to be by prior appointment. Over a third of Quinta Grande is planted with Verdelho, with almost as much of Sercial. But there is some Boal as well, together with a hectare of Malvazia Cândida, and a precious half-hectare of Terrantez.

The wines are made by Luis Pereira, who has been in charge of winemaking at Henriques & Henriques for decades. The vinification and *estufagem* cellar is up at Quinta Grande, near the vineyard, and was built in 1995. The basic Henriques &

Henriques range, **Monte Seco, Special Dry, Medium Dry, Medium Rich** and **Full Rich**, are made from Tinta Negra, and are very clean and modern. Quality leaps with the **Henriques & Henriques 10 Years Old** range, all four made from the noble white grapes, **Sercial, Verdelho, Bual** and **Malvazia**, and all savoury, woody and intense. The **Henriques & Henriques 15 Years Old** wines are even better, more intense, more complex and more concentrated. The **H & H Vintage** wines are all excellent. The **1971 Sercial** is bone-dry and intense, with savoury, lemon-lime notes. The **1964 Sercial** is ethereal and austere. The **1957 Boal** is rich, toffeed and creamy, and the **1954 Boal**, treacley and very intense. The **1954 Malmsey** is intense, treacley-sweet, and balanced by marvellous acidity. And there are two delicious **Terrantez Vintage** wines, the **1976 Terrantez** with lovely poise and greengage fruit sweetness, and the **1954 Terrantez**, soft, sweet yet savoury, with amazing intensity and high acidity. The **Solera Century Malmsey 1900** was a blend started in 1900 and finished in 1985, much more austere than the younger wines, with elegance and sweetness. Finally, there are four legendary Reserve wines, the **Henriques & Henriques 1965 Sercial** (that's just the bottling date!), the **Grand Old Boal** (bottled in 1927), the **WS Boal** (bottled in 1927) and the **1964 Malvasia** (bottling date again). These wines, of immense complexity, are said to date from before 1850, and are certainly amongst the best in Madeira.

Avenida da Autonomia 10, 9300-146
Câmara de Lobos
T +351 291 941 551
E heh@henriquesehenriques.pt
W www.henriquesehenriques.pt
Visits Mon-Fri 9-1, 2.30-5.30
Closed public hols

FUNCHAL C1

Vinhos Barbeito The company was founded in 1946 by Mário Barbeito de Vasconcelos (grandfather of Ricardo Vasconcelos Freitas, the current Managing Director). Although the first exports were of wines in bottle, as Vinhos Barbeito grew through the 1970s, it was drawn inexorably into the bulk Madeira market. Barbeito de Vasconcelos' daughter, Manuela de Vasconcelos, took over when her father died, and continued selling around the world. When Ricardo Freitas joined in 1991, two major changes happened. First, the family cemented an alliance with their longstanding Japanese distributor, Kinoshita Shoji, and sold them half the shares in the company, and second, Barbeito started thinking about stopping bulk exports.

These ceased in 1993, and Barbeito returned to what they did best, producing good wines, sold in bottle. The company owns no vineyards (the last were sold in 1978), but buys grapes from 193 growers, whom it supports with viticultural advice throughout the year. Much of the wine is aged in the *canteiro* method, in three separate warehouses, but some of the least expensive blends undergo gentle *estufagem* in modern, stainless steel vats. None of the Barbeito Madeiras has its colour adjusted with caramel, so they're all light in colour.

You can visit the winery and have a free tour and tasting, without an appointment. Alternatively, you could go to Diogo's, the wine shop owned by Barbeito (*page 417*). Here you can taste, and you can also visit their museum devoted to Christopher Columbus. This, though small, is the second-best collection of Columbus-related documents in the world (the largest is in the USA).

Ricardo Freitas, winemaker and part-owner, has pursued an amazingly innovative path in such a traditional wine region. He has been one of the pioneers of single harvest Madeira, not the traditional 'vintage' (or *frasqueira*, the word Barbeito use), with its compulsory 20 years in cask and 2 years in bottle before sale, but younger wine, aged for a minimum of five years in cask (or seven for Sercial). These are known as 'single harvest' wines, which gives an opportunity of indicating a year without trespassing on the historic territory of the term 'vintage'.

The **Barbeito 3 Years Old** wines are good for the category, made from Tinta Negra, clean and elegant. **The Barbeito Single Harvest Tinta Negra Mole** is savoury, elegant and stylish. Another innovation is the **Barbeito Medium Dry Reserva VB**, a blend of Verdelho and Boal, subtle, with savoury elegance and good length. Even the **Barbeito Boal 5 Years Old** is fascinating, with tangy, dried fruit flavours. The **Barbeito 10 Years Old** range has some very good wines, a complex, woody, elegant **Verdelho**, a spicy, intense, fragrant **Boal**, and an elegant, toffeed, long **Malvasia**. Another innovation is single-cask bottling. **1999 Barbeito Boal Colheita Casco 8a+d** is minty, elegant and very intense, the 'a+d' signifying its passage through two different warehouses to vary the ageing conditions. The **Barbeito 20**

Anos Malvasia is a magnificent symphony of dried fruit, wood, leather and toffee, complex and intense. And older Barbeito Frasqueira wines can be fabulous, the **1981 Barbeito Verdelho Frasqueira** woody, subtle, complex and intense, the **1978 Barbeito Sercial Frasqueira** smoky, elegant and intense, with length and balance, and the **1982 Barbeito Boal Frasqueira** creamy, nutty and complex. There is also a **Barbeito Lote Especial 30 Anos Malvasia**, which really is special, elegant, intense, savoury, complex and sweet.

Estrada Monumental 145,
*   9000-098 Funchal*
T +351 291 761 829
E barbeitomadeira@mail.telepac.pt
W www.vinhosbarbeito.com
Visits: Mon-Fri 9-12.30, 2-5.30 Closed
*   public hols*

Artur de Barros & Sousa Right next to D'Oliveira's lodge in Rua dos Ferreiros is Artur de Barros e Sousa. It's an entrance you might walk past (we have!) if you didn't know it was there. It's a tiny operation, and all the winemaking and maturation happens at this one small lodge. They do not export, except for the occasional bottle that wings its way to a customer who has already visited them at the lodge.

The business was started by Dr Pedro José Lomelino, who was a medical doctor as well as head of the Funchal primary school at the beginning of the 20th century. Dr Lomelino was an avid collector of good Madeira, and employed his nephew, Artur de Barros e Sousa, to sort out his collection when Artur returned from Brazil. This went so well that Dr Lomelino started a business for Artur to run, at first under the Lomelino name, then, in 1922, under the name Artur Barros e Sousa, Lda. The company is still

run by Artur and Edmundo Olim, grandsons of the original Artur de Barros e Sousa. They welcome visitors, and it really is worth the time.

Behind the discreet entrance is a slice of Madeiran wine life as it used to be. A little passage leads to the old-fashioned shop and tasting room, then the office. There's a cobbled yard behind, in which the wines are fermented in old oak barrels after harvest. And there are three floors of wine storage. That's all. Everything is done by hand. All the wines, even the less expensive ones, are aged in barrel, on *canteiros* similar to those you will see in the yard. There is no heating of the wine *(estufagem)*, even though the Olim brothers do use Tinta Negra and Complexa, as well as white grapes. They make perhaps 4,000 litres of new wine per year, from all sorts of grapes, including Terrantez, Moscatel and Bastardo, as well as the well-known ones.

And the wines are very individual; several are challenging in their austerity. The Olims don't have any really old vintage wines left, but there are Reserve wines, with no vintage marked, that are blends of much older wines than the five years demanded by law. The **Artur de Barros e Sousa Bastardo Reserva** is austere, quite robust and very dry, and the **Artur de Barros e Sousa Terrantez Reserva** is dry, light and ethereal, savoury and tangy. **ABSL Sercial 1988** is clean and toasty, with a note of orange peel and savoury concentration. **ABSL Malvasia 1988** has aromas of nut, honey and dried fruits, with length and lovely acidity balancing the sweetness.

Rua dos Ferreiros 109, 9000-082 Funchal
T +351 291 220 622
E absl@netmadeira.com
W www.vinhosmadeira.com
Visits Mon-Fri 9-12.30, 2-5.30 Closed Aug

VINHOS JUSTINO HENRIQUES, FILHOS, LDA

Colonel Sigfredo da Costa Campos was a pragmatic man (he died in May 2008). He believed most Madeira should be made of Tinta Negra, the most widely planted grape on the island, and that the old system of vintage wines is dying, to be replaced by the new, younger *colheitas*. And he was a firm advocate of the *estufagem* method of ageing Madeiras. Justino's does age its white wines in barrel, by the *canteiro* method, but they account for only 15% of production.

Justino Henriques started as a family company in 1870, and became a limited company in 1953. Colonel da Costa Campos bought it in 1981 and did a deal with the French company, La Martiniquaise, in 1993. La Martiniquaise now has a majority share, and distributes

the wines in France, where Madeira is viewed as a wine to be used in sauces, Madeira sauce, to be precise. This has led to the interesting situation of Justino's being the only shipper still to have a significant proportion of its exports (20%) in bulk. But we're talking about denatured Madeira, with salt and pepper added to make the wine undrinkable: just what French kitchens want.

To make all this cooking Madeira, and their other wines, Justino's buy about 35% of Madeira's entire harvest each year, from about 1,000 growers. A lot of effort goes into the new *colheitas*, made from Tinta Negra and other red varieties. Their large modern warehouse at the Cancela Industrial Park has long rows of ex-Cognac oak barrels, stacked four-high, most bearing the seals of the *poseima*, the EU subsidy system. All these have been through three months of *estufagem* at temperatures between 45 and 50°C. A warehouse higher in the building has

white wines ageing in barrels in warmer rooms. These are destined to be vintage wines, and are not subjected to *estufagem*.

The basic blends and Justino's 5 Years Old wines are made from red grapes. Our favourites are the tangy **Justino's Fine Rich**, with raisin and tea aromas, and **Justino's 5 Years Old Reserve Fine Rich**, quite intense, with malty, nutty intensity. There are also versions of the **Justino's 10 Years Old** wines made from red grapes, **Justino's 10 Years Old Reserve Fine Dry**, with tangy, woody length, and **Justino's 10 Years Old Reserve Fine Rich**, nutty, raisiny and elegant. Of the white grape 10 Years Old wines, our favourites are **Justino's 10 Years Old Sercial**, light, elegant and citrussy, and **Justino's 10 Years Old Verdelho**, greengagey and elegant. Likewise, some *colheita* wines are made of Tinta Negra, others of the white grapes. If there is no grape variety stencilled on the bottle, it is Tinta Negra. **Justino's Colheita 1996** is elegant, savoury and quite sweet, and **Justino's Sercial Colheita 1998**, rich, tangy and dryish. Reaching back to the older dated wines, **Justino's Terrantez 1978** is rich, complex and greengagey; **Justino's Sercial 1940**, citrussy, austere and very intense; **Justino's Verdelho 1954**, intense, toffeed and poised; **Justino's Boal 1964**, savoury, treacley and intense; and **Justino's Malmsey 1933**, nutty and intense, with amazing length.

Juan Teixeira *(right)*, the Venezuela-born winemaker, is doing a great job experimenting with Tinta Negra and the other red varieties to

maximise their potential. Unfortunately, this forward-looking company does not yet receive visitors. They are considering the possibility, in 'the near future'.

FUNCHAL C1 *(continued)*

HM Borges As you walk up the Rua 5 de Outubro, which runs down to the seafront in Funchal, you cannot fail to notice the large capital letters spelling out the company name, HM Borges, Succrs Ltda, on an imposing white lodge, details picked out in grey. The lodge is four months away, the other side of the *levada*, on the Rua 31 de Janeiro!

Henrique Menezes Borges founded the company in 1877, after amassing a large collection of old Madeiras, bought with the profits from his food importing business. For many years the business sold Madeiras to other companies, but did not export its own wines. When HM Borges died in 1916, his sons and daughter took over the company. They started to export HM Borges wines in 1922, and the company moved to its present home, an ex-flour mill. HM Borges is now run by two great-granddaughters of the founder, Helena (who looks after the commercial side) and Isabel (the winemaker and blender), both named Borges Gonçalves.

When you visit the delightfully atmospheric lodge, it is almost certainly one of these who will welcome you. The company receives quite large groups from cruise ships and travel agents, so it's wise to phone before going, to avoid a clash. The lodge lies behind and above the tasting room and office, a place of large satinwood casks and old barrels, where the wines made from white grapes mature in the traditional manner, the youngest at the hotter top of the building, and the older down on cooler floors. HM Borges uses *estufagem* only for their 3 and 5 Year Old wines. The 3 Year Old wines are all

Tinta Negra, the 5 Year Old ones moving in that direction.

Although the company was once famous for vintage wines, the stock of these had fallen almost to nothing over the years, until Isabel's father Jorge started laying some down again in 1977. But they have eagerly embraced the new *colheita* category, and have wines from 1995 and 1998. From 10 Year Old upwards, the HM Borges wines are made from the white grape varieties, and aged in barrels only. The **HM Borges 10 Year Old Boal** is complex, bright and savoury, the **HM Borges 15 Year Old Verdelho** is tangy, nutty and dryish, and the **HM Borges 15 Year Old Malmsey** is rich and raisiny, with a good balancing acidity. **HM Borges Colheita Sercial 1995** is tangy and citrussy.

Rua 31 de Janeiro 83, 9050-011 Funchal
T+351 291 223 247
E info@hmborges.com
W www.hmborges.com
Visits Mon-Fri 9-12.30, 2-5.30 Closed
*   public hols*

Madeira Wine Company The gravity of the name suggests it has always been there. Actually, the Madeira Wine Association was founded in 1913, by a group of Madeira shippers (Henriques & Camara, Wm Hinton & Sons and Welsh & Cunha) who wanted to share some of their costs to make their businesses more profitable. In 1925, Blandy Brothers & Co, Leacock & Co and Thomas Mullins joined the partnership, and John Ernest Blandy became head of the firm. Over the next 30 years, 22 other companies joined up (including Cossart Gordon in 1953). And, in 1981, the company changed its name to the present one, the 'Madeira Wine Company' (MWC). In 1989, the Blandy family, who by now had bought

out the other partners, sold a majority interest to the Symington family, in order to get better distribution of the MWC wines internationally.

Most of the companies that formed the original association had been founded much earlier than 1913 (Leacocks in 1760, Cossart Gordon in 1745, Blandy's in 1811 and Rutherford & Brown in 1814, for instance). So it's no surprise that the 'Old Blandy's Wine Lodge' is one of the unmissable visits of Madeira. It's right in the centre of Funchal, one street back from the sea-front. The building was once a Franciscan monastery. Since 1840 it has been a wine 'lodge' (warehouse), and it is still used to house some of the finest of the MWC's maturing Madeiras. As you will learn, they keep the younger wines on the top two floors, where temperatures are higher, reserving the first floor for the older wines that don't need to age so quickly. Admire the beautiful satinwood vats, breathe in the complex

smells of wood and nuts, take a look at the first-floor museum of letters, implements, labels and pictures. And then a free tasting of some of the younger wines from the MWC awaits. If you want to taste older wines, you'll have to pay.

The company owns no vineyards, but has contracts with some 800 growers. Some only bring in one 40kg box of grapes! The largest supplier delivers 35 tonnes. The winery was built in 1986, and rebuilt in 1998. They use autovinificators, relying on the pressure of the carbon dioxide formed during fermentation to pump the must over the cap, as well as open vats for the red wine. The whites are almost all fermented in open vats. Winemaker Francisco Albuquerque *(overleaf)* has made huge changes since the pre-Symington days, and the inexpensive **Dukes** range is much better-made than it used to be. It's when you get to the 5 year old wines that interest really picks up. The **Blandy's 5 Year Old Malmsey** is raisiny, intense and

savoury. **Blandy's Alvada 5 Year Old**, a blend of Malmsey and Bual, is toffeed and creamy, with a hint of greengage. **Blandy's 1999 Harvest Colheita Malmsey** is soft but tangy, with bright acidity and flavours of dried fruits – a light, fruity, well-balanced style. The **Cossart Gordon 10 Year Old Verdelho** is off-dry, with bright, tangy acidity, flavours of greengage

and nut and some complexity. The **Cossart Gordon 10 Year Old Bual** is complex, tangy and gentle, medium-sweet with toffeed, dried fruit length. Cossart Gordon has a **1995 Colheita Bual**, with a pleasantly almondy character and tangy, greengagey fruit.

But the real glories of the MWC are their Vintage wines, aged for at least 20 years in barrel before bottling. **1977 Blandy's Verdelho** is very tangy, with aromas of lime, grass and herbs, high acid and exciting length. **1976 Cossart Gordon Bual** is complex and savoury, with notes of iodine, leather and old furniture and toffeed, woody length. The **1975 Blandy's Terrantez** is amazingly tangy, with high acid and a bitter streak running through it. It seems young and aggressive, almost 30 years after being made. Delving further back, the **1960 Cossart Gordon Sercial** is fragrant, creamy and citrussy, with an amazing balance between the dry citrussy character and the creamy toffee. **1958 Cossart Gordon Bual** is gentle and mature, with aromas of wood, leather and dried fruits, balanced and delicious.

Avenida Arriaga 28, 9000-064, Funchal
T+351 291 740 110
E info@oldblandyswinelodge.com
W www.madeirawinecompany.com
Visits Old Blandy's Wine Lodge Mon-Fri
* 9.30-6.30 Sat 10-1 Closed Sun &*
* public hols €4.20*
Winery tours Sept only €12

FUNCHAL C1 *(continued)*

Pereira D'Oliveira There's an interesting story behind this modestly-sized shipper, a specialist in old vintage wines. It was started by João Pereira D'Oliveira, in 1850. He was a farmer with land and vineyards in São Martinho, a village that lay just to the west of Funchal. He started collecting wines in the 1880s, when Madeira was still suffering from the devastation caused by oidium and phylloxera. He would buy up struggling companies and their wine stocks, and then mature them. But he didn't really like selling them. Even today, the company (still run by his grandsons Aníbal and Luís, and Aníbal's son, Filipe) has some of these stocks of old wines, the oldest still on offer an 1850 Verdelho! They started exporting wines only in the 1970s.

Pereira D'Oliveira moved to their present lodge and shop at the beginning of the 20th century, and, for about 10 years, have been contemplating moving the shop to a different location, in Rua Visconde de Anadia, near the central market. Their current lodge dates from 1619, according to the engraving above the door, and is a treasure-trove of old barrels, vats, demi-johns and bottles, well worth visiting. The shop is open all week except Sunday, but to gain admittance to the lodge as well you need to make an appointment. You will be offered a free tasting of some of their wines, which might include an older vintage if you're lucky. They make their wines at their *adega* in São Martinho, now almost

part of Funchal's suburban sprawl, where they still have a few hectares of vineyard. Most of their grapes come from contracts with growers.

As well as the wonderful old *Reservas* (Pereira D'Oliveira has always used the description *'Reserva'*, rather than 'Vintage'), the company produces younger wines. Their 3, 10 and 15 Year Old wines are usually blends of different varieties, as they strive to keep the flavour consistent from one year to the next. These often contain Tinta Negra (sometimes at quite a low proportion), aged in *estufas* in the normal way. The white grapes are aged in the *canteiro* method. The 10 Years Old wines are a big step up from the younger wines in complexity and intensity, with the nutty, raisiny **D'Oliveira's 10 Year Old Medium-Dry** standing out. The 15 Years Old wines are finer and more intense still (often containing significant proportions of white grape wine). Here our choices would be the tangy, woody, complex **D'Oliveira's 15 Year Old Medium-Dry** and the rich, succulent **D'Oliveira's 15 Year Old Sweet** (which actually has 70% Malvasia in the blend).

They have several wines labelled in the modern way as 'colheita'. Oldest is **D'Oliveira's Colheita Verdelho 1981**, which they started bottling in the mid-90s, before it qualified as a vintage – or *'Reserva'*, as they would call it. It's off-dry, with gentle, greengage and nut flavours, and a creamy, tangy feel. Of the vintage wines, **D'Oliveira's Reserva Verdelho 1973** is tangy, bright and intense, with acidity that covers the sweetness. **D'Oliveira's Reserva Boal 1977** is definitely medium-sweet, savoury and tangy, with an almost salty intensity, length and complexity. **D'Oliveira's Reserva Verdelho 1966** is clean, intense and tangy, with flavours of old wooden furniture, walnuts and citrus.

Rua dos Ferreiros 107, 9000-082 Funchal
T+351 291 220 784 / 291 228 558
  Adega +351 291 228 622.
E perolivinhos@hotmail.com
Shop Mon-Fri 9-6 Sat 9.30-1 Closed Sun
  & public hols
Visits appt only

São Vicente B2

Seiçal Duarte Caldeira is a determined man. He inherited 20 little plots of land around the village of Seixal on the north coast of Madeira after his father died. The sensible thing to do would have been nothing. But he got together with a couple of friends, and their holdings came to almost a hectare. Now there are over 40 producers in the group and they own 13ha – spread over 200 plots! They started making VQPRD Madeirense with Sercial and Arnsburger, a Riesling crossing imported from Germany. The Sercial was more successful. Then they thought they would try making red wines. The Madeira Wine Institute suggested Cabernet and Merlot, which were already on the island, but Caldeira had his own ideas. He persuaded the Institute to let him plant Touriga Nacional, Tinta Roriz and Syrah, and, in 2000, the vines went in. The 2001 harvest yielded 26 bottles, and they had 4,000 from the 2003 vintage. Now they are producing a total of 43,000 bottles, of red, white and rosé VQPRD Madeirense and VR Terras Madeirenses. At the moment, all the partners are carrying on their day-jobs, and tending vines in the evenings and at weekends. But they realise that soon someone will have to start actively selling the wines.

The wines are made at the government-owned São Vicente winery, and that is where Senhor Caldeira will meet you if you want to see the winery. If not, he could meet you at a restaurant or the shop, Wines & Drinques, in Funchal. A visit to the winery is free. At a restaurant or at Wines & Drinques the price would depend on what you had. The best of the Seiçal wines so far released (and the best VQPRD Madeirense we've tasted) is the **Latadas Branco**, made from Verdelho, refreshing, fragrant and citrussy.
Adega de São Vicente, Sítio do Calhau,
  9240-018 São Vicente
T+351 965 013 168

E seical@sapo.pt
Visits appt only
Mon-Fri 9-6 Closed
public hols

Torcaz The winemaker at the Madeira Wine Company, Francisco Albuquerque, also has his own winemaking project, Torcaz (named after the protected species of dove that lives in the *laurisilva* forest). It's a chocolatey, bright-fruited red made from 2ha of Tinta Negra and Merlot vines planted in 2004, between Caniçal and Ponte de São Lourenço. So the vineyard is very dry, with poor soils and wind stress. Yields are low. His aim is to make a small quantity of good wine. It's an embryonic project at the moment: the first harvest was in 2006, when he made a mere 300 litres of Tinta Negra wine! Albuquerque is a serious winemaker, and Torcaz is certainly the best unfortified Tinta Negra we've yet tasted.
Adega de São Vicente, Sítio do Calhau,
  9240-018 São Vicente
T+351 291 840 040/1
E fma@madeirawinecompany.com
Visits appt only Mon-Fri 9-6
  Closed public hols

WATCH OUT FOR THESE WINES

Madeira
Bartholomew Broadbent, son of Michael, the wine writer and auctioneer, ships a range of Madeiras to the USA and UK under the Broadbent brand. Pick of his range are the tangy, raisiny **Broadbent Madeira Malmsey 10 Year Old**, and the elegant **Broadbent Madeira Terrantez 1978**, nutty, creamy and medium-dry , with flavours of greengage and coconut.

Unfortified wine
The only other VQPRD Madeirense wine we've met and enjoyed is **Enxurros Branco**, a blend of Verdelho and Arnsburger, made by Ricardo França at the São Vicente winery. It's fresh and citrussy, with a streak of minerality. The red version, **Enxurros Tinto**, is a blend of Touriga Nacional, Cabernet and Merlot, pleasant, light and fruity, but not quite perfect yet.

Eat in Madeira

How would you translate into Portuguese 'taking coals to Newcastle'? *'Levar bananas para Madeira'*, of course! Taking bananas to Madeira would indeed be foolish, because Madeira's bananas may be the most delicious you have ever tasted; they are small and sweet and wonderful, and they are in season all year round. Besides munching them fresh, you will eat them grilled or fried as vegetables, incorporated in dishes both sweet and savoury, and in fresh fruit salads, perhaps the best of all ways to end a Madeiran meal.

Although they are now Madeira's number one export, bananas were not natives. They arrived from Brazil, which itself had acquired them via Africa and India. When the Portuguese laid claim to Madeira in the mid-15th century, the island was covered by forest (*madeira* is the Portuguese word for 'wood') and explorers who found fennel *(funcho)* growing in wild profusion named the future capital Funchal. Slaves soon began to dig the *levada* irrigation system, and to terrace the hills and mountainsides, which still today permit the growing of fruit and vegetables over much of the island, with bananas taking precedence on the lower, warmer slopes.

First stop for any food lover (after the wine lodges, maybe...) must be Funchal's produce market, the Mercado dos Lavradores *(page 417 and pictured above)*, a buzzing,

brilliantly coloured display, of tropical fruit and vegetables, as well as fish and flowers. We bought eight different types of passion fruits at great expense (maybe we looked like tourists), only to discover that by far the best were the familiar ones we buy at home... One of the most delicious fruits is the custard apple or chirimoya *(anona)*, which grows all over the island, in private gardens as well as farms. *Anonas* have their own DOP quality designation on Madeira and are particularly important for farmers around Machico in the east. The season runs from December to April. You will be tempted too by the little red, shiny *pitangas* (Surinam cherries), guavas, mangoes, figs, peaches, and all kinds of citrus fruits... (Why, we wonder, admiring all these beautiful oranges, is the hotel breakfast juice sometimes so disappointingly processed?)

You will enjoy more salads and vegetables in Madeiran restaurants than in many parts of mainland Portugal, though here, too, local people often take their vegetables in soup form. The oniony *sopa de tomate* has a last-minute egg poached in it. Sweet potatoes *(batatas doces)* are a delicious staple, served on the side or incorporated into dishes, and into everyday bread and cakes. Chestnuts are also incorporated into dishes, especially in the north of the

THE MADEIRA KITCHEN'S E-WORDS

The *ementas* (menus) of Madeira may elicit the occasional expletive of frustration – it is so easy to order a meat kebab by accident instead of a fish! So let us eradicate the confusion – because you really should try these Madeiran *especialidades* at least once…

escabeche Things, usually fish and vegetables various, fried, then marinated in vinegar or lemon juice, served cold.

espada The black scabbard fish is the main catch on Madeira, appearing on menus as *peixe espada* or just plain *espada*, although its real name is *espada preta*. It is caught all round these islands but most comes in to the fishing port of Câmara de Lobos, just west of Funchal. Multiple weighted, baited lines plummet 800 meters into the dark, volcanic depths to attract these evil-looking creatures, which are long, thin, black-skinned and indeed scabbard-shaped, with large eyes and long, sharp teeth. They are dead by the time they reach the surface, killed by decompression. Their flesh is soft and white, not very fishy, not very anything, really. Probably that is why you will rarely see it in mainland Portugal. Sauces are its saviour, or the usual accompaniment, delicious fried bananas. And, to confuse you even more, swordfish *(espadarte)* is known as *pez espada* in Spain.

espadarte Swordfish, a big, meaty fish with good flavour, but on the dry side, and (to our taste) almost inedibly dry when over-cooked, as it all too often is in Madeira. Ask for it to be *muito mal passado*.

espetada Up in the hills, on the terraces, beside the *levadas*, it was traditional to thread chunks of garlicky meat onto bay or laurel  sticks, and grill them over fires. The idea spread to restaurants. Some still use laurel sticks. Most now thread the meat on long, metal skewers, which may, once cooked, be suspended communally above your table, the meat forked down at will. Garlic and bay are still the flavours of choice, on beef or chicken. You may also meet *espetadas* of fish, vegetables and fruit. Meat *espetadas* may be priced on menus by weight.

island. *Milho frito* is a speciality – small, rectangular chunks of cornmeal mixed with vegetables and herbs and crisply fried – it's a bit like Italian polenta. In traditional restaurants, most dishes come with potatoes or chips, and of course also with bread.

Madeira's signature bread, the *bolo do caco*, contains sweet potato and is griddle-cooked into soft but crusty flat rounds. You can buy them hot and laced with garlic butter as street food, and they will arrive, garlicky or not, to nibble before a meal.

Much of Madeira's restaurant food is simply grilled, often over wood. Chicken or beef may be on a skewer  *(espetada)*. You might be asked to select from a display of the freshest of fish, and watch it hit the grill. There are literally hundreds of species of fish off the coast, but many others are imported. Fish is often priced on menus according to weight, imported fishes and seafood unsurprisingly being the most expensive (beware the price of lobsters!). Tuna is the big thing locally – admire the huge beasts in the Mercado dos Lavradores. The main tuna port is Machico, on the east of the island near the airport. Traditional restaurants serve it simply, as tuna steaks *(bifes de atum)*, which will undoubtedly arrive thoroughly cooked, except in modern-style restaurants: ask for it *mal passado* if you prefer it pink. The unimpressive black scabbard fish *(peixe espada)* is everywhere. Look out for good, firm, flavourful sea bream *(pargo)*, delicious red mullet *(salmonete)*, gilt-head bream *(dourada)*, and swordfish *(espadarte)*, which is good if not overcooked. Even opera fans must not allow themselves to be seduced by the parrot fish *(papagaio)* – unappealing flesh lies beneath the pretty skin. The local limpets *(lapas)* are a delight, served usually in garlic butter. Salt cod

Left Passion fruit soufflé at the Quinta da Bela Vista above Funchal

Right preparing tables at the Casa da Quinta restaurant, Casa Branca

Far right Oranges in Funchal's market

(bacalhau) is as popular here as everywhere else in Portugal but since there is no local cod, they make their own version from a local fish, the *gaiado*. You will also find the fish dishes of the mainland, mixed fish stew *(caldeirada)* and various fish in rice *(arroz de…)*.

There are other dishes from elsewhere in Portugal: Minho cabbage and sausage soup *(caldo verde)*, a garlicky, soupy Alentejo bread dish with meat or seafood *(açorda)*; and still too many old fashioned dishes of the prawn cocktail school of English cooking. Truly local dishes to try are *carne vinha d'alhos*: pork marinated and then cooked in wine and wine vinegar, bay, garlic, chillies, olive oil and sometimes coriander seeds; *feijoada*: a mountain bean stew that usually contains offal and sausages including black pudding; and *picado*: a communal dish of cubes of beef fried with garlic and sometimes red peppers and served with chips from which everyone at the table picks – *picar* means 'to pick'. Up in the mountains there are stews of rabbit *(coelho)* and quail *(codorniz)*.

The sweet speciality of Madeira is the spicy *bolo de mel*. Although this means 'honey cake' it is sweetened not with honey but with molasses. *Bolo de mel* was made in Madeira for centuries as a Christmas treat, from the days when sugar and spices first began to arrive in Madeira on the trade routes from Africa and the east, even before Madeira itself was an important sugar producer. It is a round, dark, dense cake, about 5cm deep, raised by yeast, and containing walnuts, candied peel and citrus zest, prunes, ground almonds, flour, lard and butter, aniseed

and mixed spices. Families traditionally make it on 8 December in sufficient quantities to last into the coming year; they prize it even after it becomes rather hard and dry. Nowadays you will be encouraged to buy it at all times of year. Personally we feel it needs a large glass of Bual to lubricate it along its way!

EATING OUT IN MADEIRA

Eating out in Madeira can be an expensive disappointment. Funchal is full of restaurants, many cooking for tourists, who are often British or German, often retired, often with limited time to find their land legs and a decent bite to eat before their cruise ship sails again. In Funchal there is also fast food, and old-style bad British food. Amongst the traditional Portuguese/Madeiran restaurants there are some whose cooking is accomplished. There is some creative, modern, international cooking using fine local ingredients – mostly in Funchal's new hotel district, but elsewhere, too. And there are restaurants cooking fish simply and badly, or simply and well. Be wary of booking half or full board in hotels unless you are sure that the restaurant is good – and that half board customers are served in the good restaurant! As in other chapters, we began our search for the best places to eat by asking the local wine producers, as well as other friends on the island and gastronomic friends in mainland Portugal who have holidayed in Madeira. Most of the modern, creative restaurants are quite expensive by Portuguese standards, but still cheaper than you would pay for equivalent cuisine in London or Paris. Recommended restaurants with modern and traditional styles of cooking are marked separately on the map at the beginning of the chapter.

RESTAURANTS

CABO GIRÃO B1

Fajã dos Padres You can arrive by boat at the pier by the 'beach', or by a new, panoramic lift, down the cliff face. The scared-of-heights should close their eyes and think of paradise – which felicitously awaits just 250m below. The restaurant is very much open-air, with two semi-covered areas, one thatched, plus tables under the palm trees on a terrace in front of the sea. Local produce rules, shellfish and fish, fish stews *(caldeiradas)* and fish soup; the avocados and much of the fruit grew on the surrounding slopes, and they make their own Malvasia aperitif. This vineyard was famous for centuries as producer of some of Madeira's best wines. The restaurant is open for lunch only, from noon till 5pm, but the lift starts working at 11am, until 6pm on weekdays, and 7pm at the weekend. The lift costs €8 return, free for children, and is not accessible for the disabled owing to steps. You can relax by the sea, or take the vine-shaded sea-view walk. And if you miss the last lift back up the cliff, there may be rooms to let *(page 424)*.
Cabo Girão
T+351 291 944 538
E info@fajadospadres.com
W www.fajadospadres.com
€30 V 🛏 *Closed Tue; 10 Jan–1 Mar*

CAMACHA (MADEIRA) C1

O Caroto Small, friendly and rustic, in a pretty little town a few kilometres above Funchal, where traditional Portuguese dishes are always beautifully cooked from excellent, fresh local ingredients. The wine list is good. You must book.
Sítio da Nogueira,
*   Caminho Velho da Camacha*
T+351 291 922 189
€22–€25 🍷 *V No credit cards*
Closed Sun din, Mon; Aug

CÂMARA DE LOBOS B1

Churchill A small place with a lovely atmosphere: a bar and pool table downstairs, a balcony restaurant overlooking the harbour, and the boats that brought in the wonderful fish and seafood hours before. Regional dishes also include meat. Cooking is excellent, and multiple Winstons will watch you as you enjoy.
Estrada João Gonçalves Zarco 39
T+351 291 941 451
E adelima@mail.telepac.pt
€20 V!
Closed 1st 2 weeks Dec

Vila do Peixe A large, fairly new restaurant with good fish and seafood, slightly cafeteria-looking in glass and wood, but with great views out to sea. Fish, mostly imported from the mainland, includes some types rarely available on the island, grilled over wood, or served in traditional dishes.
Estrada Dr João Abel de Freitas
T+351 291 099 909
E viladopeixe@sapo.pt
€20–€30 V
Closed Mon

CANIÇO C1

La Perla Amidst the beautiful gardens of the Quinta Splendida hotel complex east of Funchal, the top restaurant has creative, modern cooking, including fresh herbs and vegetables grown on the property. A very good wine list is reasonably priced. Dinner only, and you must book.
Quinta Splendida, Estrada da Ponte da
*   Oliveira 11*
T+351 291 930 400
E luca.chiesa@quintasplendida.com
W www.hotelquintasplendida.com
€40 🍷 *V* 🛏
Closed lunch

ESTREITO DE CÂMARA DE LOBOS B1

Adega da Quinta Part of the Quinta do Estreito hotel complex *(page 424)*, this is a rustic sibling restaurant of the Bacchus *(below)*. An old winery building has been renovated and the big picture windows give great views down over the vine terraces to the sea. This is a great place to sample proper old-fashioned Madeiran cuisine, such as garlic flatbread, *espetadas* of various meats skewered on bay sticks, *milho frito*, or meat barbecued or roasted in the wood-fired oven.
Quinta do Estreito, Rua José Joaquim da
*   Costa*
T+351 291 910 530
E quintaestreito@charminghotelsmadeira.com
W www. charminghotelsmadeira.com
€25 🍷 *V* 🛏
Closed 25 Dec

Bacchus Smart restaurant with good, modern food, creative and fresh, with regional influences, and a fine wine list. The converted farmhouse forms the heart of the Estalagem Quinta do Estreito, a hotel set amidst the terraced vines above Câmara de Lobos *(page 424)*. Three fish and three meat dishes change daily, served

in an informal 'winter garden' or the more formal, old-fashioned dining rooms. Gastronomic weeks focus on specific cuisines.

Quinta do Estreito, Rua José Joaquim da Costa
T+351 291 910 530
E quintaestreito@charminghotelsmadeira.com
W www.charminghotelsmadeira.com
€55-€60 ♀ V on request
Open din only

Casa da Vinha Surrounded by well-tended vines, the Casa da Vinha was created from an old winery. Its three dining rooms are furnished with antiques, and have wonderful views, as does the terrace. The cooking is local, with modern touches. They sell their own white wine, made mainly from Verdelho grapes in the government wine cellar at São Vicente.
Rua dos Lavradores 4
T+351 291 945 505
E casadavinha@netmadeira.com
€20-€25 ♀
Closed Mon; 25 Dec & 1 Jan

Viola A simple restaurant very popular with locals for its excellent value and the quality of its *espetada*, *milho frito* and grilled meats. Try some of the local wines.
Estrada João Gonçalves Zarco 596
T+351 291 945 601
€13
Closed Mon

O Barqueiro Excellent venue for fish and seafood lovers, much appreciated by the locals. There may be queues. Prices are reasonable, unless you opt for lobster from the central focal point, a large lobster tank. The wine list is good. Definitely worth the 15-minute taxi ride from the centre.
Centro Commercial CentroMar,
*   Rua da Ponta da Cruz,*
T+351 291 761 229
€25 ♀ V
Closed 25 Dec

Casa da Quinta The restaurant of the Quinta da Casa Branca takes an accomplished, modern approach to Portuguese cooking. Wines  are good and knowledgeably served, with a generous choice by the glass. The restaurant is in the old manor house (the rest of the hotel is more modern, *page 425*), in the

city centre but surrounded by exotic gardens. A romantic terrace has views over the gardens and trees to the sea.
Rua da Casa Branca 7
E estalagem@quintacasabranca.pt
W www.quintacasabranca.pt
€60 ♀ V ⛺ Open every day, din only

A Casa do Vizinho Popular, inexpensive restaurant with a pleasant garden terrace on the ground floor of a new apartment block. It serves good local cuisine in an attractive, airy dining room filled with intriguing bric-a-brac.
Rua Imperatriz Dona Amélia 74
T+351 291 281 515
€25-€30 ♀ V Closed Sun

Casa Velha Long-established, next to the Casino Park, the charming 'Old House' serves modern Madeiran cuisine, with a decent wine list. The garden terrace is ideal for a simple lunch, and the very pretty first floor restaurant with glazed veranda is a delightful setting for dinner. Service is good and friendly. (No link with Casa Velha do Palheiro.)
Rua Imperatriz Dona Amélia 69
T+351 291 205 600
E albatroz.cvelha@mail.telepac.pt
W www.casavelharestaurant.com
€30-€35 ♀ V Open every day

Chega de Saudade Accomplished international/Portuguese/Asian cooking is backed on Friday and Saturday nights by professional live jazz – till late. Downstairs is a bar and terrace, upstairs the restaurant; decor is original and eclectic.
Rua dos Arranhas 20
T+351 291 242 289
E chegadesaudade@sapo.pt
W www.chegadesaudadecafe.blogspot.com
€17 V
Closed Sun, Mon, Tue din; public hols

Doca do Cavacas Out past the new developments of Funchal's western suburbs to the Ponta da Cruz headland, this converted gun esplanade is a place to go for delicious, very fresh shellfish and fish,

simply and beautifully cooked. The wine list is interesting, too. The little restaurant is perched above natural swimming pools in the rocks, overlooking the bay and the Praia Formosa beach. The former terrace on top of the original dining room has now been enclosed to form a second floor. Decor is white and blue, with seascapes and fishing tackle.
Rua Ponta da Cruz, Piornais
T+351 291 762 057
€20 ♀
Closed Mon; 1st 2 weeks Dec

Dom Pepe Under new management and a new chef, this restaurant is still serving very good local and continental Portuguese cuisine, based on fine quality seafood, fish and meat. *Bacalhau* appears in numerous guises. The decor is bright and pleasantly modern, on the ground floor of a new block. The wine list is excellent.
Rua da Levada dos Barreiros 86
T+351 291 763 240
E reservas@dompepe.net
€60 ♀ *V*
Closed Sun; Mon in July & Aug

É Prá Picanha Smart, new, young venue, friendly and fun, the menu based around the *picanha*, an especially tender Brazilian cut of beef, which is carved from a spit at your table. Opposite Savoy Hotel.
Avenida do Infante 60A
T+351 291 282 257
E info@eprapicanha.com
W www.eprapicanha.com
€25 Closed Sun, Mon lunch

Fora d'Água Contemporary, inventive cuisine as well as local dishes, at very reasonable prices, in an elegant, modern restaurant on the Lido promenade. The wine list is fairly good. Decor is minimalist, designer, colours black, white, lime green and mature red wine! There are sea views from the picture windows and the long, thin terrace. Find it to the rear of the Tivoli Hotel.
Tivoli Hotel building, Promenade do Lido
T+351 291 766 992
€35 ♀ *V*
Closed Sun, Mon lunch; lunch on public hols

Gallo d'Oro In the large, elegant dining room of the Cliff Bay Hotel, the food by French chef Benoît Sinthon is top class modern international, with Italian, French, local and Mediterranean influences. The wine list is good. The terrace has fabulous sea views, and there's live piano music.
Cliff Bay Hotel, Estrada Monumental 147
T+351 291 707 700
E info@cliffbay.com
W www.portobay.com
€60 ♀ *V* 🛏

Mar Brando Totally unassuming, with a friendly atmosphere, Mar Brando is ideal for a light, inexpensive, traditional-style lunch. It has an attractive terrace to the rear and serves simple Madeiran dishes from a small menu.

Rua Imperatriz Dona Amélia 130
T+351 291 232 648
€20 ♀ *V*
Closed 25 Dec, Good Fri

Quinta da Bela Vista In the Quinta da Bela Vista hotel *(page 426)*, a €6 taxi ride up from the town centre, the Casa Mãe restaurant has taken over the original 1844 manor house around which the hotel was built. Food is very good, creative and modern, with inventive but not outrageous combinations, based on fine, local raw materials. Dishes are attractively assembled, and look beautiful on the plate. The dining rooms have a bright, airy colonial feel.

Caminho Avista Navios 4
T+351 291 706 400
E info@belavistamadeira.com
W www. belavistamadeira.com
€60 ♀ *V* 🛏

Quinta Palmeira This was amongst the first of the top international-style restaurants on the island, and is still one of the very best. Cooking is inventive, but rooted in Portuguese tradition, and based on the freshest local produce. In an old white manor house between the Casino and the Savoy Hotel, west of city centre, it is grand but relaxed, with a beautiful garden terrace. The Quinta Palmeira Wine Bar has canapés, *petiscos*, five wines always available by the glass, and a wine tasting package, including port and

Madeira. There's another good but less expensive restaurant, the Quinta Palmeira Café Galeria, accessible from the main Avenida do Infante.
Avenida do Infante 17-19
T+351 291 221 814
E quintapalmeira@quintapalmeira.com
W www.quintapalmeira.com
€45 ♀ V!

FUNCHAL C1 *(continued)*

Riso A fairly new, very modern restaurant where everything comes (very deliciously) with rice. The fish is excellent. It sits out over the sea with a hanging, tent-like roof and electric sides that wind up if the weather is bad.
Santa Maria 274
T+351 291 280 360
E reservas@riso-fx.com
€45 V

Sabores do Paquete New, modern and sleek, this family-run restaurant offers mainly Portuguese/Madeiran cuisine, with a few international dishes. The quality, service and atmosphere are all good.
Edifício Casa Branca,
*   Rua da Casa Branca 34A*
T+351 291 761 292
E saboresdopaquete@hotmail.com
€25-€30 V
Open Mon-Sat din only Closed Sun; last 2
*   weeks Aug*

Tokos It is vital to book ahead for this small, atmospheric restaurant, where traditional cooking includes a good selection of fish and seafood. Smart, friendly and cosy.
Estrada Monumental 169
T+351 291 771 019
€35-€40
Closed Mon; 15 Jul-15 Aug;
*   1 week Christmas*

Villa Cipriani Much more relaxed than the restaurants actually within the Reid's Palace Hotel, the Cipriani, just 200 metres down the road, has excellent food and a summer terrace with breathtaking views of Funchal and the ocean. (Book early for a terrace table, but the dining room is pretty, too.) The cooking is Portuguese/international with an Italian accent, very much based upon island produce. The wine list has an excellent selection of Portuguese and Italian wines, at fair prices. Reid's is currently owned by Orient Express hotels, hence the Cipriani connection.

Estrada Monumental 139
T+351 291 717 171
E reservations@reidspalace.com
W www. reidspalace.com
€50 ♀ V 🛏
Open every day din only

Xôpana Within the Choupana Hills Hotel *(page 425)*, an inspired combination of Asian and Portuguese cuisines is beautifully presented by French chef Giles Galli. Decor is orientally minimalist, with lots of marble and wood, and striking architectural lines. Find it in a fabulous setting in the hills overlooking Funchal.
Choupana Hills Resort, Travessa do Largo
*   da Choupana*

T+351 291 206 020
E info@choupanahills.com
W www.choupanahills.com
€56 ♀ V 🛏

POISO C1

Casa de Abrigo do Poiso The inn at the mountain crossroads at Poiso, high in the eastern mountains, has a surprisingly good wine list to accompany the well-cooked local dishes – this is an excellent place to discover true Madeiran cooking. It's a cosy restaurant, with log fires and nourishing *espetadas*.
Poiso
T+351 291 782 269
€20 ♀
Closed 25 Dec

PRAZERES A2

O Tosco Amidst the vines right along the south-west end of Madeira, this little restaurant with only six tables serves excellent *petiscos, bacalhau, espetada*, beef ribs, and *porco preto* – delicious Alentejo pork. It has an outstsanding wine list.
Sítio da Estacada
T+351 291 822 726
€30 ♀ V
Closed Mon

SANTANA C2

Cantinho da Serra In this attractive, small town on the north east coast of Madeira, backed by steep mountains, the 'Little Mountain Hideaway' serves copious

starters followed by good roasts – chicken, kid – and well-cooked traditional dishes.
Estrada do Pico das Pedras
T+351 291 573 727
€20   Closed Mon

Quinta do Furão Good restaurant in a hotel *(page 427)* on the north-eastern side of the island, serving traditional cuisine and good wines. The Madeira ice cream with wild berries gets rave reviews, and vegetarians are unusually well served.
Achada do Gramacho
T+351 291 570 100
E reservations@quintadofurao.com
W www.quintadofurao.com
€35   ⚲ V!

SÃO GONÇALO C1
Casa Velha do Palheiro One of Madeira's best restaurants, in the hotel of the same name *(page 427)* in the hills just east of Funchal. Food is creative, Mediterranean with hints of the oriental, and comes in optional quantities, from the 'Light Menu' to a seven-course taster menu with accompanying Portuguese wines.
Rua da Estalagem 23
T+351 291 790 350
E casa.velha@palheiroestate.com
W www.palheiroestate.com
€40-€50   ⚲ V

SEIXAL B2
Restaurante Sol Mar A simple and good restaurant attached to a small hotel *(page 427)* by the bridge just before the entrance to the old harbour of Seixal, on the north-west coast of Madeira. We ate the Madeiran version of fish and chips, with freshly caught local fish, served with limpet *(lapa)* rice, salad and huge chips.
Sítio do Lombinho
T+351 291 854 854
€15

PORTO SANTO
O Calhetas Simple restaurant with two terraces in a quiet, beautiful spot at the southern end of Porto Santo's spectacular long, white beach Very good local cooking, fish and seafood, *arroz* or *caldeirada de peixe*. It's a nice walk along the beach, or if you book, they will collect you by car from the port of Vila Baleia.
Calheta, Porto Santo
T+351 291 984 380
€25   ⚲
Closed 25 Dec, 1 Jan

La Roca Fun and friendly summer-only restaurant by the Porto Santo Marina, built partly of thatched reed and sailcloth, with good fish and local cuisine mostly from the grill. The kitchen is open until 1am, and in mid-August they have 'Summer Parties' with live music. There's also a La Roca café open all year 8am-8pm serving light meals and snacks.
Marina de Porto Santo
T+351 291 982 353
E laroca.pxo@gmail.com
€30-€35 V
Closed Oct-Easter

MARKETS, WINE AND FOOD SHOPS

FUNCHAL C1
Diogos Wine & Spirits Shop Helpful shop owned by the Barbeito Madeira company *(page 404)*, with Madeiras back to the 19th century and well chosen wines from Portugal and elsewhere. After stocking up, visit the Christopher Columbus museum in the basement.
Avenida Arriaga 48

Garrafeira Espírito do Baco Wine shop in the old town. *Largo de Corpo Santo 28/30*

Garrafeira Pipa Velha Wine shop within the market hall of the Mercado dos Lavradores. *Largo Lavradores, Loja 28*

Garrafeira In the market hall of the Mercado dos Lavradores, opposite the Garrafeira Pipa. *Largo Lavradores, Lojas 15/16 T+351 291 230 479*

Loja dos Vinhos A modern shop in the Eden Mar Shopping Centre in the hotel district, spilling out on to the pavement, stocking wines from all the Madeira producers including some old and rare.
Edificio Eden Mar, Loja 19, Rua do Gorgulho

Lagar d'Ajuda Wine shop in amongst the smart hotels, built around an antique wine press, with a good range of Madeira and port, and other Portuguese wines.
Galerias Jardins da Ajuda, Estrada Monumental

Mercado dos Lavradores Art deco produce market on three levels: a stunning selection of fruit, vegetables and flowers, fish down below, meat around the side. The market is bigger on Fridays with the addition of farmers from around the island, stalls spreading into the streets and the carpark south of Rua de Carlos 1. Stop to admire the *azulejos* by the entrance. *Rua Profetas Open Mon-Thu 7-5, Fri 7-8, Sat 7-3 Closed Sun and public hols.*

Explore Madeira

Many visitors arrive in FUNCHAL on cruise ships – it was the deep, sheltered harbour that won Funchal its status as capital. Those who stay head mostly nowadays for the smart new 'Hotel Zone', along the lengthy Estrada Monumental on the western hills and cliffs. From here it is half an hour on foot to the centre of town, through sub-tropical gardens, past Baroque and Art Deco mansions, and along a wide seafront promenade to the Zona Velha. The cobbled old town is being rapidly spruced and pedestrianised. Its Mercado dos Lavradores *(page 417)* sells a stunning array of fish, meat, vegetables, fruit and flowers. East along the seafront is the base station for the new cable car.

In ten minutes, this will whisk you up to MONTE, whose grey and white church towers are a prominent landmark on the hillside way above Funchal. The railway that used to ply this route closed in 1939, having fallen from favour

Left Madeira's new roads often pass through tunnels

Right and far right Madeira's rocky coast has few beaches

Below Funchal fills the amphitheatre around its deep harbour and bay

after a fatal accident in 1919. There are views, cafés, restaurants, smart houses and gardens up here – a newer section of cable car connects to the Monte Palace Tropical Garden. You can walk along *levadas*, then return by cable car, or take the historic toboggan ride *(page 422)*.

Driving west out of Funchal along the coast, CÂMARA DE LOBOS is a pretty fishing village with a little pebbly beach and brightly coloured boats and houses, famously painted by Winston Churchill. The *'lobos'* (wolves) were

PORTO SANTO

This small island 37km north-east of Madeira is warmer and sunnier than its nearly beach-free and sometimes cloudy neighbour. It is remarkable for its 10km of white sandy beach, beside a warm, calm sea. Just 14.5km long by 5km wide, it is relatively undeveloped. Once more or less barren, it has been planted with trees and grapes to prevent erosion.

There is also a fine new golf course, and a few restaurants and hotels. Vila Baleira is the little main town. Visit the island by plane, helicopter, or ferry. But be quick – it's developing fast.

the monk seals that once used to bask on the beach. This is the main fishing port for black scabbard fish *(espada)*, which they sell on the beach too early for most visitors to watch. Banana plantations dominate the lower terraces, vines above. Up in the hills, ESTREITO DE CÂMARA DE LOBOS is one of the island's main centres for grape-growing and wine-making.

Take a scary look over the precipitous CABO GIRÃO headland before making for the FAJÃ DOS PADRES. This stretch of south-facing, terraced land at the base of a cliff, accessed by a new panoramic lift or from the sea, was renowned for its Malvasia, mentioned in despatches as long ago as the 15th century. Malvasia vines were replanted in the 1980s, and the fine old wines are soon to be bottled. Bananas and other fruit trees grow here too, and there's a good restaurant and little houses to rent.

Stop for a coffee and a quick visit to the ethnographic museum *(page 422)* in RIBEIRA BRAVA, which was important as a centre for sugar processing from the 15th century. PONTA DO SOL grows and processes bananas. Pretty seaside villages follow – CALHETA with its steep, cobbled streets, surrounded by banana terraces and vines, JARDIM DO MAR just beyond, its pebble beach renowned as a fine surfing venue in winter.

At the north-western tip of the island, PORTO MONIZ is a busy farming town, neat heather and bracken fences

protecting little fields of crops from the ocean winds. You can swim in natural rocky pools, and a new seafront has restaurants and cafés. Some of the northern coast road now passes through tunnels, but sometimes it skirts the cliff side. SEIXAL, with its dramatic vineyards on near-vertical terraces, is surrounded by waterfalls. Numerous tunnels lead to SÃO VICENTE, a neat, smart, pretty little town. Grottos *(Grutas)* just south east of town, have impressive rock pools, and a Volcanism Centre tells the story of the island's formation *(page 422)*. It's still a bit of a scary drive from São Vicente to Santana, turning the corner onto the east coast. Here, a cable car heads up into the hills, past green valleys, orchards and vegetable

terraces. Some people still live in the traditional A-framed thatched houses *(palheiros)*. Pretty PORTO DA CRUZ, down the coast, is a quiet old port town, with sheltered swimming, cobbled alleys and old wine lodges.

Round to the south-eastern side, CANIÇAL is a small tuna fishing port, its cobbled alleys dominated by a sea fortress. Apparently Gregory Peck became so seasick on location here whilst filming *Moby Dick* that the rest of the film was shot in studio. The main tuna port is MACHICO, Madeira's second largest town, where tourism is just beginning to bite. If you're there in season (December to April) buy some delicious custard apples *(anonas)*, the most important crop of the surrounding fertile valley.

The road ducks under the airport runway and round, blissfully fast and new once more, to SANTA CRUZ, a pleasant old town with a beach and cafés. Off to the right, in the hills, is the village of CAMACHA, only just east of Funchal, a destination for tour coaches laden with customers for its extraordinarily skilful wickerwork: furniture, animals and baskets.

❋ VIEW FROM THE TOP ❋

Boca da Encumeada The 'saddle' of the mountain road from Ribeira Brava on the south coast across the middle of the island to São Vicente is 1,007m above sea level. There are views of both north and south coasts, and across the mountain peaks, steep, green valleys, and the plateau of Paúl da Serra. In the middle of the day, you may be looking down at clouds...

CÂMARA DE LOBOS **Miradouro do Espírito Santo e Calçada** As you arrive from Funchal, looking down over the harbour, this spot is also known as the **Miradouro Winston Churchill.** He famously painted here in 1950.

CURRAL DAS FREIRAS **Miradouro da Eira do Serrado** From over 1,000 metres above sea level, one of Madeira's best views, down into the beautiful, deep, wide valley of **Curral das Freiras** (Nuns' Refuge), and beyond to the mountains and the sea. Tour coaches visit the viewpoint, but cannot navigate the road that tunnels down to the village. There's a safe footpath down through sweet chestnut woods, once upon a time the only access; this was the route by which nuns, long ago in 1566, fled to the remote safety of this lovely place, escaping pirate attacks on their convent in Funchal. Buy some of the local chestnut bread at the Sunday market.

QUINTA GRANDE **Miradouro da Boca dos Namorados** North of Câmara de Lobos, 1,000m up, this is one of the most beautiful views of the mountains and sea.

CÂMARA DE LOBOS **Miradouro do Cabo Girão** Cabo Girão is Europe's highest headland, 580m above the sea on the road between Câmara de Lobos and Quinta Grande. Fine views of the bays of Câmara de Lobos, Funchal, out to sea, and down onto the scary cliff-side terraces.

MONTE **Terreira da Luta** Views down to Funchal from the monument on the spot above Monte where a 15th century shepherd girl claimed to have seen the Virgin Mary.

Miradouro do Pico do Arieiro Up in the centre of the island, north of Funchal, the third highest peak on Madeira is easily accessible by road, with only a tiny climb to the true summit, 1,818m above sea level, just above the café. Spectacular views over the central mountains, and the ancient woodland, the *laurisilva*. Best views are to be had in the cloudless early morning, or late afternoon to evening. Take warm clothes. Hardy walkers could continue from here to the highest peak and the really top views – allowing six hours for the round trip.

FUNCHAL **Jardim Orquídea** Visit these exotic greenhouses and plastic tunnels in the flowering season from November to early April, and learn how orchids are propagated and grown. *Rua Pita da Silva Open every day 9-6*

Quinta da Boa Vista Lovely garden with an orchid production centre an added attraction in the flowering season, from November to early April. *Rua Lombo da Boa Vista Open Mon -Sat 9-5.30 Closed Sun*

MONTE A little tamer, healthier and safer than it used to be, the famous toboggan ride takes you down, propelled by white-clad, straw-boatered men, to Funchal (4km) or Livramento (2km) in a wicker sledge on wooden runners. Back in 1850, someone had a great idea...

SÃO VICENTE **Grutas de São Vicente/ Centro de Vulcanismo** Just south-east of the northern town of São Vicente, nearly a kilometre of 'lava tubes', grottos, with beautiful rock pools and streams. 30-minute musical guided tours. *Sítio do Pé do Passo Open every day 10-7 Closed 25 Dec*

MUSEUMS & GALLERIES

FUNCHAL **Adegas de São Francisco/Old Blandy's Wine Lodge** Evocative museum of the island's wine production and trade, within a former monastery, now the visitor centre of the Madeira Wine

Company *(page 407). Avenida Arriaga 28 Mon-Fri 9.30-6.30 Sat 10-1 Closed Sun, public hols*

Madeira Story Centre Opened in 2005, this modern, interactive museum starts with the volcanic eruption and leads you through the island's discovery and history.

There's a panoramic terrace with telescopes. *Rua Dom Carlos I 27-29 Open every day 10-6 Closed 25 Dec*

Museu de Arte Sacra The top floor of this museum, housed in the former Episcopal Court, has a remarkable collection of Renaissance Flemish paintings of the 15th and 16th centuries. *Rua do Bispo 21 Open Tue-Sat 10-12.30, 2.30-6 Sun 10-1 Closed Mon*

Museu do Vinho da Madeira The official wine museum of the Madeira Wine Institute in the former residence of 19th century British consul Henry Veitch: a collection of historic photos and vinegrowing and winemaking equipment, admission free. *Instituto do Vinho da Madeira, Rua 5 de Outubro 78 Open Mon-Fri 9.30-12, 2-5 Closed Sat, Sun, public hols*

Museu Frederico de Freitas Delightful Madeiran house, 17th century with Art Nouveau additions, bequeathed to the town 30 years ago by Funchal-born lawyer Frederico de Freitas. Apart from

the original furnishings, there is de Freitas' amusing collection of 19th century paintings, cartoons and engravings of the island. *Calçada de Santa Clara Open Tue-Sun 10-12.30, 2-6 Closed Mon*

Museu Municipal Meet Madeira's wildlife – a live aquarium as well as stuffed fish and local birds and beasts. *Rua da Mouraria 31 Open Tue-Fri 10-6 Sat & Sun 12-6 Closed Mon*

RIBEIRA BRAVA **Museu Etnográfico da Madeira** Museum of Madeiran crafts, farming, fishing, music, transport, costume and domestic life, with information in Portuguese, English and German. *Rua de São Francisco 24 Open Tue-Sun 10-12.30, 2-6 Closed Mon*

CHURCHES

CALHETA **Igreja do Espírito Santo** Impressive church with a knot-work ceiling like the one in the cathedral in Funchal *Open every day 10-1, 4-6*

FUNCHAL **Convento de Santa Clara** 15th to 17th century convent church with a fine interior cladding of white, blue and yellow *azulejos* in geometric designs. The convent now houses a school, but you can visit the pretty cloistered garden. *Calçada de Santa Clara Open every day 10-12, 3-5*

Igreja de São Pedro Started in 1590, finished in 1743, this church has beautiful gilded woodwork, chandeliers, paintings and 17th century wall-to-ceiling *azulejos. Rua de São Pedro Open Mon-Sat 9-12, 3-7 Sun 10-1*

Igreja do Colégio If your church visiting is limited, make this the one. Built in the 17th century with profits from wine

WALKING THE LEVADAS

Madeira's *levadas* irrigate the island. The first were carved from the rocks in the 15th century, many were dug by slaves, the last completed early in the 20th century. They are fed by natural springs, and from reservoirs high on the marshy moorland of the Paúl da Serra. *Levadas* have always had to be maintained, and sluices have to be opened at pre-arranged times to send water to specific parts, so paths follow the channels – which of course are more or less horizontal. The *levada* paths provide wonderful walks, some easy, some frankly perilous, all requiring footwear suitable for mossy rocks or scree. *Levadas* pass along mountainsides, through crops and gardens, and ancient woodland, by spectacular waterfalls and even past hotel pools. Guidebooks to *levada* walks are sold all over the island.

production and trade, this Jesuit church next door to the university has frescoes, *azulejos*, impressive gilded woodwork, a lovely *trompe l'oeuil* ceiling, and a carved facade. *Praça do Município*

Sé Funchal's graceful cathedral is particularly famed for its ceiling - a lovely combination of white carved ivory and carved local wood; there are some fine Flemish paintings, and gilded woodwork. *Rua do Aljube*

MACHICO **Igreja de Nossa Senhora da Conceição** One of Madeira's most impressive churches, 15th century Manueline and Gothic. *Largo do Município*

PONTA DO SOL **Igreja de Nossa Senhora da Luz** Admire the 15th century knotwork ceiling, green ceramic font, 16th century Flemish altarpiece, fine *azulejos*.

RIBEIRA BRAVA **Igreja de São Bento** 16th century church built in the late 15th century with the riches of the sugar trade; impressive stone carvings.

SANTA CRUZ **Igreja de Santa Maria** Graceful 15th to 16th century Gothic church with Manueline elements, similar in style to the cathedral in Funchal, with impressive stone carvings.

FAIRS & FESTIVALS

FEBRUARY FUNCHAL **Carnaval** In February, for three days leading up to the final parade on Shrove Tuesday, Funchal has one of the best carnivals in Portugal, everyone dresses up and floods the decorated streets until late into the night, music, dancing, parades, floats... Smaller towns and villages also celebrate *Carnaval*.

APRIL/MAY FUNCHAL **Festa da Flor** Funchal's Flower Festival was invented for the tourists, but a healthily competitive spirit between local clubs and businesses has turned this into a major fun event for the locals, too. At a weekend around the turn of the month, Funchal's streets, shops and houses are spectacularly decorated with flowers, flower carpets and flower pictures. There is a parade of flowery floats.

AUGUST **Madeira Wine Rally** The moment of the early August car rally, Madeira's biggest sporting event, is best avoided if you are after peace and quiet.

AUGUST MONTE **Feast of the Assumption** Celebrated on 15 August in towns and villages all over the islands; religious ceremonies are followed by drinking and eating, family picnics and street parties, and in Monte, pilgrims climb the 72 church steps on their knees.

SEPTEMBER CALHETA/ESTREITO DE CÂMARA DE LOBOS/FUNCHAL **Festa do Vinho da Madeira** These are the three centres attracting visitors for a Madeira Wine Festival: grape treading, dancing, street parties, fireworks, local wine and *espetadas*.

DECEMBER FUNCHAL New Year's Eve Funchal's Christmas lights are truly spectacular, the temperature a cheering 18°C. And on New Year's Eve people flock to Funchal from around the island and around the world to see one of the world's most exciting firework displays. Computer-synchronised fireworks are set off at numerous different sites around Funchal's natural amphitheatre, and cruise ships anchored in the bay make their own contribution. Hotels charge their highest prices – book well ahead.

Sleep in Madeira

CABO GIRÃO B1

Fajã dos Padres Three cottages and a former boat house have been renovated in this stunning location at the foot of a 250-metre cliff, down which a panoramic lift has been transporting restaurant guests *(page 413)* and residents since 2000. You can also arrive by boat, to the little jetty by the solid beach. Each house has one double bedroom, sitting room with sofa bed, kitchen, bathroom, terraces with stunning sea views, and extensive private grounds. Two houses have barbecues. Breakfast and lunch are available at the restaurant. All around are fruit trees – bananas, papayas, avocados… The lift is free for residents, running from 11am until 6pm on weekdays, and till 7pm at the weekend; its steps make it inaccessible for the disabled or infirm.
Below Estrada Padre António Dinis
Henriques
T+351 291 944 538
E info@fajadospadres.com
W www.fajadospadres.com
€89-€93 with breakfast
§ 4 SC 4(2+2 or 3) ✗ ⛵ *sea*

CAMACHA (MADEIRA) C1

Casas Valleparaízo Six cosy self-catering cottages to rent, all converted from farmworkers' cottages and set discreetly apart in their own small gardens. Sleeping between two and six, they have sitting rooms with open fires or wood-burning stoves, bathrooms, kitchens. This is a

family estate, with orchard and pine woods, and wonderful mature gardens, within the small hill town of Camacha. A *levada* crosses the property. The two top golf courses are within 15 minutes' drive, riding can be organised, and there's ping-pong and badminton on site. Hourly buses to Funchal run till late.
Vale Paraíso, 9135-350 Camacha
T+351 291 922 174 / 962 939 357
E info@valleparaizo.com
W www.valleparaizo.com
€90
SC *9(2, 2+2, 4+2) No credit cards*
Min nights normally 1 week

Quinta da Portada Branca Renovated in 1994, this old white house is tastefully furnished and decorated, set in a mature garden 1km from the centre of Camacha. 700m up in the hills, it has fine views down to the ocean. Bedrooms are all en-suite, and guests share a breakfast room, games room and sitting room with fireplace. Although very peaceful and rural, it is only 8km from the airport, 12 from Funchal, and convenient for golf.
Sítio dos Casais de Além,
9135-090 Camacha
T+351 291 922 119
€80-€90
🛏6 § 1

ESTREITO DA CALHETA A2

Quinta das Vinhas High in hills, not far from the coast, just north of Calheta, this delightful, wine-coloured manor house opened as a small country house hotel in 1997. It is owned by a Welsh family, and surrounded by vines. Beautifully furnished and renovated, with ecological matters in mind, the main house has six airy en-suite bedrooms, a dining room, sitting room, and a reading room in the old chapel. Breakfast is in the lovely garden or the

kitchen, dinner available. There's a pool. A separate drive leads to 14 self-catering cottages, very pretty and brightly decorated inside, sharing another pool, also with access to the main house. There is maid service, daily bread delivery, and the possibility of breakfast and meals in the main house. Find it between the picturesque villages of Calheta and Jardim do Mar, on Madeira's sunny south-west coast, 35 minutes' drive from Funchal.
Lombo dos Serrões,
9370-223 Estreito da Calheta
T+351 291 824 086
E info@qdvmadeira.com
W www.qdvmadeira.com
€70-€85
🛏6 SC 14(2+2, 3) ✗ ⛵
Min nights 2 for rooms, 7 for cottages

ESTREITO DE CÂMARA DE LOBOS B1

Quinta do Estreito Quinta do Estreito used to be a big wine producer. It is perched amidst gardens and vineyards on a hillside just west of Funchal, with breathtaking views and excellent meals as well as fine breakfasts in the Bacchus restaurant *(page 413)*. The former manor house now has the reception rooms of the hotel, beautifully renovated and furnished, while peaceful, tasteful modern rooms spill down the hillside, each with a sunny terrace with sea and mountain views. There are indoor and outdoor pools and a sauna.
Rua José Joaquim da Costa,
9325-034 Estreito de Câmara de Lobos

T+351 291 910 530
E quintaestreito@charminghotelsmadeira.com
W www.charminghotelsmadeira.com
€150-€255
🛏46 S 2 🍸 ✕ 🏊 🔥

FUNCHAL C1

Choupana Hills Resort A beautifully designed, exclusive, modern hill resort and spa, opened in 2003. The designer was French, but the feel is oriental, peaceful and luxurious. Rooms have balconies with amazing views, suites have private jacuzzis on their terraces. There's an outdoor lagoon pool, an indoor pool, exquisite spa, and the Xôpana restaurant *(page 416)* serving delicious fusion food and well-chosen wines.

Travessa do Largo da Choupana,
9060-348 Funchal
T+351 291 206 020
E info@choupanahills.com
W www.choupanahills.com
Rooms €290-€425 Suites €625-€798
🛏58 S 4 🍸 ✕ 🏊 ♨ 🏃

The Cliff Bay Well-designed, luxury modern hotel perched on a headland above a private beach just west of town centre. Large, elegant rooms have balconies with sea or mountain views. There is a high quality spa, indoor pool, gym, gardens, outdoor saltwater pool plus children's pool at beach level, tennis, kayak hire and a dive school. The formal Gallo d'Oro restaurant is very good.

Estrada Monumental 147, 9004-532 Funchal
T+351 291 707 700
E info@cliffbay.com
W www.cliffbay.pt
€230-€430
🛏186 S 14 🍸 ✕ 🏊 ♨ 🏃 🤿

Estalagem Quinta da Casa Branca
Charming, peaceful, modern hotel in the tropical gardens of the manor house that formerly belonged to the British wine family of Leacock – the hotel's excellent restaurant *(page 414)* now occupies the old house along with an upstairs cocktail bar and a romantic terrace. Rooms, all with their own patio, look out over the gardens, or to the sea. There is a heated outdoor swimming pool, health club and spa, gym, and beauty therapy. Be tempted at least once by the afternoon teas. The city centre is nearby.

Rua da Casa Branca 7
T+351 291 700 770
E estalagem@quintacasabranca.pt
W www.quintacasabranca.pt
€225-€305
🛏41 S 2 🍸 ✕ 🏊 ♨ 🏃

Estalagem Quintinha de São João
There are many reasons to choose this hotel. It is very convenient for the centre of Funchal, but peacefully set just above the city centre, the views sometimes partly obscured by the many mature trees in the grounds. Bedrooms in the modern building are unusually spacious and all (not just the suites) have a sitting area and balcony. Public rooms are comfortable and flower-filled, staff exceptionally friendly and helpful. They even offer Portuguese lessons. Breakfasts are good. There's a small but attractive outdoor pool, sauna, gym, table tennis, and a tree-shaded tennis court. Underground parking is a bonus. (Do not confuse this hotel with the Hotel São João next door.)

Rua da Levada de São João 4,
9000-191 Funchal
T+351 291 775 936
E info@quintinhasaojoao.com
W www.quintinhasaojoao.com
€145-€150 🛏34 S 9 ✕ 🏊 🔥 🏃 🤿

Hotel Quinta da Penha de França/ Penha França Mar A twofold venue: a traditional hotel built around a converted manor house is now joined to a new wing,

the Penha França Mar, by a footbridge and lift. The complex is sandwiched between other smart hotels a 15-minute walk from central Funchal, through gardens or along the promenade. Breakfasts are good, the main house cosy, in pretty country house style, set in mature gardens, the modern part smart, with sea view balconies. Swim beneath the trees in the small garden pool, or in a large new pool down by the sea, with direct sea access. There are two professional billiard tables.

Rua Imperatriz Dona Amélia 87,
   9000-014 Funchal
T+351 291 204 650
E info@hotelquintapenhafranca.com
W www.hotelquintapenhafranca.com
€77-€110
🛏*106* S*3* 🍷 ✕ 🏊

FUNCHAL C1 *(continued)*

Quinta da Bela Vista Characterful, welcoming, family-owned hotel set amidst 2ha of peaceful, mature gardens with magnificent views down over the bay of Funchal. The original manor house, now extended, was built in 1844. There are fine antiques and paintings throughout, characterful older rooms in the main

house, and modern annexe rooms, with small balconies. Two good restaurants include the Casa Mãe *(page 415)*, and light meals are served in the bar by the

pool overlooking the city. There's a small gym with sauna and jacuzzi, and tennis. Minibus service will take you in the daytime to and from Funchal, and waves permitting you could take a sunset cruise on the private yacht.

Caminho do Avista Navios 4,
   9000-129 Funchal
T+351 291 706 400
E info@belavistamadeira.com
W www.belavistamadeira.com
€190-€276
🛏*82* S*7* 🍷 ✕ 🏊 🏛 🏋 ✎ *jacuzzi*

Reid's Palace Hotel This famous, grand hotel appeals to an older market – if you enjoy old fashioned charm and dressing up for dinner, this may be the place for you. Set amidst hectares of gardens, Reids dominates a spectacular cliff top overlooking Funchal and the Atlantic. It was renovated in 2006, with the addition of a fine new spa. There are three

swimming pools, two tennis courts including one on the cliff edge, and a lift takes you down to a private 'beach'. The Villa Cipriani restaurant, also belonging to Orient Express Hotels, will probably provide the best in-house dining *(page 416)*, and tea on the beautiful terrace is not to be missed. Indeed, why not come for tea, just to imagine… but not in shorts.

Estrada Monumental 139,
   9000-098 Funchal
T+351 291 717 171

E reservations@reidspalace.com
W www.reidspalace.com
€445-€615 Suites €785-€2,395
🛏*125* S*35* 🍷 ✕ 🏊 🏊 🏛 🏋 ✎

Residencial da Mariazinha Friendly, unpretentious hotel in a narrow street in the centre of Funchal's old town. The old building has been restored to provide nine big air-conditioned rooms with en-suite bathrooms, and a suite with jacuzzi and balcony. There's a sitting room, bar and an interior patio, but no lifts. Very close to the wonderful market, the cable car and public transport, including the airport bus.

Rua de Santa Maria 155,
   9050-040 Funchal
T+351 291 220 239
E residencialmariazinha@netmadeira.com
W www.residencialmariazinha.com
€60-€70
🛏*9* S*1*

MONTE C1

Quinta do Monte In a smart hill suburb up above Funchal, this is an attractive, well-run hotel in a large, restored manor house surrounded by leafy gardens. It's a two-minute (steepish) walk from the cable car up from Funchal old town, also convenient for public bus routes and the famous toboggan run; there is also a courtesy bus and private parking. Rooms are large, all with balconies, views magnificent, staff friendly and helpful, breakfasts good. There is a delightful modern indoor pool, gym, a Turkish bath and a spa ten minutes away, to which transport is provided.

Caminho do Monte 192/194, Monte,
   9050-288 Funchal
T+351 291 780 100
E reservations@quintadomontemadeira.com
W www.quintadomontemadeira.com
€150-€255
🛏*38* S*4* ✕ 🏊 🏛 🏋

Torre Praia Friendly, comfortable, modern hotel with a sun terrace and pool just above Porto Santo's long, sandy beach, and right beside the main town of Vila Baleira. There's a serious gym and squash courts on site, and a multitude of watersports available locally. Food-wise, breakfasts are the high point.
Rua Gulart Madeiros,
*   9400-164 Porto Santo*
T+351 291 980 450
E reservastorrepraia@torrepraia.pt
W www.torrepraia.pt
€120-€230
🛏62 S4 ✕ ⛱ 🏔 ✕ 🎿 *jacuzzi*

SANTANA C2
Casa da Tia Clementina On the edge of this pretty north-eastern village, within the national park, a beautifully restored country house, set amidst flowers and vegetables, with fine views right down to the sea. Rooms are en-suite, air-conditioned or centrally-heated, breakfast is in a big living room furnished with antiques, with an open fire. There's a games room in the cellar, TV room, and barbecue.
Achada de Simão Alves, 9230-039 Santana
T+351 291 574 144
E reservas@casadatiaclementina.com
W www.casadatiaclementina.com
€50
🛏8 🏔 *No credit cards*

Quinta do Furão (The Farm of the Ferret doesn't sound quite so attractive, so let's stick to the Portuguese.) The Quinta do Furão is a large, white, three-storey hotel in the midst of vines on the edge of the village, overlooking the wild, unspoilt north-eastern coastline. Rooms are spacious, comfortable, pleasantly decorated, mostly with terraces. It's a 50-minute drive up from Funchal; the approach from São Vicente may raise a few screams and hairs. Food in the restaurant *(page 417)* is excellent, local in style, and there's a 'pub'

and a wine tasting room, as the hotel belongs to the Madeira Wine Company. Free internet access is a bonus. Relax in the indoor pool and solarium, or tread the *levadas* and scale the Pico Ruivo, Madeira's highest mountain. At harvest time, you can help pick, or even tread the grapes.
Achada do Gramacho, 9230-082 Santana
T+351 291 507 100
E reservations@quintadofurão.com
W www.quintadofurão.com
€120
🛏40 S3 SC2(4+2) ✕ ⛱ 🏔 ✕

SÃO GONÇALO C1
Casa Velha do Palheiro Once a noble hunting lodge, then a manor house belonging to the Blandy wine family, this stylish country house hotel is 9km up into the hills east of Funchal. Its semi-formal gardens and mature woodland are famous for their camellias – visit November to April to see them in bloom – and they receive coach tours up the winding road from Funchal. The golf course beside the hotel is scenically challenging. Bedrooms are luxurious and spacious, some furnished with antiques. Apart from the heated outdoor pool, there's a sauna, steam bath, games room, floodlit all-weather tennis court, badminton, billiards, croquet and table tennis. The restaurant *(page 417)* is one of Madeira's best.

São Gonçalo, 9060-415 Funchal
T+351 291 790 350
E casa.velha@palheiroestate.com
W www.palheiroestate.com /
*   www.casa-velha.com*
€195-€342
🛏32 S5 ✕ ⛱ 🏔 ✕ 🎿
♿*opening 2008*

SÃO ROQUE DO FAIAL C2
Moinho do Comandante Rooms and suites to rent in a delightful, tall mill house, or the Casa das Flores (Flower House), a pretty little cottage in the garden. It's just south of Santana. The garden has a natural spring and water garden, and the property is backed by a steep hillside, flanked by two ancient stone bridges, and surrounded by the laurisilva forest. The restored mill house has two suites, one sleeping a family of four, plus a shared sitting room, dining area and small kitchen. It can be rented as a whole house, or as separate rooms. The cottage has a double bedroom, sitting room and kitchen. There's a wood-fired sauna (€5 per person).
Fajã Grande/Fajã do Cedro Gordo,
*   9230-050 Faial*
T+351 291 575 210
E melvidal@hotmail.com
€40 (2), €80 (6)
🛏3 S3(2&4) SC2(2&6) ✕*on request*
🏔 *No credit cards*

SEIXAL B2
Residencial Sol Mar Comfortable, inexpensive, friendly hotel with good food *(page 417)* towards the western side of the north coast of Madeira. There are six simple but spacious rooms with WC but shared bathrooms. The sea views are spectacular.
Sítio do Lombinho, 9270-125 Seixal,
*   Porto Moniz*
T+351 291 854 854
€35 🛏6 ✕

Grapes of Portugal

Unfamiliar grape names may puzzle newcomers to Portuguese wines, but the wonderful flavours of some of Portugal's unique grape varieties are one of the things that make the wines of Portugal so individual and interesting. These truly are different grapes from those grown in the rest of the world – with a few exceptions, such as Alvarinho and Aragonez (Spain's Albariño and Tempranillo). Understanding is not helped by the occasional use of the same name in different regions for quite different grapes; or by the use of numerous synonyms for the same grape! We have described the grapes here under their main official name, cross-referencing to main alternative names. And we have listed only the Portuguese grapes. Of course, Portugal also grows Cabernet Sauvignon, Syrah, Chardonnay and most of the other well-known international grapes, for use mainly in their regional wine, Vinho Regional, often in characterful blends with the local grapes. We have highlighted the most interesting grapes with a ✤ symbol.

❖ Outstanding varieties

WHITE GRAPES

❖**Alvarinho** The star white grape of the Vinho Verde region can make rich, full-bodied and fragrant white wines, best drunk young. It is grown mostly around Monção in the north of the region. (The same grape grown over the border in Spain is spelt Albariño.) The Portuguese Alvarinhos have a more 'mineral' base structure, overlaid when ripe with fine, flowery-fruity notes of peaches and citrus, and sometimes tropical fruits and flowers. Yields are low, demand high, and Alvarinho wines are always expensive.

❖**Antão Vaz** Good, acid-retaining white grape from the Alentejo, which can be made into an early-picked, crisp white, or barrel-fermented for a rich, full-bodied result. Often used in blends with Roupeiro or Arinto.

❖**Arinto** This makes steely, high acid whites (even in hot climates) that age well. Although usually blended with other grapes, it makes good, lemony, mineral whites that can gain complexity with age. It is grown widely in northern Portugal as well as in the Alentejo, and is the main grape of Bucelas. In Bairrada, they use it for sparkling wines and it brings acidity to blends in the hotter south. It has various synonyms, such as Pedernã in Vinho Verde and Cerceal in Dão and Bairrada. The 'Arinto' of the Dão region is a quite different variety.

❖**Avesso** This grape inhabits a small south-eastern corner of the Vinho Verde region, close to and just north of the Douro river – warmer and drier than the rest of the Minho. It's unusual in Vinho Verde in that it makes a relatively soft, creamy wine, but gives good yields and retains its acidity in high temperatures. Its flavour is delicately peachy.

Azal Branco Late-ripening, high-acid Vinho Verde grape with a neutral flavour. Once the region's most-planted grape, it is now in decline.

❖**Bical** A grape with fresh acidity and good peachy-floral flavours, important in the Beiras (Bairrada and Dão). The wines are good young, but age well to exhibit increasingly toasty complexity. Often blended with other grapes.

Boal Madeira name for Malvasia Fina. To confuse matters, there are three other types of Boal grape in the official Portuguese lists, and various Boal names are used 11 times more as synonyms for other grapes.

❖**Cerceal** Synonym for Arinto, used in Dão and Bairrada. A different grape from the Sercial of Madeira.

❖**Côdega** Douro name for the Síria.

❖**Encruzado** Dão's white star grape. It's the balance between sugar ripeness and acidity that makes it so successful, and as capable of barrel-fermentation as of making light, fresh whites. It deserves to be more widely planted.

Esgana Cão The name in the Vinho Verde, Lisboa, Ribatejo and Bucelas regions for the Sercial of Madeira. It means 'dog strangler' – a reference to its high acidity!

❖**Fernão Pires** This aromatic grape makes it onto the most-planted lists from Beiras down to the Setúbal Peninsula. It often exhibits a slightly muscatty, floral character that can become cloying if not balanced by enough acidity. But its more elegant side (when not over-ripe) is well-suited to easy-drinking sparkling wines in Bairrada, and pleasant, dry or off-dry whites in the Ribatejo and Lisboa. Also known as Maria Gomes in Bairrada.

❖**Fonte Cal** Found only in the Beira Interior, but capable of making rich, honeyed whites with high, steely acidity. Good drunk young, but it can develop complexity.

Gouveio Part of the cocktail that can make exciting dry whites in the Douro. It is sometimes known as Verdelho in the Douro, but is different from the Madeira Verdelho.

❖**Loureiro** Along with Alvarinho, Loureiro is one of the two great white grapes of the Minho, and makes some of the best Vinhos Verdes. It has bewitching, musky, grapey, citrus, floral aromas and good acidity, and has overtaken the less exciting Azal Branco as the region's most widely planted white grape.

Malvasia There are 13 different types of Malvasia on the official Portuguese list, plus a Malvia and a Malvoeira. The most widely grown is Malvasia Fina, common in the Douro, and also known as Arinto do Dão and Assario Branco (in Beiras). Malvasia Rei (possibly related to Spain's Palomino Fino) is also found in the Douro, making fairly bland wine. On Madeira, confusingly, the Boal (or Bual) is actually Malvasia Fina. So Madeira's Malvasia (also known as Malmsey) must be one of the other Malvasias. Locals there say the finest Malmsey is made from Malvasia Cândida, but very little of this remains on Madeira.

Manteudo A relatively neutral, high-yielding white grape grown in the Alentejo region.

❖**Maria Gomes** The name given to Fernão Pires in Bairrada.

❖**Moscatel** Most of Portugal's Moscatel grapes, including the famous Moscatel of Setúbal, are Moscatel Graúdo ('great Muscat'), known elsewhere in the world

as Muscat of Alexandria. It grows all over the southern half of Portugal, with its heartland in the Setúbal Peninsula. Though it can be made into light white wines, with grapy-flowery fragrance, it is used more often in the traditional sweet, fortified Muscats. In the Douro, there is a little **Moscatel Galego Branco** – the fine Muscat Blanc à Petits Grains.

Perrum Widely grown in the Alentejo for dry white wines. It yields well, but makes neutral wines.

❧**Pedernã** The name in Vinho Verde for the Arinto of Bucelas, Lisboa and the Ribatejo.

❧**Rabigato** One of the best white grapes in the Douro. Rabigato gives generous yields and is able to retain acidity through the baking Douro summers.

Rabo de Ovelha A recommended white variety in the Ribatejo, Setúbal Peninsula and Alentejo. It ripens early and needs to be picked before its acidity plummets.

❧**Roupeiro** Southern Alentejo synonym for Síria.

❧**Sercial** One of the noble grapes of Madeira, where its very high acidity levels can keep vintage wines alive for centuries! On the mainland, it's grown in the Vinho Verde, Lisboa, Ribatejo and Bucelas regions, often in blends with Arinto.

❧**Síria** (aka Alva, Côdega and Roupeiro) Best known for the honeyed whites it produces (as Roupeiro) in the southern Alentejo, but also grown (as Alva) in Portalegre in the northern Alentejo, (as Côdega) in the Douro (for white port) and (as Síria) in the Beiras. Its high-acid grapes are very suitable for white port.

Tamarez Setúbal Peninsula and Alentejo synonym for Trincadeira das Pratas.

Terrantez One of the 'noble grapes' of Madeira, high in sugar and acidity, but now rare. It's still found in the Douro, however, as Folgasão.

Trajadura Relatively aromatic Vinho Verde grape used mostly to counteract high acidities in other varieties. Ripens early and yields well.

Trincadeira das Pratas Recommended in much of the Ribatejo more for its quantity than quality. Known as Tamarez in the Alentejo and Setúbal Peninsula.

Verdelho One of the 'noble varieties' on Madeira, where its high acidity makes it great for off-dry wines. It's not the same as the Douro's Gouveio, as was once thought.

❧**Viosinho** A really classy white Douro grape, which makes fresh, fragrant wines with high acidity, especially when planted at high altitudes

RED GRAPES

❧**Alfrocheiro** Early-ripening Dão grape, but now planted widely throughout the country. Alfrocheiro has good colour, rich tannin, a good balance of strawberry-like fruit and acidity, and is increasingly viewed as one of Portugal's high-quality red grapes.

Alicante Bouschet One of the small band of red-fleshed grapes used in winemaking. Alicante Bouschet comes originally from the South of France, and contributes

enormously to colour. It used to be an important component of Alentejo red blends, particularly at Quinta do Carmo. It fell from fashion, and is now making a come-back, valued for its intense, 'treacley' flavours (even though dry).

❧**Aragonez** Growers all over Portugal agree on the quality of this grape, one of the five recommended varieties for port in the Douro (where it is called Tinta Roriz). But it has really come to prominence as the principal component of several top Douro red wines, including Barca Velha. Aragonez is its Alentejo name. It ripens early, and produces good yields of flavoursome wine reminiscent of red fruits, plums, strawberries and blackberries, with firm tannins. It responds well to ageing in oak. Also known as Tinta Roriz in Dão (and as Tempranillo in Spain).

Azal Tinto Pale, late-ripening, high acid red Vinho Verde grape with a neutral flavour.

❧**Baga** Famous as the notoriously difficult, tannic grape of red Bairrada, ripening properly only four years in ten. The grapes are small, dark and thick-skinned. It tends to make lean, tannic reds that can be very astringent in youth, but mature to complexity with age. In hotter years, or by skilful ripening and winemaking, Baga can give rich, dense, elegant reds, with cherry and damson perfume, ageing to complex flavours of herbs, malt, cedar and dried fruit. It is widely planted in Dão as well, also in Encostas de Aire (Lisboa) and the Ribatejo.

Bastardo More of a grape for port and Madeira, but still with substantial plantings in Dão and the Douro (for table wines). It ripens early, but has low yields and low acidity. It is said to be the same as the Trousseau of the Jura in France.

❖ Outstanding varieties

❖Castelão Possibly Portugal's most widely planted red variety, dominant in the southern half of the country, though increasingly being replaced by earlier-ripening varieties. It performs best on the Setúbal Peninsula in the Terras do Sado, where it makes firm, elegant, raspberry-fruity wines that evolve to a cedary, cigar-box character reminiscent of fine, mature Cabernet. It goes under several aliases – João de Santarém in the Ribatejo, Periquita in the Terras do Sado.

Espadeiro Vinho Verde grapes with fresh acidity and good, herby flavour, often used for rosé.

Moreto Widely grown in the southern half of Portugal. It needs low yields to show at its best. The Moreto of Dão is a different grape, also known as Malvasia Preta in the Douro.

Mortágua Name used in some places for Trincadeira, whilst elsewhere, confusingly, Preto Mortágua is Touriga Nacional.

❖Moscatel Roxo The official government list has five different types of Moscatel, of which two are red (or reddish). The pink Moscatel Galego Roxo is related to the Muscat Blanc à Petits Grains, and the limited amount grown makes very fine wine in the Setúbal Peninsula.

Ramisco The legendary grape of Colares, whose plantings are declining in the fast-disappearing sandy vineyards. It's said to have made great wines in the past, though modern opinions are less kind. Let's hope some vines survive, if only in scientific collections.

Rufete Traditional Douro grape, surviving now only as part of old, mixed vineyards. Productive, but of no great quality. Also known as Tinta Pinheira.

❖Tinta Amarela Douro synonym of Trincadeira.

Tinta Barroca This is one of the five officially recommended grapes in the Douro. Tinta Barroca yields generous quantities of well-ripened grapes in cooler vineyards. And it gives dark coloured wine. Used more for port than for table wines.

Tinta Miúda Possibly the same as Spain's Graciano, Tinta Miúda is widespread in the Lisboa area, giving wines high in colour and acidity. It is more valuable for contributing these qualities to a blend than used by itself.

Tinta Negra The main grape of Madeira, used there for wines of different styles and sweetnesses. It gives soft wines without great colour (not a problem for Madeira). Formerly incorrectly known as Tinta Negra Mole it is not the same as the boring Negra Mole of the Algarve.

Tinta Pinheira Same as Rufete.

❖Tinta Roriz Name in northern Portugal for Aragonez.

Tinto Cão One of the five recommended Douro grapes, used more for ports than table wines. It is late-ripening, but resists mildew and rot owing to its thick skins, to give dense, structured wines.

❖Touriga Franca Definitely in the top trio of Douro grapes, and now planted widely in the northern half of Portugal. It may not have the structure of Touriga Nacional, but does have appealing floral fragrances and velvety tannins, and can age well. Nowadays you will find it in red table wines as far south as the Setúbal Peninsula. It was known until recently as Touriga Francesa.

❖Touriga Nacional The most highly prized grape in the Douro and in Dão, and truly a northerner, this is such a star that plantings have now spread right down to Alentejo and the Algarve. As well as firm, rich colour, its aroma is a really complex mixture of raspberries and ripe blackcurrants, herbs, flowers and liquorice. It sometimes goes by the name of Preto Mortágua.

❖Trincadeira This grape is grown almost everywhere in Portugal, but it performs best in hot climates. The best wines have wonderfully bright raspberry fruit, spicy, peppery, herbal flavours, and very good acidity. In the Douro, as Tinta Amarela, it makes fine, elegant ports. In the Alentejo and Ribatejo, rich-flavoured, balanced, spicy reds are its strength. Its propensity to rot means that the damp Minho region is not so suitable (although it's there as well). It is also a very vigorous vine, and the grapes can taste herbaceous if the vegetation is allowed to run rampant. It is also sometimes known as Mortágua or Espadeiro.

Vinhão This is what the French call a *teinturier* grape, one with red flesh, therefore red juice. As Vinhão, it's the main grape of red Vinho Verde. As Sousão, it is increasingly popular to beef up the colour of red wines in the Douro, mainly for port, to which it also brings welcome high acidity.

Architectural Heritage

Romanesque

From the 12th century on, after the expulsion of the Moors and up to the 14th century in the north, a simple, sturdy, ascetic style style rejecting the flamboyant Moorish architecture, and returning to the barrel vaults and rounded arches of the Romans. VISIT: the Sé Velha (old cathedral) in Coimbra *(pictured above, and page 201)*.

Gothic

Coexisting alongside Romanesque, this is the familiar pointing-to-heaven style of northern Europe. Gothic style arrived in Portugal from France in the 1170s. Every aspect leads the eye upwards, pointed arches, flying buttresses and lofty ceilings. It's elegant and ethereal, with ribbed vaults and soaring stonework. VISIT: the Dominican abbey of Santa Maria da Vitória at Batalha (above), the monastery at Alcobaça *(page 293)*, and the cathedral at Guarda *(page 201)*.

Manueline

A term first used in the 19th century to describe the very decorative branch of late Gothic that began in the reign of Manuel I. It is now used for the whole of the dynastic period to which he belonged (1383 to 1580). Features include twisted columns, ornate lattice-work ceilings, carvings on semicircular windows and portals, often with maritime themes, such as twisted ropes or anchors, to celebrate the era of the Discoveries. VISIT: Mosteiro dos Jerónimos in Belém *(pictured facing page and page 238)*.

Renaissance

A return to the classical Greek and Roman sense of symmetry in the 16th century brought proportion, regularity, balance and harmony, often combined with elements of Manueline, or later, Mannerism. VISIT: the chapel of Nossa Senhora da Conceição in Tomar *(page 293)*.

Azulejos

You'll find these painted ceramic tiles in and on buildings from the 15th century onwards, starting with simple

floral designs in blue *(azul)* and white, then incorporating golden yellow, finally other colours. The idea came from Seville in the 15th century, and most *azulejos* date from the 17th century. At their height, *azulejos* were used to decorate churches, palaces, kitchens, gardens and railway stations, and on murals inside and outside houses, sometimes with very grand scenes of battles and heroic endeavours, sometimes simple scenes of domestic life.

Baroque

Gold from Brazil is the key to this flamboyant late 17th century to late 18th century style. The basic forms of the buildings may have been classical, but everything was overlaid with elaborate golden decoration, and dramatic, ornate, fluid lines, suggesting movement. Rococo is a late 18th century development of baroque, lighter and more playful, ornamental and fanciful, with lots of clouds, cherubs and shells.

VISIT: Baroque Igreja dos Clérigos in Porto and Mateus Palace in Douro *(page 103)*.

Neo-classicism

A return to sobriety after the excesses of rococo, in the late 18th and early 19th centuries. More echoes of Greco-Roman architecture. Porticoes and columns are important features. Popular in Porto with Scottish port shippers. VISIT: the Factory House in Oporto, the Theatre of Dona Maria II in Lisbon, and the Santuário do Bom Jesus do Monte near Braga *(page 58)*.

Pombaline

The name given to the neo-classical style drawn up by military engineers and supervised by Marquês de Pombal after the great Lisbon earthquake of 1775. It had to be executed quickly and cheaply, to restore normality after disaster. Lisbon's Baixa, the area completely destroyed, was rebuilt on a grid system, with straight lines, wide streets and squares, and little decoration. VISIT: the Praça do Comércio with its pink arcades, and Rossio Square *(page 232)*.

Wine-speak and table-talk

Newcomers to the Portuguese language may find the spoken language impenetrable, though Spanish and French help with the reading. Spoken Portuguese presents all kinds of difficulties: a lot of nasal sounds, contorted-sounding vowels and diphthongs, cavernous 'back' sounds reminiscent of Russian, rs that may be rolled a bit like in Spanish or Italian (though a little less enthusiastically) or made at the back of the nose, even more enthusiastically than in French. And, in some regions, the Portuguese swallow a lot of syllables. If you would like to learn to pronounce Portuguese really well before you go, we would recommend the American course Pimsleur Conversational Portuguese (Continental), Simon & Schuster Audio. There is no book – this is an oral-only course, and so rather pain-free. Mutter along with the CD or tape in your car – it will really get you speaking in no time, with an accent that the locals will understand! Your library may have it. (Don't choose the Brazilian version!)

We'd like to mention just a few linguistic traps that lie in wait… The word *'no'* (pronounced 'noo') means 'in the'. So don't feel starvation coming on if you read 'no restaurante'. *'Refrigerantes'* are soft drinks. A *Frigideira* is a frying pan. And *'puxe'*, pronounced more or less like 'push' means 'pull'. (Push is *empurre*, by the way.) The days of the week may also trip you up. The Portuguese start counting on Sunday *(domingo)*, which makes Monday, confusingly, the Second-Day *(segunda-feira)* and Friday the Sixth-Day *(sexta-feira)*.

The days go like this:

domingo Sunday
segunda-feira Monday
terça-feira Tuesday
quarta-feira Wednesday
quinta-feira Thursday
sexta-feira Friday
sábado Saturday

VITAL VOCAB

…for wine lovers
água pé a mix of grape juice and a rough wine made by adding water to the skins and pips left after pressing, then re-fermenting. It literally means 'foot water'! You might meet it at fairs and festivals.
águardente brandy (from *água ardente* – burning water)
bagaçeira a white spirit, same as French *marc* or Italian *grappa*, distilled from the *bagaço* (skins, stalks and pips) left over after post-fermentation pressing.
branco white *vinho branco seco* dry white wine
colheita vintage
um copo de vinho a glass of wine
doce sweet
a lista de vinhos the wine list
rolha cork (stopper)
rosé rosé
saca-rolhas cork-screw
seco dry
tinto red *vinho tinto* red wine
vinho wine!
vinho do porto port
vinho espumante sparkling wine
vinho verde DOC wine from the Minho; the term is sometimes used, confusingly, to mean simply 'young wine', from anywhere

…for winery visitors
adega winery
ânfora traditional large clay jar used for wine fermentations, still used by some wineries
armazém (plural *armazens*) lodge, store, warehouse
balseiro large upright wooden vat for storing wine
casta grape variety
cepa vine
colheita vintage, also a style of port
cuba (de inox, de cimento) stainless steel/cement tank or vat
estufagem heating process speeding

wine ageing in Madeira
herdade large estate
inox stainless steel
lagar (plural *lagares*) stone, cement (or marble!) shallow tank used for foot-treading (or robotic plunging) and fermentation
latifúndio large estate in the south
monte farmhouse or estate in the Alentejo
patamar modern vineyard terrace without retaining stone walls
pipas casks, of varying size depending on region
pisa a pé foot-treading
poda pruning
prensa press
prova tasting
queria uma garrafa do… I'd like a bottle of the…
queria uma caixa do… I'd like a case of the…
quinta farm or estate
roga gang of pickers or foot-treaders
rota do vinho wine route
socalco walled terrace
tonel/toneis vat/vats used for storing wine
vindimas vintage time
vinha vineyard
vinho wine
uvas grapes

…for food lovers
almoço lunch
jantar dinner
pequeno-almoço breakfast
esplanada terrace
tasca cheap, sometimes tiny eating place, *(tasco)* in the north
tasquinha even smaller *tasca*
casa de chá teahouse with cakes
churrasco grilled
churrascaria, churrasqueira grill/barbecue restaurant
marisqueira seafood restaurant
ementa de degustação tasting menu, a series of small dishes
couvert bread, olives, cheese
entradas nibbles or starters
petiscos Portuguese version of

Spanish tapas, small dishes

biológico/bio organic

caseiro home made/home style

fabrico próprio home made

bacalhau salt cod, a staple food everwhere, much loved by the Portuguese

marmelada wonderful, stiff quince paste, served with cheese, or as jam

massa de pimentão paste from roasted red peppers, garlic and olive oil, eat on canapés or use to flavour dishes

doces conventuais sweets made of egg yolk, sugar and often almond, traditionally made in convents, often given as presents or eaten in cake shops/cafés. Expensive and very rich.

pasteis pastries

pasteis de nata custard tarts

queijadas small cheesecake tarts; all over the country, but a speciality of Sintra and Coimbra

queijaria artesanal a small-scale cheesemaker; you may be able to buy direct

uma sande / sanduíche sandwich

...for ordering hot drinks

CAFÉ COMES IN MANY GUISES:

uma bica a small cup of very strong black coffee, espresso-type; a southern expression – a northerner would simply ask for *um café*

um café duplo/uma bica dupla a double espresso

uma bica cheia, um café cheio a small black coffee topped up with hot water – *cheio* means 'full'

um pingo or *um café pingado* an espresso with a dash of milk

uma meia de leite de máquina (south), *um meia de leite directa* (north) a larger cup of half espresso, half milk

um galão a tall glass, maybe half milk, half coffee, maybe just a dash of coffee. You can

influence the mix by asking for *um galão claro* (pale, with just a little coffee) or *um galão bem oscuro* (dark). *Galão* literally means 'gallon'

um garoto slang word for milky filter coffee; this literally means 'small boy' or 'kid'

café com leite milky filter coffee

OTHER HOT DRINKS:

um chá de limão hot water on lemon rind

um chá preto com limão tea, which will almost certainly be weak, unimpressive, and black (with lemon). You might want it (unconventionally) *com leite*, with milk

chocolate quente hot chocolate

cacau cocoa

infusão (camomila, menta) herb tea (chamomile, mint)

...for ordering cold drinks

água sem gás still water

água com gás fizzy water

água da torneira tap water

bebidas drinks

uma cerveja (gelada) a (cold) beer

um chá gelado iced tea

com gelo with ice

um copo de leite (frio) a glass of (cold) milk

refrigerantes soft drinks

um sumo de laranja (natural) (freshly-squeezed) orange juice

...for food shopping

onde há... where is there a ...

uma charcutaria a delicatessen

uma confeitaria a cake and coffee shop, where you can eat in or take away

uma doçaria a sweet and cake shop

uma mercearia a grocer

um mercado a market

uma padaria a bakery

uma pastelaria a pastry and cake shop, also generally serving coffee, to eat in or take away

uma peixaria a fish monger

VITAL GENERAL VOCAB

...for conversing with the locals

adeus goodbye; also, more casually, *tchau*

até logo see you

bom-dia good morning

boa tarde good afternoon (used in the evening until nightfall)

boa noite good night, good evening (after nightfall)

olá hello

obrigado (if you are a man), *obrigada* (for women) thank you; the polite answer is *de nada* (it's a pleasure, literally 'it was nothing')

por favor/se faz favor please (interchangeable)

desculpe I'm sorry (apology)

sim, não yes, no

não compreendo I don't understand

fala inglês/francês? do you speak English/French?

gosto I like it

não gosto I don't like it

...for travellers

como se vai para... how do I get to...

auto-estrada motorway

autocarro bus

barco boat

bilhete de ida e volta return ticket

bilhete de ida one way ticket

carro car

comboio train

eléctrico (carro eléctrico) tram

estação station

paragem bus or tram stop

táxi taxi

...for tourists

aceitam cartões de cré dito? do you take credit cards? Worth checking, because the answer will often be *não*

a que horas está aberto? what time does it open? (It will often be shut for lunch, until 2 or 3pm)

azulejos traditional painted decorative tiles used inside and outside many buildings, traditionally blue (*azul*) and white

onde é o posto de turismo? where is the tourist office?

campo de golfe golf course

entrada gratuita admission free

igreja church

miradouro vantage point, spot with a fine view

museu museum

mosteiro monastery

paço manor house in the country

pousada one of a chain of 42 hotels, almost all in historic buildings, situated throughout Portugal *(www.pousadasofportugal.com)*

preciso de I need; you need 'of' something in Portuguese.

preciso de vinho is 'I need wine'

sé cathedral, alternatively *catedral*

solar manor house

torre tower

um supermercado a supermarket

um talho a butcher

...for reading a menu

assado roast

cozido boiled

crú raw

doces puddings/deserts

entradas starters or nibbles

escalfado poached

estufado stewed

filhós fritters

no forno in the oven, roasted

frito fried

fumado smoked

grelhado grilled

guisado braised

lagareiro (à lagareiro) 'in the style of the man who tends the olive oil press' – with lots of olive oil

meia dose half portion; often available at maybe two-thirds of the full price.

por pessoa per person; *para duas (2) pessoas* for two people minimum

prato dish; *prato do dia* dish of the day; *pratos completos* one-pot dishes – a meal in themselves

recheado stuffed

sobremesas puddings, desserts

à vapor steamed

BOM APETITE!

abóbora pumpkin; don't miss *doce de abóbora*, delicious (yes, really) pumpkin jam; pumpkin is also used in puddings

açafrão saffron

açorda thick bread soup, with meat or seafood, sometimes enriched with beaten egg, yolks or hard boiled eggs

alheiras light, garlicky sausages, Jewish originally, using chicken or turkey instead of pork; often contain bread

alho garlic

alperces apricots

ameijôas clams

ameixas plums

ameixas de Elvas Elvas plums, delicious candied greengages

amêndoa almond

amendoim peanut

ananás pineapple

arroz rice/risotto

arroz de pato duck risotto

arroz doce pan-cooked rice pudding, often with egg yolks, lemon and always cinnamon sprinkled on top

atum tuna; ask for it *mal passado* (rare) as it may be overcooked in traditional restaurants

avelã hazelnut

aves poultry

azeite olive oil

azeitonas olives come in many varieties; ask *posso provar* (may I try?) in shops or markets before buying

bacalhau salt cod

banana banana

batatas potatoes

berbigão clams, cockles

beringela aubergine, eggplant

bife steak, which might be beef *(bife de vaca)* but also tuna *(bife de atum)* or whatever

borrego yearling lamb

broa lovely corn bread (savoury), a speciality of the Minho; or small, dryish sweet potato and almond cakes with maybe citrus zest, coconut, honey or spices

cabidela soup-like rice dish with chicken, thickened with chicken's blood

cabrito kid (month old); *cabrito assado* roast kid

caça game

cação a kind of shark, not very flavoursome

calamares squid

caldeirada thick fish and potato stew

caldo clear soup, broth

caldo verde cabbage soup with *chouriço*

camarões prawns

canela cinnamon

canja chicken broth

caracóis snails, usually cooked with garlic

caranguejo (de mar) small variety of crab; *(de rio)* crayfish

carapau horse mackerel

caril curry, generally mild

carne meat

carneiro mutton

castanhas chestnuts

cataplana stew (usually fish) cooked in a sealed copper cooking pot, originally an Algarve dish; the metal dish itself is also a cataplana

cavala chub mackerel

cebolada a paste of onion and bay cooked in olive oil, added to dishes

cenoura carrot

cerejas cherries

chanfana goat or mutton stew

cherne wreckfish

chocos cuttle fish

choquinhos baby cuttlefish

hello, I'd like… *bom dia (boa tarde, boa noite, olá), queria…*

a table for (2,3,4,5,6) *uma mesa para dois/três/quatro/cinco/seis*

on the terrace *na esplanada*

inside *na sala*

please *por favor, se faz favor*

thank you *obrigado* (for a man), *obrigada* (for a woman)

bread *pão*

butter *manteiga*

nibbles *couvert* (bread, butter, maybe olives) are included in the table setting and part of the basic price of the meal; *entradas* (cheese, charcuterie, seafood, fish cakes…) may appear unordered on the table, and you pay if you eat – send back or ask for more depending on your appetite and pocket

the menu *a ementa*

the wine list *a lista de vinhos*

white wine *vinho branco*

red wine *vinho tinto*

rosé wine *vinho rosé*

a bottle *uma garrafa*

a half bottle *uma meia garrafa*

cheers *saúde!* or you might say, more colloquially, *tchim tchim*; or 'to our good health' *à nossa*, 'to your good health' *à sua* (to one person you don't know well), *à tua* (to a close friend), or *à vossa* (to more than one person)

another bottle of wine *mais uma garrafa de vinho*

cold wine *vinho fresco*

cooler/colder *mais fresco*

water *água;* still water *água sem gás;* fizzy water *água com gás*

cold water *água fresca* or *água gelada*

I'm a vegetarian *sou vegetariano* (*vegetariana* for a woman); if you want more than an omelette it might be best to phone ahead

do you have…? *tem…?*

I'm allergic *sou alérgico* (for a man) or *alérgica* (for a woman) to gluten *ao glúten;* to wheat *ao trigo;* to dairy products *aos produtos lácteos;* to peanuts *aos amendoins;* to nuts *aos frutos secos*

pepper *pimenta*, usually only white ground, not usually on the table

salt *sal;* Portuguese kitchens usually salt their food liberally, and salt is rarely on the table

well done *bem passado;* this is how it will normally arrive, except in a modern, internationally-minded restaurant

rare *mal passado;* the Portuguese traditionally like their meat and fish well cooked; in a traditional restaurant, make sure they know you really mean 'rare': insist and say *muito mal passado*

medium *médio*

enjoy your meal *bom apetite!*

the bill *a conta*

the loo? *a casa de banho?*

goodbye *adeus*

chouriço similar to Spanish chorizo, made typically from fatty pork, garlic, paprika and smoked; eat raw or cooked

chouriço de sangue blood sausage

codorniz quail

coelho rabbit

coentros coriander

cogumelos mushrooms

cordeiro lamb

costeletas cutlets

couve cabbage

cozido stew

cozido à portuguesa boiled meat and vegetables

dourada gilt-head bream, good flavour; in a market, recognise it by the gold colouring on its head

enchidos sausages, including dried and cured versions, such as *chouriço*

enguias eels

ensopado stew containing bread

escabeche marinated in vinegar or lemon juice

espargos asparagus

espardarte swordfish, can be dry if overcooked

espetada skewer, kebab

faisão pheasant

farinheira smoked sausage containing bread/flour, pork fat, wine and spices

favas broad beans

feijão dried beans

feijoada bean stew made from rehydrated dried beans with meat or fish

fiambre cooked ham

fígado liver

figos figs

framboesas raspberries

francesinha multi-layered sandwich with a tomato and beer-based sauce (Porto/Gaia)

frango chicken, young cock

frutos do mar seafood

galinha chicken

gambas prawns

ganso goose

gaspacho cold vegetable soup containing onions and tomatoes (not puréed like the Spanish version)

gelado ice cream

grão chick peas

hortaliça vegetables

hortelã mint

javali wild boar

lagosta lobster

lampreia lamprey, eel-like, strong, meaty, oily, slightly muddy (you'll love it or hate it!)

lampreia de ovos celebration cake made bizarrely in the shape of a lamprey, full of eggs, sugar and almonds and *fios de ovos* (more eggs and sugar)

langueirão razor clam

lapas limpets

laranja orange

lebre hare

leitão suckling pig, usually roasted with delicious crackling, a speciality of Bairrada

legumes vegetables; also called *hortaliça*

limão lemon

língua tongue

linguado sole

linguiças long thin *chouriço*-type sausages; sometimes used as a generic word for sausage

lombo pork fillet

lulas squid

lulas recheadas stuffed squid

maçã apple

manteiga butter

maracujá passion fruit

mariscos seafood

marmelada wonderful quince cheese, a sliceable sweet paste with lovely gritty texture, often served with (dairy) cheese

melão honeydew melon, rugby-ball-shaped, greenish-white; but *melão* is also a generic word for melon

melão branco do Ribatejo white-skinned, rugby-ball-shaped melon, very sweet, with white flesh, deep yellow around the seeds

melancia water melon

meloa canteloupe melon (round ball, sweetly aromatic), orange flesh

mexilhões mussels

migas an Alentejo dish now found everywhere – fried bread crumbs moistened with various ingredients, with meat or seafood; *migas* literally means 'crumbs'

milho corn

miolos brains

molho sauce

morango strawberry

morcela black pudding, blood sausage

nabo turnip

nabiça turnip greens, an excellent vegetable

natas cream

noz walnut

ostras oysters

ovo egg – you might like it boiled (*cozido*), scrambled (*mexido*), fried (*estrelado*) or poached (*escalfado*)

ovos moles sweet egg-paste used in cakes, a kind of thickened egg yolk custard using water rather than milk

paio thicker, leaner version of *chouriço* sausage, containing vinegar

pão bread; *pão caseiro* home baked bread; the standard bread is white, but you may find *pão integral* wholemeal bread

pargo sea bream, good, meaty, firm-textured

parracho turbot, a great flat fish, wonderfully firm-textured

passas raisins

pés de porco pigs' trotters

pato duck; *um pato bravo* is a wild duck

pastel (plural *pastéis*) cake, pie, tart

peixe fish

peixe espada scabbard fish, long, silver-skinned and good; the black fish they sell in Madeira as *peixe espada* is really *espada preta*, and is more bland

pêra pear

perceves goose-neck barnacles

perdiz partridge

peru turkey

pescada hake, not unlike cod

pêssego peach; especially good ones come from Alcobaça in Estremadura

pimento pepper (vegetable)

pimenta pepper (spice)

pimentão seasoning of hot red peppers

pinhões pine kernels

piri-piri sauce made from red-hot chillis called *piri-piri,* discovered in Angola

polvo octopus

pombo pigeon

porco pork

à portuguesa 'Portuguese style' is generally in a sauce of tomatoes, onions, garlic, herbs and olive oil – or possibly lard

presunto raw ham, cured, matured, sometimes smoked; the lovely *pata negra* version is from the *porco preto*, the black pig of the Alentejo

pudim flan egg custard, usually baked and possibly flavoured with vanilla, cinnamon, citrus zest or caramel

queijo cheese

raia skate

requeijão ricotta, soft cheese-like dairy product, often served at breakfast

rins kidneys

robalo sea bass, very flavourful and firm-fleshed

rodovalho halibut, delicate fish

rojões chunks of fried belly pork, quite fatty

safio conger eel, bony and boring unless well sauced

sal salt

salada salad

salmão salmon

salmonete red mullet, fine flavoured fish, excellent texture

salpicão thick, dark, garlicky smoked pork sausage, a thick version of *chouriço*

salsa flat-leafed parsley

santola spider crab

sapateira rock crab, an Atlantic species, very good

sarda mackerel

sardinhas grelhadas grilled sardines

sarrabulho pork and rice cooked in wine and pig's blood

sopa de coentros thick soup of coriander, bread and egg

tamboril monkfish

trigo wheat

tripas tripe

toucinho do céu 'bacon from heaven', a northern cake/dessert containing almonds, sugar, loads of egg yolks, and cinnamon

truta trout

uvas grapes

vaca beef

vinagre vinegar

vitela veal

Photo credits & Bibliography

PHOTO CREDITS

Much of the photography of wineries, vineyards and wine producers is by Luís Pais **It's not all beaches** 13 *golfers on cliff* Sheraton Algarve Hotel at Pine Cliffs Resort; *roofs* Sebastião da Fonseca; *house with flowers* José Manuel; 14 *beach* Região de Turismo do Algarve **Food in Portugal** 22 *fish* Nuno Correia, Lágrimas Hotels and Emotions; 23 *Elvas plums* imported by Bristol Merchants, sales@bristol merchants.com; *cheese* Adriana Freire; *mushroom dish* Hotel da Cartuxa, Évora; 24 *chestnuts* John Copland; *seafood starter* Vila Joya, Albufeira; 25 *olives and olive oil still life* Nuno Calvet; *bread* Adriana Freire; 26 *seafood* Vila Joya, Albufeira; 27 *asparagus fish* Varanda, Lisbon; *carne de porco à alentejana* Hotel da Cartuxa; *cataplana* Sebastiao da Fonseca; *composed starter* Vila Joya; 29 *fruit dessert with yellow sauce* Nuno Correia, Lágrimas Hotels and Emotions **Vinho Verde and the Minho** 33 *Ponte de Lima bridge* TURIHAB- Solares de Portugal; 51 *São Gião restaurant* Rui Duarte Silva; 52 *market stall* Rui Leal; 56 *Amarante bridge* Paulo Magalhães; *bridge across the River Vez* Rui Leal; 57 *Santuário de Santa Luzia* Asta d'Eça **Trás-os-Montes** 65 *squirrel* Vidago Palace Spa; *grapes* Sebastião da Fonseca; 68 *alheira sausage* João Paulo; 73 *tower in Bragança* António Sacchetti; 76 *climbing waterfall* Francisco Silva; 77 *church* António Sacchetti **Douro** 80 *Douro* José Manuel; 81 *almond blossom* Região de Turismo do Algarve; *sunset* Rui Cunha; 111 *goat engraving* Instituto Português de Arqueologia; 113 *riverside railway* António Sacchetti; *horse engraving* Instituto Português de Arqueologia **Porto & Gaia** 121 *gull* Graham St John Smith; *bridge at night* Douro Azul; 122 *bridge* CM Gaia; 124 *pillory cathedral* António Sacchetti; 126 *reading on the riverside, Mosteiro da Serra do Pilar* and *aerial shot of Gaia* CM Gaia; 127 *Porto by night* and *Palácio da Bolsa* Paulo Magalhães; 130 *aerial view of lodges* CM Gaia; 143 *white wine with rice* Degusto; *fish stew, sável* and *raw fish* CM Gaia; 144 *bacalhau* Nuno Correia-Lágrimas Hotels & Emotions; 153 *gull* Graham St John Smith **Beiras** 157 *library* António Sacchetti; 186 *mountain sheep* Sociedade Agrícola da Beira; 187 *dessert* Púcara, Viseu; 188 *market* Quinta dos Três Rios; *dessert* Praça Velha, Castelo Branco; 201 *Santa Cruz monastery* António Sacchetti **Azores** 209 *lake* Sebastião da Fonseca; *house by the sea* Adegas do Pico; *hydrangea* José Manuel; *Ponta Delgada* Associação de Turismo dos Açores; *Flores coast* Fernando Chaves; 213 *pineapple* Sandra Dart; 214 *cozido (bottom)* F Rigaud/Travel-Images.com; 218 *boats* Associação de Turismo dos Açores; 219 *São Jorge coast* and *São Jorge coast with lagoons* Associação de Turismo dos Açores; *bay on Santa Maria* Paulo Magalhães; 221 *Ponta Delgada Marina* and *lake* Associação de Turismo dos Açores; 222 *Angra do Heroísmo* and *coast with hydrangeas* Associação de Turismo dos Açores **Lisbon** 229 *modern bridge* José Manuel; *duck risotto* Varanda, Ritz Four Seasons; *man with cakes* Rui Cunha; *Restaurante Eleven* Nuno Correia-Lágrimas Hotels & Emotions; 231 *street restaurant* and *couple in restaurant* José Manuel; 234 *ruined convent* António Sacchetti; *modern arches* José Manuel; 236 *golden coach* José Manuel; 237 *barbecue* José Manuel; *Jerónimos* António Sacchetti **Lisboa and Ribatejo** 251 *palace* Junta de Turismo da Costa do Estoril; *surfing* António Sacchetti; 256 *Tagus* José Manuel; 275 *seafood* Miguel Raurich; 277 *Brisas do Liz* Região de Turismo Leiria/Fátima; 278 *olive hands* and *olive pickers* Lynn Freda; 288 *Cascais* José Manuel; *Pena Palace* António Sacchetti; 290 *Óbidos below the city walls* José Manuel; *tower* CMS/Lus Mata; 292 *Library in National Palace* António Sacchetti; 293 *monastery at Batalha* António Sacchetti; 294 *Festa dos tabuleiros* José Manuel **Terras do Sado** 302 *vines, olives and mountains* Quinta de Catralvos; 316 *church* ©Maurício Abreu **Alentejo** 321 and 344 *Elvas plums* imported by Bristol Merchants; 341 *the two large pictures,* Hotel da Cartuxa, Évora; *on black dish* Convento do Espinheiro; 343 *dairy sheep and cork trees* Jamie Goode; *dogfish soup* Hotel da Cartuxa, Évora; 344 *sericaia* Hotel da Cartuxa, Évora; 350 *bottom left* Marvão José Manuel; 353 *harvesting cork bark* APCOR; 355 *sunlit field* Francisco Almeida Dias; 358 *cathedral ceiling* António Sacchetti **Algarve** 363 *octopus* Búzio, Alvor; *chimney* Região de Turismo do Algarve; *restaurant by the water* O Sueste, Ferragudo; 366 *glass with seafood* Gigi Praia, Quinta do Lago; 367 *table above beach*

Búzio, Alvor; 370 *colourful desserts* Henrique Leis, Almancil; *fresh seafood* and *colourful peppers* Apolónia Supermarket; 371 *salt pans* and *raking salt* Região de Turismo do Algarve; *lamb dish* Vila Joya, Albufeira; *holding two fishes* Gigi Praia, Quinta do Lago; *squid* Casa do Lago, Quinta do Lago; *terrace at night* Old Coach House Restaurant, Quinta do Lago; 372 *cataplana* Casa do Lago; 380 *sand spit* Hotel da Quinta do Lago; 385 *Vilamoura Marina* Patrício Miguel; 386 *sunset* Região de Turismo do Algarve; 387 *almond blossom* Região de Turismo do Algarve; *Faro cathedral* António Sacchetti; 388 *Roman ruins* Região de Turismo do Algarve; 389 *golf course* Lusotur Golfes **Madeira** 411 *bacalhau and broccoli* Quinta da Bela Vista, Funchal; 412 *dessert with physalis* Quinta da Bela Vista, Funchal; *dining room* Casa da Quinta, Funchal **Grapes** 428 *black grapes (left and right)* Quinta do Côtto; 430 *green grapes* Paço de Teixeró; **Architecture** 433 *Coimbra cathedral (top left),* António Sacchetti; *Bom Jesus (middle right)* José Manuel **Wine-speak and table-talk** 434 *pulling the cork* APCOR; 436 *dining table* APCOR.

BIBLIOGRAPHY

Portugal with Madeira and the Azores, American Express Guide, Dorling Kindersley, London, 1997

Boa Cama, Boa Mesa, Expresso, 2006 and 2007

The Story of Port, Sarah Bradford, Christie's Wine Publications, 1978

Northern Portugal Car Tours and Walks, Paul and Denise Burton, Sunflower Books, 2004

Madeira, The Island Vineyard, Noël Cossart, Christie's Wine Publications, 1984

The Manueline – Portuguese Art During the Great Discoveries, Pedro Dias and others, published by Electa & INGO Museum With No Frontiers, Vienna, Austria, 2002

Portugal, Turismo no Espaço Rural, Direcção-Geral do Turismo, 2005

National Geographic Traveler Portugal, Fiona Dunlop, National Geographic Society 2005

Portugal, Abigail Hole & Charlotte Beech, Lonely Planet Publications Pty Ltd, 2005

Alastair Sawday's Special Places to Stay, Portugal, Laura Kinch, Alastair Sawday Publishing Co Ltd, 2005

Madeira, Alex Liddell, Faber & Faber, 1998

Port Wine Quintas of the Douro Alex Liddell & Janet Price, Sotheby's, 1992

The Wines and Vineyards of Portugal, Richard Mayson, Mitchell Beazley Classic Wine Library, 2003

Michelin The Green Guide, Portugal, Madeira, The Azores, Michelin Travel Publications, 2001

Repsol Guia Portugal 2007-2008, Repsol, 2007

Guia de Compras dos Vinhos Portugueses 2007, Luís Ramos Lopes, Revista de Vinhos, 2006

World Food, Portugal, Lynelle Scott-Aitken & Clara Vitorino, Lonely Planet Publications Pty Ltd, 2002

AA Essential Portugal, Martin Symington, 2004

The Taste of Portugal, Edite Vieira, Grub Street, 2000

Conservation and Management of Archaeological Sites, Vol. 2, pp193-206, João Zilhão, 1998

Espresso Restaurantes de Lisboa, 2007

Blue Wine, Essential Algarve, Essential Lisboa and *Essential Madeira*

www.copod3.blogspot.com; www.dn.sapo.pt; www.essential-portugal.com; www.gastronomias.com; www.ivv.min-agricultura.pt; www.lifecooler.com; www.madeirawineguide.com (Dr Peter Reutter); www.os5as8.com; www.pingasnocopo.blogspot.com; www.netmenu.pt; www.portugalvirtual.pt; www.travelandleisure.com; www.tripadvisor.com; www.vinhoverde.pt; www.viniportugal.pt; www.pt.wikipedia.org; www.wineanorak.com

Index